Workplace/Women's Place

An Anthology

Dana Dunn
University of Texas, Arlington

Foreword by
Paula England
University of Arizona

Roxbury Publishing Company
Los Angeles, California

Library of Congress Cataloging-in-Publication Data

Dunn, Dana
Workplace/women's place: an anthology/
Dana Dunn
p. cm.
Includes bibliographical references and index.
ISBN 0-935732-81-0 (pbk.)
1. Women—Employment. 2. Women employees.
I. Dunn, Dana II. Title.
HD6053.W678 1997
331.4—dc21

96-48794
CIP

WORKPLACE/WOMEN'S PLACE: An Anthology

Publisher and Editor: Claude Teweles
Supervising Editor: Dawn VanDercreek
Production Editors: C. Max-Ryan and James Ballinger
Assistant Editors: Joyce Rappaport, Colleen O'Brien, and Renee Burkhammer
Typesetting: Synergistic Data Systems
Cover: Marnie Deacon Kenney
Printed in the United States on acid-free paper that meets the standards of the
Environmental Protection Agency for recycled paper.

ISBN 0-935732-81-0

Roxbury Publishing Company
P.O. Box 491044
Los Angeles, California 90049-9044
Tel.: (213) 653-1068 • Fax: (213) 653-4140
Email: roxbury@crl.com

Table Of Contents

Foreword

Paula England, University of Arizona

Today, more undergraduate and graduate students are enrolled in courses focusing on gender than ever before. Such courses have entered the standard curriculum in sociology, psychology, women's studies, management, economics, and the humanities.

Workplace/Women's Place, an anthology assembled by sociologist Dana Dunn, is a welcome addition for those social scientists who believe that understanding gender inequality in the sphere of paid work is key to understanding much that is different in men and women's lives. The book will be a useful teaching tool for instructors who want this emphasis reflected in what they assign students to read.

Why is gender inequality in paid work so consequential for gender inequality in all spheres of life? In part it is because more women are employed for pay that ever before; over half of ever married mothers of infants in the U.S. are now employed. Also, women's own earnings are more important to them than ever because the average woman spends much more of her lifetime without a man's financial support than ever before—whether because her husband is unemployed, because she doesn't marry or marries late, because she divorces, or because she is widowed for many years. As divorce and nonmarital births have increased in all industrial societies, men's financial contributions to households with children have plummeted; many men contribute little to the financial support of their children when they are no longer coresident with them. In the United States, policy makers have lacked either the will or the means to enforce the payment of child support that would make up for this lost income. Nor have they provided state subsidies that compensate for more than a fraction of the access to men's earnings children have lost. Thus, a woman's own earnings determine her standard of living and that of her children to an extent not previously seen. But gender inequality in earnings also affects married women with employed husbands. Relative earnings of spouses affects the distribution of power in marriage, including decisions about such things as who does how much household work and who has more leisure. And money is not the only outcome of gender inequality at work. Differences in the job tasks men and women hold, and in the ways they are treated by managers, customers, and coworkers, have ongoing effects in molding their skills, mental health, and personalities. Work casts a long shadow on the person doing it, and increasingly paid work is added to household work for women. In sum, for many social scientists, gender inequality in paid work has effects that penetrate into all areas of life.

Gender inequality at work is pervasive. Women earn about 70 percent what men do, on average. Occupations remain substantially segregated by sex, with women concentrated in lower-paying occupations. Women also earn less than men within every occupation. Cultural expectations still require more of mothers than fathers in responsibility for childrearing and the home, even when most women are employed. Although the amount of segregation and the pay gap are smaller than they were several decades ago, they remain large. Few norms or laws encourage employers to make accommodations for workers' family roles, despite the fact that fewer husbands have full-time wives at home and virtually no women have a full-time homemaker partner tending the home fires. Most people claim to support equal opportunity for the sexes, and yet parents and schools, in ways subtle and overt, provide very different encouragement to boys and girls regarding their future roles as paid workers and as family members. While the law now prohibits sex discrimination in hiring or discrimination in the sense of lack of equal pay for equal work in the same job, enforcement is by no means perfect. Equally important, few changes have been legally required or voluntarily undertaken by employers in many other practices that perpetuate gender inequality at work. For example, wage scales typically devalue traditionally female jobs, even when they require as much education as a male job (so, for example, secretaries may earn little more than janitors and less than welders); yet comparable worth is not legally required. Because top managers and union officials are usually men, they often devise organizational rules that advantage men, sometimes deliberately, sometimes unwittingly. More subtle processes, like the assumption that typically male styles of management work better, may lead men to be rewarded more highly even when women are contributing as much to the bottom line of the organization. All these mechanisms perpetuate male advantage.

Despite the pervasiveness and importance of gender inequality in paid employment, most textbooks available for undergraduate courses in gender focus little on such inequality. Texts on the sociology of gender often devote only a chapter or two to the topic. And for those of us whose research and teaching have specialized in gender and paid work, these chapters often seem superficial.

Dunn's anthology will fill this gap. The entire volume focuses on gender inequality in paid employment. It can be used as a main text in an undergraduate class on gender and work, or as one of several books in a course covering many aspects of gender inequality. I will find it useful in courses on sociology of gender. The reader can also be used to bring gender questions into courses not centrally about gender, for example courses in stratification, the sociology of work, or organizational behavior.

Workplace/Women's Place offers the big picture—trends in segregation and in the sex gap in pay, explanations for both, and employer or governmental policies that could reduce inequality. It also explores links between employment and other institutions. For example, household-employment and school-employment links are considered in the chapters that discuss how girls receive less encouragement at every step in the process that might lead into the most lucrative occupations. Job and family links are also center-stage in the section on how workers who also have family responsibilities cope with these dual demands, and how it is women who often have to perform the balancing act. Links between gender, race, and class are also considered.

The reader also provides in-depth looks at women's and men's experiences in a number of specific occupations. These include management, male-dominated professions such as law, female-dominated professions such as nursing and teaching, and in traditionally female clerical and service jobs. These chapters give descriptive richness to the portrayal of gender equality, making the book more accessible and interesting for undergraduates.

Many of the readings are taken from articles or monographs and cover important recent research. They are suitably shortened and edited for simplicity, yielding a very accessible volume. The coverage is interdisciplinary, including pieces by sociologists, psychologists, and others.

In short, the book provides those of us who teach on gender with a reader that documents and describes concrete details of gender inequality in paid work, and provides some analysis of the causes and serious consequences of gender inequality. ✦

Preface

This book is designed as a reader for courses addressing women and work. The book will complement most women and work textbooks, and is appropriate for courses in diverse disciplines including the social sciences, women's studies, and management. The selections contained in this book are excerpted from recently published works of scholarly significance in both academic and trade publications. Authors represent a number of academic disciplines (e.g., sociology, women's studies, psychology, management, political science, and communication) and several employment fields (e.g., journalist, career placement counselor, educator, and government task force representative).

A wide range of issues pertaining to women and work are examined in this text including sexual harassment, hiring and pay discrimination, tokenism, job stress, work satisfaction, worker activism, occupational segregation, gender differences in management styles, and communication differences between the sexes. A number of the selections in this reader incorporate the voices of working women as they describe their own experiences. Most selections are sensitive to issues of difference among women, and several focus on the ways in which race/ethnicity and class pattern women's work experiences.

The book begins with an introductory chapter which highlights the importance of studying women and work and provides historical perspective on women's employment. Five units, focused on the themes of socialization for work, gender inequality in the workplace, the intertwining of work and family roles, women's "ways" of work-

ing, and case studies of different types of occupations comprise the remainder of the reader. Each unit is prefaced by an introductory discussion which highlights major themes and topics and addresses their relevance. The unit introduction also provides a brief overview of the chapters that follow. Food for thought and application questions are included at the end of each chapter to stimulate critical thinking.

Despite the wide coverage of issues in this book, limitations on book length resulted in some important topics not being covered. Particularly visible omissions include selections on part-time and temporary employment (disproportionately female categories of work); home-based production; women business owners; and the work experiences of women outside the United States (particularly women in developing nations), lesbian women, and elderly women. The diversity of women's work experiences today makes it impossible to provide coverage of all relevant topics. It is my hope that students will "fill in the gaps" by reading beyond the materials in this book. Those who assign this reader should consider alternate ways of providing coverage of missing topics (such as lectures, films and videos, or supplemental readings).

I am grateful to the following scholars for providing feedback on the prospectus and outline for this book: Irene Brown (Emory University), Paula England (University of Arizona), Beth Hess (County College of Morris), Ruth Milkman (University of California at Los Angeles), Irene Padavic (Florida State University), Natalie Sokoloff (John Jay School of Criminal Justice), and

Linda Waite (University of Chicago). The insightful comments of these reviewers resulted in revision and strengthening of this book. I would also like to thank three sociologists who played an important role in stimulating my initial interest in the study of women and work: Elizabeth Almquist, University of North Texas; Paula England, University of Arizona; and Janet Chafetz, University of Houston. Thanks also go to Claude Teweles of Roxbury Publishing Company for encouraging me to edit this book, RoseAnn Reddick for invaluable assistance in manuscript preparation, and to the authors of the chapters whose important work was excerpted to create this book. Finally, I must thank Thomas Mills, who sacrificed much leisure so that I could complete my work on this book. ✦

About the Contributors

Teresa Amott is a feminist economist and activist who teaches at Bucknell University.

Linda M. Blum is Assistant Professor of Sociology at the University of New Hampshire. This article is drawn from her dissertation, "Re-evaluating Women's Work: The Significance of the Comparable Worth Movement," University of California, Berkeley. Her other publications include essays on feminist theory and politics.

Joan Keller Burton is Associate Professor, Department of Sociology and Anthropology, Women's Studies Program at Goucher College in Maryland. Her current research examines office-worker discontent and activism, focusing on the incentives that attract recruits to 9 to 5, National Association of Working Women, and on the role of commitment in sustaining their participation.

Wayne Carlisle, before his untimely death, was Director of Placement and Career Services at Wichita State University. He served a three-year term on the Executive Board of the National Association of Student Personnel Administrators, served as Program Chair for the 1991 national conference, and on four occasions served as Chair of Career Services at national conferences. In 1990 he received the Fred Turner Award from the National Association of Student Personnel Administrators.

Janet Chafetz is Professor of Sociology at the University of Houston. Over the past 25 years she has written extensively in the area of sociology of gender, focusing primarily on developing theoretical understandings of stability and change in systems of gender inequality. Her most recent research concerns the impact on family structure of changes in women's relationships to the labor force in advanced industrial nations.

Nina L. Colwill is affiliated with the University of Manitoba and the University of Western Ontario, and has her own management consulting practice. Dr. Colwill is the author of two books: *The Psychology of Sex Differences*, with Dr. Hilary Lips, and, more recently, *The New Partnership: Women and Men in Organizations*. She is a member of the advisory board for the Women in Management Program, National Centre for Management, Research and Development, University of Western Ontario.

Maureen Connelly received her Ph.D. in sociology from Ohio State University in 1980. She is Associate Professor of Sociology at Frostburg State College in Maryland. She has recently received an MSW from the University of Maryland. Her areas of interest are sex roles and deviant behavior.

Yvonne Corcoran-Nantes has previously conducted research among women in Brazil and is currently lecturer in Sociology at Flinders University of South Australia.

Marian Court taught in primary and secondary schools in New Zealand and worked as an equal employment opportunities reviewer with the Education Review Office before becoming a Senior Lecturer in the Department of Policy Studies in Education at Massey University, Palmerston North. She now teaches courses on the sociology of women and girls in education, EEO, and women in educational leadership, focusing on issues of gender and work. Her current research is investigating women educators' shared leadership initiatives.

Dana Dunn is Associate Professor of Sociology and Director of the Women's Studies Program at the University of Texas at Arlington. She has authored articles on gender stratification, sex-based earnings inequality, women in political office, and gender inequality in developing societies.

Paula England is Professor of Sociology at the University of Arizona. Her research interests include occupational sex segregation; the sex gap in pay; and the integration of sociological, economic and feminist theories. She has written numerous articles on these topics, and is the author of *Comparable Worth: Theories and Evidence*.

The Federal Glass Ceiling Commission is a 21-member bipartisan body appointed by President Bush and Congressional leaders and chaired by the Secretary of Labor.

Sue J. M. Freeman is Professor of Education and Child Study at Smith College and a practicing psychologist.

Kathleen Gerson is Professor of Sociology at New York University, where she teaches courses on gender, work, family, and social change. She is the author of several books, including *No Man's Land: Men's Changing Commitments to Family and Work* (Basic Books, 1993) and *Hard Choices: How Women Decide About Work, Career, and Motherhood* (University of California Press, 1985). She is now at work on a study of how children growing up in diverse types of families have responded to the gender revolution at home and at the workplace.

Nona Y. Glazer teaches sociology and women's studies at Portland State University. She has completed a forthcoming manuscript on the "work transfer" that includes an analysis of the shift of once-paid nursing work to family members and the consequences for women as family members and as paid health service workers.

Elaine J. Hall is Associate Professor of Sociology at Kent State University. In addition to studying the way service occupations construct gender relations, she is researching the conceptualization of class, race, and gender in introductory sociology textbooks.

Sally Helgesen is a journalist whose work has appeared in national magazines and newspapers including the *New York Times*. Formerly contributing editor of *Harper's* magazine, she is also the author of *Wildcatters: A Story of Texans, Oil and Money*.

Elizabeth Higginbotham is Associate Director of the Center for Research on Women and Associate Professor in the Department of Sociology and Social Work at Memphis State University. She has written widely in the areas of race, class, and gender. In 1993, she was a co-recipient (with Bonnie Thornton Dill and Lynn Weber) of the American Sociological Association's Jessie Bernard Award and the Distinguished Contributions to Teaching Award for the work of the Memphis State Center for Research on Women.

Rita Mae Kelly is Dean of the School of Social Sciences at the University of Texas at Dallas. She has authored numerous articles on women and politics, and is the author of *The Gendered Economy: Work, Careers and Success*.

Julie Matthaei is a feminist economist and activist who teaches at Wellesley College.

Marsha Lakes Matyas conducts research on factors affecting the attrition of undergraduate women from biology majors and methods for encouraging secondary school students to continue in science. She serves as a member of the Role and Status of Women in Biology Committee of the National Association of Biology Teachers and of the special interest group, Research on Women in Education, of the American Educational Research Association.

Peggy Orenstein was formerly managing editor of *Mother Jones* magazine, and was a founding editor of the award-winning *7 Days* magazine. She has served on the editorial staffs of *Manhattan, inc.* and *Esquire*, and her work has appeared in such publications as *The New York Times Magazine, Vogue, Glamour, The New Yorker, New York Woman,* and *Mirabella*.

Harry Perlstadt is Associate Professor at Michigan State University and codirector of a cluster evaluation of health professions education initiatives funded by the Kellogg Foundation. His interests in women lawyers stems from conversations with Barrie Thorne and his sister, a partner in a major Wall Street law firm.

William R. F. Phillips is Professor of Sociology at Widener University. His research focuses on social movements and the law. In addition to the current ongoing study of women lawyers, he is working on a project concerned with ideological development in the early-20th-century city planning movement.

Jo Anne Preston is Assistant Professor in Sociology at Brandeis University. She is currently completing a book on the feminization of school teaching. Her previous publications address the relationship of millgirl narratives to collective identity and labor activism, the conflict between female apprentices and merchant-tailors in the early industrial period, and the discrepancy between female teachers' self-conceptions and 19th-century gender ideology.

Kathleen Kelley Reardon is a communication and management researcher and Director of the Leadership Institute at the University of Southern California School of Business.

Barbara Reskin is Professor and Chair of Sociology at The Ohio State University.

Her books related to gender and work include *Women and Men at Work* (with Irene Padavic), *Job Queues, Gender Queues: Explaining Women's Inroads into Male Occupations* (with Patricia Roos), and *Sex Segregation in the Workplace: Trends, Explanations and Remedies* (edited volume). Themes in her research include sex differentiation; occupational segregation by sex, race, and ethnicity; and the effects of sex and race on workers' access to promotions, authority, and other job outcomes.

Patricia Rhoton received her Ph.D. in sociology from Notre Dame in 1981. She worked at the Center for Human Resource Research at Ohio State University from 1977 to 1986. She has published several articles related to occupational choice and the interaction of work and other types of human activity. She is currently self-employed, doing marketing research and consulting.

Kenneth Roberts is Professor of Sociology at the University of Liberpool. He is a specialist in employment issues and is currently investigating the effects of the reforms on the labor markets in former communist countries.

Mary Romero a Professor at Arizona State University, is the author of *Maid in the U.S.A.* (Routledge, 1992), co-editor of *Challenging Fronteras: Structuring Latina and Latina Lives in the U.S.* (Routledge, forthcoming); *Women and Work: Race, Ethnicity and Class* (Sage Publications, forthcoming); *Community Empowerment and Chicano Scholarship* (1992) and *Estudios Chicanos and The Politics of Community* (1989) Selected Conference Proceedings, National Association for Chicano Studies. She has expanded her research on family and work, particularly paid reproductive labor, and is writing a book about the experiences of a Mexican maid's daughter.

Janet Rosenberg is Professor of Sociology at Widener University. Her recent research interests include the role of the federal courts in the reform of public institutions and the effects of gender on the stratification of professions dominated by men.

Marian Swerdlow has had a long career as a campus and workplace activist in New York City. She has taught sociology at Fordham University, Hunter College, and, most recently, Buffalo State College. She has written and spoken publicly on Marxist theory and a wide variety of its applications. She is currently preparing a book about work relations among rapid transit operatives.

Lynn Zimmer is Assistant Professor of Sociology at the State University of New York at Geneseo. Her work on female prison guards appears in *Women Guarding Men* (University of Chicago Press, 1986). Among her current interests are feminist jurisprudence, male domination in the social sciences, and gender inequality in employment. ✦

Introduction to the Study
of Women and Work

The rapid influx of women into the paid labor market is one of the most dramatic social changes of the century. Women have always worked, but much of the work they have performed has not "counted" officially as work. The best example of this uncounted work is domestic work.[1] Domestic work is nonmarket work—it is performed outside the formal economy in support of households and families, not for exchange on the market. While such work is clearly of great importance, it is not the focus of this book. The selections in this book focus on women's participation in paid work performed outside the home.

There are many reasons for examining women's increased involvement in paid work. The first reasons discussed here are economic. New information on women as paid workers is needed because women today represent over 45 percent of all paid workers (Bureau of Labor Statistics 1995). Women are a valuable economic resource in that their labor is necessary for the production of the goods and services we all consume. Traditionally, the study of work addressed primarily male workers (Acker 1988). With women representing almost one half of the workforce today, it is equally important to understand issues such as: (1) what motivates women to be productive workers, (2) what causes women to be satisfied with their work, and (3) how and if women's management styles differ from those of men.

Another economic reason for studying working women is that the majority of women who work for pay do so out of perceived economic need (Baca Zinn and Eitzen 1993). It has become increasingly difficult to support a family at what is considered to be a desirable standard of living on just one income. Further, many households today do not consist of traditional families with adult males present, and women are the only economic providers in these households. The fact that, on average, women earn less for the work they perform than men contributes to disproportionately high rates of poverty in female-headed households, a phenomenon that has come to be known as the feminization of poverty. The economic reasons for studying women and work then are that women are important producers in today's economy, as well as important economic providers for their families and households.

Studying women's increased involvement in paid work is also important for social reasons. Women's increased labor-force participation has broad social consequences that extend well beyond the economy. Families and schools provide examples of two social institutions profoundly affected by increases in women's labor-force participation. As mentioned above, women have always performed domestic work; in fact, they have typically borne the primary responsibility for such work. As women begin to spend significant numbers of hours working outside the home for pay, their ability to perform domestic work and, potentially, the quality of life of their families is affected. Families need to adapt to women's changing work roles by making other provisions for the performance of domestic work. As we will see in chapters in Unit Four, women in many families still perform a disproportionate share of domestic tasks in addition to their paid work because these needed adaptations have not taken place. Educational institutions are also affected by women working. For example, schools can no longer depend upon the unpaid labor of the employed mothers of school children (e.g., as teachers' aides to support classroom activities). Issues such as providing for the transportation of children to and from school and the compatibility of school hours with parents' work hours need to be reexamined in light of women's increased involvement in paid work.

Studying women's paid work is also warranted for what can be referred to as personal or individual reasons. Social scientists agree that work is far more than the means to an economic end. Work has personal meaning because individuals in modern society are defined, in large part, by the work they perform (O'Toole, et al. 1973, Pavalko 1988). "What do you do?" means "What type of work do you perform?" and this is typically the first thing we ask a new acquaintance. The answer to this question conveys a myriad of information, including economic status, social class, level of education, even interests, abilities, political views, and personality traits (Hedley 1992). "What do you do?" is shorthand for "Who are you?" and others respond to us on the basis of our answer. College professors are assumed to be intelligent and "bookish"; nurses, nurturing; engineers, detail-oriented; and salespersons, gregarious. These assumptions about who we are, derived from others' knowledge of our work, eventually impact our self-concept, our own perception of who we are (Dunn 1995). For this reason, we can say that work contributes to feelings of self-esteem. In order to understand who women are today and how they feel about themselves then, it is necessary to examine their participation in the workforce.

Work affects self-concept and feelings about oneself by contributing to feelings of efficacy and worth. The connection between feelings of efficacy, the power to produce effects, and work is obvious. Producing goods and services is a form of mastery over self and the environment and proof of one's ability to "get things done". If the output from one's work is valued by others, then work enhances feelings of worth. On the other hand, if one's work is not socially valued, self esteem is likely to be low. Consider, for example, the often under-valued, unpaid work performed by homemakers. The fact that domestic work has become under-appreciated causes many homemakers to respond to the "What do you do?" question with "I'm just a housewife" (Matthews 1987). That domestic work is insufficient for producing a positive self-concept is further supported by evidence of sub-standard mental health among full-time homemakers (Bernard 1972). Women's increased participation in paid work is therefore personally important because it provides an opportunity for empowerment and increased self esteem.

Finally, and perhaps most importantly, examining women's paid work is important because the type of work performed by each sex and the social valuation of that work is the best indicator, across societies and throughout time, of the degree of equality between the sexes. When women are judged to be performing valuable work, especially work for pay outside the home, on a comparable basis with men, then gender inequality is minimized.[2] It is not surprising then that many battles for gender equality have been fought in the workplace. Much women's movement activity in the 1960s and 1970s was centered around issues of hiring discrimination and equal pay on the assumption that if women could gain access to the same types of jobs as men for similar rates of pay, they would be treated equally (Daniel 1987).

The chapters that follow explore a wide range of issues related to contemporary women's involvement in paid work. Before introducing these chapters, it is necessary to provide some historical perspective on working women. The following sections of this introduction will explore the changing patterns of women's work participation and examine the causes that underlie that change. A final section will highlight important issues to consider when approaching the study of women and work.

The Changing Patterns of Women's Work

Human societies have always divided labor by sex, reserving certain work tasks for men and others for women. While a division of labor by sex has existed in all known societies, the form of the division of labor has varied. In the section below the typical sex-based division of labor in early human societies and how that division of labor changed as societies evolved will be described for four broad types of societies: hunting and gathering societies, horticultural societies, agricultural societies, and industrial societies. Next, changes in women's labor-force participation and patterns of work will be examined in more detail for contemporary, post-industrial societies.

The Sex-Based Division of Labor in Pre-Industrial Societies

The earliest human societies, hunter-gatherer societies, had a simple division of labor by sex—men hunted wild game, women gathered naturally occurring vegetation, and those too old or too young to participate in these activities stayed home

and cared for one another. The sex-based division of labor in hunter-gatherer societies was efficient because women's reproductive role was incompatible with physically demanding hunting activities that often required travel far from home (Bradley 1989). Imagine, for example, the difficulty involved in hunting large game while pregnant or nursing an infant. The gathering tasks reserved for women were compatible with pregnancy and child care—they were less physically demanding and could be performed close to home. Hunter-gatherer societies were small, and survival was often difficult in these subsistence-based groups (Lenski and Lenski 1982). For this reason, women's reproductive role was highly valued. The level of equality between the sexes was high in these societies because the work performed by women and men was judged to be of roughly equal importance (Boulding 1976; Chafetz 1984; Nielsen 1978). Men's hunting activities often yielded substantial subsistence resources for support of the group, but hunting activities were sometimes unreliable, and hunters often came back from their long hunts empty-handed (Friedl 1975; Sanday 1981). Women's work contribution became especially important in these periods. The nuts, roots, berries, and tubers gathered by women provided edible foodstuffs which enabled group members to survive during periods when the hunt was unproductive. Thus, the stability of women's economic contribution was highly valued, as was their reproductive role, and these factors contributed to a greater degree of equality between the sexes than in any subsequent period in history (Yorburg 1987; Nielsen 1990).

Over time, horticultural societies developed as a result of technological advancements and new forms of social organization. Rather than depend on hunting wild game and gathering naturally occurring vegetation, people in horticultural societies met their subsistence needs by domesticating plants which resulted in a more reliable and significant yield (Lenski

1966). Women, having established a tradition of contributing to subsistence needs by gathering plants, made the rather smooth transition to domesticating plants. Men were typically responsible for claiming the land used for planting. The resulting male ownership of land placed control over the means of production in the hands of men and began to erode women's status (Friedl, 1975; Dunn et al. 1993). Men also continued to hunt, and when successful, provided the scarce and highly valued animal protein. At some point, men also began to domesticate animals in many societies, raising small herds not only for meat, but also for milk and other animal by-products (Lenski 1966).

Horticultural societies grew in size with the advent of new technologies (e.g., more sophisticated implements, irrigation). Eventually a transition occurred from a subsistence orientation to a surplus orientation. In surplus-oriented societies, people can produce more than is required for meeting subsistence needs, making it possible for some people to be freed from food production in order to engage in other forms of work. Specialized full-time occupations emerged at this point in history. Some involved turning raw materials into handicrafted goods, others involved providing services (e.g., shopkeeper, educator). To the extent that these new occupations were performed away from the homesite, they were considered the domain of men. Domestic work, performed in and around the home, was reserved for women.

The invention of the plow marked the transition to the agricultural stage of development and the ability to produce a surplus increased dramatically. Animal-drawn plows transferred much of the hardest labor involved in producing food to animals. Having established a tradition of working with animals—first hunting them and then domesticating them—men worked behind the animal-drawn plows and produced increasing amounts of surplus (Yorburg 1987). Other men, freed

from the need to produce food, entered newly developing specialized occupations in even larger numbers. A complex market economy resulted where foodstuffs were exchanged for dollars (or other goods) which were then used to purchase goods produced by workers in the new occupations.

What were women doing while men were plowing, shopkeeping, blacksmithing, leather crafting, and so on? First, women often assisted with these activities when needed (during harvest time, for example). Their primary work responsibilities, however, remained in the home. Women were responsible for providing an array of services to their families including cooking and storing food, sewing and manufacturing clothing, medical care, education, and even religious training (Yorburg 1987). These types of work activities are referred to as use-value production because what is produced is consumed by the family unit. In contrast, the work performed by men in agricultural societies is referred to as exchange-value production because the products are intended for exchange through the market. Exchange-value production is more highly valued than use-value production because the former provides greater flexibility in terms of what can be consumed and also affords the party performing the work the opportunity to develop social networks and ties (Nielsen 1990).

An important exception to this pattern of restricting women's work to the domestic sphere occurred in cases of slavery, wherein enslaved groups performed coerced labor. Africans brought to the U.S. as slaves, for example, did not conform to the sex-based division of labor described above. While it is the case that some black women slaves were forced to work primarily in the slave owner's home, many others were forced to work alongside men in the fields, engaged in extremely physically demanding labor (Deckard 1975; Matthaei 1982).

As women became increasingly associated with domestic labor and use-value production, their status relative to men declined (Nielsen 1990). Gender inequality reached its peak in agricultural societies, not because women were no longer working hard and making an economic contribution, but because of the changed nature of their work. Men were the more visible producers, they owned the means of production (land), the product of their labor was now relatively stable, and what they produced could be exchanged for an almost infinite variety of goods and services through the market. Women, working "behind the scenes" in the less than glamorous domestic arena, supported their husbands' work by attending to his needs and those of the rest of the family (Cott 1977).

The Impact of Industrialization on Women's Work

The next major societal transition that had an impact on the nature of work and the division of labor between the sexes was the emergence of industry. Industrialization involved using forms of power other than human and animal (e.g., water, steam, mechanical, electric) to produce manufactured goods. Efficient utilization of these new forms of power meant that workers had to be located in a common work setting and resulted in the rise of the factory mode of production. During the early phases of industrialization in both Europe and the United States, some women—especially unmarried women, women from the lower classes, and minority women—worked in factories (Matthaei 1982). A sex-based division of labor developed for the specialized factory jobs. Women worked with smaller equipment and machinery, on average, and were concentrated in jobs in the textile industry. The jobs women performed paid lower wages than those performed by men (Deckard 1975). Men, with higher wages, were viewed as the primary breadwinners for families, and women's economic contributions, although often necessary, were considered supplemental. Women employed in factories continued to be respon-

sible for domestic work at home, creating for the first time a "double shift" for women consisting of eight or more hours of paid work to be followed by a night shift of use-value work in support of the family (Andersen 1988). Married women, especially white women who could afford to do so, stayed home as full-time homemakers (Matthaei 1982).

By the turn of the century (1900), just under 19 percent of all working-age women participated in paid work, and the majority of these women were under the age of 24. Less than 6 percent of married women worked for pay outside the home at this time (Kessler-Harris 1982; Costello and Krimgold 1996). Married women's rates of labor-force participation remained low during the first three decades of the twentieth century due to what has come to be known as the cult of domesticity. The cult of domesticity, also referred to as the doctrine of separate spheres, was borrowed from the English upper-middle classes and held that a woman's proper place was in the home (Reskin and Padavic 1994). Under the cult of domesticity, the homemaker's absence from the paid workforce served as a symbol of the husband's masculinity (Matthaei 1982). Married women only entered the labor force when their husbands were incapable of providing a family wage—a wage sufficient for providing for the family. The cult of domesticity encouraged married women to be economically dependent on their spouses, and thereby led to a decline in women's status.

Poor women and women of color, forced to work out of economic need, retained a higher degree of independence than white women. Ironically, for these women who could not afford the "luxury" of the full-time homemaker role, paid work resulted in somewhat more equal standing with their male peers. Even today, some minority groups have higher rates of female labor-force participation than white women, and the sexes also share resources more equally in these groups (Almquist 1987).

In the early decades of the twentieth century, women who worked outside the home had limited options. Single white women were sometimes employed in new fields as clerical workers, teachers, and nurses (Andersen 1988). Working class women and women of color worked in factories as laborers, and many immigrant women were employed as domestic servants in other women's homes. There were slow but rather steady increases in the rates of women's labor-force participation until the early 1940s, when World War II created severe labor shortages and an increased demand for female labor. Over five million more women were in the labor force in 1944 than in 1940, due to wartime efforts (Herz and Wootton 1996). During the war years, the sex-based division of labor in manufacturing broke down as many women worked—and performed well—in nontraditional jobs (Kemp 1994). However, despite their successful job performance, women were often displaced from the previously male-dominated jobs when men returned home from the war.

During the middle decades of the twentieth century, the United States economy experienced an important shift from an emphasis on the production of goods to the provision of services. More than half of the labor force was employed in service-producing industries by the 1950s (Montagna 1977). Many of the new service-oriented jobs in industries like banking, insurance, health, and education were white-collar jobs which required little demanding physical effort, were far-removed from the dirty, factory setting, and for these reasons seemed more "appropriate" for women. That, combined with the rapid rates of growth in these occupations opened the doors for many women to enter these new service-producing occupations. Women entered lower tier service-producing occupations such as retail sales, and personal services in large numbers. From this period forward, women's rates of participation in paid employment increased steadily.

Women's Labor-force Participation in Recent History

The rise in women's labor-force activity that has occurred over the last few decades has been accompanied by a decrease in men's rates of labor-force participation, causing women to represent an increasing share of all workers. Table I.1 provides an overview of changes in women's and men's rates of labor-force participation from

Table I.1
Labor-force Participation Rates by Sex and Women's Share of the Total Labor Force for Selected Years: 1900–1994

People 16 and Older, Civilian Labor Force[1]

Labor-force Participation

Year	Males	Females	Women's Share of Labor Force
1900	80.0	18.8	18.3
1910	81.3	23.4	21.2
1920	78.2	21.0	20.5
1930	76.2	22.0	22.0
1940	79.2	25.4	24.3
1950	86.4	33.9	29.6
1955	85.3	35.7	31.6
1960	83.3	37.7	33.4
1965	80.7	39.3	35.2
1970	79.7	43.3	38.1
1975	77.9	46.3	40.0
1980	77.4	51.5	42.5
1985	76.3	54.5	44.2
1990	76.1	57.5	45.3
1994	75.0	58.8	46.0

[1] Before 1947, people in the labor force included workers age 14 and older.

Source: Adapted from Kemp, Alice Abel, *Women's Work: Degraded and Devalued*. NJ: Prentice Hall, 1994:174. Her data sources include: U.S. Department of Commerce, 1975, pp. 131-132 (1900-1947); U.S. Department of Labor, 1989: Table 2 (1950-1987); U.S. Department of Labor, 1992: Table 2 (1980-1991). The 1994 data were taken from the Bureau of Labor Statistics, *Current Population Survey*, March 1994 Supplement (Washington, D.C.: Bureau of the Census).

1900 to 1994 and also indicates the percentage of the total labor force that is female.

The influx of women, especially married women, into paid employment accelerated in the 1960s and 1970s when the women's movement played a role in making paid work appear more desirable to married women (Herz and Wootton 1996). As full-time homemakers compared themselves to employed women, they recognized their comparatively dependent status and felt devalued. Further, increasing divorce rates and rising numbers of impoverished displaced homemakers were making abundantly clear to full-time homemakers the risks of complete economic dependence on a male provider (Matthaei 1982). A number of other factors also contributed to increases in women's labor-force participation during this period. The civil rights movement resulted in more opportunities and equal treatment for women and minorities in the workplace, which served to make paid work more attractive. In addition, women's educational attainment was becoming more similar to men's, allowing women more access to interesting and lucrative employment. Increased employment opportunities led to a decline in the birthrate, which meant that women spent less of their adult years with pre-school age children, and thus had more years available to spend in paid employment (Herz and Wootton 1996). While all of the above affected the supply of female labor, the most important cause of women's increased employment was the increased demand for workers resulting from economic expansion (Chafetz 1990, Daniel 1987).

Changes in occupational opportunity in the 1960s and 1970s had differential impact across groups of women (Anderson 1988; Ortiz 1994). Table I.2 provides labor-force participation rates for women by race/ethnicity for 1960 and 1970. Among the groups listed, only Mexican, Puerto Rican, and American Indian women had lower rates of labor-force participation

Table I.2
Labor-force Participation Rates for Women by Race/Ethnicity, Selected Groups, 1960 and 1970

	1960	1970
White	33.6	40.6
Black	42.2	47.5
Mexican	28.8	36.4
Puerto Rican	36.3	32.3
Chinese	44.2	49.5
Japanese	44.1	49.4
Filipina	36.2	55.2
American Indian	25.5	35.3

Source: Adapted from Vilma Ortiz, *Women of Color: A Demographic Overview*. In M. Baca Zinn and B. Thornton Dill (eds.), *Women of Color in U. S. Society*: 28.

than white women. Black, Chinese, Japanese, and Filipina women were all employed at higher rates than white women, primarily in lower tier, personal service occupations (e.g., domestic, seamstress) and as factory operatives. More recently, improved educational opportunities for women of color, combined with continued civil rights activity and legal changes have created new job opportunities for black women, especially in female-dominated, semi-professional occupations (Sokoloff 1992). (See Chapter 18 for further discussion of black women's employment in the professions.)

The rate of increase in women's participation in paid work slowed in the early 1980s due to economic recession. The impact of economic recession was greater, however, for male dominated industries and occupations (e.g., manufacturing). By 1990, the growth in women's labor-force participation had slowed even further, as continued economic stagnation and job losses in retail trade occupations took a toll on women's employment opportunities. Since that time, labor-force participation rates for women have remained relatively stable (Herz and Wootton 1996).

Women's participation in paid work today varies by age, race/ethnicity, marital status, the presence of children, and education level. These characteristics affect women's participation in paid work for two primary reasons. First, they are related to opportunities for employment and earnings and the opportunity costs of not working (e.g., age, race/ethnicity, and education level); and second, they are related to domestic/family demands on women's time that detract from the opportunity to work (e.g., marital status and the presence of children). Table I.3 presents selected population and labor-force characteristics of women in 1994. Today, women in their late thirties and early forties have the highest participation level, with over 77 percent in the labor force (Herz and Wooton 1996). This represents a change from the earlier part of the century when rates were highest for young, unmarried women (England and Farkas 1986). Through the middle part of the century, women exited the labor force in significant numbers upon marriage and especially the birth of children, causing a dip in labor-force participation rates for those under the age of 35. As these women re-entered the labor force when their children became school age, rates climbed once again, though not to a level as high as that for young, unmarried women. Women today are far more likely to work continuously, causing their labor-force participation rates to appear similar to men's, increasing through the middle years, leveling off, and then declining around retirement (Herz and Wootton 1996).

Since the 1960s and 1970s, variation in women's labor-force participation by race/ethnicity has diminished. Increases in white women's levels of participation have served to close the gap between white and black women (Ortiz 1994). Rates of participation for Hispanic women represent marked increases over previous decades, but are still about 6 percentage points lower than those for black and white women. (see Table I.3). Social scientists have long attributed the lower rates for Hispanic women to cultural patterns that emphasize traditional roles in the family. The rapid increases in participation in paid work for Hispanic women suggest that such traditions are eroding, or perhaps that increased employment opportunities and economic need compel women to deviate from tradition (Almquist 1979; Ortiz 1994; Zavella 1987). It is important to note that while labor-force participation rates vary little across racial/ethnic groups, unemployment rates are about two times higher for racial/ethnic minority women (except Asian/Pacific Islanders) (U. S. Bureau of the Census 1990).

Women's family situations continue to affect their employment, though much less so than in the past. In recent decades, the most dramatic increases in labor-force participation for women occurred for married women with preschool-age children. Between 1950 and 1980, the labor-force participation rate of married women with children under the age of 6 rose from 12 to 45 percent—a 275 percent increase (England and Farkas 1986)! While women with school-age children are more likely to be employed than those with children under the age of six, the majority of all mothers, regardless of the children's ages, are in the labor force today (Herz and Wootton 1996) (see Table I.3).

Education is an important tool that not only increases employment opportunities for women, but also increases the opportunity costs of not participating in the labor force. Today women receive about the same overall level of education as men (Sapiro 1994), and their labor-force participation rates reflect these educational gains. The most educated groups of women are those with the highest levels of labor-force activity. For example, 85 per-

Table I.3
Selected Population and Labor-force Characteristics of Women, 1994 (numbers in thousands)

Characteristic	Percentage of the Population in the Labor Force
Total, 16 years and over	58.8
Age	
16 to 19 years	51.3
20 to 24 years	71.0
25 to 54 years	75.3
25 to 34 years	74.0
35 to 44 years	77.1
45 to 54 years	74.6
55 to 64 years	48.9
65 years and over	9.2
Race and Hispanic Origin[1]	
White	58.9
Black	58.7
Hispanic origin	52.9
Marital Status	
Never married	65.1
Married, spouse present	60.6
Widowed	17.6
Divorced	73.9
Married, spouse absent	62.9
Presence and age of children	
Without children under 18	53.1
With children under 18	68.4
6 to 17 years, none younger	76.0
Under 6 years	60.3
Under 3 years	57.1
Under 1 year	54.6
Men, total, 16 years and over	75.1

[1]Details for race and Hispanic origin groups will not add up because the data for the "other races" group are not presented and Hispanics are included in both the white and black population groups.

Source: Adapted from Table 1.1 (p. 49) in D. E. Herz and B. H. Wootton, "Women in the workforce: An overview." In C. Costello and B. K. Krimgold (eds.), *The American Woman: Where We Stand*. Englewood Cliffs, NJ: Norton. "Women in the workforce: An overview." In C. Costello and B. K. Krimgold (eds.), *The American Woman, 1996-1997: Where We Stand*. Englewood Cliffs, NJ: Norton.

cent of all women with four-year degrees were in the labor force in 1994 (Herz and Wootton 1996).

Despite dramatic increases in women's labor-force activity this century, women continue to be employed in a far more narrow range of occupations than their male counterparts (Dunn 1996; Reskin and Roos 1990). One third of all employed women in 1990 worked in just ten of the 503 detailed occupations listed in the census (Reskin and Padavic 1994). The term occupational segregation is used to refer to the concentration of same sex workers in an occupational category. This phenomenon, and its relationship to the pay gap between the sexes, will be discussed in more detail in Chapters 5 and 6. For now, it will suffice to note that women are overrepresented in lower-level positions in the workplace, and especially in those occupations that have lower rates of pay. Several factors contribute to the concentration of women in a narrow range of traditional occupations. They include gender role socialization (addressed in Unit Two), constraints resulting from work-family conflict (addressed in Unit Four), and also discrimination (Dunn 1996).

Approaching the Study of Working Women

The study of women and work is an interdisciplinary endeavor. The selections included in this text incorporate theory and research from sociology, psychology, management, economics, history, women's studies, and linguistics. The disciplinary perspective most useful in understanding women's work depends upon the questions one asks. For example, if one wants to examine the causes of the wage gap between the sexes, economics and sociology may provide the most guidance. If, however, one wants to know whether communications differences between the sexes block women's movement into high level managerial jobs, linguistics or management may provide the most insight.

Within disciplines, different theoretical approaches have developed to explain women's work experiences. One important characteristic that differentiates theories in several disciplines (e.g., sociology, economics, management) is whether they view women's work experiences as primarily affected by characteristics of individual women or by structural features of social institutions (e.g., economy, family). It is not always so easy to sort out the two types of influences. For example, at first glance, it might appear that observed differences in men's and women's styles of leadership (discussed in Chapter 14) result from personality differences between the sexes (individual characteristics). Further examination, however, would reveal that because women and men are differentially situated in work organizations, they face differing structures of opportunity and constraint (structural features). The fact that women managers are disproportionately located in low-status positions lacking in authority causes them to rely on more cooperative approaches to leadership. Put simply, women with limited power cannot successfully issue directives and orders (what some call a male-oriented management style); instead, they must enlist the cooperation and support of subordinates in order to gain their compliance (Colwil 1993). This is clearly a case where differences between the sexes result, at least in part, from features of social structure, specifically the structure of work organizations. It is common for individual characteristics to interact with structure so as to impact women's work.

An additional, important feature of much recent scholarship on women and work is its feminist orientation.[3] While many academic disciplines have been producing scholarship on women and work for decades, most of this early scholarship did not *focus* on women's work experiences (Stacey and Thorne 1985). The tendency in many disciplines prior to the 1980s, and often beyond, was to examine women's work experiences only in relation to men's, and thus, to depict male experience as the norm (Anderson 1988; Ward and Grant 1985). In other words, women and their work experiences were treated as the exception to the rule or a deviant case. Clearly it is no longer valid to portray working women as an exception to the rule, given that they now comprise nearly 50 percent of all workers. Feminist approaches to women and work position women's experiences at the center of inquiry, and as a result, often generate new knowledge. A feminist orientation also involves exploring the exploitation and oppression of women and a commitment to changing those conditions (Acker, et al. 1983). As noted earlier, feminists have long viewed the workplace as a promising arena for activism for social change to improve women's status. The selections that follow vary with respect to their degree of feminist emphasis, but all are feminist in the sense that they have as their *central* subject matter women's work.

Recent feminist scholarship on women and work is also sensitive to issues of diversity among women (Guy-Sheftal 1995). Women (and women workers) are not a homogeneous group. Race/ethnicity, social class, age, and sexual orientation interact to create differences among women and result in different life and workplace experiences. Subtle and overt forms of workplace discrimination faced by women of color, lesbians, and elderly women provide examples of the impact of difference on women's lives. The selections in this reader address, to varying degrees, issues of difference among women workers, and some selections focus on the impact of race/ethnicity and social class on women's work experiences (Chapters 8, 18, and 27).

The study of women and work can be undertaken using a variety of research methods. The selections that follow employ a range of data collection methods including observation, surveys, in-depth interviews, and existing records. Each approach carries strengths and weaknesses. Field-based methods (also called qualitative methods) such as observation and in-depth interviewing have the advantage of providing rich, descriptive information. They are especially well-suited for providing an "insider's view" of women's work experiences. The downside of these approaches is that the findings they generate cannot be assumed to hold true beyond the sample of women workers studied. Survey research techniques are especially useful for studying social issues that require generalizations based on large groups of people such as all working mothers, secretaries, or black professional women. The key disadvantage of surveys, however, is that compared to field methods, they have greater difficulty obtaining situational or contextual information. This is particularly troubling for the study of women and work, because a focus on women's experience as workers was relatively rare in most disciplines until the last few decades. For this reason, more of the selections in this text, particularly those contained in Unit Six, use observational and interview techniques to capture the voices and experiences of working women.

Not all of the selections in this reader are research-based. Some address women and work issues from an applied perspective. Authors of the selections contained herein represent several employment fields including journalist, career placement counselor, educator, and government task force representative. The varied background of the authors provides a well-rounded overview of women and workplace issues, but unfortunately, results on occasion in rather abrupt transitions in writing style. A critical reading of the selections should involve an assessment of how the occupation and/or academic discipline as well as personal history and social location of the author affects the perspective of what is written.

Endnotes

1. Volunteer work and coerced work (e.g., slavery) are other forms of unpaid work.

Women have also had high rates of participation in these forms of nonmarket work.

2. This linkage between women's work and their status relative to men is complicated by the fact that work is often under-valued simply because women perform it. This issue will be addressed later in discussions of comparable worth in Chapters 7 and 8.

3. Various feminist perspectives on women and work exist, including liberal feminism, Marxist feminism, socialist feminism, and radical feminism. For a discussion of these different perspectives see Kemp, Alice A., *Women's Work: Degraded and Devalued*, (Englewood Cliffs, NJ: Prentice Hall, 1994); Donovan, Josephine, *Feminist Theory: The Intellectual Traditions of American Feminism*, (New York: Ungar, 1987); and Tong, Rosemarie, *Feminist Thought: A Comprehensive Introduction*, (Boulder, CO: Westview Press, 1989).

References

Acker, J. 1988. "Women and work in the social sciences." In A. Stromberg and S. Harkess (eds.), *Women Working* 2nd Edition. Mountain View, CA: Mayfield Publishing:10-24.

_____, K. Barry, and J. Esseveld. 1983. "Objectivity and truth: Problems in doing feminist research." *Women's Studies International Forum*, 6:423-435.

Almquist, E. 1987. "Labor Market Gender Inequality in Minority Groups." *Gender and Society*. Vol. 1, No. 4, pp. 400-414.

_____. 1979. *Minorities, Gender and Work*. Lexington, KY: D. C. Heath.

Andersen, M. L. 1988. *Thinking About Women: Sociological Perspectives on Sex and Gender*. New York: Macmillan Publishing Company.

Anderson, K. 1988. "A history of women's work in the U.S." In A. Stromberg and S. Harkess, *Women Working*, 2nd Edition. Mountain View, CA: Mayfield Publishing:25-41.

Baca Zinn, M. and D. S. Eitzen. 1993. *Diversity in Families*. New York: Harper Collins.

Bernard, J. 1972. *The Future of Marriage*. New York: Bantam.

Boulding, E. 1976. "The historical roots of occupational segregation." *Signs*, 1:94-117.

Bradley, H. 1989. *Men's Work: Women's Work*. Minneapolis: University of Minnesota Press.

Bureau of Labor Statistics. 1995. *Employment and Earnings*. Washington, D.C.: U.S. Government Printing Office.

Chafetz, J. S. 1990. *Gender Equity: An Integrated Theory of Stability and Change*. Newbury Park, CA: Sage Publications, Inc.

_____. 1984. *Sex and Advantage: A Comparative, Macro-Structural Theory of Sex Stratification*. Totowa, NJ: Rowman and Allenheld.

Colwill, N. L. 1993. "Women in management: Power and powerlessness." In B. C. Long and S. E. Kahn (eds.), *Women Work and Coping*. Montreal: McGill-Queens University Press:73-89.

Costello, C. and B. Kivimac Krimgold (eds.). 1996. *The American Woman, 1996-1997: Where We Stand*. New York: Norton.

Cott, N. 1977. *The Bonds of Womenhood: 'Women's Sphere' in New England, 1780-1835*. New Haven: Yale University Press.

Daniel, R. L. 1987. *American Women in the 20th Century: The Festival of Life*. San Diego: Harcourt Brace Jovanovich.

Deckard, B. 1975. *The Women's Movement: Political, Socioeconomic and Psychological Issues*. New York: Harper and Row.

Donovan, J. 1987. *Feminist Theory: The Intellectual Traditions of American Feminism*. New York: Ungar.

Dunn, D. 1996. "Gender segregated occupations." In P. J. Dubeck and K. Borman (eds.), *Women and Work: A Handbook*. New York: Garland Publishing:91-93.

_____. 1995. "Sociological dimensions of economic conversion." In L. J. Dumas (ed.), *The Socio-Economics of Conversion from War to Peace*. Armonk, NY: M.E. Sharp:23-44.

_____, E. Almquist and J. Chafetz. 1993. "Macrostructural perspectives on gender stratification." In P. England (ed.), *Theory on Gender/Feminism on Theory*. New York: Aldine De Gruyter:69-90.

England, P. 1992. *Comparable Worth: Theories and Evidence*. New York: Aldine de Gruyter.

_____. and G. Farkas. 1986. *Households, Employment and Gender: A Social Economic and Demographic View*. Hawthorne, NY: Aldine Publishing Co.

Friedl, E. 1975. *Women and Men: An Anthropologist's View*. New York: Holt, Rinehart and Winston.

Guy-Sheftal, B. 1995. *Women's Studies: A Retrospective*. New York: Ford Foundation.

Hedley, R. A. 1992. *Making a Living: Technology and Change*. New York: Harper Collins.

Herz, D. E. and B. H. Wootton. 1996. "Women in the workforce: An overview." In C. Costello and B. Kivimac Krimgold (eds.), *The American Woman, 1996-1997: Where We Stand*. New York: Norton:44-78.

Kemp, A. A. 1994. *Women's Work: Degraded and Devalued*. Englewood Cliffs, NJ: Prentice Hall.

Kessler-Harris, A. 1982. *Out to Work: A History of Wage Earning Women in the United States*. New York: Oxford University Press.

Lenski, G. and J. Lenski. 1982. *Human Societies: An Introduction to Macrosociology*, 4th Ed. New York: McGraw Hill.

_____. 1966. *Power and Privilege: A Theory of Social Stratification*. New York: McGraw-Hill.

Matthaei, J. A. 1982. *An Economic History of Women in America: Women's Work, the Sexual Division of Labor and the Development of Capitalism*. New York: Schocken Brooks.

Matthews, G. 1987. *Just a Housewife: The Rise and Fall of Domesticity in America*. New York: Oxford University Press.

Montagna, P. D. 1977. *Occupations and Society: Toward a Sociology of the Labor Market*. New York: John Wiley and Sons.

Nielsen, J. 1990. *Sex and Gender in Society: Perspectives on Stratification*, 2nd Edition. Prospect Heights, IL: Waveland Press.

_____. 1978. *Sex in Society: Perspectives on Stratification*. Belmont, CA: Wadsworth.

Ortiz, V. 1994. "Women of color: A demographic overview." In M. Baca Zinn and B. T. Dill (eds.), *Women of Color in U. S. Society*. Philadelphia, PA: Temple University Press:13-40.

O'Toole, J., E. Hansot, W. Herman, N. Herrick, E. Libow, B. Lusignan, H. Richman, H. Sheppard, B. Stephansky, and J. Wright. 1973. *Work in America*. Cambridge, MA: MIT Press.

Pavalko, R. M. 1988. *Sociology of Occupations and Professions*. Itasca, IL: Peacock.

Reskin, B. and I. Padavic. 1994. *Women and Men at Work*. Thousand Oaks, CA: Pine Forge Press.

_____. and P. A. Roos. 1990. *Job Queues, Gender Queues: Explaining Women's Inroads into Male Occupations*. Philadelphia, PA: Temple University Press.

Sanday, P. R. 1981. *Female Power and Male Dominance*. Cambridge: Cambridge University Press.

Sapiro, V. 1994. *Women in American Society*. Palo Alto, CA: Mayfield Publishing.

Sokoloff, N. 1992. *Black Women and White Women in the Professions*. New York: Routledge.

Stacey, J. and B. Thorne. 1985. "The missing feminist revolution in sociology." *Social Problems*, 32:4(April):301-316

Tong, R. 1989. *Feminist Thought: A comprehensive Introduction*. Boulder, CO: Westview Press.

U. S. Bureau of the Census. 1990. *Census of the Population*. CP-S-1, Supplementary Reports, Detailed Occupation and Other Characteristics from the EEO File for the States.

Ward, K. B. and L. Grant. 1985. "The feminist critique and a decade of published research in sociology journals." *The Sociological Quarterly*, 26(2):139-157.

Yorburg, B. 1987. "Sexual identity in human history." In J. Stimson and A. Stimson (eds.), *Sociology: Contemporary Readings*. Itasca, IL: F. E. Peacock Publishers.

Zavella, P. 1987. *Women's Work and Chicano Families: Cannery Workers of the Santa Clara Valley*. Ithaca, NY: Cornell University Press. ✦

Unit One

Becoming Workers: Girls' Socialization for Employment

What did you want to be when you grew up? I wanted to be a teacher—not a college professor, my current occupation, but rather, a public school teacher. Playing "school" was my favorite pastime, and I was constantly on the lookout for playmates who were willing to be my students. What was the source of my early occupational aspiration? My mother was a full-time homemaker, so my career plans did not result from modeling my mother. The fact that public school teaching is and has long been a heavily female-dominated occupation meant that my early aspirations were gender-traditional. Socialization messages from a variety of sources likely influenced my early desire to be a teacher. Television shows, the books I read, even the staffing patterns in my schools all delivered the same message— teaching is for women. I was not oblivious to these messages; I translated them into my career goals. The reading selections in this unit address how the process of sex role socialization shapes girls' work aspirations and eventual experiences.

Sex role socialization is a process that begins at the moment of birth when male and female infants are handled differently by caretakers and continues throughout the childhood years (Karraker et al. 1995; Rubin et al. 1974). Parents typically teach their children to behave in accordance with traditional sex roles. This learning is reinforced by sex role socialization in the school and peer group, by the media, and from other sources. The result is that we internalize our gender, the learned behaviors and expectations associated with our biological sex. This learning sets us on a course for adulthood and the many roles we will play, as spouses/partners, parents, and workers.

Early views on behavioral differences between the sexes did not emphasize the importance of socialization in acquiring gendered behavior. Instead, traditional understandings of differences between the sexes centered on the role of biology in creating sex differences. Even today it is not uncommon for conventional wisdom to suggest that "boys will

15

be boys" and "girls are the way they are" due to the influence of biology. For example, you may have heard explanations offered for the dearth of women in high level management jobs that center on women's natural absence of aggressiveness (often attributed to hormonal patterns) or explanations as to why women are not likely to pursue careers in math and science that focus on a presumed lack of ability (often attributed to brain structure and methods of processing visual/spatial information). Increasingly, as scientific research places these biologically deterministic explanations of behavioral differences between the sexes under scrutiny, they are revealed to be incorrect, or at best incomplete.[1] Yet, to the extent that people believe in biologically based differences between the sexes, they continue to influence job choices and opportunities. If an employer is confident that men make better managers because they are naturally more aggressive or that women won't devote adequate amounts of attention to a demanding job because of their innate desire to nurture children, then it is not difficult to predict who will be promoted to fill the next Vice President vacancy.

With the knowledge that sex role socialization encourages girls to prepare for and pursue traditional women's occupations, research began to focus on exploring the subtle, and sometimes not so subtle, processes through which this occurs. Studies have revealed how teachers' expectations of sex-linked differences in math ability lead them to encourage boys and neglect girls in math instruction (Fox, Fennema, and Sherman 1977). They have also shown how even the most well-intentioned parents, as a result of their own gender traditional upbringing, might encourage daughters to limit their aspirations and become adult women who derive rewards not from their own, but their husband's accomplishments (Lindsey 1994).

Our socialization patterns and practices are a product of our culture. Some would argue that they cannot be changed without a fundamental restructuring of society. Yet it is often true that our actions lag behind our attitudes, that we behave according to yesterday's beliefs (or even the last decade's). To the extent that this is true with respect to attitudes concerning gender and employment, it points up the importance of educating adult socialization agents (e.g., parents, teachers) about the consequences of encouraging gender stereotypes. Gender stereotypes, preset assumptions about individuals based on knowledge of their sex, commonly portray men as strong, competent, and rational and women as nurturing, weak, and emotional. Endorsing these gender stereotypes means assuming that women and men are predisposed to different types of work roles. For parents, it means shaping their children, through socialization, to fit the stereotypes. For employers, it means assuming that job candidates adhere to the stereotypes even when they do not. The end result involves artificially restricting the employment opportunities of both sexes, and, in particular, discouraging the achievement of women.

The selections that follow address how women become workers as a result of their sex role socialization. In the first reading, Kelly explores the contributions of biology and social learning to gendered behavior, with an emphasis on how these factors contribute to women's preparation for and orientation toward work. She provides specific examples of previously held assumptions of biological differences between the sexes, shows how new information has led to the rejection of these assumptions, and illustrates the impact of these understandings on the educational and work experiences of women. Kelly also provides an overview of the many different agents of sex role socialization, including the family, teachers, books, television, and the peer group and discusses how they impact the work aspirations of girls. Her contribution establishes a foundation for further exploration of sex socialization for employment as it occurs in specific settings.

In the second selection, Freeman probes, in depth, the role the family plays in socializing gender. She shows, based on her in-depth interviews with women in managerial career tracks, how parents (particularly mothers) influenced career choice and success. Interview excerpts from her research provide examples of the salience of parental expectations and perspectives on education, independence, and gender for daughters' work experiences. Freeman's research is important not only because she provides evidence of the importance of parents as role models for occupational choice, but also because she reveals that women who followed gender-traditional paths often expected more of their daughters, encouraging them to "Do as I say, not as I have done."

In the next section, Orenstein turns our attention to the schools and the ways in which primary- and secondary-level education affect girls' self esteem and levels of confidence. She begins by noting the rather depressing findings of the American Association of University Women (AAUW) survey—that the sharp decline in adolescent girls' self esteem can be attributed, in large part, to gender-biased patterns in our schools. Motivated by the AAUW survey, Orenstein spends a year interviewing and observing students, teachers, and administrators in two middle schools. She describes her observations of rampant gender bias in the classroom, providing concrete examples of teachers favoring boys and ignoring girls, and uses the students' own words to convey girls' feelings of discouragement. Orenstein also discusses her observations of how school experiences differentially impact girls in different racial/ethnic groups. Her selection informs the study of women and work in that it provides insight into the social origins of the lack of confidence and achievement orien-

tation exhibited by many talented and able women workers.

Matyas extends Orenstein's look at the role of the schools in socializing gender differences by focusing on factors that affect women's interest in and preparation for science and scientific careers. She discusses how both classroom experiences and math/science curricula contribute to low numbers of women in scientific careers. Matyas emphasizes research findings which show that girls' failure to take science courses results not from poor grades or a lack of ability, but from attrition caused by sex role stereotypes. She concludes by noting that our increasingly technological society needs the "brain power" of the many capable girls who are being discouraged from preparing for scientific careers, providing an excellent example of how the restrictions imposed by traditional sex socialization harm not only women, but also the larger society.

Endnote

1. For further discussion of the debunking of myths about biologically-based gender differences and gender bias in science, see A. Fausto-Sterling, *Myths of Gender*, New York: Basic Books, 1985; and N. Tuana (ed.), *Feminism and Science*, Bloomington, IN: Indiana University Press, 1989.

References

Fox, L. H., E. Fennema and T. Sherman (eds.). 1977. *Women and Mathematics: Research Perspectives for Change*. Washington, D.C.: National Institute of Education.

_____, D. Tobin, and L. Buedy. 1979. "Sex role socialization in mathematics." In M. A. Wittig and A. C. Peterson (eds.), *Sex-Related Differences in Cognitive Functioning*. New York: Academic Press.

Karraker, K. H., D. A. Vogel, and M. A. Lake. 1995. "Parents' Gender-Stereotyped Perceptions of Newborns: The Eye of the Beholder, Revisited". *Sex Roles*, 33(9-10):687-701.

Lindsey, L. L. 1994. *Gender Roles: A Sociological Perspective*. Englewood Cliffs, NJ: Prentice Hall.

Rubin, J. Z., F. J. Provenzano, and Z. Luria. 1974. "The eye of the beholder: Parents' views on sex of newborns." *American Journal of Orthopsychiatry*, 44(4):512-519.

Weitzman, L. J. 1979. "Sex role socialization: A focus on women." In J. Freeman (ed.), *Women: A Feminist Perspective*, 3rd Ed. Palo Alto, CA: Mayfield. ✦

1

Gender Culture and Socialization

Rita Mae Kelly

Society, it is said, is like " 'a gigantic Alcatraz,' a prison of already constructed definitions" (Berger and Luckman 1966; Farganis 1986). Humans enter into a world already shaped by gender, class, race, ethnicity, nationality, and existing sociopolitical economic systems. As Sondra Farganis (1986) notes:

> One's life is lived by learning from others—significant others, generalized others, agents of socialization—what one must do to make it through the terrain of lived experience. Who one is—that is, the already existent class and status into which one is born—determines how the terrain is traversed almost as predictably as will one's eye color, or ear length, or predisposition to a genetic problem such as Tay-Sachs or sickle cell anemia. One's socially ascribed status is pre-set, "there," a vise into which one's particular self is placed and away from which one can move with varying degrees of ease or difficulty. (p. 48)

Gender culture is a generic term for the variety of ways in which persons are shaped by socialized sex-role expectations and ways in which sex differences are manifested. Clearly, the meaning of being a man or a woman, of being masculine or feminine, has altered considerably in the 20th century. Up to the 1970s and the Women's Movement, male and female were strongly associated with bipolar notions of masculinity and femininity. In the 1970s androgyny became popular, the no-

tion that the ideal person, particularly the ideal professional, was a person who shared the instrumental masculine self with the more expressive feminine self.

In the 1980s androgyny retreated in popularity among socialization experts and a more multiplistic and pluralistic approach to gender appeared. Concern existed that androgyny produced a "hollow identity" (Mednick 1988; Morawski 1987; Sarbin and Scheibe 1983). Ascribed roles were confused with and negated by attained roles. A female's feminine identity was subsumed or totally absorbed by her worker identity. Many did not appreciate the loss of the "vive la difference" notion between the sexes. Homogeneity was not necessarily what was desired or what constituted empirical reality. Nonetheless, the parallel between androgyny and liberal equality retains appeal to many scholars, particularly liberal feminists, as well as to activists.

Although the terms of the debate change over time, consensus exists that sex and gender differences remain. Important questions are, which parts of the gender culture are malleable, and which ones are likely to be found unchangeable, due to biology or consistency in socialization processes?

Analyses of sex roles have focused on three basically different orientations: social biology, social learning, and social cognition. Biological analyses rely heavily on the reproductive, physical, and hormonal differences between males and females. Social learning theories focus on how rewards and punishments shape sex-role behaviors. Social cognition theories identify cognitive "schemas" or "scripts" as the core of sex-role development. In recent years the latter two theories have blended together in some ways (Kendrick 1987). Both stress that children learn an ill-defined, fuzzy set of sex-role schemas associated with their culture, which they then apply in their behavior and identity development. More recently, scholars have stressed the interaction among the organism, the environment, and cognition.

Biological Differences

Sex differences are associated with biological differences. Historically, it was widely believed that men and women differed sharply in intellectual and physical abilities, in addition to differing in reproductive capacities. For example, until the 1980s the stereotypical, as well as the "scientific" view, was that males were superior in their mathematical abilities, were more aggressive, and had greater visual-spatial acuity, while females possessed superior verbal ability (Maccoby and Jacklin 1974). Indeed, to be male or to be female was, for most practical purposes, to be classified into mutually exclusive categories.

By the 1990s most of these views had changed dramatically. Among scientists some consensus still exists that males more readily deal with algebra than females, but recent studies reveal no meaningful differences with regard to arithmetic or geometry (Powell 1988). In addition, it is now recognized that girls tend to do as well as boys when they take math classes; the difference is that the girls opt out of taking such classes at much higher rates than boys. By the time adulthood is attained, the percentage differences as well as the actual math abilities between the sexes are considerable (Anastasi 1985).

Males are also still thought to be more adept at selected aspects of visual-spatial ability, but it is no longer concluded that they have across-the-board superiority. Differences in verbal ability are now considered less significant (Powell 1988), although females still perform better than males at all ages in perceptual speed, the ability "to perceive details quickly and accurately and to shift attention from one item to the next rapidly" (Hyde 1985). Some social development experts still see an overall female advantage in verbal ability and a male advantage in mathematical

and visual-spatial ability (Grusec and Lytton 1988).

The gender difference found in visual-spatial ability has been projected to cognitive style in a way negative to women (Witkin 1964). From a series of experiments with a rod and a frame tilted at various angles, it was discovered that men made fewer errors than women in adjusting the rod to the true vertical without the frame. From this finding Witkin (1964) and his colleagues concluded that men had an independent cognitive style, whereas women had a field dependent style. As Hyde (1985, p. 196) notes, it would be just as accurate, perhaps more accurate, and certainly less pejorative to women, if the authors had concluded that "women are context-sensitive and men are context-insensitive."

Although it is now thought that both men and women can be equally aggressive, it appears that different stimuli trigger the aggression. Men are more likely to initiate aggression and to respond to physical challenges whereas women are more likely to get angry because of unfair treatment (Powell 1988). Girls also appear to be more likely to take steps to avoid quarrels and to self-select out of high conflict/dominance situations whereas boys are inclined to seek them out (Gilligan 1982). Reviews of multiple studies of sex differences in nurturance and aggressiveness reveal that females tend to be more nurturing as adults as well as during childhood, and that in a variety of cultures males are consistently found to be more aggressive, more physical, and more dominance-oriented (Grusec and Lytton 1988).

Other studies have found a link between nonverbal expressions of dominance and sexual attractiveness. "Dominant males were seen as more sexually attractive in three studies; no such relationship was found for females" (Kendrick 1987, p. 35).

In previous eras these differences— and many others—were thought to be biologically determined and unchangeable. Today more confidence exists that education and socialization can provide individuals with sufficient levels of skill, whether in mathematics, verbal, or analytical ability, to compete with members of either sex. As the debate over Scholastic Aptitude Test (SAT) scores makes clear, many achievement-related sex differences were created by the wording of tests, not by biological differences (Evangelauf 1989; Waters 1989). Moreover, it is now recognized that at least half of the top 1% of people with the highest IQs are female. The lack of public achievements by women are not the result of native ability. Explanations must be sought elsewhere.

Today, most sex differences are viewed as variations in degrees rather than dualistic opposites. Figure 1.1 illustrates the switch in thinking. The bell-shaped curves depicting male and female abilities overlap considerably, indicating that on average, even when differences exist between the sexes, the differences do not signify mutually exclusive abilities or skills.

Figure 1.1
Notions of Sex Differences

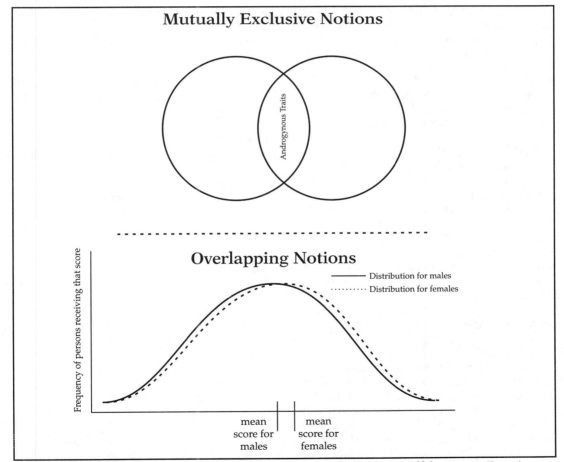

Source: The bottom figure depicting Overlapping Notions is adapted from Half the Human Experience: The Psychology of Women, 3d ed. (p.140), ed. J.S. Hyde (Lexington, MA: D.C. Health,1985). Reprinted by permission.

Even when one sex is thought to have an advantage (such as males are thought to have in algebra and coordination of most body movements), large numbers and percentages of women will still be superior to large numbers and percentages of men. Society is clearly better off using female talents than not using them and relying on less capable males. In addition, the variation in ability among males, even mathematical and visual-spatial ability, is substantially greater than the ability differences between males and females. Among females, less sharp extremes in ability and performance occur (Grusec and Lytton 1988). Group variations within each sex are sufficient to permit large numbers of women to compete on equal footing with large numbers of men. With regard to major workplace issues, at any point of the bell-shaped curve (Figure 1.1), differences between men and women are less significant than differences among women themselves and among men themselves.

As new technologies enable individuals to perform tasks previously accomplished by manual labor, the traditionally male occupations that require physical strength, like the military, will increasingly rely on people trained to operate sophisticated machinery (Witherspoon 1988). Although women are demonstrating competence in meeting these changing needs (Laboda 1990), not all women are suited to all such physically demanding jobs. The gradual movement of women into such positions has, however, helped to break down myths suggesting that women are physically inferior.

Women's migration into the military and law enforcement has accompanied an increasing support of women's participation in sports. Women were barred from entering the original Olympic Games in 1896; they now compete in most events. Five women now serve on the International Olympic Committee. Additionally, small but growing numbers of women serve at every level of international sport

(De Frantz 1988). This international competition has set a precedent for expanded participation in sports by women at all levels of the U.S. society. Title IX has also opened opportunities on school athletic teams for women. Before the passage of this law, which limits discrimination against students, faculty, and staff in federally assisted education programs, women accounted for only 7% of interscholastic athletes, and no colleges offered women's athletic scholarships. By 1982, women accounted for 35% of the interscholastic athletes, and by 1984, more than 10,000 athletic scholarships were offered to women (Bohlig 1988). Sociologist Susan Greendorfer has argued that, by playing in high school and college sports, men gain "an incredible advantage, because most workplaces are structured on a competitive model" (Bloch 1989, p. 138). *Health* magazine editor Gordon Bakoulis Bloch comments, "Sports have always been part of the glue that has kept the old-boy network alive and kicking; now women can reap the same benefits from the contacts they make through sports" (1989, p. 138). American businesswomen not only have demonstrated an interest in playing and following professional sports, they have also found that sports talk can open doors with new clients (Friedman 1989). This change in understanding of the nature of sex differences has opened important new workplace opportunities for women.

In the 1980s, even the assumption that only women can carry and nurse a child was being challenged, as efforts were made to enable men to have fetuses implanted in their abdomens and devices were developed to facilitate a baby sucking from the father. Test tube babies and genetic engineering in general have opened new doors for cross-sex behavior that once would have been considered absolutely impossible. Advances in reproductive technology, especially in birth control and abortion, have also reduced the ease with which reproductive differences can be used to establish dichotomous, mutually exclusive differences between the sexes. Only the most naive or the most rigid believers in sex differences can still argue that biology is destiny and that, because of physiological differences, males belong in one sphere of life and females in another.

Environmental Factors

Simone de Beauvoir once wrote that, "one is not born a woman, but rather becomes a woman" (1952, p. 301). We learn, we imitate, we identify. We are socialized by our parental family, school, religion, friends/peers, the mass media, and the organizations and people with whom we work. Gender differences in socialization that have relevance for career choices and success abound. These differences are thought to be particularly meaningful in terms of shaping ambition, skill development, moral development, attitudes toward power, and behavioral/leadership styles.

The Family

Imitation of same-sex models, particularly parents, is recognized as central to the socialization process. Boys will tend to imitate their fathers or a favored older male, whereas girls will tend to imitate their mothers or a favored older female. If these parents act out and believe in the traditional sex-role stereotypes, they are likely to reward boys for being leaders, encouraging competitiveness, autonomy, aggressiveness, and independence, and to discourage girls from similar behavior. Seeing that they are rewarded for being gentle, caring, nurturing, and supportive of others, girls respond increasingly in these ways until such behavior becomes habitual. To break out of this pattern is difficult.

In the 1980s, increasing numbers of parents chose a more egalitarian approach to child rearing, expecting girls as well as boys to be competitive in sports, to excel in math and science, to be independent, and to be leaders. In addition, as more and more mothers worked outside the home, it became increasingly likely that daughters would have as their mothers female role models who themselves had successful careers. Imitation of professional and managerial mothers facilitates similar career success in daughters, just as imitation of professional and managerial fathers facilitates similar career success in sons (Kelly and Boutilier 1988).

Ambition typically precedes achievement. Parents who hold egalitarian views about sex-roles tend to expect their daughters to perform well in school and to have high career aspirations. Yet, they also expect their daughters to use the family as a referent more than their sons. Beginning early in childhood, girl's play is focused on mimicking family life and responsibilities. In 1966 and in 1975, less than 6% of high school and college women did not intend to marry (Donelson 1977). Moreover, even in the 1980s, a majority of girls still gave "mother" or "wife" as their primary occupational goal; young boys seldom mentioned "father" or "husband" as their career aspiration (Greenglass and Devins 1982).

Males also use the family as a referent. The outcome is different, however, because their experience in an intact family is different. Men are assumed to need and/or deserve more leisure time and greater freedom from housework and other caretaking functions. Women are assumed to accept these family and nurturing responsibilities as central to their womanhood. These differences in orientation toward the family and the adult responsibility that women and men are expected to have within the family and in their roles as wife/husband, mother/father, daughter/son, and initiator or receiver of sexual interest strongly influence career opportunities in the workplace.

One consequence of the differential emphasis on family responsibilities is that, even in egalitarian family environments, girls more often than boys tend to opt for occupations more compatible with child care responsibilities, such as being an elementary rather than a university teacher, or being a nurse instead of a doctor, or being a science technician rather than a scientist or engineer. Societal patterns become norms to be followed rather than simply choices that other generations have made (Kendrick 1987).

To achieve one needs to be ambitious; to be ambitious means one must be motivated. Studies consistently show that "adult sex differences in cognitive abilities are motivational, and that motivational differences lead to different learning experiences" (Kendrick 1987, p. 24). This motivational difference is found to be related to the "reliably more persistent and single-minded pursuit of high levels of occupational achievement among males, but only small differences in abilities" (Kendrick 1987, p. 24). It is also found to have significant influence on girls' decisions to take or avoid mathematics in high school and college. Given that mathematics is the "critical filter" for jobs in the core economy and high-prestige professions, such as engineering, medicine, computer science, the physical sciences, and business, it is vital to reverse the decision of girls not to take math (Sherman 1982). Gender equity and parity in career success will not occur if skills to compete are not obtained.

Studies of factors affecting career choices of females in the labor force indicate that entrepreneurs and managers both:

> . . . scored higher than did secretaries in achieving motivation, locus of control, internality, and sex role 'masculinity.' . . . Women owners had more parental models, both mothers and fathers, who had engaged in occupational ownership than did either the managers or secretaries. This suggests that very early experience may be significant in determining important career behaviors that are seen later in life. (Osipow 1987, p. 274)

Two studies in 1985 show that "the motivation influences of aspiration, mastery, and career commitment are significantly related to the background, personal, and environmental dimensions" (Osipow 1987, p. 273). H.S. Farmer (1985) finds that the environmental changes are having a significant effect on girls' career and achievement motivations, reflecting again the impact of the Women's Movement and the demand for female labor. Farmer also found a change in boys; they are not anticipating playing a shared role in parenting as well as having a career. In the same study, girls were found to have higher career aspirations than boys.

The critical role of parents in sex-role development can hardly be overstated. Studies consistently show that both mothers and fathers impact their child's sex-role identity and that fathers are much more likely to be traditional in the roles and behaviors they encourage. "The process of [sex-role] differentiation is attributed to the powerful socialization pressures of the family and society through differential reinforcement and the process of identification with the same sex parent" (Shepherd-Look 1982, p. 412). The power of parental sex-role expectations on themselves and their children can be seen in several findings: a baby dressed in pink and labeled a girl will be given dolls, labeled cuddly, weaker, smaller, softer, and more finely featured than a baby dressed in blue and labeled a boy; and girls will be smiled at and parents will do things for them—rewarding them for dependent behavior. Boys, on the other hand, will be taught how to do a task and praised for their independence and ability. Fathers, in particular, are found to stress competence, task performance, achievement, careers, and occupational success for their sons, but to reinforce dependency behavior on parts of daughters (Shepherd-Look 1982). It is almost self-evident that parents who do not encourage achievement and career ambition for their daughters will be less likely to provide them with the financial, emotional, and other intellectual supports required to obtain the educational and other human capital training needed to succeed. The professional mother becomes important here, not only as a role model, but also as the source that can ensure availability of such resources (Kelly and Boutilier 1988).

According to Nancy Chodorow (1978), early childhood socialization accounts for much of the difference in adult masculine and feminine characteristics. The difference stems from the way gender identity is formed for males and females. Females achieve gender identity in the ongoing relationship with their mother. They are taught relational and empathetic skills and their identity is forged within the family relationship. In contrast, males are encouraged to develop independence and organizational skills. They must separate from their mothers in order to achieve a masculine identity, thus their individuation and self-concept are forged in relation to the larger world.

These differences in psychological development are thought to affect not only the way an individual perceives him or herself but also society's view of the individual. When societal expectations or role demands meet self-concept, the result is often individual confusion. This confusion is thought to be greater for females on the average than for males simply because their orientation to the larger world has been more limited (Chodorow 1978). By the same token, their self-image lacks individuation, as they view themselves functioning only in relationship to the whole. Female ethical concerns highlight relationship and understanding; as a result relationship often takes precedence over achievement. Socialization literature stresses that females are more cooperative, more empathetic, and emphasize interpersonal relationships much more than males—from childhood through advanced age (Grusec and Lytton 1988). A consequence of this gender difference is that, when individual achievement is highlighted, women often experience a higher degree of success anxiety when that achievement is perceived to be at the expense of another. Numerous observers argue that these differences in socialization lead to substantial differences in managerial and decision-making styles as adults.

From 1960 to 1988, the number of female-headed households (single or divorced) raising children alone more than tripled. More than one of five children live with only one parent (U.S. Bureau of the Census 1989). Usually it is the father who is absent, raising the question, "Does a father's absence make a difference in a girl's sex-role development?" Studies show that no effect is found on preadolescent girls, but that effects do appear during adolescence. Girls without fathers showed more anxiety and discomfort around males, and tended to be more sexually precocious and "inappropriately aggressive" toward males (Shepherd-Look 1982). Girls from divorced families tend to marry earlier, be pregnant when they marry, and be less satisfied with their partner, ultimately leading to more divorces.

Birth Order and Social Class

Birth order and social class have also been found to be important mediators of sex-role socialization and career success (Basow 1980; Hess and Sussman 1984; Weitzman 1975). Birth order studies show that high achievers are more likely to be first born, only children, or last born. For both sexes, family size, the number and gender of siblings, relationship to parents, and social class interact with birth order to impact career success. In general, birth order is important because, as the first or only child (or the last), the child is more likely to receive financial resources and more attention, both of which are essential for success. Many female achievers have not only been first born, they also have had no brothers, suggesting that having no competition for such resources from males was critical (Crawford 1977; Lott 1973; Mednick, Tangri and Hoffman 1975). In the 1980s, as the average number of children declined to less than 2.0, such birth order concerns undoubtedly have less impact.

Studies of successful women in the 1970s debated whether achieving women were deviants or the products of an enriched environment (Almquist and Angrist 1971). Research supported the enrichment perspective. For example, all female presidents and vice presidents of U.S. businesses in a 1977 study of managerial women were first-born children who felt special as children, had parents with high educational levels, and a mother with a strong employment record with positive feelings toward her work (Hennig and Jardim 1977). Similar patterns were found among the very highest female political leaders (Kelly and Boutilier 1988).

Adolescence, Peers, and the Opposite Sex

Adolescence has been a critical point in the development of achievement and ambition for girls. Until reaching puberty, girls are encouraged to excel as much as boys. Then, in preparation for adulthood, which historically meant wifehood and motherhood, the stress switched to the adoption of feminine attitudes and behaviors. Academic excellence, achievement, and femininity have historically *not* been viewed as being compatible (Hyde 1985). The impact on self-concept has been considerable. For example, although gender differences are small in elementary school, by the eleventh and twelfth grades girls were found to be significantly more concerned with being liked and were more self-conscious, whereas boys were more concerned with achievement and competence (Rosenberg and Simmons 1975).

Numerous studies have found that sex roles mediate intellectual accomplishments and achievement aspirations (Shepherd-Look 1982). Children, and adolescents in particular, strive to be consistent with their self-defined gender categorization. "Simply labeling a task as appropriate for either boys or girls has had the effect of increasing expectancy for success, appeal of the game, task persistence, qual-

ity of performance, and achievement level attained . . . when the task was sex-appropriate" (Shepherd-Look 1982, p. 425). Girls and women are consistently found to have higher success expectations and higher performance standards when the area of achievement was considered appropriate for females (Anderson 1988; Hoener 1969; Stein and Bailey 1973). In addition, the females showing the greatest fear of achievement were those with the strongest traditional sex-role expectations (Shepherd-Look 1982). The fear of success syndrome appears to be a fear of inappropriate sex-role behavior (Deaux 1976).

If women are to be achievement oriented and successful in careers, the female sex role needs to be perceived as more compatible with achievement-oriented behaviors, and males need to become accepting of that behavior. These data draw attention to the importance of role models of the same sex, and highlight again why having a successful mother in a positive relationship with an adult male (spouse or significant other) is so critical to the self-esteem and achievement aspirations of the daughter.

Another difficulty in developing female achievers concerns the dating game. Because girls mature at a faster rate than boys, they tend to seek and date older males who, because of their age, are more knowledgeable and more experienced. This differential establishes a pattern of deference and an assumption that men are more likely to be knowledgeable about the world than women (Hyde 1985). Historically, girls did not have the option of taking the initiative in the dating game. Rather, they had to use their appearance and "feminine wiles" to attract males. One longitudinal study of fifth- and sixth-grade girls, begun in the 1930s, found that the more attractive girls had, as women, married the most well-to-do, successful men (Elder 1969). This demonstrated that, as late as the 1960s, "a woman's status [was] determined by her appearance, a man's by his achievements" (Hyde 1985, p. 163).

In the 1980s, dating patterns changed, enabling girls to take the initiative. Relationships came to be more emphasized than marriage. In 1970, 35.8% of all U.S. women age 20 to 24 had never married; by 1987, that percentage had risen to 60.8% (U.S. Bureau of the Census 1989). The reduced interest in early marriage reflected the pursuit of more education for young women and an effort to resist the constraints associated with the wife/mother role.

Television

Children in the United States watch an average of 20 hours or more of television each week, and television plays a major role in most children's lives before they learn to read and write (Morgan and Signorielli 1990). The content of television shows can shape viewers' conception of gender roles (Durkin 1985), and television can have considerable impact on children's perceptions of gender. The influence of TV on the development of children's gender identities raised concern in the 1970s (Dambrot, Reep and Bell 1988). One 1974 study of shows popular at the time found only 34 significant female characters, "and those were presented in very traditional female roles characterized by dependence and over-emotionalism. There was not a single instance in which a married woman worked outside the home" (Shepherd-Look 1982, p. 426).

Fortunately television shows have changed substantially over the last 15 years. Women in such shows as *Murphy Brown*, *The Cosby Show*, and even *Star Trek—The Next Generation* express nontraditional attitudes and pursue careers. Nevertheless, while the number of female main characters has significantly increased over the 1980s, women are still underrepresented. A 1989 study by Signorielli found that nearly 71% of prime time characters are men, while only 29% are women (Signorielli 1989). This study also revealed that women were more likely than men to be identified by their marital status (59% of women compared to 32% of men), more likely to be engaged in housework (20% of women compared to 3% of men), more likely to be pursuing a romantic relationship, and more likely to be victimized. Although some women characters do have successful careers, "less than a third of the married women and half of the single and formerly married women are portrayed as working outside the home." Three-fourths of male characters are identified by an occupation outside the home (Signorielli 1989, pp. 350-351). Even commercials create false gender expectations by portraying successful women as primarily young and beautiful (Kimball 1988). If children's acceptance of women's advancement is to improve, the media portrayal of women must also continue to improve.

Printed Matter

Children's literature has historically been very male-centered. A 1971 study of the Caldecott Award winning books discovered that most stories were about boys, men, male animals, or male adventures (Nilsen 1971). A follow-up 1972 study found that males appeared in pictures 11 times more frequently than females and that "most of the women in picture books have status by virtue of their relationships to specific men—they are the wives of the kings, judges, adventurers, and explorers, but they themselves are not the rulers, judges, adventurers, and explorers" (Shepherd-Look 1982, p. 426).

Like television programming, children's literature has also improved its portrayal of gender roles. Follow-up studies on the Caldecott Award winners in the 1980s found that, by 1985, the ratio of male to female characters has risen from a low of 78% males to 22% females in the period from 1971 to 1975 to 57% males to 43% females in the period from 1981 to 1985 (Dougherty and Engel 1987). The ratio of illustrations of men and women also improved from 75% males to 17% females in the period from 1976 to 1980 to 63%

males to 37% females in the period from 1981 to 1985 (Doughtery and Engel 1987). Again, these statistics demonstrate that male bias continues to permeate the media socializing American children; however, this improvement can allow future business leaders to better appreciate women's contributions. Gayle Kimball, a professor of women's studies at California State University, Chico, notes that parents can help shape their children's attitudes by screening books their children read (Kimball 1988).

The Schools

Schools have been notorious for perpetuating the traditional sex-role stereotypes. Teachers consistently pay more attention to boys than girls. They also tend to reward males for independence and task performance and reward females for passivity and dependence behavior. By giving different feedback to each sex, they can instill a learned helplessness in girls (Dweck and Goetz 1977; Greenberg 1988). In the classroom setting, girls "receive less teacher attention than boys, unless girls stay physically close to the teacher and lose needed opportunities for inventive and independent experiences." Greenberg continues, "boys receive attention whether they stay near to or far from the teacher" (Greenberg 1988, p. 462).

Schools often have sex-typed tracking systems as well, with higher proportions of girls going into English, history, and the social sciences at the college preparatory track, and more males going into the physical sciences and math. In vocational areas, girls are channeled into home economics, typing, and bookkeeping, whereas boys are channeled more into mechanical and technical courses.

Textbooks and tests also perpetuate traditional sex-roles. Even in 1990, women are rarely pictured as political leaders, scientists, and public achievers. An analysis of 24 best-selling teacher education texts reveals that, as educators, teachers are not being made aware of the problem of sexism in the classroom. Of the 24 texts re-

viewed, 23 gave less than 1% of their space to the issue of sexism; one-third did not mention sexism at all; not a single text provided future teachers with curricular resources or strategies to counteract sexism in the classroom (Sadker and Sadker 1988). The content of textbooks for students gives the basic message that females are less important and less visible than males. In addition, educational achievement tests contain more male than female pronouns and references. Item content analysis of social science texts also revealed that the majority of the professors, doctors, presidents of companies, and members of professional teams, as well as famous persons in history, were male. Moreover, most biographies were about men. When women or girls did appear, they were more often portrayed in passive roles and/or sterotyped occupations (Hahn and Bernard-Powers 1988).

Conclusion

The fact that changes in many of the historically more negative patterns of socialization for girls have occurred cannot be disputed. Yet remnants of the impact of these patterns on female aspirations and achievement potential remain. The women trying to move up the career ladder in the 1990s, who are now in their mid-thirties and forties, were socialized during a more traditional period. Studies of the female identity patterns of this age group during adolescence revealed three different approaches: being traditional, anticipating no career and being a wife/mother; being achievement- and success-oriented for oneself with no intention of marrying or having children; and finally being bimodal and committed to both family and career, the "superwoman" of the 1980s (Dellas and Gaier 1975). As Hyde (1985) points out, none of these approaches really resolves the identity conflict between femininity and achievement. The first two each reject the other; the third attempts to be all things to all people. The women today who are in their fifties and sixties, who should be at the top of their careers, were raised during an even more traditional period. Sex-role ideology and traditional sex-role development patterns hang heavy on the lives of both males and females playing the 1990s' competitive game of "success." We might need to await the 21st century to witness the development of more viable options.

References

Almquist, E. M. and S. S. Angrist. 1971. "Role model influences on college women's career aspirations." *Merrill-Palmer Quarterly*, 17(3):263-279.

Anastasi, A. 1985. "Reciprocal relations between cognitive and affective development with implications for sex differences." In T. B. Sonderegger (ed.), *Nebraska Symposium on Motivation, 1984: Psychology and Gender*. Lincoln: University of Nebraska Press.

Anderson, M. 1988. *Thinking About Women: Sociological Perspectives on Sex and Gender*. New York: Macmillan.

Basow, S. A. 1980. *Sex Role Stereotypes: Traditions and Alternatives*. Monterey, CA: Brooks/Cole.

Berger, P. L. and T. Luckman. 1966. *Social Construction of Reality: A Tretise in the Sociology of Knowledge*. Garden City, NY: Doubleday.

Bloch, G. B. 1989. "Sports and your career." *Working Women* 14(6) (June).

Bohlig, M. 1988. "Women coaches/administration: An endangered species." *Scholastic Coach* 57(February).

Chodorow, N. 1978. *The Reproduction of Mothering: Psychoanalysis and the Sociology of Gender*. Berkeley: University of California Press.

Crawford, J. S. 1977. *Women in Middle Management*. Ridgewood, NJ: Forkner

Dambrot, F. H., D. C. Reep, and D. Bell. 1988. "Television sex roles in the 1980s: Do viewers' sex and sex role orientation change the picture?" *Sex Roles* 19(56):387-401.

Deaux, K. 1976. *The Behavior of Men and Women*. Monterey, CA: Brooks/Cole.

de Beauvoir, S. 1952. *The Second Sex*. Trans. H.M. Paushley, New York Modern Library. New York: Vintage Books.

De Frantz, A. L. 1988. "Women and leadership in sport." *Journal of Physical Education, Recreation and Dance*, 59(March):46-48.

Dellas, M. and E. L. Gaier. 1975. "The self and adolescent identity in women: Options and implications." *Adolescence*, 10:399-407.

Donelson, E. 1977. "Becoming a single woman." In E. Donelson and J. Gullahorn (eds.), *Women: A Psychological Perspective*, New York: John Wiley.

Dougherty, W. H. and R. E. Engel. 1987. "An 80s look for sex equality in Caldecott winners and honor books." *The Reading Teacher*, 40(4)(January):395.

Durkin, K. 1985. *Television, Sex Roles and Children: A Developmental Social Psychological Account*. Philadelphia, PA: Milton Keynes Open University Press.

Dweck, C. S. and F. E. Goetz. 1977. "Attributions and learned helplessness." In J. H. Harvey, W. Ickles, and R. F. Kidd (eds.), *New Directions in Attribution Research*, Vol. 2, Hillsdale, NJ: Lawrence Erlbaum.

Elder, G. H. 1969. "Appearance and education in marriage mobility." *American Sociological Review*, 34:519-533.

Evangelauf, J. 1989. "SAT called a 'defective product' that is biased against women." *Chronicle of Higher Education*, 35(34),3 May, A3.

Farganis, S. 1986. *The Social Reconstruction of the Feminine Character*. Totoway, NJ: Rowman & Littlefield.

Farmer, H. S. 1985. "Model of career and achievement motivation for women and men." *Journal of Counseling Psychology*, 32:363-390.

Friedman, S. 1989. "Sports helps women be 'one of the boys.'" *National Underwriter: Property & Casualty/Risk Benefits Management Edition*, 93(30) (24 July).

Gilligan, C. 1982. *In a Different Voice: Psychological Theory and Women's Development*, Cambridge, MA: Harvard University Press.

Greenberg, S. 1988. "Educational equity in early education environments." In S. S. Klein (ed.), *Handbook for Achieving Sex Equity Through Education*. Baltimore, MD: Johns Hopkins University Press.

Greenglass, E. R. and R. Devins. 1982. "Factors related to marriage and career plans in unmarried women." *Sex Roles*, 8:57-72.

Grusec, J. E. and H. Lytton. 1988. *Social Development: History, Theory and Research*. New York: Springer Verlag.

Hahn, C. L. and J. Bernard-Powers (with L. Hunter, S. Groves, M. MacGregor, and K. P. Scott). 1988. "Sex equity in social science." In S. S. Klein (ed.), *Handbook for Achieving Sex Equity Through Education*, Baltimore, MD: Johns Hopkins University Press.

Hennig, M. and A. Jardim. 1977. "Women executives in the old boy network." *Psychology Today*, 10(January):76-81.

Hess, B. H. and M. B. Sussman. 1984. *Women and the Family: Two Decades of Change*. New York: Haworth.

Hoener, M. S. 1969. "Fail: Bright women." *Psychology Today*, 3(6).

Hyde, J. S. 1985. *Half the Human Experience: The Psychology of Women*, 3rd ed. Lexington, MA: D.C. Heath.

Kelly, R. M. and M. Boutilier. 1988. *The Making of Political Women: A Study of Socialization and Role Conflict*. Chicago, IL: Nelson-Hall.

Kendrick, D. T. 1987. "Gender, genes, and the social environment: A biosocial interactionist perspective." In P. Shaver and C. Hendrick (eds.), *Sex and Gender*, Newbury Park, CA: Sage.

Kimball, G. 1988. *50-50 Parenting*. Lexington, MA: D.C. Heath.

Laboda, A. 1990. "Women with navy wings: They fly everywhere but into battle, and on that point they've just begun to fight." *Flying*, (January):39-51.

Lott, A. J. 1973. "Social psychology." In B. Wolman (ed.), *Handbook of General Psychology*. Englewood Cliffs, NJ: Prentice-Hall.

Maccoby, E. E. and C. N. Jacklin. 1974. *The Psychology of Sex Differences*. Stanford, CA: Stanford University Press.

Mednick, T. 1988. "On the politics of psychological constructs." *American Psychologist*, 44(8)(August):1118-1123.

Mednick, M. T. S., S. S. Tangri, and L. W. Hoffman. 1975. *Women and Achievement*. New York: John Wiley.

Morawski, J. G. 1987. "The troubled quest for masculinity, femininity, and androgyny." In P. Shaveranol and C. Hendrick (eds.), *Sex and Gender*. Newbury Park, CA: Sage.

Morgan, M. and N. Signorielli. 1990. "Cultivation analysis: Conceptualization and methodology." In N. Signorielli and M. Morgan (eds.), *Cultivation Analysis: New Directions in Media Effects Research*. Newbury Park, CA: Sage.

Nilsen, A. P. 1971. "Women in children's literature." *College English*, 29:918-926.

Osipow, S. H. 1987. "Counseling psychology: Theory, research and practice in career counseling." *Annual Review of Psychology*, 38:274.

Powell, G. N. 1988. *Women and Men in Management*. Newbury Park, CA: Sage.

Rosenberg, F. R. and R. G. Simmons. 1975. "Sex differences in the self-concept in adolescence." *Sex Roles*, 1:147-159.

Sadker, D. and M. Sadker. 1988. "The treatment of sex equity in teacher education." In S. S. Klein (ed.), *Handbook for Achieving Sex Equity Through Education*. Baltimore, MD: Johns Hopkins University Press.

Sarbin, T. R. and K. E. Scheibe. 1983. "A model of social identity." In T. R. Sarbin and K. E. Scheibe (eds.), *Studies in Social Identity*. New York: Praeger.

Shepherd-Look, D. L. 1982. "Sex differentiation and the development of sex roles." In B. B. Wolman (ed.), *Handbook of Developmental Psychology*. Englewood Cliffs, NJ: Prentice-Hall.

Sherman, J. A. 1982. "Mathematics, the critical filter: A look at some residues." *Psychology of Women Quarterly*, 6:428-444.

Signorielli, N. 1989. "Television and conceptions about six roles: Maintaining conventionality and the status quo." *Sex Roles*, 21(516):341-361.

Stein, A.H. and M.M. Bailey. 1973. "The socialization of achievement oriented females." *Psychological Bulletin*, 5(51):345-366.

U.S. Bureau of the Census. 1989. *Statistical Abstract of the United States, 1989*. Washington, DC: Department of Commerce.

Waters, T. 1989. "SAT bashing." *Discover*, 10(8)(August):28.

Weitzman, L. J. 1975. *Sex Roles*. New York: Oxford University Press.

Weitzman, L. J., D. Gifler, E. Hokada, and C. Ross. 1982. "Sex role socialization in picture books for pre-school children." *American Journal of Sociology*, 77:1125-1150.

Witherspoon, R. P. 1988. "Female soldiers in combat: A policy adrift." *Minerva*, (Spring):1-27.

Witkin, H.A. 1964. "Origins of cognitive style." In C. Sheerer (ed.), *Cognition: Theory, Research, Promise*. New York: Harper & Row.

Food for Thought and Application Questions

1. Develop a list of commonly held assumptions about biological differences between the sexes. Kelly noted that, even if these assumptions hold true for the "average" man or woman, group variation within each sex is such that large numbers of women and men do not fit the assumptions. Identify specific areas where rigid adherence to these biologically-based assumptions of sex differences penalizes society due to a failure to effectively utilize human resources. Now consider the costs (both economic and social-psychological) to the individual who is denied access, for example, to a job, because of sex stereotypes. Given these costs, why do you think that the erosion of gender stereotypes is such a slow process?

2. Now that you have completed your reading, go watch television. Wait! There *are* more instructions. You have read that television is an important agent of gender role socialization and that the depiction of women's roles in television has changed substantially over the last few decades. Your task is to examine the portrayal of two working women on television and to determine the extent to which these portrayals represent movement away from gender stereotypes. Examples of things to look for include: Are the types of occupations gender-traditional? Are the women portrayed as competent in their work roles? Are they portrayed as sex objects? Is there a great deal of attention focused on their physical appearance? Are they young and thin? Are the women depicted as "exceptions to the rule"? In your opinion, is what you have seen on television an accurate portrayal of working women? Why or why not? ✦

2

Parental Influence and Women's Careers

Sue Joan Mendelson Freeman

It is common knowledge that a family's environment contributes significantly to the shape of an individual's future. That environment has both external and internal components. Outside of it, a family has several sources of identity within the larger society; its race, class, religion, and ethnicity inform a family's practices, beliefs, and opportunities. Cultural heritage and social access are largely determined by the sociological circumstances of one's birth.

Beyond a sociological rubric, factors operating on the individual level shape a person's future. Internal to the family is its psychological environment. Freud awakened our consciousness to the importance of early child-rearing practices for subsequent personal development. Whether or not they accept a psychodynamic framework, social scientists since have reiterated the significance of family in molding its members' psyches.

Notions of self, relation to other, and place in a social network originate in the family. Parent-child relationships are especially critical to one's growing understanding of identity and future. Self-image is subject to many other sources of influence throughout the course of development, but the first impressions emblazoned through the intimacy of family carry considerable weight. Our relationships within the family not only become the pro-

totype for subsequent ones outside but also teach us who we are and what we might expect to do with our lives.

A family's instruction about children's personal attributes and future paths had varied by gender for more than half of this century. Males and females learned characteristics and directions that were separate and specific to their gender. Institutions representing various aspects of society fostered and reinforced gender-specific behavior, and children had firsthand models in their own homes. Mothers who served as family caretakers and fathers who went out to work were powerful role models for children's emulation (Bayes and Newton 1978). Thus, males' and females' identities and destinies were overdetermined by internal and external contributors.

It is not just behavior of role models that influences a child's development. Parents' messages about their own and their children's identities can take many forms. Influence extends beyond behavior to attitudes. For example, the operative factor in the case of mother-daughter messages may be the mother's degree of satisfaction with her role. Thus, mothers who are at home but dissatisfied with that position are more likely to encourage their daughters to do something different (Brown 1979).

Lessons conveyed verbally and behaviorally are particularly influential because of their source and recipient. Children are in a formative process and are therefore malleable, especially by the most powerful people in their lives, their parents. Parents derive their power from their position: Children are totally dependent upon them for an extended period of time. Thus, parental teachings about the child's value and potential are of extraordinary endurance.

A division of labor according to traditional gender lines would find fathers in the work force and mothers in the kitchen. If role model imitation followed expectation, girls would identify with their mothers and thereby formulate notions of themselves and their futures around domesticity. Indeed, some women, like thirty-seven-year-old Dorothy, began with such notions, which were subsequently revised as a function of career opportunity and professional experience.

> My early socialization through my family was very patriarchal, and my mother never worked. It was understood that if I went to school it wasn't for any particular reason other than it was just something to do. But not any emphasis was ever placed on career for a woman; nothing was placed on learning for a woman. It was understood in my mind to become a mother and a wife, and that was it. So when I went to school, I never really took it very seriously; I didn't study very hard; I really didn't care. And my whole reason for being there—and what I think a lot of women in my position at that time were going through—was to find a husband.

Predictions of sex role imitation ordinarily follow same-sex lines: Girls are expected to identify with their mothers and boys with their fathers. Within a context of a gender-based division of labor, however, girls would have to identify with their fathers in order to develop the characteristics requisite to career aspiration. Females who did just that—identified with their fathers and subsequently became executives—were the subject of an early study, *The Managerial Woman* (Hennig and Jardim 1977). That study also supported the association of high achievement orientation with birth order, firstborn or only children getting an inordinate share (Hennig and Jardim 1977). Among the women interviewed for this study we find more variability in birth order, in which parent is cited as being influential, and in the ways influence is manifested (Brown 1979; Epstein 1970).

Social beliefs about gender roles vary with time and context. Children born after 1960 were likely to receive very different messages about gender-appropriate iden-

tities and directions than those born two decades earlier (Brown 1979). Social change spawned by recent human rights movements has affected our attitudes and practices regarding male and female traits and behavior. Revised beliefs and economic conditions have combined to allow women's development and occupation to extend outside the home. . . . The families of the women in this study spanned an age range from early twenties through mid-fifties, the time frames of their early formative years vary. Most childhoods predated the current women's movement; yet these women developed high achievement motivation for work and career. By looking at their families, we gain insight into the shaping of these women's aspirations. . . .

This Study

The testimony presented here [about parental influence on careers] comes from interviews with forty women who were or were about to become middle managers. Interviews were conducted during a four-year period in the early 1980s. The women were diverse in class and ethnic backgrounds, although most were white Americans; included were three black and three foreign-born women.

Their organizations ranged from large to Fortune 500 companies. The women worked in financial services; retail industries; large, diversified conglomerates; media and publishing; high-technology industries; transportation; manufacturing; natural resources; and consumer products. They could be found in production on the shop floor, in regional offices in the field, and in corporate headquarters. Their positions ranged from sales representative to vice-president, with project leaders, instructors, accountants and auditors, writers and overseers of company publications represented. About half of the women already held the title of manager, and their areas included marketing, personnel and human resources, equal employment opportunity, product manufacturing and distribution, in-house education and training, sales, and legislative affairs.

These women were a special group because they had been chosen by their companies for further training at a college-affiliated management program. That these women were singled out for such support by their companies is subject to various interpretations, including the implication of professional promise, perhaps in the form of advancement within the organization. Thus, we are listening not just to female middle managers but to a select subset of that population, those to whom some kind of company commitment has been implied. . . .

Mothers as the Prime Movers

For several women, mothers were predominant influences. Sharon's mother stressed the importance of education, and at the time of the interview Sharon had already earned one graduate degree and was pursuing another.

> Absolutely from my mother. Nobody in our immediate family ever went to college, so being the oldest child . . . my mother always encouraged me to think about going to college. It was always to have a better job. There was a real big focus on having skills and being unique in that respect. And she was absolutely the prime reason. In that respect, my father was always encouraging but certainly not so much on a vocal level. It was definitely my mother.

Parents do not merely convey a "Do as I did" message to their children. In fact, mothers often use their own lives as negative examples for their female offspring. They want their children to have opportunities that they lacked. Alison's achievement orientation began early with educational strivings, and by the age of twenty-five this young woman had found herself already on the edge of managerial positions.

> My mother, from as early as I can remember, was pushing me . . . I think she always felt cheated by the fact that

she didn't go to college, and she didn't have a career and didn't have a way to be independent . . . As long as I can remember, my mother was always saying, "Get a college education so you can be independent and never depend on a husband or anybody else." I bet I heard that once a week for my entire life.

Mothers, who had been socialized according to traditional gender dicta of female domesticity and dependence, found their experience wanting and preached the opposite to their daughters. Recognizing the limitations imposed upon them by economic dependence, they encouraged their daughters to increase the possibilities for their own lives. Leigh's mother did not mince words in her explicit message, but Leigh did not begin to build a career until she joined a growing manufacturing corporation in her mid-thirties.

> She had been a support when I was young, very definitely. When I was in college, she would say things like "Prepare yourself for a job." "But I want to take all these art courses." And if I had listened to some of the things she said, I might have done things a little differently. I don't know if I would have, but she had been through [it] herself and knew where things were. Very bright woman.

When mothers recognize the many options that could be available to their daughters, they often coach them about paths to pursue. Marsha's mother described the different destinations in which various paths would culminate. This tutelage in decision making and nurtured independence prepared Marsha for a direct path to a high executive position in finance for which she had solid undergraduate training.

> I have to give her some of the credit because she did a lot of talking. We were very close. We talked quite a bit. And she would bring up comparisons: "You either do this, and this is where you may end up. But if you do this, there's

no limit to where you can go." So I have to say that she was the major factor.

The support of a close relationship is crucial to risk taking. Encouraged to make decisions and tutored in their consequences, a woman develops a strong self-image and many skills necessary for career success. Ursula, in industrial sales and a single parent by age thirty-two, also learned strengths and skills from her mother's example.

My mother was a very strong influence in our family. She was a very strong woman . . . And I think I've incorporated—I've learned from her. One of the things that's helped me so much has been being persistent, not giving up. If somebody tells me, "No," how can I make them say yes? How can I change their minds? Or what do I need to change to make it work? And I really picked that up from my mother. My mother was not in business . . . But she was strong and took responsibility for a lot of things. And I think she had a lot of influence on the choices that I've made.

The majority of women interviewed had mothers who were not employed in business. Several had never worked outside of the home, and the few who had were primarily part-time employees. A mother's participation in the labor force did not define what and how she communicated to her daughter, however. For example, some employed mothers would have preferred full-time homemaking, and others who were at home would have preferred paid work. Daughters became aware of what mothers did, said, and might have desired. Their personal characteristics evolved under a mother's watchful tutelage, others from a more subtle model. Values and a general sense of personal worth, not tied to any specific undertaking, were derived from supportive maternal environments. Daughters also learned skills and attributes essential to career from mothers who

managed not businesses but homes (Baruch, Barnett and Rivers 1983).

Where Fathers Take the Lead

Ordinarily, neither parent dictated a particular path for a child to pursue. Instead, daughters were encouraged to develop so that they were prepared to take advantage of all sorts of opportunities. Like mothers, fathers had various ways of fostering development that ranged from specific expectation to general support.

Through intellectual challenge, Connie's father sharpened her thinking ability and stimulated her assertiveness. His style of coaching reflected his own strength, which served as both a formidable model and a dependable support. By her early thirties, Connie, who had always been a high achiever, was headed for one of the top executive positions held by women of this group.

I was the oldest child, and I was given a lot of opportunity to experience things first time around. I think my father encouraged me to debate and talk: "Why do you feel this way, and how did you get to that point, and why?" [He was] interested in what I was doing. So I think my father was important, and my mother was very supportive. And I don't know that I'm through this stage yet, but I would be very secure and calm if I could go home and ask him the answer to a question, and he told me his version of it. Whatever that version was, I always felt that was the right story and that probably nobody else knew, because nobody else was as smart.

A father's authoritative expertise can work to a daughter's advantage when he not only lends her the benefit of his experience but also facilitates similar expertise in her. Connie learned that she could rely on her father as a knowledgeable consultant, but more importantly, she developed her own problem-solving abilities through his prompting.

Other fathers also emphasized cognitive skill in their daughters. To expand oneself through knowledge is useful for its own sake as well as for practical purposes. Scholastic study and achievement can promote a sense of accomplishment and self-esteem. Meanwhile, broad exposure acquaints one with prospects for the future. Through education, daughters learn more about available opportunity and about themselves and their aptitudes. Teresa's interest in school carried her through a graduate degree, which prepared her for escalating positions within her company. Her recollection of an emphasis on education is common to many.

> We had to go to school; we had to do our homework. That was just what you were supposed to do. And I always did well in school, and they kept encouraging it.

For Ina, who also held a graduate degree, the importance of education was an unquestioned given:

> [My mother's] idea of an education [as] security was the key thing that ran through my whole life—and my sisters' also. We all have professions . . . And they always encouraged it. You got one B and all the rest A's. Well, next time try for all A's. Go for the top. And even still, my mother's very proud of my career.

It is not necessarily one or the other parent who promulgates education and high achievement, but fathers, more often than mothers, are perceived as demanding. The demand may be connected to scholastic performance or to achievement more generally. Without articulating particular expectations, Leigh's father still served as a motivating force for her, although it was her mother who had instructed her to prepare for a job when she wanted to take art courses.

> I'd say my father was very demanding—a very demanding person. And it wasn't as though he was gearing me to go to work. But the person I had to

succeed for was my father . . . he's been very successful, and a very bright person. And I had to prove myself to him. So I've always had to fight hard to do that, but it's certainly been a motivation. And I wouldn't have known that many years ago. I certainly know that now.

A father's admirable characteristics can inspire his daughter's emulation. Further, his qualities make his approval all the more desirable to a daughter who strives to prove herself worthy through similar accomplishment.

Nina, who had been more interested in work than school, can now relate her father's values to her own.

> My dad's very goal-oriented. He's always instilled that in us—to get our act together and to have some goals and aspirations and to set them high, and . . . both my parents would always support us in that.

These women describe encouragement and support for achievement in a general sense. They do not speak of being groomed for a lifetime of work or career, never mind a specific occupation. Sex differences may remain, with families expecting boys to prepare for lifelong employment and coaching them toward particular careers (Hardesty and Jacobs 1986). Perhaps females born within the past two decades have received similar messages. However, the women of this study, who have spanned the old and new messages about women's lives, speak in the sketchier and broader terms of achievement.

Family Support for Achievement

Influenced by the spoken and unspoken, children are commonly unaware of the sources of motivation during their formative years. In retrospect, they can recognize family components that contributed to what they have become. The full meaning of parental example and instruction becomes clear when women connect their current selves to the past. Stella attests to the value of the interview question in stirring an integration for her.

> I like the idea of you getting me to actually talk about [my family] and to relate it somehow. I never really saw a correlation between my feelings for my family and my work and the obligations and the things like that. I always thought that this is one thing and this is another and somehow the two paths never meet, but it's almost inseparable.

Several women interviewed acknowledged the influence and support of both parents in their development. Karen, who coordinates financial planning for a retail corporation, derived different qualities from her mother and father, and their individual strengths combined to enforce a belief in her potential.

> My father was very much one of these workaholic-type people. He was also somebody that you could never satisfy . . . and so I think I probably did a lot of stuff trying to please him but never quite getting that satisfaction. My mother was a very organized person . . . I learned a lot of organizational-type things from her. I would say both parents were pretty strong. And I was never raised with any sort of feeling other than you could do whatever you wanted to do.

We see here the origins of a strong achievement orientation. Striving to do and be as much as possible begins in childhood in relation to a parent and continues in adulthood in relation to oneself. Personal attributes and concrete skills that contribute to professional success are initially acquired through family tutelage. Connie draws parallels between her behavior as a child in the family and as a professional in the corporation.

> I can remember always, as a child, having to do, to be, in order to please my parents, I would want to get all A's. Then I took up horseback riding, and I had to enter a contest, and I wanted to win, get the first prize. And immediately, when I got this prize, I turned and looked to them to see the smiles and the positive reinforcement. So it must have started there. I think that I play to the house when I work. I don't build a lot of relationships with subordinates, and I don't build a lot of relationships with peers. What I do is build relationships with superiors, and that's got to go back to wanting your parents' approval. . . . It's got to be a transferring of that. And then just being hard on yourself . . . if I have a chance of doing it perfectly, then I will do it. But if I only have a chance of being average, it's not fun anymore. . . . So it has to be that. It goes all over.

Even when women cannot trace career origins to family influence, they are aware of an unqualified support for their endeavors and for themselves. Renee's family is virtually ignorant of the technicalities of her work as a systems consultant, but she feels their pride in her accomplishments.

> My family per se has never had any kind of a part in my career . . . she [her mother] never had any idea what I did for a living. And I can't blame her. If I were not in the industry . . . I cannot explain it to anyone else. So they really didn't have anything to do with it other than just being very proud. I would always get a strong sense of that.

Thus, families vary in the ways they exert influence and in the values they choose to emphasize. Some families' influence is perceived as negligible with regard to career. Most women interviewed nonetheless acknowledged their families in the development of a strong sense of self. A general emphasis on education and preparation for employment was an integral part of many women's upbringing, but critical to development was a global feeling of parental faith in daughters' worth. Not only did parents reinforce certain values, they believed in their daughters' abilities to meet expectations. Personal strength ultimately contributes to professional growth. Specific career assistance is less vital than the gift of self that Connie's parents have given her.

> My parents are not involved right now in coaching me or giving me tips on how to be more effective. They provide a lot of love and support and encouragement and interest—in that sense, helping me form a strong self-concept. I think they did that.

Sex Roles

An environment that both supports and holds out high standards can instill in a woman the belief that she is capable of doing anything she chooses. However, open-ended options are contrary to a gender-based division of labor that prescribes what roles males and females should occupy. Many women interviewed came from homes where traditional gender lines held sway. In some instances, the explicit message about a daughter's future did not contradict the modeled one. Monica, thirty-two, believes that her choices would have been different had her family not perpetuated customary sex roles (Bayes and Newton 1978). Now a manager in human resources, she has earned a graduate degree since her secretarial beginnings in the corporation.

> In fact, I get aggravated with my parents, because my mother and father were very traditional. My father made the decisions. My mother was a full-time housewife. They talked a lot about girls do this and boys do that, though they always encouraged me. I did very well in school, and my father was very helpful to me [in] school work. There was a feeling that I should go to college, but it was for the wrong reason. It was because you'll meet a nice boy and get married. And unfortunately, no one ever gave me any other options. Had I to do it over again I certainly would have had a different view of things.

The larger cultural environment can reinforce family stereotypes of the preferred gender. The strength of inner conviction overcomes socialization that limits female potential. It is Hope's internal sense of self-worth that fully frees her.

> We had a very male-dominated environment. Boys—like they are everywhere, but specifically in the South—boys are the chosen kids. And everything centers around them. Girls are just second-class citizens. And so you never really get over that. The conflict comes when you realize that "Hey, I really am not a second-class citizen. In fact, sometimes I'm actually a better citizen than they are. I'm more capable, I'm more competent." And that brings another kind of conflict, because you don't have to prove that you're that. You have to come to terms with the fact that you're simply being as good as you can be—good, by your own definition, not good by someone else's.

Even when women grew up in homes that depicted traditional sex roles, they learned of other possibilities for their own lives. Parents, in the majority of cases, communicated prospects for their daughters that they themselves were not living. Jill reiterates an emphasis on education and values demonstrated by parents. The principle underlying specific lesson was that she could do and be whatever she pleased.

> Obviously, they have played a tremendous role in my life, as every family does. In my career development in particular, both parents contributed something differently. My mother did not work and has always been oriented toward the home and family life. My father has always directed all of his children, that we could do anything we wanted to, that as long as you worked hard, and were productive, and did your best . . . it was out there, and you just have to try. And he himself was a very hard-working individual and very dedicated to whatever he went into, so his own behavior was an excellent example of what he had to teach us. I would say that certainly helped in terms of my career development.

Parents instilled in daughters the value of conscientious effort. Moreover, parents conveyed their confidence in women's ability to attain their goals. Daughters internalize both the beliefs and the confidence originally derived from their families; hence, they formulate and fulfill similarly high expectations of themselves. Susan, a twenty-eight-year-old production manager, can feel the full weight of her personal worth and professional success as a result of this kind of family interaction.

> The environment I grew up in was pretty much middle-class. My parents were very concerned with grades for all of us, and there was really no distinction in terms of who could do what, or who was supposed to excel at what. My father's whole thing was that everybody should be a math major, everybody should be a chem or physics major. They were real pushy around achievement. I think that contributed a lot to what ultimately happened once I got into the work environment. The standards of performance that they expected became my own expectations somewhere in the later years of college. I didn't need them behind me anymore, expecting that. I expected it of myself. So they really played a critical role [in] developing those expectations and achievement levels.

These women set high standards for their professional performance. Individual variation notwithstanding, they were impressively uniform in their desire to achieve all that they might, not necessarily in terms of material reward but in relation to their sense of self. One woman spoke for several in saying that she was more apt to improve herself due to constantly questioning "whether I'm as good as I should be." There is plenty of evidence that these women have high standards for their performance, and those standards seem to originate in families where expectations for children's development are gender-free. With a background in human services and currently working as a manager in a traditionally male transportation business, Beverly learned that she could do whatever she wished as long as it was at a high level:

> But he [father] was really influential in that he truly believed that I could do anything I wanted to do. He had none of the traditional ideas about what I ought to do and what I shouldn't do. He was also a real perfectionist and expected me to be a cut above average in everything always. So there was a lot of achievement pressure and a lot of performance pressure.

Janna's family also valued cognitive strength and encouraged her career:

> My father's major value system has to do with competence and intelligence . . . reinforced for being bright. So I was never told that I really ought to consider being a nurse or a teacher. It was always expected that I would go to college; it was always expected that I would have a career. And I don't think that as a child or a young woman growing up in that family I was ever treated as a female.

The absence of a gender-linked socialization characterized Esther's childhood in the depression years.

> I can't honestly say that I was . . . brought up in an atmosphere that said women can't do this or can't do that. I just believed I could do anything I wanted to, and I never thought of it as being a woman. I did a lot of reading when I was a child, and I had a lot of role models in my own mind—people like Marie Curie, George Sand, Amelia Earhart was a great heroine of mine, Clara Barton, Elizabeth Browning. They sound like such stereotypes, but they were the women that I really did relate to.

Whether women had female role models available to them in their immediate families or from other sources, they still developed the idea that everything would be available to them regardless of gender. An "anything is possible" notion came from parents like Nina's who believed that to be so for their daughters.

> And my parents have instilled [in] us that we had the ability to do anything we wanted to and given us the opportunity to do that.

Independence

These women recall receiving both general and specific notions about themselves and their futures from their first families. For many, particular parental emphases on education and achievement were apparent progenitors of internalized high standards for their own performance. A family environment that communicated support and confidence in daughters' inherent worth was critical to their developing belief in themselves. Frequently coupled with such faith was encouragement for gender-free pursuits and a future of economic independence.

Socialization according to a gender-based division of labor would shape female identities for domesticity and economic dependence on a male. The majority of women interviewed had mothers without careers—indeed, without paid work of any kind—who spent their lives occupied with family caretaking. When their mothers did enter the labor force, it was often out of necessity as divorced or widowed women who had children to support. Daughters learned an indelible lesson from the experience of mothers who were suddenly abandoned and unprepared to fend for themselves and their families. Women whose primary occupation had been wife and mother were not equipped to take over as breadwinner. Witnessing what had happened to their mothers, women resolved not to repeat the pattern. Mary, who claimed work to be central to her identity, sees the link between her current independence and her mother's experience.

> I think [what] influenced me most is I wanted to be independent. I would never do what she did. I would never

ever want to put myself in a position where I would fall apart. I don't want to give up "I'm me" and "I'm going to support me, and I'm going to be independent." I'll give up some of my independence in other ways but not in terms of money and support and my identity.

Family tragedy exerts a powerful influence on psychological development. From the misfortune of parents' lives children infer what they must avoid in their own futures. Colleen learned early from family events and her mother's reaction to them.

> I always felt a need to be self-supporting. I never wanted to depend on a man to have to take care of me. I'm talking about financially. I think I got that because my dad died when I was young. My mother had to go out to work . . . and she was totally unprepared for that shock. The kinds of things that I saw her going through and the pain that she went through because of being totally unprepared for it was something that I never wanted to experience.

Rebecca, equipped with an advanced technical degree and a corresponding supervisory position by age thirty, drew very specific conclusions from a similar life history:

> The other significant thing was [that] my father died so young and my mother had to go back to work to raise me. I always felt that it was kind of a driving factor for me in being independent, and being able to draw on an educational background that was marketable. [I felt] that I could always draw on that strength, [having] that education behind me, that if anything similar happened in my life, whether I got married or not, . . . I would feel that I was not totally dependent on my husband and that income. And I think I've done that. As a result, I can never see myself not working. I don't abandon all other roles—I enjoy being a wife and hopefully a mother someday, but there's always that thing in the

back of my mind that says, "Well, you know you have this identity. You know you're not going to give it up."

Environmental events and circumstances are formative influences in children's psychological development. In these cases, the lessons of adversity seem to extend to earliest recollection. Women talk of "always" having wanted their independence. The long-standing convictions formed as a consequence of family circumstance become part of their identity.

It is not only death or divorce that molds daughters' resolve. Absence of economic advantage confirmed Hope's need for financial independence.

I think [there was] always the sense that I could take care of myself. I never wanted to be in a position where I had to rely on someone else and be at their mercy. I grew up without a lot of advantages. There was a lot of negative stigma to the area that I grew up in, so I was constantly overcoming obstacles, and that has something to do with what goes on in the job. By the time I was fourteen, I was already into expressing myself and becoming my own person. Certainly I have my mother's strength. And when I left home, I left because I felt like I needed my own identity . . . it got me started on the right track, because I became who I'd always been inside anyway.

Sometimes a family's main influence is not from direct teaching or parental example. Women define themselves and their aspirations in reaction against the negative model of a family's status. Stella received personal support, but inspiration for a different direction from her upbringing.

They've encouraged me in anything . . . that I want to pursue or anything that I feel that I want to do. But as far as making a decision about myself, an actual decision, I think it comes directly from me. The only thing that I can say is that I grew up in a very poor family, and I grew up knowing that I didn't want things to remain the way

they were. And that was always in the back of my mind, that I knew in order to do better I had to rely on just me. Because I can't really say that anybody in my family influenced me. They were certainly supportive of everything I did.

The development of self-reliance may be a common outgrowth of certain kinds of environments. Where a family's situation, for whatever reason, precludes deliberate individualized attention to its members, children learn independence early. Thus, socioeconomic advantage is not a necessary condition to develop personal characteristics that forecast women's career and economic independence. Roberta's ability to fend for herself grew even in the absence of family guidance. Currently a consultant in a staff operation of a *Fortune* 500 firm, she finds herself working on degree completion and developing a career path in her early thirties.

Well, with all of us kids, . . . there was never much support in terms of what we were doing with our lives or with our schooling or anything like that. So I learned very early on to be independent and just to fight for myself as best I could.

A need to be independent is communicated to daughters in several ways. Many learn from the negative example of mothers unprepared for employment. Adverse family conditions teach children to develop attributes and abilities that will insure a different adult life. Mothers might communicate the virtues of independence even when family situations do not ostensibly precipitate it. Elena, a single parent who resists dependence, remembers receiving contradictory messages that she subsequently sorted out for herself.

What I consciously know is that my mother was always very ambivalent about her dependence on my father. She said, "It's really important for you to take care of yourself." So that's something that I always had in my head. But yet, it was also very important to her that we should be feminine and that we should be attractive and that we should be looking for a husband. So, her whole message was always very, very mixed. . . . And basically what I learned [later] was that I could support myself, which was a very important thing to me, because I felt at that time that I didn't want to focus my whole life on finding somebody to marry me and support me. I couldn't possibly do it—what I was supposed to do. And that encouraged me to explore even more.

Regardless of whether they learn it as a function of early necessity or later experience, women are convinced of the importance of self-sufficiency in an economic sense. Fending for themselves, living up to high standards, and achieving gratifying work all become integral to who they are and the way they live their lives. They may become wives and mothers, but not at the expense of their identities as fully functioning independent human beings.

References

Baruch, G., R. Barnett, and C. Rivers. 1983. *Lifeprints: New Patterns of Love and Work for Today's Women.* New York: New American Library.

Bayes, M. and P. M. Newton. 1978. "Women in authority: A sociopsychological analysis." *Journal of Applied Behavioral Science,* 14:9.

Brown, L. K. 1979. "Women in business management." *Signs,* 5(Winter):287.

Epstein, C. F. 1970. *Women's Place.* Berkeley: University California Press.

Hardesty, S. and N. Jacobs. 1986. *Success and Betrayal: The Crisis of Women in Corporate America.* New York: Franklin Watts.

Hennig, M. and A. Jardim. 1977. *The Managerial Woman.* Garden City, NY: Anchor Press/Doubleday.

Food for Thought and Application Questions

1. Select the autobiography of a well-known woman who is/was accomplished in a socially valued role. Political leaders, entrepreneurs, scientists, athletes, musicians, artists, and writers provide examples of possible choices. Read the sections in the autobiography which describe childhood experiences and family upbringing. Is there evidence of parental socialization for achievement? Give examples and discuss. Are any of the specific patterns revealed in Freeman's interview study of women managers evident (e.g., "Do as I say, not as I do," role modeling)?

2. What did you want to be when you grew up? Were your early occupational aspirations "gender appropriate"? If so, who or what influenced the choice? To what extent did your parents play a role in shaping your career goals? How did they do so? If your early occupational aspirations were not gender-traditional, were you ever encouraged to change them? Did you? Why? ✦

3

Shortchanging Girls: Gender Socialization in Schools

Peggy Orenstein (in Association With the American Association of University Women)

. . . Like many people, I first saw the results of the American Association of University Women's report *Shortchanging Girls, Shortchanging America* (1991) in my daily newspaper. The headline unfurled across the front page of the *San Francisco Examiner*: "Girls' Low Self-Esteem Slows Their Progress" (Eaky 1991), and the *New York Times* proclaimed: "Girls' Self-Esteem Is Lost on the Way to Adolescence" (Daley 1991).[1] And, like many people, as I read further, I felt my stomach sink.

This was the most extensive national survey on gender and self-esteem ever conducted, the articles said: three thousand boys and girls between the ages of nine and fifteen were polled on their attitudes toward self, school, family, and friends. As part of the project the students were asked to respond to multiple-choice questions, provide comments, and in some cases, were interviewed in focus groups. The results confirmed something that many women already knew too well. For a girl, the passage into adolescence is not just marked by menarche or a few new curves. It is marked by a loss of confidence in herself and her abilities, especially in math and science. It is marked by a scathingly critical attitude toward her body and a blossoming sense of personal inadequacy.

In spite of the changes in women's roles in society, in spite of the changes in their own mothers' lives, many of today's girls fall into traditional patterns of low self-image, self-doubt, and self-censorship of their creative and intellectual potential. Although all children experience confusion and a faltering sense of self at adolescence, girls' self-regard drops further than boys' and never catches up (AAUW 1990 and 1991). They emerge from their teenage years with reduced expectations and have less confidence in themselves and their abilities than do boys. Teenage girls are more vulnerable to feelings of depression and hopelessness and are four times more likely to attempt suicide (AAUW Educational Foundation 1992).

The AAUW discovered that the most dramatic gender gap in self-esteem is centered in the area of competence. Boys are more likely than girls to say they are "pretty good at a lot of things" and are twice as likely to name their talents as the thing they like most about themselves. Girls, meanwhile, cite an aspect of their physical appearance (AAUW 1991). Unsurprisingly, then, teenage girls are much more likely than boys to say they are "not smart enough" or "not good enough" to achieve their dreams.

The education system is supposed to provide our young people with opportunity, to encourage their intellectual growth and prepare them as citizens. Yet students in the AAUW survey reported gender bias in the classroom—and illustrated its effects—with the canniness of investigative reporters. Both boys and girls believed that teachers encouraged more assertive behavior in boys, and that, overall, boys receive the majority of their teachers' attention. The result is that boys will speak out in class more readily, and are more willing to "argue with my teachers when I think I'm right" (AAUW 1991).

Meanwhile, girls show a more precipitous drop in their interest in math and science as they advance through school. Even girls who like the subjects are, by age fifteen, only half as likely as boys to feel competent in them. These findings are key: researchers have long understood that a loss of confidence in math usually *precedes* a drop in achievement, rather than vice versa (AAUW 1992; Kloosterman 1990; Fennema and Sherman 1977). A confidence gap, rather than an ability gap, may help explain why the numbers of female physical and computer scientists actually went down during the 1980s (White 1992; National Science Board 1991; Linn 1990). The AAUW also discovered a circular relationship between math confidence and overall self-confidence, as well as a link between liking math and aspiring to professional careers—a correlation that is stronger for girls than boys. Apparently girls who can resist gender-role stereotypes in the classroom resist them elsewhere more effectively as well.

Among its most intriguing findings, the AAUW survey revealed that, although all girls report consistently lower self-esteem than boys, the severity and the nature of that reduced self-worth vary among ethnic groups. Far more African American girls retain their overall self-esteem during adolescence than white or Latina girls, maintaining a stronger sense of both personal and familial importance. They are about twice as likely to be "happy with the way I am" than girls of other groups and report feeling "pretty good at a lot of things" at nearly the rate of white boys (AAUW 1990). The one exception for African American girls is their feelings about school: black girls are more pessimistic about both their teachers and their schoolwork than other girls. Meanwhile, Latina girls' self-esteem crisis is in many ways the most profound. Between the ages of nine and fifteen, the number of Latina girls who are "happy with the way I am" plunges by 38 percentage points, compared with a 33 percent drop for white girls and a 7 percent

drop for black girls. Family disappears as a source of positive self-worth for Latina teens, and academic confidence, belief in one's talents, and a sense of personal importance all plummet (AAUW 1990). During the year in which *Shortchanging Girls, Shortchanging America* was conducted, urban Latinas left school at a greater rate than any other group, male or female (U.S. Bureau of the Census 1992). . . .

Seeking the Source: Entering Girls' Worlds

When I first read about the AAUW survey, I felt deeply troubled. This was a report in which children were talking directly to us about their experience, and I didn't like what I heard. These girls had internalized the limitations of gender. As a feminist, I took this as a warning. As a journalist, I wanted to find out more. According to the survey, middle school is the beginning of the transition from girlhood to womanhood and, not coincidentally, the time of greatest self-esteem loss (AAUW 1990 and 1991). So, with that in mind, I went back to eighth grade.

I chose to work on this project in California, which has the largest school system in the country. California, along with Minnesota and several other states, has been on the cutting edge of both gender-fair and multicultural education and perhaps there is less bias here than there might be elsewhere. But I wanted to see what was working in classrooms as well as what was not.

School administrators are leery of journalists, and teachers even more so. It was not easy to find educators (or parents) who were willing to put up with a year's scrutiny, even though, since I was writing about children, I promised to change the names of everyone involved. I interviewed over one hundred and fifty girls and spoke with nearly a dozen administrators before settling on two schools, fifty miles apart, in which I would spend the 1992-93 school year. . . .

Learning Silence: Scenes from the Class Struggle

The school described in the sections that follow, Weston, is a suburban middle school with an overwhelmingly white student body and a reputation for excellence. Weston, California, sits at the far reaches of the San Francisco Bay Area. The drive from the city takes one through a series of bedroom communities, carefully planned idylls in which, as the miles roll by, the tax brackets leap upward, the politics swing right, and the people fade to white. But Weston is different: once an oddly matched blend of country folk and chemical plant workers, this is an old town, the kind of place where people still gather curbside under the bunting-swathed lampposts of Maple Street to watch the Fourth of July parade. Many of the businesses in Weston's center—doughnut shops, ladies' clothing stores, a few hard drinkers' bars, and picked-over antiquaries—haven't changed hands in over thirty years. There are a few fern bars and one cafe serving espresso here, but if people want high tone, they go to the city.

Not that Weston has remained suspended in time. The ramshackle houses downtown may still be populated by the families of mechanics, plant workers, and, in shoddy apartment complexes, a small community of working poor, but the hills that ring the town's edge have been gobbled up by tract homes where young professionals have hunkered down—a safe distance from urban ills—to raise their children. There's even a clean, modern supermarket by the freeway, built expressly for the new suburbanites, with a multiplex cinema across the street for their occasional evenings out.

The only place where Weston's two populations converge regularly is at Weston Middle School, a crumbling Spanish-style edifice just up the street from the post office, city hall, and, more important to the student body, a McDonald's. This is the town's sole middle school, and as such,

it serves nearly nine hundred students a year from this disparate population. The bumper stickers on the cars dropping off the children reflect the mix: Toyota vans advertising the local NPR affiliate pull up behind rusty pickups that proclaim: "My wife said if I buy another gun she'll divorce me; God, I'll miss her!" There is also a staunch Christian population here—Mormons, Seventh-Day Adventists, and other, less austere sects whose cars remind other residents that "Jesus Loves You!"

In recent years, Weston Middle School has fulfilled its mandate well: the school entrance is draped with a "California Distinguished School" banner, earned last year by the students' estimable standardized test scores as well as the staff's exemplary performance. The teachers are an impressive, enthusiastic group who routinely seek methods of instruction that will inspire a little more engagement, a little more effort on the part of their pupils: an eighth-grade history teacher uses a karaoke microphone to juice up his lessons; an English teacher videotapes students performing original poems to bring literature to life; a science teacher offers extra credit to students who join him in cleaning up the banks of a local river. There is also some concern about gender issues in education: Weston's history teachers have embraced the new, more inclusive textbooks adopted by the state of California; in English, students write essays on their views about abortion and read, among other books, *Streams to the River, River to the Sea*, a historical novel which recasts Sacagawea as an intrepid female hero.

Yet the overt curriculum, as fine as it may be, is never the only force operating in a classroom. There is something else as well. The "hidden curriculum" comprises the unstated lessons that students learn in school: it is the running subtext through which teachers communicate behavioral norms and individual status in the school culture, the process of socialization that cues children into their place in the hierarchy of larger society. Once used to describe the ways in which the education system works to reproduce class systems in our culture, the "hidden curriculum" has recently been applied to the ways in which schools help reinforce gender roles, whether they intend to or not.

The Daily Grind: Lessons in the Hidden Curriculum

Amy Wilkinson has looked forward to being an eighth grader forever—at least for the last two years, which, when you're thirteen, seems like the same thing. By the second week of September she's settled comfortably into her role as one of the school's reigning elite. Each morning before class, she lounges with a group of about twenty other eighth-grade girls and boys in the most visible spot on campus: at the base of the schoolyard, between one of the portable classrooms that was constructed in the late 1970s and the old oak tree in the overflow parking lot. The group trades gossip, flirts, or simply stands around, basking in its own importance and killing time before the morning bell.

At 8:15 on Tuesday the crowd has already convened, and Amy is standing among a knot of girls, laughing. She is fuller-figured than she'd like to be, wide-hipped and heavy-limbed with curly, blond hair, cornflower-blue eyes, and a sharply up-turned nose. With the help of her mother, who is a drama coach, she has become the school's star actress: last year she played Eliza in Weston's production of *My Fair Lady*. Although she earns solid grades in all of her subjects—she'll make the honor roll this fall—drama is her passion, she says, because "I love entertaining people, and I love putting on characters."

Also, no doubt, because she loves the spotlight: this morning, when she mentions a boy I haven't met, Amy turns, puts her hands on her hips, anchors her feet shoulder width apart, and bellows across the schoolyard, "Greg! Get over here! You have to meet Peggy."

She smiles wryly as Greg, looking startled, begins to make his way across the schoolyard for an introduction. "I'm not exactly shy," she says, her hands still on her hips. "I'm *bold*."

Amy is bold. And brassy, and strong-willed. Like any teenager, she tries on and discards different selves as if they were so many pairs of Girbaud jeans, searching ruthlessly for a perfect fit. During a morning chat just before the school year began, she told me that her parents tried to coach her on how to respond to my questions. "They told me to tell you that they want me to be my own person," she complained. "My mother *told* me to tell you that. I do want to be my own person, but it's like, you're interviewing me about who *I* am and she's telling me what to say—that's not my own person, is it?"

When the morning bell rings, Amy and her friends cut off their conversations, scoop up their books, and jostle toward the school's entrance. Inside, Weston's hallways smell chalky, papery, and a little sweaty from gym class. The wood-railed staircases at either end of the two-story main building are worn thin in the middle from the scuffle of hundreds of pairs of sneakers pounding them at forty-eight-minute intervals for nearly seventy-five years. Amy's mother, Sharon, and her grandmother both attended this school. So will her two younger sisters. Her father, a mechanic who works on big rigs, is a more recent Weston recruit: he grew up in Georgia and came here after he and Sharon were married.

Amy grabs my hand, pulling me along like a small child or a slightly addled new student: within three minutes we have threaded our way through the dull-yellow hallways to her locker and then upstairs to room 238, Mrs. Richter's math class.

The twenty-two students that stream through the door with us run the gamut of physical maturity. Some of the boys are as small and compact as fourth graders, their legs sticking out of their shorts like pipe cleaners. A few are trapped in the agony of a growth spurt, and still others cultivate downy beards. The girls' physiques are less extreme: most are nearly their full height, and all but a few have already weathered the brunt of puberty. They wear topknots or ponytails, and their shirts are tucked neatly into their jeans.

Mrs. Richter, a ruddy, athletic woman with a powerful voice, has arranged the chairs in a three-sided square, two rows deep. Amy walks to the far side of the room and, as she takes her seat, falls into a typically feminine pose: she crosses her legs, folds her arms across her chest, and hunches forward toward her desk, seeming to shrink into herself. The sauciness of the playground disappears, and, in fact, she says hardly a word during class. Meanwhile, the boys, especially those who are more physically mature, sprawl in their chairs, stretching their legs long, expanding into the available space.

Nate, a gawky, sanguine boy who has shaved his head except for a small thatch that's hidden under an Oakland A's cap, leans his chair back on two legs and, although the bell has already rung, begins a noisy conversation with his friend Kyle.

Mrs. Richter turns to him, "What's all the discussion about, Nate?" she asks.

"*He's* talking to *me*," Nate answers, pointing to Kyle. Mrs. Richter writes Nate's name on the chalkboard as a warning toward detention and he yells out in protest. They begin to quibble over the justice of her decision, their first—but certainly not their last—power struggle of the day. As they argue, Allison, a tall, angular girl who once told me, "My goal is to be the best wife and mother I can be," raises her hand to ask a question. Mrs. Richter, finishing up with Nate, doesn't notice.

"Get your homework out, everyone!" the teacher booms, and walks among the students, checking to make sure no one has shirked on her or his assignment. Allison, who sits in the front row nearest both the blackboard and the teacher, waits patiently for another moment, then, realizing she's not getting results, puts her hand down. When Mrs. Richter walks toward her, Allison tries another tack, calling out her question. Still, she gets no response, so she gives up.

As a homework assignment, the students have divided their papers into one hundred squares, color-coding each square prime or composite—prime being those numbers which are divisible only by one and themselves, and composite being everything else. Mrs. Richter asks them to call out the prime numbers they've found, starting with the tens.

Nate is the first to shout, "Eleven!" The rest of the class chimes in a second later. As they move through the twenties and thirties, Nate, Kyle, and Kevin, who sit near one another at the back of the class, call out louder and louder, casually competing for both quickest response and the highest decibel level. Mrs. Richter lets the boys' behavior slide, although they are intimidating other students.

"Okay," Mrs. Richter says when they've reached one hundred. "Now, what do you think of one hundred and three? Prime or composite?"

Kyle, who is skinny and a little pop-eyed, yells out, "Prime!" but Mrs. Richter turns away from him to give someone else a turn. Unlike Allison, who gave up when she was ignored, Kyle isn't willing to cede his teacher's attention. He begins to bounce in his chair and chant, "*Prime! Prime! Prime!*" Then, when he turns out to be right, he rebukes the teacher, saying, "*See*, I told you."

When the girls in Mrs. Richter's class do speak, they follow the rules. When Allison has another question, she raises her hand again and waits her turn; this time, the teacher responds. When Amy volunteers her sole answer of the period, she raises her hand, too. She gives the wrong answer to an easy multiplication problem, turns crimson, and flips her head forward so her hair falls over her face.

Occasionally, the girls shout out answers, but generally they are to the easiest, lowest-risk questions, such as the factors of four or six. And their stabs at public recognition depend on the boys' largesse: when the girls venture responses to more complex questions the boys quickly become territorial, shouting them down with their own answers. Nate and Kyle are particularly adept at overpowering Renee, who, I've been told by the teacher, is the brightest girl in the class. (On a subsequent visit, I will see her lay her head on her desk when Nate overwhelms her and mutter, "I hate this class.")

Mrs. Richter doesn't say anything to condone the boys' aggressiveness, but she doesn't have to: they insist on—and receive—her attention even when she consciously tries to shift it elsewhere in order to make the class more equitable.

After the previous day's homework is corrected, Mrs. Richter begins a new lesson, on the use of exponents.

"What does three to the third power mean?" she asks the class.

"*I know!*" shouts Kyle.

Instead of calling on Kyle, who has already answered more than his share of questions, the teacher turns to Dawn, a somewhat more voluble girl who has plucked her eyebrows down to a few hairs.

"Do you know, Dawn?"

Dawn hesitates, and begins "Well, you count the number of threes and . . ."

"*But I know!*" interrupts Kyle. "*I know!*"

Mrs. Richter deliberately ignores him, but Dawn is rattled: she never finishes her sentence, she just stops.

"*I know! ME!*" Kyle shouts again, and then before Dawn recovers herself he blurts, "*It's three times three times three!*"

At this point, Mrs. Richter gives in. She turns away from Dawn, who is staring blankly, and nods at Kyle. "Yes," she says. "Three times three times three. Does everyone get it?"

"*YES!*" shouts Kyle; Dawn says nothing.

Mrs. Richter picks up the chalk. "Let's do some others," she says.

"Let me!" says Kyle.

"I'll pick on whoever raises their hand," she tells him.

Nate, Kyle, and two other boys immediately shoot up their hands, fingers squeezed tight and straight in what looks like a salute.

"Don't you want to wait and hear the problem first?" she asks, laughing.

They drop their hands briefly. She writes 8_4 on the board. "Okay, what would that look like written out?"

Although a third of the class raises their hands to answer—including a number of students who haven't yet said a word—she calls on Kyle anyway.

"Eight times eight times eight times eight," he says triumphantly, as the other students drop their hands.

When the bell rings, I ask Amy about the mistake she made in class and the embarrassment it caused her. She blushes again.

"Oh yeah," she says. "That's about the only time I ever talked in there. I'll never do that again."

Voice and Silence

I had chosen Amy, along with two of her friends, Evie DiLeo and Becca Holbrook, as three of the subjects for this book partly because, within minutes of our first meeting—and months before I ever saw them in a classroom—they announced to me that they were not like other girls at Weston: they were, they proudly announced, feminists. Amy explained that to them "feminism" meant that as adults they plan to be economically independent of men. Until that time, though, it means "knowing that boys aren't all they're cracked up to be."

I had hoped that these girls, with their bold credo, would defy the statistics in the AAUW survey *Shortchanging Girls, Shortchanging America*. Yet although they spoke of themselves in terms of grit and independence, those qualities were rarely on display in the classroom. Whereas their male classmates yelled out or snapped the fingers of their raised hands when they wanted to speak, these girls seemed, for the most part, to recede from class proceedings, a charge they didn't deny.

"I don't raise my hand in my classes because I'm afraid I have the wrong answer and I'll be embarrassed," Becca, who is gangly and soft-spoken, explains one day during lunch. "My self-confidence will be taken away, so I don't want to raise my hand even if I really do know."

"I hate when teachers correct you," says Evie, who, dark-haired and serious, is enrolled in Weston's gifted students' program. "And it's worse when they say it's okay to do things wrong in that voice like 'It's okay, honey.' I can't handle it. I get really red and I start crying and I feel stupid."

"I think," Amy says slowly, "I think girls just worry about what people will say more than boys do, so they don't want to talk so much."

I mention to Amy that the boys freely volunteer in the math and science classes I've observed, even though their answers are often wrong. They seem to think it's okay to say "I think," to be unsure of a response.

Amy nods in agreement. "Boys never care if they're wrong. They can say totally off-the-wall things, things that have nothing to do with class sometimes. They're not afraid to get in trouble or anything. I'm not shy. But it's like, when I get into class, I just . . ." She shrugs her shoulders helplessly. "I just can't talk. I don't know why."

Girls' hesitance to speak out relative to boys is not mere stylistic difference; speaking out in class—and being acknowledged for it—is a constant reinforcement of a student's right to be heard, to take academic risks. Students who talk in class have more opportunity to enhance self-esteem through exposure to praise; they have the luxury of learning from mistakes and they develop the perspective to see failure as an educational tool. Boys such as Kyle and Nate feel internal permission to speak out whether they are bright or not, whether they are right or wrong, whether their comments are insightful, corrosive, combative, or utterly ridiculous. The important thing is to be recognized, to assert the "I am."

"I think my opinions are important, so I yell them out," Nate tells me one day after Mrs. Richter's math class. "The teacher'll tell you not to do it, but they answer your question before the people who raise their hands. Girls will sit there until the bell rings with their hands up and never get their question answered." He waves his hand in the air as if brushing the girls aside and says contemptuously, "Forget that."

According to gender equity specialists Myra and David Sadker, students who participate in class hold more positive attitudes toward school, and those attitudes enhance learning. Yet they also found that, in the typical classroom, boys overwhelmingly dominate the proceedings: they consistently command more of the teacher's time and energy than girls, receiving more positive reinforcement, more remediation, and more criticism. Nor is the difference just one of quantity: in the Sadkers' observations of one hundred classrooms in four states, they found that the boys were routinely asked more complex questions than girls, and were commended for their academic acumen, while girls were commended for social skills and docility (Sadker and Sadker 1985 and 1986).

In every class I visit at Weston there is at least one boy like Nate or Kyle, a boy who demands constant and inappropriate attention and to whom the teacher succumbs: if she doesn't, after all, she won't get much done during that period. In a straight count of who talks in Weston classrooms—who yells out answers, who is called on by the teacher, who commands the most interaction—the ratio hovers roughly around five boys to one girl. Compared to other schools, however, this constitutes progress: the Sadkers placed the rate at eight to one (Sadker and Sadker 1985; Schrof 1993). Even in English class, traditionally girls' turf, Weston boys received roughly three times the recognition of their female classmates.

The argument can be made that boys as well as girls suffer from the hidden curriculum. Boys such as Nate may be learning an unfortunate self-centeredness along with a lack of respect for their female classmates. Yet they still profit from the attention they receive. Ignored by their teachers and belittled by their male peers, girls lose heart: they may become reluctant to participate at all in class, unable to withstand the small failures necessary for long-term academic success. Even girls such as Amy, Evie, and Becca, who frequently proclaim that "guys are *so* obnoxious," have absorbed the hidden lessons of deference to them in the classroom, and, along with it, a powerful lesson in self-abnegation.

Several days after joining Amy in her math class, I visit Ms. Kelly's English class. Ms. Kelly is a second-year teacher: freckle-faced and snub-nosed, dressed in a T-shirt and khaki skirt, she barely looks older than her students. The class has been studying Greek mythology; today Ms. Kelly, who has placed the desks in clusters of six, instructs the students to write out the discussion they imagine took place between Zeus and Hera when she discovered he had fathered an illegitimate child.

"Any questions?" she asks, after explaining the assignment.

Two girls, Kathy and Amanda, raise their hands and she calls on Amanda. Amanda glances at Kathy, who sits in the group of desks next to hers. "Well, can you help me when you've answered her question?" she says politely. The teacher tends to Kathy, and then to a boy in another group who is misbehaving; she never returns to Amanda, who becomes frustrated.

"What are we supposed to do?" she mutters. "I don't get it." She puts her pencil down and looks over the shoulder of the girl sitting next to her. After a few minutes, she sighs wearily and begins to write.

I walk around the room, asking the students if I can read their works-in-progress. Amanda, who will eventually get an A on her paper, covers hers when I ask to see it.

"Oh," she says, "mine's so stupid you wouldn't want to read it."

Kathy reluctantly hands me her work. As I skim through it, one of the boys shoves his paper at me.

"Don't you want to read mine?" he asks.

I smile politely, as unwilling as the teachers to chastise him for interrupting, and take his paper. The dialogue he's written is almost incoherent and laced with misuses of the archaic forms of "you," as in "Hera, I'll whip thou butt for that."

He smirks as I read.

"Good, huh?" he says, then takes the paper back to read to his seatmates.

During an earlier lesson, the students have composed their own original myths, and have voted on the one they think is the best in the class. At the end of today's period, Ms. Kelly reads the winner, written by a wiry, sharp-featured Latina girl named Amber. The tale is surprisingly artful, the story of a young boy's search for the answers to questions that his father says are unsolvable. His quest takes him through enchanted woods, where he encounters talking animals who help him unlock the secret of a magic waterfall. He attains wisdom through risk and adventure, and, in the end, brings insight as well as treasure home to lay before his father.

After class I ask Amber why she chose to make a boy, not a girl, the central character in her story. She shrugs. "I used a boy because little girls don't go into creepy places and explore things," she says. "And it was an adventure; it wouldn't be right if you used a girl."

I ask Ms. Kelly to lend me the students' stories from all of her class periods and flip through the stack. Although many girls chose men and boys as the embodiments of bravery, strength, and wisdom, it did not surprise me to find that not a single boy had imagined a female hero.

Certainly some girls at Weston act out, demand attention, clown in class, but when they try those tactics, using disruption as a tool to gain individual attention and instruction, they are not met with the same reward as boys.

In mid-November, Mrs. Richter is giving out grades to Amy's class. The teacher sits at her desk in the back corner of the room, and the students come up one by one, in reverse alphabetical order; their faces are tense on the way up, then pleased or disappointed on the way back.

When Dawn's turn comes, Mrs. Richter speaks sharply to her.

"You're getting a B," the teacher says, "but for citizenship, you're getting 'disruptive.' You've been talking a lot and there have been some outbursts."

Dawn scrunches her mouth over to one side of her face, lowers her eyes, and returns to her seat.

"Disruptive?" yells Nate from across the room where the teacher's voice has carried. "*She's* not disruptive, *I'm* disruptive."

Mrs. Richter laughs. "You've got that right," she says.

When his turn comes, Nate gets a B plus. "It would've been an A minus if you turned in your last homework assignment," Mrs. Richter says. As predicted, his citizenship comment is also 'disruptive,' but the bad news isn't delivered with the same sting as it was to Dawn—it's conferred with an indulgent smile. There is a tacit acceptance of a disruptive boy, because boys *are* disruptive. Girls are too, sometimes, as Dawn illustrates, but with different consequences.

So along with fractions and exponents, Dawn has learned that she has to tamp down assertive behavior, that she has to diminish herself both to please the teacher and to appease the boys, with whom she cannot compete. Meanwhile, Nate has learned that monopolizing the class period and defying the teacher gets him in trouble, but he also garners individual attention, praise, and answers to his questions.

Over the course of the semester, Dawn slowly stops disrupting; she stops participating too. At the semester break, when I check with Mrs. Richter on the classes'

progress, she tells me, "Dawn hardly talks at all now because she's overpowered by the boys. She can't get the attention in class, so she's calmed down."

Nate, however, hasn't changed a bit, but whereas Dawn's behavior is viewed as containable, the teacher sees Nate's as inevitable. "I'll go through two weeks of torture before I'll give him detention," Mrs. Richter says. "But you have to tolerate that behavior to a certain extent or he won't want to be there at all, he'll get himself kicked out."

"I know his behavior works for him, though," she continues. "He talks more, he gets more answers out there, and he does well because of it. I try to tell him that we need to let others talk so they can understand too. But when I do, I begin and end with positive things about his behavior and sandwich the bad stuff in the middle. I'm never sure which part he really hears. . . ."

Endnote

1. The students who participated in the survey were drawn from twelve locations. The sample was stratified by region, and the students included were proportionate to the number of school-aged children in each state.

References

American Association of University Women (AAUW). 1990. *Shortchanging Girls, Shortchanging America: Full Data Report.* Washington, D.C.: American Association of University Women.

_____. 1991. *Shortchanging Girls, Shortchanging America: Executive Summary.* Washington, D.C.: American Association of University Women.

_____. 1992. *The AAUW Report: How the Schools Shortchange Girls.* Washington, D.C.: The AAUW Educational Foundation and the National Educational Association.

Daley, S. 1991. "Girls' self-esteem is lost on way to adolescence, new study finds." *New York Times*, National Edition, January 9, p. B1.

Eaky, K. 1991. "Girls' low self-esteem slows their progress, study finds." *San Francisco Examiner*, January 9, p. A1.

Fennema, E. and J. Sherman. 1977. "Sex-related differences in mathematics achievement, spatial visualization and affective factors." *American Educational Research Journal*, 14:1.

Kloosterman, P. 1990. "Attributions, performance following failure, and motivation in mathematics," in E. Fennema and G. C. Leder (eds.), *Mathematics and Gender*, New York: Teachers College Press.

Linn, M. C. 1990. "Gender, mathematics and science: Trends and recommendations." Paper presented at the Summer Institute for the Council of Chief State School Officers, Mystic, CT. July-August.

National Science Board. 1991. *Science and Engineering Indicators*. Washington, DC: National Science Board.

Sadker, M. and D. Sadker. 1985. "Sexism in the schoolroom of the '80s." *Psychology Today*, March.

_____. 1986. "Sexism in the classroom: From grade school to graduate school." *Phi Delta Kappan*, 67, 7.

Schrof, J. M. 1993. "The gender machine." *U.S. News & World Report*, August 2.

U.S. Bureau of the Census. 1992. *Educational Attainment in the United States: March 1991 and 1990*. Washington, DC: U.S. Government Printing Office.

White, P. E. 1992. "Women and minorities in science and engineering: An update." Washington DC: National Science Foundation.

Food for Thought and Application Questions

1. Reflect on your own primary- and secondary-level educational experiences. Identify aspects of the "hidden curriculum" which encouraged gender-traditional behavior. To the extent that teachers played a role in transmitting this hidden curriculum, do you think they did so intentionally? If not, what motivated their behavior?

   What do you believe to be the end result of the existence of this hidden curriculum? Did it affect you personally? If so, how?

2. The educational setting described by Orenstein is co-educational. How would the hidden curriculum and girls' experiences differ in a single-sex educational environment? Give specific examples and discuss the likely consequences of these differences. ✦

4

Factors Affecting Female Achievement and Interest in Science and Scientific Careers

Marsha Lakes Matyas

Research has consistently shown that, in general, girls do not achieve as well in science classes as do boys. Between ages nine and 14, girls' science achievement declines and their interest in science wanes (NAEP 1978; Hardin and Dede 1978). During high school girls do not elect to take science and mathematics courses as often as do their male peers (Dearman and Plisko 1981; NSF 1982); and, among college-bound senior high school students taking the Scholastic Aptitude Tests (SAT) in 1980, males outscored females by eight points on the verbal portion and 48 points on the mathematical portion. In college fewer girls choose science, especially the physical sciences, as their major area of study. On the other hand, the percentage of young women choosing social science as their field of study is twice the percentage of young men, and three times as many women as men select education as a college major (Butler and Marzone 1980). Although equal percentages of men and women choose biological sciences as a field of study, the percentage of men enter-ing physical science is twice that of women, entering technical majors (e.g., electronics, mechanics, data processing) is 3.5 times that of women, and entering engineering is 9.5 times the percentage of women (Butler and Marzone 1980).

These statistics should not be interpreted as an indication that women have not been interested in science and in scientific careers. Historically, women have contributed in botany, astronomy, anatomy, bacteriology, anthropology, psychology, and nutrition and, recently, opportunities have opened for them in other scientific fields. The data, however, indicate that factors still exist which significantly affect young women's science education as well as entrance and retention in a scientific career. In order to increase the number of women in science, these factors must be exposed and examined. A considerable body of work is in progress and, in general, researchers have isolated three groups of factors: educational, sociocultural, and personal. In this chapter all three types will be examined.

Educational Factors

To examine educational factors affecting girls' avoidance of science, one logically studies formal science classes, for it is expected that most students receive their first formal science instruction within a class. Florence Howe (1978) has described the critical impact of school learning on a child's future interests and career choice: "What you learn in school is not a joking matter. It forms an invisible network of belief—interfaced by the networks of church and family and now the media—that may blind you or may free you to see" (p. 21). Some believe that differential experiences within science and mathematics classes have not "freed" women to perceive future scientific careers (Skolnick, Langbort, and Day 1982; Kahle and Lakes 1983). Recent data from the 1976-77 National Assessment of Educational Progress (NAEP) provide strong support for the claim that boys and girls do not receive the same science education within the critical environment of the classroom.

Class Experiences

In 1976-77 NAEP conducted its third survey of science. Using national samples of nine, 13, and 17-year-olds, it assessed both science achievement levels and science attitudes. The student sample was balanced according to race and community type and is generalizable to the national population. The results showed that, as early as age 13, girls' science achievement was significantly lower than that of boys. In addition, the responses to attitudinal items indicated that girls, compared with boys of the same age, held less positive attitudes toward science and had participated in far fewer science activities (Kahle and Lakes 1983). Differences between boys and girls in attitudes toward and achievement in science are not restricted to the United States. A recent multi-national study explored the relationship between science attitudes and science achievement in 19 countries. The results were described by Allison Kelly (1981), who stated that ". . . pupils with favorable attitudes toward science tended to achieve better in science than pupils with less favorable attitudes. Attitudes toward science were significantly related to achievement in science even when ability . . . was taken into account." (p. 36)

In order to understand the cause of achievement and attitudinal differences, responses to two types of NAEP questions were examined. One type of question assessed the number of actual science experiences encountered by a student; the second type assessed the student's wish to participate in these same activities regardless of actual participation opportunities. Responses to this second type of question indicate whether girls' reported lack of science experiences was due to lack of interest or dearth of opportunity. Responses comparing girls' desires for typical classroom science experiences (e.g., "Would you like to see a sprouting seed?") versus their actual experiences ("Have you seen for real a sprouting seed?") revealed some surprising results. At age nine, although girls expressed interest in many science activities, the actual number of science activities they had participated in was significantly less than the number boys had experienced. For example, the NAEP survey included questions on a variety of scientific instruments, phenomena, and experiences. Girls were asked whether they would like to observe scientific phenomena (birds hatching and seeds sprouting, etc.), use scientific equipment (scales, telescopes, thermometers, and compasses) and work with experimental materials (magnets, electricity, and plants). Girls consistently reported fewer experiences with these scientific materials than did boys of the same age. However, other responses, in general, indicated that girls as well as boys wished to have these opportunities (Kahle and Lakes 1983). Other responses by 13 and 17-year-olds indicated that the disparity in science experiences between boys and girls increased with age. In addition, responses to science attitude questions indicated that girls' desires to participate in science activities diminished between ages nine and 13. This decline parallels a decline in science achievement levels and in science experiences between nine, 13, and 17 years of age. According to the NAEP data, by the time students enter high school girls, compared with boys, have had fewer science experiences with instruments and materials and score lower on science and mathematical achievement tests.

Mathematics Curriculum

In addition to fewer basic science experiences, many researchers suggest that the lack of mathematical training for girls in elementary and secondary schools is critical. A substantial body of research has investigated factors affecting girls' lower achievement levels in mathematics and lower enrollment rates in advanced high school math courses. Much of this work was inspired by early studies which indicated a large disparity between the percentages of males and females entering college with four years of high school mathematics (Sells 1973). Researchers have estimated that high school graduates with less than a full college preparative series of mathematics courses may be filtered out of three-quarters of all college majors (Tobin in Iker 1980). Since high school mathematics is a requirement for many occupations and fields of study, mathematics has often been called the "critical filter" in the training of future scientists and engineers.

Maccoby and Jacklin (1974) found that during elementary school both boys and girls enjoy mathematics. Nevertheless, by high school graduation, girls' SAT-Math scores are lower than boys' by almost 50 points. This difference does not appear to be due to differences in the math sequence taken but may result from attrition from that sequence. Recent data indicate that although comparable percentages of boys and girls (46.4 and 43.1 percent respectively) enroll in college preparatory mathematics sequences in high school (Dearman and Plisko 1981), on the average girls, compared with boys, still enter college with one-third year less high school mathematics (NSF 1982; Chipman and Thomas 1980). Girls' higher attrition rates from college preparatory math sequences cannot be attributed to poor grades. Remick and Miller (1978) found that Asian American and Caucasian American girls who continued beyond two years of college preparatory math were superior students, while their male colleagues in advanced courses were frequently average students.

Several explanations for the noted differences in enrollment patterns and achievement levels between girls and boys in math courses have been offered. Benbow and Stanley (1980, 1983) at The Johns Hopkins University suggest that boys per-

form better than girls on math achievement tests because they have greater aptitude for math, not because they enroll in more math courses. Additional studies, however, indicate otherwise. Sherman (1981) performed a longitudinal study on high school students to determine what factors were important in predicting whether students enroll in future mathematics courses. Her analysis indicates the following factors are most important for girls: (1) spatial visualization ability; (2) Quick Word Test performance; (3) perceived usefulness of mathematics; and (4) confidence in learning mathematics. The most important factor among girls in this study was spatial ability; that is, the ability to visualize objects in their spatial orientation and to rotate them within their field in one's imagination. Spatial ability has frequently been related to successful learning of mathematics. Previous studies have indicated that females, in general, have poorer spatial abilities than do males (Maccoby and Jacklin 1974; Treagust 1980). However, Fennema and Sherman (1977) and deWolf (1981) found that when the number of space-related courses taken by students was considered, differences in spatial visualization abilities and mathematics achievement scores disappeared. Recently, Linn's (1982) meta-analysis of sex differences in spatial ability research revealed no significant differences between males and females before, during, or after puberty. Furthermore, Skolnick, Langbort, and Day (1982) maintain that girls can improve their spatial abilities by relevant exercises and experiences and possibly increase their interest and achievement in math-science courses as well. Of the three other factors cited by Sherman (1981), only one, the Quick Word Test, is a measure of ability. The Quick Word Test is described simply as a vocabulary test of verbal skill and general ability. The other two factors deal with girls' attitudes toward and perceptions of mathematics. Girls' perceptions of the future usefulness of mathematics as instrumental in their decision to take advanced courses has been cited not only by Sherman (1981) but also by other researchers (Iker 1980; Fennema and Sherman 1977). The same group of researchers also found that girls have less confidence in their ability to learn mathematics and do not perceive positive parental attitudes toward them as math learners. Girls, therefore, may not lack the necessary abilities for achievement in mathematics, although they do seem to lack the prerequisite positive attitudes and personal confidence.

The relationship between mathematics coursework and achievement and the possibility of a future science career seems clear. If girls take fewer high school math courses and have lower achievement levels in them, they limit their selection of scientific or technical majors in college as well as their probable success should they elect such a major. Research shows that professionals successful in math-related careers average at the 90th percentile level on SAT-Math tests (Chipman and Thomas 1980). Those attaining these elite scores are usually males as are those students who have taken more than four years of mathematics in high school (Dearman and Plisko 1981). Accordingly, if girls do not overcome a reticence to enroll in mathematics courses, the female pool of potential professional scientists and engineers will not increase effectively.

Extracurricular Activities

Disparities between the science education of girls and boys do not end at the classroom door; for girls report fewer science experiences both within and outside the classroom. Responses to NAEP (1978) survey items showed that girls, ages thirteen and seventeen, participated in extracurricular science activities significantly fewer times than did boys. These activities included reading science articles and books, watching television shows on scientific topics, and doing science projects and hobbies. When field trip opportunities were surveyed, girls in all three age groups

reported visiting far fewer places than did boys. Although 9-year-old girls expressed more interest than boys in participating in many field trips, by ages 13 and 17 fewer girls than boys had visited 12 out of 14 field sites listed (Kahle and Lakes 1983).

Even when children are at play, their experiences may provide unequal preparation for later science instruction. Male and female children are given different toys to play with and are encouraged by parents, teachers, and peers to engage in sex-appropriate play. Boys' toys and games tend to emphasize relationships between objects, manipulation of objects in space, grouping of objects, and taking apart and rebuilding of objects, while girls' activities are more closely associated with verbal, interpersonal, and fine-motor skills (Skolnick *et al.* 1982). The play activities of boys, therefore, are more likely to provide practice at spatial-visualization tasks which are useful later in both science and mathematics courses.

These differences in types of play are common and appear to have long-term effects. In the NAEP survey, 13 and 17-year-old girls were asked how often they had done electrical or mechanical tasks (traditionally masculine tasks) and how often they had worked with an unhealthy plant or animal (traditionally feminine tasks). Girls ranked far below boys in the number of times they had performed "masculine tasks," yet above boys in number of times they had performed "feminine tasks." These findings support those of who found that third grade girls were

> . . . conditioned to accept toys as they are and not manipulate or change them. . . . By fifth grade, girls were quite reluctant to work with science toys at all and frequently protested 'I'm a girl, I'm not supposed to know anything about things like that.' Boys, even in these early grades, were about twice as good as girls at explaining ideas about toys. (Torrance 1962, p. 112)

The relationship between play and experiences and science classwork is clearly explained by Samuel (in Kelly 1981):

> Boys are often encouraged to play with mechanical, electrical or construction toys and to help with tasks around the home involving tools, but girls are less likely to have this background experience. Thus, the girls are doing something new and unfamiliar in science laboratory classes, and it is, perhaps, not surprising that they often look for reassurance and encouragement, even though they have been given and have understood the directions (p. 248).

Samuel's explanation can be easily demonstrated by means of a simple analogy. Envision the thoughts and feelings of an adolescent boy asked to enter the kitchen, recipes and definition list in hand, and to prepare a full meal on which he will consequently be graded. Realize that he is in competition with female peers who, though they also have never done this particular task, have considerably greater facility with the equipment required. Perhaps by this analogy we can understand the apprehension of the adolescent girl deciding whether or not to take high school physics. In fact, a recent study performed in Nigeria provides strong evidence that sex stereotyping of tasks significantly influences performance (Ehindero 1982). Although boys and girls perform equally well on gender-neutral Piagetian tasks, when mathematical word problems of equal difficulty but which deal with typically male or typically female situations are presented, boys perform significantly poorer on the feminine situation problems and girls perform significantly poorer on the masculine situation problems. Since the only differences in the problems are the content areas, extracurricular activities must play a role in children's familiarity with various content areas and, consequently, with their performances. The lack of familiarity with tools and techniques useful in science, many of which are available through extracurricular experiences, may be a contributing factor in girls' low enrollment levels and high attrition rates from science courses and perhaps in their lower achievement levels in science.

Socio-Cultural and Personal Factors

Research studies have explored a variety of social and personal factors which limit science as a career choice for girls. Since it is difficult to separate society's influence from personal choice, these two types of factors will be discussed together.

Sex-Role Stereotyping

Sex-role stereotyping has been cited as one of the major reasons for women's avoidance of science careers; that is, girls view science careers as masculine and, therefore, avoid them. Vockell and Lobonc (1981) tested these assumptions and found that high school girls rate science careers as masculine, especially physical science careers. Sex-role stereotyping of careers has been found as early as kindergarten (Vockell and Lobonc 1981). In addition, the stereotyped characteristics associated with women are generally not those commonly associated with scientists. According to Broverman, Vogel, Broverman, Clarkson, and Rosenkrantz (1972), women are associated with a "warmth-expressiveness" cluster of attributes such as gentleness, quietness, tenderness, emotionality, passivity, dependence, and subjectivity. Men, on the other hand, are associated with characteristics such as aggressiveness, dominance, rationality, independence, calmness, unemotionality, and objectivity (Broverman et al. 1972). These traits are readily associated with the stereotypic view of scientists. A longitudinal study by Chambers (1983) asked 4807 children, grades K to five, to draw a picture of a scientist. Of the 4807 pictures drawn, only 28 were of women, all drawn by girls. Clearly, children's stereotypic image of a scientist is masculine. Girls who are interested in science careers, therefore, must break the sterotypic mold of sex-appropriate careers, as well as accept that they will be associated with stereotypically-masculine attributes.

Not surprisingly, sex-role stereotyping of science careers is less pronounced among girls who attend single sex schools. Dale (1974) has found that girls in single sex schools have higher preferences for science and math courses than do girls in coeducational schools. This preference difference cannot be totally attributed to higher socio-economic status among girls in single sex schools. While holding socio-economic class factors constant, Dale has found that the student's choice of subject was still biased. Arithmetic and physics were favored among girls in single sex schools, while in coeducational schools girls chose French, sewing, and cooking. Perhaps girls in single sex schools do not feel some of the social pressures which affect girls enrolled in science and math classes in coeducational schools. Kelly (1981) made similar observations, finding that girls in single sex schools have better attitudes toward science than do their counterparts in coeducational classes.

With the current public emphasis on the feminist movement and on equal job opportunities for women, one would anticipate that stereotyping of occupations would decline. In fact, a recent study by Hensley and Borges (1981) found that females (age 7-8 and college age) did not sex-stereotype occupations but that males of the same age groups did. The same study also found that children of working mothers stereotyped occupations to a greater extent than did children of non-working mothers. It may be that children with working mothers have a more realistic view of the jobs to which women have ready access and, since over 50 percent of children have mothers who are currently employed (Cocks 1982), a large proportion of young girls may be confused by conflicting information. The information they are receiving from their mothers' experiences in the real world of employment opportu-nities contrasts with the information they may receive at school or through the media which indicates that professional careers in traditionally masculine areas are now open to young women. Such conflicting information leaves young women in a "triple bind":

> [T]he traditional vision of the full time wife and mother conflicts with economic realities which dictate that most women must work; the newer vision of the career women conflicts with child rearing, which is still seen mainly as women's responsibility; and the new ethic of equality inspires girls to be more independent and competent than they suspect is really acceptable and more than they have been taught to feel. To reconcile old and new demands and their own feelings, girls would have to become super-women. (Skolnick et al. 1982, p. 39)

Such conflicts are real and immediate for high school girls and may quench a girl's interest in a professional career. One 11th grade girl, when asked what she would like to do as an adult, stated that she would like a professional career, in this case, as a lawyer:

> As far as going to school, I can go to about any school I want to, but the thing is I don't know if I am going to go out and become a lawyer after law school. It's like if I become a lawyer, it's a full-time operation and maybe I'll have a husband and I'll want to have kids. I would want to spend time with them and I don't know if I can be a full-time lawyer and a full-time lover, and I don't want to take anything away from my kids or take anything away from my occupation. It bothers me so much. . . . It's just that—I don't know—I want to be somebody that people write down in history, somebody that is not forgotten. I don't want to be just another skeleton in the ground. I think I will become a housewife and it bothers me because I don't know what to do (Skolnick et al. 1982, p. 37).

These conflicts, resulting from social pressures, are experienced by many young women making professional career choices, and the social pressures are even greater for girls interested in science. Girls choosing to continue science and mathematics studies during high school may be viewed as non-conformists at a developmental period when conformity is highly valued by peers. Girls taking science courses describe themselves as ". . . less feminine, less attractive, less popular, and less sociable. That is, they appear to see themselves as less socially attractive than their peers" (Smithers and Collins in Kelly 1981, p. 166). The seriousness of this social pressure is suggested by Fox (in Iker 1980) who states that many gifted girls do not enter accelerated math courses because of negative social consequences, especially peer rejection. Horner (1972) and Stein and Bailey (1973) report that girls have lower motivation to achieve in traditionally male areas because of the perceived consequences. Finally, Ormerod (1975) summarizes this situation, stating that ". . . at an age when they are becoming acutely aware of the other sex, in co-education boys and girls are expressing preferences and, when possible, choices in such a way as to reaffirm their perceived sex role" (p. 265). Unfortunately, the socialized female sex role does not currently include scientific aspirations.

Role Models

If girls do not perceive science, math, and technological careers as appropriate for their sex, steps must be taken to change this perception. Emphasis has been placed on the use of role models to encourage girls' participation in science. Hardin and Dede (1978) point out that there is a dearth of female role models in scientific careers. In addition, many of these role models have not achieved success. Recent surveys indicate that women with advanced degrees do not obtain tenure as early and, at every degree level and age, are paid less than men (Vetter 1981).

Research on the effects of role models on student behaviors has produced conflicting results. Some studies have found role models to be an important influence on the achievement and career decisions of female students (O'Donnell and Anderson 1978; Seater and Ridgeway 1976; Stake and Granger 1978). Other studies, however, found that role models did not have a significant effect (Basow and Howe 1980; Vockell and Lobonc 1981). In addition, Kelly (1981) has found that, although the number of female role models varies from country to country, the difference in science achievement between girls and boys in various countries remains constant.

Before any effect of role models can be substantiated, researchers may need to delineate how role modeling actually works. Brush (1979) has found that the similarity between a student's self-image and her/his image of a scientist is a good predictor of whether that student chooses to take science classes. If a student attributes the same personal characteristic to her/himself as s/he does to a scientist, s/he is more likely to take optional science classes. The critical factor for role models, therefore, may be to emphasize the similarities between themselves and students. As stated by Ebbertt (in Kelly 1981), "If females in science careers are seen to require such characteristics as capability, logicality, and exactitude, there may be considerable self-selection away from science subjects by girls who do not see themselves as possessing these traits . . ." (p. 121).

One of the first science role models girls encounter is their science teacher. Many investigators agree that the importance of the teacher in developing a girl's attitude toward science cannot be overemphasized. Female scientists surveyed by Remick and Miller (1978) reported that the "encouragement of a single high school teacher was the deciding factor in their choice of a career in science. (High school counselors, on the other hand, are uniformly reported as negative influences.)"

(p. 282). Stake and Granger (1978) measured teacher influence on science career commitment and found that same-sex teachers perceived as an attractive individual by the student had a greater positive influence on science career commitment than did opposite-sex teachers. The highest science career commitment was found among students who had varied and important same-sex teacher contacts such as participation in science research projects under the direction of a same-sex role model. Unfortunately, only 24 percent of all high school science teachers nationally are female (NSF 1982); therefore, girls have fewer opportunities for this important same-sex teacher contact.

Other researchers have tried specifically to discern teacher behaviors which differentially affect boys and girls. Results indicate that boys receive more direct questions from their teachers than do girls, that boys are praised more frequently than are girls for correct answers, and overall that boys have more interactions with teachers than do girls (Brophy and Good 1970). Although a greater amount of interaction with boys is concerned with criticism and disapproval, this negative feedback is generally directed toward disciplinary aspects rather than toward academic/work-related aspects of boys' behavior (Brophy and Good 1970). Girls, on the other hand, receive more criticism of their academic performances than of their classroom actions. Negative academic interactions with teachers may be a significant reason for girls' lack of self-confidence and expectancy for success in academic settings (Fennema and Sherman 1977).

Solutions

The factors affecting girls' levels of achievement and interest in science are many and diverse. Unlike blatant sex discrimination, these differences are subtle and, taken individually, appear almost insignificant. Their collective effect, however, exerts a powerful force upon young women to think long and hard before committing themselves to a scientific career. Not only must they make important decisions about the high academic standards demanded by science, but they must also decide to face the social and interpersonal conflicts which a science career currently places on women. If girls do not receive an equal science education at the elementary school level and then receive little encouragement during high school, there is little chance that they will become scientists. It will require the combined effort of teachers, parents, and counselors to break this pattern and to offer female students the chance to excel in science, mathematics, and engineering.

Because of the importance of teacher/student interactions, it is imperative that science teachers do not unwittingly convey perceptions of science as a masculine endeavor. Bowyer (in Trowbridge, Bybee, and Sund 1981), states that boys in school are "valued for thinking logically, independently, with self-confidence, and an appropriate degree of risk taking." Girls, however, are "valued for their emotional expressiveness, sensitivity to others, dependency, and subjective thinking" (p. 97). Teachers' value judgments such as these do not increase girls' science potential and must be consciously avoided.

Some researchers have suggested that girls and boys may require different teaching methods for optimal achievement in science classes (Ormerod 1975; Treagust 1980). There may be simpler, more direct solutions to the problem, however. For example, girls' extracurricular science activities might be increased by offering more in-class activities. Classroom data indicate that for grades K-3, only 17 minutes per day and during grades 4–6 only 28 minutes per day are spent in science instruction (Weiss 1978). In addition, 36 percent of all elementary science classes are conducted in rooms with no science facilities whatsoever. School boards and administrators, therefore, need to mandate more time to be spent each day on science activities and more funding for science equipment.

This lack of classroom science activities may also be due to inadequate science training among elementary school teachers. Only 22 percent of elementary school teachers in the same survey indicated that they felt "very well qualified" to teach science, and 16 percent indicated they were not well qualified to teach science (Weiss 1978). With this in mind, the number of science activities for all students might be increased by improving the science preparation of elementary school teachers. In addition, materials are now available to help teachers at both the elementary and junior high school levels teach children basic skills in science, mathematics, graphing, and spatial visualization (Skolnick et al. 1982). These materials can provide girls with the practice needed to catch up and keep up with their male peers in science and mathematics.

Undoubtedly, a key factor in changing girls' attitudes will be science teachers and counselors and their attitudes. As stated by Skolnick et al. (1982), "Teachers' expectations are communicated to children in myriad ways, not only through what they say explicitly but also through what they do not say, what they do, and whom they call on. Indirect or covert messages constitute a hidden curriculum which is sometimes more powerful than the lessons in the textbooks . . ." (p. 17). If teachers in both elementary and high schools can convey positive attitudes toward scientific and mathematical studies and can encourage girls to pursue science course work and careers, then real changes in female achievement in and attrition from science courses might occur.

High school counselors have been cited as a negative factor in girls' choice of science as a career (Remick and Miller 1978). Counselors must convey to students the knowledge that class and curriculum choices early in high school can eliminate science career choices later on. Girls must be encouraged not only to pursue but also

to excel in mathematics; their confidence in their math skills must be bolstered, and their participation in spatial visualization activities should be stressed. Counselors must emphasize to young women the wide range of scientific occupations available to them and encourage them to keep their options open by pursuing science and mathematics electives during high school.

Finally, the role of parents in developing positive attitudes toward science cannot be ignored. Parental influence on a girl's potential as a scientist begins in the preschool years. Through toys, games, and play, parents can encourage their daughters' inquisitiveness and development of spatial visualization and problem-solving skills (Skolnick et al. 1982). During later childhood and adolescence, parents can exert a great influence on choice of extracurricular activities for their children and can affect both the number and kind of science activities girls experience outside school. As previously discussed, parental attitudes toward girls' science classwork affect girls' choices of science classes, their confidence in math classes, and their perception of science as masculine. In addition, lack of parental encouragement operates as a factor in the high attrition rate of girls from science majors in college (Graham 1978). Finally, parents must take an active interest in the science education their children are receiving.

Summary

In summary, several factors significantly contribute to lower science and mathematics achievement levels of girls as well as their higher attrition rates from scientific courses and careers. A lack of science-based experimental and extracurricular activities in the elementary school years followed by less than a full college preparatory series of mathematics and science courses places girls at a disadvantage when selecting a college major and ultimately a career. In addition, various sociocultural factors including sex-role stereotyping, peer pressure, and lack of or ineffectual role models discourage girls from science classes and careers. Interactions with teachers, parents, and counselors may fail to provide the kind of encouragement necessary to prevent or to overcome these socio-cultural factors.

Finally, it should be noted that the intent of any educational program should not be to force girls into a career unsuited to their particular talents and interests, but, as stated by Kaminski and Erickson (1979), "This is not to argue that all females need to be pushed into science careers. Rather, like high school males, more females (particularly those with higher ability) need to leave a wider variety of options open to themselves for later, more informed career decisions" (p. 15). The technological society in which we live cannot afford to lose the scientific brainpower of over one-half of its population. Girls still should be free to see themselves as scientists and engineers and to see science is a viable option by the time they reach college. It is critical that girls do not close the door to scientific success at the level of the primary or secondary school.

References

Basow, S. A. and K. G. Howe. 1980. "Role-model influence: Effects of sex and sex-role attitude in college students." *Psychology of Women Quarterly*, 4(4):558-572.

Benbow, C. P. and J. C. Stanley. 1980. "Sex differences in mathematical ability: Fact or artifact?" *Science*, 210:1262-1264.

_____. 1983. "Sex differences in mathematical reasoning ability: More facts." *Science*, 222:1029-1031.

Brophy, J. E. and T. L. Good. 1970. "Teachers' communication of differential expectations for children's classroom performance: Some behavioral data." *Journal of Educational Psychology*, 61(5):365-374.

Broverman, I. K., S. R. Vogel, D. M. Broverman, F. E. Clarkson, and P. S. Rosenkrantz. 1972. "Sex-role stereotypes: A current appraisal." *Journal of Social Issues*, 28(2):59-78.

Brush, L. R. 1979. "Avoidance of science and stereotypes of scientists." *Journal of Research in Science Teaching,* 16(3):237-241.

Butler, M. and J. Marzone. 1980. *Education: The Critical Filter. A Statistical Report on the Status of Female Students in Post-Secondary Education*, Vol. 2, San Francisco, CA., Women's Educational Equity Communications Network Far West Laboratory for Educational Research and Development.

Chambers, D. W. 1983. "Stereotypic images of the scientist: The draw-a-scientist test." *Science Education*, 67:255-265.

Chipman, S. F. and V. G. Thomas. 1980. *Women's Participation in Mathematics: Outlining the Problem.* Washington, D.C., Report to the National Institute of Education, Teaching and Learning Division.

Cocks, J. 1982. "How long till equality?" *Time*, 12 July:20-29.

Dale, R. R. 1974. *Mixed or Single Schools*, Vol. 3. London, Routledge and Kegan Paul.

Dearman, N. B. and V. W. Plisko. 1981. *The Condition of Education*. Washington, D.C., National Center for Education Statistics.

deWolf, V. A. 1981. "High school mathematics preparation and sex differences in quantitative abilities." *Psychology of Women Quarterly*, 5(4):555-567.

Ehindero, O. J. 1982. "Correlates of sex-related differences in logical reasoning." *Journal of Research in Science Teaching*, 19:553-557.

Fennema, E. and J. Sherman. 1977. "Sex-related differences in mathematics achievement, spatial visualization and affective factors." *American Educational Research Journal*, 14(1):51-71.

Graham, M. F. 1978. "Sex differences in science attrition." Doctoral dissertation, State University of New York at Stony Brook. *Dissertation Abstracts International*, 39, 2570-B (University Microfilms No. 78-21, 847).

Hardin, J. and C. J. Dede. 1978. "Discrimination against women in science education." *The Science Teacher*, 40:18-21.

Hensley, K. K. and M. A. Borges. 1981. "Sex role stereotyping and sex role norms: A comparison of elementary and college age students." *Psychology of Women Quarterly*, 5(4):543-554.

Horner, M. S. 1972. "Toward an understanding of achievement-related conflicts in women." *Journal of Social Issues,* 28:157-175.

Howe, F. 1971. "Sexual stereotypes start early." *Saturday Review,* 16 October:76-94.

_____. 1978. "Myths of Coeducation." Paper presented at Wooster College, Wooster, OH, November.

Iker, S. 1980. "A math answer for women." *MOSAIC,* 11:39-45.

Kahle, J. B. and M. K. Lakes. 1983. "The myth of equality in science classrooms." *Journal of Research in Science Teaching,"* 20:131-140.

Kaminski, D. M. and E. Erickson. 1979. "The magnitude of sex role influence on entry into science careers." Paper presented at the meeting of the American Sociological Association, Boston, August 1979 (ERIC Document Reproduction Service No. ED 184855).

Kelly, A. 1981. *The Missing Half.* Manchester, England, Manchester University Press.

Linn, M. 1982. "Gender differences in spatial ability; meta-analysis." Paper presented at Purdue University, November.

Maccoby, E. M. and C. N. Jacklin. 1974. *The Psychology of Sex Differences.* Stanford, CA., Stanford University Press.

National Assessment of Educational Progress (NAEP). 1978. *Science Achievement in the Schools.* Science Report No. 08-S-01. Denver, CO, Education Commission of the States, December.

National Science Foundation (NSF). 1982. *Science and Engineering Education: Data and Information.* NSF 82-30. Washington, D.C., National Science Foundation.

O'Donnell, J. A. and D. G. Anderson. 1978. "Factors influencing choice of major and career of capable women." *Vocational Guidance Quarterly,* 26:215-221.

Ormerod, M. B. 1975. "Subject preference and choice in co-educational and single-sex secondary schools." *British Journal of Educational Psychology,* 45:257-267.

Remick, H. and K. Miller. 1978. "Participation rates in high school mathematics and science courses." *The Physics Teacher,* May:280-282.

Seater, B. B. and C. L. Ridgeway. 1976. "Role models, significant others, and the importance of male influence on college women." *Sociological Symposium,* 15:49-64.

Sells, L. W. 1973. "High school mathematics as the critical filter in the job market." Unpublished manuscript, University of California, Berkeley.

Sherman, J. 1981. "Girls' and boys' enrollments in theoretical math courses: A longitudinal study." *Psychology of Women Quarterly,* 5(5):681-689.

Skolnick, J., C. Langbort, and L. Day. 1982. *How to Encourage Girls in Math and Science.* Englewood Cliffs, NJ, Prentice-Hall.

Stake, J. E. and C. R. Granger. 1978. "Same-sex and opposite-sex teacher model influences on science career commitments among high school students." *Journal of Education Psychology,* 70:180-186.

Stein, A. A. and M. M. Bailey. 1973. "The socialization of achievement orientation in females." *Psychological Bulletin,* 80:345-366.

Torrance, E. P. 1962. *Guiding Creative Talent.* Englewood Cliffs, NJ, Prentice-Hall.

Treagust, D. F. 1980. "Gender-related differences of adolescents in spatial representational thought." *Journal of Research in Science Teaching,* 17:91-97.

Trowbridge, L. W., R. W. Bybee, and R. B. Sund. 1981. *Becoming a Secondary School Teacher.* Columbus, OH, Charles E. Merrill.

Vetter, B. M. 1981. "Women scientists and engineers: Trends in participation." *Science,* 214:1313-1321.

Vockell, E. L. and S. Lobonc. 1981. "Sex-role stereotyping by high school females in science." *Journal of Research in Science Teaching,* 18:209-219.

Weiss, I. R. 1978. *Report of the 1977 National Survey of Science, Mathematics and Social Studies Education.* SE-78-72, Washington, D.C., U.S. Government Printing Office.

Food for Thought and Application Questions

1. Recently, a new program for teaching mathematics to fifth and sixth graders was introduced into the curriculum in a metropolitan school district. This program involved using sports statistics (e.g., batting averages, yards rushing, percent from the line) to teach basic math concepts. The program was enthusiastically received by parents and teachers, and is scheduled for evaluation at the end of the next school year. What do you predict the evaluations will reveal about the success of the new program?

2. Locate a copy of your college/university catalog. Turn to the sections for the math and science department where faculty are listed. Count, based on the identification of male and female names, the proportion of women on the math and science faculties. (Omit any gender neutral names from your analysis.) Are women under-represented on math and science faculties at your institution? If so, what does this imply for educational experiences of women students in these programs at your university? Now, do the same calculation by faculty rank. In other words, what percentage of the Full Professors in science are women? Associate Professors? Assistant Professors? Instructors? Does the percent female decrease as you descend the academic hierarchy from Professor to Instructor? Interpret your findings. (Hint: Could it be that women are now moving into these fields, but have not been there long enough to achieve the higher ranks? Or could it be that women who are the "exception to the rule" find it more difficult to achieve the highest levels in their fields? If you agree with the latter, what types of structural barriers might impede the career progress of women in math and science?) ✦

Unit Two

Workplace Inequality: Segregation, the Pay Gap, and Comparable Worth

Perhaps you have seen the bumper stickers, tee shirts, and buttons— "Equal pay for equal work," "The best man for the job may be a woman," "Oh, so that explains the difference in our salaries" (accompanied by a graphic of two toddlers, a male and a female, looking inside their diapers), "We try harder and get paid less," and "Women make policy, not coffee." These popular slogans are responses, or mass level forms of resistance, to gender inequality in the workplace which takes a number of forms, as the slogans suggest, ranging from gender-based earnings inequality to unequal access to jobs. It is often assumed that women's increased involvement in paid work has been associated with a sharp reduction in workplace inequality; but, in reality, this is not the case. As increasing numbers of women have entered the labor force, the potential for workplace inequality has escalated. No longer isolated in the domestic sphere, women work alongside men in offices, factories, and other work settings. This makes workplace comparisons between the sexes more likely and serves to highlight inequi-

ties. Federal legislation was enacted more than 30 years ago to address increasingly visible workplace inequality. The Equal Pay Act of 1963 and Title VII of the Civil Rights Act of 1964, which forbids workplace discrimination against women and other protected groups, have met with limited success because women and men are located, often by choice, in different occupations.

In recent years there has been a barrage of articles in popular magazines about the progress women have made entering management and the professions. These articles exaggerate the amount of change that has actually occurred in women's employment patterns. While women have made inroads into high-level occupations, their share of these top level jobs is still extremely small. Most studies indicate that women hold less than 5 percent of senior managerial and executive positions in large corporate organizations (Federal Glass Ceiling Commission 1995). Looking to managerial and professional occupations for an indication of levels of workplace inequality is, however, misleading because only a minority of men and women are employed in these jobs. Unfortunately, women are even more under-represented in some other types of occupations, particularly the skilled trades and other manual, blue-collar jobs.

Sex segregation is the term used to refer to the concentration of workers of the same sex in job categories. Sex segregated employment is a prevalent type of inequality in the workplace, and it often serves as the basis for a second type of workplace inequality, sex-based earnings differences. Occupations dominated by women are paid at lower rates than occupations dominated by men, causing women to earn only about 72 cents for every dollar men earn. There is much evidence that the low pay in many female jobs (e.g., nurse, teacher, secretary) cannot be explained by their demand for skill or training (Treiman and Hartmann 1981). It can be convincingly argued that rates of pay in these jobs are low simply because women hold the jobs. This type of systematic undervaluing of women's work is a prevalent form of pay discrimination commonly referred to as comparable worth discrimination.

The workplace is segregated not only by sex, but also by race. Compared to white women, women of color are concentrated in lower tier occupations with less pay. Workplace inequality, then, is patterned by both sex and race—also by social class and other group characteristics. One's placement in a job hierarchy as well as the rewards one receives depends, in part, on how these characteristics "combine."

What explains sex-based inequality in the workplace today? It is possible for workplace inequality to result from productivity-related differences between women and men. These differences might result from one sex obtaining more education than the other or from one sex having more on-the-job training. To the extent that these types of differences exist between the sexes, unequal access to jobs and unequal rates of pay are viewed as

nondiscriminatory. Studies show, however, that productivity-related differences between the sexes are responsible for only a small portion of the inequality that exists in the workplace today (Marini 1989). Educational and work experience differences between the sexes have been eroding for some time, yet these changes have done little to create more similar occupational distributions for the sexes or narrow the earnings gap.

Gender socialization forces discussed in Unit One are partially responsible for creating patterns of workplace inequality. If belief systems and cultural values support sex stereotypes, then the sexes appear suited for different types of work. Women are encouraged by parents, teachers, and other socialization agents to prepare for and pursue jobs that will utilize their presumed traits. It is by no means a coincidence that jobs which involve the care of young children (e.g., day care workers, elementary school teachers) are female-dominated. The assumption is that women, with their innate nurturing ability, will be well suited for the work. Gender stereotypes involve a very different set of traits for men, ones that equip them for high-level positions of authority in the workplace. Employers who endorse gender stereotypes will make hiring decisions accordingly, and deny jobs to the "wrong" sex. From their biased perspective, doing otherwise would jeopardize productivity and profits.

Gender socialization forces also contribute to workplace inequality by encouraging women to bear the primary responsibility for child care. Assuming these responsibilities means that women may opt for certain types of employment that facilitate the coordination of work and family roles. Some positions, like teaching, are particularly compatible with child care responsibilities (summers off and after-school hours free). Other positions, such as those that require long hours or extensive travel, prove very difficult for women with primary child care responsibilities.

Unfortunately for women, the latter category of jobs is by far the more financially rewarding one. (Women's coordination of work and family roles will be discussed in detail in Unit Three.)

Another explanation of sex inequality in the workplace is that men, the beneficiaries of sex inequality in the workplace, work to preserve their advantaged position. For reasons of self interest, men who feel that their advantage is threatened by women's progress in the workplace might fight to exclude them from particular occupations. As employers, men might simply refuse to hire women; as employees, men might refuse to work with women or treat them poorly when hired so as to encourage their rapid departure. The widely publicized harassment of a female student at a previously all male military academy provides an example of this phenomenon in an educational setting.

It is important to note that white women are a privileged group in the workplace when compared to women of color. Working to preserve their relative advantage, white women have, on occasion, worked to deny opportunities to women of color (Reskin and Padavic 1994). Patterns of workplace inequality are also shaped in this fashion.

The selections in this unit address forms of workplace inequality and their causes. In the first selection, Reskin describes stability and change in sex segregated employment patterns. After introducing a measure designed to capture the amount of occupational segregation present in the workplace, she shows that rates of decline in occupational segregation have been rather slow since the 1970s. In contrast, Reskin also demonstrates a sharp downward trend for occupational segregation by race, especially among women. The causes of workplace segregation, both cultural and structural, are then discussed and examined in light of post-1960's occupational desegregation. Given that segregated employment patterns are a major contributor to the earnings gap be-

tween the sexes, this selection provides a useful starting point for examining pay inequities.

The next selection, by England, begins with a description of trends in the sex gap in pay. England shows how the size of the pay gap varies by race/ethnicity and age. Potential causes of pay differences between the sexes are then examined systematically in light of research findings. After concluding that the sex composition of a job is one of the most important determinants of wage level, England turns her attention to a discussion of the consequences of sex-based earnings inequality. Making the case that the consequences of the pay gap extend beyond economic problems for women to impact the balance of power between the sexes in marriages, England sets the stage for examining policies designed to erode the pay gap.

The selection by Blum explores a policy remedy aimed at reducing gender inequality in the workplace, comparable worth. She describes the emergence and growth of the comparable worth or pay-equity movement, arguing that it represents a major shift in strategy for women's economic advancement—away from affirmative action strategies aimed at job integration toward a revaluing of female-dominated occupations. In-depth interviews of California public sector employees suggest that comparable worth has more appeal to low-paid, working class women than affirmative action strategies. She notes, however, that the benefits working class women would derive from comparable worth would also serve to increase the gap between these women and underclass women in the lowest tiers of the workplace. Blum's selection provides an important example of how women in the workplace are not a homogeneous group, but rather a diverse group whose workplace experiences are patterned by class and race differences.

The final selection in this unit, by Amott and Matthaei, provides a conceptual framework for understanding how social class and race/ethnicity differentiate women's work lives and economic positions. The authors argue that race, class, and gender represent intertwining systems of domination and subordination that result in different forms, as well as varying degrees of economic exploitation for women workers. Their contribution is important because it represents the type of inclusive scholarship necessary for understanding work experiences in a pluralistic, diverse society, and as they point out, for facilitating broad based movements against the oppressions experienced by women.

References

Federal Glass Ceiling Commission. 1995. *A Solid Investment: Making Full Use of the Nation's Human Capital.* Washington, D. C.: U. S. Government Printing Office.

Marini, M. M. 1989. "Sex differences in earnings in the United States." *Annual Review of Sociology,* Vol. 15.

Reskin, B. and I. Padavic. 1994. *Women and Men at Work.* Thousand Oaks, CA: Pine Forge Press.

Treiman, D. J. and H. I. Hartmann (eds.). 1981. *Women, Work and Wages: Equal Pay for Jobs of Equal Value.* Washington, D.C.: National Academy Press. ✦

5

Sex Segregation in the Workplace

Barbara F. Reskin

Sex segregation in the workplace refers to women's and men's concentration in different occupations, industries, jobs, and levels in workplace hierarchies. More broadly, sex segregation constitutes a sexual division of paid labor in which men and women do different tasks, or the same tasks under different names or at different times and places. People's race and sometimes their ethnicity and age are also bases for differentiation at work, so workplaces are segregated by sex, race, and ethnicity, as well as other characteristics. The assignment of jobs based on workers' sex, race, and ethnicity is one of the most enduring features of work in industrialized societies and a mainstay in preserving larger systems of inequality.

Because the work that people do greatly influences their pay, sex segregation contributes substantially to the gap in earnings between women and men (England and McCreary 1987). Segregation also reduces women's fringe benefits and their access to medical insurance, pensions, and Social Security income. By disproportionately relegating women to jobs with short or absent career ladders, segregation lowers women's chances of promotion. Both task and rank segregation restrict women's likelihood of exercising authority at work (Reskin and Hartmann 1986). The effects of segregation extend beyond the workplace. Men's higher incomes, occupational status, and authority preserve their power over women in private and public realms.

Ever since the Industrial Revolution removed most productive work from the home, employers have segregated the sexes, reserving better jobs for men (Goldin 1990). We can gauge the extent of sex segregation across occupations, industries, or jobs by examining the index of segregation. (An occupation refers to a cluster of related work activities that constitute a single economic role—for example, baker. In contrast, a job refers to the specific tasks performed by one or more people in a specific work setting—for example, a production baker at Oroweat's Oakland plant, or a "bake-off" baker at the Ballard Safeway store.) The index of occupational segregation shows the minimum proportion of either sex that would have to change from a sex-typical to a sex-atypical occupation for the sexes to be distributed similarly across all occupations. If sex had no effect on people's occupation, the index of segregation would equal 0. If women and men never held the same occupation, the index would equal 100.

In the United States, the amount of occupational sex segregation fluctuated slightly between 1910 (69.0) and 1970 (67.6). The century's largest drop in segregation occurred during the 1970s—by 1980, the index was 59.8 (Jacobs 1989). Segregation continued to decline in the 1980s, but at a much slower rate. The 1990 index—calculated for employed workers in 477 occupations—was 4.5 points lower than the 1980 index, indicating that out of every one 100 women about 55 would have had to switch from predominantly female to predominantly male occupations for the labor force to be fully integrated across occupations. Of course, even such an improbably wholesale redistribution would not truly integrate America's places of work because women and men in the same occupation typically work for different employers in different industries and hence hold different jobs (Bielby and Baron 1986).

Occupational segregation by race has dropped sharply in the U.S. since 1940,

Table 5.1
Trends in Sex and Race Segregation

	1940	1950	1960	1970	1980	1988 [a]
Segregation between						
Black and white women	0.618	0.649	0.640	0.474	0.326	0.293
Black and white men	0.383	0.415	0.439	0.362	0.313	0.293
Black women and men	0.772	0.738	0.697	0.694	0.532	0.609
White women and men	0.802	0.729	0.729	0.723	0.574	0.604

Source: King 1992
[a] Indexes based on 159 occupations common to census classification systems between 1940 and 1980.

when most blacks were still confined to a small number of occupations. As Table 5.1 shows, race segregation has declined more rapidly among women than men (King 1992). However, American women of African, Asian, and Hispanic descent as well as Native-American women continue to be overrepresented in the least desirable, traditionally female jobs (Smith and Tienda 1988). In sum, women are less segregated by race than are men, and as far as occupations are concerned, being female is a bigger obstacle among the employed than not being white.

In all industrialized countries, barriers restrict women's access to many jobs. The pattern of segregation for the United States resembles that in other industrialized countries, although the Scandinavian countries exhibit particularly high levels of segregation, partly because their family policies encourage women to work part time (Rosenfeld and Kalleberg 1991).

Contributing to sex segregation are the actions of employers and workers, as well as cultural and institutional forces. Occupational sex labels and sex-role stereotypes influence employers' decisions as well as workers' occupational expectations. The occupational and industrial structures (in other words, where the jobs are) set limits on the pace of integration. For example, the growth of managerial occupations during the 1980s facilitated women's entry into managerial jobs, but the explosion of service jobs involving traditionally female tasks has slowed integration.

Workers' characteristics and employers' policies also affect the extent of segregation. The human-capital explanation for segregation holds that women's family obligations (1) keep them from investing in education and experience—thus reducing their qualifications for male jobs—and (2) incline them toward traditionally female occupations that supposedly are easy to reenter and do not penalize workers for work interruptions. This theory has little support (England and McCreary 1987). Considerable evidence shows the importance of employers' and male workers' actions—including discrimination and stereotyping—in segregating workers (Reskin 1993).

The small decline in segregation during the 1960s stemmed more from men's entry into customarily female "semiprofessions" than from the integration of traditionally male occupations (Reskin and Hartmann 1986). The 1970s brought the first large-scale movement by women into the predominantly male occupations (of which there are more than 300). The 1980s brought increased understanding of what factors maintain and reduce it (Reskin and Hartmann 1986). Three factors contributed to the post-1970 decline in sex segregation. The first was "structural" changes in American occupations. The growth of several integrated occupations and the shrinkage of some highly segregated occupations redistributed jobs from segregated to integrated occupations.

The second component of desegregation resulted from women's gradual entry into many sex-atypical occupations (for example, statistician, groundskeeper). Several factors fostered women's increasing share of many male occupations. The more egalitarian values popularized by the women's liberation movement, later marriage and more divorce, and a recessionary economy meant that more women supported themselves and their families. These changes paved the way for laws and regulations barring sex discrimination in educational institutions and the workplace. Changing attitudes, bolstered by new regulations, encouraged many large employers to adopt equal-employment policies. As women's opportunities expanded, they increasingly resembled men in college major, job aspirations, attachment to the labor force, and paid work experience. A growing number of women entered occupations that had been reserved primarily for men, and occupations' traditional sex labels weakened and became less binding on labor-market participants. These factors reinforced small to moderate increases in the representation of women—mostly white women—in many customarily male occupations. Rarely did men replace white women in traditionally female jobs; instead, shortages created opportunities for women of color, contributing to the decline in race segregation among women.

The third component of occupational desegregation stemmed from women's substantial headway into a few male occupations such as insurance adjuster and bank manager. However, their substantial shifts in sex composition did not necessarily produce integration. Instead, some traditionally male occupational specialties such as residential real-estate salesperson and public-relations specialist, became resegregated as women's work. Employers hired thousands of women for these occupations when doing so would save money. Regulations that barred discrimination or required affirmative action contributed to women's large inroads into broadcast reporting, bank management, and bartending (Reskin and Roos 1990). So too did enormous job growth in a few customarily male occupations that outpaced the supply of qualified male applicants. Finally, employers resorted to women for occupations that could not attract enough men because their earnings had declined or they had deteriorated in other ways. In other words, employers turned to women when they needed to cut costs and when a deteriorating occupation did not generate an adequate supply of men (Reskin and Roos 1990). Women flocked to these formerly male occupations because they offered better pay and opportunities than the traditionally female occupations open to equally qualified women.

At the beginning of the 1990s, the majority of both women and men still worked in jobs in which the other sex was underrepresented, if not completely absent. Nonetheless, the work force was less sex segregated than at any earlier time in the twentieth century. How much has occupational desegregation enhanced workplace equity? Although the wage gap has declined, employers still pay a premium to workers in male-dominated jobs, so men and women in customarily male occupations usually outearn women in predominantly female jobs. And job segregation in mixed-sex occupations ensures that women rarely earn as much as their male counterparts (Reskin and Roos 1990). Moreover, while the tens of thousands of women who entered occupations and specialties that men were abandoning averaged higher pay than they would get in "women's" jobs, few earn as much as their male counterparts, and their wage advantage is unlikely to last in occupations that resegregate as "women's work."

The stalled pace of sex integration has three crucial policy implications. First, enforcing existing current programs to bar discrimination and implement affirmative action in training and employment is essential for continued declines in segregation. Second, the prevalence of job-level segregation within nominally integrated occupations means that we must find other solutions to the economic disadvantage under which women labor. One possible solution is pay equity (comparable worth)—the policy of compensating workers for the skill, effort, and responsibility their jobs require rather than for the sex composition of their workforce. However, pay equity cannot eliminate the wage disparity between the sexes so long as women are disproportionately consigned to jobs that society defines as low skilled and denied the opportunity to exercise workplace responsibility. Finally, women's continued responsibility for most family work hampers their access to some jobs. A more egalitarian division of domestic work and family-work policies that takes into account employees' family roles is needed to redress this disadvantage.

To achieve these goals, women must return to the tactics that fostered the pro-equality political climate of the 1960s and 1970s: They must act politically, applying pressure on employers, politicians, and regulatory agencies. Without such action, we will begin the twenty-first century with a workforce in which sex and race rather than talents continue to determine the jobs people do.

References

Bielby, W. T. and J. N. Baron. 1986. "Men and women at work: Sex segregation and statistical discrimination." In *American Journal of Sociology*, 91:759-99.

England, P. and L. McCreary. 1987. "Gender inequality in paid employment." In H. Hess and M. Ferree (eds.), *Analyzing Gender.* Newbury Park, CA: Sage:286-320.

Goldin, C. 1990. *Understanding the Gender Gap: An Economic History of American Women.* New York: Oxford University Press.

Jacobs, J. A. 1989. *Revolving Doors: Sex Segregation and Women's Careers.* Stanford: Stanford University Press.

King, M. C. 1992. "Occupational segregation by race and gender." *Monthly Labor Review,* 115:30-37.

Reskin, B. F. 1993. "Sex segregation in the workplace." *Annual Review of Sociology,* 19:241-70.

_____ and H. I. Hartmann. 1986. *Women's Work, Men's Work: Sex Segregation on the Job.* Washington, D.C.: National Academy.

_____ and P. A. Roos. 1990. *Job Queues, Gender Queues.* Philadelphia: Temple University Press.

Rosenfeld, R. and A. L. Kalleberg. 1991. "Gender inequality in the labor market: A cross-national perspective." In *Acta Sociologica,* 34:207-25.

Smith, S. A. and M. Tienda. 1988. "The doubly disadvantaged: Women of color in the U.S. labor force." In A. H. Stromberg and S. Harkess (eds.), *Women Working.* Mountain View, Calif.: Mayfield, 61-80.

Food for Thought and Application Questions

1. Gender-segregated employment is reinforced by the selective evaluation of what stereotypical women and men can contribute to the workplace. For example, it might be argued that men are better physicians and engineers because they are more logical and interested in science. Similarly, women might be

judged as better suited for positions as librarians or clerical workers because they are detail oriented. Although such traits may indeed be beneficial for the performance of these work roles, they represent a selective interpretation of women's and men's qualifications for the jobs. Isn't it likely that the detail-oriented stereotype commonly applied to women would be an equally important asset to the physician?

Gender stereotypes are problematic, not only because they represent gross overgeneralizations, but also because they are applied selectively to limit the occupational choices of women and men. Select any highly gender segregated occupation (e.g., auto mechanic—98.7% male, architect—95% male, registered nurse—96% female) and explain how gender stereotypes contribute to segregation in the occupation by creating the expectation that one sex or the other is better suited for the work. To illustrate the selective application of gender stereotypes to employment categories, discuss how the stereotypical gender traits might be reinterpreted as beneficial to nontraditional employment. For example, what female traits might prove useful in auto repair? Or what masculine traits would be valuable to a registered nurse?

2. Identify three occupations that have become increasingly gender-integrated over the last few decades. Why have these changes occurred? Is the increased representation of women (or men) the result of a greater supply of non-traditional sex workers ready to perform the job? Or do the changes result from an increase in employer demand for non-traditional sex workers? ✦

6

The Sex Gap in Pay

Paula England

In the United States, as in most nations, women earn substantially less than men. For manufacturing workers, the female/male earnings ratio moved from 0.35 in 1820, to 0.50 in 1850, to 0.58 in 1930 (Goldin 1990). For all workers, the ratio rose from 0.45 to 0.60 between 1890 and 1930 (Goldin 1990). Table 6.1 shows little change between 1955 and 1980 for whites. During most of this period the ratio was about 0.59. Among blacks, Table 6.1 shows that the sex gap in pay narrowed considerably between 1955 and 1980, with women's relative earnings moving from 0.55 to 0.79. Thus, when it comes to women's pay relative to that of men, there have been eras of progress and eras of stagnation, and the timing of such change has differed by race.

Since 1980, white, black, and Hispanic women have made progress relative to men of their own racial or ethnic group,

Table 6.1
Median Annual Earnings of Women and Men Employed Full-Time, Year-Round, by Race and Hispanic Origin, 1955-1987[1]

	White			Black			Hispanic[2]		
	Women	Men	Ratio[3]	Women	Men	Ratio	Women	Men	Ratio
1955	12,110	21,431	0.565	6,220	11,292	0.551	NA	NA	NA
1960	12,988	21,431	0.606	8,804	14,165	0.622	NA	NA	NA
1965	14,155	24,468	0.579	9,612	15,367	0.625	NA	NA	NA
1970	16,187	27,623	0.586	13,637	19,409	0.703	NA	NA	NA
1975	16,323	27,918	0.585	16,030	21,416	0.748	NA	NA	NA
1976	16,719	28,487	0.587	15,737	20,914	0.752	NA	NA	NA
1977	16,642	28,852	0.577	15,848	20,707	0.765	NA	NA	NA
1978	16,955	28,502	0.595	15,855	22,549	0.703	NA	NA	NA
1979	16,624	28,144	0.591	15,454	21,218	0.728	NA	NA	NA
1980	16,142	27,200	0.593	15,055	19,138	0.787	13,637	19,021	0.717
1981	15,381	26,473	0.581	14,298	18,730	0.763	13,646	18,726	0.729
1982	16,310	26,186	0.623	14,577	18,598	0.784	13,384	18,362	0.729
1983	16,741	26,348	0.635	14,860	18,786	0.791	13,578	18,246	0.744
1984	17,040	27,162	0.627	15,357	18,537	0.828	14,253	18,790	0.759
1985	17,404	27,131	0.641	15,407	18,977	0.812	14,279	18,315	0.780
1986	17,721	27,582	0.642	15,507	19,447	0.797	14,706	17,625	0.834
1987	17,775	27,468	0.647	16,211	19,385	0.836	14,893	17,872	0.833

Source: Figart, Deborah, Heidi Hartmann, Eleanor Hinton Hoytt, and Janice Hamilton Outtz. 1989. "The Wage Gap and Women of Color." Pp. 25-33 in *Proceedings from the First Annual Women's Policy Research Conference.* Washington, D.C.: Institute for Women's Policy Research.

Notes:
[1]Earnings are in constant 1987 dollars. Thus, these figures are adjusted for changes in the cost of living (as measured by the Consumer Price Index) such that they reflect real trends in before-tax purchasing power. NA, data not available.
[2]Includes all Hispanics, regardless of race. Hispanics are also included in "white" or "black" categories according to their race.
[3]Ratio of women's annual earnings to men's annual earnings.

and relative to white men. As Table 6.1 shows, the sex ratio for whites moved from 0.59 to 0.65 between 1980 and 1987. For blacks the sex ratio moved from 0.79 to 0.84, and for Hispanics from 0.72 to 0.83. For the most part, women made these relative gains because their earnings showed slight (inflation-adjusted) absolute gains during the 1980s, while white and black men's wages were relatively stagnant and Hispanic men's wages declined.

The figures referred to so far (in Table 6.1) are based on annual earnings of full-time workers. Another way to look at trends in the pay gap is to examine usual weekly earnings of full-time, year-round workers. Figures in the left two columns of Table 6.2 show these trends for black and white men and women. For some reason the female/male ratios are slightly higher in such data, but they show the same basic trends in the sex gap in pay-steady decreases among blacks and decreases among whites since 1980.

One limitation of the statistics in Table 6.1 and in the left two columns of Table 6.2 is that all workers who work at least 35 hours a week are considered full-time. Yet among these full-time workers, men average slightly more hours per week than women. Thus, when figures on the sex gap in pay are adjusted for differences in hours worked within full-time workers, the ratios are several percentage points higher, although the *trends* in sex gaps are similar, as the right two columns of Table 6.2 show.

One set of statistics that can mislead as an indicator of women's progress is comparisons between the sex gap in pay for different age groups. Table 6.3 gives female/male earnings ratios separately by age group, for 1973, 1978, 1983, and 1988. The table shows that, in each year, the gap is much smaller among younger workers. For example, in 1988, the female/male earnings ratio among those 20-24 was 0.96, whereas it was 0.85 among those 25-34, and 0.75 among those 35-44. Some interpret this to mean that the sex gap in pay is disappearing. This optimistic interpre-

Table 6.2
Female-Male Ratios of Median Usual Weekly Earnings Among Full-Time Wage and Salary Workers, by Race, 1967-1989

Year[3]	Unadjusted for Hours Worked[1]		Adjusted for Hours Worked[2]	
	White	Black	White	Black
1967	0.608	0.700	0.676	0.732
1971	0.607	0.707	0.669	0.747
1973	0.606	0.718	0.669	0.756
1974	0.598	0.731	0.659	0.768
1975	0.613	0.751	0.672	0.789
1976	0.615	0.738	0.676	0.781
1977	0.606	0.731	0.669	0.775
1978	0.599	0.732	0.660	0.773
1979	0.611	0.747	0.673	0.790
1981	0.635	0.775	0.694	0.817
1982	0.639	0.794	0.698	0.838
1983	0.646	0.790	0.703	0.832
1984	0.670	0.798	0.731	0.842
1985	0.674	0.829	0.736	0.874
1986	0.679	0.827	0.742	0.866
1987	0.682	0.844	0.745	0.890
1988	0.684	0.830	0.746	0.877
1989	0.693	0.865	0.758	0.914

Source: U.S. Department of Labor 1967-1989.
Notes:
[1]Includes only full-time workers, i.e., those working at least 35 hours per week.
[2]Includes only full-time workers, i.e., those working at least 35 hours per week, and adjusts for sex differences in average hours worked among these workers.
[3]Data for 1967-1978 are for the month of May only.

tation hinges on assuming that the differences in a given year across age groups result entirely from a cohort effect and not at all from a life cycle effect. Another way to put this assumption is to say that each cohort (i.e. people born in a given year) will retain the same sex ratio of pay it currently has as it ages. If this is true, as the older cohorts with the larger sex gap retire, the overall sex gap in pay will decrease. If, on the other hand, we interpret the age differences as entirely a life cycle effect, experienced by every cohort, the figures have no implications as to the future of the sex

Table 6.3
Adjusted[1] Female-Male Ratios of Median Usual Weekly Earnings among Full-Time Wage and Salary Workers, by Age, 1973-1988

Age	1973	1978	1983	1988
Total, 16 years and older	0.68	0.67	0.72	0.77
16-19	0.86	0.91	0.96	0.93
20-24	0.83	0.80	0.89	0.96
25-34	0.72	0.73	0.80	0.85
35-44	0.61	0.59	0.66	0.75
45-54	0.62	0.59	0.63	0.67

Sources: Figures for 1973 to 1983 from Table 3, O'Neill, June. "The Trends in the Male-Female Wage Gap in the United States." *Journal of Labor Economics* Vol. 3, No. 1, pp. S91-SI16. Copyright © 1985. Reprinted with permission. Figures for 1988 from U.S. Department of Labor 1989a (Table 33) and 1989b (Table 41).
Note:
[1] Adjusted for sex differences in hours worked among workers classified as full-time (i.e., 35 hours/week or more). For 1988 figures only, data on hours used for the adjustments come from a slightly different age group than was used for the figures on earnings because of unavailability of data on narrow age groups in published sources. For 1988, hours for those 25-44 were used to adjust earnings ratios of those 25-34 and 35-44, and hours of those 45-64 were used to adjust earnings ratios of those 45-54.

gap in pay. They simply reveal that the sex gap in pay increases with age. This results in part because the sex gap in experience increases as women go through the childbearing years, and in part because even those women who are employed continuously usually work in jobs low on prospects for mobility and raises. For both these reasons, women's earnings fall further and further behind men's across the life cycle. Further complicating matters is the possibility of period effects. Period effects refer to changes over time, for example, decreases in discrimination, that affect all employed cohorts and age groups approximately equally.

In reality, all three effects (cohort, life cycle, and period) are probably operative, as suggested by Table 6.3 (and by Bianchi and Spain 1986). In each of the years shown, younger workers have a higher female/male ratio of earnings. We can also follow one cohort across the years. To take one example, consider those who were aged 25-34 in 1973, with women earning 0.72 of men's earnings. Ten years later, in 1983, when this same cohort was aged 35-44, the women were earning only 0.66 of what men earned. For this cohort, women's relative losses across the life cycle were great enough to override any period gains between 1973 and 1983. But, if we look at the cohort 25-34 in 1978, women earned 0.73 of men's earnings in 1978, but had decreased the sex gap slightly to a ratio of 0.75 by 1988 when the cohort was 35-44. Here the period progress accruing to the cohort appears to have been large enough to override any relative losses of women across the life cycle. This suggests that favorable change in women's relative pay is occurring via both period and cohort effects. However, net of these changes, women's relative position deteriorates across the life cycle. Thus, the progress is not as fast as would be indicated by interpreting all of the age differences in sex ratio for any given year as cohort effects.

Explanations of the Sex Gap in Pay

What factors explain the sex gap in pay? Here I will consider evidence for the role of a number of factors . . . Some of these factors have their effects on the sex gap in pay via their effects on segregation.

Sex Differences in Productivity or Effort?

Are women less productive than men? We seldom have measures of productivity, so there is litle direct evidence on this. Yet there is much speculation and some indirect evidence. Becker (1985) speculates that, because of their domestic responsibilities, women exert less intense effort on the job, saving energy for domestic pursuits. The fact that women who are employed do more household work than their husbands is well documented (Berk and Berk 1979; Ross 1987; Hochschild 1989). But despite this, tests of differences in effort have, if anything, suggested that women expend *more* effort than men in their paid jobs. Bielby and Bielby (1988) analyzed data from a national survey that asked respondents how "hard" their jobs require them to work, how much "effort, either physical or mental" their jobs require, and how much "effort" they put into their jobs "beyond what is required." Women reported slightly *more* effort than men. One might wonder whether this finding simply results from women "bragging" more than men about their effort level. This is doubtful, since socio-psychologists' experiments show that men generally overestimate and women underestimate their own performance (Colwill 1982). Evidence on time allocation also suggests that women's effort is higher that men's; national survey data show that women report less time than men in coffee breaks, lunch breaks, and other regularly scheduled work breaks (Stafford and Duncan 1980; Quinn and Staines 1979). Thus, research indicates that sex differences in effort explain none of the sex gap in pay.

Industries and Firms

While the most obvious form of segregation is at the occupational level, there is some segregation by industry and firm as well, and this contributes to the sex gap in pay. Unlike occupations, many of which are nearly all male or female, almost all firms (and their industries, since they are a collection of firms all selling the same product) employ both men and women. Yet, although sex segregation by firm and industry is not nearly as extreme as by occupation, there are, nonetheless, systematic tendencies for women to be employed in those firms and industries with low average wages (Blau 1977; Beck, Horan and Tolbert 1980; Hodson and England 1986; Aldrich and Buchele 1989, Coverdill 1988;

Ferber and Spaeth 1984). For example, Blau (1977) examined cases where men and women in the same very detailed occupation (like accounting clerk, payroll clerk, or computer programmer) had different wages, and found that this was usually a matter of women working in a lower-wage firm. Often the entire industry the lower-paying firms were in had lower average wage scales.

However, even when women move to higher-wage firms and industries, their wages do not go up as much as men's do. The wage premium associated with being in a high-wage firm or industry goes disproportionately to male jobs (Aldrich and Buchele 1989).

Amount of Human Capital Investment and Expected Human Capital Investment

Are women in jobs requiring less skill, and, if so, does this affect the sex gap in pay? Here, let us confine our attention to *amount* of skills or training rather than *types* of skill. Amount of schooling, one type of human capital, explains virtually none of the sex gap in pay, since men and women in the labor force have virtually the same median years of formal education, as Table 6.4 shows. Among whites, women had 1.3 years more education than men in the labor force in 1952, and men did not close this gap until 1969. By 1979, white men's median was a trivial 0.1 year more education than white women's. For blacks the trends are somewhat different, but black women have had slightly more education than black men in all years since 1952, as Table 6.4 shows, although by 1983 this female advantage in median education had declined to a relatively trivial 0.2 year.

There *is* a sex difference in another sort of human capital: years of job experience. Because many women spend some years rearing children and keeping house full-time, the average woman in the labor force has fewer years of experience than the average man. Early studies had shown that this difference explains between one

Table 6.4
Median Years of School Completed by Men and Women in the Labor Force, by Race,
1952-1983

	White			Black		
	Men	Women	Difference	Men	Women	Difference
1952	10.8	12.1	-1.3	7.2	8.1	-0.9
1959	11.8	12.2	-0.4	8.1	9.4	-1.3
1969	12.4	12.4	0.0	10.8	11.9	-1.1
1979	12.7	12.6	0.1	12.2	12.4	-0.2
1983	12.8	12.7	0.1	12.4	12.6	-0.2

Source: From: O'Neill, J. "The Trends in The Male-Female Wage Gap in the United States." *Journal of Labor Economics* Vol. 3, No. 1, pp. S91-SI16. Copyright © 1985. Reprinted with permission.

quarter and one half of the sex gap in pay (Polachek 1975; Mincer and Polachek 1974, 1978; Sandell and Shapiro 1978).

A 1979 study by Corcoran and Duncan will be discussed in some detail since it is the best available for assessing the effects of various types of human capital on the sex gap in pay. They used a standard method of regression decomposition in which the amount that any variable contributes to the sex gap in pay is a function of (1) the rate of return of the variable (how much an additional increment contributes to earnings for both men and women) and (2) the size of the difference between men and women's average on this variable. They found that the regression coefficients or slopes—the rates of return—to different types of human capital were not terribly different for men and women. Their results do show that the *overall* rate of return to experience is higher for white males than other groups. (Hoffman 1981 also found this.) But when experience is divided into subcomponents according to whether the experience was with one's current employer (called "tenure") and whether it involved on-the-job training, rates of return for the subcomponents did not differ much by race or sex. This implies that the overall group differences in rates of return to experience came from groups spending different proportions of their employed years in different types of expe-

rience, which in turn offer varying rates of return. For example, white men are likely to have a higher portion of their experience in a job that provides on-the-job training, and years of tenure during which training was provided have a higher rate of return than other years of tenure in one's current firm or than years of experience in prior firms.

A striking . . . [finding in the research of Corcoran and Duncan (1979)] is the amount of the sex gap in pay among whites that comes from men having more tenure (seniority with one's firm), including periods during which the employer was providing training. The training portion of tenure explains 11% of the gap between white men and white women. Although . . . this same factor explains 8% of the gap between white men and black women, and 15% of the gap between black men and white men, . . . on-the-job training is a relatively minor factor in the sex gap in pay between black men and women, explaining only 2%. It is also a trivial part of the pay gap between black women and white women (1%). Whether or not differences between groups in time spent in jobs with training are themselves explained by discrimination in job assignments or by job choices is a separate question that Corcoran and Duncan's analysis cannot answer.

White women also earn less if they have been out of the labor force. (See also

Mincer and Ofek 1982.) This is shown by the net effects on wages of (1) years of work experience before present employer and (2) years with current employer prior to current position. The first of these two factors explains 3% of the gap between white men and white women but has no effect on the sex gap among blacks. The second factor explains 12% of the sex gap among whites and 7% of the sex gap among blacks. The proximate cause of these portions of the sex gap in pay is women's lesser employment experience. However, discriminatory job and wage differentials may be behind some proportion of these sex differences in years of employment experience, since women have less motivation to stay employed if they are paid less. It is interesting that none of the measures of experience contribute to the pay gap between white and black women; black women have more experience but lower earnings.

Overall, . . . Corcoran and Duncan (1979) found human capital (broadly construed to include all measures of education, employment continuity, and labor force attachment) to explain 44% of the pay gap between white men and women and 32% of the gap between white men and black women.

. . . [Their study] also reveals some facts about the interaction of race and gender. Overall, a much smaller proportion of the sex gap in pay between black women and black men is explained by human capital than is explained for either the gap between black and white women or between black women and white men. In particular, black women's higher average education than black men's makes a large *negative* contribution to the sex gap for blacks. That is, black women have higher education than black men, but lower earnings. In contrast, education makes significant contributions to the pay gap between black and white women (76%), between black women and white men (11%), and between black and white men (38%).

Let us now turn our attention to the question of whether women's *intentions* or *expectations* for less employment continuity at the time they first enter employment might explain some of the subsequent sex gap in pay. To the extent that job experience provides skill accumulation, this can be seen as relevant to the amount of human capital one accumulates. There are two versions of how expectations about continuity of experience might affect earnings. One posits that, if there is a trade-off between starting wages and steep wage trajectories (i.e., high returns to experience and/or tenure), women who plan intermittent employment will be more apt to choose jobs with relatively high starting wages than will either men or women planning continuous employment. This could possibly create an average sex gap in pay, despite the fact that it would produce higher lifetime earnings for women than if they chose jobs similar to men. However, as mentioned above, no study to date has found higher average starting wages for women or in women's jobs, even when other factors are controlled (England 1984; England, Farkas, Kilbourne, and Dou 1988). A milder version of this thesis might say that women will be more motivated to choose jobs with steep upward wage trajectories the longer they plan to be employed. I find this a more plausible claim, although we lack research on how much this has affected women's choices.

A second way that women's plans for intermittent employment may affect the sex gap in pay is via employers' statistical discrimination. . . . If women have higher turnover rates, and employers know this, then based on this sex difference in turnover they may engage in what economists call statistical discrimination. That is, employers will be reluctant to hire women in jobs where turnover is especially expensive, particularly jobs that provide much on-the-job training. What evidence is there for this as a factor in the sex gap in pay? First, let us look at the evidence about sex differences in turnover. It is equivocal

(Price 1977, p. 40). Several studies based on recent national probability samples of young workers (mostly in their twenties) found no sex differences in turnover, even when wage was not controlled (Waite and Berryman 1985; Donohue 1987; Lynch 1991). At first glance this seems extremely counterintuitive since we know that women leave the labor force for childrearing more often than men. The seeming anomaly is explained by the fact that men change firms more often than women (Barnes and Jones 1974). Other studies find gross differences, with women having higher turnover rates, but after statistically adjusting for wages or wage-related job characteristics, these differences disappear or reverse (Viscusi 1980; Blau and Kahn 1981; Haber, Lamas, and Green 1983; Shorey 1983). In general, workers of any sex or race are more likely to quit a job when it is low paying or has low opportunity for advancement (C. Smith 1979; Osterman 1982; Haber et al. 1983; Shorey 1983; Grounau 1988; Kahn and Griesinger 1989; Light and Ureta 1989). Thus, if women are placed in less desirable jobs through discrimination, this could explain part of their higher turnover in studies that do find gross sex differences in turnover. If this is true, then women's disadvantageous job placements may explain their higher turnover rather than vice versa. However, if the job placements result from statistical discrimination based on real exogenous turnover differences, then statistical controls for job characteristics are inappropriate in studies designed to assess exogenous sex differences in turnover propensity. Thus, the "chicken and egg" question of which is exogenous, the higher turnover or the discrimination, is virtually impossible to assess statistically. My best guess is that, except in the most recent cohorts (to which Waite and Berryman's 1985, Donohue's 1987, and Lynch's 1991 analyses were confined), exogenous sex differences in turnover existed but were very small and not present in all workplaces or occupations. However, it is important to note that among young cohorts in the recent period, turnover differences disappeared. Thus, if employers continue favoring men for jobs providing much training, it cannot be explained rationally via statistical discrimination but must reflect erroneous perceptions or other discriminatory motivations.

Thus far I have discussed how much of the sex gap in pay can be explained by human capital or anticipated human capital at any one point in time. But what of the trends in the sex gap in pay? Can these be explained by trends in human capital? Let us look at this question first in terms of the post-World War II period up until about 1980, a period during which the sex gap in pay was relatively unchanging. Were there trends in human capital that we would expect to have reduced the sex gap in pay? Several studies suggest not. For example, women's education relative to men's has not increased in the last 50 years (Goldin 1990; Smith and Ward 1984). Thus, based on education trends, we would not expect the sex gap in pay to change. Of course, during all this time, both men's and women's levels of education were increasing, and women had as much or more education than men (Jacobs 1989). Thus, the point is not that at any one time education can explain the sex gap in pay, but rather that trends in the sex gap in education were not changing favorably to women, so we would not expect a change in the sex gap in pay on the basis of trends in education alone.

Similarly, prior to 1980, women's experience did not increase relative to men's (Smith and Ward 1984; Goldin 1990). At first this seems counterintuitive. One might think that as the percentage of women who are employed increases, this would lessen the sex gap in experience. But, in fact, the upward surge in women's employment affects the average experience of employed women in two conflicting ways: (1) On the one hand, the fact that fewer currently employed women have left the labor force (at all or for as long a time) increases the average experience of employed women. (2) On the other hand, the entrance of new female workers with little experience depresses the average years of experience of employed women. Thus, whether the average experience of employed women goes up, down, or stays the same as women's employment increases depends upon the relative strength of these two conflicting forces. Recent research (Smith and Ward 1984; Goldin 1990) suggests that they canceled each other out, so that women's average experience did not rise, and the sex gap in experience did not begin to close, until about 1980. Since 1980, however, women's relative experience has increased, and this is one factor in the declining sex gap in pay (Smith and Ward 1984; Goldin 1990; O'Neill 1985). However, this does not mean that experience completely "explains" the sex gap in pay. As we have seen, experience explains less than one half the sex gap in pay at any particular point in time.

Values and Preferences

Do women's values and preferences help explain the sex gap in pay? In one sense, I have already considered this question above. I argue that gender-specific socialization orients both men and women toward kinds of jobs and skills typical for their gender. Insofar as women's jobs then pay less, values have played a part in the sex gap in pay. In a formal analysis of this type, Filer (1983) uses a large number of measures of tastes and personality characteristics to predict earnings and finds that they explain some of the sex difference in pay. Much of this, I would argue, is an indirect effect. Values are affecting occupational choice and occupations are affecting earnings, but Filer's (1983) study does not make clear the mechanism through which occupational characteristics affect earnings. One such mechanism is the sort of wage discrimination against female jobs at issue in comparable worth, to be discussed below.

A thesis claiming a more direct causal line from values to earnings posits that men simply place a higher value on earnings when they decide which occupation to select, while women trade these off for other job characteristics. A number of studies have asked people what they value in jobs, and find that men rank earnings more highly than women (Brenner and Tomkiewicz 1979; Lueptow 1980; Peng et al. 1981; Herzog 1982; Major and Konar 1984). However, one study by Walker et al. (1982) found no such difference. Moreover, research on job satisfaction has found that women's satisfaction is more affected than is men's by the pay in their job (Glenn and Weaver 1982; Crane and Hodson 1984). In addition, studies of turnover find that the extent to which wage increases affect whether women will quit a job is as large or larger for women than for men (Shorey 1983; Kahn and Griesinger 1989; Light and Ureta 1989). Thus, if we look at responses to job characteristics, it appears that women may place more importance than men on earnings. In short, existing evidence provides no clear answer to the question of whether or not there is a sex difference in the value placed on money contributing to the sex gap in pay.

Sex Composition Effects and Comparable Worth

The call for comparable worth is based on the finding that a job's sex composition affects its wage level. This is a very consistent finding coming from a wide range of studies. . . . One type of study has taken U.S. Census detailed occupational categories as units of analysis and used national data. Such studies have controlled for occupational characteristics, such as average requirements for education, and an array of occupational demands, with measures typically taken from the Dictionary of Occupational Titles (DOT). In general, such studies have found that, net of these measures, both men and women earn less if they work in a predominantly female occupation. This has been found for 1940, 1950, and 1960 with controls for education (Treiman and Terrell 1975), for

1970 with controls for education, DOT skill measures, and other variables (England and McLaughlin 1979; England, Chassie, and McCormick 1982), and for 1980 with similar controls (Parcel 1989). . . .

Sorenson (1989) has assembled most of the published studies investigating the net effect of occupations' percentage female. (She includes studies using either census occupations or individuals as units of analysis.) In general, these studies find that moving from an all-male to a comparable all-female occupation is associated with a wage penalty equivalent to between 10 and 30% of the sex gap in pay. . . .

Other studies that have also analyzed how change over time in jobs' sex composition affects change in their pay find that when a job changes its sex composition, the wage for both men and women goes up if more males come into the job, and the wage for both men and women goes down if more women come into the job (Ferber and Lowry 1976, p. 384; Pfeffer and Davis-Blake 1987). We cannot be sure if the changing sex composition affected the wages, as these authors suggest, if the change in wage affects sex composition (as suggested by Reskin and Roos 1990), or if both effects are operative.

Types of Skills and Working Conditions in Jobs: Indirect Gender Bias

Another factor affecting the sex gap in pay is the kind, rather than amount, of skills and working conditions jobs require. Some view this as a part of the comparable worth issue. The studies above implicitly do not. That is, they take as given the returns to different job characteristics, and, controlling for these factors, estimate the adverse effect on wages of being in a predominantly female occupation.

However, the types of skills common in women's jobs may have lower returns than the types of skills common in men's jobs *because* of gender discrimination. That is, if a type of skill or working condition has traditionally been associated with

women's work in either the household or paid employment, it may come to be devalued via stigma that gets institutionalized into wage systems, so that this skill or working condition comes eventually to carry a low rate of reward, or a penalty, whether it appears in a male or female occupation. However, since such skills and working conditions are more common to female occupations, this devaluation has a disparate and adverse impact on women's wages. . . . There is substantial evidence that women's concentration in jobs with different kinds of skills affects the sex gap in pay. Daymont and Andrisani (1984) show that one's college major has an important effect on pay, and women are in the majors associated with lower pay. Women are more often than men in jobs involving nurturant social skills, and these not only have lower returns than other skills, but actually have net negative returns (Kilbourne, England, Farkas, and Beron 1990; Steinber et al. 1986; Jacobs and Steinberg 1990; Steinberg 1990). . . .

Overall, I conclude that the *kinds* of skills traditionally exercised by women are valued less in wage determination than are traditionally male skills. This more indirect form of gender bias is seen by many advocates as part of the discrimination to be redressed by comparable worth.

Consequences of the Sex Gap in Pay

What are the consequences of the sex gap in pay? A person doubting the importance of the issue might argue that if marriage is nearly universal and husbands and wives pool their income, the sex gap in pay has little consequence for the economic well-being of either women or children. This would be a mistaken conclusion, however. The sex gap in pay has important consequences within marriage as well as for those women who are not married.

Not all women marry, and some women divorce. Many never-married and divorced women have children. Indeed, rates of both divorce and out-of-wedlock births have increased dramatically. About half of the cohort born in the early 1950s (Cherlin 1981; Preston and McDonald 1979), and two thirds of those marrying today (Martin and Bumpass 1989) are projected to experience divorce. Many divorced women have children. Out-of-wedlock births rose from 5% of all births in 1960 to 18% in 1980 (Preston 1984). Unmarried women with children—whether divorced or never married—typically have custody of their children and must support them on some combination of their own earnings, any child support they receive from the children's fathers, and government subsidies. Child support awards are typically small. For example, awards to divorced women averaged $2500 per year per family in 1981, and less than half the mothers received the full amount awarded (U.S. Bureau of Census 1983). While it is true that many divorced women remarry, both age and the presence of children inhibit women's remarriage probabilities (Mott and Moore 1983), so a significant minority of women with children do not remarry (Preston 1984). Thus, the sex gap in pay, in combination with the fact that divorced and never-married women generally have financial responsibility for their children after divorce, is a crucial part of why such a high proportion of female-headed families is in poverty (McLanahan, Sorensen, and Watson 1989, p. 120).

There is a paradox here. To some extent the increase in divorce is probably itself a result of women's increased economic independence (England and Farkas 1986, pp. 64-65). The fact that more women than previously have jobs means that more can afford to leave marriages they consider unhappy and at least minimally support themselves and their children. Yet, because of the continued sex gap in pay and men's failure to support their children after divorce, the economic consequences of divorce for women and children are still grave (Preston 1984).

But what of marriages that remain intact? For married women, does the sex gap in pay have adverse consequences? Yes. A long line of research on marital power (reviewed in England and Kilbourne 1990) has shown that women's employment and the relative earnings of husbands and wives affect the balance of power in marriages. When women's earnings are lower, even when they are making valuable contributions in the form of home management and child rearing, their bargaining power vis-à-vis their husbands is substantially lower than that of women with higher earnings. The fact that women's economic fate is more adversely affected by divorce than men's is part of why men can retain disproportionate bargaining power within marriages. The ability to leave a relationship with relatively few losses implies the power to hold out for a better bargain without risk of a big loss. Thus, the sex gap in pay has profound consequences for the degree of informal democracy in marriages. It adversely affects women's ability to negotiate for what they want in marriage on a wide range of issues, including intimacy, purchasing decisions, the sharing of household work, and geographical moves. The sex gap in pay is a part of what prevents equality in husbands' and wives' bargaining power over all these issues. . . .

Conclusions

This chapter examined research on the sex gap in pay. Education and effort, the two "all-American" routes to economic success, do have payoffs for both men and women. Yet neither is particularly relevant to the sex gap in pay since women have as many years of education as men, and studies show women expend as much or more effort as men on their jobs. Women's fewer years of seniority and overall employment experience, and the intermittency of such experience, explains some proportion (between one quarter and one half) of the sex gap in pay.

Much of the sex gap in pay results from segregation itself. Some of this segregation is interfirm, with women concentrated in lower-paying firms and industries. This aspect of the sex gap in pay would not be touched by comparable worth reforms unless we envisioned a national wage setting board whose authority spanned the entire economy, something no American advocates of comparable worth have suggested.

A large component of the sex gap in pay comes about because women are segregated into lower-paying occupations within every firm. Proponents of pay equity reforms allege that at least some portion of the pay differences between male and female jobs arise *because* the jobs are filled by women or entail skills that are traditionally female. Evidence abounds that, controlling for a number of measures of skill and other occupational requirements, jobs with more women in them offer lower wages to both men and women than do jobs containing more men. I refer to this as direct gender bias in wage setting. There is also evidence that, net of this direct effect of jobs' sex composition, kinds of skills traditionally done by women, such as nurturant social skills, have lower (sometimes even negative) returns than other kinds of skills (such as cognitive skills). I refer to this as indirect gender bias in wage setting. Comparable worth is about both of these types of gender bias in wage setting: direct gender bias based on the sex composition of the job, and indirect gender bias in which the returns to jobs' requirements for various types of skill and working conditions differ according to whether the job characteristic is traditionally associated with women's or men's spheres.

References

Aldrich, M. and R. Buchele. 1989. "Where to look for comparable worth: The implications of efficiency wages." In M. A. Hill and M. Killingsworth (eds.), *Comparable Worth: Analyses and Evidence*. Ithaca, NY: ILR Press:11-28.

Barnes, W. and E. Jones. 1974. "Differences in male and female quitting." *Journal of Human Resources*, 9(4):439-451.

Beck, E. M., P. M. Horan, and C. M. Tolbert II. 1980. "Industrial segmentation and labor market discrimination." *Social Problems*, 28:113-130.

Becker, G. 1985. "Human capital, effort, and the sexual division of labor." *Journal of Labor Economics*, 3:S33-S58.

Berk, R. A. and S. F. Berk. 1979. *Labor and Leisure at Home: Content and Organization of the Household Day*. Newbury Park: Sage.

Bianchi, S. and D. Spain. 1986. *American Women in Transition: The Population of the United States in the 1980s*. New York: Russell Sage Foundation.

Bielby, D. D. and W. T. Bielby. 1988. "She works hard for the money." *American Journal of Sociology*, 93:1031-1059.

Blau, F. 1977. *Equal Pay in the Office*. Lexington, MA: Heath.

Blau, F. D. and L. M. Kahn. 1981. "Race and sex differences in quits by young workers." *Industrial and Labor Relations Review*, 34:563-577.

Brenner, O. C. and J. Tomkiewicz. 1979. "Job orientation of males and females: Are sex differences declining?" *Personnel Psychology*, 32:741-750.

Cherlin, A. J. 1981. *Marriage, Divorce, Remarriage: Social Trends in the United States*. Cambridge, MA: Harvard University Press.

Colwill, N. 1982. *The New Partnership: Women and Men in Organizations*. Palo Alto, CA: Mayfield.

Corcoran, M. and G. J. Duncan. 1979. "Work history, labor force attachments, and earnings differences between the races and sexes." *Journal of Human Resources*, 14:3-20.

Coverdill, J. E. 1988. "The dual economy and sex differences in earnings." *Social Forces*, 66:970-993.

Crane, M. and R. Hodson. 1984. "Job satisfaction in dual career families: Gender differences in the effects of job and family characteristics and personal expectations." Univeristy of Texas-Austin. Mimeo.

Daymont, T. and P. Andrisani. 1984. "Job preferences, college major, and the gender gap in earnings." *Journal of Human Resources,* 19(3):408-428.

Donohue, J. J. 1987. "The changing relative hazard rates of young male and female workers." Northwestern University School of Law, American Bar Foundation. Chicago, IL: unpublished paper.

England, P. 1984. "Wage appreciation and depreciation: A test of neoclassical economic explanations of occupational sex segregation." *Social Forces,* 62:726-749.

England, P., M. Chassie, and L. McCormick. 1982. "Skill demands and earnings in female and male occupations." *Sociology and Social Research,* 66:147-168.

England, P. and G. Farkas. 1986. *Households, Employment, and Gender: A Social, Economic and Demographic View.* Hawthorne, NY: Aldine de Gruyter.

England, P., G. Farkas, B. S. Kilbourne, and T. Dou. 1988. "Explaining occupational sex segregation and wages: Findings from a model with fixed effects." *American Sociological Review,* 53:544-558.

England, P. and B. S. Kilbourne. 1990. "Markets, marriages, and other mates: The problem of power." In R. Friedland and A. F. Robertson (eds.), *Beyond the Marketplace: Rethinking Economy and Society.* Hawthorne, NY: Aldine de Gruyter:163-189.

England, P. and S. McLaughlin. 1979. "Sex segregation of jobs and male-female income differentials." In R. Alvarez, K. Lutterman, and Associates (eds.), *Discrimination in Organizations.* San Francisco: Jossey Bass:189-213.

Ferber, M. A. and H. M. Lowry. 1976. "The sex differential in earnings: A reappraisal." *Industrial and Labor Relations Review,* 29:377-387.

Ferber, M. A. and J. L. Spaeth. 1984. "Work characteristics and the male-female earnings gap." *American Economic Review,* 74:260-264.

Figart, D., H. Hartmann, E. Hinton Hoyt, and J. Hamilton Outtz. 1989. "The Wage Gap and Women of Color," pp. 25-33. In *Proceedings from the First Annual Women's Policy Research Conference.* Washington, D.C.: Institute for Women's Policy Research.

Filer, R. 1983. "Sexual differences in earnings: The role of individual personalities and tastes." *Journal of Human Resources,* 18(1):82-99.

_____. 1989. "Occupational segregation compensating differentials and comparable worth." In R. T. Michael, H. I. Hartmann, and B. O'Farrell (eds.), *Pay Equity: Empirical Inquiries.* Washington, D.C.: National Academy Press:153-170.

Glenn, N. and C. Weaver. 1982. "Further evidence on education and job satisfaction." *Social Forces,* 61:46-55.

Goldin, C. 1990. *Understanding the Gender Gap: An Economic History of American Women.* New York: Oxford University Press.

Gronau, R. 1988. "Sex-related wage differentials and women's interrupted labor careers—the chicken or the egg?" *Journal of Labor Economics,* 6(3):277-301.

Haber, S. E., E. J. Lamas, and G. Green. 1983. "A new method of estimating job separation by sex and race." *Monthly Labor Review,* June:20-27.

Herzog, A. R. 1982. "High school students' occupational plans and values: Trends in sex differences 1976 through 1980." *Sociology of Education,* 55:1-13.

Hochschild, A. 1989. *The Second Shift.* New York: Viking Penquin.

Hodson, R. and P. England. 1986. "Industrial structure and sex differences in earnings." *Industrial Relations,* 25:16-32.

Hoffman, S. D. 1981. "On-the-job training: Differences by race and sex." *Monthly Labor Review,* July:34-36.

Jacobs, J. 1989. *Revolving Doors: Sex Segregation and Women's Careers.* Stanford, CA: Stanford University Press.

Jacobs, J. A. and R. J. Steinberg. 1990. "Compensating differentials and the male-female wage gap: Evidence from the New York State Comparable Worth Study." *Social Forces,* 69(2):439-468.

Kahn, S. and H. Griesinger. 1989. "Female mobility and the returns to seniority: Should EEO policy by concerned with promotion?" *American Economic Review,* 79(2):300-304.

Kilbourne, B. S., P. England, G. Farkas, and K. Beron. 1990. "Skill, compensating differentials, and gender bias in occupational wage determination." Paper presented at the Annual Meetings of the American Sociological Association.

Light, A. L. and M. Ureta. 1989. "Panel estimates of male and female turnover behavior: Can female non-quitters be identified?" Department of Economics, State University of New York at Stony Brook, Working paper.

Lueptow, L. B. 1980. "Social change and sex-role change in adolescent orientations toward life, work, and achievement: 1964-1975." *Social Psychology Quarterly*, 43:48-59.

Lynch, L. M. 1991. "The role of off-the-job vs. on-the-job training for the mobility of women workers." *American Economic Review*, 81(2):151-156.

Major, B. and E. Konar. 1984. "An investigation of sex differences in pay expectations and their possible causes." *Academy of Management Journal*, 27:777-792.

Martin, T. C. and L. L. Bumpass. 1989. "Recent trends in marital disruption." *Demography*, 26(1):37-50.

McLanahan, S. S., A. Sorensen, and D. Watson. 1989. "Sex differences in poverty: 1950-1980." *Signs*, 15(1):102-122.

Mincer, J. and H. Ofek. 1982. "Interrupted work careers: Depreciation and restoration of human capital." *Journal of Human Resources*, 17:3-24.

Mincer, J. and S. Polachek. 1974. "Family investments in human capital: Earnings of women." *Journal of Political Economy*, 82:S76-S108.

_____. 1978. "Women's earnings reexamined." *Journal of Human Resources*, 13:118-134.

Mott, F. L. and S. Moore. 1983. "The tempo of remarriage among young American women." *Journal of Marriage and the Family*, 45:427-436.

O'Neill, J. A. 1985. "The trend in the male-female wage gap in the United States." *Journal of Labor Economics*, 3(January Supplement):S91-S116, Tables 3 and 5.

Osterman, P. 1982. "Affirmative action and opportunity: A study of female quit rates." *Review of Economics and Statistics*, 64:604-612.

Parcel, Toby. 1989. "Comparable Worth, Occupational Labor Markets, and Occupational Earnings: Results from the 1980 Census." Pp. 134-152 in *Pay Equity: Empirical Inquiries*, edited by Ropbert Michael, Heidi Hartmann, and Brigid O'Farrell. Washington, D.C.: National Academy Press.

Peng, S. S., W. B. Fetters, and A. J. Kolstad. 1981. *High School and Beyond: A Capsule Description of High School Students*. Washington, D.C.: National Center for Education Statistics.

Pfeffer, J. and A. Davis-Blake. 1987. "The effect of the proportion of women on salaries: The case of college administrators." *Administrative Science Quarterly*, 32:1-24.

Polachek, S. W. 1975. "Discontinuous labor force participation and its effect on women's market earnings." In C. B. Lloyd (ed.), *Sex, Discrimination, and the Division of Labor*. New York: Columbia University Press:90-124.

Preston, S. 1984. "Children and the elderly: Divergent paths for America's dependents." *Demography*, 21:435-458.

Preston, S. H. and J. McDonald. 1979. "The incidence of divorce within cohorts of American marriages contracted since the war." *Demography*, 16:1-25.

Price, J. L. 1977. *The Study of Turnover*. Ames: Iowa State University Press.

Quinn, R. P. and G. L. Staines. 1979. *Quality of Employment Survey, 1977: Cross Section*. Ann Arbor, MI: Interuniversity Consortium for Political and Social Research.

Reskin, B. F. and P. Roos. 1990. *Job Queues, Gender Queues: Explaining Women's Inroads into Male Occupations*. Philadelphia: Temple University Press.

Ross, C. E. 1987. "The division of labor at home." *Social Forces*, 65:816-833.

Sandell, S. H. and D. Shapiro. 1978. "A re-examination of the evidence." *Journal of Human Resources*, 13:103-117.

Shorey, J. 1983. "An analysis of sex differences in quits." *Oxford Economic Papers*, 35:213-227.

Smith, C. B. 1979. "Influence of internal opportunity structure and sex of worker on turnover patterns." *Administrative Science Quarterly*, 24:362-381.

Smith, J. P. and M. P. Ward. 1984. *Women's Wages and Work in the Twentieth Century.* R-3119-NICHD. Santa Monica: Rand.

Sorensen, E. 1989. "The wage effects of occupational sex composition: A review and new findings." In M. A. Hill and M. Killingsworth (eds.), *Comparable Worth: Analyses and Evidence.* Ithaca, NY: ILR Press:57-79.

Stafford, F. P. and G. J. Duncan. 1980. "The use of time and technology by households in the United States." In R. G. Ehrenberg (ed.), *Research in Labor Economics*, Volume 3. Greenwich, CT: JAI Press:335-375.

Steinberg, R. 1990. "Social construction of skill: Gender, power, and comparable worth. *Work and Occupations*, 17:449-482.

Steinberg, R. J., L. Haignere, C. Possin, C. H. Chertos, and D. Treiman. 1986. *The New York State Pay Equity Study: A Research Report.* Albany, NY: Center for Women in Government, State University of New York Press.

Treiman, D. J. and K. Terrell. 1975. "Women, work and wages—trends in the female occupational structure since 1940." In K. C. Land and S. Spilerman (eds.), *Social Indicator Models.* New York: Russell Sage Foundation:157-200.

U.S. Bureau of the Census. 1983. *Child Support and Alimony: 1981.* Current Population Reports, Special Studies, Series P-23, No. 124. Government Printing Office.

U.S. Department of Labor. 1983. *Time of Change: 1983 Handbook on Women Workers.* Women's Bureau, Bulletin 298. Washington, D.C.: Government Printing Office.

Viscusi, W. K. 1980. "Sex differences in worker quitting." *Review of Economics and Statistics*, 62:388-398.

Waite, L. and S. Berryman. 1985. "Women in nontraditional occupations: Choice and turnover." The Rand Corporation, Santa Monica, CA. Rand Report R-3106-FF.

Walker, J., C. Tausky, and D. Oliver. 1982. "Men and women at work: Similarities and differences in work values within occupational groupings." *Journal of Vocational Behavior*, 21:17-36.

Food for Thought and Application Questions

1. An oversimplification of trend data on the sex gap in pay suggests that over the last 10 years the pay gap has narrowed by a little more than half a cent per year. Assume for just a moment that this rate of decline in the sex-based earnings gap represents a linear trend that will continue into the future. If you were a woman earning the average wage for all women, how long would it take for your earnings to be equal to those of the average male?

2. The average 26-year-old woman earns more relative to her male peer than does her 50-year-old mother. Why is this the case? Discuss the role of life cycle and period effects in creating the difference between the wage gaps experienced by this mother and daughter. Is it safe for the 26-year-old woman to assume that by the time her infant daughter enters the labor market, the wage gap will have disappeared? Why or why not? ✦

7

Possibilities and Limits of the Comparable Worth Movement

Linda M. Blum

In spite of two decades of agitation by the feminist movement in the United States for women's equality, including the enactment of major antidiscrimination legislation, the majority of employed women remain in low-paid, highly gender-segregated work. Remedial strategies for occupational gender stratification have shifted from affirmative action to comparable worth or pay-equity demands. Affirmative action proved successful primarily for more privileged women, as it opened professional and managerial job opportunities. It also brought women into some new civil service positions, and a very limited number of craft positions, but affirmative action did little for most women working in lower-level white- or pink-collar jobs. Pay equity will certainly not bring full economic equality but it does address the concerns of those low-paid women who still represent the majority of women workers. In this article, I will discuss both the challenge and the limitations of the comparable worth movement.

Academic literature on comparable worth has been primarily concerned with pay-equity implementation, its legal status (Blumrosen 1979; Nelson et al. 1980), methodologies for comparing different jobs (Beatty and Beatty 1984; Northrup 1980; Schwab 1985; Treiman 1984), and the determinants of the gender wage gap (summarized in Treiman and Hartmann 1981, pp. 13-68). Alternatively, I examine comparable worth as a social and political movement, asking what it represents to those involved and to their interests.

This article is drawn from a study of two California public sector cases, Contra Costa County and the city of San Jose. I conducted 60 interviews with participants and examined archival and documentary evidence. From these two case studies, I make three claims:

(1) Comparable worth can better advance women economically and challenge the economic structure because it emerged out of affirmative action's limitations.

(2) Comparable worth appeals to women whose interests were not furthered by affirmative action and whose job conditions would not necessarily have been bettered by occupational change or an attack on gender boundary lines in the labor market.

(3) Comparable worth is itself limited by tensions underlying its formulation. A strategy that is gender-specific yet collectively oriented has led to an awkward, perhaps contradictory, combination of affirmative action-civil rights and collective bargaining-labor union strategies.

Comparable Worth and Affirmative Action

Affirmative action's purpose is the creation of equal employment opportunities for women and minorities. Originating as an integral part of the U.S. black civil rights movement of the 1960s, affirmative action policies recommend deliberate recruitment, hiring, and promotion of underutilized groups, with goals and timetables for job integration. Women were originally secondary to policies for racial integration, but affirmative action was increasingly used by the feminist movement throughout the 1970s to promote women's occupational advancement.

In the United States, affirmative action has directly benefited women who have been able to move into highly rewarded professional, managerial, and craft jobs dominated by men. However, such categories account for a small percentage of women in the U.S. labor force. Women's representation in managerial jobs increased from 18 percent to 30 percent in just one decade, but these jobs account for only 7 percent of women in the U.S. labor force (Bianchi and Spain 1983). Similarly, while the proportion of professional degrees awarded to women in law and medicine has gone from under 10 percent to one-third (Greer 1986; U.S. Department of Labor 1983), on an aggregate level, very few women are employed in these elite fields in the United States. Such gains have contributed to a popular impression that all barriers to women's advancement have been removed, but the tenacity and pervasiveness of the gender segregation of work, even in the face of affirmative action efforts, is well documented (Bielby and Baron 1984; Roos and Reskin 1984). Clearly any notion that job integration policies would benefit large numbers of low-paid women has proven to be overly optimistic.

Although it had limited results, affirmative action legitimated women's specifically gender-based moral claim to improved economic treatment and created political opportunities for raising such a claim. The emergence of the comparable worth strategy can, in fact, be seen as the result of the rising expectations and political opportunities created by affirmative action, in the face of the lack of material gains for most employed women. Comparable worth aims to upgrade the wage scales for jobs that employ large numbers of women and therefore has the potential to provide benefits on a far broader scale than affirmative action. Comparable worth expands the collective character of affirmative action class-action suits based

upon employers' patterned discrimination. While affirmative action challenged the allocation of jobs on the basis of stereotypical gender traits, comparable worth challenges the allocation of rewards on the basis of such traits. It thus extends the notion of discrimination to include the systematic underevaluation and underpayment of the work women do.

The pay-equity suit against the state of Washington, argued on behalf of 15,000 state employees in the federal courts, provided the first clear legal victory for comparable worth. This victory was short-lived, but the political effects have been more resilient. The 1983 ruling of Judge Tanner called for the distribution of nearly one billion dollars in damages and back pay, in addition to 30 percent pay adjustments for jobs in which women predominate (*New York Times* 1985), but this decision was overturned by the Federal Appeals Court in 1985. Nevertheless, Washington State still agreed to spend $42 million for pay-equity adjustments in the next contract year (Kirp 1985), and when employees agreed not to appeal the case any further, state officials consented to pay over $100 million in future adjustments (Turner 1986). By battling this case for the past decade, employees had built up political power and popular backing so that despite its legal victory, the state government was willing to negotiate a substantial settlement.

Many other public employers are being faced with the pay-equity issue. Several major cities, including Chicago, Los Angeles, and San Francisco, have agreed to implement wage adjustments (*National NOW Times* 1986, 1987). The California State Employees Association has a wage discrimination suit pending against that state (*New York Times* 1984), and all but four states have taken some form of action. New York State, for example, although facing a contentious political situation, has moved haltingly forward. In 1986, unions negotiated a three-year contract that allocated funds for comparable worth adjustments to more than 50,000 employees in jobs predominantly held by women (Lawson 1985).

Many of these efforts have progressed to preliminary stages only and are merely documenting the existence of wage disparity. And other efforts that have succeeded in winning some wage adjustments may still face a difficult political future, in which opposing interests may be able to cut into initial gains. Yet the comparable worth argument has changed feminist thinking about advancement strategies and has demonstrated a strong appeal to low-paid women who want their contributions recognized. As one California activist stated: "Comparable worth has been called the issue of the '80s, and it may not be. It may be the issue of the '90s. But comparable worth is here to stay—it's not just yesterday's fashion!" (Finney 1986).

The Appeal of Comparable Worth

In two comparable worth cases, I have been able to trace the emergence of the issue from the limits of affirmative action. San Jose, located 50 miles south of San Francisco, is often considered the prototypical case of comparable worth. After a much-watched strike in 1981, it became the site of one of the first victories for pay equity in the United States. San Jose, the fourth largest city in California, employs approximately 900 women, 700 of whom received pay equity adjustments (Farnquist et al. 1983). Over half of the women employees work in clerical jobs, and the majority of the rest are in the women's semiprofessions (City of San Jose 1984).

Contra Costa County, located on the northeastern edge of San Francisco Bay, has recently begun to implement an incremental pay-equity program. Contra Costa employs approximately 3,500 women, 2,300 of whom are covered by the pay-equity program. As in San Jose, the women covered work in clerical and semiprofessional jobs (Finney 1983).

In 1975, Contra Costa County settled a sex and race discrimination lawsuit with an affirmative action consent decree that set goals and timetables to increase the representation of women and minorities. San Jose implemented a similar affirmative action plan in the early 1970s. In both cases affirmative action significantly increased the representation of women in management, but a larger number of low-paid women experienced a frustrating lack of mobility.

In San Jose, this frustration led directly to several confrontations between clericals and personnel officials and to the clericals' first attempts at autonomous collective action in a group they called City Women for Advancement. In an interview, one of the early activists explained why clerical women were frustrated by affirmative action. She said:

> In spite of affirmative action, the city did not allow any kind of experience substitution for the education requirement for the professional-level jobs. And it was very obvious to some of us, the clerical people who were working next to professional people, that we were really more competent than they, and there was no reason that we couldn't handle those jobs just as well. So they made a new classification, called administrative aide, that was supposed to be an entry-level professional position. And they worded requirements such that they didn't really tie in that you absolutely needed the four-year [college] degree. So we applied for the jobs, about 20, maybe 30 clericals, we all applied for the job. We actually had several informal meetings and we decided to apply for the job. And we were all turned down—they disqualified all of us from taking the exam. So we appealed to the Civil Service Commission. And in appealing to the Commission, I drafted a letter to various women's groups in the area, NOW, the Santa Clara County Commission on the Status of Women, the Human Relations Commission, and asked that they send letters of support.

We outlined that we have over 300 years of clerical experience and that we felt that this was sufficient qualification for the position. And that we should at least be allowed to test. And so several groups did respond, which I'm sure helped. And the Civil Service Commission ultimately did decide that in certain clerical classifications experience could be equated for the education—mine was not one of them however!

After this attempt to gain upward mobility, the members of City Women for Advancement focused on the low wages of clerical jobs compared with many jobs held by men. In 1977, however, the clericals' group still presented comparable worth as an affirmative action recommendation. Their report to the city council, "Affirmative Action for City Women," included among traditional affirmative action concerns a new request, for women's jobs to be paid on other than marketplace criteria. A year later, as a somewhat symbolic gesture, City Women, now working with the union, an affiliate of the American Federation of State, County and Municipal Employees, requested 27.5 percent increases for all clericals based on rough comparisons with men's pay scales.

In Contra Costa County, women clericals also struggled for promotions, but union activism, perhaps arising from the area's working-class culture, came much earlier. In San Jose, clerical activism had coincided with the emergent comparable worth issue; in Contra Costa, an autonomous clerical union had been demanding both wage and career-ladder changes since 1970, but the official affirmative action plan adopted in Contra Costa in 1975 did little to meet these demands.

Like the clericals in San Jose, the Contra Costa clerical union had pressed for affirmative action strategies to increase their mobility out of low-paid work. These strategies included increased career ladders within clerical series to create some higher-paid positions and opportunities for promotion. Another strategy was the creation of bridge classifications, intermediary positions to bridge clerical women into some professional job classes, primarily in accounting. These demands were so important that, as one union staff member put it, among women workers "*the* buzzword prior to comparable worth was bridge class." A Contra Costa activist said ruefully, "One of the clerical union's proudest accomplishments is that a few of our older members made it into the accounting series. But this was our only real success with affirmative action." Mobility opportunities for clerks were still very limited. An accounting clerk explained why:

The number of openings is very few, so even if you're now eligible to apply, your chances are very slim. I've taken all the night courses, and have waited years, but I still haven't even made it into the bridge class.

As in San Jose, frustration with blocked mobility provoked comparisons with the wages in the jobs held by men and led the Contra Costa union to embrace comparable worth after the success of the San Jose strike. As a leading clerical activist in the County explained:

I joined the union as soon as I took a county job. But I had been fairly naive regarding male/female differentials. The comparable worth issue came up when San Jose went on strike. I became a lot more enlightened, and pretty outraged.

The other major occupational group involved in the comparable worth efforts are the women semiprofessionals (Etzioni 1969); in San Jose, librarians and recreation supervisors; in Contra Costa, nurses and social workers. College-educated or credentialed, and thus relatively more privileged than clericals, women semiprofessionals nonetheless face career trajectories and earnings that dead-end at low levels. Affirmative action, with its suggestion that mobility is achieved only by moving into traditional men's occupations, has a pejorative connotation to those who have invested in traditional women's fields. As one San Jose librarian explained:

> The city has said: "What we really think we need to do in the long run is to get all the women into these male occupations." Well, then *who the heck* is gonna do all the other jobs that are important! What they're really saying is that our jobs are not important, whereas we say they are!

In a similar vein, a Contra Costa social worker had this to say:

> I believe in affirmative action, but they say women should move into male jobs if they want more pay. I like being a social worker. I just don't want to be a truck driver!

The appeal of comparable worth for women semiprofessionals is thus very clear. As one comparable worth activist told me:

> I started in the library ten years ago. We'd say we wanted to raise our salaries, and they'd say [and here she imitated the feigned innocence of city administrators]: "Okay, sure, fine. What are librarians in the next jurisdiction getting?" [She laughed softly.] Well, of course, we are all getting coolie wages, so there was no sense comparing me to another coolie in another jurisdiction!
>
> I don't want to leave librarianship to make an adequate salary. Why is that [other] field more financially rewarding and less emotionally satisfying, less intellectually satisfying? The only explanation I can come up with is because it's [library work] run by women, and that's why it's not valued.

Traditional Jobs and Women's Interests

Comparable worth may be more attractive than affirmative action to many working women because they may stand to lose from greater job integration. Giving up the monopoly of semiprofessional and clerical jobs could entail negative consequences, and some women may prefer traditional jobs.

The semiprofessions have been viewed as desirable jobs for women. Teaching, nursing, librarianship, and social work supposedly reflect women's altruism and nurturing talents. While women in these fields may want to discard the pejorative aspects of such stereotypes, many enjoy the positive aspects of such work. Its fulfilling nature, the variety and autonomy on the job, and the sense of significant human interaction were personally important to the semiprofessionals I spoke with. Even when promotions might have been possible, several said that they would not be interested in giving up the direct involvement with their clients in exchange for administrative duties. That women, under current gender arrangements, may have a less instrumental moral orientation and stronger preference for nurturant, humane work than men is suggested by the work of several feminist theorists, notably Nancy Chodorow (1978) and Carol Gilligan (1982).

As Rosabeth Moss Kanter (1977) has noted, many women in traditional secretarial positions also gain a sense of fulfillment from the one-on-one relationship between boss and secretary. The secretary to the director of a large convention facility run by the city of San Jose said she enjoys her job very much, which she describes as: "keeping track of him [the director] and his calendar, filling in for him because he's gone a lot, and speaking for him." She told me that she knows her boss well, and that the one-on-one relationship with him is the best part of her job; yet she and 12 other women vociferously protested the question on the test for promotion that asked: "Would you run errands for the boss' wife?"

Another clerical worker also told me how much she likes the office environment, but how underpaid she has been for her skills. She explained that a lot of the men she worked for had not been aware of how little the women made. When the comparable worth issue came up, they were shocked by their secretary's low pay scales, because, as she remarked: "We take something with poor grammar and no punctuation, and we make it into something wonderful. We make them look good, and they know it."

Of course, many clerical workers do not work in situations of enriching one-on-one relationships, but in pools bearing closer resemblance to production work. However, even jobs with a high degree of intrinsic job satisfaction do not compensate for low pay. The comparable worth movement has, in fact, been most successful among women public agency workers who have such satisfying jobs.

Women may also feel comparable worth is in their interest while affirmative action is not, because with job integration they would have to compete with men for jobs they now monopolize. Women's jobs represent an increasing share of the economy, while sectors providing traditional men's jobs are contracting (Cain 1985; Sacks 1986; Smith 1984). As in the past, fluid boundaries between men's and women's work could end with men supplanting women (Milkman 1981). Two recent case studies of affirmative action indicate that such displacement of women workers is a possibility (Hacker 1982; Kelley 1982). In contrast, there is evidence that rigid gender segregation has in the past protected women from being displaced in times of economic contraction (Milkman 1976).

Job integration, the goal of affirmative action, may lead to subtle forms of domination and occupational gender typing (Bielby and Baron 1984). For example, a public health nurse said she would prefer that men stay out of nursing altogether and that the current gender segregation continue. The male nurses she has known act just like "little doctors," and she went into public health primarily to get away from that type of domination. She added:

"I don't want to compete with men. I just don't want them to be around." For this nurse, the integration of her field threatens the autonomy she enjoys in her work, and the respect with which her group of co-workers, all women, treat each other. A librarian explained that the few male librarians tended to specialize in business reference or audiovisual departments, leaving women to the supposedly less important areas such as the children's department. Such internal gender stratification is difficult to address when concealed within newly integrated job categories.

Job integration may not lead to upward mobility if an occupation is downgraded as women enter. Clerical work in the early part of this century is the classic example (Davies 1979; Massachusetts History Workshop 1984), and teaching and librarianship have followed similar patterns (Feldberg 1984). Occupations in the insurance and computer fields, which many women entered in the 1970s are also undergoing deskilling and loss of status (Donato 1986; Phipps 1986). A rise in the proportion of women and concurrent job degradation may even be occurring within management, law, and medicine (Carter and Carter 1981). Comparable worth can be a defense against the feminization-degradation trend by keeping wages stable when the gender composition of an occupation shifts and by making transparent the degree to which any job is undervalued if it is performed predominantly by women.

In sum, job integration, even if it were to occur on a larger scale, might not lead to improved conditions for many women workers at this time. It might result in job loss, more subtle forms of gender typing and domination, and even job degradation. For some women, to change occupations might require the sacrifice of job satisfaction. Comparable worth has become an attractive strategy for low-paid women workers because, I argue, it resonates more deeply with their interests. Better pay for a stable, satisfying, long-accepted type of work may be a wiser strategy for many women workers than a direct attack on the gendered occupational structure.

The Limitations of Comparable Worth

As it has struggled toward more effective strategies, the comparable worth movement has employed a range of approaches, from litigation and legislation to collective bargaining. These approaches produce tensions and contradictions, especially as comparable worth proponents move beyond the limitations of affirmative action. There are three contradictions in the current comparable worth movement: the problem of universalizing women's gender-based interests, the problem of universalizing a classlike interest in comparable worth, and the problem of hierarchy.

Gender-Based Interests

Like affirmative action, comparable worth claims to be in the interests of all women, as women. While this claim is enormously appealing, it often breaks down in practice. In both San Jose and Contra Costa County, many nonmanagement women initially allied with management women and women in elective offices and expected these more powerful women to lead the way in implementing comparable worth. In each case, when pay-equity activists tried to act politically on the assumption that all women have a common interest in comparable worth, they met with frustration and disappointment.

In San Jose, when comparable worth was first debated, there was a woman mayor, a woman assistant city manager for personnel and labor relations, and seven of the ten members of the city council were women (Keppel 1981). In fact, Mayor Janet Gray Hayes was fond of referring to San Jose as "the feminist capital of the world" (Beyette 1981). From the union women's viewpoint, neither she nor the council acted on behalf of "women in general" during the prolonged battle for comparable worth. The mayor and council did not want to conduct the comparable worth job evaluation study, and they resisted bargaining on implementation when the results were released. When bargaining broke down after months of recalcitrance and the strike ensued, those who had walked off their jobs over comparable worth were threatened with firing. Naturally, they questioned women city officials' feminist convictions. A union leader stated to the press: "The City wanted tokenism. . . . It was dragged kicking and screaming along the path to equality by the union" (Johnston 1981, p.165). And one sign carried on the picket lines declared: "If I hear the Mayor say this is the feminist capital of the world just once more, I'll puke!"

In the interviews, the contradiction of trying to retain the general interest of women was often alluded to. A recreation center director and union activist explained to me that because the assistant city manager, Sally Reed, had come up through the ranks of city employment:

A lot of the older gals out on the picket line were [saying]: "And where in the hell did you come from?" It's like all of a sudden you got up there, and now you have to play the game that there just wasn't enough money, and that's all it [opposition] was. So, it's funny because there were women with the power at that time. It wasn't a real male trip. So, on the one hand, they couldn't be putting down the plight of women's jobs, but yet they have the dollars and cents of the city budget to look out for. So there wasn't a lot of bad-mouthing of the issue, and nobody ever came out and said "Hey, that's all you should get paid."

Just recently the *This Week* [San Jose Sunday paper feature] had a thing on Sally Reed, and I read it. She was the cover article, and now she's the top county executive [in Santa Clara County]. I guess I expected just plain old empathy, a little bit more empathy. From the mayor, and from her. Wouldn't you just naturally assume that there'd be a little bit more empathy? I mean, *was she* born with a silver spoon in her mouth?

Tensions also emerged in Contra Costa County between women in power and lower-paid women employees. Because their comparable worth effort followed the San Jose strike, politicians, management, and activists in Contra Costa avoided a dramatic confrontation. In addition, Contra Costa has proportionally fewer women at the top levels of government. With the two women members of five on the board of supervisors and no women at the highest levels of management, it could hardly be considered a feminist capital. Not only were there fewer women politicians to be disappointed by, but the conservative and sometimes blatantly sexist men in the county government were a more obvious target.

Women politicians who did fight for comparable worth were not, however, trusted by lower-level women employees. One of the women supervisors, who made comparable worth "her issue" on the heels of the San Jose strike, became very visible statewide as an advocate of pay equity. A union activist and member of the labor side of the joint labor-management comparable worth task force told me that although she first saw Sunne McPeak as a strong ally, she now views her with suspicion. She explained:

> There's a lot of a sense of ownership of the comparable worth issue. Women in management and political leadership feel they're special and do not accept collective action. They don't want to be contaminated with a labor association. Women in politics see their own political futures in comparable worth. Sunne is going around the country claiming her success on this issue when, by the county's own figures, there's still a 33 percent wage gap.

Women in powerful management and political positions have often been credited with the success of pay equity. In contrast to the labor women quoted above, Carol Mueller (1985) and Janet Flammang (1985) have specifically argued that without a network of women in leadership positions throughout the San Jose area, the comparable worth contract in that city would not have been possible. Similarly, Elaine Johansen (1984) claims that the development of a core of elite women, sophisticated in using political resources, has led to the success of the comparable worth issue in other cases. Although elite women may truly support the ideal of pay equity, this "elite female network" perspective ignores the potential for competing definitions of success, as it overlooks the conflicting interests among women in different institutional and class locations. Problems can arise over the difficult realities of implementation, and, as is evident in these two cases, all sides may not agree on what constitutes a successful comparable worth policy. Women managers and elective officials, for example, may need to claim success for political and organizational purposes. However, it is not their paychecks that are at issue. As the labor activist from Contra Costa made clear, the "ownership" of comparable worth can be problematic when the differing interests among women are overlooked.

Class-Based Issues

Another point of tension within the comparable worth movement involves the attempt to construe pay equity as a labor issue and to draw a classlike alliance in contrast to a solely gender-based alliance. Comparable worth activists in both San Jose and Contra Costa tried to build alliances with male nonmanagement employees, maintaining that pay equity could be in their interests as well. However, much of the women's anger was directed against these same men, with whom they were comparing their jobs and wages. Generally, comparable worth advocates reject any suggestion to cut men's wages, but men's future wage increases may be limited or frozen. Comparable worth proponents argue that when a man has a working wife, mother, or daughter, he should realize the significance of pay equity and strongly support it, but men may feel they are targets of comparable worth, not beneficiaries, regardless of their family situation. One woman in my study separated from her husband over her involvement in the San Jose strike, and I interviewed several others who had experienced serious conflicts at home.

The anger of some women at men of the same class came across strongly in the interviews. A woman who had worked her way up over the past 20 years from a clerk-typist job to a supervisorial position in Contra Costa County told me that she had had no idea what men were actually being paid until she became a member of the negotiating team for her union. Then she said, "It really gets to you!" She continued on quite vehemently:

> Window washers for the county make more than I do! A second-line supervisor of men makes $600 a month more than I do! There's no excuse that a janitor makes more than an eligibility worker! Local One [the union for most men's jobs in Contra Costa] owns this county. And they're real male chauvinist pigs. And they've been kissed royally this year. They've been fed from my trough, mine and every other female-dominated job.

When I asked a San Jose secretary her opinion of comparable worth, she stalked out, seized her classification handbook, and began to read the specifications for concrete finishers to me. Then she proceeded to read the specifications for executive secretary, and their respective wages. When she was through reading she nearly screamed: "If this is comparable worth, someone's not doing their job!" She accused all men of trying to undermine existing policies, and saw the union, because it represented both men and women, as a weak ally at best. She maintained that only women could be expected to really work for comparable worth.

Hierarchy

As discussed above, some analysts have viewed comparable worth primarily as a reform "from above," implemented by networks of women political and organizational elites. Others have argued that since it involves significant collective activity by labor and subordinate women, comparable worth has radical possibilities (Amott and Matthaei, 1984; Feldberg, 1984; Moore and Marsis, 1983). Yet comparable worth's radical possibilities have been limited by its liberal, equal-treatment framework, as well as by contradictory gender and class conceptions of general interest. As Feldberg (1984) points out, while comparable worth questions the legitimacy of the market and the value of labor, it is not an attack on occupational inequality. Comparable worth reinforces the legitimacy of skillbased hierarchies of rewards. Although the movement raises the idea that the judgement of skill is politically and ideologically based (Feldberg 1984, pp. 321-24), its objective is a new hierarchy, based on a more just evaluation of work, rather than the abolition of hierarchy, or even its narrowing or compacting. In this respect, comparable worth is a striking contrast to, for example, the solidaristic wage policies pursued by Swedish labor unions (Cook 1980). In Contra Costa, the comparable worth coalition refused to accept offers that included adjustments only to the lowest end of the wage scale. In San Jose, adjustments were based on the amount of discrepancy within each point-factor score grouping, not on a job's location in the overall wage hierarchy.

In several interviews, on the other hand, I did hear stronger, egalitarian sentiments expressed. There were certainly some who said they felt comparable worth had implicit socialist or utopian goals of equality. There also was some concern for the lowest-paid clericals, not so much for the unrecognized worth of the jobs they perform, as for the fact that wages may simply fall below any decent standard of living. This egalitarian tendency did not seem to be the predominant view, nor is it in any way part of the explicit rhetoric of the comparable worth movement. Indeed, the use of the term pay equity itself implies the more restricted objective of an equitable or just hierarchy, as opposed to the term equality.

Conclusion

What are the possibilities and limits of comparable worth as a collective advancement strategy for women? Comparable worth moves beyond more individualistic affirmative action strategies of upward mobility toward an objective of collective mobility. By focusing on economic advancement for women in traditional occupational categories, comparable worth may appeal to larger numbers of working women than affirmative action did. However, comparable worth, like affirmative action, assumes a commonality of interests among women, sets up antagonism between women and men, and falls short of attacking inequality itself.

Comparable worth has the potential to be a feminist issue that appeals to working-class, low-paid women whose interests have not been directly addressed by affirmative action. However, because it also points to the divergence of interests between working women in traditional jobs and those in highly rewarded positions dominated by men, it may contribute to the declining significance of gender. In *The Declining Significance of Race*, William Julius Wilson (1978) argued that economic and political changes have led to a division between the new black middle class and the black underclass that remains impoverished. Because of this division, class is increasingly more critical than race in determining life chances. A similar development may be occuring for women—not in the sense that gender no longer matters, nor that all gender discrimination has been eliminated—but, in the class-based divergence of interests among women in the labor force, as well as between employed women and women not in the paid labor force.

Comparable worth may bring clericals and semiprofessionals employed in the public sector and core sector private firms up to middle-income levels. In the process, however, it may leave a larger gap between these new middle-class women and underclass women employed in peripheral firms, in low-paid service sector jobs, in domestic work, or unemployed. From a more pessimistic view, comparable worth might, by attracting men into better-paid women's work, push some women out. In addition, raising wages of women workers creates incentive for employers to subcontract work, use part-time and temporary workers, or eliminate jobs entirely. The structure of the capitalist economy may, in the end, erode some of the material benefits of comparable worth, and strategies other than comparable worth will be needed to work toward greater economic equality. Nonetheless, comparable worth does question the ideology of the marketplace in the setting of wages, it reveals the systematic devaluation of the work women do, and it does promote collective action by working-class women. For these reasons, and because it may improve the life chances of many working women, it is a policy worthy of feminist support.

References

Amott, T. and J. Matthaei. 1984. "Comparable worth, incomparable pay: The issue at Yale." *Radical America*, 18(September-October):21-30.

Beatty, R. W. and J. R. Beatty. 1984. "Some problems with contemporary job evaluation systems." In H. Remick (ed.), *Comparable Worth and Wage Discrimination*. Philadelphia: Temple University Press:59-78.

Beyette, B. 1981. "Dispute in San Jose: Equal pay for comparable worth." *Los Angeles Times*, July 13.

Bianchi, S. and D. Spain. 1983. *American Women: Three Decades of Change*. Special

Demographic Analysis CD 3-80-8, August. Washington, DC: U.S. Bureau of the Census.

Bielby, W. T. and J. N. Baron. 1984. "A woman's place is with other women: Sex segregation within organizations." In B. F. Reskin (ed.), *Sex Segregation in the Workplace: Trends, Explanations, Remedies*. Washington, DC: National Academy Press:27-55.

Blumrosen, R. G. 1979. "Wage discrimination, job segregation and Title VII of the Civil Rights Act of 1964." *Michigan Journal of Law Reform*, 12:399-502.

Cain, P. S. 1985. "Prospects for pay equity in a changing economy." In H. I. Hartmann (ed.), *Comparable Worth: New Directions For Research*. Washington, DC: National Academy Press:137-165.

Carter, M. J. and S. B. Carter. 1981. "Women's recent progress in the professions, or women get a ticket to ride after the gravy train has left the station." *Feminist Studies*, 7:477-504.

Chodorow, Nancy. 1978. *The Reproduction of Mothering*. Berkeley: University of California Press.

City of San Jose. 1984. "Affirmative Action Plan," December 6.

Cook, Alice. 1980. "Collective bargaining as a strategy for achieving equal opportunity and equal pay: Sweden and West Germany." In R. Steinberg Ratner (ed.), *Equal Employment Policy for Women*. Philadelphia: Temple University Press:53-78.

Davies, M. 1979. "Women's place is at the typewriter." In Z. Eisenstein (ed), *Capitalist Patriarchy and the Case for Socialist Feminism*. New York: Monthly Review Press:248-266.

Donato, K. M. 1986. "Social and economic factors governing the changing composition of computer specialties." Paper presented at the American Sociological Association Annual Meeting, New York.

Eisenstein, Z. R. 1981. *The Radical Future of Liberal Feminism*. New York: Longman.

England, P. 1984. "Socioeconomic explanations of job segregation." In H. Remick (ed.), *Comparable Worth and Wage Discrimination*. Philadelphia: Temple University Press:28-46.

Etzioni, A. (ed.). 1969. *The Semi-Professions and Their Organization*. New York: Free Press.

Farnquist, R. L., D. R. Armstrong, and R. P. Strausbaugh. 1983. "Pandora's worth: The San Jose experience." *Public Personnel Management*, 12:358-68.

Feldberg, R. 1984. "Comparable worth: Toward theory and practice in the United States." *Signs: Journal of Women in Culture and Society*, 10:311-28.

Finney, Lee. 1986. Presentation to the Comparable Worth Project Conference, Laney College, Oakland, CA, April 12.

_____1983. "Closing the wage gap in Contra Costa County: Strategies for action." Unpublished report of the Contra Costa Comparable Worth Coalition, September 20.

Flammang, J. A. 1985. "Female officials in the feminist capital: The case of Santa Clara County." *Western Political Quarterly*, 38:94-118.

Gilligan, C. 1982. *In a Different Voice*. Cambridge, MA: Harvard University Press.

Greer, W. 1986. "Women gain a majority in jobs." *New York Times*, March 19.

Hacker, S. 1982. "Sex stratification, technological and organizational change: A longitudinal case study of AT&T." In R. Kahn-Hut, A. K. Daniels, and R. Colvard (eds.), *Women and Work: Problems and Perspectives*. New York: Oxford University Press:248-266.

Johansen, E. 1984. *Comparable Worth: The Myth and the Movement*. Boulder, CO: Westview Press.

Johnston, D. 1981. "Issues: Will they lead the way in San Jose?" *Working Women*, 6:162-65.

Kanter, R. M. 1977. *Men and Women of the Corporation*. New York: Harper & Row.

Kelley, M. 1982. "Discrimination in seniority systems: A case study." *Industrial and Labor Relations Review*, 36:40-55.

Keppel, B. 1981. "Equal pay for comparable work: San Jose on new ground in women's wage debate." *Los Angeles Times*, June 30.

Kirp, D. 1985. "Comparable worth: Take it out of courts." *Los Angeles Times*, September 9.

Lawson, C. 1985, "Women in State jobs Gain in Pay Equity." *New York Times*, May 20.

Massachusetts History Workshop. 1984. *They Can't Run the Office Without Us: Sixty Years of Clerical Work.*

Milkman, R. 1981. "The reproduction of job segregation by sex: A study of the changing sexual division of labor in the auto and electrical manufacturing industries in the 1940s." Unpublished Ph.D. dissertation, University of California, Berkeley.

———— 1976. "Women's work and economic crisis: Some lessons of the Great Depression." *Review of Radical Political Economics*, 8:73-97.

Moore, R. and E. Marsis. 1983. "What's a woman's work worth?" *The Progressive*, 47(December):20-22.

Mueller, C. 1985. "Comparable worth in Santa Clara County." *Radcliffe Quarterly*, 20(March):14-15.

National NOW Times. 1987. "Mass NOW leads all-out effort for pay equity." 20(April):6.

———— 1986. "Pay equity gallops across America in 1985." 18(January):2.

NCPE *Newsnotes.* May 1985 and Summer 1986. Washington, DC: National Committee on Pay Equity.

Nelson, B. A., E. M. Opton, Jr., and T. E. Wilson. 1980. "Wage discrimination and the comparable worth theory in perspective." *Michigan Journal of Law Reform*, 13:233-301.

New York Times. 1985. "Ruling on pay equity for women upset by federal court on coast." September 5.

———— 1984. "California suit charges sex discrimination on pay." November 22.

Northrup, H. R. 1980. "Wage setting and collective bargaining." In R. E. Livernash (ed.), *Comparable Worth: Issues and Alternatives*. Washington, DC: Equal Employment Advisory Council:107-136.

Phipps, P. A. 1986. "Occupational resegregation: A case study of insurance adjusters, examiners and investigators." Paper presented at the American Sociological Association Annual Meeting, New York.

Roos, P. and B. Reskin. 1984. "Institutional factors contributing to sex segregation in the workplace." In B. Reskin (ed.), *Sex Segregation in the Workplace: Trends, Explanations, Remedies*. Washington, DC: National Academy Press:235-260.

Sacks, K. B. 1986. "Women's wages: Essential to preserving middle income jobs. The telecommunications industry example." Unpublished Report, Oberlin College.

Schwab, D. P. 1985. "Job evaluation research and research needs." In H. I. Hartmann (ed.), *Comparable Worth: New Directions For Research*. Washington, DC: National Academy Press:37-52.

Serrin, W. 1984. "Women still working for meager pay." *Oakland Tribune*, December 10.

Smith, J. 1984. "The paradox of women's poverty: Wage-earning women and economic transformation." *Signs: Journal of Women in Culture and Society*, 10:291-310.

Steinberg, R. 1986. "The debate over comparable worth." *New Politics*, 1:108-24.

Treiman, D. J. 1984. "Effect of choice of factors and factor weights in job evaluation." In H. Remick (ed.), *Comparable Worth and Wage Discrimination*. Philadelphia: Temple University Press:79-89.

Treiman, D. J. and H. I. Hartmann (eds.). 1981. *Women, Work and Wages: Equal Pay for Jobs of Equal Value*. Washington, DC: National Academy Press.

Turner, W. 1986. "Drive seen as gaining pay equity for women." *New York Times*, January 27.

U.S. Department of Labor. 1983. *Time of Change: 1983 Handbook on Women Workers*. Women's Bureau, Bulletin 298. Washington, DC: Government Printing Office.

Van Beers, L. B. 1981. "The effects of implementing comparable worth pay criteria in the city of San Jose." Unpublished master's thesis, University of California, Berkeley.

Wharton, A. S. 1984. "Blue collar segregation: A demand-side analysis." Unpublished Ph.D. dissertation, University of Oregon, Eugene.

Wilson, W. J. 1978. *The Declining Significance of Race*. Chicago: University of Chicago Press.

Reprinted from: Linda M. Blum, "Possibilities and Limits of the Comparable Worth Movement," in *Gender and Society* 1(4), pp. 380-399. Copyright © 1987 by Sage Publications, Inc. Reprinted by permission.

Food for Thought and Application Questions

1. Discuss several reasons why women working in highly segregated occupations do not always favor job integration.

2. What is the status of pay equity/comparable worth in your city/state? Has a pay equity study been undertaken for public sector jobs? If so, has there been any attempt to implement wage adjustments based on the study findings? If not, are any wage discrimination suits pending against your city/state?

3. Discuss why private sector firms might be reluctant to implement comparable worth. How might one make the case that comparable worth is in the best interest of work organizations? ✦

8

Race, Class, Gender, and Women's Works: A Conceptual Framework

Teresa L. Amott and Julie A. Matthaei

What social and economic factors determine and differentiate women's work lives? Why is it, for instance, that the work experiences of African American women are so different from those of European American women? Why have some women worked outside the home for pay, while others have provided for their families through unpaid work in the home? Why are most of the wealthy women in the United States of European descent and why are so many women of color poor? In this chapter, we lay out a basic conceptual framework for understanding differences in women's works and economic positions.

Throughout U.S. history, economic differences among women (and men) have been constructed and organized along a number of social categories. In our analysis, we focus on the three categories which we see as most central—gender, race-ethnicity, and class—with less discussion of others, such as age, sexual preference, and religion. We see these three social categories as interconnected, historical processes of domination and subordination. Thinking about gender, race-ethnicity, and class, then, necessitates thinking historically about power and economic exploitation.

There is a rich and controversial body of literature which examines the ways in which economic exploitation, ideology, and political power create and, in turn, are created by, gender, race-ethnicity, and class; we cannot do justice to the complexity of these issues here (Omi and Winant 1986; San Juan 1989; Spelman 1988; Matthaei, forthcoming). Rather, in this chapter, we develop a basic conceptual framework for thinking about the racial-ethnic histories of women's work. . . .

Gender, Race-Ethnicity, and Class Interconnected

The concepts of gender, race-ethnicity, and class are neither transhistorical nor independent. Hence, it is artificial to discuss them outside of historical time and place, and separately from one another. At the same time, without such a set of concepts, it is impossible to make sense of women's disparate economic experiences.

Gender, race-ethnicity, and class are not natural or biological categories which are unchanging over time and across cultures. Rather, these categories are socially constructed: they arise and are transformed in history, and themselves transform history. Although societies rationalize them as natural or god-given, ideas of appropriate feminine and masculine behavior vary widely across history and culture. Concepts and practices of race-ethnicity, usually justified by religion or biology, also vary over time, reflecting the politics, economics, and ideology of a particular time and in turn, reinforcing or transforming politics, economics, and ideology. For example, nineteenth-century European biologists Louis Agassiz and Count Arthur de Gobineau developed a taxonomy of race which divided humanity into separate and unequal racial species; this taxonomy was used to rationalize European colonization of Africa and Asia, and slavery in the United States (Gould 1981; Omi and Winant 1986). Class is perhaps the most historically specific category of all, clearly dependent upon the particular economic and social constellation of a society at a point in time. Still, notions of class as inherited or genetic continue to haunt us, harkening back to earlier eras in which lowly birth was thought to cause low intelligence and a predisposition to criminal activity.

Central to the historical transformation of gender, race-ethnicity, and class processes have been the struggles of subordinated groups to redefine or transcend them. For example, throughout the development of capitalism, workers' consciousness of themselves as workers and their struggles against class oppression have transformed capitalist-worker relationships, expanding workers' rights and powers. In the nineteenth century, educated white women escaped from the prevailing, domestic view of womanhood by arguing that homemaking included volunteer work, social homemaking careers, and political organizing. In the 1960s, the transformation of racial-ethnic identity into a source of solidarity and pride was essential to movements of people of color, such as the Black Power and American Indian movements.

Race-ethnicity, gender, and class are interconnected, interdetermining historical processes, rather than separate systems (Sargent 1981). This is true in two senses, which we will explore in more detail below. First, it is often difficult to determine whether an economic practice constitutes class, race, or gender oppression: for example, slavery in the U.S. South was at the same time a system of class oppression (of slaves by owners) and of racial-ethnic oppression (of Africans by Europeans). Second, a person does not experience these different processes of domination and subordination independently of one another; in philosopher Elizabeth Spelman's metaphor, gender, race-ethnicity, and class are not separate "pop-beads"

on a necklace of identity. Hence, there is no generic gender oppression which is experienced by all women regardless of their race-ethnicity or class. As Spelman puts it:

> . . . in the case of much feminist thought we may get the impression that a woman's identity consists of a sum of parts neatly divisible from one another, parts defined in terms of her race, gender, class, and so on. . . . On this view of personal identity (which might also be called pop-bead metaphysics), my being a woman means the same whether I am white or black, rich or poor, French or Jamaican, Jewish or Muslim. (Spelman 1988, p. 136)

The problems of "pop-bead metaphysics" also apply to historical analysis. In our reading of history, there is no common experience of gender across race-ethnicity and class, of race-ethnicity across class and gender lines, or of class across race-ethnicity and gender.

With these caveats in mind, let us examine the processes of gender, class, and race-ethnicity, their importance in the histories of women's works, and some of the ways in which these processes have been intertwined.

Gender

Over the past 20 years, feminist theorists have developed the concept of gender as central to understanding women's lives and oppression. As we will see, while the concept of gender is invaluable, the gender process cannot be understood independently of class and race-ethnicity. Further, there is no common experience of gender oppression among women.

Gender differences in the social lives of men and women are based on, but are not the same thing as, biological differences between the sexes. Gender is rooted in societies' beliefs that the sexes are naturally distinct and opposed social beings. These beliefs are turned into self-fulfilling prophecies through sex-role socialization: the biological sexes are assigned distinct and often unequal work and political positions, and turned into socially distinct genders.

Economists view the sexual division of labor as central to the gender differentiation of the sexes. By assigning the sexes to different and complementary tasks, the sexual division of labor turns them into different and complementary genders. The work of males is at least partially, if not wholly, different from that of females, making "men" and "women" different economic and social beings. Sexual divisions of labor, not sexual difference alone, create difference and complementarity between "opposite" sexes. These differences, in turn, have been the basis for marriage in most societies.

Anthropologists have found that most societies, across historical periods, have tended to assign females to infant care and to the duties associated with raising children because of their biological ability to bear children. In contrast men usually concentrate on interfamilial activities, and gain political dominance; hence gender complementarity has usually led to political and economic dominance by men (Levi-Strauss 1971; Rosaldo 1974).

The concept of gender certainly helps us understand women's economic histories. Each racial-ethnic group has had a sexual division of labor which has barred individuals from the activities of the opposite sex. Gender processes do differentiate women's lives in many ways from those of the men in their own racial-ethnic and class group. Further, gender relations in all groups tend to assign women to the intrafamilial work of childrearing, as well as to place women in a subordinate position to the men of their class and racial-ethnic group.

But as soon as we have written these generalizations, exceptions pop into mind. Gender roles do not always correspond to sex. Some American Indian tribes allowed individuals to choose among gender roles: a female, for example, could choose a man's role, do men's work, and marry another female who lived out a woman's role. In the nineteenth century, some white females "passed" as men in order to escape the rigid mandates of gender roles. In many of these cases, women lived with and loved other women.

Even though childrearing is women's work in most societies, many women do not have children, and others do not perform their own child care or domestic work. Here, class is an especially important differentiating process. Upper-class women have been able to use their economic power to reassign some of the work of infant caretaking—sometimes even breastfeeding—to lower-class women of their own or different racial-ethnic groups. These women, in turn, may have been forced to leave their infants alone or with relatives or friends. Finally, gender complementarity has not always led to social and economic inequality; for example, many American Indian women had real control over the home and benefitted from a more egalitarian sharing of power between men and women.

Since the processes of sex-role socialization are historically distinct in different times and different cultures, they result in different conceptions of appropriate gender behavior. Both African American and Chicana girls, for instance, learn how to be women—but both must learn the specific gender roles which have developed within their racial-ethnic and class group and historical period. For example, for white middle-class homemakers in the 1950s, adherence to the concept of womanhood discouraged paid employment, while for poor black women it meant employment as domestic servants for white middle-class women. Since racial-ethnic and class domination have differentiated the experiences of women, one cannot assume, as do many feminist theorists and activists, that all women have the same experience of gender oppression—or even that they will be on the same side of a struggle, not even when some women define that struggle as "feminist."

Not only is gender differentiation and oppression not a universal experience which creates a common "women's oppression," the sexual divisions of labor and family systems of people of color have been systematically disrupted by race-ethnic and class processes. In the process of invasion and conquest, Europeans imposed their notions of male superiority on cultures with more egalitarian forms of gender relations, including many American Indian and African tribes. At the same time, European Americans were quick to abandon their notion of appropriate femininity when it conflicted with profits: for example, slave owners often assigned slave women to backbreaking labor in the fields.

Racial-ethnic and class oppression have also disrupted family life among people of color and the white working class. Europeans interfered with family relations within subordinated racial-ethnic communities through rape and forced cohabitation. Sometimes whites encouraged or forced reproduction, as when slaveowners forced slave women into sexual relations. On the other hand, whites have often used their power to curtail reproduction among peoples of color, and aggressive sterilzation programs were practiced against Puerto Ricans and American Indians as late as the 1970s. Beginning in the late nineteenth century, white administrators took American Indian children from their parents to "civilize" them in boarding schools where they were forbidden to speak their own languages or wear their native dress. Slaveowners commonly split up slave families through sale to different and distant new owners. Nevertheless, African Americans were able to maintain strong family ties, and even augmented these with "fictive" or chosen kin (Gutman 1976). From the mid-nineteenth through the mid-twentieth centuries, many Asians were separated from their spouses or children by hiring policies and restrictions on immigration. Still, they maintained family life within these split households, and eventually succeeded in reuniting some-

times after generations. Hence, for peoples of color, having children and maintaining families have been an essential part of the struggle against racist oppression. Not surprisingly, many women of color have rejected the white women's movement's view of the family as the center of "women's oppression."

These examples reveal the limitations of gender as a single lens through which to view women's economic lives. Indeed, any attempt to understand women's experiences using gender alone cannot only cause misunderstanding, but can also interfere with the construction of broad-based movements against the oppressions experienced by women.

Race-Ethnicity

Like gender, race-ethnicity is based on a perceived physical difference and rationalized as "natural" or "god-given." But whereas gender creates difference and inequality according to biological sex, race-ethnicity differentiates individuals according to skin color or other physical features.

In all of human history, individuals have lived in societies with distinct languages, cultures, and economic institutions; these ethnic differences have been perpetuated by intermarriage within, but rarely between societies. However, ethnic differences can exist independently of a conception of race, and without a practice of racial-ethnic domination such as the Europeans practiced over the last three centuries.

Early European racist thought developed in the seventeenth and eighteenth centuries, embedded in the Christian worldview. Racial theorists argued that people of color were not descended from Adam and Eve as were whites. Later, in the nineteenth century, with the growth of Western science and its secular worldview, racial-ethnic differences and inequality were attributed directly to biology. According to the emerging scientific worldview, human beings were divided into biologically distinct and unequal races. Whites were, by nature, on top of this racial hierarchy, with the right and duty to dominate the others ("white man's burden") (Omi and Winant 1986; Cox 1959; Banton and Harwood 1975). In this racist typology, some ethnic differences—differences in language, culture, and social practices—were interpreted as racial and hence natural in origin. The different social and economic practices of societies of color were viewed by whites in the nineteenth century as "savage," in need of the "civilizing" influence of white domination. We use the term "race-ethnicity" in this book to grasp the contradictory nature of racial theories and practices, in particular the fact that those people seen as belonging to a particular "race" often lack a shared set of distinct physical characteristics, but rather share a common ethnicity or culture.

European racial theories were used to justify a set of economic and social practices which, in fact, made the "races" socially unequal. In this way, racism and the practices which embody it became self-fulfilling prophecies. Claiming that people of color were inherently inferior, whites segregated and subordinated them socially, economically, and politically. Furthermore, by preventing intermarriage between people of color and whites, whites perpetuated physical and ethnic differences as well as social and economic inequality between themselves and people of color across the generations. Although few scientists today claim that there are biological factors which create unequal races of human beings, racist practices and institutions have continued to produce both difference and inequality.

Does the concept of race-ethnicity help us understand the economic history of women in the United States? Certainly, for white racial-ethnic domination has been a central force in U.S. history. European colonization of North America entailed the displacement and murder of the continent's indigenous peoples, rationalized by the racist view that American Indians were savage heathens. The economy of the South was based on a racial-ethnic system, in which imported Africans were forced to work for white landowning families as slaves. U.S. military expansion in the nineteenth century brought more lands under U.S. control—territories of northern Mexico (now the Southwest), the Philippines, and Puerto Rico—incorporating their peoples into the racial-ethnic hierarchy. And from the mid-nineteenth century onward, Asians were brought into Hawaii's plantation system to work for whites as semi-free laborers. In the twentieth century, racial-ethnic difference and inequality have been perpetuated by the segregation of people of color into different and inferior jobs, living conditions, schools, and political positions, and by the prohibition of intermarriage with whites in some states up until 1967.

Race-ethnicity is a key concept in understanding histories. But it is not without limitations. First, racial-ethnic processes have never operated independently of class and gender. In the previous section on gender, we saw how racial domination distorted gender and family relations among people of color. Racial domination has also been intricately linked to economic or class domination. As social scientists Michael Omi (Asian American) and Howard Winant (European American) explain, the early European arguments that people of color were without souls had direct economic meaning:

> At stake were not only the prospects for conversion, but the types of treatment to be accorded them. The expropriation of property, the denial of political rights, the introduction of slavery and other forms of coercive labor, as well as outright extermination, all presupposed a worldview which distinguished Europeans—children of God, human beings, etc.—from "others." Such a worldview was needed to explain why some should be "free" and others enslaved, why some had rights to land and property while others did not. (Omi and Winant 1986, p.58)

Indeed, many have argued that racial theories only developed after the economic process of colonization had started, as a justification for white domination of peoples of color (Cox 1959). The essentially economic nature of early racial-ethnic oppression in the United States makes it difficult to isolate whether peoples of color were subordinated in the emerging U.S. economy because of their race-ethnicity or their economic class. Whites displaced American Indians and Mexicans to obtain their land. Whites imported Africans to work as slaves and Asians to work as contract laborers. Puerto Ricans and Filipinas/os were victims of further U.S. expansionism. Race-ethnicity and class intertwined in the patterns of displacement from land, genocide, forced labor, and recruitment from the seventeenth through the twentieth centuries. While it is impossible, in our minds, to determine which came first in these instances—race-ethnicity or class—it is clear that they were intertwined and inseparable.

Privileging racial-ethnic analysis also leads one to deny the existence of class differences, both among whites and among people of color, which complicate and blur the racial-ethnic hierarchy. A racial-ethnic analysis implies that all whites are placed above all peoples of color. . . . But in fact, as European American economist Harold Baron (1975) points out, a minority of the dominated race is allowed some upward mobility and ranks economically above whites. At the same time, however, all whites have some people of color below them. For example, there are upper-class black, Chicana, and Puerto Rican women who are more economically privileged than poor white women; however, there are always people of color who are less econonically privileged than the poorest white woman. Finally, class oppression operates among women of the same racial-ethnic group.

A third problem with the analysis of race domination is that such domination has not been a homogeneous process.

Each subordinated racial-ethnic group has been oppressed and exploited differently by whites: for example, American Indians were killed and displaced, Africans were enslaved, and Filipinas/os and Puerto Ricans were colonized. Whites have also dominated whites; some European immigrant groups, particularly Southern and Eastern Europeans, were subjected to segregation and violence. In some cases, people of color have oppressed and exploited those in another group: some American Indian tribes had African slaves; some Mexicans and Puerto Ricans displaced and murdered Indians and had African slaves. Because of these differences, racial oppression does not automatically bring unity of peoples of color across their own racial-ethnic differences, and feminists of color are not necessarily in solidarity with one another.

To sum up, we see that, as with gender, the concept of race-ethnicity is essential to our analysis of women's works. However, divorcing this concept from gender and class, again, leads to problems in both theory and practice.

Class

Radical economists stress class as the most important category for understanding economic life. Following Marx, these economists have focused on the ways in which individuals' relationships to the production process are polarized, such that one class reaps the benefits of another class' labor (a process which Marx called "exploitation"). Struggle between the classes over the control of the production process and the distribution of its output, Marx claimed, was the key to economic history. Thus, Marx characterized different societies as involving different "modes of production," each with its own class relations. In the feudal system of medieval Europe, for example, nobles owned the land and serfs were forced to work it, giving over a portion of their product and labor to the leisured nobility. In slavery, slaveowners, by virtue of property rights in slaves, owned the product of their slaves' labor, living and enriching themselves through their exploitation of the slaves. In capitalism, the owners of the machines and factories are able to live off the labor of the workers, who own nothing but their own labor and hence are forced to work for the owners. In the century since Marx wrote, radical economists have further developed Marx's conception of class, making it into a powerful concept for understanding economies past and present.

We believe that the concepts of class and exploitation are crucial to understanding the work lives of women in early U.S. history, as well as in the modern, capitalist economy. Up through the nineteenth century, different relations organized production in different regions of the United States. The South was dominated by slave agriculture; the Northeast by emerging industrial capitalism; the Southwest (then part of Mexico) by the *hacienda* system which carried over many elements of the feudal manor into large-scale production for the market; the rural Midwest by independent family farms that produced on a small scale for the market; and the American Indian West by a variety of tribal forms centered in hunting and gathering or agriculture, many characterized by cooperative, egalitarian relations. Living within these different labor systems, and in different class positions within them, women led very different economic lives.

By the late nineteenth century, however, capitalism had become the dominant form of production, displacing artisans and other small producers along with slave plantations and tribal economies. Today, wage labor accounts for over 90 percent of employment; self employment, including family businesses, accounts for the remaining share (U.S. Bureau of the Census 1990). With the rise of capitalism, women were brought into the same labor system and polarized according to the capitalist-wage laborer hierarchy.

At the same time as the wage labor form specific to capitalism became more prevalent, capitalist class relations became more complex and less transparent. Owners of wealth (stocks and bonds) now rarely direct the production process; instead, salaried managers, who may or may not own stock in the company, take on this function. While the capitalist class may be less identifiable, it still remains a small and dominant elite. In 1996, the super-rich (the richest one-half of one percent of the households) owned 35 percent of the total wealth in our country, over 70 times the share they would have had if wealth were equally distributed. The richest tenth of all households owned 72 percent of all wealth, over seven times their fair share. This extreme concentration of wealth conveys a concentration of leisure and power over others into the hands of a small number of households, a concentration which is perpetuated through the generations by inheritance laws and customs.[1]

At the other end of the hierarchy, in 1986, the poorest 90 percent of households owned only 28 percent of total wealth, and had to send at least one household member out to work for the household's survival. Among these waged and salaried workers, a complicated hierarchy of segmented labor markets gives some workers greater earnings and power over the production process than others. Indeed, there are many disagreements over how to categorize managers, professionals, and government workers—to name only a few of the jobs which seem to fall outside the two-class model. . . .[2]

Class can be a powerful concept in understanding women's economic lives, but there are limits to class analysis if it is kept separate from race-ethnicity and gender. First, as we saw in the race section above, the class relations which characterized the early U.S. economy were also racial-ethnic and gender formations. Slave owners were white and mostly male, slaves were black. The displaced tribal economies were the societies of indigenous peoples. Independent family farmers were whites who farmed American Indian lands; they organized production in a patriarchal manner, with women and children's work defined by and subordinated to the male household head and property owner. After establishing their dominance in the pre-capitalist period, white men were able to perpetuate and institutionalize this dominance in the emerging capitalist system, particularly through the monopolization of managerial and other high-level jobs.

Second, the sexual division of labor within the family makes the determination of a woman's class complicated—determined not simply by her relationship to the production process, but also by that of her husband or father. For instance, if a woman is not in the labor force but her husband is a capitalist, then we might wish to categorize her as a member of the capitalist class. But what if that same woman worked as a personnel manager for a large corporation, or as a salesperson in an elegant boutique? Clearly, she derives upper-class status and access to income from her husband, but she is also, in her own right, a worker. Conversely, when women lose their husbands through divorce, widowhood, or desertion, they often change their class position in a downward direction. A second gender-related economic process overlooked by class analysis is the unpaid household labor performed by women for their fathers, husbands, and children—or by other women, for pay.[3]

Third, while all workers are exploited by capitalists, they are not equally exploited, and gender and race-ethnicity play important roles in this differentiation. Men and women of the same racial-ethnic group have rarely performed the same jobs—this sex-typing and segregation is the labor market form of the sexual division of labor we studied above. Further, women of different racial-ethnic groups have rarely been employed at the same job, at least not within the same workplace or region. This racial-ethnic-typing and segregation has both reflected and reinforced

the racist economic practices upon which the U.S. economy was built.

Thus, jobs in the labor force hierarchy tend to be simultaneously race-typed and gender-typed. Picture in your mind a registered nurse. Most likely, you thought of a white woman. Picture a doctor. Again, you imagined a person of a particular gender (probably a man), and a race (probably a white person). If you think of a railroad porter, it is likely that a black man comes to mind. Almost all jobs tend to be typed in such a way that stereotypes make it difficult for persons of the "wrong" race and/or gender to train for or obtain the job. Of course, there are regional and historical variations in the typing of jobs. On the West Coast, for example, Asian men performed much of the paid domestic work during the nineteenth century because women were in such short supply. In states where the African American population is very small, such as South Dakota or Vermont, domestic servants and hotel chambermaids are typically white. Nonetheless, the presence of variations in race-gender typing does not contradict the idea that jobs tend to take on racial-ethnic and gender characteristics with profound effects on the labor market opportunities of job-seekers.

The race-sex-typing of jobs makes the effects of class processes inseparable from the effects of race-ethnicity and gender. Not only is the labor market an arena of struggle in which race-ethnicity and gender, as well as class, are reproduced. In addition, the race-sex typing of jobs has been central in determining the job structure itself. For example, secretarial work developed in the late nineteenth century as a white woman's job; hence, in contrast to the white male job of clerk which it replaced, secretarial work cast white women in the role of "office wives" to white men, and involved no path of career advancement into management.

. . . White workers, not just white capitalists, helped impose this race-ethnic hierarchy. White capitalists—wealthy landowners, railroad magnates, factory owners—imported blacks, Asians, and, later, Puerto Ricans and Mexicans as a low-wage labor supply. The entrance of these workers of color into the labor force was met with hostility and violence by both white workers and small producers such as farmers and craftsmen. Since employers used immigrant workers of color as strike-breakers or low-wage competition, white workers trying to organize for higher wages resisted this immigration. The threat of competition from workers of color and an ideology of white supremacy kept most white workers from recruiting workers of color into their emerging trade unions on equal terms. European immigrants who spoke languages other than English also faced economic and political discrimination. Thus, in an environment of nativism and racial hostility, jobs came to be increasingly segmented along racial-ethnic lines as the result of combined capitalist and worker efforts (Bonacich 1976). Furthermore, as people of different racial-ethnic groups were drawn out of the many different labor systems from which they had come into wage labor, they were also segregated within the developing labor market hierarchy.

The processes which have perpetuated the sex-typing of jobs have, for the most part, been less overt and violent. White male unions, in the late nineteenth century, fought for the passage of "protective legislation" that, by excluding women from dangerous or unhealthy jobs and from overtime work, had the effect of denying them highly paid factory jobs and confining them in lower-paying (and also hazardous) sectors such as apparel and textile manufacture. Women were also confined to low-paid, servile, or care-taking jobs by the sexual division of labor in the home, particularly married women's assignment to the unpaid work of caring for children and serving their husbands. Many employers simply refused to hire married women, with the view that their place was in the home. Domestic respon-sibilities also limited women's ability to compete for jobs requiring overtime or lengthy training. Professional associations and schools, dominated by white men, restricted the entry of women of all racial-ethnic groups well into the twentieth century. When individual women gained the qualifications and tried to break into jobs monopolized by men of their racial-ethnic group, or into elite, white men's jobs, they were rejected or, if hired, sabotaged, ridiculed, and racially and sexually harassed. These processes have been extremely costly to women in terms of lost wages and job opportunities. This combination of race- and sex-segregation in the labor market meant that, in general, only white men were able to earn a "family wage," adequate to support oneself and a family.

In these ways, the racial-ethnic and gender processes operating in the labor market have transposed white and male domination from pre-capitalist structures into the labor market's class hierarchy. This hierarchy can be described by grouping jobs into different labor market sectors or segments: "primary," "secondary," and "underground." The primary labor market—which has been monopolized by white men—offers high salaries, steady employment and upward mobility. Its upper tier consists of white-collar salaried or self-employed workers with high status, autonomy, and, often, supervisory capacity. Wealth increases access to this sector, since it purchases elite education and provides helpful job connections. . . .

The lower tier of the primary sector, which still yields high earnings but involves less autonomy, contains many unionized blue-collar jobs. White working-class men have used union practices, mob violence, and intimidation to monopolize these jobs. By World War II, however, new ideologies of worker solidarity, embodied in the mass industrial unions, began to overcome the resistance of white male workers to the employment of people of color and white women in these jobs.

In contrast to both these primary tiers, the secondary sector offers low wages, few or no benefits, little opportunity for advancement, and unstable employment. People of color and most white women have been concentrated in the secondary sector jobs, where work is often part-time, temporary, or seasonal, and pay does not rise with increasing education or experience. Jobs in both tiers of the primary labor market have generally yielded family wages, earnings high enough to support a wife and children who are not in the labor force for pay. Men of color in the secondary sector have not been able to earn enough to support their families, and women of color have therefore participated in wage labor to a much higher degree than white women whose husbands held primary sector jobs.

Outside of the formal labor market is the underground sector, where the most marginalized labor force groups, including many people of color, earn their living from illegal or quasi-legal work. This sector contains a great variety of jobs, including drug trafficking, crime, prostitution, work done by undocumented workers, and sweatshop work which violates labor standards such as minimum wages and job safety regulations.

White women and people of color have waged successful battles to gain admittance to occupations from which they once were barred. Union organizing has succeeded in raising jobs out of the secondary sector by providing higher wages, fringe benefits, a seniority system, and protection from arbitrary firing for workers. Similarly, the boundaries of the underground ecomomy have been changed by struggles to legalize or make illegal acts such as drug use and prostitution—for example, by women's successful struggle to prohibit the sale of alcohol during the early twentieth century—as well as by immigration and labor laws.

Conclusion

Women throughout the United States have not experienced a common oppression as women. The processes of gender, race-ethnicity, and class—intrinsically interconnected—have been central forces determining and differentiating women's work lives in U.S. history. Thus, while the explanatory power of each concept—gender, race-ethnicity, and class—is, in itself, limited, together they form a basis for understanding women's work. . . .

Endnotes

1. This represents an increase for the top 0.5 percent, from 25.4 percent of total wealth 20 years ago; 20 years ago, the poorest 90 percent of all households had 34.9 percent of all wealth, 6.7 percentage points more than they have presently. There has been a controversy over these numbers; after these data, collected by the Federal Research Board, were publicized by the Joint Economic Committee of Congress, the Federal Reserve claimed that a mistake had been made in the original survey, and that actually there had been no increase in the share of wealth held by the top 0.5 percent. See "Scandal at the Fed? Doctoring the Numbers on Wealth Concentration," *Dollars and Sense*, No. 125 (April 1987):10.

2. For good discussions of this process, see David Gordon, Richard Edwards, Michael Reich, eds., *Segmented Work, Divided Workers: The Historical Transformation of Labor in the United States* (New York: Cambridge University Press, 1982); and Eric Wright, "Class Boundaries and Contradictory Class Locations," in *Classes, Power, and Conflict*, ed. Anthony Giddens (Berkeley: University of California Press, 1982):112-129.

3. Marxist-feminists did attempt to analyze this work as "domestic labor" in a theoretical debate in the 1970s; for a review of this debate, see Wally Seccombe, "Reflections on the Domestic Labor Debate and Prospects for Marxist-Feminist Synthesis," in *The Politics of Diversity*, ed. Robert Hamilton and Michele Barrett (Canada: Book Center Inc., 1986). Some claim that

the household is part of a different mode of production which coexists with capitalism; see Harriet Fraad, Stephen Resnick, and Richard Wolff, "For Every Knight in Shining Armor, There's a Castle Waiting to Be Cleaned: A Marxist-Feminist Analysis of the Household," *Rethinking Marxism* 2 (Winter 1989):10-69; and the comments by Julie Matthaei, Zillah Eisenstein, Kim Lane Scheppele, Nancy Folbre, Heidi Hartmann, and Stephanie Coontz in the same issue.

References

Banton, M. and J. Harwood. 1975. *The Race Concept*. Ch. 1. New York: Praeger.

Baron, H. 1975. "Racial domination in advanced capitalism: A theory of nationalism and divisions in the labor market." In R. Edwards, M. Reich, and D. Gordon (eds.), *Labor Market Segmentation*. Lexington, MA: D. C. Heath and Company.

Bonacich, Edna. "Advanced Capitalism and Black/White Race Relations in the United States: A Split Labor Market Interpretation," *American Sociological Review* 41(Feb. 1976): 34-51.

Cox, O. C. 1959. *Class, Caste and Race: A Study in Social Dynamics*. New York: Monthly Review Press.

Ferguson, A. 1983. "On conceiving motherhood and sexuality: A feminist materialist approach." In J. Treblicot (ed.), *Mothering: Essays in Feminist Theory*. Totowa, NJ: Rowman and Allanheld.

Gould, S. J. 1981. *The Mismeasure of Man*. New York: W. W. Norton and Company:42-51.

Gutman, H. 1976. *The Black Family in Slavery and Freedom, 1750-1925*. New York: Pantheon Books.

Hodges, J. et al. 1975. *The Cultural Bases of Racism and Group Oppression*. Berkeley: Two Riders Press.

Levi-Strauss, C. 1971. "The family." In A. Skolnick and J. Skolnick (eds.), *The Family in Transition*. Boston: Little Brown.

Matthaei, J. forthcoming. "Marxist contributions to radical economics." In S. Feiner and B. Roberts (eds.), *Radical Economics*. Norwell, MA: Kluwer-Nijhoff.

Omi, M. and H. Winant. 1986. *Racial Formation in the United States: From the 1960s to the 1980s*. New York: Routledge & Kegan Paul.

Rosaldo, M. Z. 1974. "Women, culture, and society: A theoretical overview." In M. Rosaldo and L. Lamphere (eds.), *Woman, Culture, and Society*. Stanford: Stanford University Press.

San Juan, E. 1989. "Problems in one Marxist project of theorizing race." In *Rethinking Marxism*, 2 (Summer):58-80.

Sargent, L. (ed.) 1981. *Women and Revolution*. Boston: South End Press.

Spelman, E. V. 1988. *Inessential Woman: Problems of Exclusion in Feminist Thought*. Boston: Beacon Press.

U.S. Bureau of the Census. 1990. *Statistical Abstract of the United States: 1990*. Washington, D.C.:GPO:386.

Food for Thought and Application Questions

1. Select any two of the following racial/ethnic groups: African Americans, American Indians, Chinese Americans, Filipinos, Japanese Americans, Mexican Americans, Puerto Ricans, and Anglos/Whites. Collect information on the labor-force participation rates and average earnings for women in the two groups you selected. How have racial/ethnic processes operated to create any differences you find in work experiences between the two groups? (In order to answer this, you should read about the economic history of the groups you selected. The book this chapter was excerpted from is one good source; the sources cited in the bibliography for this chapter provide others. You may also find useful information in textbooks on race and ethnic relations.)

2. In your opinion, has gender, race/ethnicity, or class had the most impact on your work aspirations and experiences? Ask the same question to people from different racial/ethnic and classgroups. Also ask a member of the opposite sex. Are their responses similar to yours? Do any patterns begin to emerge in the responses you receive? ✦

Unit Three

Work and Family: A Delicate Balance

The breakdown of family values, rising juvenile crime rates, declining educational achievement, teen pregnancy, latchkey children, the drug problem, and the high divorce rate are all social problems that the public, politicians, the popular media, and even academicians have blamed on working women and the resulting neglect of families. Why have working women become a popular scapegoat for so many social ills? Several reasons exist. First, increases in women's employment this century represent rapid social change, and rapid social change is disruptive to society, at least in the short-run. It takes time for social institutions to adapt and adjust to change, and, as we will see in the selections that follow, accommodations to women's employment have been slow in coming. Relatedly, because rapid social change is often disruptive in the short-run (even though it may have very positive long-run consequences), social values and individual beliefs typically support the status quo. The public clamor over the breakdown of family values provides a good example. Family values are not breaking down, they are simply changing in order to accommodate new family forms (e.g., single parent families, dual

worker families, gay and lesbian partnerships). Sit-down dinners, seven days a week with all family members present, may be a thing of the past, but there are many indications that commitment to the family is as strong as ever (Lasch 1977).

Another reason for attributing the cause of social problems to working women is related to the definition of scapegoat. A scapegoat is a "safe goat"; that is, blame can be placed on a scapegoat without fear of retribution. Women, as a disadvantaged group, are relatively powerless to respond; thus, it is convenient to blame them. Many of the problems listed above (e.g., youth crime, declining educational achievement, teen pregnancy, drug use) are caused to varying degrees by economic inequality. It is very difficult, however, to blame the economically advantaged for depriving others and thus contributing to social problems.

Laying the blame for social problems on women's paid work is problematic not only because women's work is seldom the cause of the problems, but also because our economy depends on women working, as do families who require the income generated by their employment. Unless unanticipated, broad-based changes in our economy occur, women will continue to work outside the home for pay, so blaming this phenomenon for social problems does little to provide solutions. A more fruitful approach to strengthening families, improving the lives of youth, reducing crime, and enhancing educational achievement involves adapting social arrangements so as to make work and family roles more compatible. This could be done by increasing men's responsibilities in the family (e.g., domestic work, child care), providing government subsidized assistance to families (e.g., subsidized parental leave), and a vast array of workplace accommodations (e.g., flex-time, on-site day care, work at home). These avenues for achieving the delicate balance between work and family are discussed at length in the selections that follow.

Working women are the ones most negatively affected by social disruptions resulting from their employment and society's failure to evolve adaptive structures for accommodating their paid work. Not only must women bear the burden of responsibility for causing social problems, they must also disproportionately bear the responsibility for minimizing the disruption that results from their work. For example, regardless of how one defines or measures housework, it is quite clear that wives still do more of it than husbands (Feree 1991; Thompson and Walker 1991). The adage that "men work from sun to sun, but women's work is never done" rings true today in dual worker families where women work full-time outside the home and then come home to what Hochschild (1989) calls a "second shift." In a study of 50 dual worker couples, she found that the second shift results in employed women performing about an extra month of full-time work each year. Most studies show that the housework contribution of husbands does not change much when their wives begin working, and that husbands of working wives spend only about one third as much time on housework as their wives (Baca Zinn and Eitzen 1993).

Child care and elder care tasks are also performed disproportionately by women in dual worker families; thus exacerbating the role overload they face. LaRossa and LaRossa (1981) find that while new fathers are willing to assist with child care tasks, they view the primary responsibility for caring for the baby as the mother's. This difference explains why mothers experience more stress in adapting to parenthood than do fathers. Women's care provider responsibilities often do not diminish significantly when the children leave the nest, because that is the point in time at which aging parents and parents-in-law are in need of care. In this society, the bulk of the care of old people is provided informally by women relatives (Aronson 1992), thus constraining women's employment opportunities and their access to resources and independence.

Gender gaps in housework and care-giving contribute to a gender gap in marital satisfaction. Studies indicate that a fair division of family work between husbands and wives is associated with higher levels of marital satisfaction for women, and that over-burdened wives are less satisfied with their marital relationships. In contrast, husbands are more satisfied with their marriages and less critical of their wives if their wives do more than their fair share of family work (Thompson and Walker 1991).

The burden of family work also falls disproportionately to single women. Over 25 percent of all families with live-at-home children are single parent families, and the overwhelming majority of the families are headed by women. The incidence of mother-only families among blacks and Hispanics is especially high—49 percent for blacks and 29 percent for Hispanics (U. S. Bureau of the Census, 1991). Women who head mother-only families must perform the work of two parents—breadwinning, housework, and child care, resulting in high stress levels. Single mothers are especially likely to be blamed for the problems of today's youth; rarely does attention turn to the responsibility of fathers.

The selections in this unit focus on issues of work-family conflict, emphasizing the consequences for women, their family lives, and their work. The first selection by Chafetz provides an overview of the strains present in dual worker families and explores strategies for reducing them. Her selection is important because it shows that there is much that can be done to minimize work-family conflict, but that the United States lags behind many other nations in providing support to dual worker families. Chafetz recommends a number of strategies that involve shifting some of the "double burden" away from women to partners, work organizations, and other sources of family support.

The selection by Carlisle focuses on women's experiences in a particular type of dual worker family, the dual career family. Dual career families are those where both adults have, not just jobs, but demanding, satisfying careers. Adults in these families earn higher incomes in intrinsically rewarding positions, but must invest well beyond the standard 40-hour work week in their jobs. Carlisle surveys professional and entrepreneurial women in these families to determine what they perceive to be the major advantages and disadvantages of dual career families and how they cope with role overload.

In the next selection, Gerson presents findings from in-depth interviews with women she labels "reluctant mothers"— women who are career-committed, perceive children as costly to their careers, but choose to become mothers nonetheless. The interview excerpts provide insight into the factors that go into the "cost-benefit" analysis these women perform in order to make the important decision about parenthood. Gerson finds that reluctant mothers are those who give disproportionate weight to the costs of not having children (e.g., loneliness, discontinuation of the family line, feelings of having "missed something"). She finds it is necessary for these women to lower the costs of having children so that they can retain their commitment to work and explores the strategies they employ for doing so.

The final selection in this unit explores how working women are expected to meet a male-centered standard in the workplace, yet at the same time conform to their traditional family roles. Kelly's essay supports the earlier argument of Kanter (1977), that working women are pressured to conform to a limited number of gender traditional stereotypes in the workplace, all of which reflect poorly on ability to do the job. Kelly describes how wife/girlfriend, mother, daughter, and sex partner/object roles spill over into work and impede women's career progress.

References

Aaronson, J. 1992. "Women's sense of responsibility for the care of old people: 'But who else is going to do it?'" *Gender and Society*, 6:8-20.

Baca Zinn, M. and S. D. Eitzen. 1993. *Diversity in Families*. New York: Harper Collins.

Feree, M. M. 1991. "Feminism and family research." In A. Booth (ed.), *Contemporary Families: Looking Forward, Looking Back*. Minneapolis: National Council on Family Relations:103-121.

Hochschild, A. (with A. Machung). 1989. *The Second Shift*. New York: Viking Press.

Kanter, R. M. 1977. *Men and Women of the Corporation*. New York: Basic Books.

LaRossa, R. and L. LaRossa. 1981. *Transition to Parenthood*. Beverly Hills, CA: Sage.

Lasch, C. 1977. *Haven in a Heartless World: The Family Besieged*. New York: Basic Books.

Thompson, L. and A. Walker. 1991. "Gender in families." In A. Booth (ed.), *Contemporary Families: Looking Forward, Looking Back*. Minneapolis: National Council on Family Relations:275-296.

U.S. Bureau of the Census. 1991. "Marital status and living arrangements: March 1990." *Current Population Reports*, Series P-20, No. 450. Washington, D. C.: U.S. Government Printing Office. ✦

9

'I Need a (Traditional) Wife!': Employment-Family Conflicts

Janet Saltzman Chafetz

Labor force roles require substantial time and energy commitments five days each week. Homes and families, especially when they include young children, also require substantial time and energy, seven days a week. When people combine a commitment to a spouse and children with a full-time occupation, the potential for conflict and strain is very real. This is especially true in a nation, such as the United States, that defines family problems as private matters to be worked out by the individuals involved, and therefore offers few public resources to mitigate employment-family conflicts.

First I will look at strains and conflicts created within the family when both parents are employed, or when there is only one parent present and she is employed. Secondly, I will examine how being married, and especially being a parent, can cause problems on the job. In both cases, because of traditional gender expectations associated specifically with the wife/mother roles, the strains and problems women confront by combining family and employment are far greater than those experienced by men. Finally, I will discuss some public, employer and private mechanisms

that can help to reduce some of the conflicts and strains discussed.

Family Strains

Only a generation ago, married women and mothers in all but the poorest families rarely participated in the labor force, and when they did, it was usually on a temporary basis. Their full-time job was to take care of the home and its occupants, meeting their physical, social and psychological needs. Beginning in the 1950s, and rapidly escalating by the 1970s, first wives and mothers with older children, subsequently even married mothers of pre-school aged youngsters, flooded the labor market. In addition, divorce rates were rising and the number of single, employed mothers increased also. By 1990, 58 percent of all married women in the U.S. were employed, and approximately 60 percent of all mothers with pre-school aged children were as well. In fact, 52 percent of mothers with children under age two were employed (data source U.S. Depts. of Labor and Commerce, as reported by Lindsey, 1994). A rapid increase in the number of married women and mothers of young children, regardless of marital status, participating in the labor force is a trend characterizing all highly industrialized nations during the last 20 to 30 years.

When homemaking is a full-time job, women usually work far more than the traditional 40-hour, five-day work week. Some estimates are as high as 70 to 80 hours spread over seven days. Moreover, when married women and single mothers enter the labor force, they do not relinquish responsibility for their gender-traditional domestic and childrearing work. Repeated research in the United States and many other industrial nations clearly demonstrates that, on average, the husbands of full-time employed wives do very little more domestic work than the husbands of full-time homemakers. Moreover, employed wives average two to three times the number of hours of domestic/childrearing work as their husbands (South and Spitze 1994; Reskin and Padavic 1994). When women divorce, their domestic work load actually decreases somewhat, suggesting that husbands create more work than they do. Arlie Hochschild (1989) coined the term second shift to describe the extra workload of employed married women, who return home from the office, shop, factory, hospital or school each evening and weekend, to several hours of mostly unshared cooking, cleaning, laundry and childcare work.

However, research also consistently demonstrates that employed wives and mothers do substantially less domestic work than full-time homemakers. Some purchase domestic and childcare services by hiring others to do the work (e.g., maids and nannies), by eating out more often and buying take-out meals, by sending clothes out to be laundered, and by placing pre-school children in daycare (Bergmann 1986). However, most families are not able to purchase many of these services, beyond the necessary one of providing care for young children, which takes a substantial bite out of all but the highest paychecks. Domestic chores, such as looking after younger siblings, cooking or laundry, are often delegated to older children. Sometimes the mothers of employed women are available and willing to help out also. The primary way that employed women reduce the heavy drain on their time and energy that the second shift entails is to reduce their standards of domestic work (Reskin and Padavic 1994). Meals are less elaborate, and laundry, ironing, cleaning and dusting are simply done less often. When women are full-time homemakers, they may enhance their self-esteem by setting exceptionally high standards of domestic work (e.g., ironing bed linens, laundering daily, sewing clothes for the family) which can be easily reduced upon employment.

It is likely that in many families, tired employed mothers end up devoting less time and attention to their children than do full-time homemakers. While married fathers appear to be increasing their involvement in childcare more than in other forms of domestic work, children in dual-earner and employed single-parent families probably average less parental attention than those whose mothers are not participating in the labor force. However, there is no evidence that this is harmful to the children (unless the attention deprivation is extreme). In fact, such children have been found to be more independent than the children of full-time homemakers, a trait normally highly valued in U.S. society. Moreover, the daughters of employed women have, on average, higher career aspirations than other girls, and their sons as well as their daughters tend to hold more gender equalitarian norms (Wilkie 1988).

Regardless of the strains produced by the second shift, research has indicated that employed married women generally enjoy better mental health than full-time homemakers. A busy life that includes diverse roles, the opportunity to interact with other adults on a daily basis, a paycheck of one's own, and other, intrinsic rewards from work roles, apparently more than compensates psychologically for whatever strains may result from a very long work day and week. The problem remains, however, that relative to their husbands, employed married women confront a serious deficit of leisure.

As long as men escape full participation in the second shift, their wives (and, all too often today, former wives) will continue to confront strain from a too-heavy workload. The reason why men do not become more involved in domestic work is currently subject to debate among sociologists. Some contend that both women and men choose a gender-traditional division of household labor as a means of expressing and reaffirming their own and their partner's gendered self-concepts (Berk 1985). Others argue that husbands continue to exercise more power within the family than their wives and can thus enforce their preference to do very little second shift work (Chafetz 1990). Regardless of the reason(s), the facts of the situation are clear and undisputed, and it is likely that the inequity of the situation is contributing to the high divorce rates characteristic of the U.S. and other industrial nations (Sanchez 1994). Nonetheless, because mothers overwhelmingly gain custody of their children upon divorce, the second shift problem is not solved for women by divorce.

Employment Conflicts

Over a century ago, the industrial revolution created a sharp separation between the places where people perform work for pay, and those where they perform work that maintains and reproduces the family. As paid work moved out of households, men followed. Married women remained in a separate sphere at home, and engaged in unpaid domestic and childrearing work. Given that most women married and divorce rates were low, most paid employment came to be defined as men's work. Jobs of all kinds were structured on the assumption that workers could and would concentrate full attention on their work, able to do so because they had someone else to worry about maintaining their homes, their wardrobes, feeding them, and taking care of their children. That is, employers assumed that workers had wives. The husband/father roles became defined as virtually synonymous with bread winner (and little else). By and large, this set of assumptions has not changed. Paid work for all but a few is conducted away from the home, precluding the simultaneous care of children, who are not welcomed at work sites for anything beyond a quick visit. Specific work days and hours are relatively inflexible for most workers, and often overlap almost completely the times when pediatricians see sick children, teachers confer with parents, or any number of other domestic errands must be run. In the last 20 to 30 years

supermarkets and most retail stores began to stay open nights and/or weekends to accommodate employed people, but most service providing organizations still do not.

Not only do employed women not have wives to take care of their needs and those of their children, many are wives (or at least mothers) with familial and domestic responsibilities. Some men, whose wives are employed, may not be able to count on them to provide domestic/childcare services, or they may wish to participate more fully than men traditionally have in the care of their children. A small number are also single, custodial parents. Such men will confront the same types of problems and conflicts as employed wives and mothers. Moreover, given traditional gender expectations, women may be somewhat forgiven by employers for allowing family-related needs to interfere with their job, because employers are likely to stereotypically assume that family is more important than job for women. However, it is a rare employer who will be equally understanding of a man who wishes to exercise the same option, rather assuming that men have wives who should be responsible for such matters.

Employer demands on workers vary by occupation. Therefore, the extent and kinds of problems people confront in the workplace, contingent upon their familial statuses, vary somewhat by occupation. Looking first at professional, managerial and other high-level white collar occupations, employers of such personnel are often quite greedy in the time and energy they demand. They may expect committed employees to regularly work more than 40 hours per week at the office, to take work home, to entertain nights and weekends for business purposes, to travel extensively, to accept geographic transfers, etc. Clearly, these kinds of expectations directly conflict with family responsibilities. If both spouses work in occupations with such demands, family-related strains are virtually unavoidable, short of one or both refusing to comply with expectations beyond a routine work week. For single, custodial parents such expectations may be all but impossible to fulfill, given childcare considerations. If, as is the case more often for women than men, family commitment is regarded as at least equally valued as career commitment, employees may be loath to conform to the requests or demands of greedy employers. Partners in a dual-career family confront especially serious conflicts when one is offered a better job or a promotion entailing a geographic transfer, when the other may not be able to find a job in the new location that is equal to, or better than the one she/he already has. A small number of couples, both of whom have demanding careers, live in cities separated by hundreds, even thousands of miles and see each other only on (some) weekends and vacations. This practice, referred to as a commuter marriage, clearly extracts a toll on family life, especially if there are children still in the home, as evidenced by high divorce rates for such couples. Refusal to become involved in extra work, to accept a geographic transfer, or to convert their personal life into an extension of their jobs may lead employers to define such employees as insufficiently committed to their work, with the result that the employees fail to gain promotions and raises they would otherwise merit.

A few years ago the term mommy track was bandied about in the popular media. This term referred to a suggestion that employers should explicitly develop a slow track designed specifically for professional and managerial women who wanted to devote time and attention to their families yet still maintain their careers. Expectations on the job would be reduced, but the women were to expect fewer and slower raises and promotions, if any. The suggestion was met with cries of sexism by feminists and most managerial and professional women. These women felt that such a plan simply reinforces the idea that family responsibility is women's work, not work to be shared equally by both fathers and mothers. While the term was quickly abandoned, a slow track for actively parenting employees still exists in numerous places of employment. In fact, a recent *New York Times* article (Oct. 13, 1994) reported research findings documenting a daddy penalty for men involved in dual-career marriages. Among a sample of managerial men with Master's degrees in Business Administration, the average 1993 salary for those with employed wives was $95,140, compared to $124,510 for men married to full-time homemakers. Moreover, the former had received salary increments averaging 43 percent between 1987-93, compared to 67 percent for the latter.

Although they may pay the price of being defined as uncommitted, many salaried white collar workers have sufficient autonomy and flexibility in their jobs to allow them to take some time off during the day for family matters. Hourly wage workers, especially those who punch a time clock, may find it much more difficult to get medical attention for a sick child or run an important personal or family errand during normal work hours. If they do get time off for these purposes, their pay is typically docked for that time, which is a serious problem given their generally low wages. Employers of such workers usually do not expect more than a 40-hour work week, although during times of especially heavy demand for their product or service, employers may pressure workers to work overtime hours, for which they are paid higher hourly wages. Salaried employees, by contrast, are usually not docked pay for taking a few hours off from their job, nor are they paid extra when they work more than a 40-hour week.

Some occupations are characterized by being heavily female in composition (e.g., primary and secondary school teaching, nursing and many allied health professions, secretarial and clerical work). Employers of these kinds of personnel often expect workers to need time off for family matters (Coser and Rokoff 1982). Such occupations usually pay less than those occupations that require comparable levels of education and skill but are not female dominated. In choosing such work, women may sacrifice some income in return for more freedom to fulfill domestic obligations. For instance, for generations public schools have had a unique system of substitutes who were on call to come in to work on very short notice. This system reflects an assumption that, given an overwhelmingly female labor force, absentee rates for family emergencies will be high (Coser and Rokoff 1982). The growth in recent years of businesses that provide temporary secretarial and clerical workers to employers may reflect this same set of expectations, as many more such workers are married and mothers now than in the past, when these jobs were filled mostly by young, single women before marriage. For school teachers, there is the added incentive that their hours and months of employment match those of their school aged children, thereby solving child-care problems and reducing employment-family conflicts.

Regardless of type of employment, when added to a 40-hour work week, substantial domestic and familial obligations make it extremely difficult for people to pursue additional training or education during their non-employment hours. In foregoing additional training or education, workers also forego the promotions and raises that might accompany it.

Finally, in any type of job domestic or familial crises may negatively impact the quality of work performed by employed persons. Workers can scarcely be expected to forget family problems upon entering the door of their workplace. If a crisis is prolonged (e.g., a seriously ill child), or they are too frequent (e.g., a child who regularly gets into trouble at school requiring a parent-teacher conference each time), serious problems can result with employers who may not be overly sympathetic to frequent requests for time off, or

excuses for inadequate performance. Raises, promotions, even job security may be jeopardized.

Reducing Employment-Family Conflict

Conflicts between employment and family work obligations can be reduced without necessarily returning to the traditional system in which most workers have wives who do not work outside the home. Millions of dual-earner couples attempt to work out their own techniques for doing so every day, with varying levels of success and equity between the spouses. More importantly, some employers have developed practices that reduce such conflicts, and some agencies of government have established policies that do so as well.

At the level of individual families, I have already mentioned several strategies for reducing work overload and the resultant strain: 1) reducing the standards of domestic work; 2) purchasing domestic and childcare services; 3) having other family members (e.g., husbands, children, parents) perform more domestic work; 4) refusing to comply with the demands or requests of greedy employers (with a cost to one's career success, probably most often the woman's); and 5) choosing an occupation (e.g., school teaching) which allows more time for the family (with a cost to one's income, usually the woman's). Couples can add time to their day by shortening the time required to commute between home and employment. They may move closer to one (or both) partner's job site, or one (or occasionally both) can seek employment specifically based on proximity to home. In the latter case, it may entail foregoing a better job to take one more conveniently located, and again, this is a more likely choice for women than men. Employment-family conflicts can also be reduced by assuming a part-time job. The overwhelming majority of part-time workers are married women, both in the U.S. and in other industrial nations, who not only earn less, but usually receive no fringe benefits. As should be clear, most strategies developed by dual-earner couples to reduce employment-family conflicts inequitably reduce the wife's income and/or career mobility prospects. Employed wives and mothers therefore tend to be doubly disadvantaged: by assuming the bulk of the second shift, and by making most of whatever employment-related sacrifices the couple deems necessary. Both of these inequities could be abolished if we, as a nation, began to take women's employment commitments as seriously as men's, and to take men's domestic and familial responsibilities as seriously as women's. Either one without the other will not suffice.

Many employers have instituted policies in recent years that help reduce family-employment conflicts. Many of these policies have not been developed explicitly for this purpose, however. Flex-time allows workers to choose to begin and end the work day earlier (or later) than normal (e.g., 7:00 a.m. to 4:00 p.m. rather than 8 to 5). By working slightly different hours, one parent can be available at each end of their children's school day. This type of policy was initially designed to reduce rush hour traffic congestion in urban areas. Many employers have shift workers because their normal hours of operation are many more than eight (e.g., factories, hospitals, some types of retail stores such as 24-hour drug stores and supermarkets). By working different shifts (e.g., one the day shift, another a swing or night shift) spouses can arrange to have someone home at all times to look after young children and to be available for both domestic work and family emergencies. Such couples may have very little time together, however, probably to the detriment of marital satisfaction and stability. A few employers (e.g., J.C. Penney's and some governmental agencies) have recently begun to cut office expenses by having part of their workforce telecommute. Connected to their employer by computer, fax and telephone, they conduct their paid work in their own homes and are therefore available for family emergencies and the care of somewhat older children who do not require constant supervision. Some other large employers have also developed daycare facilities, attached to or in the vicinity of the work site (e.g., many universities), that allow parents to see their children at lunch, for them to spend their commuting time with their children, and to be close by if their children become sick or injured. Finally, employers increasingly grant workers personal or family leave time for family crises and emergencies, not just sick leave time for themselves. However, such leave is often unpaid.

Government efforts to cope with employment-family conflicts have been sparse in this nation. Until 1993, when the U.S. government mandated that all but very small employers must grant parental leave upon the birth or adoption of a child, we were one of the only industrial nations to lack a guaranteed maternity leave policy. Before that, some employers granted it, some did not. Even now, while employers must reserve a person's job (or equivalent one) who is on parental leave, they do not have to pay the employee while on leave. In many European nations, either the employer or the government pays for one new parent to take a leave of absence. Whether paid or not, when offered parental leave most new parents who take advantage of the offer are women. Whether they personally prefer not to, or because of cultural constraints that define it as inappropriate, few men do so, even in Sweden which, among all Western nations, has had the longest history of such leaves, and the strongest governmental encouragement of men to use them. Some local school districts have begun to offer pre-school for 3–5-year-old children and extended day or after-school programs to elementary school-aged children, which help to alleviate child-care problems for employed parents.

What else could be done to reduce employment-family conflicts and strains? In some European nations (e.g., Sweden and Germany), workers are beginning to demand a six-hour work day, which would provide more time for the family and/or less reason for women to accept part-time jobs. Greedy employers could rethink their criteria for assessing the commitment level of their employees. Work hours in many types of jobs could be made more flexible, and much more desk work could be conducted at home, reducing workers' hours at a central work site. Family-related service providers, such as pediatricians and dentists, could shift their work hours on a couple of days each week to begin and end several hours later (e.g., noon to 8:00 p.m.), thereby accommodating parents who work normal hours without too much sacrifice of their own familial responsibilities. Teachers could be required and paid to be available for parental conferences for a couple of hours per week either on Saturday or one evening. Pediatric medical and dental clinics could be housed in public schools, minimizing the burden on parents to get such attention for their children. With little medical cost, special rooms could be set aside in schools for moderately ill children (e.g., those with the flu or German measles) who, instead of staying home could be cared for by school-based nurses. Parents could pay fees for school-based medical services, pre-schools, and extended day programs according to their means, thus not over-burdening tax-payers, while insuring decent care to all children. Beyond aiding employed parents, other, long-term social benefits could result from such programs, such as enhanced productivity for employers, employment stability for parents, better health care for poor children, a reduction in the number of latch key children, and perhaps even less juvenile crime. Taken together, the various employer and governmental policies and practices discussed here, if widely adopted, would not magically eliminate all employment-family conflicts, but they would reduce the total amount considerably. Unfortunately, it is unlikely that many of the policies and programs discussed above will be adopted on a wide-scale in the U.S. in the foreseeable future, either by employers or by governmental units. Global economic competition is encouraging employers to increase productivity with fewer employees, thereby pressuring workers to work longer hours than was true several years ago. In short, to compete, employers believe they must become increasingly greedy. Nor are they likely to institute employee benefits that increase their short-term costs, even if they result in long-term benefits to worker morale and productivity. At all levels local, state and national governmental units in the U.S. have been cutting budgets and personnel, in response to citizen demands to reduce taxes and the national deficit. Since at least 1980, there has been an increasing mood of political conservatism which de-emphasizes governmental solutions to most social problems (except crime control) and re-emphasizes private ones. As a nation, we have become increasingly suspicious of the capacity of governmental agencies to develop programs that enhance our collective well-being. In short, the prevailing national mood is in the direction of emphasizing family solutions to the kinds of employment-family conflicts discussed here, and it should be clear by now that such solutions are often inadequate and usually inequitable to women.

Conclusion

Domestic and familial obligations *are* work, and hard work at that. The tasks required of those who run a household and raise children are time, attention and energy-consuming. Full-time jobs also consume substantial time, attention, and energy some more so than others. Conflicts arise in the family largely because domestic work is not shared equitably by women and men. On the job, conflicts arise because family needs often do not neatly confine themselves to non-work hours, because some employers are greedy of their employees' time and energy, and because family-generated stresses and problems cannot easily be forgotten while on the job.

In recent years some employers have begun to develop policies that, whether designed for these purposes or not, ease employment-family conflicts somewhat. In this nation, unlike many others, the government has contributed little to helping to solve such conflicts and strains. For the vast majority of single employed parents and dual-earner couples, strains and problems inevitably arise from the fundamental facts that employment in industrial societies is largely and inflexibly based on a standard work day and located outside the home. For most couples and single parents, the solution cannot be found by women opting out of the labor force, both because their income is essential to meet family needs and because many do not want to quit work. Moreover, our economy today is highly dependent upon the labor of millions of women who are also wives and/or mothers. In the absence of governmental policies and widespread employer practices designed to ease employment-family conflicts, spouses and parents are left largely on their own to devise solutions. Some, especially among those with a high income and/or reasonably flexible employment conditions, are able to so with relative ease. Many, however, end up paying a high personal price on the job, within the family, or both. Moreover, women are apt to pay a much higher price in both contexts than men. Employed single parents and dual-earner couples can be forgiven if they conclude: I need a (traditional) wife!

References

Bergmann, B. 1986. *The Economic Emergence of Women*. New York: Basic Books.

Berk, S. F. 1985. *The Gender Factory*. New York: Plenum.

Chafetz, J. S. 1990. *Gender Equity: An Integrated Theory of Stability and Change*. Newbury Park, CA: Sage.

Coser, R. L. and G. Rokoff. 1982. "Women in the occupational world: Social disruption and conflict." In R. Kahn-Hut, A. Kaplan Daniels and R. Colvard (eds.), *Women and Work*. New York: Oxford University Press.

Hochschild, A. 1989. *The Second Shift*. New York: Viking Press.

Lindsey, L. 1994. *Gender Roles: A Sociological Perspective*. Englewood Cliffs, NJ: Prentice-Hall.

Reskin, B. and I. Padavic. 1994. *Women and Men at Work*. Thousand Oaks, CA: Pine Forge Press.

Sanchez, L. 1994. "A panel study of the association between the gender division of housework and marital dissolution." Paper presented at the Annual Meeting of the American Sociological Association. Los Angeles.

South, S. and G. Spitze. 1994. "Housework in marital and nonmarital households." *American Sociologic Review*, 59: 327-347.

Wilkie, J. R. 1988. "Marriage, family life and women's employment." In A.H. Stromberg and S. Harkess (eds.), *Women Working Theories and Facts in Perspective*. Mountain View, CA: Mayfield., pp. 149-166.

Food for Thought and Application Questions

1. Chafetz notes that employed wives and mothers do substantially less domestic work than full-time homemakers, and that this reduction in hours is accomplished, in part, by purchasing domestic and childcare services. In order to gain insight into the market value of domestic work, estimate the annual cost of contracting out the services listed below. (Note that the items listed below do not represent an exhaustive list of all

domestic work required by a typical family.)

Task	Amount per Year
Daycare (for one preschool-aged child)	_____
Daycare (summers only for a 6-year-old, school-aged child)	_____
Housecleaning (once a week, thorough cleaning)	_____
Eating out (five meals per week for two adults and two children)	_____
Laundry (work/school clothes only)	_____
TOTAL	_____

In your opinion, is it likely that a middle-income, dual career family will be able to afford to purchase all of these services? What about a lower-middle income, dual-worker family?

2. List five things employers can do to minimize work-family conflict. Employers often argue that implementing the kinds of measures in your list is too costly for their organization. For each of the items you listed, prepare an argument addressing the costs of *not* taking the action. Focus on costs to the work organization, but also consider costs to individual workers and the larger society. ✦

10

Women in Dual-Career Marriages

Wayne Carlisle

My interest in dual-career issues springs from my role as a career placement professional and as a partner in a dual-career marriage. Like many other career placement professionals, I have sought information to better assist career aspirants in preparing for the "balancing act" that seems to complicate women's and men's careers and relationships, as well as to apply this understanding to my professional and personal roles. Although issues relating to dual-career/two-income couples have been examined and discussed in the academic and popular press for at least the past two decades (Price-Bonham and Murphy 1980; Sekaran 1986), I was eager to see whether I could gain new insights by studying dual-career relationships from the perspective of business and professional women considering dual-career issues in the context of their lives, rather than in the context of organizational or professional expectations. [The findings in this chapter are based on a survey of business, professional and entrepreneurial women in Wichita, Kansas. The survey, conducted by the Research Group on Women and Work at Wichita State University in 1986, was designed to examine the lives of women employed in non-traditional occupations.] The 70% of participants in this study who described themselves as part of dual-career relationships provided interesting insights into the advantages and challenges of such relationships.

Pleck (1987) noted that women in career positions view their work much differently from those who have "jobs." Although the distinction between a career and a job is blurred and is probably best self-defined, participants in this study can be regarded as career oriented, particularly on the basis of their preference for individualistic resolution of problems and their determination to forge a successful life through hard work. Participants' responses to dual-career issues expressed their commitment to extraordinary individual effort, their satisfaction with overcoming obstacles, and their rejection of the need for structural changes to accommodate their needs. Although they acknowledged societal and personal problems involved in dual-career relationships, they fully endorsed the advantages they experience in dual-career relationships.

Dual-Career Advantages

Participants involved in dual-career relationships had very positive responses to what they saw as six potential advantages to dual careers. These six advantages were provided as options because they have been noted in previous research (Cramer and Herr 1984; Hall and Hall 1979; Voydanoff 1984; Walls and Krieshok 1987). Although these items have been listed before, they have not been compared with each other or with other possible advantages. About 10% of the respondents added unsolicited comments to the prepared advantages section of the questionnaire. These added comments do not suggest another category, but do support the view that the advantages make the dual-career relationship a positive experience. Whereas most previous research has shown primarily strains and disadvantages of dual-career relationships, especially for the woman in the relationship (Hunt and Hunt 1982; Rapoport and Rapoport 1977), results of this study confirm the view of Pendleton, Poloma, and Garland (1982) that the dual-career relationship basically is rewarding and that the net gain in satisfaction is worth the costs.

More than 91% of the participants acknowledged larger income as the biggest advantage. Also 58% responded positively to items suggesting greater respect from the partner and greater cohesion due to shared experience, confirming the possibility that relationships are enhanced by dual careers. And 48% responded positively to items suggesting increased balance of power and increased autonomy as advantages. A consideration of demographic variables contributes further insight into participants' perceived advantages in dual-career relationships. Business owners (73%) were more likely than women in all other career categories combined (55%) to see relational cohesion as a positive attribute.

Respondents with high incomes were more likely than those with low incomes to cite relational cohesion as an advantage, although equal power, autonomy, and self-esteem were not cited more frequently by this group than by those with lower incomes. When total income for the couple was considered, the lowest income groups were less likely to view greater respect from their partner as an advantage.

Although age was not a factor in self-esteem, respect, or income, age did influence some perceptions: 58% of women over age 40 saw autonomy as an advantage, while only 42% of those under 40 did so, indicating that autonomy may be valued more with the advancement of age. Cohesion within the relationship due to shared experience was valued more for women aged 30 to 39 than by women aged 40 to 49. These findings contribute to interesting speculation about the movement from valuing cohesion to valuing autonomy as stages of adult development. It is also possible that cohesion is more available than autonomy during the earlier life stage.

Dual-Career Disadvantages

The disadvantages of dual-career relationships have been classified as everything from significant to insurmountable in most popular press articles and in some research (Nadelson and Nadelson 1980). Rapoport and Rapoport (1977) listed five disadvantages—role conflict, work overload, slowed or leveled career progress, societal pressure/attitude, and little time for relationships—as potentially significant problems. Their results acknowledge disadvantages, but respondents' responses to disadvantages were much lower than their responses to advantages. In fact, only two of the five issues were rated at levels predicted from previous research. Respondents seemed to see advantages outweighing disadvantages while still acknowledging the presence of disadvantages.

In the study, 82% of the participants saw overload as a disadvantage; 63% cited little time for relationships as a disadvantage. These responses show the clear problem of time availability to women respondents. Although it is important to exercise caution in making inferences from the data, these responses may suggest that women assume primary responsibility for multiple functional tasks. Although the definition of time for relationships does not specify the type of relationships, respondents may refer to relationships beyond the family. If less time is available for friendships, quality of life may be diminished.

Whereas some previous research has cited role conflict as a major dilemma for women, only 28% of this sample cited role conflict as a disadvantage for dual-career relationships. Although respondents saw role overload (too much to be done) as a disadvantage, they did not necessarily see a conflict between roles. This result supports Konek's (1994) finding of integrative leadership strategies among respondents. Only one respondent saw role conflict as a disadvantage.

A further surprising indication that the dual-career relationship presents few strong disadvantages is the fact that only 21% of the women thought their career progress had been slowed or leveled. The finding that a dual-career relationship required the woman to accept career leveling (Hunt and Hunt 1982) is not supported by these data. The common assumption that the partner's career and the woman's multiple roles will take priority over the woman's career seems unfounded for this group. Finally only 14% noted societal pressure as a disadvantage. Perhaps pressure for women to give primary focus to partner, home, and/or family is much less now than it was previously, or perhaps women in this sample were unusual in their ability to ignore or cope with pressure. There is also a possibility that these responses reflect the participants' reliance on rugged individualism to overcome adversity, whether presented as work demands or social pressure.

There were few variations on the disadvantages of dual-career relationships when demographic variables were crosstabulated. Few business owners saw their careers slowed or plateaued. More women in professional roles rated less time for relationships as a disadvantage than cited slowed or plateaued careers as a disadvantage. A consideration of this issue in relation to couple income level shows that the higher the income, the less the time for relationships. This finding may have more to do with time commitment at work than with the income level itself. Although participants, in general, did not cite role conflict as a major disadvantage, 44% of the youngest group (aged 20 to 29) rated role conflict as a disadvantage. This finding may indicate an adult development stage of trying out and learning various roles, or it may show a frustration with the discrepancy between expectation and reality.

Women with BA/BS, MA/MS, or PhD degrees were more likely than those with associate or law or medical degrees to cite slowed or leveled career progress as a dual-career disadvantage.

Coping Strategies

When participants were asked about their most effective coping strategies, many indicated that simply learning to live with the disadvantages was the best choice, especially in light of the advantages. There are some clear indications of coping strategies: 65% suggested encouraging partners to share the workload, while 44% suggested hiring household help as a coping strategy. More individualistic coping strategies included improvement of time management skills (45%), giving higher priority to leisure and relaxing activities (42%), and exercise (35%).

By far the least used coping strategy cited (19%) was locating support from others in a similar situation. Although participants acknowledged lack of time for relationships as a disadvantage, it seems that social support and shared experiences either were not available or were not viewed as viable by these women. It is possible that the focus on the partner relationship itself may provide support. The complexity of coping emotionally was noted by Wilcox-Matthew and Minor (1989), Gilbert and Rachlin (1987), and Voydanoff (1984). The strain of worrying about ways to cope may be as difficult as actual overload for women who viewed the possibility of seeking support beyond that of the partner as either unavailable or ineffective.

Women in law and medicine were less likely to encourage their partners to share responsibilities and more likely to hire help than were women in other careers. Also, hiring help was an increasingly popular coping strategy as individual or joint income increased. Younger women were more likely to report encouraging their partners to share work and using leisure and exercise as coping strategies than were older women.

Voydanoff (1984) and Sekaran (1986) noted in two of the very few research studies of coping strategies that the responsibility for finding ways for the family or couple to cope is often assumed by the woman. This finding is consistent with the finding that, even in relationships in which partners share the workload, planning for the completion of tasks often is done by the woman. Comments made by participants in this study support the perception that arrangements for home and/or child care are the woman's responsibility. This study supports the general consensus that coping with dual-career issues is possible but is basically an individualized response. Participants made few suggestions that could be generalized to most relationships. The comments of many participants stressed the acceptance of disadvantages, rather than the expectation that coping strategies will be very effective.

Women in this study indicated that the pressure of role overload and less time for relationships are disadvantages in dual-career relationships, but they also placed a higher value on the advantages than on the disadvantages of the dual-career relationship. They evidently found that benefits outweigh sacrifices. Time for relationships cannot be delegated, purchased, hired, or accomplished by the partner. The other disadvantages presented in the research can be seen as individual responses to external pressures. The loss of time for relationships may deprive women of enjoyment and a coping strategy for handling other disadvantages. This limitation also may contribute to preferring individualistic, rather than structural, strategies for perceived inequities. Women may be individualistic if relationally deprived or disconnected.

Partner's Contribution

More than one in four of the respondents in this study indicated that their partner shares equally in all areas of responsibility. Another 56% said their partner shares significantly, and only 13% said their partner provides insignificant or no

support. The level of partners' actual contribution to child rearing, housework, and the woman's career reported by these participants was greater than that reported in previous research (Hall and Hall 1979; Rapoport and Rapoport 1977). This sample reported a much higher rate of contribution than was reported by working married women in general. It is impossible to know how much of this difference is related to the woman's expectations and negotiated sharing and how much is related to partners' willingness to contribute. It is possible that the women and perhaps the couples in this study differ from the general population. The high level of partner contribution may be related to the general positive response to the advantages of dual-career relationships. It must be noted, however, that a woman still may be expected to plan housework and child care while her partner is "helping" with what are perceived to be her responsibilities. The difference between "helping" and actually "sharing responsibilities" is not clearly defined.

Another question in this section raises the deeper concern of sexist beliefs and behaviors on the part of some partners. Only 63% of participants saw their partner as giving emotional support and encouragement. That percentage should be higher, considering the level of perceived partner contribution. Some partners are evidently more willing to contribute to tasks than they are to give emotional support.

The level of a partner's contribution could not be distinguished by women's career categories, although income level did contribute to such a distinction, with women earning incomes in the $40,000 to $50,000 range reporting more equal sharing of responsibility than did women earning less. As might be expected, women over age 50 reported less equality of sharing than did younger women. Women with AA, BA/BS, and law degrees noted less contribution from partners than did women with MA/MS, PhD, or medical degrees. Emotional support was consistent across all variables.

Effective Preparation

Participants were asked how women might more effectively prepare for and cope with disadvantages of dual-career relationships. The one area of preparation that was suggested by over half of the participants was reading, an individual form of preparation. Most of the participants evidently believed that preparation is impossible or is the responsibility of the individual.

In their comments, a large number of women suggested early negotiation with partners regarding dual-career issues: 55% of the women recommended reading advice, 39% recommended taking courses, 36% recommended advising in school settings, and 38% of respondents endorsed employer-provided advice and flexibility. It seems clear that just over a third of respondents saw an educational approach to addressing disadvantages as effective. Respondents seem to have seen individual preparation and responsibility as more effective than structured or organizational solutions. Comments provided by 32% of the sample reinforce this impression. Comments were primarily of two types: (a) Participants suggested that there is no good preparation for dual-career relationships and that the advantages, disadvantages, and coping strategies are learned only in process; and (b) participants saw dual-career experiences as so individualized on the basis of human differences, expectations, demographics, family circumstances, and so forth that "packaged advice is probably not very effective."

Demographic cross-tabulations with effective preparation variables provided little noteworthy information, although women managers and women with less education were more likely to see courses and advice as effective than were others.

Career Interruption for Child Rearing

In this study 37% of the women interrupted their careers for childbearing or child rearing. Others in the sample may yet make a similar decision, so this percentage reflects the timing of the study, rather than the life cycle of the women included in it. Those who did interrupt their careers were asked what effect the time away had on their careers: 26% returned to the position they had left, 22% found that they had lost responsibility and had to rebuild their reputation, 38% made a career change on reentry, and 36% sought additional education. It is obvious that the career interruption associated with childbearing or child rearing had a major effect on the careers of these women, but in many cases women used this experience as an opportunity for change and education, suggesting that they created career advantages for themselves. This finding may provide an additional indication of the way respondents perceived the advantages of choices and minimized disadvantages.

Women in couples with a combined income over $40,000 were much more likely to return to education after the interruption than those with incomes of less than $40,000 (44%, compared with 6%). The small sample size and the inappropriateness of age and education variables make other cross-tabulations meaningless.

Single Women

In this study 30% of the women included were single. This group was asked two questions: (a) Are the issues faced in a dual-career relationship a concern for you if you consider marriage? (76% responded positively) and (b) If divorced, were dual-career issues a contributing factor in the divorce? (61% responded positively). Dual-career issues were seen as an important part of a marriage relationship by the single respondents. Because those in relationships saw few avenues for effective preparation, the gap between concern and ability to prepare is a problem. Perhaps awareness of the issues involved will be enough to encourage individuals and couples at least to discuss potential problems prior to the crisis management approach often referred to in the literature (Gilbert and Rachlin 1987; Sekaran 1986).

Conclusions

Women in this study provided a collective view of the dual-career relationship as a positive experience. Advantages include more income, increased self-esteem, and greater respect from and cohesion with partners. They identified as disadvantages work overload and little time for relationships. Fewer women than expected noted role conflict, career leveling, and societal pressure as disadvantages.

Participants offered few encouraging coping strategies. Rather, the general response seemed to be "Learn to live with the disadvantages." According to the group, the advantages compensate for the problems, and the disadvantages will not change. Respondents recommended extra work and self-management as a way of designing the life-work structure they desire. Although participants might prefer a more equitable personal and work environment, they found their current situations preferable to alternatives, and perhaps as equitable as they could expect. Their coping behaviors included encouraging partners to share the workload, improving their own time management skills, and hiring housework help. Surprisingly, seeking support from others was not frequently noted as an effective strategy.

Participants in this study reported a more balanced contribution from partners for child rearing, housework, and support of their careers than expected from previous studies: 26% of those surveyed reported equal sharing of responsibility with their partner, while 56% reported significant, but not equal, sharing from their partner.

Also 37% of the participants had interrupted careers for childbearing or child rearing. Although a mere 27% of these women returned to the same position, only 20% thought they had "lost ground." Frequently the women returned to education and/or changed careers after the interruption.

The only preparation for dual-career relationships that was suggested by this group of women was to read literature and advice on dual-career issues. Their comments and advice for other women urged them to expect problems but to enjoy the many advantages of dual-career relationships. They did not see structured courses in academic or employment settings as very effective in contributing to their coping strategies.

The career women viewed dual-career relationships as positive but expressed resigned acceptance of the problems involved. They apparently rely on the dual-career relationship or on themselves for effective coping strategies. These findings contribute to an emergent view of participants in this study as self-reliant, seeking individualistic solutions to career challenges.

References

Cramer, S. H. and E. L. Herr. 1984. *Career Guidance and Counseling Through the Lifespan* (2nd ed.). Boston: Little, Brown.

Gilbert, L. A. and V. Rachlin. 1987. "Mental health and psychological functioning in dual-career families." *Counseling Psychologists*, 15:7-49.

Hall, P S. and D. T. Hall. 1979. *The Two-Career Couple*. Reading, MA: Addison-Wesley.

Hunt, J. G. and L. L. Hunt. 1982. "Dual career families: Vanguard of the future or residue of the past?" In J. Aldous (Ed.), *Two Pay Checks: Life in Dual-Earner Families*. Beverly Hills, CA: Sage:41-59.

Konek, C. W. 1994. "Leadership or empowerment? Reframing our questions." In C. W. Konek and S. L. Kitch (Eds.), *Women and Careers*. Thousand Oaks, CA: Sage:206-233.

Nadelson. C. and T. Nadelson. 1980. "Dual-career marriages: Benefits and costs." In F. Pepitone-Rockwell (Ed.), *Dual-Career Couples*. Beverly Hills, CA: Sage:91-109.

Pendleton, B. F., M. M. Poloma, and T. N. Garland. 1982. "An approach to quantifying the needs of dual-career families." *Human Relations*, 35:69-82.

Pleck, J. H. 1987. "Dual-career families: A comment." *Counseling Psychologists*, 15:131-133.

Price-Bonham, S. and D. Murphy. 1980. "Dual-career marriage: Implications for the clinician." *Journal of Marital and Family Therapy*, April:181-187.

Rapoport, R. and R. N. Rapoport. 1977. *Dual-Career Families Reexamined*. New York: Colophone.

Sekaran, U. 1986. *Dual-Career Families: Contemporary Organizational and Counseling Issues*. San Francisco: Jossey-Bass.

Voydanoff, P. 1984. *Work and Family: Changing Roles of Men and Women*. Palo Alto, CA: Mayfield.

Walls, C. and T. Krieshok. 1987. *The Rise of the Dual-Career Family: Stresses, Strains, and Gains*. Paper presented to the American College Personnel Association, Chicago, IL.

Wilcox-Matthew, L., and C. Minor. 1989. "The dual-career couple: Concerns, benefits, and counseling implications." *Journal of Counseling and Development*, 68:194-198.

Food for Thought and Application Questions

1. Carlisle lists six advantages and five disadvantages of dual-career relationships (see lists below). Rank order the items in each list in terms of their importance to you (1 = most important, 5 or 6 = least important). Then compare the highest ranked (most important) items in each list. If forced to choose between the two, which is *most* important to you? Ask yourself the same question for the two items ranked in second place, in third place, and so on. When you have completed this task, do you find the advantages or the disadvantages to be most important overall? Imagine a partner going through the same exercise. Is it likely that their results would be identical to yours? How would the final decisions about work be made in the case of disagreement?

Advantage	Importance Rank	Disadvantages	Importance Rank
Income	☐	Work overload	☐
Self Esteem	☐	Relationships	☐
Greater respect	☐	Role conflict	☐
Greater cohesion	☐	Career leveling	☐
Equal Power	☐	Societal pressure	☐
Autonomy	☐		

2. Why do you think women with higher incomes report more equal sharing of household responsibilities than women earning less? In your opinion, is this fair? Keep in mind the size of the earnings gap between the sexes and evidence presented in Unit Two suggesting that many female-dominated occupations are paid less, not because of the contributions and skills of the workers, but simply because women perform the work. ✦

11

Combining Work and Motherhood

Kathleen Gerson

This chapter . . . [examines the views and experiences of women] who chose to combine committed work with parenthood. . . . [The findings are based on in-depth interviews with a sample of women drawn from both a list of alumnae at a four-year university and a list of enrollees at a community college.] Unlike domestically oriented women, these women were committed workers who viewed children as potentially costly to their work careers. Unlike permanently childless women, however, they decided over time that childlessness held greater costs than motherhood. These women thus neither wholeheartedly embraced motherhood nor rejected it completely. Rather, they approached parenthood reluctantly, aware of the problems it posed, yet fearful that a different course would hold even greater dangers. This chapter analyzes the process by which this group of work-committed women became, or planned to become, "reluctant mothers."

The reluctant mother's approach to childbearing was one of deep ambivalence, which is well illustrated by this thirty-year-old married worker's struggle to develop enthusiasm for childbearing amid fears that motherhood would upset the delicate balance of her professional and personal life:

Q: Over the next five to ten years, do you plan to work, raise a family, or do both?

A: I think I plan to combine working with raising a family. And the reason I say I *think* is that, if I want to have a family, I'm sure I'll want to combine working with a family. I'm having a little trouble wanting a family. I'm not quite sure where that's coming from.

Q: Where do you think it's coming from?

A: I'm not sure that I like children. It's more than that. I'm stretched so many ways now, in terms of demands on my time. And I feel that a baby, if I commit myself to a baby, I can't let it go for a week like I can the garden. I'm a little afraid of that extra commitment. That's just going to be a little more than I can take. I'm not sure yet what has to give where. I'm afraid of having kids, and yet that's hard because I know I'm going to hate myself when I'm sixty if I don't have any kids. . . .

In contrast to those whose ambivalence about children led them toward childlessness, however, these women planned to add, or had already added, children to their lives.

Reluctant Motherhood

Reluctant mothers confronted different constraints and brought different resources to bear on the decision to have a child than did their childless counterparts. They were more likely to find themselves in relationships that would be seriously jeopardized by childlessness. They were also in a better position to minimize the negative impact children threatened to have on their lives. This group thus faced cross-pressures that lowered the perceived costs of childbearing and raised the costs of childlessness above a tolerable level. Childlessness became harder to choose and less attractive, leading these women to add children to their already established commitments at the workplace.

These features of their situation also made reluctant mothers less inclined to discount and more inclined to focus on the potentially dire long-term consequences of childlessness. They then developed coping strategies to reduce the perceived costs of motherhood and discounted instead the costs of combining work and family. In contrast to their childless counterparts, they came to believe that they could integrate mothering into their lives without significant sacrifice to themselves, their work, or their children. This upwardly mobile office manager concluded, for example, that bearing a child would pose no major obstacle to achieving her rapidly rising work aspirations:

Q: Why do you plan to have children and work at the same time?

A: I don't want to have to give up anything to have children. I don't want to have to change my life-style at all. I look at it as an addition to my life. I'm not planning on changing anything.

Several factors led these women to decide that they could successfully combine work and motherhood without "giving up anything." First, as in the cases of childless women, men played a critical role in shaping these women's responses to the motherhood dilemma. Unlike the pressures men exerted on childless women, however, the pressures exerted on reluctant mothers by their male partners pushed them toward motherhood rather than away from it. Second, given the social and emotional pressures they faced, reluctant mothers were less able than childless women to discount the costs of childlessness. They were also better positioned to develop contextual supports for combining work and motherhood.

Men's Parenting Motivations

The women who chose childlessness lacked a committed relationship or, paradoxically, had a valued relationship that children threatened to undermine. Reluctant mothers generally faced the contrasting situation: Forgoing children threatened to undermine a relationship more than did having them. Reluctant mothers typically had partners who, directly or indirectly, encouraged and pressured them to bear children. In contrast to the stereotype of the manipulative and overanxious wife coaxing her reluctant husband into parenthood, these respondents found themselves being pushed toward childbearing by husbands impatient to become fathers. This computer programmer explained:

Q: So you're feeling a lot of pressure at this point to have a child?

A: Mostly it's from my husband. Not because he's deliberately doing it, but because I know he wants to make babies, and he has been very serious about talking about it. When are we going to do it, this and that, until finally I said, "Please back off because I'm not ready for this yet."

Q: Do you think it would affect your marriage if you decided to never have children?

A: Yes, because if I decide I won't have children, my husband has to decide if he wants to keep me. . . . Because he wants a family, and I think that's really important to him. I would prefer not to do that, having a baby just because the husband wants it, simply to please him. If I'm to go through being pregnant, I prefer to be deliriously happy about it.

The male desire to have children and the prospect of losing a spouse or partner if one opposed this desire were often decisive in opting for motherhood. In the context of personal ambivalence, pressure from her spouse pushed this secretary to decide in favor of parenthood:

Q: What are your plans regarding children?

A: Doug and I are really at odds over it. He has always said he wants children. I never really see children in the future, but I don't see them *not* in the future either. The few times we have really talked about it, he's said they are very important to him; so I don't know. If I were to get pregnant now, I would be, I'm sure, unhappy about the situation when I first found out, but I would deal with it and make the best of things.

Q: So you feel that your husband is a major factor?

A: He could be maybe a *deciding* factor. If I'm getting closer to it, he might bring me over nearer the edge. I think if I were with a man who did not want them, it would be definitely no. But the more we have talked about it, and it has been recurring more often, Doug has said he really *does* want children; so I think that would be a major factor in our relationship. . . .

Such male pressures did not apply solely to those who planned to become parents. Reluctant motherhood was often a fait accompli because a spouse had already succeeded in his circuitous, but effective, efforts to gain his wife's acquiescence. Although unable to consciously decide to get pregnant, this thirty-one-year-old office worker abandoned contraception in the face of her husband's pressure:

Q: Was this child planned?

A: Not exactly. As you probably gathered, I have difficulty making some of these decisions. My husband wanted to have kids. I was unwilling to make a conscious decision to have one, but between all the scary things they say about being on the pill, I was willing to take chances. My number came up much sooner than I ever expected. I made a decision only to the extent that I wasn't absolutely going to prevent it from happening.

Q: So your husband was important in the decision to "take chances?"

A: Well, if he wasn't really all that interested in having a kid, I probably would have had less ambivalence about *not* having one. You know, my ambivalence,

my thinking that I might regret it if I don't.

Pressure from a spouse also operated in more subtle ways. Just as an uninterested partner pushed some women away from motherhood, mild forms of support pushed others toward it. Male support became especially powerful when it led a woman to equate a committed relationship with children. In this context, children implied costs and problems, but they also expressed the value of the relationship itself. Thus, at twenty-seven, this lawyer viewed child rearing not as a form of individual fulfillment, but rather as a biological and emotional extension of her commitment to a man:

Q: What would you say are your main motivations for having a child?

A: I see it closely as an identification with my husband. He wants them. He's *very* family-oriented. It's never been discussed, but it would bother him if he didn't think he was going to have them. But if I found I was biologically unable to have them, I don't think I would adopt. Having kids will really be a hassle and complicate life. It's going to be very inconvenient, and I think a strong reason I want children is to have a child with my husband rather than to have children per se.

Finally, even though reluctant mothers did not define children as the fulfillment of their identity or nurturing needs, they often viewed them as a way of fulfilling their spouses' needs. Depriving their partners of children meant depriving themselves of the pleasure of giving something important to the person they valued most. Her spouse's enthusiasm for parenthood assuaged this secretary's ambivalence:

Q: Is there anything about not having children right now that bothers you?

A: I miss parts. Children can really be a job, but I miss [it during] the times Steve is with other children, and I watch him. He's really good with them, and that makes me feel sad or whatever that he does not have a child of his own. I think he would be very, very good, and that part does bother me at times. That would be a major thing for me. I would feel a lot of satisfaction for him to have satisfaction in that type of relationship.

Just as an uninterested or openly hostile spouse dampened the desire for children, so an encouraging or assertive one led other nondomestic women to overcome or at least act against their ambivalence toward childbearing. These accounts suggest, furthermore, that theories that picture men as universally uninterested in children and uniformly underdeveloped in their nurturing needs, capacities, and desires oversimplify both men's orientations toward parenting and women's experiences with men. These male partners' parenting motivations went beyond the desire to reproduce offspring merely to prove manhood or to perpetuate the family name and genetic structure. At least in the eyes of their female partners, these men possessed a genuine desire and ability to nurture children. (Recent research by Pruett 1983, on a sample of primary caretaking fathers supports this conclusion.) Were these parents or would-be parents not of the male gender, one might be tempted to label their motives as a need or desire to mother. Similarly, reluctant mothers' reasons for wanting babies resemble those commonly attributed to men for wanting to father children.

As the strength and legitimacy of the nondomestic path for women have grown, men have faced added pressure to acknowledge their parenting motives and to push for children in their marriages. Because men do not typically view their options as a choice between work and family, they are less likely to focus on the negative consequences children might exact from their work careers than are their nondomestic female partners.

If we credit these reluctant mothers' perceptions, we must conclude that both men and women vary significantly in their desires to bear children and in their reasons for doing so. We must also conclude that men's and women's parenting motivations are related and interactive. Reluctant mothers appear to have responded as much to their partners' desires to procreate and nurture as to their own. Despite their own ambivalence, reluctant mothers were propelled by their partners slowly and haltingly toward motherhood. These accounts challenge the tenacious view held by social theorists, psychoanalysts, and ordinary people alike that women uniformly become mothers primarily to fulfill strongly felt needs to nurture and men typically seek parenthood grudgingly.

Perceived Consequences of Childlessness

Because these respondents experienced strong contextual pressures favoring motherhood, they were less able to insulate themselves from their fears of what childlessness implied in the long run. They therefore tended to focus on the negative consequences of childlessness rather than discounting them.

As pressures mounted, reluctant mothers were increasingly haunted by the costs of permanent childlessness: social disapproval, consignment to a lonely and desolate old age, and the loss of a major life experience with intrinsic value beyond its social measure. The fear of these costs had powerful psychological ramifications for childless women facing pressures to parent. An upwardly mobile worker facing pressure from her spouse worried:

Q: How do you think you'd feel if you never had children?

A: Guilty, guilty. I really think that my approach toward having children at this point in my life is more based on what is expected of me than what I expect of myself. I think the only reason I'm considering having children right now is because it's heresy not to consider having children. . . .

Although childlessness had been the path of least resistance in early adulthood, fears of the negative consequences of never having children took on greater significance as respondents entered their thirties. At thirty, this same respondent conceded:

Q: But the negative consequences of not having a child also bother you?

A: That's right. I'm going to hate myself when I'm sixty. I won't have any grandchildren, nobody to take care of me in my old age, all that kind of stuff.

Thus, although children were not welcomed in the present, the long-term consequences of childlessness grew increasingly more ominous for these reluctant mothers. They gradually came to see parenting as their best chance for establishing intimate, enduring interpersonal bonds. Some even concluded that rejecting motherhood would foreclose the possibility of meaningful human relationships altogether. A lawyer, for example, viewed children as her only protection against an otherwise impersonal world:

Q: What are your main reasons for wanting children?

A: I think it would be really sad to be forty or fifty years old and not have a family. I think families are extremely important. Our society is getting so splintered as it is that I think it's really nice to have this close group of people, besides just your spouse.

Despite parenthood's drawbacks, reluctant mothers began to switch their focus from its costs to its intrinsic benefits. These included not only the continuation of the family unit but also the experience of creating a human being and adding balance, fullness, and renewed purpose to a life skewed too heavily in favor of work. Although strongly committed to work, this

accountant came to view child rearing as the ultimate challenge:

A: When you go into life and everything, you're living day to day. You can have one or another job, you can do something, but whatever you do is not an influence as much as raising a family. So I think it's really important. It's the most challenging thing that anybody can do.

And this lawyer rejected the traditional imperative that would deny her the right to build a life structured around both work and family:

Q: What are your main reasons for wanting children?

A: It's more of a family unit, a continuation of life. I don't think it's fair that professional women can't have kids. They make things fuller, more complete. I think it rounds out your life better.

In conclusion, reluctant mothers responded to social and personal cross-pressures by focusing on the costs of childlessness rather than discounting them. Torn between fears of the disruption that children would cause and offsetting desires to please their spouses and affirm their interpersonal commitments through children, these women mustered a variety of reasons, some positive and some negative, to bolster their halting commitment to motherhood.

Consciously and unconsciously, they developed coping strategies designed to lower the costs of children and ease the way toward childbearing. Some strategies rebounded on male partners who exerted pressures in favor of parenthood. Because their partners desired children, reluctant mothers could bring more leverage than their childless counterparts to the process of negotiation with their partners about how to rear their shared offspring. Spouses and male partners thus found themselves pulled more fully into the parenting process and pushed to redefine both their beliefs about proper child-rearing practices and the actual sexual division of labor within the home. Reluctant mothers acted back upon the dilemma they faced, using whatever material and ideological leverage they could muster to control and limit the costs of motherhood.

Coping Strategies

Reluctant mothers rejected childlessness and were unable or unwilling to loosen their work commitments, so only one viable response remained: lower the costs of children. This group developed three strategies to accomplish this task. They decided to limit the number of children they bore; they struggled to bring their male partners into the parenting process; and they redefined their traditional notions about how to rear children. Each of these strategies represented some form of change how they organized their lives, in how they dealt with the people around them, or in how they theorized about mothering.

Limiting Family Size

A common strategy for holding down the costs of children was to hold down the number. Historically, this response has led to the rise of the so-called typical family of 2.5 children, with a concomitant decline in the percentage of larger families (Masnick and Bane 1980). Reluctant mothers joined this trend despite their earlier hopes of having larger families. Some stopped at two children even though they originally planned for more:

A: Two is a manageable number. My husband would have liked a larger family, but at that point, for financial reasons, I would have not been able to work. And I would not have felt right having three of them.

Despite the historical decline in family size, until recently, a pervasive aversion to families with fewer than two offspring has prevailed. Many following a nondomestic path, however, found themselves settling not just for smaller families but for one-child families. Fifty-three percent of those who planned to combine work and family

also planned to limit their family size to one child. This decision was reached by a number of routes, but it was usually made for the same reason: One child became a convenient compromise between a reluctant mother's determination to avoid a life defined primarily by domestic responsibilities and the pressure she felt to bear a child. This alternative became especially attractive when motherhood appeared foreboding, but childlessness looked even worse. Many reluctant mothers agreed with this thirty-three-year-old academic that one child would round out their lives, but more than one would overcrowd them:

Q: How do you respond to a woman who has decided to never have children?

A: When I look at *them*, I feel like they've missed something. I don't know if it's necessary to have a child to have a fulfilled life, but somehow I see that they could have another dimension in their life they didn't have.

Q: So you don't want to never have children any more than you want to be a full-time homemaker?

A: I don't think so. Actually, when it comes down to it, I probably want to have one, just so I can have that experience, too. In a way, it seems more attractive to me than having two because there are fewer complications. . . . It's not that I don't like children. It's that life is complicated by so many other things. It would be hard to pay enough attention to more than one.

. . . The decision to limit fertility to one child almost always involved a downward readjustment from earlier plans. This change required letting go of old beliefs about the need for siblings and the pitfalls of being an only child. This change allowed reluctant mothers to reconcile their rising work ambitions with their similarly high standards for mothering. This office worker concluded that there were offsetting economic benefits for only children:

A: I feel I can be just as good a mother working as staying home. That's why I want only one child. Before I felt you can't just have one; they need a little brother or sister. I feel now that one child can be just as well adjusted, and a person should have what they can afford.

For some, the decision to bear only one child was part, and often an unintended part, of a strategy of postponement. As time passed and work ambitions rose, deadlines for childbearing neared and the previously unthinkable became not only a probability but a likelihood. This administrative assistant past thirty unwittingly backed into the one-child strategy:

A: I've always thought you should have at least two children. But the chances are strong we'll have one. I'm too old, and work is too important.

Others found that the experience of motherhood itself sparked the decision to impose a permanent moratorium on childbearing. The experience of rearing her son alone convinced a divorced mother that one child was enough:

A: The kid has influenced me to the point that I don't want any more kids . . . with just the responsibility, the burden of raising kids. It's kind of held me back to a certain degree, being a single parent, not getting to do what I want to do, having to worry about him first.

In some of these cases, the decision to curtail childbearing plans after only one birth reverberated within the marriage itself. As frustrated mothers clashed with disappointed fathers, marital discord ensued. This high school-educated single mother, for example, chose to divorce rather than to fulfill her husband's desire for more children:

A: I had my daughter from my first marriage, and [I was] haphazardly wondering if I could hang on to the marriage like everybody did. I was raised Catholic, and we didn't believe in divorces. My husband wanted [me] to stay in the marriage, but he wanted a lot of children and I didn't; so we made an understanding that eventually, when I can financially support myself and my daughter, that's what I want to do. And if he wants more children, we would have to think about separating, and his continuing his life with more children, which he has.

Divorce also limited family size even when more children had been planned. Divorce curtailed childbearing not only for childless women but also for those with one child. Mothers who were invariably left to care for the first child concluded that another child would erode the financial security, personal autonomy, and work prospects they had fought so hard to gain:

Q: What are your main reasons for having only one child?

A: I wouldn't want to raise one out of wedlock, not because of the social stigma it's nobody's business but mine but I couldn't see raising two kids on the salary I'm making. It costs a lot of money to raise a kid. Also because I have things that I want to do. I have plans.

As the number of women exposed to increased work opportunities, affected by divorce, or engaged in a strategy of postponing childbearing grows, the one-child alternative appears likely to grow as well. The one-child family has never been a popular choice, and some experts (such as Blake 1966, 1974) argue that neither childlessness nor having only one child is likely to increase substantially with this generation of women. Certainly, many who plan to limit their fertility to one child may find that, once a child arrives, earlier ambivalence and reluctance subside with the pleasant reality of motherhood. The opposite, however, may also occur, as some who plan for two or more children ultimately decide to stop with one after the first is born.

The larger forces at work make the family a sensible choice. As long as growing numbers of reluctant mothers find themselves caught between the costs of children and the costs of childlessness, a substantial number will be motivated to keep the costs of motherhood down without rejecting it altogether. (Bird 1979, makes the same prediction.) Having only one child, whatever the historic social biases against doing so, is a reasonable and readily accessible strategy for accomplishing this end.

Bringing Men In

Reluctant mothers also lowered the cost of children by bringing men into the parenting process and the domestic work of the household. Although this entailed a conflictual process that typically produced mixed results, many reluctant mothers made male participation a precondition to accepting the responsibilities of parenthood. Without a participatory father, this professional reasoned, the benefits of parenthood would not be worth the price:

Q: What if Phillip were not willing to participate equally?

A: I don't know that I would want children under those circumstances. I want the emotional support. I want it for the children, for myself. I want the participation, and without it I don't want children. I don't think it would be a fulfilling experience. Without two people doing it, I think it would be a burden on one person. It's no longer a positive experience; it has lots of negative aspects to it.

Of course, wanting—and even demanding—a partner's equal participation does not guarantee securing it. Inequality in the household division of labor has persisted despite the rise in the proportion of committed women workers with young children. Time budget studies collected over the last thirty years unanimously attest to the intransigence of an unequal sexual division of labor in the home. Recent studies confirm what older studies also found that whether or not they work, married women tend to perform most of the tasks associated with running a modern household. Working wives generally get more help from their husbands than do full-time homemakers, but the couple that shares household tasks equally remains rare (Berk 1980; Blumstein and Schwartz 1983; Hofferth and Moore 1979; Huber and Spitze 1983; Pleck 1975; Scott 1974; Szalai 1972; Vanek 1974; Wilensky 1968). Male participation in housework and child care does appear, however, to be on the rise, and the trend is toward increased participation (Badinter 1981; Shinn 1983).

With historical precedent and structural arrangements organized against it, the struggle to bring men into the process of parenting and caring for a home is thus not likely to succeed unless a woman is both sufficiently motivated to struggle and armed with enough leverage to extract consent from her partner. Domestically oriented women had little reason to push for fuller male participation, and childless women generally lacked the leverage.

Reluctant mothers, however, were more motivated and better positioned to carry out this struggle. These women gained leverage primarily from two sources: their spouses' desire for children and the benefits male partners gained from having a work-committed wife. The husband who pushed his reluctant wife toward childbearing usually found he had to give something to get something. This reluctant mother expecting her first child explained:

Q: Will you be able to depend upon your husband's participation when the baby is born?

A: I think so. We're in the process of changing. We're even now starting to switch the load, and I think it will be shared much more equally when the baby comes. I was kind of cocky when we first got married, and I thought I could be the perfect wife that I envisioned my mother being and also work. We're having to retrain each other's psyches on that.

Q: And he's going along with that?

A: With the kid, he really is. He wanted this kid more than I did.

The financial benefits men gained from work-committed wives gave reluctant mothers additional leverage in the negotiation of domestic equality. Their important contributions to the economic stability of their households provided a base for demanding fuller male participation in parenting. This accountant found that mutual financial dependence promoted mutual arrangements at home:

Q: How does your husband feel about whether you should work, raise a family, or do both?

A: He feels that you can combine both, and he's willing to help and stuff. I think probably, too, he's thinking of the monetary end of it.

In one rare case, the wife was able to command a greater income as a lawyer than her husband did as a house painter and aspiring novelist. Because she was the primary wage earner, they were preparing for an arrangement once considered unthinkable a father as primary caretaker:

A: I sort of entered law thinking this is the kind of work you can do on a part-time basis, but I think I might have been wrong. But I'm sure by the time we have a child, Larry should be in a situation where he's mostly writing, and he should be at home. So theoretically, it ought to work out fine. I think he realizes that I will have to work, and I think he also thinks it's important to have one of the parents around most of the time. . . .

Although unusual, their situation demonstrates the powerful impact economic arrangements have on domestic organization. Mothering "predispositions" aside,

when economics makes exclusive motherhood too costly, fuller participation by fathers is likely to follow. Analyses that define male interests primarily in terms of male dominance via breadwinning supremacy generally overlook the fact that economically independent women such as these offer men benefits they often cannot afford to ignore. Reluctant mothers, moreover, could convert these benefits into increased decision-making power within the home. The husband of this upwardly mobile high school-educated woman, for example, supported her independence because it increased his independence as well:

A: My husband is very understanding. I never try to listen to anything about "Oh, you're never home; you don't cook for me seven days a week." He's very happy that I'm accomplishing what I'm accomplishing. He doesn't want to be burdened by having to make me happy. When I met him, he knew I had a lot more ambition. He helped me along. He's a manager, and I'm a manager, and we just share ideas and help each other out.

Male partners were thus enlisted in what was once considered "women's work." Few reluctant mothers expected to gain complete domestic equality or to shift the primary child-care responsibility to their spouses, but all became involved in a negotiated process to garner increased male participation in parental caretaking. The more responsibility their partners assumed, the less costly children appeared. Negotiating greater male participation in child care and household work was often an unpleasant process, but it was essential to making motherhood an acceptable choice. Initial male resistance confronted female determination. This aspiring linguist explained:

A: When we were first living together, I did most of the housework. But I think I changed more and more. I feel like [I wanted to be] very, very certain that nothing happens to me again like what happened in the past with other men, including my father. So at first I would ask him to do half the housework. We would argue about it, and finally I would get him to do half of it. And now I can usually get him to do it, by asking him about five times, but we don't have to argue so much about it any more. It's coming to be more fifty-fifty.

Q: Do you think you'll be able to depend upon him for help rearing the children?

A: I think by then we'll have those kinds of things worked out to the extent that he will do half. I don't ask him to do anything alone, including financially, to support the child, but I want half. It's going to be a struggle for me to get him to do it.

Thus, despite transit resistance and the intractable nature of old habits, grudging, but nonetheless significant, male partners' behaviors and assumptions usually followed. As these men confronted the terms of the implicit bargain they had struck with their work-committed partners, they began to accept and even take pride in their new responsibilities. This manager described the process of change:

Q: How do you think he'll feel about helping out?

A: I think he'll learn to love it. It's been a shock for him. He never expected to marry anybody like me; but he was attracted to me because of the things I am, which is not the little woman who is barefoot and pregnant in the kitchen. His initial response is to rail against it because he never grew up thinking he was going to have to fold his own underwear. As soon as he understands that that's part of the bargain, he even gets to the point where he develops some pride in doing for himself; but it really takes a while. I am sure that with a baby it will also be an educational, development time called, "You want me to do

what? No, okay, all right." We go through that.

Of course, powerful barriers also made change difficult and limited the degree and type of male participation. Because structural and social supports for male parental caretaking remain weak and because men have little reason to voluntarily forgo prerogatives at home, reluctant mothers faced protracted and exhausting battles to secure their partners' participation. These battles invariably seemed worth the effort, but over time they took an emotional toll. Exhaustion and self-doubt occasionally accompanied the efforts of reluctant mothers to secure male support:

Q: So you've made demands and he's responded to them?

A: I guess I've gone through periods of getting really depressed about it, because I feel, like I'm the evil person. If I complain or ask or demand or get mad, I feel like it's all classified as bitching. . . . I don't like being put in the position of having to make the marriage an equal one and always to have to be willing to struggle. Sometimes I think maybe I'd rather be single than struggle. But I think I've gotten more out of the marriage than the struggle. I think that the positive parts have made it worth it. . . .

Because most reluctant mothers inherited household responsibilities and attempted later to shift them, victories were often limited in scope. Most retained primary responsibility for seeing that things ran smoothly, even when domestic tasks were divided more evenly. Although male participation increased, it was not equal participation, no matter how much a male partner agreed to do under protest. Despite her desire for children and efforts to change, an upwardly mobile computer programmer still feared that the weight of domestic responsibilities would rest on her shoulders:

Q: What about your husband? You said he really wants children, but you don't feel comfortable about asking him to share in the child care?

A: I think he is willing to do any job that needs to be done, but I think both of us are still looking too much at what he does as helping the little woman out in the home. If we have kids, it's going to be my primary responsibility and my worry, and he helps out. And I notice this when he does work around the house or just the cooking; I still feel guilty. When he doesn't do the dishes, I'm the one who's embarrassed if someone comes over and walks into my kitchen. It's very hard to work this thing through.

Full-time work requirements often barred men from greater parental participation. Even reluctant mothers did not endorse an arrangement that would bring a father more fully into the home if it also pulled him out of the workplace. Few, even among the well-remunerated, commanded incomes that compared favorably with their partners. This earnings disparity made role reversal impractical as well as unattractive to female as well as male partners. Thus, despite the rise in the number of women workers, the economic system continues to promote sexual inequality in household labor. Because these men generally earned more than their wives and rarely retained the option *not* to work, they could more easily justify their comparatively low participation in domestic chores. And because the workplace itself remains so impervious to change, even men who wished to be active fathers faced considerable barriers to high parental participation. As a result, although nondomestic women took great pride in their own self-sufficiency, they rarely equated personal independence with traditional male breadwinning responsibilities. Even the most work-committed women approached the idea of male domesticity, and resultant dependence on their own earnings, with trepidation and resistance. This professional woman explained:

Q: How would you feel about being the sole breadwinner so your husband could stay home with the children?

A: I've thought about that before and feel that one of the luxuries I allow myself is that I'm working and I don't have to. It's a real screwy little backwards knob in there somewhere; I know that, if he quit and I was the sole support, there'd be a different feeling, if I had to work. It is not something I'm unwilling to do, be the mainstay of the family for a while which is different from forever, though.

Even the most conflicted reluctant mothers thus rarely viewed gender role reversal as a palatable or possible alternative. Few wanted or expected fathers to remain home with the children during the day. A "catch-22" of sorts worked to discourage male partners from trading their briefcases or tool boxes for aprons. First, domestically oriented homemakers had no incentive to induce their husbands to withdraw from the workplace to care for children; this group depended on a committed male breadwinner to support their own domesticity. Nondomestically oriented women, however, were also reluctant to challenge traditional models of appropriate male work behavior even as they pushed for new definitions of appropriate female behavior. Those who were unwilling to stay home with their young children were equally reluctant to request or demand of their partners what they refused to do themselves. The great importance they attached to work made it difficult for them to accept the legitimacy of domesticity for male partners as well as for themselves. These women supported dual-earning household arrangements (and the delegation of child care to a paid caretaker), but they generally rejected full-time male domesticity as an acceptable alternative to the traditional household.

In sum, numerous obstacles limited what a woman could extract from her partner in order to shift the costs of childbearing. Reluctant mothers could gain the help and support of their partners, but this generally produced a form of equality more accurately described as less mothering than as more fathering. (The words "less" and "more" refer only to the amount of time spent at home and focused specifically on child care. These respondents distinguished between quantity and quality of care. From their perspective, less time devoted to child care did not imply a lower quality of parenting.) These women supported an arrangement in which they would spend less time at home; they were reluctant, however, to support an arrangement in which their partners would spend more. Although male parental participation was expected, paid care was considered the cornerstone of a workable arrangement:

Q: Will your husband help care for the children on a regular basis?

A: I think we'll have somebody do it, since I'll keep working. But the time we're together, we'll more than share.

Although reluctant mothers were more motivated and in a better position to secure their partners' help than were either childless or traditional women, they faced considerable barriers to fully integrating men into the work of parenting. Indeed, some combiners found it easier to do without a spouse than try to secure the help of one. Single mothers, especially, saw men as a hindrance rather than a help in combining work and motherhood:

A: I've been on my own since 1973, and I miss having a mate around, I guess for companionship. But then I think, Is it really worth it, having a male around the house, having to put up with the hassles of, as soon as you come home, having to cook dinner, picking up his clothes, washing them, being like a maid?"

A strategy of equal male participation was therefore often viewed as the path of last resort, when all other alternatives had been tried and failed:

A: I think that any really different kind of arrangement, different in terms of nontraditional, would only come as a result of my not being able to find a more traditional resolution to the problem. Because otherwise, he won't see that there's a need for it.

Because the conditions that support equal male participation, although becoming somewhat more widespread, remain comparatively rare, reluctant mothers also looked elsewhere for strategies to retain their footing in the workplace, reduce the costs of motherhood, and resolve the contradictions of their situation. If structures were unyielding, there remained another, more accessible avenue for change in the realm of ideas and personal standards about how best to rear a child.

Altering Child-Rearing Ideologies

In their search for a way to combine committed work with motherhood, reluctant mothers typically changed their beliefs about the nature of proper child rearing and early childhood development. These ideas were more malleable than the relatively intransigent and slowly responding structures of work and marriage. Bereft of viable structural alternatives, ideological change became the path of least resistance. Caught between pressures to procreate and to achieve at work, reluctant mothers surrendered traditional beliefs that their own mothers had lived by and passed on to them:

A: I'm the opposite extreme of where I came from . . . where I felt you had to be home full-time in order to raise a child in terms of what the *child* needs. I don't think that's true anymore. Before, I felt a mother, to be a good mother, should be home with her children. Not only is it not necessary, but it might not even be best. Besides, those are the terms on which I'm willing to have a family.

The emerging beliefs of this group of women contrasted sharply with the views and behavioral patterns of their mothers, currently domestic women, and women committed to childlessness. They also represented a break from reluctant mothers' own earlier views. To ease the integration of work and family, reluctant mothers rejected traditional views and challenged the widely espoused notion that working mothers have a deleterious impact on their offspring. This process offered an escape from an otherwise irresolvable double bind, but it also required a difficult break from past assumptions and parental messages. A respondent with high work aspirations explained:

Q: What brought about the change in your attitude that work and child rearing couldn't be combined?

A: I just don't think it's true. I don't think it was true for [my mother]. I believe that I can manage to combine anything I want to, and I can do it well. I feel like a lot of the messages I got growing up were that, in fact, you couldn't combine career and family, that if I were to marry and have a family, that would be the end of my life. And I think I adopted them without understanding that, and I acted on them. Now that I have begun to separate from my parents' views, and particularly my mother's, I don't think that those are valid for me.

For some, ideological change occurred after their children were born. Faced with the experience of domesticity, they realized that, regardless of the dangers they had been told their return to work would entail, staying home was not acceptable. They thus developed new notions of good mothering that better fit their needs. Ambivalent emotions that included both guilt and a certain fragile confidence that their children would not be harmed emerged side by side. A biologist and mother of three returned to work after the birth of her first child despite her concerns and doubts:

A: I'd never held a baby in my life, and just the idea of this individual being in my charge was overwhelming. And then I found out there's nothing to it. I went back to work with guilt feelings that I should be home, but I could see that [my children] were great.

Q: Why did you decide at that point that it was okay to work?

A: At that point, I wasn't sure if the children were fine. I was still having tremendous guilt feelings, and I did for the next couple of years. But staying home was not for me. I loved my children dearly, and I felt I was a very good mother. I loved my husband dearly. But I wasn't going to sacrifice my life for these individuals. I wanted something for myself, too.

Fear, guilt, and doubt were especially common among those who lacked the moral and financial support of a male partner. This clerk and single mother, for example, considered desperate measures when divorce left her perched on an economic and emotional precipice:

Q: Did you ever worry that Laurie would suffer from your working?

A: I did. She was about two when I first separated. She started getting hyper attacks. It really scared me. I thought, "Oh, what have I done?" I was going through a very depressed, worried period, and I wrote my brother and asked if maybe I should give her up for adoption, giving her to a family, because maybe I'm not giving her enough. He said, "No. Your daughter, you keep." I think I would have regretted it. My ideal isn't the way it happened, but I don't regret the way it happened, either. . . .

Given their lack of other acceptable alternatives, guilt and doubt, however deeply experienced, did not thwart reluctant mothers' determination to combine work and child rearing. Instead, they emphasized the benefits working mothers offer their children. They turned the traditional ideology on its head and began to develop a new philosophy of mothering that hinged upon the conviction that, at least in some instances, full-time mothering can actually harm children. Inherited beliefs and prevailing theories notwithstanding, reluctant mothers concluded that their own children would be better off because they would be mothered less.

Reluctant mothers came to believe, first, that an unhappy mother would produce an unhappy child. If full-time mothering produced disastrous consequences for the mother, it would produce disastrous consequences for the child as well. This divorced bank officer concluded that a tired, but happy, caretaker was preferable to a miserable full-time mother:

Q: Has working interfered with your ability to raise a family?

A: No, because if Janet and I had stayed home together, we would have driven each other nuts. I would not have been as good a mother as I am now. Thank God there are all these lovely people who are willing to watch my child when I'm gone and give her certain things that I'm not ready or able to give.

Work-committed mothers also argued that they would bring energies, ideas, experiences, and resources to child rearing that full-time mothers could not offer. An accountant reasoned:

A: Also, I think that, if I'm challenged and alert, it's something I could probably communicate to my children.

Reluctant mothers thus believed that their absence could and would be offset by benefits they were uniquely positioned to provide.

Third, reluctant mothers focused on money. If full-time homemaking would impose financial strains on the household, they reasoned, then a child would suffer more from economic deprivation if its mother stayed home than it would from maternal deprivation if its mother worked.

The fact that a working mother could provide money in place of time also justified the choice to work. This lawyer offered the same rationale for working full-time that men have historically relied on to justify their absence during the day:

A: I plan to have children, probably two, and my idea is to take off work, maybe four months, and then go back. I might want to work part-time, but that's just not feasible; so I don't even think about it. I think about going back to work full-time. And you also have to have enough money to make it comfortable, because if you've got economic strains [the child will suffer].

Fourth, reluctant mothers argued that by working they would protect their offspring from the dangers of "overmothering." They directly challenged the belief that children need constant care and attention from one primary care-taker, preferably their biological mother. Instead, they argued that children can be overindulged and overprotected by an ever-present, overzealous mother lacking other major commitments. Reluctant mothers came to believe that their children would actually have a better chance for healthy development precisely because their mothers would be occupied elsewhere:

A: I'm not sure I'm right in saying there's *no* bad in all that comes from being gone all the time during the day. But I had the opportunity to see both families where the parents are at home and the parents aren't at home. To tell you the truth, the kids are better off if they don't have Mommy home all the time, keeping them babies. And I think in a way, too, it might help them to learn responsibility and self-reliance and things like that.

This work-committed mother with another child on the way agreed that her job as a clerk protected her children from the dangers of mothering:

Q: Has working interfered with your ability to raise your family?

A: No. I think I've been a much better mother, and also he's around other people, not just me. I think it's a lot better; his adjustment is better. I think it's worked out better than I thought it would.

Finally, reluctant mothers questioned the widely accepted assumption that mothers who do not work shower their children with attention and affection. They argued instead that housework and other activities so preoccupy most full-time homemakers that they are no more likely to attend to their children's needs than are working mothers.

Q: So you don't think the children will suffer if you work?

A: No, I don't think so. You figure that a mother that is home all the time, even though she might be around, is still preoccupied with something else. She spends a lot of her time doing housework or whatever; so I don't see the difference. When a family gets together at night, their main concentration right then is on each other; so I think it's something that *would* work out.

This argument may not be as farfetched as it superficially appears. Bane (1976:15-17) reports that television has become a major babysitter for most children, including preschoolers, and that the difference in the amounts of time working and home-making mothers spend exclusively with their children is "surprisingly small." The average preschooler, for example, watches television about one-third of his or her waking hours, regardless of who is caring for the child. Reluctant mothers concluded that the quality rather than the quantity of time spent with offspring was the decisive criterion for defining good mothering and responsible child rearing. In their view, working did not seriously compromise the overall texture of the relationship between parents and children.

They argued instead that working actually improved the quality of familial bonds. This rather simple substitution of quality for quantity of time a mother spends with her child opened up the otherwise inaccessible option of combining motherhood with committed work:

Q: You said that when you were younger, you saw working and raising children as incompatible. Why don't you feel that way any more?

A: Because it's the quality of time that you spend with them, I think. That's where I was a little bit confused. I thought you had to spend all your time with them and be a mother and housewife or just full-time working, but you can do both.

Ideological change required not only a leap of faith into uncharted territory, but a considerable amount of discounting as well. Confronted with a traditional set of beliefs (however ill-supported by evidence) that argues that mothers of young children who indulge their "selfish" desires to work run the risk of producing damaged offspring, reluctant mothers had to struggle to minimize such a possibility in their own minds. Because they were experimenting but would not know the results for some time, they found themselves waiting and hoping that all would turn out well. But they also braced themselves for unanticipated contingencies. Reluctant mothers chose to travel an uncertain path, the outcome of which they knew they could not foresee:

Q: Will working interfere with your ability to raise a family?

A: I'll try very hard not to let it. But clearly it will be different for my kid than it was for me having a mother at home all the time. Whether that's going to be a positive thing or a negative thing, only time will tell.

Reluctant mothers also discounted the costs children threatened to exact from workplace accomplishment. Although the fear of work costs remained, they struggled to minimize such threats as well:

Q: Do you think having children will affect your progress at work?

A: I think that is in the back of my mind. . . . Probably the reason why I've never actively gone out to have a kid is that concern. But again, I keep pushing that concern aside and saying that it's not going to affect [anything], which may be foolish.

Whatever their qualms, the process of ideological change lowered the perceived costs of children to a level that made the choice for motherhood possible. In the midst of uncertainty, reluctant mothers developed a strong commitment to creating new ways of integrating work and family life. For this group, there was no other acceptable choice. They concluded, unlike both their domestic and their childless counterparts, that responsible mothering and committed work are not incompatible. As this aspiring worker declared:

Q: What are the main reasons you plan to work and raise a child at the same time?

A: Because I don't think just raising kids would be fulfilling for me. If I had to give work up, I don't think I would have children. But I don't see why I would have to give it up. I don't think they're incompatible.

Psychoanalytic theory notwithstanding, beliefs about what constitutes correct child rearing and good mothering are as much ideological constructs as established scientific "fact." There are, of course, some demonstrably wrong ways to rear a child, such as extreme abuse, deprivation, or neglect; but that leaves much room for variety in terms of who cares for the young, how much time is focused upon them exclusively, and how many caretakers are actively involved. Caretaking by the biological mother is neither the only safe option nor a guarantee of a "successful" outcome. It is thus difficult to resist the conclusion that persistent beliefs about the harmful effects of working mothers serve more to control women's behavior than to protect their children. These beliefs can be considered ideologies in the truest sense of the word: important control mechanisms that prevent some women from acting in their own behalf and that induce guilt in those who do (Schur 1984).

The argument that modern theories of child rearing are ideologies that serve, to some extent, as mechanisms of social control is supported by the historical record. Full-time mothering is a relatively rare and historically recent social construction, as are the beliefs that support and justify this particular family form. Before the industrial revolution, children were afforded neither maternal indulgence nor constant adult attention, and they were not deemed to need them (Aries 1962; Ryan 1981; and Shorter 1975). Because these children appear to have developed into healthy, functioning adults, these examples call into question the scientific basis for concluding that all children require a specific and universal form of mothering for proper development.

Despite the power of ideological prohibition, however, reluctant mothers were compelled to change the terms of the discourse about motherhood. They rejected the received wisdom of their childhood and many of their peers and substituted a set of beliefs that better fit their own needs and circumstances.

A vivid illustration of how "theories" of correct child-rearing practices tend to change with social circumstances can be found in the American "bible" for parents, Dr. Benjamin Spock's *Baby and Child Care*. Although this book championed full-time motherhood when it was first released in the late 1940s, the most recent edition rejects Spock's earlier claims that working mothers harm children. It argues instead that women should feel free to work and that men make good parents, too (Spock 1976). Perhaps Spock has been as much influenced *by* women as he has influenced them.

This process of ideological change among reluctant mothers shows clearly how beliefs about child rearing serve as imperfect mechanisms of social control. Traditional child-rearing ideologies supported some women's preference of domesticity and led others to reject motherhood. Those committed to combining work and parenthood, however, were influenced, but not controlled, by traditional beliefs. Traditional ideologies made their task more difficult, but ultimately these beliefs did not and could not prevent reluctant mothers from breaking the rules they had been reared to believe in.

Armed with the support of a growing group of like-situated women and fearful of the hazards of domesticity, these women brought the weight of collective social change to their struggle. Emerging support groups neutralized the impact of the disapproval they faced and legitimated new alternatives in spite of the structural and ideological forces opposed to change. Eroding supports for domesticity gave strength to those, such as this accountant, committed to change:

Q: What are the main reasons you plan to work and raise children at the same time?

A: I think in our society the whole attitude has changed. There aren't the social groups or anything for nonworking mothers. When I was growing up with my mother being home all the time, she did have a lot of social contact. But that was a different situation from what I'm in. Right now, with most of the women working anyway, there aren't that many women staying home. Like in this apartment building, there isn't anybody who stays home. You would be basically by yourself.

Ideological change, then, helped reluctant mothers cope with the motherhood dilemma. The pressure to challenge traditional beliefs and values, however, would not have been present if larger historical forces had not created a dilemma in the first place. Pressure from changing social structures gave impetus to change in ideas. Once confronted by these structural dilemmas, reluctant mothers had little recourse but to alter their beliefs to better fit their circumstances. This mental reformulation subsequently affected behavior, easing the way toward motherhood while simultaneously justifying a continued attachment to work. . . .

References

Aries, P. 1962. *Centuries of Childhood: A Social History of Family Life.* Translated by Robert Baldick. New York: Knopf.

Badinter, E. 1981. *Mother Love: Myth and Reality.* New York: Macmillan.

Bane, M. J. 1976. *Here to Stay: American Families in the Twentieth Century.* New York: Basic Books.

Berk, S. F., ed. 1980. *Women and Household Labor.* Beverly Hills, CA: Sage Publications.

Bird, C. 1979. *The Two-Paycheck Marriage.* New York: Pocket Books.

Blake, J. 1966. "Ideal family size among white Americans: A quarter of a century's evidence." *Demography,* 3(1):154-173.

_____. 1974. "Can we believe recent data on birth expectations in the United States?" *Demography,* 11(February):25-44.

Blumstein, P. and P. W. Schwartz. 1983. *American Couples: Money, Work, Sex.* New York: Morrow.

Hofferth, S. L. and K. A. Moore. 1979. "Women's employment and marriage." In R. E. Smith (ed.) *The Subtle Revolution: Women at Work.* Washington, D.C.: Urban Institute.

Huber, J. and G. Spitze. 1983. *Sex Stratification: Children, Housework, and Jobs.* New York: Academic Press.

Masnick, G. and M. J. Bane. 1980. *The Nation's Families: 1960-1990.* Cambridge: Joint Center for Urban Studies of M.I.T. and Harvard University.

Pleck, J. H. 1975. "Work and family roles: From sex patterned segregation to integration." Paper presented at the annual meeting of the American Sociological Association, San Francisco, August.

Pruett, K. D. 1983. "Infants of primary nurturing fathers." *Psychoanalytic Study of the Child*, 38:257-77.

Ryan, M. P. 1981. *The Cradle of the Middle Class: The Family in Oneida County, New York, 1790-1865*. New York: Cambridge University Press.

Schur, E. M. 1984. *Labeling Women Deviant: Gender, Stigma, and Social Control*. New York: Random House.

Scott, H. 1974. *Does Socialism Liberate Women? Experiences from Eastern Europe*. Boston: Beacon Press.

Shinn, M. 1983. "Well-being and the relationship between work and family." In *New York City Area Study Proposal*. New York: Consortium for University Research.

Shorter, E. 1975. *The Making of the Modern Family*. New York: Basic Books.

Spock, B. 1976. *Baby and Child Care*, rev. ed. New York: Pocket Books.

Szalai, A. 1972. *The Use of Time*. The Hague: Mouton.

Vanek, J. 1974. "Time spent in housework." *Scientific American*, 231(November):116-121.

Wilensky, H. L. 1968. "Women's work: Economic growth, ideology, and structure." *Industrial Relations*, 7(May):235-248.

Food for Thought and Application Questions

1. Gerson argues that pressures resulting from changing social structures have given rise to new beliefs and values regarding working mothers. These new ideas are visible in popular culture in television programs, media advertising, magazines, novels, movies, and song lyrics. At the same time, vestiges of traditional beliefs about women's proper role remain visible in popular culture. Select any one of the "elements" of popular culture listed above and look for examples of both traditional and non-traditional messages about working mothers. Reflect on how the messages you find are likely to affect reluctant mothers.

2. Visit a toy store or examine the toy section of a major catalog. How many toys can you find that encourage girls to be mothers/homemakers (e.g., dolls, tea sets, ovens)? How many toys can you find that encourage girls to be paid workers (e.g., work-related costumes or equipment)? Now complete the same exercise for boys. What are the implications of what you found for women making decisions about work and family roles? For men? ✦

12

Sex-Role Spillover: Personal, Familial, and Organizational Roles

Rita Mae Kelly

Americans have traditionally equated the role of "worker" with the roles of breadwinner, father, and husband. As women enter the work force, they have been expected to meet this male-centered standard. At the same time, women also have been expected to follow their traditional roles of wife or girlfriend, mother, daughter, and sex partner/object. The intertwining of women's expanding economic power and less rapidly evolving sex roles has produced the gendered dimension of the U.S. segmented labor market.

In 1986 more than 80% of women in the work force were of childbearing age (Hardesty and Jacobs 1986). A large proportion of employed women experienced significant conflicts between their roles as workers, wives, mothers, daughters, and family caretakers, all of which they were expected to play simultaneously (Lewis and Cooper 1988). These concurrent demands caused many women to suffer from two conditions: role overload, which results when a person is expected to fulfill more roles than she or he can handle; and

role strain, which results from conflict between two or more roles. Table 12.1 contrasts the traditional family and organizational roles of men and women.

Working Women and the Home

The Wife Role (Housekeeper/Homemaker/Hostess)

In the 1950s and 1960s wives employed outside the home to augment their husbands' income gradually gained acceptance in the role of supplemental workers. By the 1980s, middle-class women had become more than just guardians of their family status and lifestyle; many had also launched careers. At the same time, many couples found that both spouses needed to work to maintain a middle-class standard of living (Pleck 1985). Wives were not the only women entering the paid labor force; 45% of all employed women were single, separated, or divorced (U.S. Bureau of the Census 1988). Further, 23% of all households consisted of nonmarried, single women (Blank 1988). The median weekly earnings in 1989 for a male-supported household without an employed wife were $486. For families with both spouses working, the median earnings were $668; yet, for a female-supported household, median weekly earnings totaled only $334 (U.S. Department of Labor 1989). These statistics indicate that increasing numbers of women have fallen into or have barely escaped poverty.

Regardless of income or marital status, female workers must deal with home and hearth in ways that male workers do not. In *The Second Stage*, Betty Friedan recognized that, while women were pulled into the public realm, men were not enticed into the private domain (Friedan 1981). The resulting lopsided division of familial responsibilities led to a condition Friedan termed the "superwoman" syndrome. While women attempted to excel at both the traditional female sex roles and the male role of paid laborer, men avoided the women's tradi-

Table 12.1
Comparison of Traditional Family and Organizational Roles

Wife	Husband	Employee	Manager
• homemaking	• provider of living wage	• subordinate follows policy	• makes and administers policy
• consumer-family goods	• initiating sex partner	• must be pleasant and receptive to clients and management	• is staff's link to organization
• attractive, receptive sex partner	• key decision maker		
• supportive— "little woman behind big man"	• family's link to political/economic system		

Mother	Father	Employee	Management
• childbirth	• provides means for rearing (education, etc.)	• complete loyalty to organizational needs—	• controls staff's movement through merit system
• childrearing	• nurturer for whole family	• continuous, uninterrupted, productive work	• complete loyalty to company policy/ goals
• always available for children's needs	• key discipliner		

Daughter	Son	Employee	Management
• respect and honor of mother	• heir apparent	• complete trust in superiors	• finds talented staff and grooms for management
• adoration of father	• "chip off the old block"	• loyalty to superiors and organization	• carries on "legacy" through protege
• "daddy's little girl"			
• attractive—good "catch" for promising son-in-law			

Girlfriend/ Sex Partner/Object	Boyfriend/ Male Sex-Actor	Employee	Management
• attractive: potential wife/mother	• successful: potential provider	**Woman** • attractive, pleasant, supportive	**Woman** • attractive, interpersonal, managerial
• passive: waits to be asked out	• assertive: makes the date	**Man** • aggressive, jocular, dominant	**Man** • successful, assertive, commanding

tional role of housekeeper/homemaker/ hostess. Consequently, women entering the paid labor force encountered a Herculean task that only a mythical "superwoman" could have completely fulfilled.

Empirical studies demonstrate the burden this condition places on women. Arlie Hochschild's (1989) study of couples and housework shows that this imbalance of roles requires women to put in a "second shift" as housekeeper, consumer, and caregiver. Skow (1989) reports that working wives spend 15 fewer hours at leisure each week than their husbands, and when faced with scheduling conflicts, women tend to reduce leisure time before reducing time spent on child care. A study reported in *The American Woman* compared married men and women who spend equal hours in the paid work force. This study found that women put in an additional 18 hours per week doing home labor (Blank 1988). Fathers average only 12 minutes per day in primary child care (Blank 1988). Even women who claim to have egalitarian arrangements at home still put in more energy, time, and labor during this second shift than do their spouses (Hochschild 1989; MacCorquodale 1986).

Although custom has decreed that women be more available for family care, this role expectation has not been viewed positively in the workplace. Ten executive men were asked by *Executive Female* magazine to participate in a roundtable discussion about the strengths and weaknesses of female peers. One executive claimed:

> "People have to have families—you can't argue that—but within the business environment, it's a negative. A woman always wants to go home at 5:00 to be with her family. Men have families too, but they don't leave. . . ." (Heller 1983, p. 102)

Men make sacrifices in order to make money and to gain power. These executives suggested that women may be hitting the glass ceiling because they are not ready to make the same sacrifices for their careers.

This perception shifts the blame for women's difficulties in the workplace to women, rather than on recognizing socially institutionalized and individually internalized stereotypes. In addition, reports indicate that this type of perception about women is becoming increasingly inaccurate. A roundtable discussion of ten successful female executives by *Nation's Business* indicates women are not only "ready to make the sacrifice" but also are making the personal concessions necessary for career advancement (Nelton and Berney 1987). One IBM executive found that her 10 to 12 hour workdays made it impossible to keep a commitment to a family evening meal. "I took a close look at that ritual and decided it had to go" (Nelton and Berney 1987, p. 18). Letting go of time-honored practices is one of the many sacrifices women, especially those in the primary labor market, have to make.

To be most competitive, especially in the primary job sector, requires not being a "wife," but actually having an effective substitute. Many careers command complete loyalty and submission to organizational goals with total submersion into corporate culture. Most management and executive careers are project-driven. Deadlines are not flexed to accommodate family or personal schedules. High-powered careers blur the lines between the personal and private realms. Work often takes place with a client over dinner, with the boss at a show, with co-workers on the golf course, and frequently out of town. It is assumed a babysitter is available, that the children are always well, or that there are no children at all.

Companies frequently expect employees will not be burdened with responsibility for cleaning the home, purchasing consumer goods, and caring for children. In addition, the higher level professional is expected to have a partner who serves as hostess to the boss and clients, stands in line to buy the theater tickets, makes reservations for the restaurant, packs the luggage for out-of-town meetings, and drives the higher status spouse (usually the man) to the airport in mid-workday. Without the help of "wives," married career women and career women with children suffer a real disadvantage competing for important contracts, key line positions or out-of-town jobs.

The Mother Role (Childbearing and Child Rearing)

In 1990 more than 70% of women age 25 to 34 were in the labor force. In 1950, there were only 35%. Lenhoff reports that 80% of all women in the workplace are of childbearing age, and 93% of them will become pregnant while working (Lenhoff 1987). Overall, approximately three-fourths of women in the work force will be affected by pregnancy and motherhood. Given that about 50 million women are in the labor force, that means about 37.2 million women will be directly affected by pregnancy and child-care policies. This estimate does not include the millions of children, elderly relatives, and spouses that are indirectly impacted.

The number of working mothers has increased sharply since the 1950s, when only 12% of women with children under the age of six worked. In 1988, approximately six of every ten mothers with a child under age six were employed. Half of all married mothers with infants younger than one year were in the labor force. In 1990, fewer than 5% of families had a father who worked and a mother who stayed home caring for the children. By 1995 it is estimated that two-thirds of all preschool children will have mothers in the work force, and that four of five school-age children will have employed mothers (U.S. Department of Labor 1988).

Neither U.S. employers nor the government have been quick to respond to these radical changes. In 1987 the Bureau of Labor Statistics estimated that only 2% of businesses with 10 or more workers sponsored child-care centers; an additional 3% provided financial assistance for day-care services; and only 6% offered help in the form of information, referral, or counseling services (Thompson 1988). AT&T reported in 1989 that families juggle up to four different kinds of child-care arrangements each week (Allen 1989). Although the number of day-care centers built in or near the workplace increased from 110 in 1979 to 4,000 in 1989 (Garbarine 1989), most workers have to rely on other family members, neighbors, religious institutions, or personally devised arrangements. In 1989, churches provided one-third of the child-care services (Hochschild 1989). In 1989, only 14% of U.S. corporations offered child-care benefits to their employees, arguing that the bottom line costs outweighed benefits.

The options for integrating the roles of mother and career woman have not been great. Women have been expected to fit into the male model of work, which forces them to either avoid being a mother, adopt a "father's" approach to child care, or seek alternative work hours and work forms. Table 12.2 presents a summary of some of the employment alternatives developed to date with a brief assessment of the advantages and disadvantages of each.

A common solution to the motherhood conflict for ambitious career women has been avoidance. Whereas 90% of male executives age 40 and under are fathers, only 35% of their female counterparts are mothers (Wallis et al. 1989). As the biological clock ticked close to menopause, more and more career women of the 1980s sought alternative approaches to the work force. Women who put off having children until the last possible moment were not rewarded for their sacrifice. Instead, their choices regarding pregnancy and maternity leave became a test of organizational loyalty (Hardesty and Jacobs 1986). The more seniority and/or responsibility a woman has, the more childbirth is likely to be viewed as an organizational disruption. Employers often want reassurance that the motherhood role will not supersede the employee role.

Large numbers of women, especially those with well-paying jobs, addressed the

Table 12.2
Advantages and Disadvantages to Alternative Work Styles

Alternative	Advantages	Disadvantages
Flextime		
Flexible arrival/exit time: can arrive at work anytime during a 2-3-hour grace period.	The most stressful time of day is the "rush hour" getting to and from the workplace—flexibility reduces this stress.	Studies indicate single women are the users, not parents. Flextime is not considered appropriate for supervisors and managers of personnel.
Compressed work week: most common ones are 40 hours in 4 days or 32 hours over a weekend.	Allows parents one or more full days of access to businesses, schools, and medical facilities. Weekend shifts popular among nurses.	High fatigue among workers. Adds the need for special child care arrangements for the extended working days.
Part-time work		
Part-time professionals: works less than 32 hours per week yet receives pro-rated amount of benefits afforded to full-time employees.	A parent spends more time on child care without losing "professional status."	May not have access to the more important projects and tasks given to those who are available through the entire work day.
Part-time partnership tracks: accomplished based on total number of billable hours, total amount of income, or total number of hours worked.	Allows professionals like doctors and lawyers to keep on a partnership track during child-rearing years.	May take twice as long to gain partnership as a traditional track. Many professions are project-oriented so may often work more hours than contracted.
Job sharing: two or more people share one job either simultaneously or alternatively.	Well received by helping professionals like teachers and counselors—avoids burn-out and helps maintain creativity. Affords the most flexibility in time spent at work.	Must be done on a voluntary basis. With professionals, employer will get more than "half" of their energy and talents—employee gets half the pay.
Extended leave		
Maternity leave: extended leave for mothers of newly born or adopted children.	Helps women make the adjustment to motherhood while still guaranteeing her job at work.	Does not offer men the opportunity to learn and practice primary child-care responsibilities.
Paternity leave: same as maternity leave but for fathers.	Promotes bonding of father to child at birth and fosters new role development for fathers.	Although the job is guaranteed, maternity or paternity leave may result in loss of positioning for key positions.
Parental leave: same as maternal and paternal.	If each spouse could take turns, the time period for which a full-time parent is available is doubled.	This system can work only if both have access to leave—an unlikelihood today.
Homework		
Telecommuting	Allows women to combine homecare, childcare, and work for pay in the home. Saves time and cuts the cost of commuting and day-care tuition. Also allows flexibility of scheduling.	The isolation of home-based work keeps women from networking and prevents positioning for key opportunities. Also, without physical boundaries, can result in even more role strain and overload.

stress of role overload and role strain due to motherhood as single working fathers have previously done. They hire other women to assist in mothering and family chores. This "fatherly" approach to child care, house care, and family consumption is a major factor in the rise of the service economy and self-employment of women in the peripheral sector of the labor market (Beattie 1984).

Although the need for child care has led to more jobs for women and greater flexibility for women owners and managers of such services, the resulting businesses and jobs have also contributed to pay inequities and employment of women in jobs that lack career growth potential. Although nearly one-half of all day-care teachers have bachelor degrees or at least some college training, the average salary of these professionals—mostly women—was only $5.35 per hour in 1988, a salary that amounts to about $9,363 a year. This sum is less than the $9,431 federally defined poverty level for a family of three (Lewin 1989). As the need for day care increased in the 1980s, the average salary of day-care teachers declined by 27% from 1977 to 1988 (Lewin 1989).

The low salaries reflect a dilemma facing U.S. women. Day care services bear large price tags. In 1986, the estimated cost of purchasing in-home care was $8,000 per year, $5,000 for day care per year, and $2,500 for a year of full-time preschool tuition—costs comparable to college tuition (Elrich 1986). Women who must hire other women to watch their children typically do not earn salaries high enough to pay day-care providers higher wages.

Working women still earn only 74 cents to every working man's dollar (Blank 1988). Even the highest level executive women suffer dramatic pay gaps. According to the U.S. Chamber of Commerce in May 1987, "corporate women at the vice-presidential level and above earn 42% less than their male peers" (Wallis et al. 1989, p. 85).

In addition to the burden of affordability, a shortage of licensed day-care centers makes it unlikely that a good center will be conveniently located. Many centers cater to those who work a regular day shift. Women who work odd shifts, who are going to school, or who often have after-hour meetings find themselves struggling to find additional home care and solutions to the restrictive drop-off and pick-up hours at the day-care center. And those few centers that can accommodate parents after 6:00 p.m. often charge an additional fee for these "off hours."

Many licensed day-care centers have age restrictions preventing enrollment of young babies. Often maternity or pregnancy leaves are not long enough to meet the age requirements for enrollment. In addition, care for physically challenged or sick children is rare and very expensive. In 1987, approximately 67% of all child care still took place in a home (Blank 1988).

School-age children pose additional problems. While public schools dismiss students in early afternoon, the average workday ends at 5:00 p.m. Lack of transportation to a care center or prohibitive costs of two to three hours of care per child often results in children caring for themselves after school.

Family work alternatives, like those in Table 12.2, put women—especially mothers—on a separate "Mommy Track." This Mommy Track reinforces the superiority of the present male career model, preventing married women and mothers from developing a more appropriate female work model. These alternatives relieve the conflict between work and home but typically become formidable barriers to long-term career success.

At the Workplace: Workers as Surrogate Daughters, Wives, Girlfriends, and Sex Partners/Objects

Career women suffer role stress in two directions. Not only does the public role of worker create overload and conflict within the home, but the spillover of traditional sex-role expectations into the workplace is a critical career barrier to women (Gutek 1985). Unlike their male peers, women are often perceived in the limited roles of surrogate daughters, wives, or mothers rather than as workers. Working women may find that they are judged by their presence, attractiveness, and attitudes rather than their talents and skills as professionals. One reason for this spillover may be that institutions adhere to a family model. In fact, with divorce so prevalent, the corporation may be a more stable institution than marriage (Berstein 1985).

For a man, the apprenticeship role may be the first of many stages in his career. For a woman, however, the novice role may be the "end of the line." As "daddy's little girl" female proteges are granted the privileged inequality of the little girl, a privilege their male peers don't have—to fail and to lean on someone. However, "as long as her need for approval is stronger than her need for self-expression, a woman may always be trapped in this subordinate daughter role" (Berstein 1985, p. 139), also called the "office daughter syndrome." A study of 18 California families owning businesses found that none of the fathers of daughters had planned on their daughters succeeding them (*Wall Street Journal* 1990). Unexpected events led to the daughters entering the business. Once in the business, 44% felt obliged to be nurturing of their fathers as well as of the business. The daughters reported feeling it necessary to kiss their dad and to continue being "daddy's little girl." Most daughters helped their fathers remain at the head of the company longer, rather than pushing him out as soon as possible, as sons often do. So few fathers assume their daughters will take over that almost no studies have been done on the topic. In one study reported in 1990, 78% of the fathers interviewed "had difficulty handling their daughters' dual family and business roles—as did 89% of the daughters. Unlike sons, daughters find themselves competing at work in their fathers'

eyes with male managers from outside the family" (*Wall Street Journal* 1990, B12). One woman interviewed shared that her father would not listen to her evidence regarding the behavior of the hired male manager.

The difficulties daughters have with their own fathers often carry over to male mentors. With less than 10% of top executive positions being held by women, it is rare that an aspiring woman finds a female mentor. Therefore, a woman's mentor will more likely be a man. Executive men who adhere to using a family model for relating to their co-workers may hesitate to invest in females as proteges because "daughters" have a tendency to grow up, go away, get married, and have babies. The organizational "sons" are viewed as a better bet to become the "heir apparent."

In addition to the daughter role, significant numbers of women also must cope with the girlfriend role. In 1980, Mary Ann Cunningham made the headlines of all the major newspapers, not because she was a graduate of Harvard and the executive vice president of a Fortune 500 corporation, but rather because she was perceived by her male co-workers to be "sleeping her way to the top." Interestingly enough, she never denied having sex with the president but rather insisted they were "truly in love" (Cunningham 1984).

The occasional headlines about office romances reflect a change that occurred in the 1980s. The office became a place for professionals and career-oriented individuals to "meet, date, and relate." Workplaces, not unlike the sex-segregated dormitories of the 1960s, had become "co-ed."

Being a successful professional often means working long hours under tight deadlines, being available on an on-call basis, and working long stints out of town. The same institutions that afford little time for house and child care make it equally difficult for singles to develop and nurture romantic relationships. According to Lisa A. Maniero's latest report on office romance, the sexual revolution that exploded on college and university campuses in the 1960s and 1970s had moved to the workplace in the 1980s (Maniero 1989). Although Maniero finds romance at work a positive influence on worker morale and productivity, Barbara Gutek (1985) finds that sex in the workplace actually reduces productivity and is generally detrimental to women workers.

Perhaps the most central traditional role for women is that of sex partner (or sex object) and procreator. When this role supersedes appropriate worker roles, the work environment becomes "eroticized." *Playboy* pin-ups in the workplace, off-color graffiti, teasing and flirting behaviors, and physical touching are all manifestations of the spillover of inappropriate sex-role expectations into the workplace.

Women in such workplaces may be accused of capitalizing on their abilities as sex partners/objects rather than as creative employees. Like Mary Ann Cunningham, they may be charged with sleeping their way to the top. Gutek suggests that one may use her "feminine wiles" to get a better typewriter, a free out-of-town excursion, a car phone, or an office with a window, but Cunningham's notoriety stands testament to the fact that sex will not necessarily take you to the top.

The spillover of sex roles into the business environment can become the career woman's nightmare—sexual harassment. Survey research has indicated that from 45% to 90% of all working women experience sexual harassment (Stambaugh 1989). This wide margin in estimating the prevalence of sexual harassment is due to an inability of the scientific, business, and legal communities to reach a consensus on a precise definition of this problem. Although it is true that harassers can be of either sex, reports of female harassment of males is rare. According to a recent study of Arizona upper-level government employees (grades 23-30), only 7% of the males surveyed had experienced requests for sexual favors—contrasted with 21% of the women (Hale and Kelly 1989). Women

at lower levels experience higher rates of harassment. Probably the most famous sexual harassment case of the 1980s has been the Jim Bakker-Jessica Hahn affair. In this case, both Bakker and Hahn claim to be victims of harassment.

Fifteen years of case law indicates three conditions that must be proved before sexual harassment is charged: (1) the behavior must be *unwelcomed,* (2) it must be *repetitive,* and (3) it must be considered *offensive* by the subject of the action (Cohen 1987).

Typically, male victims assert that they are targets of a much younger, provocatively dressed, attractive "girl" (Backhouse and Cohen 1981). In these cases, the young women refuse to take a "hint"; the "victims" of sexual harassment typically see to it that the young women are transferred or dismissed. The most prevalent sexual harassment cases, however, involve male superiors who press female subordinates for sexual favors.

A more subtle form of harassment stems not from any one person's behavior but from a *hostile environment.* Hostile behaviors often develop at office parties, picnics, and other "fun" activities where drinking and unprofessional behavior are encouraged. Workplaces where flirting and sexual touching are accepted are highly "eroticized" and are more likely to harbor sexual harassers than environments free of sexual expectations (Gutek 1985).

Such sexual harassment of women in traditional male careers by co-workers may be the result of the defensive posture of the men. Sexual harassment is used to remind the invading women that their primary role is that of a sex object, not of a professional.

There is evidence that sexual harassment occurs across all industries, including the Fortune 500 companies (Sandroff 1988). Employees in all occupations are harassed—supervisors have been harassed by their staff (Clarke 1986) and teachers often endure harassment by their students (Herbert 1989). It is prevalent in the military (Reily 1980), in the government (U.S. Merit Systems Protection Board 1987), and in academic institutions (Dziech and Weiner 1984). The scope of the problem is difficult to assess because most cases go unreported (Markunas and Brady 1987). This fact may reflect a fear held by victims that nothing will be done to address the problem adequately. One case that has become an important exception to this rule occurred in Arizona. Leta Ford, a manager for Revlon, brought suit against her employer (*Ford v. Revlon* 1987). The courts ruled in Ford's favor because she was able to produce a "paper trail" of complaints and grievances over a 13-month period and to demonstrate that Revlon had not taken action to stop the harassment.

The 1986 Supreme Court opinion in the case of *Meritor Savings Bank v. Vinson* has been widely used by organizations to formulate their sexual harassment policy (Cohen 1987). In the *Vinson* decision, victims of sexual harassment won the battle but lost the war. In the first year after *Vinson*, the courts ruled against the plaintiff and in favor of employers in 20 of 31 federal district court cases (Bureau of National Affairs, Inc. 1988). The majority of appeals court decisions have also favored the employer (Bureau of National Affairs, Inc. 1988). Therefore, it appears that the judicial opinions on sexual harassment have served to create effective sexual harassment policies that *avoid liability*. However, it is not clear to what degree these policies actually prevent sexual harassment.

In October of 1989, the House Ethics Committee found representative Jim Bates (D-Calif.) guilty of sexually harassing two members of his staff (Associated Press 1989). The women claimed his behavior created a hostile environment. Bates apologized to the two women but stated: "Times are changing. Members of Congress are going to be scrutinized for their personal and professional behavior . . . sexual harassment is very serious and

not to be taken lightly. *I did not know what sexual harassment means until this came up*" (Associated Press 1989, A13).

It is clear from Rep. Bates's last remark that, even though sexual harassment has been a long-standing problem for women and a political issue for more than ten years, many still are not aware of the basic dimensions of the problem: (1) of what sexual harassment is, (2) that it is harmful, and (3) that the consequences can be harsh. Increased media attention would do much to increase the public's awareness of the problem.

Conclusion

Establishing a successful career in the 1990s requires integrating one's private and public lives. The task is much more than an individual or even an organizational matter. It involves a reconceptualization of sex-role ideology; the acceptance of this new ideology by both men and women; and the adoption of this way of thinking by the nation's political, economic, and judicial institutions.

References

Allen, R. E. 1989. "It pays to invest in tomorrow's workforce." *The Wall Street Journal*, 6 November: A16.

Associated Press. 1989. "Lawmaker harassed two women on staff, is rebuked by panel." *Arizona Republic*, 19 (October):A13.

Backhouse, C. and L. Cohen. 1981. *Sexual Harassment on the Job*. Toronto: Prentice-Hall.

Beattie, L. E. 1984. "Battling another bias in business lending." *Business Week*, 31 (October):14-16.

Berstein, P. 1985. "Family ties, corporate bonds." *Working Women*, 10(S) (May):85-87; 138-139.

Blank, R. M. 1988. "Women's paid work, household income and household well-being." In S. E. Rix (ed.), *The American Woman 1988-1989*. New York: W. W. Norton.

Bureau of National Affairs, Inc. 1988. "Sexual harassment." In *Corporate Affairs, Nepotism, Office Romance and Sexual Harassment.* Washington, D.C.: Bureau of National Affairs.

Clarke, L. W. 1986. "Women supervisors experience sexual harassment, too." *Supervisory Management,* 31(4) (April):35-36.

Cohen, C. F. 1987. "Implications of *Meritor Savings Bank, FSB v. Vinson et al.*" *Labor Law Journal,* 38 (April):243-247.

Cunningham, M. 1984. *Power Play.* New York: Simon & Schuster.

Dziech, B. W. and L. Weiner. 1984. *The Lecherous Professor.* Boston: Beacon.

Elrich, E. 1986. "Child care, the private sector cannot do it alone." *Business Week,* (October):52-53.

Ford v. Revlon. 1987. Arizona State Supreme Court.

Friedan, B. 1981. *The Second Stage.* New York: Summit.

Garbarine, R. 1989. "Building workplace centers to reduce turnover." *New York Times,* 15 (October):32.

Gutek, B. A. 1985. *Sex and the Workplace.* San Francisco: Jossey-Bass.

Hale, M. M. and R. M. Kelly. 1989. *Gender, Bureaucracy and Democracy.* Westport, CT: Greenwood.

Hardesty, S. and N. Jacobs. 1986. *Success and Betrayal: The Crisis of Women in Corporate America.* New York: Franklin Watts.

Heller, L. 1983. "The last of the angry men." *Executive Female,* (September/October):33-38.

Herbert, C. 1989. *Talking of Silence: The Harassment of School Girls.* New York: Palmer.

Hochschild, A. 1989. *The Second Shift.* New York: Wiley.

Lenhoff, D. 1987. "Family medical leave act." In L. Tarr-Whelan and L.C. Isensee (eds.), *The Women's Economic Justice Agenda: Ideas for the States.* Washington, D.C.: Center for Policy Alternatives.

Lewin, T. 1989. "Study finds high turnover in child care workers." *New York Times,* 18 October:A10.

Lewis, S. N. C. and C. L. Cooper. 1988. "Stress in dual-earner families." In B. Gutek, A. Stromberg, and L. Larwood (eds.), *Women*

and Work, An Annual Review, Vol. 3, Newbury Park, CA: Sage.

MacCorquodale, P. 1986. "The economics of home and family." In J. Monk and A. Schelgle (eds.), *Women in the Arizona Economy.* Tucson: University of Arizona Press.

Maniero, L. A. 1989. *Office Romance: Love, Power and Sex in the Workplace.* New York: Rawson of McMillan.

Markunas, P. V. and J. M. Joyce-Brady. 1987. "Underutilization of sexual harassment procedures." *Journal of the National Association for Women Deans,* (Spring):27-32.

Nelton, S. and K. Berney. 1987. "Women: The second wave." *Nation's Business,* (May):18-22.

Pleck, Joseph H. 1985. *Working Wives, Working Husbands.* Beverly Hills, CA: Sage.

Reily, P. J. 1980. "Sexual harassment in the Navy." Unpublished master's thesis. U.S. Navy Post Graduate School, Monterey, CA.

Sandroff, R. 1988. "Sexual harassment in the Fortune 500." *Working Woman,* (December:69-73.

Skow, J. 1989. "The myth of male housework." *Time,* (August):62.

Stambaugh, P. 1989. "Sexual harassment: The politics of discourse." Unpublished paper, School of Justice Studies, Arizona State University, Tempe, Arizona.

Thompson, R. 1988. "Caring for the children." *Nation's Business,* 76 (May):20.

U.S. Bureau of the Census. 1988. *Current Population Survey Report.* Washington, D.C.: U.S. Government Printing Office.

U.S. Department of Labor. 1988. *Child Care: A Work Force Issue,* Table B-21. Washington, D.C.: U.S. Government Printing Office.

U.S. Department of Labor. 1989. *Handbook of Labor Statistics.* Washington, D.C.: U.S. Government Printing Office.

U.S. Merit Systems Protection Board. 1987. *Sexual Harassment in the Federal Workplace: Is It a Problem?* Washington, D.C.: U.S. Government Printing Office.

Wallis, C., S. Brown, M. Ludtke, and M. Smiligis. 1989. "Onward women!" *Time,* 4 (December):80-89.

Wall Street Journal. 1990. "A daughter heir apparent isn't heir." *Wall Street Journal,* 9 February:B12.

Food for Thought and Application Questions

1. Kelly lists four different family-related roles for women that often "spill over" into the workplace—daughter, wife, girlfriend, and sex partner/object. Have you ever been pressured at work to conform to any of these roles? Why do you think this particular role was selected? Were there any drawbacks associated with the role? Consider how each of the traditional stereotypes discussed by Kelly is detrimental for women's careers.

2. Select a popular "women's" magazine and examine the advertisements which portray women in a work role. Are there elements of the daughter, wife, girlfriend, and/or sex object roles present in the ads? What messages do these advertisements deliver about working women? ✦

Unit Four

Women's Ways of Working

Who would you rather work for, a man or a woman? Responses to this question are divided, but when the "votes" are tallied, men get the majority. What is interesting about this is not that a majority of the public prefers men managers but the reasons underlying this preference. Preferences for men (or women) managers are rooted in assumptions of differences between the sexes. Some attribute these differences to biology (e.g., men are naturally more aggressive, women's hormonal fluctuations make them ill-suited for the rational decision making); others attribute the differences between men and women managers to gender socialization (e.g., men are socialized to be competitive, women are socialized to nurture). The merits of these two explanations continue to be explored by researchers. Increasingly, scientific research suggests that biology may result in slight patterned differences in behavior for the sexes, but that these differences are by no means sufficient for explaining workplace inequality (Fausto-Sterling 1985).[1] Research on gender socialization continues to show different patterns for the sexes, but also indicates some movement away from traditional models that equip men for positions of mastery and simultaneously discourage women (Karraker, Vogel, and Lake 1995; Lindsey 1994).

The most important explanation for preference for male managers and for the more general perception that "women's ways of working" differ fundamentally from men's is, interestingly, one that often escapes public attention. Workplace performance, "styles" of managing and communicating, and even evaluations of success or failure are determined in large part by the structure and culture of the organization itself. In other words, women's careers (and men's) are affected less by individual traits (whether socialized or resulting from biology) than by structural variables (e.g., the proportion of women in the work position, organizational rules and policies, hierarchical management structures) (Ashburner 1991, 1994; Brown 1988; Cockburn 1991; Kanter 1977).

A now classic example of research addressing the influence of organizational structure on women's work experience is Kanter's research on tokenism. Kanter (1977) argues that women's success in organizations and others' perception of their success is influenced by the proportions in which women find themselves. When women are present in *skewed* groups in organizations (i.e., groups in which there is a great preponderance of men) they are *tokens*, and group dynamics develop to inhibit their success. Tokens, according to Kanter, stand out in relation to the majority group (men), and as a result face numerous performance pressures. Their "difference" serves to marginalize them and causes co-workers and superiors to view their abilities as suspect. Faced with this situation, tokens respond in a variety of ways. Some may overachieve to prove that their "different" status does not impact their ability to perform. Others may flaunt their uniqueness, highlighting that they are the only representative (or one of a few) of their group in the work position. A third possibility is to attempt to assimilate into the dominant group; that is, to downplay differences. For women tokens in the workplace this might mean dressing like men, attending the "impromptu meetings" on the golf course, or joining in the telling of jokes that denigrate women. The problem is that each of these responses requires an expenditure of time and energy that could otherwise be spent on getting the job done. These responses are also problematic because overachievement can lead to burnout or resentment by co-workers, flaunting difference can be viewed as seeking special treatment, and assimilation reinforces the view that to do the job well, one has to be "like a man."

Structural variables like tokenism constrain women's opportunities and limit their success in two key ways. First, they highlight sex differences and make them appear salient when they are irrelevant for job performance (Andersen 1988). Second, they result in differential treatment of the sexes which, in turn, generates real work differences between women and men. The example described in the introduction to this text of women managers being denied organizational resources to back up their authority and thus developing more cooperative management styles illustrates how organizational structure contributes to sex differences.

The selections in this unit examine communication and management style differences between women and men workers that are created, at least in part, by the structure and culture of work organizations. As you read the selections, consider whether the differences being described preceded the worker's entry into the organization or were more likely shaped by their experience in the organization. Also consider whether the differences under discussion serve to advantage or disadvantage working women. Interestingly, two models addressing women in management, the equity model and the complementary contribution model, disagree on the impact of viewing the sexes as different (Adler and Izraeli 1988). From the perspective of the equity model, viewing women as different from men results in their being seen as inferior (Brown 1988; Epstein 1991). The complementary contribution model, in contrast, argues that masking difference serves to negate women's identity and thus their contribution to organizations (Marshall 1984, 1985). Another way of characterizing the two models is to say that the former views difference as a problem, the latter views it as a resource (Adler and Izraeli 1988). It is the opinion of this writer that while difference has the potential to enrich work organizations, the values that currently infuse the cultures of organizations do not often tolerate, much less value, difference. Changing those values and the associated structures of opportunity is a difficult task. Legal mandates (e.g., affirmative action) alone are insufficient to accomplish the change. Highlighting the benefits work organizations can derive from difference, one objective of the complementary contribution model, can help to speed up the pace of change.

The first selection in this unit examines communication differences between the sexes, focusing on dysfunctional patterns of male-female interaction in the workplace which cause women to feel ignored, excluded, patronized, insulted and/or undermined. Reardon refers to these communication patterns as subtle forms of discrimination which inhibit women's ability to succeed in the workplace. After providing examples of dysfunctional communication patterns, she describes both effective and ineffective ways of responding to them. She acknowledges that a number of factors must be considered when attempting to alter communication patterns, including the status of the other party and whether they intentionally communicate so as to disadvantage women. Her suggestions for changing communication patterns that are negative for women include both conforming to a "male" communication style and confronting men about the problems inherent in that style of communicating.

The second selection, based on case studies of four successful women leaders, suggests that women managers exhibit qualities that are both different from those exhibited by male managers and more beneficial to modern work organizations. The women leaders in Helgesen's study describe themselves as "being in the middle of things" or at the center of a weblike structure of leadership. This web extends to roles outside the organization, making it possible for women to integrate their work and private lives. The web structure is in sharp contrast to the hierarchy of authority present in traditional work organizations. Those at the top of traditional management hierarchies, typically men, are required to sacrifice their private lives so as to be successful in the workplace. Helgesen's selection is important because it makes the case that a management style that is disproportionately female is one that is well suited to our information society.

In the next selection, Colwill examines three distinct dimensions of power—personal power, interpersonal power, and organizational power—and discusses them with respect to sex differences. She ac-

knowledges the role of structure in creating power differences between the sexes by noting that when women and men are in similar circumstances, personal power (locus of control) differences disappear. Interpersonal power, the ability to influence others, is suggested by Colwill to be more commonly associated with men. She argues that men's interpersonal power advantage is created and maintained through communication. The dysfunctional patterns of communication described in Chapter 13 provide an illustration of how men use language to tip the power balance in their favor. Surprisingly, Colwill suggests that women have greater organizational power (the ability to get things done) than men, despite the fact that their access to organizational resources and interpersonal power is limited.

The final selection in this unit uses interview data from a sample of women administrators in the field of education to describe an alternative to "macho" management. Court argues that the managerial traits and style of management typically valued by work organizations are not associated with effective management in educational organizations. She concludes that the "holistic" management style employed by the women educators in her study results in improved organizational cultures and enhanced teaching and learning. Her arguments, like those of Helgesen in Chapter 14, point to the value of replacing traditional "masculine" models of management with new models incorporating "feminine" values.

Endnote

1. Biological differences between the sexes are inadequate for explaining workplace inequality not only because they result in very slight behavioral differences, but also because intra-group variation is such that all women and men do not conform to the "typical" pattern. For more information, see the discussion of "overlapping notions" in selection 1 of this text.

References

Adler, N. J. and D. N. Izraeli. 1988. *Women in Management Worldwide*. Armonk, NY: M. E. Sharp.

Andersen, M. 1988. *Thinking About Women: Sociological Perspectives on Sex and Gender*, 2nd Edition. New York: Macmillan.

Ashburner, L. 1994. "Women in management careers: Opportunities and outcomes." In J. Evetts (ed.), *Women and Career: Themes and Issues in Advanced Industrial Societies*. London: Longman.

_____ 1991. "Men managers and women workers: Women employees as an under-used resource." *British Journal of Management*, 2:3-15.

Brown, L. K. 1988. "Female managers in the United States and in Europe: Corporate boards, M.B.A. credentials, and the image/illusion of progress." In J. J. Adler and D. N. Izraeli (eds.), *Women in Management Worldwide*. Armonk, NY: M. E. Sharp:265-274.

Cockburn, C. 1991. *In the Way of Woman: Men's Resistence to Sex Equality in Organisations*. Basingstoke, U.K.: Macmillan.

Epstein, C. 1991. "Debate: Ways men and women lead." *Harvard Business Review*, Jan-Feb:150-152.

Fausto-Sterling, A. 1985. *Myths of Gender*. New York: Basic Books.

Kanter, R. M. 1977. *Men and Women of the Corporation*. New York: Basic Books.

Karraker, K. H., D. A. Vogel and M. A. Lake. 1995. "Parents' gender-stereotyped perceptions of newborns: The eye of the beholder revisited." *Sex Roles*, 33(9/10):687-701.

Lindsey, Linda. 1994. *Gender Roles: A Sociological Perspective*. Englewood Cliffs, NJ: Prentice Hall.

Marshall, J. 1985. "Paths of personal and professional development for women managers." *Management Education and Development*, 16(2):169-179.

_____. 1984. *Women Managers: Travellers in a Male World*. Chichester: Wiley. ✦

13

Dysfunctional Communication Patterns in the Workplace: Closing the Gap Between Women and Men

Kathleen Kelley Reardon

Reginald Strongbrow arrived at his office at 8:02 a.m. The traffic had been heavy. As he sat down at his desk, his boss, Bill Simmons, V.P. of operations, stopped in the doorway. "Strongbrow, you're looking tired today," he said, more as an observation than an expression of concern. "Family problems?" Reginald was taken aback. He didn't feel tired, and there were no family problems. Bill awaited a reply. "No. I'm fine," Reginald said. "Okay," Bill replied as he started to move on. "Get some rest." Reginald sat at his desk wondering whether he looked tired and what Bill's comment about his family had meant.

Reginald glanced up at the clock. It was now 8:30. Attempting to put the remark behind him, Reginald began to peruse the mail on his desk. He came across a copy of the division's newsletter. The front page carried a photo and story about his project team. Reginald was not included in the photo, nor was he mentioned

in the story. Newsletter in hand, he walked down the hall to the office of John Smith, project coordinator. "If you have a moment," Reginald said, "I just saw the story in the newsletter." Smith looked at the newsletter in Reginald's hand and quickly replied, "Oh, that spur-of-the-moment thing. The editor wanted a photo of the team, so we got together and let them take one. I think you were away that morning. We had to meet a print deadline. No big deal though. Right?" This wasn't the first time Reginald had been overlooked, but he decided not to belabor the issue. "No big deal," he said. "Yeah," Smith added, "it isn't even a good photo, and the story is worse. You're lucky you got out of it."

As Reginald returned to his office, he met the division secretary, who said, "You have a meeting with Frank Pillar in ten minutes." Pillar, the CEO, wanted an update on the project team's progress. Reginald entered the conference room early so he could prepare his thoughts. Pillar entered with Bill Simmons at his side. "Hey there, Reginald," Pillar said, smiling. "Bill, check out Reginald's new suit . . . and what a tie! We must be paying him too much." Simmons laughed aloud. Reginald smiled. He could take a joke. Yet he wondered what Pillar had meant. They certainly weren't paying him what he deserved. He considered himself to have good taste and he never bought anything too stylish. Reginald decided to let the comment pass, thinking, "It was probably harmless—no real meaning or message."

During the meeting, Reginald offered his opinion on a project item with which he was intimately familiar. He no sooner began his comment than Bill interrupted him. "Let me just finish this point," Reginald said. The interrupter yielded and Reginald began again to explain his position. Again Bill interrupted him with "I want to be sure we get some closure on this today." Reginald didn't hear much of Bill's remarks beyond that point. He was busy dealing with his annoyance and frustration.

The rest of the day was uneventful. Reginald finished some work between thoughts about what Bill had meant by his early morning comments, about having been excluded from the team photo and story, and then being interrupted. At 6 p.m. he prepared to leave for the day. Bill appeared in the doorway. "Before you go, I want to mention you don't have to worry about the Japan trip. Mike will be going." Reginald's mouth fell open. He had planned on making the trip to Japan, an important one for the company. "What do you mean?" was the only response Reginald could think of at the moment. "Well, with your two kids and Mary working, we didn't think you'd want to be away for a week. Don't give it another thought. It's a done deal. See you tomorrow."

As Reginald walked to his car, he felt drained. "This can't go on," he told himself. "Another day like this and I'm out of here."

Reginald Strongbrow had just experienced what is, for many women, a typical day at work. There is, of course, no Reginald Strongbrow, but if men were to experience the subtle put-downs and frequent quips that keep women feeling unwelcome and devalued, they too would be leaving organizations in large numbers.

As Brenda Snyder, the twenty-eight-year-old outspoken president of US West Women, a lobby for the company's 36,148 women, explained in 1992, "On a surface level for the majority of the corporations, not discriminating against women is rewarded. You just don't hear certain kinds of things. We have come far. But the next mountain is harder to climb, and that is all the stuff you can't see, can't feel, can't touch, but it's there. It's the subtle, subliminal discrimination."[1]

The stuff women can't see, feel, or touch are interactions that leave them feeling ignored, excluded, patronized, insulted, or undermined. Bringing what now seems subliminal out into the open for evaluation and revision is what this chapter is about. Dysfunctional communication patterns (DCPs) are at the heart of the

"stuff" working women can't see, feel, or touch. Identifying and altering them is the only way women will reach leadership positions in significant numbers.

To do so, women must take control over what is said to them and how they're treated. It's time women countered some one-up moves with one-up moves of their own. No more waiting for younger men to be different from their fathers. No more smiling at offense. It is time to confront the obvious: Women will not be welcomed into senior-level positions until and unless they start acting like they belong there. No one expects U.S. Olympians Bonnie Blair or Nancy Kerrigan to walk onto the ice thinking they don't belong there and hoping they won't offend the people who do. That is not a winning posture. Yet it's one many women still cling to—the "grateful to be here" approach.

It bears repeating that women are not only valuable to business, they are indispensable. They have reached critical mass. What remains is for them to believe it and to develop the communication skills for success. It's time to stop wondering about disparaging remarks and to start responding on the spot. It's time to cease worrying about being thought humorless for rejecting offensive jokes. And it's time to expect to be included in important events and selected for key assignments, whether or not you've decided to be a mother.

Dismissive DCPs

The most common dysfunctional pattern of male-female interaction at work involves dismissing women by interrupting, talking over, or ignoring them. "It's as if I'm not there much of the time," a female marketing manager explained to me during a presentation I was making on women reaching the top of their organizations. "I'll say something. They'll look at me and move on as if I hadn't said anything. It's unbelievable." Another woman in the same company described a similar pattern: "I start to say something and they just interrupt. They might say, 'I get the picture, so . . .' and go on with their thoughts or just dismiss what I'm in the process of saying with 'That's not going to work.' How does he know? If he'd let me finish he might learn something. It infuriates me."

Research indicates that men interrupt women more than women interrupt men.[2] It's habit. Women often contribute to the pattern by not insisting upon regaining the floor. They also speak more softly and sometimes take longer to get to the point, so men get impatient. Men are accorded greater credibility as a rule, so people are willing to hear them out. These factors culminate to create environments where women are not heard. They are invisible at some meetings. Tired of being talked over and dismissed, many resort to silence.

Silent retreat perpetuates the problem. It's important to speak up. "I'd like to finish my thoughts" is one possibility. "You may not have meant to interrupt me, Al, but you did" is another. Some women regain the floor by saying, "Let's get back to what I was describing earlier" or "This is important, so I'm not letting it drop."

Nonverbal displays of dominance and status are important here. Men are used to violating the personal space of women. Research shows that women have smaller zones of personal space than men, are touched more often than they touch, sit in "ladylike" ways. Men have a wider range of possible stances indicative of higher status and greater comfort. Women are also more tolerant of personal space violations. They are usually smaller than men, speak in higher pitches, show greater receptivity through eye contact often associated with lower status, and they smile more often.[3]

There are times when these "feminine" ways of communicating are effective. Velma Moore, a real estate agent, told me, "I find that my supportive, understanding approach pays off with my bosses. The two of them are often at each other's throats. They argue all the time. I listen to them and then say, 'Now wait a minute. The two of you aren't disagreeing as much as you

think.' I help them reach an understanding. They appreciate it."

I asked Moore, "Do you think this will get you promoted?" She paused and then said, "You know, I don't know. Maybe it won't." As we later discussed, it's important for women to realize that while the short term rewards for "feminine" ways of communicating are often appealing, the real question is whether relying exclusively on them might lead to misinterpretations of your ability to handle difficult situations, including conflict.

The ways we communicate convey meaning. To the extent that a boss sees a woman subordinate's actions as indicative of nurturance and kindness but not of assertiveness and leadership capability, he is likely to treat her ideas as not deserving of attention and fail to seriously consider her for promotion as well. If his misinterpretation of her communication style is not brought to his attention, she is denied access to senior levels.

Xerox Corporation found that women were being talked over in what several of their employees described to me as a command-and-control environment. It's a top-down, hierarchical, respect-upward-but-not-across-and-downward type of work environment. Xerox senior management decided to give all their people the right to be heard. As one female manager explained, "I can now tell a senior manager who interrupts me, 'You just shut me out.' He'll stop talking and let me finish. He knows that's expected of him now. So, no matter who he is, he has to respect my right to express my opinion."

At Xerox, this practice brought a common pattern of interaction to the forefront of people's minds. Northrop Corporation instituted a similar procedure. At meetings managers who interrupted had to put a few dollars into a charity fund. Shirley Peterson, Northrop Grumman vice president for ethics and business conduct, believes that the process really helped: "People didn't realize they were interrupting each other. They'd just get carried away with their own ideas. We had times when someone would throw his money onto the table and say, 'I can't take it, I have to interrupt.' It put some humor into the learning process."

Corporate rules for altering DCPs may prove useful. But in time, as happened at Northrop, the charm wears off and people return to their old ways. In such cases, the responsibility rests on the shoulders of individuals. Women and men must make concerted efforts to disallow Dismissive DCPs. The best way is to develop a repertoire of phrases that allow people to regain the floor. For example, "I'd like to hear Frances finish her thought" or "You're like a bull in a china shop, Jack. Let Madeline complete her sentence" can be used to assist others. For the person whose allies are absent or quiet, the following floor-regaining phrases are useful: "You guys can hear me out now or never hear the end of it. Your choice," "Sit back, Bill, I plan to finish my thought this time," or "Take a breath, Larry, I'd like to get a word in edgewise."

Style preferences, status of the offender, degree of offense, intentionality, and fear of retaliation enter into women's response choices. Most women prefer to avoid alienating coworkers with direct comebacks to interruptions and dismissals. Some are even willing to wait for the retirement or death of the offenders to bring an end to sexism. Life is much too short for that. Besides, there is a wide range of responses to offensive behaviors. Among them, demure silence is the least effective.

Passed Over

Women are also dismissed when they are overlooked for promotion. "It happened to me," said Marion Spicer, a thirty-two-year-old manager at a small executive search company. "One time they promoted a guy to manager of the division I'd been holding together. He lacked experience. Every time he made a decision, he had to come to me first. I was the invisible manager making all the decisions but getting none of the pay. It was crazy. In time they figured it out. By then we had more women and they had to promote some of us. But many good people left in the process, and the rest of us still remember and wonder if those days won't return."

Notice the phrase "In time they figured it out." Why wait for that? When I ask that question, many women say, "It just doesn't sound right to whine about a situation like that" or "You don't want to be labeled a complainer." There is truth to the common belief that people don't like chronic complainers and whiners. But it isn't necessary to whine. And a legitimate complaint worded in a nonpersonal manner is better than silence. Marion could have refused to help the fledgling manager look good. I haven't met many men who provide constant assistance to former peers promoted to positions they wanted. Yet many women do this. What the company gets is a two-for-one deal. They get the woman's expertise and a satisfied male. Spicer was concerned that she would appear a "spoilsport" if she did not help. And she might have had she refused to help at all. But she didn't have to prop him up on a day-to-day basis.

Losing Credit

Another means of dismissing women involves stealing their ideas. To women it seems amazing, but Clara Ferris, training director for a high-tech firm, thinks men often don't see it as stealing: "Women are very careful to include other people in their proposals. They'll say, 'As Mark mentioned earlier' or 'Chuck's idea is key here.' They give credit. Sometimes to a fault. Men don't go to great lengths to make sure people are credited, so it looks like they're stealing an idea when they don't mention the original source."

Here's an alternative explanation: They're so used to not listening to women that they probably half hear an idea when a woman presents it. They think it came from their own brain. In other cases they know she won't speak up to retrieve ownership, so they usurp her thoughts and call them their own. Whatever the reason, it is infuriating.

Whether ideas are stolen from women purposely or inadvertently is less important than how women respond when it happens. When I ask women, "What did you do about it?" most reply, "At the time I just fumed" or "You can't blurt out, 'That was my idea.' It sounds like you're grabbing individual attention." These are dysfunctional responses. They merely perpetuate a bad situation.

Here are a few functional responses.

"Hey, Tom. That was my idea. Hands off. You're ruining it."

"Tom, get your own idea, that one was mine. When I proposed that plan I had something slightly different in mind."

"I'm taking that idea back. You guys are butchering it."

"That plan sounds a lot like the one I mentioned earlier."

There are times when retrieving stolen ideas is not worth the effort. But when big stakes are involved, it is unwise to let ideas pass quietly into the hands of others. For those who abhor what some women have described to me as "making a scene," there is always the behind-closed-doors approach. A visit to the office of the person who stole the idea might work just as well as exposing his folly in public. The following repertoire of approaches ranges from direct to subtle.

DIRECT: I have just five words to say about your usurping my idea in there today: Don't let it happen again!

STRONG: We can work well together, Jim. Just remember to give credit where it's due. By the end of the meeting, I think everyone thought my project upgrade was yours. You know, two can play that game.

MODERATE: I don't know what you were thinking in that meeting today,

Jim. I'd appreciate at least a footnote next time you borrow one of my ideas.

MILD: Jim, you might have directed some credit my way in that meeting.

Idea stealing and credit grabbing are on the increase. It's important to learn how to handle such situations. According to the *Wall Street Journal*, competition for jobs is fostering conditions conducive to back stabbing.[4] Idea and credit snatching is a form of back stabbing when it is purposeful. You have to locate the source and end it quickly. The price of doing anything less can be high.

Retaliatory DCPs

During a task force meeting I'd been invited to attend as a consultant, the mostly female group of managers from across the country focused their discussion on the slow pace of female promotions in this stereo products company. A male manager in his mid-thirties who had been conspicuously silent for hours finally spoke up. Apparently tired of watching his female colleagues struggle to identify reasons why women had not reached the top of this mid-sized international company, he said, "Let me tell you what's really bothering a lot of us. Most of the men I know got burned one time or another by a woman. They haven't forgotten that. Women may have dumped them in elementary school or in college. Whenever it happened, it hurt. I remember when a girl came up to me in the fifth grade and said, 'Kate doesn't want to be your girlfriend anymore, so don't call her.' That was cruel, but it wasn't unusual—not where I grew up. After a while, you started distrusting girls and later women. I know women get hurt too. But men are more fragile than they appear. They remember."

Another male manager provided additional support by saying, "I don't think most men are willing to admit the degree to which women are a threat. If a man criticizes or beats you, that's one thing. But when a woman does it, you're more humiliated. We're talking emotional reactions here. Men know women are equally competent on a rational level, but they don't want to deal with it on an emotional level."

As these men spoke, I was reminded of a conversation I'd had some weeks earlier with a male colleague. Walking across campus to an executive education program we were to deliver together, the conversation turned to racquetball. He had just won a game. I told him I hadn't played in a while. Before I could utter another word, he said, "I'd challenge you to a game, but you might win." I told him that was not likely given that I hadn't played in two years. "Nevertheless," he said, "can't do it. It's bad enough when one of the guys beats me, I don't want to suffer the grief I'd get if you won." Losing to a woman on the racquetball court was frightening to this man. When I ran this story past a male business associate of mine who is a successful real estate lawyer, I half expected he would say, "That guy needs help." Instead he said, "I can see his point. I wouldn't want to play racquetball with you either. Men don't like to lose to women. I should know. I'm one of them."

As a rule, women are aware of and fearful of men's discomfort with their competence. At a *Daily News* Conference where I was a speaker, a female sales manager raised her hand. In response to my comments on the hesitancy of women to speak up when they disagree with male peers and bosses, she said, "I used to think that they really wanted me to debate the issues with them, to play the devil's advocate, but more often than not, they don't. If I have recommendations that might make prior practices look questionable, they want to hear about them in private. At first I thought this was just a company culture thing, but it's not. They criticize each other in public and debate. With me, it's different. I have to introduce my thoughts gently or they ignore me. No one wants a woman to make him look bad."

Women who come into jobs hoping to prove themselves worthy of promotion are the ones most likely to inadvertently make one or more men look bad. Focused on getting ahead, they don't notice the havoc created by their abilities. It's a double bind for women. Male colleagues tell women, "We're the best, and we expect the best. It won't be easy for you. You'll have to work long and hard." When the new female recruit does exactly as advised, she jeopardizes relationships with those around her who consider her "overly gung ho" or a "pitbull."

This, too, is a dysfunctional communication pattern. Not all DCPs are conversations. Some, like this one, are long-term ways of relating to each other. Men tell women that they will have to be the best in order to keep up with them. But they are expected to do so quietly. They are not supposed to disagree. If they do, they risk retaliation because, in many cases, a disagreeing woman is a threat. In the not-so-distant past, women had little to say publicly about work. Now they do. And in many cases, it reminds men that their territory is being encroached upon by people who shouldn't know more than they do.

In 1983 Eugene Koprowski turned to mythology for his *Organizational Dynamics* article prediction that there would be considerable "footdragging and resistance on the part of the male power structure" in the quest for female social equity at work. He explained that "historically, men have developed very ambivalent feelings toward women and the powerful elements in nature that they symbolize. Men currently hold the upper hand in terms of power in our society, and they are not likely to relinquish that power to women without a struggle."[5] The basis for male ambivalence comes, Koprowski argued, from long-held views of women.

While the status of women in myths suggests they have historically held a secondary role, the symbolic value of women in myths suggests that they have been historically feared as well as desired and possessed by men. Jung, who spent much of his professional career studying the psychological meaning of symbols and myths, suggests that women through the ages have come to symbolize the following: maternal solicitude and sympathy; magic authority; wisdom and spiritual exaltation that transcends reason; helpful instinct or impulse; all that is benign; all that cherishes and sustains; all that fosters growth and fertility; magic transformation and rebirth; the underworld and its inhabitants; anything that is secret, hidden, dark; the abyss; the world of the dead; anything that devours, seduces, and poisons or that is terrifying and inescapable like fate or death.[6]

If Jung was correct, that men respond to women not only as people but as symbols, men are both attracted to and fearful of them. The fear is increased at work, where the presence of women as equals or bosses is relatively new. There are those who will say that this is a lot of nonsense. But such nonsense is at the heart of the subtle stuff women trip over on their path to the top. Women know that one way to elicit fear and retaliation is to challenge men who still have one foot, or two, squarely entrenched in historical symbols of femininity.

Ann Wilk, a forty-five-year-old insurance company senior vice president, has a solution. "I do a lot of behind-the-scenes discussions of ideas," she says. "Rather than surprise men with an idea that they may not agree with, I talk to them before the meeting. Two benefits come from this approach: I learn the weaknesses and strengths of my idea and, when the idea is good, I gain support for it prior to the meeting."

I've shared Wilk's approach with other women. Some think it is too demure. "Why should a woman have to go behind the scenes to sell her ideas?" is one reasonable question. If a woman cannot express herself without fear of retaliation, then she isn't really equal to men, is what some

women think when they consider the behind-the-scenes approach. As with most strategies for changing DCPs, some are more comfortable than others. Most women who make it as far as Ann Wilk has do so because they save their major thunder for situations that count.

Another approach is to let the person most likely to disagree know that you expect him to be disappointed in your decision to oppose him but that you must do so for reasons that you then describe. The following example was taken from a conversation between a female and a male computer products manager. The male manager had proposed a strategy for expediting product launches. The female manager, Elise, had some reservations.

> *Elise*: You may find what I have to say unsettling, Jeff, but I can't support this proposal. It doesn't address the role outside vendors play and the slow-ups we have working with our own subsidiaries. If there is a way to address those, I'm open to it.

The success of this approach depends to a large extent on the corporate culture and the relationship between the two people involved. Elise spoke with conviction and avoided personalizing this issue by saying "this proposal" rather than "your proposal." She laid out objective criteria for judging the proposal and expressed willingness to reconsider if her concerns were met. It worked. Jeff took her comments as they were intended and entered into a discussion with Elise about outside vendor and subsidiary challenges.

If Elise had been subordinate to Jeff, her approach might have been different. If men do not like being corrected or challenged by women who are their equals, they like it even less when the woman is a subordinate. As Felice Schwartz wrote in her book *Breaking with Tradition*: "Women know from their first entrance into the gleaming headquarters of the company that although male senior managers pay public tribute to the need for women in the work force, their underlying feelings are more ambivalent."[7]

For many men, lurking beneath the surface rhetoric is a readiness to treat a female subordinate's disagreement as an indication of ingratitude for the acceptance they and the company have shown by letting her take a management position. There is still a perception that men are "letting" women into companies. It is an antiquated notion but one with a considerable afterlife.

With a boss who thinks like this, Elise should word her response in a nonpersonal manner and speak with conviction while avoiding the impression that she has disregarded the status difference between herself and her boss:

Elise: We need to get this project on the road, Jeff, but it is in the interests of the company to consider outside vendor buy-in and slow-ups at subsidiaries. If we ignore those, we destine this project to failure.

Here Elise is using the company's interests as a frame for her position. She says "we" rather than "I," suggesting a team concern. She recognizes the need to get the project on the road, but implies that speed, while important, is secondary to a comprehensive, potentially successful plan. She is speaking in business language and doing so with conviction in a manner likely to avoid personal affront.

A second alternative is for Elise to skip the idea that the boss is missing the point and offer assistance in making his idea work:

Elise: In order to make this a foolproof plan we'll need vendor buy-in and subsidiary support. I'd be glad to take that on with some help, Jeff.

Elise has moved to the solution rather than introducing the problem. Instead of asking for permission to help out, she has offered to take charge of a team to solve the problem. He may choose to deny her offer. If he does, she hasn't lost anything.

If he accepts her offer, she has turned what could have been construed as criticism into an opportunity to work more closely with Jeff on an issue important to him.

Another option is the "cease-to-care" approach. Here the decision to disagree with a male superior or peer is made with full knowledge that he might not like it. Most women find this difficult. They manage their language to avoid personal affront and conflict. They sense what research confirms: although aggressive behaviors may be perceived as more competent, they are less likable.[8] What women often fail to recognize is that men come to expect them to tiptoe around important issues. But they also wonder if the tiptoer has anything substantive to offer.

Lisa Hill Fenning, a U.S. Bankruptcy judge, concurs. "Female lawyers often want to be liked," she says. "Respect and some fear is usually more effective. There's a mismatch of expectations for women. Men tend to look outside the workplace for emotional support. Women still believe they can get support at work if they do a good job. I'm not advocating dislike. You don't need to make enemies, but you don't need to constantly seek approval either. Trying to give everyone what they want is a subordinate, supportive role. Do this enough and male partners can't envision you as a potential equal who can make competent decisions."

Worrying too much about men being offended is dysfunctional. Besides, many of the senior women I meet have come to the conclusion that women overestimate the extent to which men devote time to considering their own communication styles and those of others. Clara Ferris of Hewlett-Packard believes that women forget that most men don't notice all the subtle nuances of language that women fear they'll find offensive. "Words have more levels of meaning for women than they do for men," says Ferris. "Women read into things and wonder what men meant. They discuss the possibilities and imagine that men do the same. They don't. Men are straighter, more direct. Women have learned to watch carefully how they phrase things. They agonize over words and they think men do too."

What women see as the subtle meanings of words, which they manage carefully to avoid affront, are often not received as such by men. Agonizing over how a male peer or boss might take something can be counterproductive. While the woman is worrying, men are stepping up and being heard. In such circumstances, it is better to be heard if it means saying, "Please excuse the following absence of eloquence, but this plan is on a fast track to nowhere without vendor support and subsidiary buy-in."

Patronizing DCPs

Women find themselves left out of important decisions quite frequently. Then they are told, "Don't worry about it" or "It was nothing personal. We just had to make a decision." Time and again they are given the impression that their contributions are secondary; their opinions afterthoughts. Patronizing behaviors deny the value of women's contributions.

Before discussing ways to prevent and terminate patronizing behavior, it's important to note the role women often play in perpetuating it. Research indicates that differences in nonverbal behaviors occur not only as a function of the sex of the person but a function of the sex of those around that person. For example, women tend to smile less in the presence of women than in the presence of men. Women are more likely to behave in "in-role" or stereotypical ways when they are with men. Whether men have more latitude is not known. But anecdotal evidence suggests that they also rely more on "in-role" stereotypically male modes of conduct when in the presence of women.

In her educator role at a top office products company, Clara Ferris shares with women what she sees as a tendency for men to relate to women as wives, mothers, or daughters. "Colleague is a hard category for many men to apply to women. Men become paternal, flirtatious, or dependent in the presence of women. They convey expectations to women by acting in these ways." But Ferris warns, "Women often respond to such expectations without thinking. Women find father figures, knights, big brothers, and confessors in men. Their language expresses this. When they do this, women mess up men's heads too." What Ferris has identified is the reciprocal nature of any pattern. It is always important to ask: Am I contributing to the recurrence of this way of relating? If the answer is affirmative, the first step is to change your own behaviors.

The following conversation is an example of a patronizing DCP.

Kelly: The meeting time you're suggesting isn't going to work for me.

Edward: We have to schedule it then.

Kelly: Why?

Edward: Kelly, everybody knows you have a lot of outside demands with your family, so if you miss the meeting it won't be a problem.

Kelly: My family has nothing to do with this.

Edward: You know, you look stressed and tired.

Kelly: My fatigue level is irrelevant.

Edward: I think it would be better if we talk about this after you've rested up.

A close look at Kelly and Edward's conversation reveals how women end up frustrated by patronizing DCPs. Edward is pressing his agenda without regard for Kelly's input. In fact, he is rejecting her input since, he explains, it comes from a person with too many family demands and a high stress and fatigue level. Unfortunately, Kelly defends her family involvement, fatigue level, and stress level. She tries to get Edward back on track, but he resists. In her efforts to revise his image of her, she neglects to notice that what he said is inappropriate and unworthy of a cordial reply. By continuously using one-down defense moves Kelly is yielding control of the interchange to Edward. She is letting him play the knowledgeable big brother or dad and contributing to a way of relating that is dysfunctional.

In hindsight, one of Kelly's options was to direct the conversation back to a nonpersonal track. The following is an example.

Kelly: That meeting time won't work for me.

Edward: We have to schedule it then.

Kelly: Why?

Edward: Listen, Kelly, everybody knows you have a lot of outside demands with your family, so if you miss the meeting it won't be a problem.

Kelly: Your concern for my family is noted, Edward, but let's stick with the subject of the meeting time. I have my calendar here. I see you have yours.

This is abrupt. But it gets the conversation back onto a business track. It is better than Kelly allowing Edward to define her personal life as a reason for not attending a meeting she clearly wishes to attend. At least this approach cuts off the personal aspect of the prior interaction and gets Kelly out of a defensive stance.

Patronizing can also center on work ability. Catalyst, a New York-based research organization devoted to women's business issues, conducted a study focused on female engineers in thirty corporations. One of their conclusions was that communication becomes very important at senior levels. As one female engineer explained,

Once you've gotten past the second or third level of management . . . even for men, that's the level where things may be based more on the comfort factor and on whether you went to the same school, whether you have a Mason's ring on, than it is based on your technical expertise. They feel if you've reached that level already, you've got to be technically qualified. So that's the point at which your management skills and your style have to meld better with the people you're working with—it becomes more important than your technical skills—that's the point at which I think women experience greater problems.[9]

This same study indicates that women face a "double-edged sword" when they attempt to meld with men by communicating like them. An authoritative management style is viewed negatively in women, yet a more humanistic, participatory style is not respected. Women engineers in this study advised other women to "smile a lot" to avoid offending men.[10] This may avoid offense, but it sends the message that the smiler is not angry—a green light to continue patronizing her.

In most cases, the best response to patronizing communication is a refusal to honor it. The means being unwilling even to talk about personal matters and refusing to allow pats on the back and hugs to hide the fact that someone is not listening and not caring about your input. The emotion must fit the seriousness of the situation. Quips about motherly duties and family obligations must be nipped in the bud. Consider the experience of a female high-technology manager:

Before I started a new assignment my boss said, 'Oh, by the way, I want you to know that you've got a couple of trips coming up. I thought I should let you know so you could cook up some meals and freeze them.' I just started laughing, and told him that my husband does 80 percent of our cooking and grocery shopping. After a while you learn how to deal with those kinds of comments, but there is no way that would have ever been said to a man coming into a job.[11]

Rather than laugh and explain her husband's duties, why not say what she is thinking: "You wouldn't say that to a man, would you, Will?"

Some women consider demure, pleasant reactions to patronizing remarks as a way of "rolling with the punches." They are rolling themselves right out of senior management. A consulting firm associate believes sometimes you have to be direct if the comment is condescending. One recommendation: "I'm letting that comment pass this time." A less abrupt alternative is "You buy the tickets, Frank, I'll take care of my family's menu." If he cares, he'll give it some thought. If he doesn't at least you know where you stand and you haven't affirmed it by letting another DCP slip by.

Pregnant and Patronized

The time when women feel most patronized is during pregnancy. In 1993 pregnancy-related complaints to the Equal Employment Opportunity Commission reached a six-year high, which the *Wall Street Journal* described as "reflecting the impact of widespread layoffs and mounting workplace tension over sex roles."[12] The popular trend of downsizing even when companies are profitable has magnified the impact of pregnancy. Add to this the increasing number of women becoming pregnant in their late thirties and early forties and the fact that the salaries of many of these women are equal to or above those of spouses. The result is comments like the one I received recently from a program director whose college-aged children, he admits, were principally raised by their mothers: "I know I'm not supposed to say this, but pregnant women are getting to be a real problem for us. Each time one of them gets pregnant, the whole program is upset."

I heard this same sentiment expressed one week later in a different department of the same company. Closer scrutiny revealed that the source of these directors' problem was not so much pregnant women as penny-pinching superiors expecting them to get by without hiring temporary help during the pregnant women's leave. They were focusing their antagonism in the wrong direction. The woman was the easier target.

Such attitudes toward pregnant women enter into workplace communication. Even if the woman keeps her job, the communication climate she experiences during and after pregnancy is different from any she had previously known.

"I did everything to hide it," Miranda Simonson, regional manager for a Los Angeles-based mid-sized company, explained. "But I gained a lot of weight and my stomach entered the room long before I did. Back then there were more men in the company. They talked to me differently after my pregnancy became visible. I felt like all the work I'd done to build my credibility went out the window. They treated me like I was barefoot and pregnant. My body told them my brain wasn't working anymore. And even after the baby was born, I couldn't regain the credibility I'd lost. My body and my life had become public domain. People came in to ask me questions that weren't their business. Everyone was so focused on my condition that they forgot to notice that my brain was still intact."

Even those women who breeze through pregnancy without illness find that their credibility is compromised. "You look like a boat. There are a few dresses that look good, but not many," a working mother with a newborn told me. "But worse than that, men talk to you in silly ways. They say things like 'You're glowing now,' which is supposed to mean pregnancy suits me. Or they start planning my life after the baby's birth—'You won't want that assignment. It means some travel. We'll give it to Jim.' The irony is that Jim has three little kids. He doesn't want to be away from home."

Miranda Simonson doesn't view the way men treat you when you're pregnant as just a product of forgetting to think about what they say. "To me it's sabotage," she says. "People are so busy validating their own weaknesses, they are pleased to consider someone's ability compromised. They write you off as if all the work you did was for nothing. It leaves more room for them. They also say things like 'You don't really expect to work full time?' or 'Who will take care of the baby?' None of these things are any of their business. It's just a way to make women feel guilty. None of the men have to listen to that stuff when they become fathers. So why should I?"

Combining career and baby is certainly demanding. But not half as demanding as dealing with thoughtless comments about maternal demands. Children can make their very accomplished adult parents feel insecure. When little people are depending on you, all the advanced degrees and impressive credentials in the world are often insufficient to assure you that you're doing right by them. Child rearing is filled with questions: Am I feeding them well? Have I encouraged them enough? Do they know how much I love them? Under such circumstances "cheap shots" and uninvited advice can cause considerable harm.

One of my male colleagues is the father of triplet toddlers. He is very involved with them. But he readily admits that people do not treat him as any less committed to his job. They don't act as if his brain is functioning less efficiently, although he'll also admit that he is balancing a lot of details. He believes that "it's just different if you're a woman. To many people, women aren't the same after children. It's ridiculous but true."

The long-term solution to this problem is enlightened companies viewing family as the responsibility of both men and women. This could be a long wait. Until division-of-labor stereotypes become more balanced, women must decide whether they wish to contribute to DCPs that undermine their career goals. The following patronizing DCP is a case in point.

Steve: Boy, it must be difficult for you to work and raise your child too.

Mary: It's a challenge at times.

Steve: A while back my wife and I decided we wouldn't pass the responsibil-

ity of raising our children on to strangers.

Mary: We haven't done that.

Steve: Oh, of course you haven't. I didn't mean to imply that you aren't a good mother.

Mary: Mark and I share the responsibility and it works out.

Steve: Sue and I share a lot too, but she is at home with the children so both of us can focus on what we need to do.

This conversation places Mary in the position of defending her decision to work. It elicits guilt and implies that doing well means being able to totally focus on home and family. In the first place, Mary's childcare decisions are not Steve's business. To discuss them with him, especially after he has implied that strangers bring up the children of working mothers, gives Steve the impression that it is okay to make derogatory comments about a woman's career/family decisions. Mary's reactions are defensive—"We haven't done that"—or explanatory/defensive—"Mark and I share the responsibility and it works out." She could have avoided this interaction by responding to Steve's comment about the decision he and his wife made with "I have to run to a meeting" or "Best of luck with that decision, Steve. See you later."

These comments cut off further discussion. Impolite? Perhaps. But he isn't exactly Mr. Etiquette. For Mary, the important thing is to exit the conversation or say something that brings the discussion to an early termination. If she wants him to know that she considers his comments insulting, she might try silence as a response to his comment about children being raised by strangers. Or she might say, "I don't see it that way, Steve. But this is no time to discuss child-rearing practices." This last option is useful because it lets Steve know that she does not agree with him. It dismisses the interaction as inappropriate. It does not attack Steve on a personal level. If Steve is educable, some benefits might accrue from encouraging him to consider the appropriateness of his comments.

Patronizing patterns of communication survive as long as there are willing participants available. Whether they are about children, work commitment, loyalty, capacity to lead, or absence of "real experiences," they do little other than place the female participant in a defensive or apologetic posture. Neither is beneficial to her career.

Exclusionary DCPs

In the course of my interviews with senior executives for this book, a CEO told me in confidence that there is a solution to "the problem of women working with men." He explained, "The answer is to have two standards of communication: one used when women are present and one when they're not. When I was younger, that is what we had. When you were in the presence of women, you knew not to say certain things. You didn't swear or make off-color remarks. You didn't comment on women unless it was to praise their looks or clothes. You treated them with what we thought was respect. Now things are all jumbled up. But we still need two standards. When you're with men, you can let loose. With women you have to be more careful."

As I explained to this CEO, the double-standard approach is destined to failure. Most women do not like double standards and they are not blind to them. A female senior marketing director for a major toy manufacturer had an experience that was still infuriating her when she told me about it. "The other day the CEO was describing some new plans at a directors meeting. He got annoyed with some idea and started swearing. Two seconds into his tirade, he turned to me and said, 'I'm sorry, Sue.' I looked around. Everyone was looking at me. He hadn't apologized to any of them. Why to me? All that does is separate me out. I didn't care for it one bit," she said.

Women consider this kind of treatment a form of exclusion from the club. It underscores that they are not entirely one of the group. Even those who believe the person doing it is attempting to be polite don't care for it. Many women reject the polite theory. The female marketing director believes that "they do it to remind you and everyone there that you are not 'in' and that your presence shouldn't delude anyone into thinking that you are."

Another reason for rejecting the double-standard approach is that in all likelihood one of the standards will be considered superior to the other. Usually it is the male one. Double standards, even ones that seem to address difficulties, perpetuate inequities. Treating women differently from men, rather than trying to address similarities and differences, only serves to perpetuate the discomfort men often feel when women are around. The double-standard answer is too simplistic a solution for a complex problem.

Exclusion takes many forms—physical and verbal. Women are excluded physically or verbally from important interactions. A female law partner of a prestigious New York-based law firm told me of a situation where two male lawyers were discussing aloud their plans to arrange a gathering with important clients. Two other male lawyers and two female lawyers were in the room. "The male lawyers planning the client gathering invited the male lawyers along. Nothing was said to the females. The expenses were being covered by the firm. The two female lawyers came to my office to complain. They had clearly been excluded from an important event. I went straight to the most senior partner, explained the matter, and told him this kind of thing has to stop. We've been losing female lawyers left and right and they're still pulling this stuff."

At another law firm, a female partner confided to me what she described as the ultimate environment of exclusion: "There is one barrier we'll never break through and that is the men's room door. When you pee next to someone, it has a certain bonding effect. Status lines break down at the urinals."

I've studied the exclusion of women in various types of organizations. Much of it is neither purposeful nor vengeful on the part of men. Instead men have grown up with what Erving Goffman, author of *Interaction Ritual*, terms "involvement rules." According to Goffman, expectations regarding involvement are learned and conventional. They vary across cultures. They also vary across genders. On a less-than-conscious level, men simply do not believe women warrant the same level of involvement as men. Women pose what Goffman refers to as subordinate rather than dominant involvement demands.[13]

Men have learned to tune out the words of women because women are usually considered peripheral to the "dominating activity" at hand. What women have to say is assumed to be of less value because women have historically been excluded from important nondomestic decisions. In many companies, women who reach the top are ones whose competence is beyond question. They are women who leave no doubt that they can make it in a man's league.

Prior to making a dinner presentation at a company launching a diversity program, I was introduced by the CFO. In his remarks he praised the group and discussed at some length the company's commitment to promote women despite their admitted less-than-impressive track record in that area. As he was completing his remarks, an idea came to his mind. "I just thought of something," he said, eyes wide and smiling with discovery. He added words to this effect: "There is a woman who should be here tonight. She should be on our diversity team. She represents what we're looking for. Alison Cray is a manager in our European office. Now there is someone women can look to as a role model. Alison has a Ph.D. in physics, she is an accomplished pianist and violinist. She made the Olympic pretrials as an equestrian and has won numerous skiing championships. She should be here, she'd be perfect."

I watched as the women around the table looked down at their napkins, reached quickly to sip from their glasses, exchanged furtive glances, or rolled their eyes. "She sounded perfect all right," one of them later said to me. "Apparently that is what they're looking for. Any females who don't measure up to Ph.D. Olympians, playing concert violin when not conducting physics experiments, winning equestrian medals, or skiing down death-defying slopes aren't senior management material. Do you believe he said that at a diversity meeting? What planet is he on?"

Often diversity committee members are selected by men who think this way. Poorly devised diversity committees are worse than none at all. In such environments women either express anger or remain silent. The ones who do the former often leave. Those who do the latter eventually give up any ambition to succeed or leave. This is a waste of time and talent. If a woman is being excluded, what does she have to lose by bringing it to the attention of the excluder? She is already being left out. She might as well take the initiative to speak up for herself. If the excluder isn't responsive, it's time to be less responsive to his needs. It may be necessary to spell that out for him too. "I'd be glad to help with that, Phil. And I'd be glad to be at the top of the list for the Parker project. Is it a deal?"

A male colleague of mine turns nearly everything he does for people into a deal. I've cringed at times listening to him get a payback for what I considered a minor favor. But he has done well for himself. He may overdo it at times. No one likes to be indebted to someone for the loan of a pencil. But there is something to be said for assuming that you are included in important events. When exclusion is purposeful, the task of inserting oneself into important events is more difficult. Kate Watson, marketing manager for the research division of a top office products company, found that it was easy for her to be excluded from important international trips to meet major customers. "If I complained, it went in one ear and out the other. One of my colleagues suggested a different approach. He advised me to assume I will be included in the trip. He suggested that I stop by my boss's office a few months before the trip with my calendar in hand. Then I should say, 'Bill, when is that trip to Japan? I want to clear my calendar in advance.' It worked."

This is a case of nipping an Exclusionary DCP before it happens again. Rather than address the problem in a way that men may interpret as female "whining," it is sometimes better just to assume that you are included, plan on it, make the arrangements, and let them go to the trouble of explicitly excluding you. Then their actions are not deniable. They cannot be attributed to forgetting or a minor oversight.

Being able to identify and respond effectively to "the subtle stuff" is imperative if women and men are to change the way they interact at work. It is, after all, the day-to-day interactions between people that constitute the communication climate of an organization. Family-friendly programs cannot make up for daily attacks on women's credibility and competence.

Being overlooked, underpaid, dismissed, passed over, ignored, and undermined on a daily basis takes its toll. It accounts, in large part, for the significant number of women leaving traditional organizations to become entrepreneurs. . . .

Endnotes

1. "The New Old Boy," *Glamour*, February 1992, p. 197.

2. A. Mulac and J. J. Bradac. 1995. "Women's style in problem solving interactions: Powerless, or simply feminine?" In P. J. Kalbfleisch and M. J. Cody (Eds.), *Gender, Power, and Communication in Human Relationships*. Hillsdale, NY: Erlbaum.

3. I. H. Frieze, J. E. Parsons, P. B. Johnson, D. N. Ruble, and G. L. Zellman. 1978. *Women and Sex Roles: A Social Psychological Perspective*. New York: W. W. Norton.

4. T. Lee. 1993. "Competition for jobs spawns backstabbers and a need for armour." *Wall Street Journal*, p. B1.

5. E. J. Koprowski. 1983. "Cultural myths: Clues to effective management." *Organizational Dynamics*, Autumn:43.

6. Ibid., p. 42.

7. F. N. Schwartz. 1992. *Breaking with Tradition*. New York: Warner Books.

8. D. J. Canary and B. H. Spitzberg. 1987. "Appropriateness and effectiveness perceptions of conflict strategies." *Human Communication Research*, Fall.

9. Catalyst, "Women in Engineering: An Untapped Resource." New York, 1992, p. 35.

10. Ibid., p. 24.

11. Catalyst, "On the Line." New York, 1992, p. 28.

12. "As more pregnant women work, bias complaints rise." 1993. *Wall Street Journal*, December 6:B1.

13. E. Goffman. 1967, 1982. *Interaction Ritual: Essays on Face-to-Face Behavior*. New York: Pantheon Books.

Food for Thought and Application Questions

1. Reardon suggests that women face a dilemma when they communicate with male co-workers. If women exhibit a "masculine" communication style, they are viewed as overly aggressive, domineering, and are not liked by their male co-workers. If, on the other hand, they communicate in a "feminine" way, they are perceived as weak, less capable, and are not respected. How can this dilemma be resolved? Will confrontation work? Silence? These two responses result in quite different stereotypes for the

woman using them. What are the stereotypes, and how are they detrimental to workplace success?

2. Analyze the interaction that occurs in a mixed sex group for the presence of dysfunctional communication patters (DCPs). If you are participating actively in the interaction, the group should consist of at least two additional members, one male and one female. (It is difficult to simultaneously analyze and communicate, so it is best to observe others communicating.) Which, if any, of the DCPs described by Reardon were present? Did the participants in the mixed sex group conform to typical "masculine" and "feminine" communication patterns? If so, what impressions did these styles create of the participants? If not, did nonconformity by one participant result in a negative or surprised reaction from the other participant(s)? Explain. ✦

14

Women's Ways of Leading

Sally Helgesen

It is lunchtime in the pink-and-green garden dining room of the Cosmopolitan Club in upper Manhattan, the all-women's club started by Abigail Rockefeller when the Union, her husband's club, refused to serve her. The atmosphere is genteel, with stone planters trailing petunias and women mostly over fifty, some even wearing hats with veils.

It seems an unlikely place in which to be discussing modern leadership and management techniques, but I am with Frances Hesselbein, chief executive of the Girl Scouts, a woman who bridges the paradox with ease. With her low, well-disciplined voice, Hermes scarf and bag, and grooming so perfect you expect that, like the Duchess of Windsor, she must polish the soles of her shoes, Frances Hesselbein clearly belongs to the world represented by the Cosmopolitan Club. Yet she is also the woman who brought modern management to her organization with such success that Peter Drucker called her "perhaps the best professional manager in America."

I am attempting to interview her, despite the club's rather archaic ban on "visible paper"; apparently ladies are not to engage in business over lunch. So I am balancing my notebook on my knees under a napkin and scribbling without looking while an elderly waitress serves Parker House rolls with silver tongs. Frances Hesselbein is describing the management structure she devised for the Girl Scouts, a replacement for the old hierarchical pyramid.

The new system is circular, she explains; positions are represented as circles, which are then arranged in an expanding series of orbits. "I use circles," she says, "because symbolically they are important. The circle is an organic image. We speak of the *family* circle. The circle is *inclusive*, but it allows for flow and movement; the circle doesn't box you in! I've always conceived of management as a circular process. When I was head of my regional organization, I devised a structure similar to the one I'm using now. It wasn't something I'd read I should do, it was just something I felt. These days, there are all these theories about the circular management model, but with me it was intuitive—this attraction I've always had to the circle."

Suddenly, Frances Hesselbein seizes a wooden pepper mill and sets it in the middle of our table. "This is me," she says, "in the center of the organization." She moves a glass of iced tea and several packets of sugar to form a circle around the pepper mill. "And this is my management team, the first circle." Using cups and saucers, Frances Hesselbein constructs a second circle around the first. "These are the people who report to the first team. And beyond this outer circle, there's another, and another beyond that. And they're all interrelated." She picks up knives and forks and begins fashioning radials to link up the orb lines. "As the circles extend outward, there are more and more connections. So the galaxy gets more *interwoven* as it gets bigger!"

The table at the Cosmopolitan Club is a mess, but I am fascinated. Frances Hesselbein has created the perfect image of a spider's web. And the image of the web has been haunting me lately, for I have been thinking about structure. More specifically, about how women structure things differently from men—companies, office spaces, human relationships, even their own presumed place in the universe.

The Web as Structure

[This chapter explores how many women lead differently than men. The information about women's leadership style described in the following pages is based on in-depth observations of four successful women leaders: Frances Hesselbein, National Executive Director of the Girl Scouts; Barbara Grogan, President of Western Industrial Contractors; Nancy Badore, Director of Ford Motor Company's Executive Development Center; and Dorothy Brunson, President of Brunson Communications. Each woman was observed as she carried out her day-to-day work activities. The data on each woman is referred to as a "diary study."]

While doing the diary studies, I became aware that the women, when describing their roles in their organizations, usually referred to themselves as being in the middle of things. Not at the top, but in the center; not reaching down, but reaching out. The expressions were spontaneous, part of the women's language, indicating unconscious notions about what was desirable and good. Inseparable from their sense of themselves, as being in the middle was the women's notion of being connected to those around them, bound as if by invisible strands or threads. This image of an interrelated structure, built around a strong central point and constructed of radials and orbs, quite naturally made me think of a spider's web—that delicate tracery, compounded of the need for survival and the impulse of art, whose purpose is to draw other creatures to it.

The image of the web not only imbued the language of the women in the diary studies; it was also evident in the management structures they devised, and in the way they structured their meetings. Frances Hesselbein's "circular management chart," drawn with cutlery and sugar packets, was the most obvious example, and perhaps the most fully articulated. Jokingly called the Girl Scouts' "Wheel of Fortune" by Peter Drucker, the wheel actually *spins*; most management staff jobs are rotated every two or three years. Frances Hesselbein explains that job rotation used in conjunction with the circular chart is ideal for team-building. Teams can be formed to address needs as they arise—for example, the devising of an eighteen-month plan—then disbanded once the task has been accomplished. People serve both on different teams and in different positions, which offers staff people wide experience in the organization. In addition, being rotated into different jobs instills a feeling of common enterprise, cuts down on the tendency to form cliques and fiefdoms, and helps managers understand firsthand both the difficulties that face and the priorities that drive their fellows. "But the reason we have such team-building freedom is because of our circular chart," says Frances Hesselbein. "When someone gets shifted, he or she is simply moved around or across—it doesn't feel like a demotion because there is no up or down. There's no onus attached to being moved."

Nancy Badore's entire career has been built on the notion that management is best done by interrelating teams; she helped to develop the model for training Ford's top executives in this style on the factory floor, and then brought it, to the chagrin of some, to the executive suite. She runs the Executive Development Center along participatory lines; the management chart shows her in the center, with team members (who head the various programs for executives) branching out like the arms of a tree, rather than in a wheel configuration. Her monthly team meetings, at which the program managers make their progress reports, are not, she explains, "about them reporting to *me*. They're about *them* getting exposure to one another's projects and ideas." Thus she appears not so much to be chairing the meeting, but acting as facilitator, extracting and directing information. This is very much like Dorothy Brunson's view of her role as "a transmitter," absorbing information, then beaming it out "to wherever it needs to go."

Similarly, when Barbara Grogan chairs a meeting of the governor of Colorado's Small Business Advisory Council (which she had founded), she focuses attention on encouraging the participants to exchange ideas with one another, and forge new alliances among themselves. She describes the process of using her central position to promote interchange as "encouraging the flow," echoing Frances Hesselbein's language.

Implicit in such structurings is the notion of group affiliation rather than individual achievement as having the highest value. This emphasis was obvious in the ways the women described their notions of success. "I never wanted success if it meant clawing my way over other bodies," said Barbara Grogan. "I always knew that would make it pretty lonely once I got there." Frances Hesselbein expressed a similar notion. "I don't have the pressure on me that people have who think of themselves as being out there alone. I think of myself as part of a long continuum. That continuum includes my family, but also all of the fifty-six million women who have ever been in the Girl Scouts—a long green line going back in time and giving me support. Thinking of yourself as part of something larger frees you. You don't feel this sense of individual burden. It's been the source of so much of my energy."

The web of concern may be very large, as Nancy Badore notes. "The Executive Development Center trains Ford executives all over the world, so I try to think in global terms. I don't just see Ford as this company, an entity unto itself, it's a piece of the world, interrelated by politics, history, and economics. And I'm part of that. So while I'm asking myself what role the company can play, I'm also asking what role I can play, particularly as a woman. I'm asking it in terms of the world: where can I make my best contribution? The question really gets down to *why was I born?*" Thus thinking in terms of the larger group is an important component of the "ecological" focus that I found among the women in the diary studies. This enlarged consciousness derives in part from the women's awareness of themselves as women, in the vanguard of a movement that is changing history. Thus a kind of hidden agenda informs their actions and decisions, manifesting itself as a mission both to improve the status of women and change the world.

This sense of having a larger concern—a concern for the group or whole—is of course implicit in the imagery of the web. The orb and radial lines bind the whole together; every point of contact is also a point of connection. The principle, as Frances Hesselbein observed about the circle, is *inclusion*. You can't break a web into single lines or individual components without tearing the fabric, injuring the whole.

From Hierarchy to Web

Carol Gilligan, in *A Different Voice*, consistently opposes the image of the hierarchy to that of the "web of connection" in describing the difference between what women and men view as valuable in this world. She writes, "The images of hierarchy and web, drawn from the texts of men's and women's fantasies and thoughts, convey different ways of structuring relationships, and are associated with different views of morality and self" (Gilligan 1982). She notes that these images are in their way mirror opposites, because *the most desirable place in the one is the most feared spot in the other*. "As the *top* of the hierarchy becomes the *edge* of the web, and as the *center* of the network of connection becomes the *middle* of the hierarchical progression, each image marks as dangerous the place which the other defines as safe" (Gilligan 1982). In the hierarchical scheme of things, "reaching the top"—where others cannot get close—is the ultimate goal; in the web, the top is too far from the center. The ideal center spot in the web is perceived in the hierarchical view as "being stuck" in the middle—going nowhere.

The contrasting models also reveal different notions of what constitutes effective communications. Hierarchy, emphasizing appropriate channels and the chain of command, discourages diffuse or random communication; information is filtered, gathered, and sorted as it makes its way to the top. By contrast, the web facilitates direct communication, free-flowing and loosely structured, by providing points of contact and direct tangents along which to connect.

The women in the diary studies, eager to be "in the center of things" and chilled by the notion of being "alone at the top," echo the values, principles, and presumptions that Carol Gilligan found to be characteristic of women in general, that indeed she believed to be structured into the female psyche. These values have long been restricted to the private sphere, but that is dramatically changing; the women in the diary studies, having attained positions of authority and influence in the public realm, are able to structure their principles into the way they do business. Thus, using the model of the web to design management charts and apportion office space, to construct meetings and evolve more direct means of communication, they are participating in an *institutionalizing of the web*.

In *Reinventing the Corporation*, Naisbitt and Aburdene propose the lattice or grid as the structural model for the new corporate economy (Naisbitt and Aburdene 1986). It is interesting to note that these structures, with their interconnecting points and intersecting lines, are quite similar to the web—except that they are bound by boxlike shapes rather than circles. Thus the structure of the reinvented corporation is far closer to the female perception of what is desirable, though it retains an essential "male" angularity. The grid of interlocking pieces facilitates direct communication, can shift to meet changing demands, and hastens the flow of information. The image recalls that of the microchip—making quick connections, breaking information into bits, processing, rearranging the units: energy moving in pulses rather than being forced to run up and down in channels.

Such a model is obviously more suited to the information age than the hierarchical structure, which found its most widespread application in the industrial era (Naisbitt and Aburdene 1986). Yet hierarchical concepts have continued to influence institutional structures because they represent a particular manifestation of male psychology, meeting male needs for limits and boundaries on relationships in the workplace, and satisfying the male value for ends over means. But as women continue to assume positions of influence in the public sphere, they are countering the values of the hierarchy with those of the web, which affirms relationships, seeks ways to strengthen human bonds, simplifies communications, and gives means an equal value with ends. . . .

References

Gilligan, C. 1982. *In a Different Voice*. Cambridge: Harvard University Press.

Naisbitt, J. and P. Aburdene. 1986. *Reinventing the Corporation*. New York: Warner Books.

Food for Thought and Application Questions

1. Does Helgesen endorse a structural or an individual approach to leadership differences between the sexes? Present evidence that she supports one position or the other. Now develop an argument in support of the opposite position.

2. Examine articles from the business section of a major metropolitan newspaper or a business periodical (e.g., *Harvard Business Review, Businessweek*) in or-

der to locate reports of new trends in management or alternative management styles. When you locate such an article, answer the following questions: (a) Is the management style being described similar to the "web" approach discussed by Helgesen? If so, how? If not, how does it differ? (b) Is there reference made to the approach as a "female" style or one that incorporates "feminine" values? (c) If specific man-

agers are mentioned in the report, are any of them women? (d) What benefits to the organization are reported as associated with the new approach?

3. The fact that higher levels of management are male-dominated creates an obstacle to implementing the "web" management style discussed by Helgesen. Why might some male managers oppose this alternative management style? ✦

15

Women in Management: Power and Powerlessness

Nina L. Colwill

Women form about one-third of the management work force in Canada and the United States, depending on the source of information that one cites and the definition of "manager" that one is willing to accept. One cannot accurately assume that a manager is a manager is a manager, however. The large majority of women who are classified as managers make little money and exert little authority (Hymowitz and Schellhardt 1986). At the board level, only 44 percent of the Fortune 1000 companies have even one female director (Friedman 1988). Among the Fortune 500, only 3.6 percent of directors and 1.7 percent of corporate officers are women (Von Glinow and Krzyczkowska-Mercer 1988).

I cannot remember a time when I was not bothered by the obvious paucity of women in management. In my twenties, I believed that education was all that was needed to rectify the situation—more university education and technical training for women and more formal and informal strategies for change in attitude aimed at men. It was all a matter, I believed, of educating women to fill the managerial positions and educating men to accept women as their managers. Men did not believe that women could manage organizations. Women only had to demonstrate their competence. Life was simple then. The task was clear.

Today, I am less naive. Women are not finding it difficult to work their way into management because they have spent too few years in universities and community colleges. Women are not dead-ended in lower positions because there are too few books to guide them or because there has been too little research to document their dilemma. Women have not failed to educate themselves and they have not failed to explain their situation to others articulately and eloquently. If women have failed at anything, they have failed merely to understand power.

During the fifteen years that I have been working in the area of power, at least one fact has become clear: there is no one way to define it. Thus, in this chapter, I examine power from three different perspectives: (a) personal power—feeling in control of one's environment, feeling good about oneself; (b) interpersonal power—the ability to influence another; and (c) organizational power—the ability to mobilize resources, the ability to get things done.

Personal power is a belief—the belief that one is or is not in control of one's own environment—and it is virtually synonymous with Rotter's (1966) notion of Internal-External Locus of Control. Personal power is, therefore, the belief that one is powerful. Interpersonal power is power viewed at a more macro, dyadic level. It is the ability to influence another. Whether that influence stems from a property of the individual, a property of the interpersonal relationship, or a property of the organization (Ragins and Sundstrom 1989), it is the ability to influence rather than the antecedents of influence that forms the definition of interpersonal power. Organizational power is viewed as occupying the most macro position in this analysis. It is, in Kanter's (1977) words, "the ability to mobilize resources." Again, that ability can stem from many sources, including personal power, interpersonal power, or any of their antecedents. But organizational power, as discussed here, simply refers to one's ability to accomplish things, to "get things done" as Kanter (1977) says, to conduct the business of the organization effectively. Thus, personal power is a belief, interpersonal power is an ability (the ability to influence another), and organizational power is another ability (the ability to mobilize organizational resources).

In this chapter I examine these three perspectives on power as they apply to women in management and conclude that male and female managers face a power differential. As managers, women and men do not appear to differ in personal power; they are equally likely to feel in control of their own environment. In the realm of interpersonal power, the research suggests that women are less effective than men—that they are less able than men to influence others. In the area of organizational power, the latest research indicates that women are more effective than men at doing the business of these organizations (Tsui and Gutek 1984). Having thus argued that women and men face a complex power imbalance in their organizations, I then examine the strategies that female managers employ for coping with this imbalance.

In writing this chapter I explore, not the vast literature on gender differences that has been generated in the past thirty years, but merely the organizational literature since 1980. Thus, I have attempted to combat the accusation that "things" have changed too dramatically in the past few decades for us to consider the literature of the 1960s and the 1970s in the analysis of the problems facing today's managerial women. Fortunately for my argument and unfortunately for women in management, the literature of the 1980s and 1990s appears to reinforce the literature of the past. The story of women in and out of management is not merely a story of increased education, demonstrated competence, and logical progression. The story of women in management is a story of pain and frustration, a story of trust and mistrust, a story of power and powerlessness.

Personal Power

Personal power is a belief—the belief that one is in control of one's own environment. To have personal power is to feel good about oneself, to feel comfortable in one's own skin. The concept of Internal-External Locus of Control (I-E) probably comes closest to the notion of personal power. Internality, according to Rotter (1966), who brought us the concept and the measure twenty-five years ago, is the belief that one's destiny is determined by one's own efforts and endeavours; externality is the belief that one's fate is in the hands of luck or chance or powerful others. Although Rotter and his followers have conceptualized I-E as a personality characteristic (see, e.g., Lefcourt 1982), I see personal power merely as a belief that is as subject to change as are the circumstances or the insights that created that belief in the first place. When one views I-E in this way, it comes as no surprise to learn that women tend to be less internal than men, a finding that has been replicated in many cultures (Lefcourt 1982). The reality of women's lives in most countries is that the situations in which they often find themselves are situations that foster a feeling of "learned helplessness" (Lips 1981; Seligman 1975)—situations in which their actions do not produce the expected outcomes (Lefcourt 1991). Neither should it come as a surprise that women and men who find themselves in similar circumstances exhibit no such gender differences in locus of control. Over the past ten years, I have measured the I-E of hundreds of Bachelor of Commerce students, MBA students, and managers in Canada and abroad, and have never found consistent gender differences among these groups.

Nor have consistent gender differences in other personality traits been found among managers or would-be managers, and the similarities between men and women increase as their tenure in the managerial role increases (Gomez-Mejia 1983; Harlan and Weiss 1982; Miner and Smith 1982). The similarity between male and female managers is usually attributed to the fact that female managers, female entrepreneurs, and female management students all demonstrate more masculine personality characteristics than do women in less male-dominated fields (Brenner 1982; Miner and Smith 1982; Steinberg and Shapiro 1982; Sztaba and Colwill 1988). Even among female managers, those in the higher-echelon, male-dominated positions tend to demonstrate more masculine characteristics than do their sisters in less prestigious managerial positions (Moore and Rickel 1980). The jury is still out on this topic, however; there is a need for more systematic and controlled research comparing men and women in male-dominated and female-dominated occupations, before one can conclude that female managers are more like men than male managers are like women.

There are many specific sex differences in the general population that have not been found among managers, because people differ by circumstance as surely as they differ by sex. People with similar characteristics seek similar education and similar occupations, and these self-chosen circumstances render them even more similar (Colwill 1990). Whether men become more like their female colleagues or women merely become more like men has yet to be examined thoroughly. The attitudes, values, beliefs, and personalities of male and female managers are more similar than different, however, and there appear to be no consistent and significant differences in personal power between these two groups. The fact that female manager's are no more external than are their male counterparts has positive implications for the coping strategies of women in management. The literature on self-efficacy, which is a cognate of I-E (Lefcourt 1991), suggests that people who consider themselves able to affect their environment are those

most likely to persist with whatever coping strategies they employ (Bandura 1977). In the following section, I examine some of the many issues with which managerial women must cope daily—the myriad issues surrounding interpersonal power.

Interpersonal Power

Paula Johnson provides a good definition of interpersonal power through her definition of power: "the ability to get another person to do or to believe something he or she would not necessarily have done or believed spontaneously" (Johnson 1976, 100)—in short, "the ability to influence another person." At this more macro level, the dyadic level, power becomes more visible, and other people are more clearly able to detect and articulate its presence.

People exert interpersonal power through communication—through their verbal, nonverbal, and paraverbal communications. They convey their relative status through the words they speak (verbal), the way they speak these words (paraverbal), and the ways in which they communicate without words (nonverbal). Thus, interpersonal power goes beyond mere persuasion, which psychologists usually consider to be the ability to influence verbally (Stang and Wrightsman 1981). Neither the influenced nor the influencer need be aware of the process in order for influence to be exerted, in order for interpersonal power to be demonstrated. Whether communicated verbally, nonverbally, or paraverbally, the communication of status can define, maintain, or even change the balance of interpersonal power in a relationship (Spinner and Colwill 1982). Do men and women differ in their interpersonal power—in their ability to influence others? And, more important for the purposes of this chapter, do male and female managers differ in this ability? There is some evidence among Israeli union leaders that women perceive themselves to be less influential than men (Izraeli 1985)—to have, in the language of this chapter, less interpersonal power than men. If organizational recognition, compensation, and perquisites are considered to be a measure of a person's ability to influence others, then women in organizations clearly have less interpersonal power than men do. They are paid less than men, even in female-dominated occupations (Abella 1984), a fact that women tend not to recognize (Major and Konar 1984). Women are, in fact, more than twice as likely as men to earn less than $15,000 a year for full-time work (Abella 1984). Even as managers, women are paid significantly less than men are, regardless of their educational backgrounds (Larwood, Szwajkowski, and Rose 1988), and, all things being equal, women move up the organizational ladder more slowly than do men (Stewart and Gudykunst 1982). Women are offered fewer remaining opportunities in their organizations and are less likely to be granted time off for educational purposes (Cahoon and Rowney 1984; Colwill and Josephson 1983).

At the presidential and vice-presidential level, where one would assume that interpersonal power is at its highest, women's salaries are 42 percent of the salaries of their male counterparts (Nelson and Berney 1987). Furthermore, women at the top are significantly less likely than men to receive other organizational perks such as stock options and bonuses. In one study (Kosinar 1981), male senior corporate officers received an average of six such perks, whereas no female senior corporate office received more than two.

But these data are drawn primarily from corporate North America. Surely one would expect that there are pockets of our working society in which women and men experience interpersonal power equally—in unions, for example, or in their own small businesses. But even in these areas, a gap exists. North American women are grossly underrepresented among union executives, and are, in fact, rarely found in those positions unless the union represents a female-dominated occupation

(Chaison and Andrappan 1982). As for entrepreneurs, women tend to receive less favourable treatment from their banks than do men (Hinrick and

O'Brien 1982). Although there is one study showing that men and women are equally likely to be offered funding by their lending institutions (Butner and Rosen 1989), women are more likely to be required to provide collateral for their loans (Swift and Riding 1988).

Moreover, the working lives of women extend beyond the realm of what we traditionally call "the workplace," and into the home. If interpersonal power is measured by the extent to which people can influence others to do work for them, then the family situation of most men renders them interpersonally powerful. The female sex role in at least thirty countries holds women responsible for work in the home, and this is true in our society even in families in which men's "help" is substantial (Bem 1987; Williams and Best 1982). The Basset Report (Basset 1985), an in-depth study of Canadian dual-career families, showed that substantial housework among husbands is anything but the norm, however; in only half of Basset's households did men *ever* do cleaning and grocery shopping; in only one-third did they share cooking and laundry.

One might assume that the frustration of such inequitable treatment would prove to be extremely stressful for any woman, yet only 56 percent of Basset's dual-career women reported that responsibility for housework caused stress in their families. It is difficult to imagine why this might be the case. Perhaps there are many women who do not consider the unequal distribution of household labour to be inequitable, so the situation is not a source of frustration to them. In Yogev's (1981) study of married female professors, for instance, many of these women acknowledged that they spent less time on their careers and more time on child care and housework than did their husbands; yet they did not consider the division of labour in their homes to be inequitable.

Women's and men's relative positions of interpersonal power are reinforced at home by women's and men's relative positions of interpersonal power in the workplace, and are reinforced in the workplace by their relative power positions at home. It is known, for example, that many family decisions are made on the basis of financial contribution—that the spouse who earns the lowest salary, for instance, is the spouse who stays home with sick children (Friedman 1988). Since women are more likely to earn less than their husbands, their bargaining power is lower, and they are usually left with the lion's share of family responsibilities. By assuming greater home responsibilities, a woman can place herself in a precarious organizational position, allowing her energy to be sapped and reinforcing the sex-role stereotype of the poorly committed female worker (Blau 1984).

Prejudice and discrimination against women clearly pervade today's organizations, but the situation is more complicated than psychologists and sociologists had previously supposed. It is known, for instance, that gender is most likely to be used as a basis for discrimination in hiring and promotion situations in which insufficient information about the competence of the applicant has been provided (Hodgins and Kalin 1985). Even in such male-dominated fields as engineering, women are more likely to be treated objectively when information about their competence is provided (Gerdes and Garber 1983). As Drazin and Auster (1987) point out, however, it is not always the people who have objective information about the competence of a female manager who are making decisions about her promotional opportunities and financial remuneration; such decisions are often made above the head of the direct supervisor, by people who have little daily contact with the incumbent. As long as a general bias against women prevails in our organizations, indi-vidual decisions will continue to be biased toward men (Nieva and Gutek 1981), and men will continue to gain interpersonal power at the expense of women.

There is some evidence that prejudice against women, per se, may not be as strong as a prejudice against the things that women do—that it is doing womanly things rather than being a woman that renders one relatively powerless. In a series of in-basket studies conducted at the University of Manitoba, both women and men elicited greater compliance when they used traditionally masculine language, or traditional male power strategies, or when they were employed in a male-dominated occupation (Colwill, Perlman, and Spinner 1982, 1983; Colwill, Pollock, and Sztaba 1986; Sztaba and Colwill 1986). The latter study is particularly telling: subjects (home economics students) did not rate home economists as less powerful than engineers, but regardless of the sex of the would-be influencer, engineers elicited greater compliance with their requests than did home economists. This finding suggests that the factors determining interpersonal power may operate below the awareness of the people interpreting that power. Taken together, the University of Manitoba studies suggest that there is a perceptual differentiation between the stereotypes of and attitudes toward "women" and "the things that women do."

Although the distinction between "women" and "the things that women do" may appear initially to be trivial, it is, in fact, an extremely important distinction. As sex roles begin to change, or as people perceive that they change, "the things that women do" will not be as easily distinguished from "the things that men do" as they were three, two, or even one decade ago. The distinction between "men" and "women" is an obvious one—an obvious basis for allocating interpersonal power—but the distinction between the male and female sex role has the potential to disappear over time. If "the things that women do" and "the things that men do" begin to blend, then the entire gender-determined basis for allocating interpersonal power also has the potential to disappear. As a society, however, we do not seem to be ready to allow ourselves to be influenced by others on the basis of their competence and their arguments rather than their sex or their sex role. On the dyadic level, on the level at which managers must interact hundreds of times daily, men have a clear edge, an edge that is reinforced in their roles of husband and father as surely as it is reinforced in the workplace. Little is known about the ways in which female managers cope with this inequity through explicit attempts to exert interpersonal power. Persuasion, or interpersonal power gained through verbal appeal (Stang and Wrightsman 1981), is an obvious coping strategy for study, being one of the most easily measured routes to interpersonal power. The collection of such data is a complex matter, however, because of the difficulty in separating gender and organizational status. In Mainiero's (1986) study of organizational empowerment strategies, for instance, women were found to be more acquiescent than were men; yet Mainiero's reanalysis of her data showed job dependency to be a better predictor of acquiescence than was gender. Ironically, the greatest hope for gender equality in the interpersonal power of managers may lie in the area of organizational power.

Organizational Power

Rosabeth Moss Kanter (1977) has defined power as "the ability to get things done, to mobilize resources, to get and use whatever it is that a person needs for the goals he or she is attempting to in meet" (166). It is this definition that I have adopted, not to define "power" as Kanter has done, but to define the third, most macro level of power in this analysis, organizational power. It is to this level of power—the level of mobilizing resources of "getting things done"—that most management texts are addressed, with personal power and interpersonal power being discussed only as they have bearing upon organizational power (see, e.g., Mintzberg 1983).

Dipboye's (1987) review of the area of managerial effectiveness is the literature most closely related to organizational power, for it examines the extent to which male and female managers are able to and are perceived to "get things done" in their organizations. This literature on managerial effectiveness shows a definite edge for women. Female and male managers are evaluated by their subordinates as being equally effective (Terborg and Shingledecker 1983), but female managers are viewed by their immediate supervisors, and by their peers as being more effective than their male counterparts (Tsui and Gutek 1984). This positive evaluation of women as managers is particularly strong among women—among female MBA students (Mickalachki and Mickalachki 1984) and among female managers (Jabes 1980). In Jabes' study, in fact, female managers rated their managerial sisters as more intelligent, more likeable, more successful, and more able than their male counterparts.

The discrepancy is an obvious one: when organizational power is defined as the ability to mobilize resources, women have greater organizational power than do men, in a world in which their access to organizational resources (Stewart and Gudykunst 1982) and interpersonal power is more limited than that of their male counterparts. In the fairest and most rational of systems, today's top executives would recognize this discrepancy and women would be skyrocketed into upper management with the tools to affect even greater change. While awaiting this event, it might be interesting to examine the coping strategies of today's managerial women.

Women in Management

The thesis of this chapter is a simple one that will provide no startling revelation for even the most naive. The lack of women in management is an issue, not of education and training, but of power. Time, patience, and women's self-improvement do not appear to be the solution. The solution, in fact, is similar to the problem: power.

Now, to review the power scores of male and female managers. In personal power, in beliefs about one's own control of one's environment, there are no consistent sex differences among managers. In interpersonal power, the ability to influence others, there are large and many sex differences, with men enjoying greater influence than women at home and in their organizations. And finally, in the area of organizational power, in the ability to mobilize resources, it is beginning to appear that managerial women are perceived by more people as being more effective than their male counterparts.

This beginning research raises as many questions as it answers. Foremost among them is the obvious question: "If women are less interpersonally powerful than men—if they are less able to influence others—how are they better able than men to mobilize resources?" or more simply, "How can women be more effective than men, while being less influential?" Although I know of no clear answer to this question, I find myself returning, when I consider it, to the concept of personal power—feeling in control of one's environment. Personal power or internal locus of control is an important organizational concept, because it is strongly related to organizational power. It is known, for instance, that internals are better than externals at negotiation and at solving difficult job-related problems, and that their workers tend to be more satisfied than are the subordinates of externals (Brousseau 1984; Johnson, Lathans, and Hennesey 1984; Stolte 1983). Furthermore, within supportive organizational environments, internals take more active roles in their career management than do externals and are more likely than externals to be pro-

moted (Hammer and Vardi, 1981). Although there are no consistent sex differences in locus of control among managers and managerial students, it is possible that locus of control and gender interact in some way, so that for women even moderate levels of internal locus of control may result in high levels of managerial effectiveness.

In any case, women's organizational effectiveness will, in the long run, undoubtedly increase their status, which will, in turn, increase their interpersonal power. As their interpersonal power increases, women cannot fail to become even more organizationally effective, for the ability to mobilize resources is often dependent upon the ability to influence others. In the short run (and the short run, Morrison, White, and Van Velsor [1987] predict, will span several decades), there are day-to-day inequities in interpersonal power to address. It is to these inequities that people usually refer when speaking of sex discrimination in the workplace. And it is women's techniques for coping with these inequities that are of interest here.

Women learn to cope with discrimination in a variety of ways. One of these methods, which researchers are only beginning to address, has come to be known as "the denial of personal discrimination." There is strong evidence that women, while clearly recognizing the fact of sex discrimination in the workplace, fail to see how they, personally, have experienced discrimination (Crosby 1984). Against all evidence to the contrary, individual women tend to see themselves as being justly treated (Abbondanza 1982; Guimond, Dube, and Abbondanza 1984). How is this possible? Abbondanza's (1982, 1983; Abbondanza and Dube-Simard 1982) research indicates that women, striving to perceive their world as a just and fair place, compare their situation, not to the situation of men in comparable positions, but to the condition of other, less fortunate women.

Although denial is usually considered to be an ineffective coping strategy, it may have some advantages. Denial of personal discrimination may prevent individual women from solving their unseen problems, but it has not prevented women in large numbers from fighting for the rights of women in general. Denial of personal discrimination may make it possible for women to get on with the day-to-day business of effective and competent work behaviour. Perhaps, by refusing to accept the possibility that they are the objects of discrimination, individual women are creating a new reality for themselves, and, by association, for women in general.

Another way in which women cope with an inordinately difficult climb up the organizational ladder and an inability to strike a fair bargain at home is to eschew marriage and family. In Canada, 91 percent of male managers but only 62 percent of female managers are married. Of these married managers, 73 percent of the men have children living at home, but only 41 percent of the women do (Nakamura and Nakamura 1989). In the United States, women without children tend to experience slight upward mobility by the age of thirty-two, whereas women with children experience slight downward mobility by that age (Sewell, Hauser, and Wolf 1980). Even for childless women, however, upward mobility is slower than for men, whether those men have children or not.

One rational way in which women could cope with their family and managerial lives would be to leave their organizations. Whether or not they are really making this choice in large numbers, however, is open to debate. Taylor's (1986) study of 1,039 female MBAs from seventeen American business schools shows that 30 percent of these fast-trackers left their jobs ten years after their graduation for self-employment or unemployment, and Fraker (1984) argues that female managers are quitting at a faster rate than are men. However, Karen Korabik's (personal communication) more recent research suggests that these preliminary data were not representative, and that the picture is more complex than it appeared initially. Whether or not women are leaving their corporations at a faster rate than men, as recent magazine articles (DeGeorge 1987) and books (Bools and Swan 1989) suggest, they are certainly starting their own businesses at an unprecedented rate—at five times the rate of men (Statistics Canada 1988).

Whatever the organizational problems facing them, women, like men, learn to cope with the stress of their working lives through the support of other people. However, there is increasing evidence that the nature of this support differs for males and females. Women, in general, are known to have emotionally richer relationships than men, characterized by greater emotional sharing and intimacy, and less activity-orientation, task-orientation, and interest-orientation, than are the relationships of men (Aries and Johnson 1983; Caldwell and Peplau 1982). Although women tend to value their co-worker relationships more highly than men do and tend to form same-sex networks, they often find themselves excluded from the informal, male-dominated networks of their organizations, a process that bans them from the power strongholds of the organization, even to the extent of lowering their probability of promotion (Brass 1985; Forisha and Goldman 1981). Instead, women are more likely than men to rely on sources of support that are external to the organization—family and non-co-working friends (Etzion 1984; Schilling and Fuehrer 1987).

Research and writing in the area of women in management has been classified as being of two types—person-centred and organization-centred (Fagenson 1988; Gregory 1988). In this chapter, as in most of the literature in this area, I have taken a person-centred approach, addressing those things that women can do and have done in order to cope with the situation they face as managers. Clearly, the organization-centred approach has received less attention than it deserves, perhaps because it is less gratifying and more difficult for researchers to address these macro issues of organizational restructuring and massive economic social change than it is for them to study the behaviours of women and men as they play their managerial roles with other women and men. Few organizations but many individual women have contributed greatly to change; few organizations but many individual women seek information to affect change. Yet, however new and underdeveloped the field of women and management (Sekaran 1988), it is beginning to tackle the big issue— "the 'genderedness' of organizational management practices and conditions" (Calas and Smirchich 1989, 3)—the issue of power.

References

Abbondanza, M. 1982. *Categorization, Identification and Feelings of Deprivation: A Multidimensional Study of the Homemaker and Employed Mothers' Social Perceptions.* Paper presented at the International Congress of Applied Psychology, Edinburgh. July.

———— 1983. *Cognitive Barriers to Intergroup Equality Between the Sexes.* Paper presented at the meeting of the Canadian Psychological Association, Winnipeg, June.

Abbondanza, M., and L. Dube-Simard. 1982. "La mère au travail et la mère au foyer: deux realites cognitives et evaluatives." *Revue Quebeçoise de Psychologie*, 3(3):3-16.

Abella, Judge R. S. 1984. *Equality in Employment: A Royal Commission Report.* Ottawa: Supply and Services Canada.

Aries, E. J., and E. L. Johnson. 1983. "Close friendship in adulthood: Conversation content between same-sex friends." *Sex Roles*, 9:1183-1196.

Bandura, A. 1977. "Self-efficacy: Toward a unifying theory of behavioral change." *Psychological Review*, 84:191-215.

Basset, I. 1985. *The Basset Report: Career Success and Canadian Women.* Toronto: Collins.

Bem, D. 1987. "A consumer's guide to dual-career marriages." *H.R. Report*, 25(1):10-12.

Billings, A. G., and R. H. Moos. 1982. "Stressful life events and symptoms: A longitudinal model." *Health Psychology*, 1:99-117.

Blau, F. D. 1984. "Occupational segregation and labor market discrimination." In B. F. Reskin (ed.), *Sex Segregation in the Workplace: Trends, Explanations, Remedies.* Washington, DC: National Academy Press:117-143.

Bools, B., and L. Swan. 1989. *Power Failure.* New York: St. Martin's Press.

Brass, D. J. 1985. "Men's and women's network: A study of interaction patterns and influence in an organization." *Academy of Management Journal*, 28:327-43.

Brenner, O. C. 1982. "Relationship of education to sex, managerial status, and the managerial stereotype." *Journal of Applied Psychology*, 67:380-383.

Brousseau, K. R. 1984. "Job-person dynamics and career development." In K. M. Rowland and G. R. Ferris (eds.), *Research in Personnel and Human Resources Management.* Greenwich: JAI Press 2:125-154).

Butner, H., and B. Rosen. 1989. "Funding new business ventures: Are decision makers biased against women entrepreneurs?" *Journal of Business Venturing*, 4:249-261.

Cahoon, A. R., and J. I. A. Rowney. 1984. *Variables Influencing Job Satisfaction and Stress in Female Managers.* Paper presented at the meeting of the Canadian Psychological Association, Ottawa, June.

Calas, M., and I. Smirchich. 1989. *Using the "F" Word: Feminist Theories and the Social Consequences of Organizational Research.* Meeting of the Academy of management, Washington, DC, August.

Caldwell, M. A., and L. A. Peplau. 1982. "Sex differences in same-sex friendship." *Sex Roles*, 8:721-732.

Chaison, G. N., and P. Andrappan. 1982. "Characteristics of female union officers in Canada." *Industrial Relations*, 37:765-778.

Colwill, N. L. 1990. "Gender differences in management: The study of sex and circumstance." *Women in Management*, 1(4):8.

Colwill, N. L., and W. L. Josephson. 1983. "Attitudes toward equal opportunity in employment: The case of one Canadian government department." *Business Quarterly* 48:87-93.

Colwill, N. L., D. Perlman, and B. Spinner. 1982. *Effective Power Styles for Women and Men: A Test of Johnson's Model.* Paper presented at the meeting of the Canadian Psychological Association, Montreal, June.

Colwill, N. L., M. Pollock, and T. I. Sztaba. 1986. "Power in home economics: An individual and professional issue." *Canadian Home Economics Journal*, 36(2):59-61.

Crosby, E. 1984. "The denial of personal discrimination." *American Behavioral Scientist*, 27:371-386.

DeGeorge, C. 1987. "Where are they now? Business Week's leading corporate women of 1976." *Business Week*, June 22:76-77.

Dipboye, R. L. 1987. "Problems and progress of women in management." In K. S. Koziara, M. H. Moskow, and L. D. Tanner (eds.), *Working Women: Past, Present Future*. Washington, DC: Industrial Relations Research Association Series, the Bureau of National Affairs:118-153.

Drazin, R., and E. R. Auster. 1987. "Wage differences between men and women: Performance appraisal ratings vs. salary allocations as the locus of bias." *Human Resource Management*, 26:157-418.

Etzion, D. 1984. "Moderating effect of social support on the stress-burnout relationship." *Journal of Applied Psychology*, 69:615-622.

Fagenson, E. 1988. *On Women in Management Research Methodology: Your Theory Is Showing*. Proceedings, Women in Management Research Symposium, Mount Saint Vincent University, Halifax, NS, April.

Forisha, B. L., and B. H. Goldman. 1981. *Outsiders On the Inside: Women and Organizations*. Englewood Cliffs, NJ: Prentice-Hall.

Fraker, S. 1984. "Why women aren't getting to the top." *Fortune*, April 16, 109:40-45.

Friedman, D. E. 1988. "The invisible barrier to women in business." *Inside Guide*, 2(5):75-79.

Gerdes, E. P., and D. M. Garber. 1983. "Sex bins in hiring: Effects of job demands and applicant competence." *Sex Roles*, 9:307-319.

Gomez-Mejia, I. R. 1983. "Sex differences during occupational socialization." *Academy of Management Journal*, 26:492-499.

Gregory, A. 1988. *Where Are We Coming From and Where Are We Going? Theoretical, Research and Methodological Perspectives on Women in Management*. Proceedings, Women in Management Research Symposium, Mount Saint Vincent University, Halifax, NS, April.

Guimond, S., L. Dube, and M. Abbondanza. 1984. *Representations Cognitives des Inegalites Entre les Hommes et les Femmes en France et au Quebec: I. Le Domaine de L'education*. Paper presented at the meeting of the Canadian Psychological Association, Ottawa, June.

Hammer, T. H., and Y. Vardi. 1981. "Locus of control and career self-management among nonsupervisory employees in industrial settings." *Journal of Vocational Behavior*, 18:13-29.

Harlan, A., and C. L. Weiss. 1982. "Sex differences in factors affecting managerial career advancement." In P.A. Wallace (ed.), *Women in the Workplace*. Boston: Auburn House:59-100.

Hinrick, R., and M. O'Brien. 1982. "The woman entrepreneur as a reflection of the type of business." In K. Vesper (ed.), *Frontiers of Entrepreneurship Research*. Wellesley, MA: Babson College:54-67.

Hodgins, D. C., and R. Kalin. 1985. "Reducing sex bias in judgments of occupational suitability by the provision of sex-typed personality information." *Canadian Journal of Behavioural Science*, 17:346-358.

Hymowitz, C., and T. D. Schellhardt. 1986. "The glass ceiling." *Wall Street Journal*, March 24:1D, 4D-5D.

Izraeli, D. N. 1985. "Sex differences in self-reported influence among union officers." *Journal of Applied Psychology*, 70:148-157.

Jabes, J. 1980. "Causal attributions and sex-role stereotypes in the perceptions of female managers." *Canadian Journal of Behavioural Science*, 12:52-63.

Johnson, P. 1976. "Women and power: Toward a theory of effectiveness." *Journal of Social Issues*, 32(3):99-110.

Johnson, A. L., F. Lathans, and H. W. Hennesey. 1984. "The role of locus of control in leader influence behaviour." *Personnel Psychology*, 37:61-75.

Kanter, R. M. 1977. *Men and Women of the Corporation*. New York: Basic Books.

Kosinar, S. 1981. "Socialization and self-esteem: Women in management." In B. L. Forisha and B. H. Goldman (eds.), *Outsiders on the Inside*. Englewood Cliffs, NJ: Prentice-Hall:31-41.

Larwood, L., E. Szwajkowski, and S. Rose. 1988. "Sex and race discrimination resulting from manager-client relationships: Applying the rational bias theory of managerial discrimination." *Sex Roles*, 18:9-29.

Lefcourt, H. M. 1982. *Locus of Control*. Hillsdale, NJ: Erlbaum.

_____ 1991. "Locus of control." In J. P. Robinson, P. R. Shaver, and L. S. Wrightsman (eds.), *Measures of Personality and Social Psychological Attitudes: Volume I of Measures of Social Psychological Attitudes*. New York: Academic Press:413-499.

Lips, H. M. 1981. *Women, Men, and the Psychology of Power*. Englewood Cliffs, NJ: Prentice-Hall.

Mainiero, L. A. 1986. "Coping with powerlessness: The relationship of gender and job dependency to empowerment-strategy usage." *Administrative Science Quarterly*, 31:633-653.

Major, B., and E. Konar. 1984. "An investigation of sex differences in pay expectations and their possible causes." *Academy of Management Journal*, 27(4):777-792.

Mickalachki, D. M., and A. Mickalachki. 1984. "MBA women: The new pioneers." *Business Quarterly*, 49:110-115.

Miner, J. B., and N. R. Smith. 1982. "Decline and stabilization of managerial motivation over a twenty-year period." *Journal of Applied Psychology*, 67:297-305.

Mintzberg, H. 1983. *Power In and Around Organizations*. Englewood Cliffs, NJ: Prentice-Hall.

Moore, L. M., and A. V. Rickel. 1980. "Characteristics of women in traditional and nontraditional managerial roles." *Personnel Psychology*, 33:317-333.

Morrison, A. M., R. I. White, and E. Van Velsor. 1987. *Breaking the Glass Ceiling*. Reading, MA: Addison-Wesley.

Nakamura, A., and M. Nakamura. 1989. *Children, Work and Women: A Managerial Perspective*. Working Paper Series No. NC 89-18, National Centre for Management

Research and Development, University of Western Ontario, July.

Nelson, S., and K. Berney. 1987. "Women: The Second Wave." *Nation's Business*, 18-27 May.

Nieva, V. E., and B. A. Gutek. 1981. *Women and Work: A Psychological Perspective*. New York: Praeger.

Ragins, B. R., and E. Sundstrom. 1989. "Gender and power in organizations: A longitudinal perspective." *Psychological Bulletin*, 105:51-88.

Rotter, J. 1966. "Generalized expectancies for internal vs. external control of reinforcement." *Psychological Monographs*, 80:1-28.

Schilling, K. M., and A. Fuehrer. 1987. *Sex Differences in Social Support in the Workplace*. Paper presented at the meeting of the Midwestern Psychological Association, Chicago, IL, May.

Sekaran, U. 1988. *Methodological and Theoretical Issues in Women in Management Research*. Proceedings, Women in Management Research Symposium, Mount Saint Vincent University, Halifax, NS, April.

Seligman, M. E. P. 1975. *Helplessness: On Depression, Development and Death*. San Francisco: Freeman.

Sewell, W. H., R. M. Hauser, and W. C. Wolf. 1980. "Sex, schooling, and occupational success." *American Journal of Sociology*, 86:551-583.

Spinner, B., and N. L. Colwill. 1982. "Power." In N.L. Colwill (ed.), *The New Partnership: Women and Men in Organizations*. Palo Alto, CA: Mayfield:113-134.

Stang, D. J., and L. S. Wrightsman. 1981. *Dictionary of Social Behavior and Social Research Methods*. Monterey, CA: Brooks/Cole.

Statistics Canada. 1988. *Business Owners in Canada, 1981-1986*. Small Business and Special Surveys.

Steinberg, R., and S. Shapiro. 1992. "Sex differences in personality traits of female and male Master of Business Administration students." *Journal of Applied Psychology*, 67:306-310.

Stewart, L., and W. Gudykunst. 1982. "Differential factors influencing the hierarchial level and number of promotions of males and females within an organization." *Academy of Management* 97:586-597.

Stolte, J. F. 1983. "Self-efficacy: Sources and consequences in negotiation networks." *Journal of Social Psychology* 119:69-75.

Swift, C., and A. Riding. 1988. *Giving Credit Where It's Due: Women Business Owners and Canadian Financial Institutions.* Paper presented at the International Council for Small Business Annual Meeting, Helsinki, Finland.

Sztaba, T. I., and N. L. Colwill. 1986. *Genderlect and Perceptions: Does it Pay to Be a Lady?* Unpublished manuscript, University of Manitoba.

———— 1988. "Secretarial and management students: Attitudes, attributes, and career choice consideration." *Sex Roles*, 19:651-665.

Taylor, A. 1986. "Why women managers are bailing out." *Fortune*, 114, August 18:16-23.

Terborg, I. R., and P. Shingledecker. 1983. "Employee reactions to supervision and work evaluation as a function of subordinate and manager sex." *Sex Roles*, 9:813-824.

Tsui, A. S., and B. A, Gutek. 1984. "A role set analysis of gender differences in performance, affective relationships, and career success of industrial middle managers." *Academy of Management Journal*, 27:619-635.

Von Glinow, M. A., and A. Krzyczkowska-Mercer. 1988. "Women in corporate America: A caste of thousands." *New Management* 6 (Summer):36-42.

Williams, J. E., and D. L. Best. 1982. *Measuring Sex Stereotypes: A Thirty-Nation Study.* Beverly Hills, CA: Sage.

Yogev, S. 1981. "Do professional women have egalitarian marital relationships?" *Journal of Marriage and the Family*, 43:865-871.

Reprinted from: Nina Colwill, "Women in Management: Power and Powerlessness," in B.C. Long and S.E. Kahn (eds.), *Women, Work and Coping*, pp. 73-89. Copyright © 1993 by McGill-Queen's University Press. Reprinted by permission.

Food for Thought and Application Questions

1. In her discussion of power differences among the sexes, Colwill cites research which finds " . . . that female managers, female entrepreneurs and female management students all demonstrate more masculine personality characteristics than do women in less male-dominated fields." Why do you think this is the case? Are certain types of women, those possessing more masculine traits, self-selecting into the roles, or is it more likely that the male-dominated position is shaping their personality (and behavior)? Describe a hypothetical example of the latter and discuss it in relation to the structuralist perspective.

2. Colwill asks the following questions: "If women are less interpersonally powerful than men—if they are less able to influence others—how are they better able than men to mobilize resources?" "How can women be more effective than men, while being less influential?" How do you account for these seeming discrepancies? Evaluate the following possible answers: (a) Due to discriminatory barriers and obstacles faced by working women, those who attain high-level, male-dominated positions are exceptionally qualified, more so than the "average" male manager; and (b) Men who manage by "getting others to do what they would not have otherwise done" (interpersonal power) do not motivate the same degree of enthusiasm in their employees as women who manage by involving their employees in decision-making. ✦

16

Removing Macho Management: Lessons From the Field of Education

Marian Court

Within a rapidly growing international body of literature on women in management, the question of whether men and women manage in different ways has become a focus of debate. Some state that there is a need for women to manage more like women (Loden 1985; Rudolph 1990; Rosener 1990), while others argue that it is inappropriate to focus on so-called male or female styles (Powell 1990; Sonnenfeld 1991; Epstein 1991).

In her discussion of the ways women lead, Judy Rosener (1990, p. 19) states that although some women have adopted a "command-and-control style of managing others," a style which she sees as "generally associated with men in large, traditional organizations," a new generation of women managers is drawing on skills and attitudes developed from their shared experience as women. Her research echoes the findings of other studies which describe the approaches of many women managers as emphasizing collaboration and participation through building relationships, sharing information and valu-

ing the views and contributions of all organizational members (see, for example, Marshall 1984; Shakeshaft 1989). These approaches have been described as employing a different kind of teamwork from those which draw on "macho" stereotypes and stress hierarchy, structured roles and functions and motivation driven by competition and individualism (Harragan 1977, 1983; Ellis and Wheeler 1991, pp. 79-80).

Taking an opposing view, Jeffrey Sonnenfeld points out that research has "identified a range of leadership styles among men" and it is wrong "to collapse all varieties of male leaders into one militaristic style" (1991, p. 160). Gary Powell writes that "There are likely to be excellent, average and poor managerial performers within each sex" (Powell 1990, p. 72), and Cynthia Epstein maintains that when we are talking and writing about managers, "The category should be 'people' not 'men and women'" (1991, p. 150). Epstein warns that research which focuses on gender differences reinforces gender stereotypes and downplays the similarities between men and women.

Although these three writers make some important points in their arguments that it is time to stop talking about gender differences in styles of management, we need to think carefully about the implications if, in our analyses of work relations, we stop examining differences in gendered *power relations*. We could fall into the trap of mistakenly assuming that men and women are now interacting on a social and organizational "level playing field" where the qualities and abilities of each person can be equally recognized and valued. This kind of thinking overlooks the ways in which the values of particular groups (in western societies mainly white, middle class, heterosexual men) have become embedded in the structures and practices of organizations and of society itself, helping (mainly these kinds of) men to maintain their positions at the top of most public corporations and public institutions.

When we consider what qualities have been commonly accepted as necessary for leadership, characteristics such as those described in Tom Wolfe's profiles of astronauts have held widespread appeal, creating an "influential macho stereotype of the qualities needed to excel . . . and whatever 'the right stuff' was, it could only be possessed by men" (Ellis and Wheeler 1991, p. 80). As British consultant Rennie Fritchie has pointed out, until very recently, the "tests given to choose people for management were the tests developed to stream young men into the forces in World War Two. Not surprisingly, women and people from other cultures dipped out" (quoted in McLeod 1990, p. 15).

In this article therefore, I do not wish to focus on the topic of *difference* in men's and women's management styles. Rather, I explore how the dominance of particular sets of assumptions about, and practices of, leadership and management has resulted in other ways of working being overlooked and undervalued. I argue that it is the persistence of hegemonic linkings between particular kinds of masculinity and leadership that underpins the marginalizing of women in management.

These issues are examined in relation to the field of educational administration in New Zealand. To "set the scene," I first of all outline some debates that have emerged within the restructuring of education in this country and overseas, then relate these debates to an analysis of leadership and gendered teaching/management hierarchies in schools. I draw on my study of a group of women middle managers in some New Zealand schools to analyze their affiliatory approach to leadership. Some of the difficulties women can encounter as they attempt to work as leaders in ways which they feel "fit" with their identities as women, while being located in schools which are organized within masculinist management cultures, are identified here.

Educational Administration and Hidden Agendas

In New Zealand, many educators have become concerned that within the recent restructuring of education (Ministry of Education 1990; Lough 1990), there have been attempts to impose an inappropriate business model of management on schools. Similar concerns have been voiced overseas; for example, Stephen Ball has stated that in the British educational system, "a transformation has begun to shift the governance of schools from professional/collegial in style to managerial/bureaucratic . . . the task of schooling is increasingly subject to the logic of industrial production and market competition" (Ball 1990, p. 153).[1] It is feared that this model could set up an organizational culture that is "hierarchical, competitive, individualist and highly task oriented . . . an instrumental culture in which ends are separated from means and people are valued only for what they produce" (Codd 1990, p. 22)—an organizational culture antithetical to the maintenance of democratic and socially just educational institutions.

The competitive market model of administration has been superimposed on an educational managerial model that has always been concerned with efficiency and control, however. As Stewart and Prebble (1985, p. 79-80) point out, in educational administration there has been "a prevailing ideology of technical rationality [that] steers the administrator to concentrate on issues of efficiency, output, productivity and systems maintenance" with this being cloaked by the use of more acceptable terms such as "facilitating," "motivating," "persuading" and "leading." Although the latter leadership discourse also exists, stated in the form of valuing the skills of teachers and collegial, collaborative decision making, in practice a bureaucratic model of hierarchically structured and authoritive leadership has been predominant in New Zealand's educational systems.

In this country, debates about what constitutes democratic, effective and efficient administration and leadership continue. However, one important fact is seldom acknowledged or seen as problematic. In schools it is mainly *male* administrators who control the work of what is predominantly a *female* teaching force.

Gender and Educational Leadership

Although 75% of New Zealand primary teachers are women, only 25% of the primary principals' positions are held by them. In secondary schools, women comprise 50% of the teachers, but only 19% of the principals. Despite a commonly held perception that the position of women has improved over the last ten years, Ministry of Education research shows that "Since 1985, there has been little change in the proportions of men and women primary and secondary teachers who are principals" (Slyfield 1991, p. 13).

The persisting under-representation of women in principals' positions and the lack of analysis of gender factors that impinge on educational leadership structures and practices are of particular concern when research findings show that schools with female principals have fewer discipline problems, higher faculty and student morale and higher student achievement (Sadker, Sadker and Klein 1986). Collegial decision making and collaborative ways of working have been shown to be effective in developing schools where staff, students and parents are well motivated towards learning (Chapman 1990), and gender has been identified as a significant factor here (Shakeshaft 1989). For example, an American analysis of principals' decision making styles and strategies found that:

> . . . in large and small schools alike, more decisions than were expected were of the collegial variety under female principals, while more decisions were made by the principal alone under male principals. . . . It was because

of the female principals' leadership qualities that their faculties exhibited higher levels of job satisfaction. Presumably if the male principals had been able to establish such close personal relations with teachers, and had exerted as much influence over the educational affairs of the school as the women did, their faculties would have shown equally high levels of satisfaction. (Charters and Jovick 1981, pp. 316, 328)

In a recent New Zealand study of decision making in innovative schools, Ramsay and his colleagues found that "women tended to be more open minded than men," more often initiating collaborative approaches (Ramsay et al. 1991, p. 22). If we agree, firstly, that collaborative approaches are likely to enhance the potential and the contributions of all members of a school, and secondly, that schools need to constantly monitor and be prepared to adapt their practices to ensure that the best possible learning environments are developed, it would seem from these studies that there are some vital lessons that could be learned from studying women principals' ways of working.

Yet women remain under-represented in school leadership. Why?

Male Hegemony

It is beginning to be acknowledged by some in the field of educational administration that the androcentric (male-centered) nature of theory, research and practice has contributed to assumptions ("so thoroughly internalized as to be virtually invisible to the individual who holds them") that women are not as able as men to be effective in administration, while there is instead, a "distinct possibility that women may, in fact, be better suited to the elementary school principalship than men" (Owens 1991, pp. 89, 98). Significantly, Robert Owens adds that "this has been well known for many years, but little discussed."[2] The processes of male hegemony are evident here.

There is an increasing body of literature investigating the ways in which the male domination of school leadership reflects male hegemony in society as a whole (see, for example, Connell et al. 1982; Connell 1987; Shakeshaft 1989; Blackmore 1989). Sociological and feminist studies have shown how in western societies our so-called private and public worlds are permeated with a culturally produced, and materially based, system of values and beliefs that reinforces the dominance of particular groups of men (Cox 1987). Their positions of power have enabled their values, attitudes, beliefs and practices to become established as the best or normal way to do things, while the views and practices of other groups have become defined as not only different, but inferior.

In these processes, particular constructions of masculinity have won ascendancy over other kinds of masculinity and over forms of femininity. Bob Connell argues that although nuances of this "hegemonic masculinity" may alter over time and place, in Western cultures it is presently organized around qualities of technical rationality and calculation, with its power sustained by a hypermasculine ideal of toughness, power and strength. This kind of masculinity exhibits competitiveness and confidence in personal abilities, especially in an ability "to dominate others and face down opponents in situations of conflict" (Connell et al. 1982, p. 73).

Perhaps influenced by this dominant social definition of what it is to be "masculine," and despite different economic and social realities, many people still seem to consider that men are the people best suited to be the actors and leaders in the public sphere. Women, on the other hand, are still assumed to be the people best suited for the work of childrearing and caring, and therefore, will need to place priority on their work in the home.

These assumptions feed in to the maintenance of the subordination of many women to men. Although the character and experience of this subordination will vary across time and place and according to the class and ethnicity of different groups of women, Bev James and Kay Saville-Smith (1989, p. 32) argue that in New Zealand's "gendered culture" there persists the "cult of domesticity." This is a set of commonsense beliefs that women naturally possess qualities of nurturance, caring and emotionality which best suit them to the activities and relationships that are most closely associated with the "private" world of the home. In cultures which differentiate between masculinity and femininity in these kinds of ways there are significant consequences for divisions of labour and for leadership. Links between authority and masculinity have accorded men a measure of cultural capital, building in them and in others an expectation of their "natural" ability and right to lead organizations. In schools for example, a hegemonic linking between physical force and masculinity has worked to create beliefs that principals need to be strong men who can control and discipline disruptive boys. Under the present "New Right free market" managerial paradigms, there are culturally produced links between masculinity and an authority grounded in skills of numeracy, technical logic and business competitiveness that can be seen to equip men as the people best suited to running schools as business enterprises. While these kinds of (shifting) associations resource men for leadership, they simultaneously "cool out" women, both in their own and in others' perceptions of their fitness for leadership positions in schools. Within the persisting domestic and material ideologies, women's primary place is more likely to be seen to be in the private world of the home or in the classroom as teachers where they can use their so-called feminine skills of caring and nurturing.

It is important to emphasize here that although ideas about what counts as masculinity or femininity vary and shift according to the culture, social conditions and expectations of a time, that which is associated with and accepted as masculine remains *valued* above that which is seen as feminine.

Affiliation, Autonomy and Educational Leadership

In 1970, Abraham Maslow's opinion that women are inferior to men is made clear in his introduction to his model of human motivation and needs:

> It is possible for a female to have all the specifically female fulfillments (being loved, having the home, having the baby) and then, without giving up any of the satisfactions already achieved, go on *beyond femaleness to the full humanness she shares with males*, for example, the full development of her intelligence, of any talents she may have, and of her own particular idiosyncratic genius. (Maslow 1970, p. xiv) (Emphasis added)

Such an analysis legitimates gender dichotomies and, implicitly, women's noninvolvement in leadership. Although Maslow's work on motivation has been strongly criticized, it has been very influential within educational administration (Shakeshaft 1989, p. 158; Owens 1991, pp. 106-114), supporting the liberal political conceptualizing of leadership as a quality exercised by autonomous, authoritative and masculine individuals.

Although such discourses work against all those who aspire to leadership positions while valuing close and warm relationships with others,[3] these linkings are particularly damaging and problematic for women, many of whom may feel they must submerge their definitions of self as a woman and conform to male norms. Other people may have difficulty seeing a woman as a "good" leader if she behaves according to a culturally defined femininity (being nurturing, intuitive or emotional); but if she is strong and behaves in a forceful, competitive or logically rational manner, under existing dominant definitions of

femininity she is likely to be seen as aggressive, hard or cold—"unfeminine." (Blackmore 1989)

These kinds of dilemmas have been overlooked in many past studies of women's aspirations to leadership, though some studies have suggested that affiliation is a women's need that may be hindering their promotion aspirations (Malcolm 1978; Neville 1988). I have argued that this view demeans women teachers (Court 1992), and Charole Shakeshaft (1989) draws on her analysis of over 200 dissertations, 600 research articles and her own research on women in administration, to show that these women leaders define excellence and fulfillment quite differently from the definitions propounded by theorists such as Maslow. Rather than seeking success in an individual autonomy, the women studied emphasized the importance of relationships and intimacy in their work as leaders.

In Mollie Neville's New Zealand study of successful women administrators, an awareness of, and emphasis on, relating to other people was not seen by them as a constraint on their ability to lead; rather, leadership was expressed as strong values of concern for people and the wish to work through cooperation rather than competition. These values were also seen by the sixteen women as part of their identities as women: they were "emphatic about the necessity to retain their sense of gender and to take their love and care of people into their managerial roles." (Neville 1988, p. 144)

However, in Neville's report of her research there is a worrying inconsistency. She writes that the women had: ". . . *broken through* what Malcolm calls 'affiliative needs' to take roles which other women do not see as traditional and *beyond where* so many women are *content* to operate" (ibid, p. 102) (Emphasis added). This wording gives a low status to qualities of affiliation, despite the fact that the quality of caring for people is described as one of the strengths of the women managers' styles (ibid, pp. 142-144). Further comments about the "successful" woman in education are that "Her major achievement has been to avoid the 'stuck' female roles in institutions, the nurturing caring roles that do not lead to promotion." (ibid, p. 149)

The inconsistency in what is reported as successful women's ways of working ("taking their love and care of people into their managerial roles") and the ways they actually achieved their positions (by avoiding the "stuck" nurturing roles), can be understood when it is remembered that most of the women in Neville's study rose to the top of a male-dominated institution by following what could be described as a male career pattern. They had gained experience in the technical tasks seen as important for promotion, and if married, they did not take time off for having children, having a supportive partner who was willing to move for their job promotions. Single or married, they often "bought" home help to help them keep on top of the inevitable housework.

It could seem from Neville's study that this is the way women are required to behave if they wish to attain management positions. But if the emphasis remains on finding ways for women to change themselves and to cope with what have been male-defined requirements for "success," these requirements and indeed, the hierarchical structures, career patterns and expectations about management that keep men in the majority of the top positions of educational leadership will not be challenged nor changed for a long time yet.

That a few women can reach top administrative positions if they fit into male norms as defined by those in power, is clear. Some would say that the Maggie Thatcher type of woman leader works within a dominant male style and there have been several books written to teach women how to succeed within this kind of management paradigm (see, for example, Harragan 1977). This approach has been criticized however, for accepting that women need to fit into what Sally Hel-

geson believes is "an alien culture" for many women (1990, p. xvii). She, and other writers, point out that many women are not attracted by traditional authoritarian management models and this is the reason why they choose not to apply for management positions. Elizabeth Al-Khalifa (1989, p. 89) argues that this is a resistance grounded in women's "positive valuation of their own 'femininity' and alternative perspectives on valued and effective behaviours in school management."

There is a need then, to change the dominant authoritarian, "macho" and overly technical, rational, economic paradigms of management and leadership. The next section of this paper aims to contribute to this work through a discussion of an affiliatory model of leadership espoused by a group of women educational administrators.

Aims of the Study and Research Stance

In 1989 I interviewed six women who were working in some primary and secondary schools in Taranaki (Court 1989a). My aim was to investigate their perceptions about their gender relations in their home and school situations to discover whether they thought these were influencing their work as educational administrators. This research developed out of a study of 30 women who had participated in a series of management training seminars. (Court 1989b)

Although it is seldom articulated, an author's own gender and gendered experiences are likely to colour any research and subsequent discussions of it. It is important to acknowledge here that my research questions and interpretations have been framed within my own world view and shaped by my past experiences as a woman educator and administrator in primary, secondary and tertiary institutions where men have been in the "top" positions with (varying degrees of) power to direct and control my work. Within "scientific" positivist views of research, acknowledging these facts could raise doubts about the objectivity of my research, opening up space for dismissing my discussion as biased and subjective. However, it has been pointed out that "The old distant voice of the objective observer/writer is now seen as a fiction, as a mechanism of power" (Jones 1992, p. 18). I agree with the opinion that, as researchers and writers, we need "to reveal our own partiality, self-consciously exposing the particular theoretical/cultural spectacles which determine our view and shape our accounts" if our texts are to open up "possibilities for others to bring their view to a dialogue" (ibid, p. 6). This, Jones argues, "invites response rather than simple acceptance or rejection" of the arguments we put forward.

Thus, my stance in the study on women teacher/managers was that of a (partial) "insider." As a Pakeha[4] I was a typical member of the original group of 30 women, and although these women unlike myself were neither married nor had children, we had all taught in either primary or secondary schools. We had also all attended the management training seminars to enhance our promotion chances. I may have shared some of the experiences of the other women, but as I carried out this research I was aware that "no matter how much our past personal experience figures and feeds into the research programme, we cannot assume it necessarily corresponds in any way to that of the research 'subjects'" (McRobbie 1982, p. 52). I knew that there was a need to "stand off" as much as possible from my own experience and try to treat "the familiar as strange" (Barton 1988, p. 112), while also treating my own experience seriously, as the "ground of my knowledge." (Smith 1974, p. 11; Strauss 1987, p. 11)

Research Methodology

At the end of the original questionnaire survey of the 30 women course members, I asked for volunteers to participate in a follow-up case history study of women's gender relations. From those who responded, I chose six women who represented as wide a range of home and school situations as possible, although they were of a similar age, between their late thirties and late forties. Pauline Chapman[5] was an assistant principal of a large rural primary school, Nichola Adams a teaching principal in a two-teacher rural primary and Susan Baker a teaching principal in a six teacher primary school. The three secondary women were heads of departments: Robyn Hunt in a co-educational rural high school, Dorothy Anselm in a city girls' school and Mary Ross in a city boys' school. Thus all of the women's school positions combined teaching and administration responsibilities.

There were both married and single women in the group I chose. Robyn was married, but she had chosen not to have children as she "was not the maternal type" and she wanted a career. Of the three other married women, Dorothy and Nichola had had time out of teaching to care for young families, while Susan had to continue teaching when her children were small as she was at that time the sole income earner in her family. Pauline and Mary had both remained single after facing dilemmas of choosing between a career or marriage and a family: at the time of this research they had both decided that under current expectations surrounding women's role in the family, they could not do justice to both.

The study used a conversational interview methodology (Oakley 1981). I was concerned to try to understand the worlds of the women as they constructed them, "grounding" any theory in their concepts and theorizing (Glaser and Strauss 1967). Thus the interviews did not adhere to a set of structured questions, but largely followed the women's own concerns within the broad focus of the research. At the beginning of the first interviews I explained to each woman that I was interested to hear her perceptions about what it was like to be a woman working in a position of leadership. I asked them to talk about this in any way they wished, though I was particularly interested in whether they thought their home and work gender relations had impacted on their experiences as women teachers and administrators.

Between two and four interviews were carried out with each woman, with the interviews being recorded, transcribed and then analyzed. To do this, I read and thought about the transcripts as a series of stories, looking for significant episodes and themes, which I then categorized. The transcripts were colour coded following the method outlined by Middleton (1988), and sent back to the women with my list of codes for them to check their comments and my interpretations. These were discussed during follow-up interviews, at which stage the concept of male hegemony always needed explanation. The draft chapters were also sent back to the women for comment as they were completed. Throughout the research, none of the women wished to withdraw any of their original statements, or alter the analysis that was developed.

Themes in the Study of Women in Educational Leadership

As I thought about the women's comments and stories, four main themes emerged as significant in their experience: the sexual division of labour in both their home and school situations; their struggles to "win" authority and the "right" to lead; their varying responses to their anger when meeting prejudice and discrimination; and the importance of the idea of affiliation in their holistic management philosophies and styles (Court 1989a, 1990, 1992). In this article I am focusing on the last of these themes.

It is important to note here that not all women experience the work of leadership and administration in the same ways; nor do all women manage one way and all men another. In even this small group of women a variety of experiences and opinions were evident. They were working through the contradictions and expectations surrounding nurturing and leadership in individual ways that did not neatly fit stereotypes of femininity but reflected their different positions, personalities and backgrounds. However, there was clear agreement on some ideas, approaches and experiences.

The views presented by the women support Charole Shakeshaft's (1989, pp. 195-198) suggestion that five factors might conceptualize the work of women educational administrators: *relationships* with others are central; *building community* is an essential part of their style; *teaching and learning* are their major foci; the line separating the *public and private worlds blurs* for them and *marginality* overlays their daily work as a result of their token status and of sexist attitudes towards them. Each of these elements emerged within the women's accounts.

A Holistic, Affiliatory Approach

What became clear to me as I analysed the women's comments was that they were describing an *holistic* approach to educational administration, weaving together what have traditionally been seen as dichotomies. These women were taking the values, beliefs and skills they had developed within their private *caring/nurturing* positions in the home into their "public" positions of *managing/leading*. Comments reflecting qualities of caring and emotionality are threaded through their descriptions of what is important in instructional leadership and participatory management and *affiliation*—in the sense of building relationships, a sense of group belonging and shared decision making—emerges as an important concept to describe leadership.

I have chosen Mary Ross's words to illustrate this perspective. As a head of department in a boys' secondary school she said she wanted to:

. . . involve people in goals that aim to create stimulating, enjoyable learning environments for kids. As teachers, I believe we are here to 'serve' the kids. I try to do this through involving people in goals and the sharing of ideas and resources. Cooperation and respect for one another are important, and I think it is really important for kids to feel loved and wanted and for teachers to be open and warm.

Mary's descriptions of her style of teaching and ways of relating to other staff reflects a bringing together of her "private" and "public" selves. She described this as:

. . . being real. With my kids I talk about what I do at the weekends or my friends. If I'm hungry I ask them what they've got to eat—and they love that. There are friends I can go to on the staff and say, 'I want a cuddle—give me a cuddle, quick!' and I cuddle my boys. The senior administration know I do that and they don't mind. I still get on my father's knee and give him a kiss and a cuddle, and probably that background has a lot to do with the way I function at school.

In this group's descriptions of their ways of working, affiliation is not merely a seeking out of relationships; it is also a quality that looks to being aware of others' needs. For Mary, this empathy is founded in a trust in herself:

It doesn't matter who you are, male or female, if you come in and you're really strong at something, people are automatically on the back foot. It comes down to being yourself and being able to see where other people are coming from. It's accepting people for who they are.

Susan Baker's description of her attitude towards a man who had rudely challenged her authority as a primary school principal also illustrates this kind of integration of empathy, affiliation and self esteem. She said:

I think he has found the changes in education very hard to take and I really feel very sorry for him. He comes from the old system and he's just got to the stage where he isn't able to accept change. He is an old chap and he is seeing his power eroded. It doesn't hurt me to perhaps pander to his ego a bit to make it easier for him. And I don't feel I have to have power like that. It's more important to develop a sharing, family atmosphere in the school.

Susan's attitude illustrates the kind of rationality described by Gould (1983) who argues that in a society where one must live with others, rather than valuing competitiveness and individuality, empathizing and connecting with others should be valued to allow the development of collective action.

Leadership and Nurturance, Mothering and Managing

Some of the women in my study saw their ways of working as leaders and managers as a logical extension of their identities as women. For Dorothy Anselm (a head of department in a girls' secondary school and a mother of four children) being a woman was closely linked with being a "nurturer." She described this as: "that sharing of yourself with others that you learn to do as you are growing up." She pointed out though, that this does not mean that all women are necessarily or essentially caring and nurturing in their ways of working, nor that men cannot or do not work in these ways. (As Lynne Segal [1987, p. 143] writes, "The soft and gentle man is not such a rare creature.")

Some studies of women in management have tended to suggest that women's use of participatory styles is natural (Rosener 1991). This can imply that women somehow have a biologically determined quality that programmes them to be sharing and caring. It is wrong to attribute socially learned and developed values and ways of behaving to any such biological essence however. As Dorothy reiterated:

> Women's nurturing skills are *learnt* and learnt very quickly if they are bringing up children. It's a 24 hour a day, seven days a week job where you are giving out all the time. I can remember Sam watching me one time—answering the phone, stepping over the baby, making the dinner and folding the washing—and him saying, 'How do you do it all?' He finds it difficult to put a meal on and get it timed to the right time. And it's just practice. It's not being clever. It's just long practice at sharing yourself. . . . If some little voice is calling you in the night, you wake up and share your sleeping time—that need that has to be met. . . . I guess I carry on being a mother all the time really, at school nurturing my HOD, carrying him and acting as a go-between with him and the rest of the staff.

It is also wrong to assume such skills can be learnt only by women, or only by women who are mothers. Pauline Chapman (an assistant principal in a primary school, who is single with no children), commented:

> I get treated as a mother if I let myself be. People would like to say that I was the comfortable person over in the B Block who the children could come to if they were hurt. Whereas in fact I'd like someone else to look after them because I'd like to read some papers at lunchtime or plan some strategy so I can get something to happen in the educational area at school. I think every woman has the expectation that she will be the caregiver laid on her though.

There are some significant consequences associated with this expectation. When women are the people always associated with responsibilities for caring, this can lay heavy demands on them. For example, they are more likely than men to be required to help and support other staff and this work can often extend beyond professional support into supporting staff in their private lives. Many women will not object to undertaking this support, in fact will argue that it is very important, both for the people involved and for the organizations in which they work. However, such "people" work is open to being overlooked and undervalued by those who assume that it is a part of women's nature to care about others' welfare.

Margaret Malcolm has also pointed out that within commonly accepted stereotypes, women administrators face *contradictory* expectations: As women, they are "supposed to be subservient, nurturant and maintain effective relationships, yet as administrators they are supposed to be independent, assume leadership and be task oriented" (1978, p. 2). Women who move into management positions in schools can thus be enmeshed in a kind of "schizophrenic" existence. Whether they are married or single, they can be viewed as "mothers" trying to be "fathers," without the authority of "fathers." They are surrounded by expectations that they will fill nurturant rather than authoritative leadership roles (Johnston 1986, pp. 216-219), yet are also expected to lead. Their leadership is expected to employ consultation and democratic decision making strategies, yet these ways of working can often be interpreted as the leader "not having an opinion of her own"—perhaps she can't make up her mind? Such contradictory expectations undermine confidence, to say the least!

Dorothy lacked confidence in her ability in public roles. Although she felt she had been successful as a mother and her husband Sam was always telling her that when it came to being a leader and manager at school, "Of course you can do it . . . whatever makes you think you can't?," she still doubted her abilities. As I listened to her telling me about her work, it seemed clear to me that at the level of thinking about her own qualifications and experience for management, Dorothy had not given herself credit for having developed within her mothering responsibilities skills which she was using in her work as an educational manager.

That she hadn't made this connection is not surprising when we consider how the links between the roles of mother/caregiver and manager are ignored in management manuals and academic literature, as well as in common leadership discourses. Although links between mothering and teaching are often made, such as in the statement "Being a mother has made me a much better teacher," it is not generally accepted that being a mother (or caregiver) and housekeeper develops management skills as diverse as budgeting and conflict resolution. We have to turn to the work of socialist feminist scholars to find an analysis that will tease out what Shelagh Cox and Bev James describe as a: "curious conflation of attributes that constitute the 'ideal' housewife and mother. She manages the house, does its menial work and provides moral and psychological guidance. She combines roles that are seen to be quite separate in the public world—administrator, charwoman, counsellor, teacher and priestess" (1987, p. 10).

A significant area of common skills can be found in the juggling of tasks and demands. Dorothy's description of concentrating on several things at once is a common experience for caregivers working in the home, and many studies of school principals have described the need for administrators to work on the run, carrying several tasks at various stages of completion without letting constant interruptions distract them (see, for example, Wolcott 1973). Male hegemony however, is evident in the commonly held perceptions that the juggling skills used by women working (unpaid) in their homes are different from, and less important than, those required in management work in the public (and paid) sphere.

The academic theorizing of school management has become increasingly surrounded by a mystique of techniques that are described in "scientific" and economic terminology—"hygiene motivators," "an-tecedent transactions," "techno-structural intervention strategies," "inputs and outputs." The women in this study were rejecting the notion that this emphasis on technical kinds of expertise was all that their management and leadership jobs required. They talked about building school communities where people felt happy and supported and they stressed the importance of working in instructional leadership roles that developed collegial relationships with their staff.

Integrating Instructional Leadership, Technical Management and Affiliation

In educational administration, instructional leadership has been seen as a most important role for a principal to fulfil if learning environments are to be improved. It is interesting to note that many studies have shown that more women emphasize the educational leadership parts of their work, while more men view the principal's job from a managerial/industrial perspective (Shakeshaft 1989, p. 171; Pitner 1981). In considering these findings, it has been suggested that men are more likely to see themselves moving through teaching into a management position than women, whose primary motivation is a focus on teaching. If this is so, it seems logical that women who do move into school leadership positions are likely to take with them their focus on teaching and learning.

Most of the six women in this study had decided early to make teaching their chosen career, and when they were asked what they enjoyed most about their management jobs, all of them were still placing teaching and student contact highly. Robyn Hunt summed up their feelings in this comment: "I really enjoy the delight most students have in learning and the process of being involved in their development." Like the women in Neville's study who described the motive in their management work as "to improve education for children" (1988, p. 140),[6] these six women were linking the work of the classroom to the management tasks they needed to accomplish. Robyn, who was fairly new in her job as head of department in a coeducational rural secondary school, explained her goals like this:

> The department can't run efficiently without good, well organized resources which the staff know where to find and how to use. And schemes of work are essential for staff sanity and student learning and enthusiasm. Just now I'm having to put a lot of time into doing this kind of organizing, but once done, it should run itself and give me and my staff the time and energy to support each other and update our knowledge and pass this on to our students.

It could be argued that Robyn's position as head of department is one most closely associated with instructional leadership and therefore it would be expected that she would give it these kinds of emphases. What is interesting in her view of the job though, is the way the instructional, technical and afflictive aspects of educational management are integrated. The technical tasks (such as this example of cataloguing and organizing resources) were not being seen as an end in themselves, but their accomplishment seen as necessary to give her and her staff "the time and energy to support each other" and to have time to update their subject knowledge for their students.

Dorothy Anselm had a similar approach. When she was asked what were the most important things she did as a manager, she said:

> I don't know how I could rank them—I would prefer to bracket them as of equal importance—like getting more equipment and developing better methods of teaching, alongside listening to staff and encouraging them to solve their problems themselves, and especially encouraging women to have a try—and attempting to modify

school procedures like prizegiving and uniforms.

Building a Community for Learning Through Team Work and Open Communication

Improving learning environments was the main aim for all the women in this study. To achieve this goal the women emphasized the need to work *alongside* teachers and parents. Susan said, "All people working in a school need to feel they are important and necessary."

Pauline Chapman demonstrated her belief in teamwork by giving her staff some of her own administration time to help them. She said: ". . . I go into their rooms and teach so that they can have thinking time—and time to take out one child who needs social teaching or counselling." This is a different kind of teamwork to that which has been described as a male sports/militaristic approach where every team member knows his role and function and the importance of sticking to the rules and obeying the captain (Ellis and Wheeler 1991). Pauline's approach flattens hierarchy, encourages flexibility and places her as a co-worker who is enabling teachers to generate directions and strategies.

Nichola Adams, a primary school principal, showed a similar orientation. Sharing information as openly as possible was an important part of involving her colleagues in decision-making processes. In their study of women principals, Charters and Jovick (1981) found that this way of working built high levels of job satisfaction for teachers. However, Nichola said that she was not working in these ways just to build a happy working environment for teachers, though she did point out that: ". . . openness in decision making and openness to ideas and suggestions will in turn develop people who are involved and likely to be happier in their teaching." She was wanting to stress that: "The learning environment will be better if there is harmony between the principal and staff in the directions they take for children's learning. I've tried to let Helen and Claire know everything that's going on as I feel that's the only way to operate in a small school like this." Nichola commented on what she saw as gender differences here, stating: "The past principal who was a man didn't share things, but I want it to be an equal thing, with us all planning things together." She added that many of the men she had known in education had been: ". . . selfish about sharing information and power . . . some got themselves in awful knots as a consequence. One man actually got very sick in the end."

It needs to be pointed out though, that rather than being selfish, the kind of behaviour Nichola describes is as much a consequence of social expectations that men should display independence (an aspect of the "masculinist" leadership paradigm), as the expectation that nurturing and sharing should be a woman's way of working. Within western social practices, many boys and men learn to be independent and to speak with "a voice of authority" as part of becoming "masculine."

For Nichola, being the one to make the decisions was not as important as empowering others to share this process. She recognized here that her sharing stance was not just altruism; it was also a way of empowering herself. She said: "When there's a difficulty for example, we can support each other. . . . I want to give the other staff the opportunity to be part of making the school go. I find Helen's insight exciting: I can only see things from my own perspective and they can see things differently." Here she was working from a recognition of her own limitations as well as from a wish to draw others into planning and decision making. Her aim was to enable each member of the group to grow from exposure to the others' ideas and strengths.

The other women in this study had similar views and believed that in their communication and relationships it was important "to be open and honest and admit you don't know everything—I'm no cleverer than anybody else," as Dorothy said. Ramsay and his colleagues report a similar stance in their description of the style of an innovative woman principal who: ". . . encouraged staff to air their own concerns (and) voiced her own concerns . . . She continued to be open to learning new skills and showed her willingness to accept criticism without feeling the need to defend herself in the school" (1991, p. 7).

Mary took her frankness about her own limitations into her teaching as well as her management work and her "private" life:

> I don't like being with people who can't admit their mistakes. I'm not perfect but I'm willing to say, 'Hey, this is where I'm at. I've got some problems in this area—can you help me?' And I say this to my kids as well as to my friends and to the staff. It's about being real and being able to admit your faults and weaknesses and build on those. Face your fears. They watch me face my fears. If I get something that I don't know I say, 'Look you guys, I'm not really sure what I'm doing now. Just hang on a tick.' Or I'll say, 'I'm not up to that bit myself yet! Let me go home tonight and check it out and I'll let you know tomorrow.' Or, 'What do you think we should do here?'

The women highlighted the place of this kind of open communication in their strategies for building consensus and trust. In all aspects of management communication skills are important; as Peter Gronn (1982, p. 30) has pointed out: "Talk *is* the work and talk *does* the work." Shakeshaft (1989, p. 185) suggests that women's asking questions of others is a way of involving them in discussion and of facilitating group problem solving. That style emerged in both Nichola's wanting to ask, "Shall we?" rather than saying "We will," and in Mary's use of questions, such as "What do you think we should do here?"

This is a view of leadership that doesn't see a need for the leader to present an image of infallibility. Rather, it emphasizes a belief in authenticity and honesty and a bringing of a sense of "wholeness" (warts and all?) to the work of teaching and leadership, a wholeness orientation that was also observed by Judy Marshall (1984, p. 113) in her study of women managers—though this is not to build an argument that all women necessarily take this view or work in these ways as part of some innate kind of femininity.

Leadership and Followership: Dilemmas and Resolutions

In thinking about these issues and about how to build positive working relationships that eschew hierarchy, some feminists have rejected the notion of leadership. Nancy Hartsock has warned that there is a danger here; she argues that this can result in:

> . . . a submersion of the identity of the individual, thereby falling into a form of female pathology of loss of self. . . . It is better to have an understanding of power for the individual which stresses both its dimensions of competence, ability and creativity and does not lose sight of effective action. (1983, p. 253)

In her discussion of this area, Judy Marshall bases her ideas on the theories of Bakan to argue that there are "two fundamental tendencies, or principles in human functioning, 'agency' and 'communion'" (1984, p. 61). She suggests that an adequate model of women's identities would need to see tendencies towards interdependence balanced and enhanced by forces towards independence (ibid, pp. 81-2). Describing dualities such as "agency" and "communion" however, runs the risk of reinforcing the splits underlying other dichotomous ways of viewing experience, such as the dividing of experience into "private" and "public" spheres and dividing work into that which is men's and that which is women's. There needs to be a perspective which takes a more holistic approach.

This is difficult though within the present structures which split administration and teaching, leading and following. For women who are trying to develop an affiliatory model that works against such dichotomies as well as against cultural expectations about men's and women's so-called different work roles and capabilities, dilemmas such as the following can result.

Nichola said she wanted the decision making in her school "to be an equal thing, with us all planning things together." Here, she saw a need for someone to initiate the group processes and ensure that the decisions are made and implemented at the end, and she was working within these roles as principal. She also said that what she enjoyed in her leadership situation, was "the challenge—the chance to be part of a team, yet I have to take responsibility for my own decisions." She is hinting here at a dilemma which can confront leaders who want to share power, but who may not always agree with a decision made by the group. Collaborative decision making requires the reaching of consensus, something that can at times be difficult (and time consuming!) to attain. In Nichola's case it was usually possible, as hers was a small school and her three staff also wanted a "co-operative sharing group" who would make decisions together; they were willing to work through to a consensus on most issues. This had enabled Nichola to move into professional areas where she said she was: ". . . taking the lead in lots of things. Like an IQ testing issue. I talked it all over with Helen because you are responsible for motivating your staff's thinking."

Robyn had a similar view of leadership to Nichola's. She saw the HOD as a researcher for the department, the person who finds out what has to be read and passes material on. She said: "For proper consensus, the department has to be as literate as you are." Robyn had a clearly thought through philosophy behind her determination to manage through consensus:

> If you are the dominant and authoritarian decision maker, you expend an awful lot of energy on: 1) making the decisions, 2) justifying them, and 3) making sure they are carried through. If you expend that time and energy on developing a consensus point of view, you're likely to have a much more motivated department because they've all been involved with the decision and agreed to it. It's less energy sapping. It's not necessarily less time consuming. But you're not IT. You might be the initiator, you might put forward an idea, but if they are really into consensus, they'll come up with six others, so you'll get more ideas out of it too.

However for her the dilemma was that she was meeting resistance here.

> I wanted all of it discussed—the setting of priorities, ordering of which resources, the best way to set out the resource room. I wanted it discussed and a consensus reached. And I wanted to make sure everyone spoke to each topic, with no reneging. But I haven't been able to implement that at the moment. That concept is totally foreign to the people in my department—they're not really sure about it. Two agreed, but you can't manage a consensus on two, you've got to have everyone.

The problem of finding out which decisions teachers want and need to be involved in is not one unique to Robyn: there is a large literature that discusses this issue. But she was finding it difficult to get two of the men on her staff to even consider her way of working as a team: "One of them just laughed, and another said, 'That's what you're paid to do.' I haven't worked out how to get around that one yet." One of the challenges here is to find ways to change the present bureaucratic

structuring and cultures which create hierarchical and fixed distinctions (both in salary and status) between teachers and administrators. Democratic ways of working such as Robyn describes could perhaps become more accepted if, for example, job sharing or team project strategies were used, with payments being made to the individuals or groups involved for the duration of the task or responsibility.[7] Obviously, paying some people more than others when we expect all to become fully involved in the task is inequitable.

For Dorothy the dilemmas were more personal. She said that "consensus decision making and dealing with [confronting] sticky problems" were both important aspects of her management work. She revealed that she had to work hard to hold these two elements in a sometimes uncomfortable tension. Although like the other women in this study she strongly emphasized the importance of team-building, this did not mean that she would allow herself to renege on making tough decisions on her own when she thought this was necessary. In her comments she showed that she was willing to confront power and take responsibility for "sorting out" difficult situations, even when this might cause her personal stress or anxiety: "I don't want people to not like me, and when I'm confronting someone, my heart beats like mad and I feel tired afterwards. But I feel very firmly that it's kinder to people in the long run to have honesty." Working within bureaucratic school structures had meant for Dorothy (as for the other women) that she had to "stand alone" at times. Learning that she would have to do this if she was to be seen not merely as a token woman but as a person in authority, had been a difficult and important step for her: "You have to stand up and take responsibility. That was a big learning thing for me—can't blame God, can't blame Sam, nor the children—it's got to be me responsible for that lot. I've got to keep plugging away at changing people's minds and educating people."

The women's comments about leadership and shared decision making revealed that they "held the reins" to varying degrees. Both personality and factors such as group support were influences here. When Susan took up her principal's position, she met resistance and antagonism from the staff, and although their actions made her feel angry, she said she knew she needed to control her anger if she was to be able to work with them towards a goal of establishing collegial ways of working and greater community involvement in the school. Her attitude here was not a meek one: she said, "I knew I couldn't let them break me . . . and I'm an extremely determined person." She was planning strategies that would enable her to confront the resistance while protecting her own position and her situation: "Co-operation, consensus and delegation are all important, but there is also a need for a principal to quietly and firmly hold the reins and make decisions when this is required."

Pauline's leadership style was a little different and perhaps was a response to an acute awareness of being in a position of minority status (Kanter 1977). She preferred to: "lead from behind, planting ideas," that she was happy to see others take up. When asked for an example of how that worked, she said: "I suppose getting the principal to write and post up agendas for staff meetings was one example. I just kept showing him my agendas for the Junior School meetings, and one day he said he thought he'd try doing that for staff meeting, so I offered to help him." This strategy of "leading from behind" can be seen to avoid the glare of being "out front," initiating from a position of high visibility. For many women leaders, such a position can result in problems of isolation. Pauline's strategy however is also one which fits a philosophy that values team, work and co-operation. It is a non-hierarchical approach that can empower staff to take action themselves and is based in a different kind of authority from that founded on the tradition and status of a position "at the top."

Jill Blackmore argues that hierarchical authority is associated with *power over* others and she points out that:

> . . . leadership 'skills' can be used in a different way. Rather than privileging the individual who is often already in a position of status and power because of the possession of specialist knowledge, capacities, skills or role allocation, expertise can, in a co-operative environment, empower the individual and the group. Leadership, and the power which accompanies it, would be re-defined as the ability to *act with* others. (1989, p. 123)

The women in this study made distinctions between what they saw as traditional male definitions of authority, and their own kinds of leadership which they saw as based in relationships with, and responsibility towards, others. Dorothy said:

> If you are defining authority in the way that it is seen in a competitive male world, I'd say it was probably recognition, and the power to enforce your will. But as a leader I don't see myself wanting to work that way. I see the wisdom thing as more important, being sensible and showing wisdom.

Robyn said that traditionally, authority was probably defined as: ". . . power—the ability to have people do the things you want them to do, the way you want them to. But leadership should be doing things the way the group wants them done."

Susan summed up this view of leadership by making a link with the Maori concept of *mana*: "I think authority is based in a person having mana—the Maori concept sums it up for me. It is earned, and then what a person says will be listened to with respect and treated as being of value to the group." Their views of leadership emphasize acting with others and basing authority in "a skill and knowledge . . . which demonstrates its force to those concerned in terms they can grasp" (Blackmore 1989, p. 123).

The findings of this study make it clear though, that taking this stance is not always easy, or perhaps even possible, for women who work as leaders in male-dominated organizations.

Responses to Resistance

My discussion has revealed some of the difficulties women can experience as they seek to establish themselves and their own kinds of authority when they move into leadership positions in schools (see also Court 1989a, pp. 109-130, 1992). I have discussed elsewhere the place of anger in the responses of this group of women to discrimination and experiences of, for example, sexual harassment and bullying (Court 1990). The women's responses ranged from disappointment, through feelings of fear, frustration and fury.

As they talked about their experiences each of the women said that in her work with some men and women, she had to avoid being threatening. In particular they had to be careful about *what* they said and *how* they said things. The need to avoid different kinds of retaliatory responses is one of the factors lying behind these perceptions. Pauline described some of her experiences while working in her teachers' union; she thought that:

> A woman's strongest way of working is sitting down and talking things out, so that I know your needs and we can work things out. But I have had experience of women's ways of working like this being seen as a 'power play' by men, where they have seen the women as 'locking themselves away', and this is threatening to men. They have become very bitter at times.

In this situation, Pauline's description of her style of "leading from behind" as: "planting ideas with others and letting them grow," suggests that she was using a strategy of *nudging* people towards change

(May 1988). Such nudging can be an effective technique of transformation; it holds fewer risks of retaliation than more confrontational methods of demanding or imposing change and works through a building of alliances and an initiating of slow changes.

However, like Dorothy, Pauline had also learnt that there were times when she had to be the one to stand up front. She was working to change male dominance in both structural and attitudinal areas and despite her preference to "work from behind," here she had found that:

> . . . there is a need to be political; to be really well-prepared, to know my facts and have them right and be able to quote them calmly. I've learnt to be ready, to dig in and not be afraid of getting knockbacks, to make sure I ask the questions I want to know the answers to, no matter who it is I am talking to . . . and to have no fear of hierarchical structures.

Nichola pointed out however, the difficulties for her of trying to change the conservative attitudes of the rural community where she worked:

> You've got to think about how much energy you've got. When you want to create change, you have to say to yourself, 'Can I cope with the conflict it's going to cause? Have I got the energy at this stage?' You can create your own conflict or you can hold it off. Right now I'm planning for the camp I'm taking the whole school on, and then there's all the management changes under Tomorrow's Schools. What I'm saying is that it's learning priorities. There are so many things one could pursue but there are only so many hours in the day.

Women like these who place a high store on working for change can end up burning the candle at both ends. In particular, it is clear that unequal power relations between women and men were taking a toll on the energies and emotions of the group of women I studied.

Some Further Considerations

Resistance to women's views about, and practices in, management does not only come from those people with whom they work however. It is also evident among academics who are researching and theorizing in the field of educational administration.

At the beginning of this article I stated that in education in New Zealand at the present time, alongside the current revised "Taylorist" educational management discourse with its emphasis on technical systems of control, costeffectiveness, staff rationalization, performance and outcomes, there exists an awareness of the significance of team-building in educational leadership, in the processes of decision making, of motivation and in job satisfaction. It is clear from my research, and other studies on women in management, that such team work requires the skills of affiliation, the ability to build and maintain relationships and a sense of belonging. These are the very skills that have traditionally been learned by girls and women within socializing processes. Most educational administration theories about consultative and participatory management do not make this gendered link however. Researchers and writers who do recognize these skills as important are likely only to see a need for them to be taught in management training programmes (see, for example, the analysis offered in Johnson and Snyder 1988, pp. 315-330) and team- work is commonly framed within a model that stresses tasks and functions in ways that do not challenge or alter hierarchies of control.

It is encouraging to note that there are the beginnings of an awareness of the effects of such male hegemonic processes in the work of some mainstream theorists. For example, in a recent interview with Tom Sergiovanni (a prominent researcher and theorist in the field of educational administration), he states:

When I first began to read feminist literature, I thought, 'Who are these arrogant people?' But it turns out they are right. Management literature traditionally was written by men for men, and its values—individualism, competition—define success in a masculine way. Maslow's theory exults self-actualization; self this self that. As a group, women tend not to define success and achievement that way. They are more concerned with community and sharing. (quoted in Brandt 1992)

In recognizing that many women are working in ways that do not fit within the dominant management discourses, it must also be acknowledged though that women are not a unitary group: not all women will choose to work in affiliatory styles such as I have described in this article. Dorothy, for example, commented that she had experienced a woman principal who worked in hierarchical ways and did not share power easily. She explained this by saying that: "They are the Maggie Thatcher types—possibly they think that's the only way to work. . . . Possibly it's also worse for women in principals' positions; because of the struggle women have to get there and to stay there, perhaps they must cover up their vulnerabilities."

Zillah Eisenstein has argued that in cultures where men and certain kinds of masculinity are dominant, women are faced with three options. Firstly:

. . . agreeing to compete in the male-defined world of politics on its own terms, in the manner of Maggie Thatcher. Second, there is the option of withdrawing from that world, out of pessimism as to its essentially patriarchal nature. . . . Finally there is the option of entering the world and attempting to change it, in the image of the women-centered values at the core of feminism. (1981, p. 144)

As I have argued, discussion of gender inequalities needs to move beyond a narrow focus on gender differences. When male standards, values and practices are seen as the norm, a focus on women's sameness or difference from men allows women to be labelled as the problem. "A more useful political analysis would draw attention to the way in which the current economic system encourages certain behaviours and discourages others" (Bacchi 1990). We need to consider how we can best reconstruct not only our schools and organizational work relations, but society and culture itself, so that:

> Any society we set out to organize anew would surely be a celebration of multiplicity and individual difference. . . . The good qualities deemed masculine—courage, strength and skill, for instance—and the good qualities seen as feminine—tenderness and the ability to feel and express feelings—should be the qualities available to all and recognized and acclaimed wherever they occur. (Cockburn 1985, p. 254)

Conclusion

In education, critical theorists such as John Codd (1990, p. 20) argue that a new model of leadership is needed to avoid the waste that results from hierarchical systems that cut out participation and collaboration. The affiliative leadership style described in this article offers an approach which eschews hierarchical control in favour of sharing of information and power through mutually supportive team decision making and problem solving. The primary goal for the women in this study was the development of positive, stimulating and caring learning environments for children through working with teachers and parents as colleagues and equals.

It is time for school staffs, boards of trustees and academic educators to give this approach wide support, along with the recognition that this kind of leadership is favoured by many of the women who have achieved leadership positions in schools. Such support and recognition will contribute to the removal of persisting gender inequalities in school administration and to

the building of school communities which will value diversity and the strengths and contributions of all. If educational institutions are to be transformed in these ways, some more far reaching changes are also required. Shifts in attitudes and practices at the levels of policy, curriculum, teaching and learning environments and interactions, management theory and practices—in fact, social interactions across a wide range of sites in both our private and public worlds—are needed. What must change is the hegemony that reinforces ideas and structures that maintain certain kinds of male individuals as the leaders of society and the definers of culture.

Endnotes

1. Rebore's (1985) American text on "how to manage the educational enterprise" is an example of a technocratic human resource management model applied to education, defining sets of roles, tasks, rights and responsibilities for specialist administrators in community relations, administrative support services, facilities, personnel/employee relations, pupil-personnel relations and building management.

2. In specifying that women could be more "suited" to elementary principalships there are some underlying assumptions that need questioning. Is there an implication here that women's "nature" only qualifies them for nurturing jobs in schools where young children are taught? Such assumptions can be traced back to ideological arguments that use the biological differences between men and women to support claims that women are more emotional and nurturing and less rational and authoritative than men. This in turn is used (often unconsciously) to justify the male domination of influential higher status, higher paid decision-making positions in the public sphere.

3. There are also class, race and sexuality factors involved here as the norms of leadership are based on the cultural assumptions of men who are mainly middle class, white and heterosexual. A recent example of research that illustrates the

persisting influence of Maslow's model of motivation on ideas about leadership is Moorhead and Nediger (1990).

4. The women who attended the course were all Pakeha (white New Zealanders). This reflects the marginalized status of Maori women in education in this country. Although there is a growing literature exploring this issue, Maori women's viewpoints about educational administration have yet to be documented.

5. The women's names are pseudonyms.

6. Mollie Neville notes that two of the women administrators in her study had continued teaching, though they had attained positions where they could free themselves from a teaching load (1988, p. 140).

7. Such strategies are presently possible within, for example, the New Zealand primary school regulations for job sharing and for the senior responsibility scheme (Court 1993).

References

Al-Khalifa, E. 1989. "Management by halves: Women teachers and school management." In H. DeLyon and F. Widdowson Mignuiolo (Eds.), *Women Teachers: Issues and Experiences*. Philadelphia: Open University Press.

Bacchi, C. L. 1990. *Same Difference*. Sydney: Allen and Unwin.

Ball, S. 1990. "Management as moral technology." In S. Ball (ed.) *Foucault and Education*. London: Routledge.

Barton, L. 1988. *The Politics of Special Educational Needs*. London: Falmer Press.

Blackmore, J. 1989. "Educational leadership: A feminist critique and reconstruction." In J. Smythe (ed.), *Critical Perspective in Educational Leadership*. London: Falmer Press.

Brandt, R. 1992. "On rethinking leadership: A conversation with Tom Sergiovanni." In *Educational Leadership*, 49, 5 (February).

Chapman, J. 1990 (ed.). *School Based Decision-Making and Management*. London: Falmer Press.

Charters, W. W. and T. D. Jovick 1981. "The gender of principals and principal-teacher relations." In P. Schmuck et al. (Eds.), *Educational Policy and Management: Sex Differentials*. New York: Academic Press:316-328.

Cockburn, C. 1985. *Machinery of Dominance: Women, Men and Technical Knowhow*. London: Pluto Press.

Codd, J. 1990. "Managerialism: The problem with today's schools." *Delta*, 44.

Connell, R., D. Ashendon, S. Kessler, and G. Dowsett. 1982. *Making the Difference: Schools, Families and Social Division*. Sydney: George Allen and Unwin.

Connell, R. W. 1987. *Gender and Power: Society, the Person and Sexual Politics*. Cambridge: Policy Press.

Court, M. 1989a. *Winning a Voice in Educational Administration: A Study of Women Working in Middle Management*. Unpublished M.Ed.Admin. thesis, Palmerston North: Massey University.

_____. 1989b. *Women in Educational Administration: An Evaluation of a Self-Help Training Strategy*. Unpublished paper, Palmerston North: Department of Education: Massey University.

_____. 1990. *Anger, Affirmation and Action: Empowering Women in Educational Administration in Mana Wahine*. Papers of the 12th Annual Conference of the Women's Studies Association, New Zealand Inc. Rotorua.

_____. 1992. "Leading from behind: Women in educational administration." In S. Middleton and A. Jones (Eds.), *Women in Education in Aotearoa,*, vol. 2. Wellington: Bridget Williams Books.

_____. 1993. *Women transforming Leadership: A Study of Shared Leadership and Career Development*. Palmerston North: Massey University, ERDC.

Cox, S. 1987 (Ed.). *Public and Private Worlds: Women in Contemporary New Zealand*. Wellington: Allen and Unwin/Port Nicholson Press.

Cox, S. and B. James. 1987. "The theoretical background." In S. Cox (Ed.), *Public and Private Worlds: Women in Contemporary New Zealand*. Wellington: Allen and Unwin/Port Nicholson Press.

Eisenstein, Z. 1981. "Reform and/or revolution: Towards a united women's movement." In L. Sargent (Ed.), *The Unhappy Marriage of Marxism and Feminism*. New York: Pluto Press.

Ellis, G. and J. Wheeler. 1991. *Women Managers: Success on Our Own Terms*. Auckland: Penguin Books.

Epstein, C. 1991. "Debate: Ways men and women lead." *Harvard Business Review*, January/February:150-152.

Glaser, B.J. and A. Strauss. 1967. *The Discovery of Grounded Theory: Strategies for Qualitative Research*. New York: Aldine.

Gould, C. 1983. *Beyond Domination: New Perspectives on Women and Philosophy*. Totowa, N.J.: Rowman and Allenheld.

Gronn, P. 1982. "Neo-Taylorism in educational administration." *Educational Administration Quarterly*, 18, 4.

Harragan, B. L. 1977. *Games Mother Never Taught You*. New York: Warner Books.

_____. 1983. "Women and men at work: Jockeying for position." In J. Farley (Ed.), *The Woman in Management: Career and Family Issues*. Cornell University: ILR Press.

Hartsock, N. 1983. *Money, Sex and Power: Towards a Feminist Historical Materialism*. New York: Longman.

Helgeson, S. 1990. *The Female Advantage: Women's Ways of Leadership*. New York: Doubleday.

James, B. and K. Saville-Smith. 1989. *Gender, Culture and Power: Challenging New Zealand's Gendered Culture*. Auckland: Oxford University Press.

Johnson, W. L. and K. J. Snyder. 1988. "Updating skills for effective leadership." *The Canadian Administrator*, XXIV, 8.

Johnston, J. 1986. "Gender differences in teachers' expectations for primary school leadership." *Educational Management and Administration*, 14:219-216.

Jones, A. 1992. "Writing feminist research: Am 'I' in the text?" In S. Middleton and A. Jones (Eds.), *Women in Education in Aotearoa*, vol. 2. Wellington: Bridget Williams Books.

Kanter, R. 1977. *Men and Women of the Corporation*. New York: Basic Books.

Loden, M. 1985. *Feminine Leadership: Or How to Succeed in Business Without Being One of the Boys*. New York: Times Books, Random House.

Lough, N. V. 1990 (Chairperson). *Today's Schools* (Lough Report), *A Review of the Education Reform Implementation Process*. Wellington: Government Printer.

Malcolm, M. 1978. "The almost invisible woman." *SET* 2. Wellington. New Zealand Council for Educational Research.

Marshall, J. 1984. *Women Managers: Travellers in a Male World*. Chichester: Wiley.

Maslow, A. H. 1970. *Motivation and Personality*. New York: Harper and Row.

May, H. 1988. "Motherhood in the 1950s: An experience in contradiction." In S. Middleton (Ed.), *Women in Education in Aotearoa*. Wellington: Allen Unwin/Port Nicholson Press.

McLeod, M. 1990. "Cracking the glass ceiling." Listener and TV Times, 30 July:15-16.

McRobbie, A. 1982. "The politics of feminist research: Between talk, text and action." *Feminist Review*, 12 October.

Middleton, S. 1988. "Researching feminist educational life histories." In Sue Middleton (Ed.), *Women and Education in Aotearoa*. Wellington: Allen and Unwin.

Ministry of Education. 1990. *Tomorrow's Schools*. Wellington: Government Printer.

Moorhead, R. and W. G. Nediger. 1990. *Process Components of Effectiveness: A Holistic Study of Four Secondary Principals*. Paper presented at the Annual Meeting of the Canadian Society for Education, Victoria, British Columbia, June 3-6.

Neville, M. 1988. *Promoting Women: Successful Women in Educational Management*. Auckland: Longman Paul.

Oakley, A. 1981. "Interviewing women: A contradiction in terms." In H. Roberts (Ed.), *Doing Feminist Research*. London: Routledge and Kegan Paul.

Owens, R. 1991. *Organisational Behaviour in Education* (4th Edition). New Jersey: Prentice Hall.

Pitner, N. J. 1981. "Hormones and harems: Are the activities of superintending different for a woman?" In P. Schmuck et al. (Eds.), *Educational Policy and Management: Sex Differentials*. New York: Academic Press.

Powell, G. 1990. "One more time: Do female and male managers differ?" *Academy of Management Executive*, 4,3.

Ramsay, P., B. Harold, K. Hawk, T. Kaai, R. Marriott, and J. Poskitt. 1991. *'There's No*

Going Back': Collaborative Decision Making in Education. C.R.R.I.S.P. Hamilton: University of Waikato.

Rebore, R. W. 1985. *Educational Administration, A Management Approach*. New Jersey: Prentice-Hall.

Rosener, J. B. 1990. "Ways Women Lead." *Harvard Business Review*, November/December:119-125.

_____. 1991. "Debate: Ways Men and Women Lead. Judy Rosener Replies." *Harvard Business Review*, January-February: 151-152.

Rudolph, B. 1990. "Why can't a woman manage more like . . . a woman?" *Time*, Summer:55.

Sadker, M., D. Sadker and S. Klein. 1986. "Abolishing misconceptions about sex equality in education." *Theory into Practice*, 25:4.

Segal, L. 1987. *Is the Future Female?* London: Virago.

Shakeshaft, C. 1989. *Women in Educational Administration*. London: Sage Publications.

Slyfield, H. 1991. *Position of Women in Education 1990*. Wellington: Ministry of Education.

Smith, D. 1974. "Women's perspective as a radical critique of sociology." *Sociological Enquiry*, 44,1:7-13.

Sonnenfeld, J. A. 1991. "Debate: Ways men and women lead." *Harvard Business Review*, January-February:159-160.

Stewart, D. and T. Prebble. 1985. *Making it Happen: A School Development Process*. Palmerston North: Dunmore Press.

Strauss, A. L. 1987. *Qualitative Analysis for Social Scientists*. Cambridge: Cambridge University Press.

Wolcott, H. F. 1973. "A Day in the Life." In *The Man in the Principal's Office: An Ethnography*. New York: Rinehart, Winston.

Food for Thought and Application Questions

1. Discuss why the "macho" management style described by Court is *particularly* inappropriate for educational organizations.

2. Court opens with a brief summary of both sides of the debate about whether men and women manage in different ways. One of the arguments presented in opposition to "difference" is that both sexes exhibit a range of management styles. Relate this idea to the discussion of "overlapping" gender traits in Chapter 2. How are women and men who do not conform to the "appropriate" gender-linked management style affected by the presence of gender stereotypes? ✦

Unit Five

Women Workers Across the Spectrum

There are over 20,000 different occupations in the United Stated today (U.S. Employment and Training Administration 1977), and women are employed in almost all of them (Herz and Wootton 1996). A person's location in the occupational structure is an important characteristic of their employment because occupational status is associated with job satisfaction and working conditions; earnings and other extrinsic rewards; and even where one lives, how one lives, personal tastes and values. You read, in fact, in the introduction to this text, that the type of work one performs is one of the most important indications to others of "who we are." It is for this reason that occupational information has been included in the U.S. decennial census since 1850 (Rothman 1987). The structure of occupations has changed markedly since that time; technology has resulted in an increasingly complex and specialized division of labor. The broad scheme currently in use by the Bureau of Labor Statistics (BLS) for classifying occupations groups jobs on the basis of skill level and type, and working conditions. These occupational categories and the percentage distributions of women working within them are presented on the next page. An examination of these data show that while women are present in each broad occupational category, there is much variation in the percent of women employed across categories. The patterns revealed here support the descriptions of occupational segregation provided in Unit Two.

Women's work experiences are affected by the type of occupation they hold, and thus vary dramatically across occupational categories. The presence of women in occupations affects occupations as well, especially in terms of the nature of the work, how it is performed, and how others—male workers, employers, and clients—experience the occupation. The selections in this unit provide "case studies" of specific occupations, illustrating both how women are affected by their work and how they affect it. Variation in the work experiences of different groups of women (e.g., racial/ethnic groups and social classes) in the same occupation is also addressed in several of the selections. The scheme used for classifying the occupational case studies that follow is somewhat different from the one employed by the Bureau of Labor Statistics. The Bureau of Labor Statistics categories are informative,

Employed Women by Occupation, 1994
(percent distribution)

Occupation	Total
Total employed women (in thousands)	56,610
Total percentage	100.0
Managerial and professional specialty	28.7
Executive, administrative, and managerial	12.4
Professional specialty	16.3
Technical, sales, and administrative support	42.4
Technicians and related support	3.6
Sales occupations	12.8
Administrative support, including clerical	26.0
Service occupations	17.8
Private household	1.4
Protective service	0.7
Service, except private household and protective	15.7
Precision production, craft, and repair	2.2
Operators, fabricators, and laborers	7.7
Machine operators, assemblers, and inspectors	5.2
Transportation and material moving occupations	0.9
Handlers, equipment cleaners, helpers, and laborers	1.6
Farming, forestry, and fishing	1.2

Source: Bureau of Labor Statistics, 1994.

but because they focus on the technical as opposed to social dimensions of work, they are not ideally suited for examining women's work experiences (Rothman 1987).

Managerial and professional jobs are the first occupations examined in this unit. These occupations are located at the top of the job hierarchy; they are high status jobs associated with relatively high levels of reward. Interestingly, women's level of representation in these jobs is reasonably high and has increased sharply over the last two decades. Before you become too encouraged by this news, it is important to note that jobs within these broad occupational categories are vertically sex-segregated, with women concentrated in the lower tiers. Consider, for example, the high status profession of lawyer. There are many types of lawyers, employed in commercial, charitable, educational, and government organizations. The highest paying positions, commonly situated in large corporate law firms in the commercial sector, are disproportionately held by men. Women, by contrast, are concentrated in government positions, small private practices, and family law—all associated with lower pay and less prestige (Harrington 1995). Management positions are also very sex-segregated, with women clustered in low level managerial jobs in small establishments in the service sector.

The first selection in this unit, authored by a presidential-appointed committee charged with identifying barriers for women's and minority's progress up the management hierarchy, describes how few women have made it to the "helm" of corporate organizations. After documenting the virtual absence of women from these elite positions, the Commission details the obstacles confronting managerial women. An important contribution of this highly visible report is the suggestion that the integration of high-level management positions is good for business. Such arguments are important for motivating profit-minded corporations to "shatter the glass ceiling."

The next selection explores black women's experiences in the professions and management, debunking myths about their progress. After providing historical perspective on black women's employment, Higginbotham shows that black women today are not only concentrated at the lower levels of both of these occupational categories, but are also disproportionately represented (compared to white women) in lower paying, public sector positions. She emphasizes that "double minority" status for black women in management and the professions leads to cumulative disadvantage as opposed to the preferential treatment posited by opponents of affirmative action (Frye 1996).

The final selection in the first part of this unit examines the sexist work experiences of women in the legal profession. Rosenberg, Perlstadt, and Phillips' survey of women lawyers reveals minimal hiring discrimination, but rampant discrimination on the job in terms of pay, promotion, and job assignments. The experience of sexual harassment is also found to be commonplace among women lawyers. Surprisingly, the authors do not find an association between having a feminist orientation and heightened perceptions of sexist behavior in the legal profession. Women today represent 50 percent of all law school graduates (Harrington 1995). This selection provides much insight into how these "intruders" into the profession are treated by their male counterparts.

Male-dominated, blue-collar occupations (precision production, craft and repair, and operators, fabricators, and laborers in the BLS scheme described on the previous page) comprise the next category of jobs examined in this unit. With the exception of farming, forestry, and fishing occupations, this job grouping employs the smallest number of women. Compared to other jobs, the work performed in blue-collar occupations is more likely to be physically demanding, hazardous, and performed outdoors or in "dirty" work environments. These distinguishing features of blue-collar work are not compatible with feminine stereotypes and are responsible for the development of male-oriented work cultures in blue-collar occupations. Women who enter these male-dominated occupations have been referred to as pioneers on the male frontier (Walshak 1981).

The first selection focusing on male-dominated, blue collar occupations explores how women's presence as rapid transit operatives generates tensions for men by threatening assumptions of male supremacy. Swerdlow, the author of this selection, worked as a conductor for a major rapid transit system in order to observe the strains generated by the arrival of women in the job. She finds that men develop a number of accommodative patterns that allow them to accept women as co-workers without compromising the male-oriented work culture and its assumptions of female inferiority. Swerdlow argues that, while often insulting to women, these accommodations enable more women to retain their jobs.

The next selection in this part uses evidence from interviews with women in management, engineering, technician, craft, and production occupations in five different British manufacturing companies to explore whether women in non-traditional jobs are obstructed by workplace culture. Corcoran-Nantes and Roberts find that women in management and craft, technician, and production occupations are marginalized by patronizing work cultures. Women engineers, equipped with educational credentials to serve as symbols of their qualifications, report fewer problems with being taken seriously by their male co-workers. All categories of women workers, however, view demands for career commitment in male-dominated occupations as incompatible with women's domestic responsibilities.

In the final selection in this part, Zimmer describes how women prison guards develop innovative job performance strategies as a means of coping with discriminatory barriers in their male-dominated jobs. Interviews with prison guards and officials reveal that women's approaches to performing their work are just as effective as, and in some cases more effective, than those employed by men. Zimmer finds, however, that the "male" approach is used as a standard for evaluating work performance, causing women to receive substandard reviews. This selection is important because it illustrates how gendered workplace culture creates structural barriers to women's success.

After examining male-dominated occupations, attention turns in the next part of this unit to the female-dominated semi-professions. Compared to the high status professions described above and explored in the selections in the first part of this unit, semi-professions are situated at a lower level in the occupational hierarchy. These occupations possess many of the characteristics of "full" professions, including the requirement of specialized knowledge and training/education, but lack the power necessary to win widespread recognition as a "full profession" and the rewards associated with that status (Reiss 1955). What prevents semi-professions from achieving "full" professional status? Sociologists suggest that the major obstacle is the fact that the jobs are female-dominated. Female-dominated semi-professionals often work under the supervision of male professionals (e.g., nurses/physicians; teachers/principals), which also serves to detract from autonomous professional status (Ritzer and Walczak 1987). The semi-professions are included in the BLS occupational category "professional specialty." These jobs are responsible for the reasonably high level of representation by women in the broad occupational category.

The selection by Glazer addresses the female-dominated semi-profession of nursing and explores attempts by professional registered nurses to resist the deskilling of their occupation. She finds that upper-level women in the occupation employ exclusionary strategies to prevent inroads by women of lower social classes and women of color. Ironically, these exclusionary strategies are described as similar to those used by male professionals to prevent the full professionalization of nursing. This selection shows how workers, women or men, who perceive threats to their job security and/or status, engage in resistance strategies that serve to reinforce patterns of occupational inequality.

Preston presents historical data on public school teaching, in the second selection in this part, to explore how inferior status and wages get associated with fe-male-dominated professions. She argues that male-dominated structures of supervision and bureaucratic control are key factors inhibiting the professionalization of teaching. Sex-segregated administrative positions are described as limiting the autonomy of female teachers and preventing collective control over the profession. This selection also provides an example of the selective application of gender stereotypes in the development of job requirements. Specifically, Preston shows how the gender-typed traits of nurturance and high moral character became central to definitions of the "ideal" teacher.

The final section of Unit Five focuses on the occupational categories, "clerical, service and sales," jobs with high levels of female representation, especially at the lower levels. Each of these categories contains a broad range of stratified occupations: clerical work occupations range from file clerks to executive secretaries; sales positions are divided between retail sales clerks and wholesale or direct sales representatives; and service occupations run the gamut from police officers to private household workers (domestics or maids). Demand for workers in these occupational categories, particularly service occupations, is largely responsible for the large numbers of women employed within them.

In the first selection in this part, Burton uses participant observation to examine the conditions that facilitate or hinder office worker activism in a local union chapter. Deteriorating work conditions and low wages in clerical occupations have fueled union membership over the last two decades. Burton, exploring how discontent is transformed into heightened consciousness and union activism, finds that job security and supportive bosses increase the likelihood of activism. The recruitment activities of women union members are found to play a less important role in increasing women's union membership. These findings highlight the importance of structural conditions in the workplace for influencing workers' behavior.

The second selection, by Hall, focuses on the gendered nature of table serving in establishments that employ both sexes. Behavioral scripts associated with the work roles of waiters and waitresses are suggested to cause the incumbents of those roles to "do gender" as they interact with customers. The male-typed script or gender display is found to be a higher status one, and for this reason Hall finds that female table servers sometimes employ it by adopting male styles of dress and interaction. This selection illustrates that the structure of work roles, not the personality traits of individuals, gives rise to the gendered performance of work.

The next selection turns attention, once again, to the work experiences of minority women. Romero describes how gender and race/ethnicity combine to limit the job opportunities of Chicana women and lead to their clustering in domestic service work. Participant observation and interview data suggest that Chicana domestic service workers are restructuring the occupation so as to maximize its benefits (wages) and reduce its disadvantages (degrading nature). The end result is described as a transformation for domestic service workers from the role of servant to that of "expert," providing an example of how workers can have an impact on the nature of their job.

In the final selection in this unit, Connelly and Rhoton document and contrast the experiences of women involved in direct sales work in two different work organizations. The compatibility of direct sales work with the domestic roles of women (e.g., flexible schedules and the opportunity to work at home) is described as a feature of the occupation that attracts women. The authors suggest that the distinctive female work culture in one of the organizations they study results in more positive work experiences for the women employed there. Interestingly, the level of monetary reward associated with the occupation is often reported to be low, yet satisfaction with the work is generally high. The authors conclude that the high levels of social interaction associated with these jobs are valued by the women workers and serve to offset the low wages.

References

Frye, J. C. 1996. "Affirmative action: Understanding the past and present." In C. Costello and B. K. Kringold (eds.), *The American Woman 1996-1997: Where We Stand.* New York: W. W. Norton:44-78.

Harrington, M. 1995. *Women Lawyers: Rewriting the Rules.* New York: Penguin.

Herz, D. E. and B. H. Wootton. 1996. "Women in the workforce: An overview." In C. Costello and B. K. Kringold (eds.), *The American Woman 1996-1997: Where We Stand.* New York: W. W. Norton.

Reiss, A. 1955. "Occupational mobility of professional workers." *American Sociological Review,* 20:693-700.

Ritzer, G. and D. Walczak. 1987. *Working: Conflict and Change.* Englewood Cliffs: NY: Prentice-Hall.

Rothman, R. A. 1987. *Working: Sociological Perspectives.* Englewood Cliffs, NJ: Prentice-Hall.

U. S. Employment and Training Administration. 1977. *Dictionary of Occupational Titles.* Washington, D.C.: U.S. Government Printing Office.

Walshak, M. L. 1981. *Blue Collar Women: Pioneers on the Male Frontier.* Garden City, NY: Anchor Books. ✦

17

The Glass Ceiling

The Federal Glass Ceiling Commisssion

The term glass ceiling was popularized in a 1986 *Wall Street Journal* article describing the invisible barriers that women confront as they approach the top of the corporate hierarchy.

The Federal Glass Ceiling Commission, a 21-member bipartisan body appointed by President Bush and Congressional leaders and chaired by the Secretary of Labor, was created by the Civil Rights Act of 1991. Its mandate was to identify the glass ceiling barriers that have blocked the advancement of minorities and women as well as the successful practices and policies that have led to the advancement of minority men and all women into decisionmaking positions in the private sector. . . .

The Federal Glass Ceiling Commission systematically gathered information on barriers, opportunities, policies, perceptions, and practices as they affect five target groups that historically have been underrepresented in private sector top-level management—women of all races and ethnicities, and African American, American Indian, Asian and Pacific Islander, and Hispanic American men. . . .

The Commission research and information-gathering process included the following:

Five public hearings held in Kansas City, Kansas; Dallas, Texas; Los Angeles, California; Cleveland, Ohio; and New York, New York, at which 126 employers and employees from a broad spectrum of industries and institutions testified about their experiences and perceptions of the glass ceiling.

The commissioning of 18 research papers on the status and problems of minorities and women and on other specific aspects of the glass ceiling such as the impact of downsizing on diversity, comparative compensation, and law enforcement.

A survey of 25 chief executive officers (CEOs) from white- and minority-owned businesses regarding their perceptions and experiences in recruiting, developing, and promoting minorities and women into decisionmaking positions.

Six racially homogeneous focus groups of Asian and Pacific Islander American, African American and Hispanic/Latino male executives in New York, Chicago, and Los Angeles to determine the perceptions, opinions, beliefs, and attitudes of minority men on the key issues related to the glass ceiling barriers. (With each racial/ethnic group, two sessions were held, one of younger men (30-45) and one older (46-65). All respondents were college graduates with a mix of bachelor's, master's, and Ph.D. degrees. All were full-time employees of U.S. companies in the following industries: communications, legal, electronic, health care, aerospace, utility, airline, financial/banking, travel, transport, publishing, realty, employment services, personal products, and beverage.)

Two focus panel groups with American Indian men and women in Washington, D.C. (All members of the groups were college graduates with a mix of bachelor's, master's, and law degrees, a mix of government and private sector employment, and a mix of ages and tribal afffliations. The majority were based in Washington but others came from as far away as California.)

Analyses of special data runs of U.S. Bureau of the Census data conducted expressly for the Federal Glass Ceiling Commission to establish as clearly as possible the educational achievement, status, and compensation levels of the target groups.

Analyses of special data runs of U.S. Bureau of the Census data to identify the status of minorities and women by industrial sector.

Highlights of the Research

What Is the Glass Ceiling?

Federal Glass Ceiling Commission research papers, as well as testimony presented at the public hearings, clearly document that today's American labor force is gender and race segregated—white men fill most top management positions in corporations.

According to surveys of Fortune 1500 companies conducted by Korn/Ferry International and Catalyst over the last decade, 95 to 97 percent of senior managers—vice presidents and above—were men. A 1989 Korn/Ferry survey found that 97 percent of male top executives are white. A 1992 survey of Fortune 1500 companies found that 95 percent of the three to five percent of the top managers who were women were white non-Hispanic women. In 1994, two women were CEOs of Fortune 1000 companies.

The representation of women and minorities on Fortune 1500 boards of directors is also limited. Cox and Smolinski point out that less than 10 percent of the largest employers have women on their board of directors. According to a 1992 Heidrick and Struggles survey, *Minorities and Women on Corporate Boards*, non-U.S. citizens held 2.85 percent of the board seats of 806 Fortune companies, slightly less than the 3.11 percent combined total held by all racial and ethnic minorities.

Conversely, the American work-force is increasingly diverse. In 1950, white men comprised 65 percent of the labor force; in 1990 white male representation had dropped to 43 percent. During the same period, representation of white women in the labor force increased from 24.2 percent to 35.3 percent. At the same time, mi-

nority representation in the labor force doubled, to 15.2 percent. Over the last decade, the size of the Asian and Pacific Islander American population has doubled, becoming the fastest growing of minority groups in the United States.

A larger proportion of women and minorities are locked into low wage, low prestige, and dead-end jobs, which according to Harlan and Bertheide (1994), are not connected to any career ladder.

The Current Status of Minorities and Women Managers

Most female and minority professionals and managers do not work in the private-for-profit sector. They hold jobs in the public sector and "third sector"—nongovernmental agencies in health, social welfare, and education; legal service, professional service, membership organizations and associations; libraries, museums and art organizations. According to Burbridge (1994), 90 percent of black male professionals, 70 percent of black male professionals, and 83 percent of white and Hispanic women professionals work in the government or the third sector, compared to 56 percent of white male non-Hispanic professionals.

The exception to this pattern of employment is Asian and Pacific Islander Americans (API) who rely heavily on the for-profit sector. Contrary to the popular image of API Americans, only a small percentage are entrepreneurs or managers of small businesses (9.8 percent).

Federal Class Ceiling Commission research also analyzed salaries as an indicator of advancement. In 1992, U.S. Census data reported the ratio of female to male earnings in management jobs ranged from a low of 50 percent in the banking industry to a high of 85 percent for managers in human services. An analysis of 1990 U.S. Census data shows that black men who hold professional degrees and top management positions earned 79 percent of what white men earn. Black women, also with professional degrees and in top management positions, earn 60 percent of what white men in comparable positions earn.

Despite identical education attainment, ambition, and commitment to career, men still progress faster than women. A 1990 *Business Week* study of 3,664 business school graduates found that a woman with an MBA from one of the top 20 business schools, earned an average of $54,749 in her first year after graduation, while a comparable man earned $61,400—12 percent more. Wernick reports that a 1993 follow-up study of the Stanford University Business School class of 1982 found that 16 percent of the men were CEOs, chairmen, or presidents of companies compared to only 2 percent of the women. At the level below those top posts, 23 percent of the men in the 1982 class were now vice presidents and 15 percent were directors, compared to 10 percent and 8 percent, respectively, of the women.

Some data support the optimism that the 25 CEOs expressed about the progress of women. For example, between 1982 and 1992 the percentage of women who held the title of female executive vice president increased from 4 percent to 9 percent; the percentage who held the office of senior vice president increased from 13 percent to 23 percent. In comparison, between 1982 and 1992, the percentage of African Americans who held the title of vice president or above increased from 1 percent to 2.3 percent. During the same period, the percentage of Hispanic top managers increased from 1.3 percent to 2 percent, and the percentage of Asian senior managers increased from .4 percent to 1.8 percent.

The small numbers of minorities and women throughout management makes statistics on the rate of change in representation misleading. For example, if two out of three black male managers take early retirement, a firm experiences a 67 percent decline in representation.

The Business Imperative

Another reason for optimism is the growing body of evidence which indicates shattering the glass ceiling is good for business. Organizations that excel at leveraging diversity (including hiring and promoting minorities and women into senior positions) can experience better financial performance in the long run than those which are not effective in managing diversity.

Cox cites a Covenant Investment Management study to prove this point. The Covenant study rated the performance of the Standard and Poor's 500 companies on factors relating to the hiring and advancement of minorities and women, compliance with EEOC and other regulatory requirements, and employee litigation. Companies which rated in the bottom 100 on glass ceiling related measures earned an average of 7.9 percent return on investment, compared to an average return of 18.3 percent for the top 100.

Cox offers several other explanations about why some businesses are motivated to eliminate the glass ceiling. In the U.S., Asians, blacks, and Hispanics collectively represent more than $500 billion a year in consumer spending. In the automobile industry explicit recognition of cultural differences within the U.S. market is paying off. In 1987, by targeting advertising, hiring bilingual sales people, and holding special events, a Miami Toyota dealer gained more than 50 percent of the local Hispanic market and his sales increased 400 percent over a six-year period. On the West coast, a San Francisco Volkswagen dealership credited improved sales to Asian and Pacific Islander Americans for a five-fold increase in overall sales per month. Sales people learned through cultural sensitivity training that among Chinese Americans, family elders often are the ultimate decision makers for major purchases.

To a lesser degree than competition for market share, turnover costs are also factors motivating companies to address issues related to glass ceilings. Cox (1994) cites a published report of Ortho Pharmaceuticals that stated yearly savings of $500,000 mainly from lower turnover among women.

These savings are not surprising. Recent studies estimate the turnover costs range between 150 and 193 percent of a manager or professional's annual salary, compared to 75 percent for lower level employees. Corning Glass reported that during the period from 1980 to 1987 turnover among women in professional jobs was double that of men. During the same time period, the turnover rates for blacks were almost two and a half times those of whites. Another study of male and female managers of large corporations found that the major reason for women quitting was a lack of career growth opportunity or dissatisfaction with rates of progress.

The Pipeline

The research monographs and testimony that examined the preparedness of minorities and women to advance to top management positions considered preparedness in terms of corporate development of minorities and women and educational credentials.

As Wernick (1994) explains, the development of business executives is a long, complicated process. Chief executive officers (CEOs) are generally in their 50s or 60s when they assume the top position. Furthermore, they have usually spent 20 to 25 years "in the pipeline."

It is also worth noting that career paths to CEO positions vary by industry. Certain functional areas are more likely than others to lead to the top. The "right" areas are most likely to be line functions such as marketing or production or a critical control function such as accounting or finance. Studies across industries find certain factors common to successful executives, regardless of gender, race, or ethnicity. They include: broad and varied experience in the core areas of the business; access to information, particularly through networks and mentoring; company seniority; initial job assignment; high job mobility; education; organizational savvy; long hours and hard work; and career planning.

Minorities and women have limited opportunity to obtain broad and varied experience in most companies. They tend to be in supporting, staff function areas—personnel/human resources, communications, public relations, affirmative action, and customer relations. Movement between these positions and line positions is rare in most major companies. Furthermore, career ladders in staff functions are generally shorter than those in line functions, offering fewer possibilities to gain varied experience.

Education is also an important part of an executive's preparation. According to a 1993 Korn/Ferry International UCLA report, almost 90 percent of executives are college graduates. U.S. Census data show that Asian and Pacific Islander Americans and women have the largest percentage of the work force with college or graduate degrees, with 42 percent and 35 percent respectively. The same source shows that college attendance is increasing for black men and women of all ages. Between 1982 and 1991, there was a 36 percent increase in the number of African Americans, ages 20 to 44, with a college degree or more.

The picture for American Indians and Hispanic Americans is less encouraging. Only 9 percent of American Indians in the workforce hold college degrees. Between 1980 and 1990, the number of Hispanic Americans with bachelor's or graduate degrees increased from 7.7 percent to 10 percent. Furthermore, the opposition to bilingual education discourages the acquisition of one of the assets that business values. According to a 1994 *Hispanic Business* magazine survey of 169 Hispanic senior managers, the majority of managers work in line positions in international divisions using their bilingual and bicultural skills. However, only 4 percent of Hispanic high school students gain bilingual capability by taking the minimum requirement for Spanish literacy, according to a Department of Education longitudinal study.

Where Are the Opportunities?

Federal Glass Ceiling Commission research on the opportunities for minorities and women to advance to top management positions in corporate America focused on two areas: 1) identification of growth industries and businesses and high-demand occupations and their relation to opportunities for advancement and 2) identification of possibilities resulting from changes in the structure of work, new technologies, and the demands of a global economy.

Gender distribution is more prominent than race distribution across industries. Women are more likely than men to be clustered in services; finance, insurance, and real estate (FIRE), and in the wholesale/retail trade industries. Nearly 75 percent of employed women work in these industries.

Growth Industries

The industries expected to grow the most between 1990 and 2005 are service/retail trade; FIRE; wholesale trade; transportation, communications, and public utilities; and construction.

Those areas which are expected to have growing needs for general managers and top executives include wholesale; retail trade, especially eating and drinking establishments; finance and real estate (but not insurance carriers); and services, particular business services, auto services, health services, education, social services, and engineering and management services.

Women appear to have the best opportunity for advancement into management and decisionmaking positions in three types of industries: those which are fast-growing (business services); those like telecommunications where change, i.e., deregulation, restructuring has occurred; and those with a female intensive work force (insurance, banking).

Restructuring

A review of research on recent changes in the organization of work identifies seven ways in which downsizing and restructuring can limit opportunities for all managers, professionals, and administrators. They are: 1) an increase in external recruiting which reduces the number of internal career ladders; 2) elimination of layers of management and staff positions; 3) hiring of independent contractors or small businesses to perform some staff functions; 4) more stringent performance measures on those managers who remain; 5) more geographic mobility required of managers; 6) increased importance of team work; and 7) a shift of employment from manufacturing to services.

As Hamlin's (1994) research on the impact of downsizing and restructuring in nine companies found, in more than half the companies, white women and—to a somewhat lesser extent—minority men have increased their representation in management both in absolute numbers and in proportion to white men between 1900 and 1994. Restructuring can present problems as well as opportunities for minorities and women in management. In some cases the last hired are the first fired. On the other hand, when early retirement is part of the restructuring process, higher level positions may become available, thereby increasing advancement opportunities. Hamlin's study showed that white male managers who had seniority and were eligible for relatively generous buy-out packages were most likely to take early retirement or choose other forms of severance during downsizing.

Comparison of Industries—Women

The industries with the highest percentage of women managers were FIRE (41.4 percent), services (38.9 percent), retail trade (38.5 percent), transportation, communication, and public utilities (25.6 percent), and wholesale trade (20.9 percent). Manufacturing (15.9 percent), agriculture (14.5 percent), construction (10.4

percent), and mining (9.8 percent) had the lowest percentages.

The proportion of women employees who are managers is the closest to that of men who are managers in transportation, communications, and public utilities (10.1 percent; 15.2 percent), with the construction industry second (6.4 percent; 9.9 percent). Manufacturing and FIRE showed the biggest proportional differences.

Predominately female industries have larger percentages of women in at least midlevel managerial positions than do predominately male industries. Furthermore, women appear to be advancing best in industries with relatively high growth, those undergoing change with regard to regulation, and those highly competitive and thus dependent on marketing and flexibility.

Comparision of Industries—Minorities

Department of Labor analyses of 1990 EEOC data for minorities (men and women) find that the industries with the highest percentage of minority managers are retail trade (13 percent), transportation, communication, and public utilities (12 percent), services and FIRE (11 percent). Agriculture (1.3 percent), wholesale trade (0.9 percent), manufacturing (0.8 percent), mining (0.7 percent), and construction (0.6 percent) had the lowest percentages.

The proportion of minority employees who are managers is the closest to that of non-minorities who are managers in transportation, communication, and public utilities (7.7 percent; 15.0 percent), with the retail trade industry second (9.2 percent; 21.0 percent). Agriculture and construction had the biggest differences between the proportions.

However, a study of Hispanic executives in the Fortune 500 industrial and 500 service industries (HACR 1993) found the highest percentage of Hispanic officers in beverages (3.8 percent), soaps and cosmetics (2.4 percent), building materials (1.9 percent), and motor vehicles and parts (1.1

percent). These sub-industries are all in the manufacturing sector. Officer representation for Hispanics in all other industrial sectors was below 1 percent, and has the lowest percentage of FIRE and transportation, communication, and public utilities.

An analysis of the 30 companies listed as best places for blacks to work in the February 1992 edition of *Black Enterprise* found 8 of the 30 companies were in the consumer products industry. Telecommunications, automobiles, other manufacturing firms, oil, chemical companies, and banking/financial services had 3 mentions each.

Representation of minorities in an industry is not directly related to their advancement to management as is the case with women. However, like women, minorities have the best chance of advancement in industries with relatively high growth, those undergoing change with regard to regulation, and those highly competitive and thus dependent on marketing and flexibility.

Research Papers

Bell, E. L., J. Edmundson and S. M. Nkomo. 1994. *Barriers to Work Place Advancement Experienced by African-Americans.* Ella Louis J. Bell, Sloan School of Management, Massachusetts Institute of Technology and Stella M. Nkomo, Belk College of Business Administration, University of North Carolina at Charlotte. Paper prepared for the Glass Ceiling Commission. On file.

Braddock, D. and L. Bachelder. 1994. *The Glass Ceiling and Persons with Disabilities.* University of Illinois at Chicago. Paper prepared for the Glass Ceiling Commission. On file.

Burbridge, L. 1994. *The Glass Ceiling in Different Sectors of the Economy: Differences Between Government, Non-Profit and For-Profit Organizations.* Wellesley College Center for Research on Women. Paper prepared for the Glass Ceiling Commission. On file.

Catalyst 1993. *Successful Initiatives for Breaking the Glass Ceiling to Upward Mobility for Minorities and Women.* Paper prepared for the Glass Ceiling Commission. On file.

Cox, T. and C. Smolinski. 1994. *Managing Diversity and Glass Ceiling Initiatives as National Economic Imperatives.* The University of Michigan. Paper prepared for the Glass Ceiling Commission. On file.

Golen, A. 1994. *The Impact of the Glass Ceiling on the Professions.* Draft working paper prepared for the Glass Ceiling Commission. On file.

Hamlin, N., S. Erkut and J. P. Fields 1994. *The Impact of Corporate Restructuring and Downsizing on the Managerial Careers of Minorities and Women: Lessons Learned.* Paper prepared for the Glass Ceiling Commission. On file.

Harlan, S. L. and C. W. Bertheide. 1994. *Barriers to Workplace Advancement Experienced by Women in Low-Paying Occupations.* Colorado State University. Paper prepared for the Glass Ceiling Commission. On file.

James, K. et al. 1994. *Barriers to Workplace Advancement Experienced by Native Americans.* Paper prepared for the Glass Ceiling Commission. On file.

Leonard, J. 1994. *Use of Enforcement in Eliminating Glass Ceiling Barriers.* School of Business, University of California, Berkeley. Paper prepared for the Glass Ceiling Commission. On file.

Mauricio Gastón Institute for Latino Community Development and Public Policy, University of Massachusetts. 1994. *Barriers to the Employment and Work-Place Advancement of Latinos.* University of Massachusetts at Boston. Paper prepared for the Glass Ceiling Commission. On file.

Schwartz, D. B. 1994. *An Examination of the Impact of Family-Friendly Policies on the Glass Ceiling.* Paper prepared for the Glass Ceiling Commission. On file.

Shaw, L. B. et al. 1993. *The Impact of the Glass Ceiling and Structural Change on Minorities and Women.* Paper Commissioned for the Glass Ceiling Commission. On file.

Thomas, Roosevelt et al. 1994. *Impact of Recruitment, Selection, and Compensation Policies and Practices on the Glass Ceiling.*

Morehouse College. Paper prepared for the Glass Ceiling Commission. On file.

Tomaskovic-Devy, T. 1994. *Race, Ethnic and Gender Earnings Inequality: The Source and Consequence of Employment Segregation.* North Carolina State University. Paper prepared for the Glass Ceiling Commission. On file.

Wernick, E. 1994. *Preparedness, Career Advancement, and the Glass Ceiling.* Paper prepared for the Glass Ceiling Commission. On file.

Woo, D. 1994. *The Glass Ceiling and Asian Americans.* University of California, Berkeley. Paper prepared for the Glass Ceiling Commission. On file.

Woody, B. and C. Weiss. 1994. *Barriers to Work Place Advancement Experienced by White Women Workers.* University of Massachusetts at Boston. Paper prepared for the Glass Ceiling Commission. On file.

Analyses and Commentaries

Bell, E. L., J. Edmondson and S. M. Nkomo. 1992. *The Glass Ceiling vs. The Concrete Wall: Career Perceptions of White and African-American Women Managers.* Unpublished working paper.

Hispanic Policy Development Project. 1994. *A La Cumbre. A Latino Perspective on the Corporate Glass Ceiling.* Paper prepared for the Glass Ceiling Commission. On file.

Lee, Y. Y. 1994. *An Asian Pacific American Perspective on the Glass Ceiling.* Lee Consultants. Paper prepared for the Glass Ceiling Commission. On file.

Special Analyses of U.S. Bureau of the Census Data

Asian and Pacific Islander Center for Census Information and Services. 1994. *Reference Documentation: Datasets of U.S. Bureau of the Census Public Use Microdata Sample Files.* Prepared for the Glass Ceiling Commission. On file.

Institute for Policy Research and Education of the Congressional Black Caucus Foundation. 1994. *The Impact of the Glass Ceiling on African American Men and Women.* Reference documentation: Datasets of U.S.

Bureau of the Census Public Use Microdata Sample Files. Prepared for the Glass Ceiling Commission. On file.

The Tomás Rivera Center. 1995. *Wage Differentials Between Latinos and Anglos: A Statistical Portrait and Its Implications to Glass Ceiling Issues.* Reference documentation: Datasets of U.S. Bureau of the Census Public Use Microdata Sample Files. Prepared for the Glass Ceiling Commission. On file.

Surveys and Focus Groups

Henderson, L. S. III et al. 1994. *Report on Six Focus Groups with Asian, Black and Hispanic Executives in Three Cities on Issues Related to The Glass Ceiling in Corporate America.* Paper prepared for the Glass Ceiling Commission. On file.

————. 1995. *Final Report on Two Focus Groups with American Indians on Issues Related to the Glass Ceiling in Corporate America.* Paper prepared for the Glass Ceiling Commission. On file.

McGuire, G. and S. Nicolau. 1994. *In Their Own Words: CEO Views of Diversity at the Top.* Paper prepared for the Glass Ceiling Commission. On file.

Reprinted from: *A Solid Investment: Making Full Use of the Nation's Human Capital.* The Federal Glass Ceiling Commission. November 1995.

Food for Thought and Application Questions

1. The Glass Ceiling Commission argues that diversifying management is "good for business." Assume that you are a management consultant arguing the benefits of diversified management to high level corporate executives. How would you convince them that filling more senior management positions with women and minorities is in the best interest of their organization?

2. How can corporate "downsizing" create opportunities for women in management? Do you think that women's movement into management positions in firms that are downsizing is associated with the perception that women are taking jobs away from men? If so, how are male employees likely to react to this perceived "threat" to their jobs? How will their reaction affect women managers? ✦

18

Black Professional Women: Job Ceilings and Employment Sectors

Elizabeth Higginbotham

Myths and stereotypes about the success of educated black women, many promoted by misleading news reports of major trends, mask important employment problems faced by members of this group (Sokoloff 1992). The limited social science research on the plight of middle-class black women makes fertile ground for myths about their success and stereotypes about their abilities to handle all situations. In reality, this is not a population exempt from problems on the job. Research on the employment status of educated black women can be important in addressing the nature of contemporary racism in America and how it impacts people of color who are members of the middle class.

This chapter explores the employment status of black professional women.[1] Throughout the twentieth century, there has been a tiny elite of educated Afro-American women employed in professional and managerial positions. Since the 1970s, this population has experienced significant growth. In 1984, 14.3 percent of full-time, year-round employed black women were in professional, technical, and kindred specialties, and 5.4 percent were managers, officials, and proprietors (U.S. Department of Labor, 1984). They constituted nearly a fifth of all full-time, year-round employed black women 16 years and older. They are employed in a variety of occupations, but the majority—even today—are primary and secondary teachers, social workers, librarians, school counselors, and nurses. Since the 1970s, the number of black women in traditionally male professions, such as attorney, accountant, physician, dentist, and minister, has increased, but the majority continue to be clustered in traditionally female professional and managerial positions (Kilson 1977; Sokoloff 1987, 1992; Wallace 1980).

The more education a woman has, the more likely she is to be employed. Thus, while a minority of black women have college educations—about 5 percent of black women over twenty-five years of age—this is the group most likely to be in the labor force (Jones 1986).

Some scholars might argue that the size of this group of black women in professional and managerial positions is evidence that racial and sexual barriers can be scaled by the talented. From another perspective, educated black women's employment patterns reveal a history of racial discrimination. During most of this century, the majority of employed professional and managerial black women have worked either in the public sector (city, county, state, and federal government) or for small independent agencies and employers in the black community (Higginbotham 1987; Hine 1989).

This chapter provides details of the contemporary employment patterns of black and white women to illustrate segmentation or clustering of professional and managerial women along racial lines. It addresses the question: What form does racial stratification take in this post-Civil Rights era? The concepts of job ceilings and employment sectors are used to illustrate shifting patterns of racism in the labor market options of professional and managerial black women. These concepts are useful in evaluating the recent progress made by black women.

The Black Middle Class

The traditional social science practice is to view social class as status rankings. New scholarship offers a definition that views social class as opposing structural positions in the social organization of production. Different social classes do not represent different ranks in a social hierarchy but denote shared structural positions with regard to ownership of the means of production, level and degree of authority in the workplace, or the performance of mental or manual labor. From this perspective, the middle class is defined to include the small traditional groups of self-employed shopkeepers and independent farmers, and the numerically larger group of professionals, managers, and administrators. This group, frequently referred to as the professional-managerial class (see Walker 1979), performs the mental labor necessary to control the labor and lives of the working class. In the modern industrial capitalist state, it is designated as middle class because of its position between labor and capital. The primary role of the middle class is to plan, manage, and monitor the work of others. Its members have greater incomes, prestige, and education than other workers, but the social relations of dominance and subordination are key in defining their social class position (Braverman 1974; Poulantzas 1974; Ehrenreich and Ehrenreich 1979; Vanneman and Cannon 1987).

While black women and men in middle-class positions enjoy many class advantages, they are still members of a racially devalued group. Understanding the middle class of a racially oppressed group requires a perspective that can investigate how both race and class interact to shape the lives of males and females. Racial oppression may be shared within the racial minority community but mediated by one's position within the class hierarchy (Barrera 1979). Both working-class and middle-class Afro-Americans are segmented and limited to the least remunerative and prestigious occupations, relative to whites within their social class. Working-class black men and women were denied access to many industrial, clerical, and sales jobs because these positions were reserved for whites. Black men and women were readily able to find work in jobs that white people did not want. In the case of black women, in the first half of the century they were employed primarily as domestics, and later gained access to service work, factory work, and some clerical and sales jobs (Amott and Matthaei 1991; Jones 1985).

Historically, black middle-class men and women who occupied professional positions served their racial communities. These positions are often shunned by white professionals. Even today, most middle-class black people teach and provide health and human services, and professional and managerial services to other black people. The size and affluence of the black community is a factor in the growth of the black middle class (Drake and Cayton 1970; Landry 1987). Gender also plays a significant role in access to professional occupations.

Gender Differences in Job Ceilings for Black Americans

As noted above, patterns of discrimination are evident in the history of employment for educated black women and men. The concept of job ceilings helps clarify practices prior to the 1960s. Contrasting employment patterns between the public and private sectors best describes discriminatory patterns after the passage of Civil Rights legislation.

Job ceilings are the racially specific caps or ceilings placed on the occupational mobility of targeted groups. This form of economic oppression can be maintained by formal or informal practices. The results are the same. Black people are denied the opportunity to fill certain jobs, even if they are qualified, because employers have decided that this particular work is closed to black Americans. Over the years, black Americans have learned to watch for subtle changes or cracks in this ceiling.

Job ceilings, institutionalized early in this century, were instrumental in excluding black people from many industrial jobs—both positions they might have held in the past and new jobs that were opening up. Job ceilings were very effective means of keeping black people in low-wage manual jobs—the lowest of all working-class employment.

In *Black Metropolis*, St. Clair Drake and Horace Cayton (1970) talked in detail about the job ceiling in Chicago in the 1920s and 1930s:

> Between the First World War and the Depression, the bulk of the Negro population became concentrated in the lower-paid, menial, hazardous, and relatively unpleasant jobs. The employment policy of individual firms, trade-union restrictions, and racial discrimination in training and promotion made it exceedingly difficult for them to secure employment in the skilled trades, in clerical and sales work, and as foremen and managers. Certain entire industries had a "lily-white" policy—notably the public utilities, the electrical manufacturing industry, and the city's banks and offices. (p. 112)

The job ceiling was not unique to Chicago. It was a fundamental part of the labor market in urban and rural communities, both in the North and in the South (Hine 1989). Its existence prohibited black males and females from following occupational mobility patterns open to both native-born white Americans and white immigrants. Over time, even first- and second-generation white immigrants were able to move from menial jobs into un-

skilled and semiskilled factory work. The next generation might proceed into skilled industrial work and sometimes eventually into white-collar positions.

With this established channel closed to them, black American men and women had to find alternative routes out of the low-wage jobs in private household work, janitorial and custodial services, laundry work, and the other positions in which they could seek employment. A few black men and women, with the support of their families or through their own efforts, were able to carve out an alternative course to better employment. They struggled to get an education, most often in traditionally black institutions.

Acquiring a college education was often a route around the job ceiling for black males and females. An education gave the credentials to qualify for middle-class positions. In this way, some black people could bypass the ceiling and move to the next floor. That floor consisted of white-collar professional and managerial positions, primarily within the minority community.

For black women, a college education did not guarantee a better livelihood than domestic or other low-wage service work. The black females who obtained a college education, even an advanced degree, found another layer of obstacles in front of them. In a racially segmented society, even middle-class occupational positions are shaped by racism (and in the case of women, also sexism). So black women who had the education to merit employment in middle-class professional jobs still faced race and sex barriers to securing satisfying and economically rewarding work in the middle class.

Prior to World War II, gender restrictions shaped the professions for which black women could prepare and practice. Black women seeking higher education were steered into primary and secondary school teaching, nursing, social work, and library sciences (Hine 1989; Jones 1985). Gender also shaped the options of black men. They were directed into medicine and dentistry, the ministry and business, as well as teaching. These gender-specific trends were noted by earlier social science researchers (Cuthbert 1942; Johnson 1969; Noble 1956). Black males and females were expected to practice their gender-specific professions within a racially segregated society.

On the whole, educational training equipped black men for professional occupations in which they could be self-employed or work within black institutions. With medical or dental training, they could set up independent or joint practices as physicians and dentists, in which they saw mostly black patients—and in large communities, they were able to develop successful enterprises. As ministers, black men were directly responsible to a congregation—if it was a large congregation, they could gain economic security. Some black men moved into providing insurance and other services to the black population. And other black men found employment in traditionally black educational institutions, where they were somewhat removed from the racist policies and practices in the white-dominated labor market.

College-educated black women faced a different prospect. They were discouraged from pursuing traditionally male occupations and directed into developing female professions (Hine 1989). Thus, black women were not educated for professions that enabled them to set up their own businesses or independent practices. Nurses do not set up individual practices; they are hired to work for doctors or employed in hospitals or clinics. Teachers do not recruit their own students; they are hired by public or private school systems. Librarians do not run their own institutions; they are hired to work in libraries operated by the city, the county, or an educational facility. And social workers do not go into business for themselves; they are hired by human service agencies in the private or public sector. Gender barriers, along with race and class obstructions in both educa-

tional institutions and the labor market, complicated black women's securing professional employment (Higginbotham 1987; Hine 1989; Jones 1985). A college education often prepared them for occupations where they still faced a racial job ceiling.

And black women did confront rigid job ceilings. Many Northern cities did not hire black people for professional positions in their schools, clinics, hospitals, libraries, and other agencies. In the South, some public sector jobs were set aside for black people, because Jim Crow policies dictated segregated facilities. This was particularly the case in the teaching field, where Afro-Americans had a monopoly on positions in black schools, and during the Depression in public health and voluntary health operations (Hine 1989). North of the Mason-Dixon Line, city and county employment policies regarding black professionals were very mixed. De facto segregation was usually the rule for designating where children were schooled, but cities differed in whether they would hire black teachers to staff the facilities used to educate black children (Tyack 1974). Black nurses could not find employment outside of black hospitals and private homes. Because they were not trained for professions that could be translated into independent entrepreneurial practices, black females were dependent on salaries and wages. Thus, employment prospects for educated black women were contingent upon city and county hiring policies to staff public institutions.

For these reasons, the numbers of black professional and managerial women remained small and lagged behind the percentages of white women in these occupations. The percentage of black women employed as professional, technical, or kindred workers increased from 4.3 percent in 1940 to 5.3 in 1950, 7.7 in 1960, and to 15.3 percent by 1980. Despite the increase among professionals, the number of black women in managerial positions did not exceed 1.4 percent until 1980, when it reached 4.2 percent (Higginbotham 1987).

Employment Sectors: Black Professional Women's Place

Legislation against race and sex discrimination challenged many of the arbitrary practices, such as job ceilings. Since the mid-1960s, more educated black people have found jobs in the professions for which they have credentials. This has meant an increase in the numbers of black women in professional and managerial positions, as well as their employment in a wider range of occupations (Kilson 1977; Sokoloff 1992; Westcott 1982). Yet, Civil Rights legislation did not dismantle the racism that is a critical part of the labor market. Empirical research indicates that the occupational positions of educated black women are still problematic (Higginbotham 1987; Sokoloff 1987, 1988, 1992). They continue to face employment barriers, but the discrimination has taken a new form. Now black women find themselves limited to employment in certain sectors of the labor market.

Recent scholarship, especially work by Sharon Collins (1983), indicates that black employees in professional and managerial positions are concentrated in the public sector. When they are in the private sector, black middle-class employees are in the marginal areas of production (such as personnel, public relations, and the like). These observations are supported by reports from black managers in the private sector (Bascom 1987; Fulbright 1986).

In an earlier work (Higginbotham 1987), I discussed how contemporary professional black women remain concentrated in the traditionally female professions of teacher, social worker, nurse, librarian, and so forth. Recently, a significant number of black women, as well as their white sisters, have broken into new occupations—those traditionally dominated by males. Today, there are more black and white women who are physi-

cians, dentists, lawyers, accountants, and managers in both small and large firms. Indeed, if one looks at broad occupational categories, the degree of sex segregation in the professional labor market has declined since the 1970s (Sokoloff 1987, 1988, 1992). If one looks below the surface, one can identify how racism remains embedded in the social structure. Instead of being evenly split between the private and public sectors, the majority of professional and managerial black women are employed in the public sector. Census data reveal that in fourteen of the fifteen Standard Metropolitan Statistical Areas (SMSAs) with the largest black populations, the majority of black professional and managerial women are employed in the public sector (see Table 18.1).[2] In each of the same fifteen metropolitan areas, the majority of white professional and managerial women were employed in the private sector.[3]

For example, in the Memphis metropolitan area, black women are about 25.3 percent of the females employed in professional and managerial occupations, and 71.7 percent are employed in the public sector; only 34.5 percent of white professional and managerial women are so employed. Likewise, 60.4 percent of white professional and managerial women work in the private sector, while only 27 percent of black women in those same occupations do so. This is a common pattern for both Northern and Southern cities.

In the metropolitan area of Newark, New Jersey, black women constitute 15 percent of women employed in professional and managerial occupations. In 1980, 55.2 percent of these black women worked in the public sector, while only 33.7 percent of white professional and managerial women did so. And 61.8 percent of white women worked in the private sector, while only 43.6 percent of the black professional and managerial women did. This is very interesting, in light of the fact that about the same percentages of black and white professional and managerial women in the Newark metropolitan area are

Table 18.1
Sectoral Distribution of Women Managerial and Professional Specialty Workers
for Fifteen SMSAs, 1980

		Black				**Non-Black**		
SMSA	N	Public (%)	Private (%)	Other (%)[a]	N	Public (%)	Private (%)	Other (%)
Atlanta	18,479	55.7	42.5	1.8	81,998	34.8	60.3	4.9
Baltimore	19,902	72.3	26.9	0.8	79,351	40.4	55.1	4.4
Chicago	44,066	53.8	44.8	1.4	268,359	26.6	69.0	4.4
Cleveland	10,835	53.8	44.0	2.1	65,049	30.0	65.9	4.1
Dallas	11,308	54.8	42.6	2.6	122,666	32.2	62.0	5.8
Detroit	24,257	59.3	39.1	1.5	127,661	33.7	62.1	4.2
Houston	19,418	55.5	42.4	2.1	114,954	30.8	63.5	5.7
Los Angeles	36,119	47.6	49.3	3.1	299,395	27.3	64.9	7.9
Memphis	9,040	71.7	27.0	1.3	26,633	34.6	60.3	5.1
Miami	9,679	60.3	38.2	1.5	59,261	26.7	66.9	6.4
Newark	14,208	55.2	43.6	1.2	78,532	33.5	62.1	4.4
New Orleans	11,446	65.8	32.8	1.4	36,259	31.5	63.7	4.9
New York	67,026	49.3	48.8	1.8	697,395	34.4	59.8	5.8
Philadelphia	25,273	56.0	42.2	1.8	164,890	29.2	65.6	4.6
St. Louis	12,939	58.2	40.3	1.4	81,959	29.3	66.3	4.4
Mean Percentage	15.4	57.9	40.3	1.7	84.6	31.7	63.2	5.1

[a]Includes self-employed and unpaid family workers.
Source: U.S. Bureau of the Census, *Census of the Population 1980*, vol. 1, *Characteristics of the Population* (Washington, D.C.: U.S. Government Printing Office, 1983), ch. D, "Detailed Population Characteristics," Table 220.

teachers, counselors, and librarians (34 percent)—they are just employed in different sectors. While 82.1 percent of the black teachers, librarians, and counselors in Newark are employed in the public sector, 70.3 percent of the white women in the same occupations are employed there (Higginbotham 1987).

In the New York City metropolitan area, black professional women are more evenly distributed in public (49.3 percent) and private (48.8 percent) sector work. With many corporate headquarters and larger numbers of private schools, social service agencies, and hospitals, one might expect that black women would have more options in the private sector than might be found in either Newark or Memphis. But white women also have these options. In the Big Apple, only 26.6 percent of white professional and managerial women were employed in the public sector and 66.5 percent were in the private sector. New York ranks third, behind Chicago and Miami, in the concentration of white professional and managerial women in the private sector. The figures for other cities in the nation are similar, with only a slight regional variation—Southern cities have somewhat higher concentrations of black professional women in public sector employment. Los Angeles is the only city where the majority of black professional women are in the private sector.

The 1980 census indicates that many educated black women are working as professionals and managers, but they are mostly likely to be public school teachers, city and county health advocates, city welfare workers, public librarians, city attorneys, public defenders, city and county managers and administrators, and faculty members of public community, and four-year colleges and universities. Professional black women are less likely to work for major corporate law firms, teach at private educational institutions on any level, or serve on the medical staff of private hospitals than are their white counterparts. These data encourage us to ask questions about the nature and extent of progress for black professional women.

The search for explanations of the continued clustering of black professional and managerial women in the public sector reveals two major factors. First, educated black women continue to be concentrated in traditionally female occupations—jobs that are primarily dependent upon the public sector for employment. Indeed, the majority of our teachers, librarians, social workers, and so forth are employed by city, state, and county governments. In Southern cities, outside of Atlanta and Miami, professional and managerial women, both black and white, are clustered in traditionally female occupations, especially primary and secondary school teaching.

The second factor is racism—a racism that persists from an earlier era but takes on new forms in this post-Civil Rights age (Omi and Winant 1987). The distribution of employed black and white professional and managerial women in public and private sectors provides the means for examining differences in the structural barriers women face in the labor market.

A Decade of Progress?

An examination of 1970 census data on the sector distribution of black and

Table 18.2
Sectoral Distribution of Women Managerial and Professional Workers for Fifteen SMSAs, 1970

		Black				Non-Black		
SMSA	N	Public (%)	Private (%)	Other (%)[a]	N	Public (%)	Private (%)	Other (%)
Atlanta	6,973	68.5	29.0	2.5	37,105	43.0	50.6	6.1
Baltimore	10,461	72.6	24.4	2.9	45,591	45.0	49 .2	5.8
Chicago	21,239	59.2	38.0	2.7	162,771	34.3	60. 5	5.2
Cleveland	6,390	59.4	36.2	4.4	45,162	37.3	57. 6	5.1
Dallas	4,709	51.8	42.9	5.3	40,668	34.9	56.8	8.4
Detroit	12,920	57.8	39.2	3.0	80,224	41.3	53.3	5.4
Houston	7,516	53.0	41.1	5.9	47,090	35.7	55.4	8.9
Los Angeles	17,429	58.0	37.4	4.6	194,433	36.2	54.8	9.0
Memphis	4,772	76.8	20.0	3.2	14,742	43.1	49.5	7.4
Miami	3,120	68.9	27.7	3.4	30,161	34.0	57.8	8.2
Newark	6,550	55.9	40.7	3.4	46,450	40.4	53.9	5.7
New Orleans	5,450	68.5	28.6	2.9	21,331	34.4	57.1	8.5
New York	41,131	49.2	47.5	3.3	317,389	36.5	57.1	6.3
Philadelphia	14,772	58.7	38.3	3.1	106,796	35.2	58.4	6.4
St. Louis	7,357	63.8	33.2	3.0	54,666	36.0	56.0	5.9
Mean Percentage	13.7	61.5	34.9	3.6	86.3	37.8	55.2	6.8

[a]Includes self-employed and unpaid family workers.
Source: U.S. Bureau of the Census, *Census of Population 1970*, vol. 1, *Characteristics of the Population* (Washington, D.C.: U.S. Government Printing Office, 1973), "Detailed Population Characteristics," Table 173.

non-black women for the same fifteen SMSAs reveals that in fourteen of the fifteen SMSAs used in the previous analysis, the majority of black professional women were employed in the public sector, while the majority of non-black women were found in the private sector (see Table 18.2). In 1970, it was New York, not Los Angeles, that was the exception. For the same fifteen SMSAs, the mean percent of black women in the public sector was 61.5, 3.6 percentage points higher than the 1980 mean. In 1970, the mean percentage of non-black professional and managerial specialty women in the public sector was 37.8, 6.1 percentage points higher than the 1980 figures for non-blacks.

Thus a comparison of the 1970 and 1980 census figures, even with the limitations of the data, indicates that a smaller percentage of professional and managerial women, both black and white, are employed in the public sector.

Table 18.3 reports the percentage point change in the sector distribution of women in professional and managerial specialty occupations between 1970 and 1980 for the fifteen SMSAs. The last column reveals that there have been small but significant gains in the percentage of black women employed in professional and managerial positions. These data reinforce other findings about the progress black women made during the decade (Sokoloff 1988, 1992; Westcott 1982). But a closer look at the percentage increases and decreases in the public and private sectors indicates that change is not uniform for all professional and managerial women.

In the majority of the metropolitan areas, the percentages of non-black women (the majority of this population is white, but it includes Asian American, Latina, and Native American women) in the private sector have grown considerably. This

Table 18.3
Percent Change in the Sectoral Distribution of Women Managerial/Professional Specialty Workers for Fifteen SMSAs, 1970-1980

| SMSA | Public | | Private | | Other[a] | | Total Change |
	Black	Non-Black	Black	Non-Black	Black	Non-Black	Black[b]
Atlanta	-12.8	-8.2	+13.5	+ 9.7	-0.7	-1.2	+2.6
Baltimore	- 0.3	-0.6	+ 2.5	+ 5.9	-2.1	-1.4	+1.3
Chicago	-5.4	-7.6	+ 6.8	+ 8.3	-1.3	-0.8	+2.6
Cleveland	- 5.6	-7.3	+ 7.8	+ 8.3	-2.3	-1.0	+1.9
Dallas	+ 3.0	-2.7	- 0.3	+ 5.2	-2.7	-2.6	-0.7
Detroit	+ 1.5	-7.6	- 0.1	+ 8.8	-1.5	-1.2	+2.1
Houston	+ 2.5	-4.9	+ 1.3	+ 8.1	-3.8	-3.2	+0.6
Los Angeles	-10.4	-8.9	+11.9	+11.1	-1.5	-1.1	+2.6
Memphis	- 5.1	-8.5	+ 7.0	+10.8	-1.9	-2.3	+0.9
Miami	- 8.6	-7.3	+10.5	+11.1	-1.9	-1.8	+4.6
Newark	- 0.7	-6.9	+ 2.9	+ 8.2	-2.2	-1.3	+2.9
New Orleans	- 2.7	-2.9	+ 4.2	+ 6.6	-1.5	-3.6	+3.7
New York	+ 0.1	-2.1	+ 1.3	+ 2.7	-1.5	-0.5	-2.7
Philadelphia	- 2.7	-6.0	+ 3.9	+ 7.2	-1.3	-1.8	+1.1
St. Louis	- 5.6	-6.7	+ 7.1	+10.3	-1.6	-1.5	+1.7
Mean Percentage	- 3.2	-5.9	+ 5.4	+ 8.2	-1.8	-1.6	+1.7

[a]Includes self-employed and unpaid family workers. [b]Represents percentage point change in Black/non-Black composition of all women managerial and professional specialty workers.

progress is due to the entrance of women into traditionally male occupations, which are more likely to be found in the private sector, and increasing opportunities to perform traditionally female work in the private sector (private schools, private hospitals, and private colleges and universities).

Even in Memphis, private sector employment for white professional and managerial women increased by 10.8 percentage points.[4] A few other cities also witnessed significant growth in the percentages of non-black women in the private sector: 10.3 percentage points for St. Louis, 11.1 percentage points for Miami, 8.8 in Detroit, and in many other metropolitan areas, increases in the range of five to nine percentage points. The mean percentage point increase in private sector employment for non-black women across the fifteen SMSAs was 8.15.

Black professional and managerial women have also made serious inroads into the private sector since 1970. Yet, in all but two metropolitan areas, their progress lags behind their non-black sisters. Only in Atlanta and Los Angeles did black women have larger percentage point increases in private sector employment than did non-black women. Both of these are Sunbelt cities where there were large increases in private sector employment for non-black women as well.

The more common pattern saw smaller changes for black women than non-black women. Houston, another Sunbelt city, had a small increase for black women (1.3 percentage points), but a significant shift of 8.1 percentage points for non-black women. In Baltimore, Newark, New York, and Philadelphia, black professional and managerial women had percentage point increases below 4. In the metropolitan areas of Chicago, Memphis, and Cleveland, black professional women increased their percentages in private sector employment by 6.8, 7.0, and 7.8, respectively. Table 18.3 provides evidence that black women are moving out of public

sector employment in many metropolitan areas, but that movement is slower than that of their non-black counterparts. The mean percentage point increase in private sector employment for black women across the fifteen SMSAs is 5.4, considerably lower than the figure for non-black women of 8.2.

In two SMSAs, the concentration of black managerial and professional specialty women in the private sector declined. In Dallas, the percent of black women in these occupations who were employed in the private sector declined by 0.3 percentage point while non-black women increased by 5.2 percentage points. In Detroit, black women's concentration in the private sector declined by 0.1 percentage point while non-black women's concentration in the private sector increased by 8.8 percentage points. It is evident that educated white women made more significant progress than educated black women. Racism does not disappear when one gets an education and a middle-class occupation. These data provide one means of detailing the racial constraints faced by black women in professional and managerial employment.

Conclusion

Black women as well as white women are gaining access to education in traditionally male fields. Once they finish this training, they enter a racist and sexist labor market. With only one major discriminatory barrier, more white than black women are able to enter the private sector. Thus, some research indicates that dominant culture women are moving into the upper levels of the middle class while black women are lagging behind (Landry 1987). Black women, even with advanced degrees, still struggle with racial discrimination and informal barriers to occupational advancement. Instead of the myth of the advantages of being a double minority, both black and female (Epstein 1973), Fulbright's (1986) research indicates that there are no advantages to being both black and female for managers; instead, there are additional constraints. The case can also be made for black women in traditionally female fields. Even when women remain in traditionally female occupations, white women are able to practice these professions in the private sector, especially private schools and agencies (Higginbotham 1987).

Both gender and racial discrimination play a role in the occupational distribution of black women. First, black women continue to be steered into training for traditionally female occupations and discouraged from attempting innovative careers. Thus, their professional training keeps them dependent upon the public sector for employment as teachers, social workers, nurses, and librarians. Second, rigid racial barriers that limit black people's employment options in the private sector, in both male- and female-dominated occupations, keep their numbers in the private sector low. Therefore more black women, even those trained in traditionally male fields, find jobs in the public sector because there is less discrimination in hiring in this segment of the labor market.

These data prompt many other questions about the quality of work life for black professional and managerial women. What does it mean to be employed in the public sector in metropolitan areas today? In the light of city, county, and state fiscal problems and reduced commitments to human services, the prospects appear grim. Many public school teachers are demanding more police protection in the schools and the institutionalization of faculty and student identification cards, as well as insisting upon smaller class sizes and more materials. In many urban communities there are additional demands to raise teachers' salaries and provide greater fringe benefits, but on the whole, working conditions are equally critical work issues for many primary and secondary public school faculty members.

In the light of these tensions and the decreasing desirability of public schools as places to work, many black teachers are finding they have few alternatives in the labor market. Many are returning to universities for retraining to increase their employment options. Others are redefining their goals and planning to work their twenty, twenty-five, or thirty years until retirement—with the hope that the financial cushion of a pension will enable them to begin second careers.

Similar issues confront human service workers in health and social service agencies. Budget cuts have resulted in significant reductions in staffing—leaving the remaining employees with high caseloads and impossible tasks. Such individuals are lucky to be able to keep their jobs during an era when the delivery of services to poor and working-class people is not a priority. Yet they face daily frustrations on the job. As the data suggest, many of professional and managerial people working under such conditions are black women and other people of color.

These current realities suggest that public sector professional employment, especially for women in traditionally female occupations, is not the prize it appeared to be in the 1950s and 1960s (Block et al. 1987). In an earlier age, women employed as teachers, social workers, and nurses in public schools and city agencies had excellent salaries, decent fringe benefits, and vacations. They also could easily return to their professions after their childbearing years. Even where professional public sector employees have been able to keep their wages on a par with private sector employees in their metropolitan areas, the conditions of work have deteriorated. These realities may provide the motivation to leave the public sector. If so, we must ask if each public sector professional employee has the same chance of securing comparable work in the private sector. These data suggest that white women might be more successful in seeking new employment options outside the public sector.

These data should encourage detailed investigations of the progress of black, white, Latina, Asian American, and Native American professional and managerial women in the private sector. As a nation, we celebrate the impact of the Civil Rights and women's movements and the passage of federal guidelines in opening corporate doors for women and racial minorities, yet these gains are fragile in the face of indifferent federal administrations (Collins 1983). Given these shifts, how do professional and managerial women survive in the private sector? Perhaps a major obstacle for many is gaining access to private sector jobs.

The racial barriers faced by educated black women are different from the blanket opposition to hiring black people in professional and managerial positions that characterized the early part of this century. There has been significant progress in both access to higher education and employment options. The persistence of racism can result in a middle class that is segmented along racial lines. Black professionals, managers, and administrators are clustered in the public sector. In their positions they serve clients in public schools, local welfare agencies, public hospitals, public defender's offices, and other human service agencies. Many of these clients are poor and working class, and many are black people or other people of color. Meanwhile, non-black women (especially white women) are increasing their numbers in private sector employment. Are black professionals, particularly women, trapped in public sector employment? In these middle-class positions, are they professionals relegated to jobs, wages, and working conditions that mirror the racial segmentation in traditional working-class occupations?

I addressed the persistence of racial restrictions in the employment options for black professional and managerial women. Indeed, the findings suggest that one way to explore racial discrimination is to observe racial differences in access to jobs in employment sectors. There are many other issues that merit exploration, especially the day-to-day experiences of black and other women of color in professional and managerial positions in different occupations and sectors.

With a grounding in theory—especially a theoretical approach that recognizes that racism is still with us—and with solid empirical tools, we can build an exemplary scholarship of people of color across social class lines. Armed with both theory and data, we can uncover evidence that highlights the intersection of race, gender, and class. This scholarship can praise the diligence and persistence of female and male members of the Afro-American community. It can also portray the costs of racism for this population. Knowledge such as this will help us know ourselves and understand the larger problems that we confront as we continue to struggle against racism and sexism in all their forms.

Endnotes

Acknowledgments: I wish to thank Lynn Weber, Betty Wiley, Jobe Henry, Jr., and Sandra Marion for their help in preparing this chapter. I would also like to acknowledge the comments of Maxine Baca Zinn and Bonnie Thornton Dill.

1. This discussion does not include black women who are in the middle class solely by virtue of marriage. Black women married to professional and managerial men but not employed in the labor force, faced different circumstances.

2. This study does not include the District of Columbia because it is a major metropolitan area where a significant number of all residents are employed in the public sector.

3. In 1970, the data on occupational distribution by SMSA categorized workers as either black or non-black; thus, the non-black figures included Asian American,

Latina, and Native American women as well as white women. This makes the status of non-racially oppressed white women difficult to ascertain. Better data on white and black women are available for 1980 and those data are used here in the text. In Table 18.1, data for black and non-black women are used to facilitate comparisons with 1970 data.

4. Memphis has a small Asian American, Latino, and Native American population; thus we can assume that the vast majority of the non-black population is white.

References

Amott, T. and J. A. Matthaei. 1991. *Race, Gender and Work: A Multicultural Economic History of Women in the United States.* Boston: South End Press.

Barrera, M. 1979. *Race and Class in the Southwest.* Notre Dame, Ind.: University of Notre Dame Press.

Bascom, L. 1987. "Breaking through middle-management barrier." *Crisis,* April/May:13-16, 61, 64.

Block, F., R. Cloward, B. Ehrenreich, and F. F. Piven. 1987. *The Mean Season: The Attack on the Welfare State.* New York: Pantheon.

Braverman, H. 1974. *Labor and Monopoly Capital.* New York: Monthly Review Press.

Collins, S. 1983. "The making of the black middle class." *Social Problems* 30(April):369-382.

Cuthbert, M. 1942. *Education and Marginality.* New York: Stratford Press.

Davis, G. and G. Watson. 1982. *Black Life in Corporate America.* Garden City, N.Y.: Anchor Press/Doubleday.

Drake, S. and H. Cayton. 1970. *Black Metropolis.* New York: Harper Torchbooks.

Ehrenreich, B. and J. Ehrenreich. 1979. "The professional and managerial class." In P. Walker (ed.), *Between Labor and Capital.* Boston: South End Press:5-25.

Epstein, C. F. 1973. "The positive effect of the multiple negative: Explaining the success of professional black women." *American Journal of Sociology,* 78(January):912-933.

Fulbright,K. 1986. "The myth of the double-advantage: Black female managers." In M. C. Simm and J. Malveaux (eds.), *Slipping Through the Cracks: The Status of Black Women.* New Brunswick, N.J.: Transaction Press:33-45.

Higginbotham, E. 1987. "Employment for black professional women in the twentieth century." In C. Bose and G. Spitze (Eds.), *Ingredients for Women's Employment Policy.* Albany: State University of New York Press:73-91.

Hine, D. C. 1989. *Black Women in White: Racial Conflict and Cooperation in the Nursing Profession, 1890-1950.* Bloomington: Indiana University Press.

Johnson, C. 1969. *The Negro College Graduate.* College Park, Md.: McGrath.

Jones, B. A. P. 1986. "Black women and labor force participation: An analysis of sluggish growth rates." In M. C. Simm and J. Malveaux (Eds.), *Slipping Through the Cracks: The Status of Black Women.* New Brunswick, N.J.: Transaction Press:11-31.

Jones, J. 1985. *Labor of Love, Labor of Sorrow: Black Women, Work and the Family from Slavery to the Present.* New York: Basic Books.

Kilson, M. 1977. "Black women in the professions." *Monthly Labor Review,* 100(May):38-41.

Landry, B. 1987. *The New Black Middle Class.* Berkeley: University of California Press.

Noble, J. 1956. *The Negro Women's College Education.* New York: Teachers College, Columbia University.

Omi, M. and H. Winant. 1987. *Racial Formation in the United States.* New York: Routledge.

Poulantzas, N. 1974. *Classes in Contemporary Society.* London: New Left Books.

Sokoloff, N. 1987. "Black and white women in the professions: A contradictory process." In C. Bose and G. Spitze (Eds.), *Ingredients for Women's Employment Policy.* Albany: State University of New York Press:53-72.

_____. 1988. "Evaluating gains and losses of black and white women and men in the professions, 1960-1980." *Social Problems,* 35(February):36-53.

_____. 1992. *Black Women and White Women in the Professions.* New York: Routledge.

Tyack, D. B. 1974. *The One Best System: A History of American Education.* Cambridge, MA: Harvard University Press.

United States Bureau of the Census. 1973. *Census of Population 1970.* Vol. 1, *Charac-*

teristics of the Population. Washington, D.C.: U.S. Government Printing Office.

———. 1983. *Census of Population 1980.* Vol. 1, *Characteristics of the Population.* Washington, D.C.: U.S. Government Printing Office.

United States Department of Labor, Bureau of Labor Statistics. 1984. *Employment and Earnings,* 31(December). Washington, D.C.: U.S. Government Printing Office.

Vanneman, R. and L. W. Cannon. 1987. *The American Perception of Class.* Philadelphia: Temple University Press.

Walker, P. (ed.). 1979. *Between Labor and Capital.* Boston: South End Press.

Wallace, P. 1980. *Black Women in the Labor Force.* Cambridge, MA: MIT Press.

Westcott, D. N. 1982. "Blacks in the 1970s: Did they scale the job ladder?" *Monthly Labor Review,* 105(June): 29-38.

Food for Thought and Application Questions

1. Higginbotham describes changes in black women's professional employment from 1970 to 1980 and compares those changes to the same information for white women. Gather information on black and white women's employment in the professions in 1990. (1990 Census data is the best source for this information and is available in most college/university libraries.) Describe how black women's representation in professional employment compares to that of white women in 1990. Do the patterns described by Higginbotham apply to the 1990 data?

2. Why are black women disproportionately concentrated in the public sector? How do jobs in the public and private sectors compare in terms of wages, job security, working conditions, and opportunities for promotion?

3. Higginbotham debunks the myth of "the advantages of double minority status" for employment in the professions. What are the implications of her arguments for relations between black and white women? ✦

19

'Now That We Are Here': Discrimination, Disparagement, and Harassment at Work and the Experience of Women Lawyers

Janet Rosenberg
Harry Perlstadt
William R. F. Phillips

The Clarence Thomas-Anita Hill hearings and the Tailhook scandal involving sexual assaults on women naval officers have focused the nation's attention on the gender-based discrimination and harassment experienced by professional women. This article analyzes the reported experiences of a sample of women lawyers in a midwestern city. We use these data to explore patterns of discrimination and their relationship to women's professional experience in diverse work settings.

Studies indicate that, although women are an increasingly large proportion of practicing attorneys, the legal profession continues to be stratified by gender (Curran 1986). Regardless of where

they work, women tend to occupy lower status positions. In private practice, they are concentrated in less remunerative specialties (Heinz and Laummann 1982), are less likely than men to become partners during the course of their careers (Curran 1986), and have little decision-making power in firms and typically, earn approximately two-thirds the income of men (Chambers 1989; Hagan et al. 1991).

In addition to discrimination, lawyers, like other professional women, are subject to a range of deprecating and harassing behaviors that affect their morale and the degree to which they have power in professional arenas (Couric 1989; Epstein 1981; Kanter 1978; Menkel-Meadow 1989; Morello 1986). Anecdotal accounts from women lawyers suggest that these events are related and indicative of gender stratification, which may be sharper and more durable in the legal profession than in many others (Hagan et al. 1991). Nevertheless, little attention has been paid to how discrimination, disparagement, and harassment are related; typically, they are studied as independent events.

This article explores patterns of sexist behavior in several ways. First, is the incidence of discrimination the same in recruiting and hiring as it is once women are working in an organization? The employment of an ever larger number of women lawyers, particularly in large firms, suggests inclusiveness and some sort of progress toward more egalitarian work environments. But recent theoretical work (Acker 1990; Hearn and Parkin 1987) indicates that fair hiring practices can mask continuing on-the-job discrimination. If so, women would report less discrimination in recruitment and hiring than on the job.

Second, we examine the possibility that women's reports of sexist behavior may be subjective accounts of experiences that vary with their professional orientation. As newcomers in the legal profession, women have come under extraordinary pressure to conform to professional norms, to defer to authority, and to avoid confrontations concerning women's issues (see Rhode 1988). As a result of these pressures, coupled with socialization to ideologies that equate political neutrality with professionalism, many women have developed assimilationist and individualistic approaches to their professional roles; thus, they focus on individual strategies to be successful regardless of the systematic roadblocks they may encounter. A career orientation of this kind may account, in part, for the reluctance of many professional women to report or acknowledge the existence of sexism at work (Hochschild 1973; LaFontaine 1983). It may also indirectly account for a tendency to attribute aggressive behavior to the overwhelming power of men's sexual needs (see MacKinnon 1979) or the characterological flaws of individuals rather than to the structural features of organizations (LaFontaine and Trudeau 1986).

In contrast, some women in law have taken a far more critical and reformist approach. They have challenged gender discrimination and recommend collective action to alter the organizational arrangements that handicap them (Rosenberg, Perlstadt, and Phillips 1990). To these women, individual success is believed to be contingent on the success of women as a class. This orientation should lead to a different way of understanding gender relations at work and, consequently, to different accounts of their experiences. Theoretically, women with this feminist orientation should have a heightened sensitivity to expressions of male hostility and sexist behavior (see Alexander and Rudd 1984) and should closely monitor their relationships with men in the workplace (see Erdelyi 1974). Thus we would expect feminists to report more frequent occurrences of discrimination, disparagement, and harassment regardless of the types of organizations in which they work.

We also examine the incidence of discrimination, disparagement, and harassment to see if they are perceived as occurring more frequently in public or private sectors and in specific workplaces. A substantial amount of research examines the experiences of women in private practice, despite the fact that, compared to men, women lawyers are overrepresented in public sector positions (Curran 1986). This distribution is often attributed to women's interest in pursuing careers in public sector jobs, where the demands of family and professional life are more easily reconciled, and a desire to avoid discrimination. Still, research suggests that patterns of gender stratification are similar in the public and private sectors (Bridges and Nelson 1989; Hale and Kelly 1989). Consequently, whether or not women lawyers find that government and other nonprofit settings are less hostile environments in which to work remains an open question.

Recent contributions to the literature on gender stratification suggest that sexist behavior is most likely to occur where organizational culture specifically values characteristics traditionally attributed to men and where power is supported by instrumental and social cliques (Acker 1990; Hearn and Parkin 1987; U.S. Merit Systems and Protection Board 1988). On the other hand, when professional women work in organizations where access and opportunity are supported by well-established affirmative action policies, they are less likely to report harassment than are their counterparts in organizations without such programs (Hale and Kelly 1989; LaFontaine and Trudeau 1986). Because lawyers work in a variety of settings within both the public and private sectors, we would expect differences in patterns of discrimination between sectors, and possibly among organizations within the sectors as well.

Finally, we ask if token women perceive themselves to be more vulnerable to victimization than those women who work in environments where women lawyers are more numerous. Kanter (1977) described the effects of unbalanced sex ratios, including isolation and behavioral distortion. Other authors suggest that tokenism is also associated with sexual harassment (Konrad and Gutek 1986; LaFontaine and Trudeau 1986). After nearly 20 years of affirmative action, tokenism remains an indication of the resistance of organizations to the inclusion of women. Therefore, we would expect women in token situations to experience more incidents of on-the-job discrimination and to be more frequent targets of harassment and disparagement.

Data and Method

Sample

The data were collected from a questionnaire examining the occupational experiences of a group of women lawyers who work in a state capital, a medium-sized city located in a midwestern metropolitan area. Mailed questionnaires were sent to all women lawyers in the area (350); and 220 were returned for a response rate of 59 percent.

Unlike the respondents in a number of previous studies, the majority of the women did not go to elite law schools and do not practice in large firms nor in major legal and financial centers. More than 80 percent went to regional law schools with unexceptional prestige ratings and found jobs close to home in government and relatively small firms. Of those responding, 93.4 percent were white (non-Hispanic); 4.2 percent were African Americans. We suspect that the level of education and the work life of the respondents are typical of thousands of women lawyers working in state capitals and other medium-sized cities. The experiences of these practitioners have been virtually ignored in the current research on women in the legal profession. Nevertheless, given the small size of the population and the unique characteristics of a state capital, we hesitate to generalize our results.

Measures

Discrimination
Respondents were asked to indicate whether they believed that because they were women they were treated differently from men and if the differences benefitted or harmed them. Questions addressed recruitment hiring and on-the-job experiences including income, promotion, and work assignments.

Gender disparagement
Included are items concerning verbal acts that call attention to women's gender and that tend to demean or reduce the status of women. These include allusions to a woman's gender characteristics or to her sexuality, the use of infantalizing terms of address (*honey, dear, doll, girl*) or of her first name when men are not addressed in that way. One item concerns whether or not the respondent was asked to act as a secretary. Disparagement, which lowers esteem or standing, refers here to verbal behavior meant to be slighting and containing invidious references. It is more specific than the term *hostile environment*, as used by MacKinnon (1979), and narrower in scope than the specifications listed in the Equal Employment Opportunity Commission guidelines (1980).

Sexual harassment
Respondents were asked if they had received unwanted sexual advances in a professional setting during the past year. In the sections of the questionnaire on disparagement and harassment, questions concerning the perpetrator of the acts and the number of times such acts occurred during the year prior to the study were included.

Professional role orientation
This is a complex variable measured on the basis of 68 items. Factor and cluster analysis were used to identify groups of women with distinctive orientations to their professional roles (see Rosenberg, Perlstadt, and Phillips 1990). The orientations have three dimensions: first, political

identity (including self-assigned political labels and measures of feminist opinion and activity); second, definitions of professional interests reflected in the respondents' choice of policies to be pursued by the local women's bar association; third, participation in professional, women's, civic, and cultural organizations (including positions on boards of directors of these and other organizations).

Clusters of women having different orientations were identified. Of the 220 questionnaires returned, only 169 could be used for the analysis of role orientation. For our analysis of role orientation in this study, the responses of 16 women who had mixed-type orientations unsuitable for our purposes were not used, resulting in a reduced sample of 153 women. Although a subsample is used in this analysis of role orientation, it matches the full sample on all demographic, political, and professional characteristics. Consequently, we are reasonably certain that the two orientations as described here fairly represent the major professional perspectives of our population.

The subjects belong to one of two clusters labeled *feminist* or *careerist*. The feminists ($N = 64$) give overwhelming support to traditional feminist positions, are members of women's organizations, and take a feminist-based view of the position of women in the legal profession. They believe in the necessity of collective action to alter the distribution of power, tend to support only candidates for bar and bench offices who espouse feminist objectives, and believe that women's bar associations should provide pro bono services to ensure the civil rights of all women. This feminist perspective is fundamental to their professional identity.

In contrast, the women we have labeled careerists ($N = 89$) support basic economic rights for women but reject feminist labels; they are less inclined to support feminist candidates, to provide pro bono services to protect women's rights, or to make a political issue of the subordinate

status of women lawyers. Rather, they believe that their position could be improved by refining their skills to compete more effectively in the legal marketplace. This orientation is compatible with an institutional ethos that denies the importance of gender in stratifying the profession. It assumes that there is an equitable return to human capital investment regardless of gender; careerists believe in the essential fairness of the competitive process. The labels feminist and careerist do not imply different levels of professional aspiration or commitment. They refer exclusively to a political-professional orientation that includes views of the structure of the legal profession, the status of women within it, and related courses of action.

Workplace

Our primary focus is the comparison of public and private sector experiences. However, given varying characteristics of workplaces within these categories, further distinctions are made. Workplaces are arranged in a hypothetical order from those most likely to those least likely to be associated with high levels of sexist behavior. Private sector workplaces include solo practice, firms, and in-house counsel. Public sector locations include government agencies, courts, and a residual category in which the majority of respondents are academics.

Briefly, our rationale for this ordering is as follows. Overall, women in private sector workplaces will be more vulnerable than women in the public sector. Within the private sector, solo practitioners are ranked first. They are believed to be subject to high levels of discrimination because of their professional isolation, a lack of collegial support, and organizational protections that inhibit offensive behavior (see Epstein 1981; Hagan 1990; Tangri, Burt, and Johnson 1982). Working in private law firms is ranked second. Until recently, private firms have been resistant to the inclusion of women and clearly dominated by men. The evidence of discrimination in private firms is weighty and convincing (Couric 1989; DeBenedictus 1989; Hagan 1990; Taber et al. 1988). Given the conflicting data on the status of women working as in-house counsels in business settings (Chambers 1989; Roach 1990), these positions are ranked third. These three private sector workplaces are followed by public sector locations; government agencies, which have been more receptive to women and in which women's positions and earnings are somewhat protected by formalized hiring procedures and salary scales, are ranked fourth. Courts follow agency positions. Although the literature suggests that women working in courts do experience forms of discrimination and disparagement (New York Task Force on Women in the Courts 1986), like other government employees, they should be protected by standardized hiring practices and salary scales. Further, the relatively small size of legal staffs working as employees of courts and the intensive nature of the interaction among members of these staffs may inhibit more flagrant forms of sexist behavior. Other nonprofit work settings, including academic positions and union offices, are included in a residual category and ranked last. The validity of the ordering was tested using Kendall's tau *B*, an ordinal measure of association that can be used to measure the goodness of fit of preinterpreted data (Ott, Larson, and Mendenhall 1983).

Token status

Respondents who worked in offices where fewer than 20 percent of the lawyers were women were classified as having token status; all others were designated nontokens.

Control variables

Age and marital status are related to disparagement and harassment (Tangri, Burt, and Johnson 1982; U.S. Merit System and Protection Board 1988) and are used as controls in appropriate sections of the analysis.

Results

Table 19.1 indicates the responses of the women lawyers to questions asking if they were treated differently because of being a woman in a variety of situations and if the difference personally benefitted or harmed them. The latter is referred to here as discrimination. Across all situations, including those at the front door and on-the-job, the majority of women believed they were treated the same as men or actually benefitted from differential treatment. But, there is a clear pattern in the responses pertaining to the consequences of being treated differently in particular situations. Among those reporting differential treatment in recruiting and hiring, more women reported personal benefits from such treatment than reported discrimination. Consequently, being treated differently during the hiring process was more likely to be an advantage than a disadvan-

Table 19.1
Discrimination—Comparing Own Treatment to the Treatment of Men (Percentages)

Treatment	Treated the Same	Treated Differently	
		Beneficial	Discriminatory
Recruitment	52.4	27.1	20.5[a]
Hiring	45.0	35.0	20.0
On-the-job			
Rewards			
Salary	57.7	1.5	40.8
Promotion	61.5	5.7	32.8
Activities			
Legal			
assignments	61.2	3.8	34.9
Settlements	58.0	10.2	32.3
Court room	59.4	9.4	31.1
Pretrial	65.6	6.2	28.1
Research	70.0	3.8	25.5

NOTE: *N*=200. The number of responses to these items varies slightly. Not all items, particularly those listed under activities, are relevant to jobs in all work settings.
[a] Rows may not add to 100% because of rounding.

tage. In contrast, once the women lawyers were on the job, in salary, promotion, or task allocation, very few (from 1.5 percent to 10.2 percent) said they benefitted from different treatment based on gender. Consequently, we find that more women experienced discrimination once on the job than in the recruiting and hiring process. The data suggest that the apparent willingness of employers to hire women does not necessarily mean that they will be treated equally.

This idea is strengthened when we examine the proportion of women who reported being verbally disparaged, that is, being addressed in ways that call attention to gender characteristics or sexuality. Although some blatant forms of disparagement, such as being assigned the role of secretary, have been effectively repressed (if not totally eliminated), the women in this study were continually exposed to more egregious, if subtle, forms of disparagement.

Approximately two-thirds of our respondents reported being addressed as "honey" or "dear" and being the butt of remarks emphasizing gender and sexuality ("nice to have a pretty face") in professional situations (Table 19.2). Other lawyers were named most frequently (36 percent) as the perpetrators of disparaging behavior, followed by clients (27 percent), judges (16 percent), and a variety of other professionally related personnel.

As would be expected, a significantly greater proportion of women under 35 reported being the victims of such behavior compared to their older colleagues (75 percent to 55 percent; $p = .02$). In contrast, marital status, a factor that we also expected to affect the reported frequency of these experiences, was unrelated to disparagement. On average, single and married women reported approximately the same incidence of disparagement (64.1 percent to 67.3 percent). Further, disparagement is not a one-time event. Of those reporting inappropriate forms of address or sexual allusion, four-fifths experienced both forms more than once and one-half experienced them more than five times during the past year. Consequently, regardless of whether or not they found these remarks offensive, merely annoying, or even innocuous, many of the women lawyers had to cope with frequent reminders of gender differences that are demeaning and call the legitimacy of their claims to professional equality into question.

Overall, one-fourth (24.5 percent) of the lawyers reported being sexually harassed, that is, receiving unwanted sexual advances in a professional situation. Of the

Table 19.2
Percentage Reporting Disparagement and Harassment by Workplace

		Private Sector			Public Sector		
	N[a]	Solo	Firm	In-House	Government	Court	Other
	100	11.8	~ 26.1	9.9	37.3	7.5	7.5
Treatment	(161)	(19)	(42)	(16)	(60)	(12)	(12)
Disparagement							
Act as secretary	17.5	22.2	17.6	25.0	16.3	0.0	25.0
Inappropriately addressed	66.0	75.0	73.7	68.8	66.6	61.5	30.8
Gender-sex emphasis remarks	64.5	78.9	78.6	68.8	65.0	33.3	33.3[b]
Addressed by first name	32.0	29.4	28.9	33.3	39.2	25.0	16.7
Harassment							
Unwanted advances	24.0	26.3	43.6	25.0	18.4	0.0	15.4[ab]

[a] The number of responses to these items varies slightly.
[b] Kendall's tau *B:* $p = .01$.

women reporting harassment, 85 percent said that it occurred more than once in the past year. The primary perpetrators were other lawyers (45 percent), followed by clients (31.3 percent), judges (17.6 percent), and other legal personnel. The incidence and perpetrators reported here are similar to the frequency and source reported in another study of women lawyers (De-Benedictus 1989) and in studies of other women professionals as well (LaFontaine and Trudeau 1986, Loy and Stewart 1984; Schneider 1985). As with disparagement, age was related to the frequency of harassment. Women under 35 reported being harassed more frequently than did older women (52.8 percent to 17.9 percent; p = .02) and in this sample, although married women were less likely to be harassed, that status did not provide the expected protection against unwanted sexual advances (married, 20.2 percent; single, 29.8 percent).

Role Orientation and Reports of Sexist Behavior

Contrary to theoretical expectations, women labeled feminists were not more likely to report sexist behavior than careerists were. The latter reported slightly more disparagement and significantly more harassment (27.3 percent to 12.5 percent; p = .01) than feminists (see Table 19.3). These results are not related to age or marital status. In fact, older careerists, (32.3 percent), compared to older feminists (8.3 percent), reported sexual harassment. Nor can the results be attributed to workplace effects, because equal proportion of careerists (23.8 percent) and feminists (23.3 percent) work in private firms, where, as we shall see below, women lawyers are most at risk of being sexually harassed.

Given the small size of the subsample used (N = 153) in the analysis of role orientation, we have to be cautious about interpreting these results. Nevertheless, the data indicate that lawyers in this community whose careerist identity, age, and marital status would lead us to expect reports of a low incidence of harassment, re-

Table 19.3
Role Orientations by Harassment, Workplace, Age, and Marital Status (Percentages)

	Careerists (N = 89)	Feminists (N = 64)
Reporting harassment by age	27.3	12.5
Under 35	29.0	18.7
35+	32.3	8.0
Workplace		
Solo practice	9.5	6.7
Private firm	23.8	23.3
In-house counsel	11.9	3.3
Government agency	42.9	35.0
Court	6.0	10.0
Other	6.0	21.7
Under 35	47.7	51.5
Married	65.3	51.2

ported significantly more harassment than did their colleagues with a feminist orientation. Whatever the reason for the results, it is clear that the proportion of women who report having been victims of harassment is unrelated to the heightened political sensitivities of feminists or to the vigilance with which they monitor and, subsequently, report their relationships with men at work.

Workplace and Sex Ratios

Tables 19.3, 19.4, 19.5, and 19.6 show that, although discrimination at the front door is unrelated to workplace, as we expected, variations in the proportion of on-the-job discrimination, disparagement, and harassment are related to where the women worked and the sex ratio of lawyers on legal staffs. When comparing themselves to men, women in the private sector—that is, in solo practice, in firms, and in the offices of in-house counsel—reported significantly more discrimination relative to salaries, promotion, and work assignments than did women in public sector workplaces (Table 19.4). Courts, however, are a special case. As anticipated, women enjoy protection in hiring and salary in courts, but larger proportions complain of discrimination in the distribution of work.

Not all types of disparagement are related to workplace (Table 19.2). Nevertheless, the most demeaning form of disparagement, being the target of remarks that emphasize gender characteristics and sexuality, occurred more often in private sector workplaces. A further analysis of the data indicates that virtually all women under 35 working in the private sector were vulnerable to this type of disparagement; 85.7 percent in solo practice, 92 percent in private firms, and 100 percent of the in-house counsels compared to 65.3 percent of the younger women in government agencies and only 33.3 percent in court settings.

As expected, women who were most likely to experience discrimination and disparagement were more often the targets of sexual harassment as well (Table 19.2), with significantly more reports from lawyers in private sector jobs. The frequency of harassment was particularly high in private firms, where 43.6 percent of the lawyers reported having been harassed during the past year. This is more than double the proportion reporting harassment in governing agencies (18.4 percent). No harassment was reported by women in court positions. Age had no significant interaction with workplace, but marital status did. Although marital status was unrelated to reports of harassment in the public sector (single, 20 percent; married, 14 percent), single women in the private sector, as compared to married women were clearly at greater risk. In solo practice, never-married and divorced women compared to their married colleagues were five times as likely to have been harassed (66.0 percent to 13.3 percent), and, in private firms, they were twice as likely (62.5 percent to 30.4 percent) to have been harassed.

Token Status and Sexism

The disadvantages related to working in settings where men make up 80 percent

---

Table 19.4
Percentage of Discrimination Reported by Workplace

	Private Sector			Public Sector		
	Solo	Firm	In-House	Government	Court	Other
Treatment	(n = 20)	(n = 51)	(n = 19)	(n = 72)	(n = 16)	(n = 13)
Front door						
Recruitment	n.a.[a]	20.8	15.7	16.6	33.3	30.7
Hiring	n.a.	22.4	21.0	13.6	18.7	30.7
Rewards						
Salary	55.0	48.9	55.5	32.8	25.0	26.6[b]
Promotion	n.a.	37.5	37.5	28.1	20.0	23.0[c]
Activities						
Legal assignments	n.a.	42.8	22.2	27.9	46.1	40.0
Pretrial	n.a.	37.7	13.3	17.2	33.3	30.0
Courtroom	n.a.	34.7	35.2	24.5	37.5	20.0
Settlement	n.a.	31.2	37.5	16.9	20.0	40.0[c]
Research	n.a.	25.5	11.1	22.3	0.0	20.0

NOTE: The number of responses to these items varies slightly. Not all items, particularly those listed under Activities, are equally relevant to jobs in all work settings.
[a] Not applicable. [b] Kendall's tau B: $p = .02$. [c] Kendall's tau B: $p = .05$.

or more of a legal staff are clearly evident (Table 19.5). Although women in the private sector are more likely to have token status, regardless of work setting, token women are roughly twice as likely to report differential treatment with regard to salary (51.8 percent to 28.9 percent), promotion (42.5 percent to 22.3 percent), and office facilities (34.6 percent to 15.3 percent). They also report significantly more discrimination in legal assignments (41.9 percent to 29.1 percent) and pretrial work (36.6 percent to 17.8 percent), probably reflecting their typically low status and concentration in less remunerative specialties. Although no differences are evident in terms of disparagement between tokens and nontokens (Table 19.6) tokens are more likely to report unwanted sexual advances (34.6 percent to 20.5 percent). Being older or married protects both tokens and nontokens.

To sum up, women in the private sector, particularly in firms, were most likely to experience the full brunt of sexism at work, that is, to report the coexistence of discrimination, disparagement, and harassment. As compared to nontokens, women in token positions were more likely to experience discrimination and harassment. Neither age nor marital status had consistent effects when crossed with workplace. Nevertheless, in the private sector, being young virtually ensured that women would be disparaged, and being married provided protection from unwanted sexual advances.

Discussion

It is ironic, as others have observed (Hale and Kelly 1989; Rosenbaum 1985), that legal and social developments that have effectively opened the door for professional women may indirectly reinforce patterns of gender stratification and inequality. This seems to be the case in the community we studied. The relatively good experiences of these lawyers on their way into the profession have not been sus-

Table 19.5
Percentage of Net Discrimination Reported by Token and Nontoken Status

	Token	Nontoken
	37.5	62.5
Treatment	(61)	(102)
Front door		
Recruitment	24.6	16.6
Hiring	23.4	15.8
Rewards		
Salary	51.8	28.9[a]
Promotion	42.5	22.3[b]
Office	34.6	15.3[a]
Activities		
Legal assignments	41.9	29.1[a]
Pretrial	36.6	17.8[a]
Courtroom	35.6	24.1
Settlement	28.3	22.8
Research	28.9	15.7

NOTE: The number of responses to these items varies slightly. Not all items, particularly those listed under Activities, are relevant to jobs in all work settings. Solo practitioners are not included.
[a] X^2: p = .02. [b] X^2: p = .01.

tained. In private sector workplaces, almost one-half report inequities in salary and promotion and believe that their assignments, and therefore their opportunities, are restricted. Regardless of where they work, disparagement is pervasive, and, for certain women, the risk of being harassed is high. Consequently, within the context of their daily work, many are forced to cope with situations in which their aspirations are thwarted and their professional standing subverted.

As we expected, on-the-job discrimination and other forms of sexist experience tend to be concurrent, higher in private as compared to public sector workplaces, and higher among women who are structurally isolated. It is not surprising that women in token positions and in solo practice are more frequently the victims of

Table 19.6
Percentage Reporting Disparagement
and Harassment by Token/Nontoken
Status

	Token	Nontoken
	37.5	62.5
Disparagement	(57)	(98)
Treatment		
Act as secretary	22.9	15.0
Inappropriately addressed	70.7	64.2
Gender-sex emphasis remarks	69.0	62.9
Addressed by first name	31.4	32.6
Harassment		
Unwanted advances	34.6	20.5[a]

NOTE: The number of responses to these items varies slightly due to missing data. Solo practitioners are not included. [a] X^2: p = .06.

discrimination and harassment. The environments in which they work promote their visibility, thereby exaggerating gender distinctions, and provide few institutional constraints that might inhibit rejection or hostile overtures. It may be that, in the private sector, a professional ethos that embodies competitive models of achievement and masculinized ideals of lawyerly behavior exists that account for the reports of stronger resistance to women than evidenced in public sector workplaces. Or formal rules and the enforcement of affirmative action policies may be even less effective means of protecting women in private settings than in the public sector, where, as public disclosures have demonstrated, rules, policy, and public scrutiny do not guarantee civility and equal treatment.

Increasing numbers of women are being recruited into the private sector (Curran 1986), and this is precisely where the careers of women are most in jeopardy. Overall, younger women are also more subject to both disparagement and harassment than are older women, a finding consistent with most past research. But in private firms, older women were as likely to be harassed as younger women were. Despite cultural norms that should protect older women in this setting, they were as vulnerable as young colleagues (32.3 percent to 29 percent). On the other hand, being married, which for this sample overall was unrelated to harassment, did prove to be a protection for those women working in the private sector. How might we interpret these curious results? One possible view is that harassment is not primarily sexual behavior but, rather, a form of aggression aimed at stabilizing gender stratification. Should this be the case, the age of the target would be immaterial. On the other hand, being married may provide protection for those women regarded as already "taken" by other men who have legitimate claims to them as sexual property.

With the increased number of women in private sector locations and changing values, we might have expected less resistance to women than is reflected in these data. But, more than a decade ago, Epstein (cited in Yoder 1991) worried that increasing numbers of women in law and other professions might be viewed as intruders and a formidable threat to men who then evoke subtle but effective strategies for protecting the boundaries of their domains. One of the ways this might be accomplished is the systematic use of on-the-job discrimination, ubiquitous disparagement, and harassment described here.

If aggression is a defensive response to women as intruders, that does not necessarily mean that all women are equally vulnerable. Some women may appear to be safer targets than others. A safe-target explanation may apply to women in structurally isolated positions, such as tokens and solo practitioners. But it may also explain why twice as many women with careerist as compared to feminist orientations report that they have been harassed. The explanation may lie in the public persona and the messages unintentionally conveyed by women with different professional orientations. As we have indicated, the women categorized as careerists reject feminist objectives and labels. They behave as if the fiction of the gender neutrality of the lawyer's role is a reality, as if gender is inconsequential to their careers, and as if it does not shape their relationship to men and other women at work. Their willingness to view the class structure of the profession as a meritocracy resulting from open competition without acknowledging the handicaps of being women, may in fact, be inadvertently sending the wrong message to men, making these lawyers more, rather than less, vulnerable to sexual overtures.

In the absence of a moderating organizational climate in which affirmative action is enforced and universal principles for the allocation of rewards applied, men may believe that careerists, anxious to compete and observant of other professional rules authored by men, have too much at stake to publicly expose them, that they will go along with the professional and social norms that encourage tacit compliance and discourage women from reporting harassment. Simply put, careerists could be vulnerable because they appear to be safe victims.

On the other hand, men might avoid those women whose feminist position is taken as a signal to colleagues that they will not be complicit in sexual games at work, that there will be costs to men who behave in sexually offensive ways. Should this be the case, ironically feminists would be protected because they express their view that gender, independent of competency and talent, accounts, in part, for the class structure of the legal profession.

The different levels of harassment reported by feminists and careerists could be the product of special circumstances in this one community. But the data suggest that different ways of behaving, related to different professional orientations, evoke more or less restraint on the part of men as they attempt to maintain the system they have controlled for so long. It is clear that, among our respondents, a feminist identity does not invite higher levels of aggression or lead to exaggerated perceptions or increased reports of sexist behavior on the job.

The issue of the relationship of women's professional orientation to the experience of sexism at work is worth pursuing in further research. For years, women entering the profession have been advised to be patient, to play down women's issues, and to take on the values of the men who have preceded them (Rhode 1988). But those women who play the careerist game may unintentionally reinforce those aspects of organizational and professional culture that encourage men to believe they can control women or drive them out through discrimination and sexual manipulation. This throws quite a different light on the decisions that women make concerning their professional relationships and on their strategies for addressing issues of gender equality.

This study finds that reports of sexism at work are not subjective accounts that have been filtered through an ideological lens, with feminists more sensitive to men's offensive behavior than are women with other orientations. Rather, different levels of sexist experience are grounded in the relationship of men to women who seem more or less vulnerable and in structural features of the workplace. The data support the views of many observers that sexism in organizations has little to do with sex, but a great deal to do with the politics of gender. In this community, in some settings more than in others, it has distorted professional relationships and has had restrictive consequences for the careers of many of the women who participated in this study.

References

Acker, J. 1990. "Hierarchies, jobs, bodies: A theory of gendered organizations." *Gender and Society*, 4:139-58.

Alexander, C. N. Jr. and J. Rudd. 1984. "Predicting behavior from situated identities." *Social Psychological Quarterly*, 47:172-77.

Bridges, W. P. and R. L. Nelson. 1989. "Markets and hierarchies: Organizational and market influences on gender inequality." *American Journal of Sociology*, 95:616-58.

Chambers, D. L. 1989. "Accommodation and satisfaction: Women and men lawyers and the balance of work and family." *Law and Social Inquiry*, 14:251-87.

Couric, E. 1989. "Women in the large firms: A high price of admission?" *National Law Journal*, 11:10-12 (Supplement).

Curran, B. A. 1986. "American lawyers in the 1980: A profession in transition." *Law and Society Review*, 20:19-52.

DeBenedictus, D. J. 1989. "California women lawyers surveyed." *American Bar Association Journal*, December, 26-27.

Epstein, C. Fuchs. 1981. *Women in Law*. New York: Basic Books.

Equal Employment Opportunity Commission. 1980. "Guidelines on discrimination because of sex," 29 CFR Part 1604. *Federal Register*, 45:210.

Erdelyi, M. H. 1974. "A new look at the new look: Perceptual defense and vigilance." *Psychological Review*, 81:1-25.

Hagan, J. 1990. "The gender stratification of income inequality among lawyers." *Social Forces*, 68:835-55.

Hagan, J., M. Zatz, B. Arnold, and F. Kay. 1991. "Cultural capital, gender, and structural transformation of legal practice." *Law and Society Review*, 25:239-62.

Hale, M. H. and R. M. Kelly. 1989. *Gender, Bureaucracy, and Democracy*. Westport, CT: Greenwood.

Hearn, J. and P. W. Parkin. 1987. *Sex at Work: The Power and the Paradox of Organization Sexuality*. New York: St Martin.

Heinz, J. P. and E. O. Laummann. 1982. *Chicago Lawyers: The Social Structure of the Bar*. New York: Russell Sage.

Hochschild, A. R. 1973. "Making it: Marginality and obstacles minority consciousness." In R. Knudsin (Ed.), *Women and Success*. Totawa, NJ: Littlefield, Adams.

Kanter, R. Moss. 1977. *Men and Women of the Corporation*. New York: Basic Books.

————. 1978. "Reflections on women and the legal profession: A sociological perspective." *Harvard Women's Law Journal*, 1:1-17.

Konrad, A. M. and B. A. Gutek. 1986. "Impact of work experiences on attitudes toward sexual harassment." *Administrative Science Quarterly*, 31:422-38.

LaFontaine, E. 1983. "Forms of false consciousness among professional women." *Humbolt Journal of Social Relations* 10:26-44.

LaFontaine, E. and L. Trudeau. 1986. "The frequency, sources, and correlates of sexual harassment among women in traditional male occupations." *Sex Roles*, 15:433-42.

Loy, P. N. and L. P. Stewart. 1984. "The extent and eff- ects of the sexual harassment of working women." *Sociological Focus*, 17:31-43.

MacKinnon, C. A. 1979. *Sexual Harassment of Working Women*. New Haven, CT: Yale University Press.

Menkel-Meadow, C. 1989. "Feminization of the legal profession: The comparative sociology of women lawyers." In R. Abel and P. Lewis (Eds.), *Lawyers in Society*. Berkeley: University of California Press.

Morello, K. B. 1986. *The Invisible Bar: The Woman Lawyer in America, 1638 to the Present*. Boston: Beacon.

Ott, L., R. F. Larson, and W. Mendenhall. 1983. *Statistics: A Tool for the Social Sciences*, 3rd ed. Boston: Duxbury.

New York Task Force on Women in the Courts. 1986. *Gender Bias Study Report*. New York: Unified Court System Office of Court Administration.

Rhode, D. L. 1988. "Perspectives on professional women." *Stanford Law Review*, 40:1164-1207.

Roach, S. L. 1990. "Men and women lawyers in in-house legal departments: Recruitment and career patterns." *Gender and Society*, 4:207-19.

Rosenbaum, J. E. 1985. "Persistence and change in pay inequalities: Implications for job evaluation and comparable worth." In L. Larwood, A. H. Stromberg, and B. A. Guted (Eds.), *Women and Work: An Annual Review*, Vol. 1. Beverly Hills, CA: Sage.

Rosenberg, J., H. Perlstadt, and W. R. F. Phillips. 1990. "Politics, feminism and women's professional orientations: A case study of women lawyers." *Women and Politics*, 10:19-48.

Schneider, B. E. 1985. "Approaches, assaults, attractions, affairs: Policy implications of the sexualization of the workplace." *Population Research and Policy Review*, 4:93-113.

———. 1991. "Put up and shut up: Workplace sexual assaults." *Gender and Society*, 5:533-48.

Supreme Judicial Court of the Commonwealth of Massachusetts. 1989. *Gender Bias Study of the Supreme Judicial Court*. Boston.

Taber, J., M. T. Grant, M. T. Husser, R. B. Norman, J. R. Sutton, C. C. Wong, L. E. Parker, and C. Picard. 1988. "Gender, legal education, and the legal profession: An empirical study of Stanford law students and graduates." *Stanford Law Review*, 40:1209-97.

Tangri, S., M. R. Burt, and L. B. Johnson. 1982. "Sexual harassment at work: Three explanatory models." *Social Issues*, 38:33-54.

U.S. Merit System and Protection Board. 1988. *Sexual Harassment in the Federal Government: An Update*. Washington, D.C.

Yoder, J. D. 1991. "Rethinking tokenism: Looking beyond numbers." *Gender and Society*, 5:178-92.

Reprinted from: Janet Rosenberg, Harry Perlstadt, and William R. F. Phillips, "Now that we are here: Discrimination, Disparagement and Harassment at Work and the Experience of Women Lawyers," in *Gender and Society* 7(3), pp. 415-433. Copyright © 1993 by Sage Publications. Reprinted by permission.

Food for Thought and Application Questions

1. Find the listings for attorneys in your local yellow pages. If you live in a large metropolitan area with extensive listings, examine only the display ads for attorneys and law firms. If there are relatively few attorneys and firms listed, examine both the display ads and the regular listings. Answer the following questions: (a) For those attorneys or firms who list first names, what is the ratio of males to females? (Do not count gender neutral first names in your analysis.) (b) Given these numbers, would you say that women have token status in these firms? If so, how will this status be likely to affect their work experiences? (c) In the display ads that contain the names or photographs of women attorneys and list types of law (e.g., criminal, family, bankruptcy) practiced, does it appear that women are more likely to practice certain types of law? If so, which ones? (d) If patterns of gender segregation by field of law are evident, how would you explain them?

2. In the previous selection, Higginbotham shows that black women professionals are more likely to be employed in the public sector, and she discusses disadvantages associated with public sector employment. In this selection, Rosenberg et al. report disadvantages associated with private sector employment for women attorneys. Considering the information presented in both these selections, list the advantages and disadvantages for women of both public and private sector employment. Weigh the importance to you personally of each item in your list. Where would you prefer to work? Explain your choice. ✦

20

Men's Accommodations to Women Entering a Nontraditional Occupation: A Case of Rapid Transit Operatives

Marian Swerdlow

The effectiveness of women's entry into nontraditional fields depends, first, on whether employers will hire women. Once that is resolved, the second set of barriers, the problems that discourage retention of women in nontraditional jobs, still remain. An important problem of this type has been the responses of male co-workers, including their harassment of women entering blue-collar work (Baker 1978; Enarson 1984; Gruber and Bjorn 1982; Meyer and Lee 1978; O'Farrell 1982; O'Farrell and Harlan 1982). Male workers have refused to teach crucial skills or other knowledge necessary to job success to women (Deaux 1984; Enarson 1984; Jurick 1985; Kanter 1977; O'Farrell and Harlan 1982),

and have sexually harassed them (Enarson 1984; Gruber and Bjorn 1982; Meyer and Lee 1978; Silverman 1976; Walshok 1981). These forms of harassment may have a chilling effect on women workers' job satisfaction and thus upon retention and even possibly upon their recruitment (Gruber and Bjorn 1982; O'Farrell and Harlan 1982). O'Farrell and Harlan (1982) speculated that the reason men wish to exclude women is to safeguard insecure jobs. Based on this view, they further suggest that it is possible that "in an industry where every worker's job was secure . . . resentment and hostility between men and women" might be absent (p. 263).

Although the occupations formerly closed to women are generally better paying than the service and clerical jobs held by the overwhelming majority of women workers, they are not homogeneous. They include such prestigious occupations as law, medicine, and high-level management, all of which pay, in general, well above the average male income in skilled trades and semiskilled occupations. Although not as well paying, prestigious, or autonomous as the first two, semiskilled blue-collar jobs usually pay better than do most jobs held by mostly women at a similar skill level. These far more numerous jobs therefore represent the greatest potential opportunity for women in the United States.

The literature that has examined women in nontraditional semiskilled occupations has focused upon harassment and hostility from male co-workers (Gruber and Bjorn 1982), difficulties in "fitting in," (Enarson 1984), and blockages to promotion (Deaux 1984). The usual conclusion is that blue-collar men are especially hostile and actively resistant to "new women," and that their resentment constitutes an important problem, if not the most important problem, in female retention in nontraditional blue-collar jobs (Baker 1978; Gruber and Bjorn 1982; Meyer and Lee 1978; O'Farrell 1982; O'Farrell and Harlan 1982).

This researcher, in a four-year, participant-observer study of a blue-collar workplace, found that men as well as women developed accommodative practices when "new women" arrived. Although the men's job security was not threatened, their deeply held belief in male superiority was challenged by the increasing evidence that women could perform their jobs competently. They responded not by attempting to oust women through harassment, but by adapting collective interpretations of experience and practices that allowed them to preserve their ideology of male supremacy while accepting the entrance of women. At the same time, individual women could be accepted as equals by their work partners and even, by proving themselves over time, win the respect of the body of men on the job and become to some degree exempt from their collective accommodative practices.

Method

For four years, beginning in August 1982, I worked as a conductor for a major rapid transit system. I am a white woman, and at the time I took the job, I was in my early thirties. During this time, I maintained extensive field notes and collected such pertinent materials as leaflets, bulletins, and publications. In addition to observing the workplace, I was involved with the union as a shop steward. I also became friends with many subway workers and socialized with them and their families. These encounters were recorded in my field notes.

The system I worked in employs approximately 6,000 semiskilled operatives. About half are conductors, whose main job is to operate the doors of the trains. The other half are train operators, who drive the trains. (Before 1983, the latter were known as motormen, and this title remains common usage among the workers themselves.) Until 1976, only men were accepted as applicants for either title. Within three years, women were working in both titles. By 1986, they constituted about 4 percent of the workers in both titles combined.

Over three-quarters of the women in these titles were black. Most of the rest were white, with a few Hispanic women. Most women on the job were not married, and many were single parents. Subway workers' pay is topped only by pay in the traditional professions, management, skilled trades, and uniformed services—occupations almost entirely closed to women, especially women from outside the upper class and without special education and training. In 1985, a conductor's gross pay was over $25,000 before overtime. Opportunities for promotion and medical and other benefits also made subway work much more attractive than traditional pink-collar jobs.

Hiring for conductors was through an open civil service examination, which is almost entirely a reading test. The examination is widely and effectively advertised. It was taken by 16,000 people in 1981 and by 44,000 in 1985. Although it is quite easy to pass, the large number of people taking it make it competitive.

Application for train operator is open only to those already employed in the system, although not necessarily as operatives. Hiring for this position is based on a promotional exam that tests knowledge of train operation, usually offered once a year. Promotion is also dependent on the employee's record. These procedures have made it fairly easy for women to obtain either job. Since a no-layoffs policy has been in effect for over 30 years, subway jobs are extremely secure. Therefore, the research setting offered an opportunity to explore O'Farrell and Harlan's speculation that hostility and resentment between men and women may be absent in cases in which male workers have no reason to fear for their jobs.

Findings

Direct Resistance and Hostility

Women entering the titles of train operator and conductor certainly did experience resistance and hostility from some male co-workers and supervisors. The most direct form of hostility was conduct that, intentionally or not, undermined feelings of competence.

A conductor's first five weeks are mainly spent in classes at training school. The classes are taught by supervisors in the title, motor instructor. One in particular singled out women:

> Lucia R. has a lot of trouble with the instructor's attitude . . . which comes across in 100 anecdotes and illustrations . . . that women are dithery, featherbrained, a distraction. He constantly gives examples of conductors not paying attention to the job by saying, "And if the conductor's talking to some chick or something." (field notes)

Especially when we were new, male co-workers told us horror stories about the riders and especially what riders, would do to us as women:

> Tony C. (a union representative) said he doesn't think women should be conductors or motormen, "because it's just a matter of time before one of those animals out there takes advantage." (field notes)

The least aggressive form belittling of competence took was an insulting officiousness that manifested itself in the form of explaining to us things we knew well and did regularly:

> We went out of service and Train Operator F. felt he had to explain to me how to discharge a train. I took it patiently. I think he doesn't like women on the job. I can't win and there's no sense taking it personally. (field notes)

Sometimes something real or imagined in our style of work was denigrated as feminine:

> My motorman was saying ". . . she's a fantastic conductor." Motorman L. said, "Yeh, I know, I had her Saturday." My motorman went on, "She's got the greatest timing . . . " "Well, of course," broke in Motorman B., "women have it, that's how they get pregnant." (field notes)

Another example:

> Of course, the ridership is performing their usual ritual of holding the doors. My motorman gets on the public address system: "Don't wait, conductor, the next train is right behind us." "I am not waiting, motorman, the riders are holding the doors." "Don't wait for them, just close the doors." "I have closed the doors, the riders are holding them open." Then when we got to Utica, this genius says to me, "It's just that a lot of the lady conductors like to wait for people coming up the stairs." When I told this to Conductor Anne S., she commented, "A lot of the [male conductors] like to wait for a lot of the ladies." (field notes)

Sometimes the criticism did not appear to be related to gender, but was undeserved, exaggerated, done on pretext, or was abusive. The times I worked with a woman train operator, we experienced an unusual amount of harassment:

> Yesterday, Assistant Train Dispatcher F. said to me, "You were on the wrong train yesterday. You and your motorman were so busy talking. . . ." At first I was bewildered. Then I began to ask some questions and it dawned on me that if we were on the wrong train, it was his fault, and as I began to imply that, he quickly got out of the conversation. (field notes)

But a week later, the same supervisor brought up the same spurious criticism.

Women were singled out for minor infractions that would have been ignored if committed by men. If we did not give the men on the job the exact behavior they wanted, but stood up for ourselves or acted to safeguard our own interests, a small minority might quickly turn threatening or abusive. Once, when I was working with a woman, we had train troubles and were forced to discharge passengers and to take the train to the yard for repairs:

Then at Mott, we saw near the leaving end a big guy with the standard motorman's gear and G. decided to stop for him. . . . He asked us were we going to the 180 St. Yard? "No." "Well, all your side signs say 'Dyre.' " Well, G. and I laughed, because wasn't that just the frosting on the cake? But he started busting G.'s chops, "You're responsible for the signs in this car, you know." She got defensive, but he wouldn't let up. . . . So finally I broke in, "You know we did you a favor letting you on now."

I left the car and returned after we passed the yards:

G. said, "After you left, he said, 'Who is that white bitch?' I told him I agreed with you and he ended up cursing me, calling me a bitch and getting off at Simpson Street . . .—he had an attitude—that's what I said to him, 'You've got an attitude.'" (field notes)

In this case, we were not sufficiently deferential nor did we take the criticisms of our operation seriously, so he turned abusive.

Occasionally, male hostility threatened our ability to do our jobs. A male train operator once refused to work with me. The dispatcher obligingly "jumped him ahead" so he could work with a male conductor. Women train operators sometimes felt they were harassed when they radioed reports that their trains were having mechanical problems. One woman related to me:

"I kept calling in. Finally, he said, 'All right, we've got your slow-accelerating train, now clear the air.' He don't say nothing, then he gets all nasty. The way that man talks to me! Every time! It makes me not want to call command, you know. . . . So nasty! He has an attitude—it's sexism." (field notes)

Sometimes supervisors expected extra "secretarial" chores from women. One conductor complained of being singled out to do personal errands for a supervisor: "With all these guys in the crewroom, why does he send me to get coffee?" These acts of subtle sabotage, although not unique, were nevertheless not common enough to dominate women's experience of the job.

Sexualization of the Workplace

Sexual harassment is by no means peculiar to nontraditional occupations, but it has been argued that men in nontraditional occupations use it as a weapon to drive women out of their fields (Gruber and Bjorn 1982; MacKinnon 1979; Silverman 1976; Waishok 1981). Sexual harassment usually has been defined by its impact on the victim (Gruber and Bjorn 1982; Nivea and Gutek 1981), that is, discomfort, humiliation (Working Women United Institute 1978, quoted in Gruber and Bjorn 1982) or negative work performance (EEOC, quoted in Nivea and Gutek 1981). This common way of defining sexual harassment raises the problems of inferring the intent of the harasser. A woman may feel discomfort and humiliation, and it is certainly legitimate to place sanctions upon the behavior that causes such anguish, but such an effect may not have been the goal of the behavior. It may be more useful analytically to examine most of the behaviors generally categorized as sexual harassment, as examples of what Enarson (1984) has called "the sexualization of the workplace." Enarson says:

The term "sexual harassment" seems to mean too much and too little. When it refers to dirty jokes or pin-ups, for instance, it is better seen as part of the sexualization of the workplace and work relations. On the other hand, it does not fully convey the reality of sexual violence against women workers. . . . Together, these different problems constitute a continuum of abuse, founded on women's fundamental economic and sexual vulnerability and reflecting a cultural tradition which sexualizes, objectifies and diminishes women. (p. 109)

As one of the three or four female shop stewards in the subways, I was in good position to hear women's complaints of sexual harassment. However, I heard only one: A woman conductor reported that a co-worker undressed in front of her (there were no separate locker rooms for women and men) in "a hostile and provocative way." So far as I could tell, there was no physical aggression against women by co-workers: no attacks, assaults, or molestations. This in itself is an important datum. However, the near absence of hostile physical aggression against women was in contrast to the overwhelming sexualization of the workplace. The crewroom itself was rife with sexual symbolism exemplifying the objectification of women and of sex itself. This atmosphere most certainly predated the arrival of women co-workers, and possibly was reduced by it. The use of profanity was constant, with "fucking" being the ubiquitous modifier, although it is possible that for most present, the word as expletive had lost any connection with sexual activity. Nevertheless, at least one woman found this usage so offensive that she rarely entered the crewroom. Sexual narratives were sometimes related in the presence of women, which was at least occasionally a source of discomfort for them. A few men had erotic postcards or centerfolds taped to their lockers and occasionally pinups appeared on walls, or "adult" magazines on tables, only to quickly vanish.

The ubiquitous television in the crewroom, occasionally tuned to adult movies on cable channels, also sexualized the workplace. One of my worst experiences with my co-workers came one evening, when, worn out and facing hours of additional involuntary overtime on hot trains, I was on my only twenty-minute break in what promised to be an eleven-hour night:

> About six guys I didn't know were in the crewroom, watching a rape scene in a *Death Wish* movie. I was so beside

myself that I just walked over and changed the channel. One changed it back and someone said, "That's the best part we're missing . . . ." I went towards the television again, and someone, it may have been the same guy, physically pushed me away from the television. I left my food, I couldn't keep eating. I started crying and walked out of the crewroom. One of the guys followed me, "I know how you must feel, but you shouldn't have just changed the channel." (field notes)

Sexualization of Work Relationships

Shortly after I got the job, the following experience gave me some insight into what our arrival in the crewrooms meant:

> Conductor Hannah S. told me that Monday when she was at Lenox, the train dispatcher called the crewroom: "Someone told me you've got a woman in there." (field notes)

This suggested to me what "a woman in the crewroom" had meant up to the time we arrived there as employees: something utterly forbidden, but more than that, something sexual. Thus before we arrived, a woman's presence in the workplace had already been defined as having, above all, a sexual connotation.

A new woman was immediately viewed sexually. The first information men sought about a new woman was her marital status, usually under the flimsy cover, "What does your husband think of you taking the job?" Our looks were the talk of the crewrooms. We were propositioned so endlessly that I finally joked about giving a civil service test for the position, with a $15 application fee, a multiple-choice exam to test knowledge of the job, and a physical.

Generally, men took gentle and light demurrals gracefully, but occasionally proved difficult to discourage, and some turned verbally abusive when rejected. The men were not interested in making our lives miserable or in pushing us out of the workplace with their endless propositions.

Their propositions and even persistence after rebuff were by no means proof of any conscious intent to degrade women. They may indeed have been aimed at achieving what was in their view a mutually acceptable relationship. Men occasionally showed signs of having tender feelings for the women who rejected them, and genuinely regarding the woman as special:

> Anne S. read me a sad letter of farewell from P. He would always love her . . . —when she was born, "the angels were singing." (field notes)

On the other hand, the unequal balance of power between men and women often meant women got "the worst of the bargain." For instance, in two cases that I knew of, women had relationships lasting over a year with men on the job, which ended in both cases when the woman found out that her lover was married.

It would not be accurate to conclude, however, that since women often got the worst of such relationships, they did not either welcome them or even at times seek them out. Men's advances were not always unwelcome, and many relationships developed on the job. Nor were men invariably the pursuers and women the pursued. Train Operator Mary D. was proud of her aggressiveness and known to initiate relationships, although she angrily denied that she was "easy," that is, willing to "put out" for any that asked. My own experience with a co-worker demonstrated that men were not always comfortable with such role reversals:

> I asked if he would like to get together. He assented in such a matter-of-fact fashion . . . then he asked, "You mean just to talk about the union, right?" "I'd like to go out with you, but if you don't want to, or aren't in a position to, I'd still like to see you to talk. . . ." "I'm living with someone . . . —you have a very direct approach," he said, as if slightly unsettled. "I guess it's the job," I was apologetic, "so many guys are direct with me." (field notes)

Men's Modes of Accommodation

Enarson (1984) has emphasized that when "new women" enter a situation dominated by men, it is the women themselves who must invent and adopt patterns of accommodation. My participant observation in the subways led me to conclude that men, too, found it necessary to find new modes of behavior to allow the acceptance of women as co-workers and still maintain a belief in male superiority. Sexualizing work relationships was one of a number of modes of accommodation on the part of men. That is, the very behaviors that most researchers have depicted as presenting difficulties for women workers in male-dominated jobs can be viewed as one of men's modes of accommodating those same women.

Men have a status stake in the sexualization of work relationships when the division of labor itself renders women equal to men. By forcing sexual identities into high relief, men submerge the equality inherent in the work and superimpose traditional dominant and subordinate definitions of the sexes. Men have a stake in seeing women as sexual beings because in no arena is male domination less ambiguous for working-class men than sexuality. One man told me:

> "Until I got this job, I never realized how much men hate women. The way they talk in the crewroom—women to them are just sex. . . . They may see their girlfriends, wives or family as exceptions. But, in general, women are just to fuck. . . . I always wondered why they say that someone 'got fucked' when they got ripped off. Because the man does the fucking, the woman gets fucked. To get fucked is to be like the woman, to get ripped off." (field notes)

This sexualization and objectification of women was a way of accepting us into the workplace, although, crucially, not as equals. For many men, it was the chief means of accommodating to women's presence in the workplace, especially when they were not crewing trains with us. Those who worked directly and continually with a woman were able to develop another mode of relating, of friendship or at least of nonsexual peers. But until familiarity reduced their discomfort, men accommodated women through sexual objectification and attempts at asserting sexual domination.

Another way of minimizing the threat produced by women's presence was the wide and constant discussion of women's errors, embroidered upon and repeated with relish. Mary D. was one of the first women conductors, and then one of the first women train operators. She was a train buff, tiny, blonde, and foul-mouthed. All of these made her especially visible even among the visible minority of token women. Like many male train operators, Mary D. committed the serious offense of backing up a train. The tower operator had lined up the tracks in such a way as to send the train en route to the wrong terminal. Mary failed to examine sufficiently the way the tracks were "lined up"—in subway slang, she "didn't read her iron"—and moved the train across the switch on to the wrong track. Like many of the males, she was found out and penalized by being demoted back to conductor. Predictably, Mary D.'s mistake was far more widely discussed, and discussed for far longer, than were identical mistakes made by men. Discussion of the men's errors was generally limited to the terminal in which the man worked, and rarely lasted longer than a few days after the event. Mary D.'s mistake was discussed in many terminals and for literally years afterwards, even after she was reinstated to train operator. Mary D.'s mistake was seen as a woman's mistake, and she was seen, almost literally, as a symbol for all women on the job:

> The Woodlawn motorman, talking to his conductor, started laughing at me, "Keep it open! Open it up now! You know better than that now. You've been up front!" Huh? Well, I opened up. "You should know," he went on,

> "that after the power is off Command has to tell you to resume." I just shrugged. He was really laughing at me, "So when are you coming back to motors?" "Back? I've never been to motors!" I snapped. "Oh, I'm sorry. I thought you were Mary." (field notes)

While the support and encouragement discussed earlier was directly helpful to women's integration, women were also commonly given exorbitant praise for routine competence, dubbed "the talking platypus phenomenon" (Abramson et al. 1977, quoted in Nivea and Gutek 1981). An example was one of my first motormen:

> His first reaction on shaking my hand in the 4 a.m. twilight was, "Can you open the doors with such small hands?"

> By the end of the day, Motorman G. had nothing but praise for me. (field notes)

Initially, he voiced doubts I could do the job at all. When I proved competent, the praise was lavish.

In my case, my work was often cited approvingly, but what seems to have stood out to my male co-workers was that I was "not afraid":

> Conductor D. said . . . "She's not afraid of the job. You wouldn't think it—she looks kind of timid and quiet. But she's not afraid of the job." (field notes)

> My motorman said, "What I like about you is that you kept cool through the whole thing. You didn't get excited." (field notes)

Paradoxically, this behavior was also helpful in integrating women. "The talking platypus phenomenon" was a way in which men could accommodate the arrival of women and still preserve their self-esteem. They kept their expectations that women could not do the job as well as men, and in particular, could not handle the stress and hazards of the job. Since stories of women's mistakes and shortcomings were exaggerated in crewroom scuttlebutt, their view of women was continually reinforced. The man's own female conductor or train operator then became the glowing exception. This attitude might be epitomized in words often heard by "tokens" of all kinds: "You are different from the rest of 'them.'" At the same time, individual women did receive recognition and validation of their competence.

Another subtle way in which men accommodated the arrival of women was through a myth of "preference." The essence of this myth, accepted almost universally by subway men, was that women workers received favored treatment over men, and that even the job itself had been made easier so that women could do it. For example, it was widely believed that the way in which a motorman fastened down the trip arms on some signals had been made easier because women weren't strong enough to do it the old way. It was also believed that any woman conductor who wished to do so could get one of the "cushy" clerical jobs for conductors at the transit headquarters. One conductor who was most fond of complaining that "all the women go down to Jay Street," was able to land one of these jobs himself, where I discovered him, much to his discomfort! Rumors and stories circulated that women could get the hours and jobs they wanted, that women were getting higher pay than men were, and that women had trips "dropped" more often than men had.

In sum, men accommodated to the idea that women were doing their jobs successfully by rationalizing that women were not actually doing the same work men did or had done in the past, and that women got certain "breaks" that they as men did not enjoy. The logic was that if women did not get these breaks, if the job had not been made easier, women would not be able to do the job. Therefore, although women were doing the job, they were, appearances to the contrary, not really as competent as the men on the job, not really equal.

Support and Positive Response

Male co-workers did not always undermine women; they also supported us and encouraged us. They did not always sexualize our interactions with them; they also treated us as peers. Most important, women in the subways were taught the ropes by their male co-workers. From the time I arrived on the job, male co-workers encouraged me:

> Conductors usually say things like, "You'll like it," "You'll do alright," or "You'll get used to it." (field notes)

The last part of training, "break-in," is made up of a day on each of the subway lines with a different operating conductor. Each of my "break-in" conductors was conscientious, patient, and supportive. On many other occasions, I found my co-workers eager to answer my questions and to share their special "tricks of the trade." Beyond a willingness to teach us the ropes, male co-workers often tried to reassure us and assuage our occasional discouragement. When I was forced to pick evening hours on a line with a very rough reputation (it was called "The Beast"), my co-workers reassured me over and over:

> "You'll be okay, just don't look for trouble." "It's not really that bad, everyone talks about it, but. . . ." "I did it for years. It wasn't anything." (field notes)

If I expressed doubts about my own competence, I was generally given support:

> I worked with Motorman D., and after our first trip was over, he said, "You do good work." I thanked him and said, "But I still don't do very well in emergencies." "That will come in time," he said. (field notes)

To some extent, different behaviors came from the same individuals, depending upon the situation. Significantly, a man was far less likely to relate sexually to a woman who was his regular conductor or train operator. If he worked with her only for the day or the week, and especially if he merely encountered her in the terminal or crewroom, a sexual overture was more likely. Thus, in my first few months on the job, I was approached sexually by far more conductors than train operators. Two reasons suggest themselves. As a conductor myself, I was perceived as a more direct threat by male conductors than train operators, since the latter could still reassure themselves that I could not perform their jobs. Second, I was not going to "go down the road" with another conductor, so I was not a potential work partner who had to be treated somewhat carefully.

A man and a woman who repeatedly crewed a train together usually developed a relationship of mutual respect. Since train operators have somewhat more control of the work, and slightly higher status and pay, it is striking than men conductors generally did not resent working with women train operators, and usually praised their operation.

> Conductor D. said, "They say G. is a hot-rodder, but I've worked with her and she's good. She's fast, but she gives you a smooth stop every time." (field notes)

Train Operator H., who asked to be "jumped ahead" to avoid working with me, eventually did work with me several times, although we never spoke much. Another train operator kept a Polaroid snapshot of me taped inside his locker, until we began to work together regularly as a crew. We did not like each other's operation, and sometimes had words. This was a different "twist" to the same dynamic. Once Train Operator J. had to work with me, he could no longer elevate me as an idealized object. I had become just a difficult conductor.

However, I usually developed good relations with the men with whom I regularly worked. My first encounter with Train Operator 0. was while he was laughing at my attempts to get all the men out of the terminal toilet facility so I could use it (there were no separate facilities for

women, nor any doors on the toilet cubicles). Yet when we began to work together regularly, we soon became friendly and able to talk together about the job, our families, and union politics.

The development of nonsexual, egalitarian relationships among work partners was typical. Yet men persisted in regarding women workers, as a group, as inferior workers and sexual objects. It was also possible for an individual woman, after working with a large number of men and proving herself over time, to be accepted by the men on her shift, in her terminal, and perhaps even beyond that. In part because I had been on the job for a relatively long time, and because I was involved in the politics of the union, I became accepted in this fashion. When I had been on the job for almost three years, I ran for delegate to the convention of the international union on an opposition slate.

The convention was held in Las Vegas:

> Conductor H. said to me, as if speaking for the whole PM crowd, "So you're running to go to California." I said, "Only as far as Nevada." He said, "The terminal is going to vote for you. The terminal is going to send you to California." (field notes)

After getting to know us, and especially after working with us, men could begin to see us as co-workers, train operators, and conductors, not as women first. They could talk with us about the job, about politics, about their families. Eventually, I found most male co-workers were willing to support me when I had run-ins with hostile individual men. By and large, they seemed to accept and enforce a norm against unwanted touching, especially when the culprit was a "junior" man: they publicly rebuffed a new conductor who put his arm around me. They were to some degree willing to support me on union issues and support me in my role as shop steward.

Discussion

These findings tend to support O'Farrell and Harlan's insight that where jobs are secure, men are less threatened by the entrance of women workers. In this case, there was no evidence that the men attempted to oust the women from the job. Willingness to "teach the ropes," encouragement, and support were by far the most common attitudes of subway workers toward "new women." However, women's arrival created strains and conflict even in the absence of job insecurity. These problems arose from men's status stake in an ideology of male supremacy. The myth of supremacy is based in important part upon the view that the work that men do is beyond the inferior capacities of women. Women's arrival, even when it does not threaten jobs, creates strains by threatening this assumption. But these kinds of strains are not dealt with by attempts to oust women from the job. Instead, the men adopted practices and interpretations of experience that reconciled the fact that women were successfully performing their jobs with a continuing belief in their own superiority. These practices and interpretations took the form of the sexualization of work relationships, the exaggeration of women's errors, depicting women's routine competence as exceptional, and perpetuating a myth of "preference." These enabled men to be comfortable with women co-workers and even, once the women had established themselves, to treat them individually as coequals.

Job security may indeed be a key variable in how blue-collar men deal with "new women" in nontraditional occupations. Job security may not eliminate hostility and resentment, but if women threaten not men's jobs but only their male supremacist beliefs, men may respond by accommodating rather than by attempting to oust women from their jobs. Such accommodations on the part of men, however insulting they may be to women, do leave space for women to learn and retain such jobs.

References

Baker, S. H. 1978. "Women in blue-collar and service occupations." In A. H. Stromberg and S. Harkness (eds.), *Women Working*. Palo Alto, CA: Mayfield:339-376.

Deaux, K. 1984. "Blue-collar barriers." *American Behavioral Scientist*, 27:287-300.

Enarson, E. 1984. *Woodsworking Women: Sexual Integration in the U.S. Forest Service*. Birmingham: University of Alabama.

Gruber, J. E., and L. Bjorn. 1982. "Blue-collar blues: The sexual harassment of women autoworkers." *Work and Occupations*, 9:271-98.

Jurick, N. 1985. "An officer and a lady: Organizational barriers to women working as correctional officers in men's prisons." *Social Problems*, 32:375-88.

Kanter, R. M. 1977. *Men and Women of the Corporation*. New York: Basic Books.

MacKinnon, C. 1979. *Sexual Harassment of Working Women*. New Haven, CT: Yale University Press.

Meyer, H. and M. D. Lee. 1978. *Women in Traditionally Male Jobs: The Experience of 10 Public Utility Companies*. R and D Monograph Number 65, U.S. Department of Labor, Employment and Training Administration. Washington, DC: U.S. Government Printing Office.

Nivea, V. F., and B. Gutek. 1981. *Women and Work: A Psychological Perspective*. New York: Praeger.

O'Farrell, B. 1982. "Women and non-traditional blue collar jobs in the 1980s: An overview." In P. A. Wallace (ed.), *Women in the Workplace*. Boston: Auburn House:135-165.

O'Farrell, B. and S. L. Harlan. 1982. "Craftsworkers and clerks: The effect of male co-worker hostility and women's satisfaction with non-traditional jobs." *Social Problems* 29:253-65.

Silverman, D. 1976. "Sexual harassment: Working women's dilemma." *Quest*, 3:15-24.

Walshok, M. L. 1981. *Blue Collar Women: Pioneers on the Male Frontier.* Garden City, NY: Doubleday.

Reprinted from: Marian Swerdlow, "Men's Accommodations to Women Entering a Nontraditional Occupation," in *Gender and Society,* 3(3), pp. 373-387. Copyright © 1989 by Sage Publications. Reprinted by permission.

Food for Thought and Application Questions

1. Swerdlow argues that women's employment in male-dominated occupations threatens assumptions about male supremacy. She suggests that men in these jobs sexualize work relationships in order to "submerge the inequality" inherent in the work arrangements. Compare this phenomenon among rapid transit operators to the harassing behaviors of male attorneys described in the previous selection. Are there similarities? Differences? Explain.

2. Swerdlow's work suggests that men in heavily male-dominated occupations are more accepting of women co-workers when they can rationalize that the women are not as competent as the men. What does this imply for how women should perform their work in order to win the acceptance of their male co-workers? If women choose to minimize conflicts with male co-workers by "living up to their expectations," how will employers evaluate women's job performance? Could this strategy for minimizing conflicts serve to close doors for other women who wish to enter the occupation? ✦

21

'We've Got One of Those': The Peripheral Status of Women in Male-Dominated Industries

Yvonne Corcoran-Nantes and Ken Roberts

Introduction

Women in the Labour Market in the 1990s

W ill there be a trend towards gender equality in employment in Britain during the 1990s? There is no dispute, firstly, that for many decades women have been a growing proportion of all employees, but secondly that, until the 1980s at any rate, sex segregation did not decline (Hakim 1979; Martin and Roberts 1984). Achieving the legal rights to equal pay for equal work and equal opportunities in hiring and promotion in the 1970s did not lead immediately to a more equal gender balance in all or even most occupations.

There have been repeated campaigns for and forecasts of greater gender equality. More females have been gaining the qualifications to embark on careers formerly dominated by men. More women have been stepping onto the lower rungs

of such careers and acquiring post-entry professional credentials (Crompton and Sanderson 1990; Crompton et al. 1990). Up to the 1980s, most of the growth in female employment was in part-time jobs (Jonung and Persson 1993) whereas since the mid-1980s, in Britain, there has been a marked rise in the number of full-time female employees (Hakim 1993). Genuine equality, or at least a clear movement in this direction, has been envisaged as a sequel to these recent developments. Moreover, it has been argued that during the 1990s skill shortages will act as a catalyst. According to this argument, the economy's need for a better-qualified and more highly skilled workforce should lead to employers making greater use of female talent. Our evidence, however, from case studies of skill formation in five large private sector companies, casts doubts on whether any such trend is either in process or imminent.

The Research

Of the five case study firms, one was an oil company (the oil refineries), another was a vehicle manufacturer (Auto Co), the third manufactured telecommunications products (Electronic), the fourth made motor car components (Motor Parts), while the fifth was a formerly nationalized service industry (Service Co). In each of these companies, except Motor Parts which had only one UK establishment, we studied pairs of northern and southern England sites. Information was obtained during 1991 from the company managements on trends in the numbers employed and the gender composition of different grades, sources of recruits, internal career paths and training provisions. However, the fieldwork was primarily qualitative and comprised interviews with managers and employees within selected units and departments, the aim being to discover how skill formation policies were actually being implemented. In Auto Co we concentrated upon production units and operative grades, on process and craft workers in the oil refineries and at Motor Parts, on research and development engineers in Electronic, and on the technical grades in Service Co. Altogether 269 interviews were conducted, of which 228 were with men (See Table 21.1).

We had originally planned to interview equal numbers of male and female em-

Table 21.1
The Sample

	Males		Females		Males		Females		Total
	<29	≥29	<29	≥29	<29	≥29	<29	≥29	
Oil Refineries									
		North				South			
Management, engineers	4	6	-	-	1	11	5	-	27
Craft, technicians	4	5	-	-	4	6	1	-	20
Production	-	11	1	-	5	5	-	-	22
	8	22	1	-	10	22	6	-	69
Electronic									
		North				South			
Management, engineers	2	4	3	-	7	12	3	3	34
Craft, technicians	4	-	1	-	-	-	-	-	5
Production	-	-	-	-	-	-	-	-	-
	6	4	4	-	7	12	3	3	39
Service Co									
		North				South			
Management, engineers	-	7	-	-	1	9	1	2	20
Craft, technicians	3	12	1	1	7	15	2	3	44
Production	-	-	-	-	-	-	-	-	-
	3	19	1	1	8	24	3	5	64
Auto Co									
		North				South			
Management, engineers	1	9	2	-	1	8	2	-	23
Craft, technicians	1	11	-	-	6	3	-	-	21
Production	5	10	-	-	3	11	2	2	33
	7	30	2	-	10	22	4	2	77
Motor Parts									
		North							
Management, engineers	5	4	-	-					9
Craft, technicians	5	-	-	-					5
Production	-	-	-	6					6
	10	4	-	6					20
All Firms									
		North							
Management, engineers	22	70	16	5					113
Craft, technicians	34	52	5	4					95
Production	13	37	3	8					61
	69	159	24	17					269

ployees; we had presumed that gender parity was a proper aim and that the production of skilled women and skilled men deserved equal attention. However, this was not how things worked out because of the competing claims of another guiding principle in the fieldwork; to study key sections of the sites' workforces. Our presumption here was that to grasp serious skill problems, and to encounter the latest trends in skill formation, we should get into units and work groups that were of particularly vital importance, where the firms were investing most heavily in plant and people, on the "crackers" rather than in dispensable manufacturing units in the oil refineries for example. The sex imbalance in our interviews is probably a better indication of the extent to which the firms were male dominated than the overall proportions of men and women on their payrolls. Women always tended to be best represented in more peripheral occupations. They were typically the secretaries, the ancilliaries, and performing the most routine assembly operations.

We always interviewed some, and typically all the females who were employed in the departments and grades that we studied, and in these interviews we always asked about their experiences as women. Men were questioned about gender only when this was relevant to whatever else was being discussed. So women's presence or absence from various sections of the workforces was always discussed with the senior company managers. Otherwise it depended on whether the issue was raised either because of trends in the particular workplace, or by the male employees spontaneously. Also, needless to say, we learnt a great deal about gender relations in the workplaces simply by being around, and overhearing or becoming participants in informal conversations.

The next section supplies more detail on the positions of women in the organizations that were studied. Women's positions were usually peripheral and on closer inspection most of the apparent excep-

tions turned out to be less exceptional than their surface appearances. This is followed by a section which analyses the company cultures, specifically the cultures of mainstream career occupations in the organizations, by examining the attitudes of male employees. This evidence is used to identify the barriers to women's progress within "equal opportunity" companies. While overt sexism was rare among males in the management and professional grades it was equally rare for these senior staff to have any intention of changing their organizations' career rules for the sake of gender parity. Refusal to countenance such changes was not seen as discriminating against women. Among shop-floor males there was more blatant sexism, always patronizing, and sometimes seeking women's exclusion. The next section presents the experiences of the women who were embarking on careers in management, as professional engineers, and in the skilled manual grades. Experiences in these occupations had made them all aware of the limits to their equal opportunities. The final section summarizes the women's experiences. Their experiences had taught them that to be given genuine equal opportunities they needed to do it "their way." In conclusion, it is argued that even cautious optimism that the trends are towards a more equal future in the workforce is probably over optimistic.

Women's Status in the Organizations

All the firms could report that the proportions of women on their staffs had increased. However, when they were in core occupations the women tended to be doing relatively peripheral jobs and when they had core jobs in core occupations they tended to be in the more junior grades. In so far as women were breaking in, this seemed to be due almost entirely to changes on the supply side of the labour market, meaning that women were changing (see also Crompton et al. 1990). None of the firms was actively seeking more women in response to skill shortages. Indeed none of the firms was experiencing or envisaging skill shortages. All the companies had reduced their workforces during the 1980s. Dispensing with rather than attracting labour had been the more typical problem. Rather than widening their recruitment the companies were becoming more selective and upward progress through internal labour markets was becoming more difficult. These trends in employment were tending to reinforce rather than break down the peripheralization of women.

Women's under-representation in key sections of the firms' workforces was not uniform. For instance, around a third of the chemical engineers at one of the oil refineries were female; one refinery manager claimed to have never seen so many. Also, women were much better represented on the production lines at Auto Co's southern plant than on the firm's northern site. Women's prominence in production at the southern site dated from the 1960s when the plant was expanding, had recruitment problems, sought women and eventually gained the trade unions' acceptance. This instance of women breaking-in was not a product of the 1970s' equal opportunities legislation. At the oil refinery where a third of the chemical engineers were women they were concentrated in the research and development units. The other refinery which had very few females was simply a production base. At neither of the sites with significant numbers of women in key occupations—on the assembly line at the southern car plant and in research and development at one of the oil refineries—was women's presence in these occupations having a generalized impact on the site cultures. Women were no better represented in line management, and those who were trying to break in were finding it no easier, than elsewhere.

However, there were at least token women in virtually all grades and departments. "Yes, we've got one of those," be-

came a familiar reply to our queries. Nevertheless, in the really key workforce sections on all the sites, especially in the craft grades, women were very tiny proportions of all employees. Skill shortages had not forced changes in this situation during the 1980s. Nor did they appear likely to do so in the 1990s. Whether women themselves would force such changes was a different matter. Most of the women that we interviewed were young, aged under 30, in the pre-child rearing life-stage. This was the case among managers, professional engineers, and in the craft and relatively skilled production grades. Sometimes, the only females in the latter groups were apprentices and trainees. The presence of young women in these areas seemed to be a product of women changing and applying in greater numbers than in the past combined with the firms' recent sensitivity to equal opportunities. All the managements felt that they needed to break up male enclaves if they were to appear credible as equal opportunity employers. A crunch question, of course, was whether the young women would remain to increase their gender's representation in the older age groups, particularly in supervisory and senior management positions, thereby providing more role models for the next generation and gradually leading to a more equal gender balance. The evidence from our interviews suggests that such developments were most unlikely.

Company Cultures and Equal Opportunities Policies

Intolerance of Overt Sexism

In very lightly structured interviews what is never or rarely mentioned can be as noteworthy as remarks that are made frequently. Only one woman reported what could be construed as a mild form of sexual harassment which she had been able to handle. Except at Motor Parts none of the women, and only a small number of men, complained of having been blatantly

disadvantaged by their gender in their recruitment to, or training or promotion
within their present companies. Motor
Parts was the only company where there
was any organized resistance by male employees via their workplace trade union organizations to the employment of women
in their occupations. At Motor Parts this
resistance was confined to the manual
grades. The shop floor trade union representatives justified their stance in terms of
the need to protect males' job opportunities in a high unemployment area, and fear
that the entry of women would depress
their terms and conditions of employment. These local stances were not receiving support from the wider trade unions,
and at the time of our research were being
actively challenged by the site management. Elsewhere such rigid, formal gender
segregation of the workforces had disappeared many years previously. Equal opportunities policies had achieved this,
though the effects had usually been little
more than token as far as women's actual
presence in key jobs was concerned. However, none of the women who had entered
the relevant occupations complained of
outright sex discrimination during their
recruitment, or when they had applied for
training or been considered for promotion, though some women made it clear
that their own equal treatment had depended on them standing up for themselves.

All the interviews with women staff
were conducted by a female fieldworker
which should have maximized the chances
of such complaints being expressed. All
the firms were officially equal opportunity
employers. Their managers were aware of
the law's demands and knew that it was
important to comply. Whether the sites always offered equal pay for equal work was
sometimes debatable. At the time of the research one of the companies (not Motor
Parts) was being prosecuted by the Equal
Opportunities Commission. However, all
the sites offered equal pay for the same
work, and monitoring, at least on paper,

was always ensuring that female applicants for jobs at every level had at least
equal and sometimes better chances of
success than men. The same applied in access to training and promotion opportunities. Overt sexism was not tolerated in any
company. At one of Auto Co's plants we
witnessed a male shop floor employee being reprimanded publicly by a middle
manager and threatened with future dis-
missal following a ribald remark to a female worker. Women were not under-represented in the key sections of the workforces that we studied primarily because the
firms were flouting or even tacitly circum-
venting equal opportunity laws. The overwhelming majority of the applicants for all
the relevant jobs were male. Women were
especially poorly represented in the older
age groups, and in supervisory and senior
management positions, because female recruitment had been even lower in the past,
but also because if they wished to take advantage of equal career opportunities
women still needed to pursue what, up to
the time of our enquiry, had typically been
the male career pattern. This was one reason why the workforce sections seemed
likely to remain male dominated for the
foreseeable future, and why the workplace
cultures would continue to be experienced
as harsh or patronizing by female entrants,
which was likely to continue to suppress
female interest and applications. These
sources of the gender imbalances that we
encountered were not under attack in existing equal opportunity policies (see also
Cockburn 1990, 1991).

Male Managers and Engineers: 'It's Equal Opportunity Here'

The most frequent type of remark
about the gender balance at work by males
in the management and professional
grades was that things were changing, and
the implication in these remarks was usually that change was overdue and would
turn out to be a good thing for all concerned. This applied to all the industries.
"It's (engineering's) not oily rags any more,

it's mostly brain work." Several managers commented on how female applications had risen when technical rather than craft apprenticeships had been offered. "The image is changing and women might see it (engineering) as a more attractive career option." "It's quite usual now to see a woman driving a van. We're certainly recruiting more into what used to be a man's world. I can now safely say that everything's open right across the board. If they're the best candidates they get the jobs" (Service Co). "There's probably no difference. It's equal opportunity here. It could work the other way. We're trying to get more females in, positive discrimination if you like" (Electronic). Some of these male respondents appeared to be exaggerating, or maybe they just misperceived the extent to which women were breaking in. For example, they would talk about there being "loads" of women when company records showed that the actual percentage was in single figures. However, even such modest levels of female employment often represented a vast increase, in percentage terms, from the situation that had prevailed in a not too distant past. There had been no tradition of female employment in most of the workforce sections that we studied. All the work environments remained heavily male dominated. The presence of any women was still regarded as "new," and sometimes as sufficient evidence that equal opportunity had arrived at last.

Some male managers and engineers recognized that the changes that had already occurred were either minute, token, or patchy, but the implication in these remarks was usually that even greater efforts were needed to achieve a more equal sex balance. "As far as apprenticeships go we're still all male. We've never had much response from girls" (Auto Co). "We have a scheme for promoting female clerical staff into engineering but no one from here has gone. There have been a few applicants but they weren't up to standard. It's a big problem for a woman particularly if she's married because the course is based in another part of the country" (Service Co). "On the engineering side we really have no women, just a token gesture towards it. Just two of our staff graduates are female and they're both in personnel" (Auto Co). "There's still a lot of bias and prejudice against women. Men have better chances of promotion but I think this is a wider social problem, not specific to this industry. It's better to be a man here. Most of the senior managers are male. One talks their language, cracks the right jokes, has the right attitude to football and that sort of thing" (Electronic).

A large number of remarks were made about how well the women were doing who had been recruited into what were traditionally men's jobs in either professional engineering, management or on the shop floor. Some of these male respondents explained that their firms were adopting proactive stances, even positive discrimination, because this was believed to be in the companies' interest. "We had the first female apprentice here some years ago when I was in training management. She did exceptionally well. In maintenance and installation she was excellent and above-average in everything" (oil refinery). "The females are among our best quality apprentices. Those we get are first class with more commitment than the boys. If anything we're now pro-active in female recruitment" (Electronic). "Not enough women apply but those we have are excellent. My previous boss encouraged me to take on more girls. When you have people of equal ability I think you should take the female" (Service Co).

Only one male respondent from the non-manual grades, an engineer at Electronic, expressed any hostility towards women entering his occupation: "I think they've promoted some women to get the numbers right rather than on ability. I had a bad experience with a female engineer who just didn't know what I was talking about." This type of remark was exceptional from non-manual males. Among the male managers and professional engineers the cultural norm was to approve of female entrants and to favour equal opportunity.

Were they sincere? It is never easy to tell. The males knew about the legislation with which their companies had to comply. However, the interviews were conducted with the usual guarantees of confidentiality, and the answers did not vary depending on whether the interviewer was male or female. Collective discrimination against any categories of workers appeared to be contrary to the men's personal and professional ethics, and the fact that some women were being recruited to all grades was often seen as proof that both sexes had the same opportunities. However, while condemning collective discrimination, the fact that individuals could be victimized for failing to meet universally applied criteria was not considered unfair. These were the regimes to which our male respondents were subject. If higher proportions of people in certain social categories met the universal criteria when these were applied impartially to individuals, this was not seen as evidence that the criteria were wrong or unfairly discriminatory. Employees in academic institutions are well aware that men can speak eloquently and persuasively in favour of equal opportunities while tolerating and even justifying unequal outcomes in the social composition of their workforces.

Gendered Organizations

The managers whom we interviewed, even those who were pro-equal opportunities, rarely saw any reason even to change, let alone lower their companies' standards for the sake of gender parity. Most male managers who argued for pro-activity were in training or personnel. They had influence, but usually not the final say in recruitment, and even less in promotions. Only one of the companies that we studied, the oil company, could be described as making a real drive to increase recruitment and retention of women at all levels including the craft grades, and even in this firm the effects up to the time of our research had been modest. The other firms were doing everything that was necessary to call themselves equal opportunity employers, which basically meant giving women an equal chance under the men's rules. The organizations were not really gender neutral. It was not just the workforces but the organizations themselves that were gendered and, in certain senses, sexualized. Male assumptions underlay normal organizational thinking and structures (Acker 1990).

The males seemed to feel that they were being fair and reasonable in expecting females to be "superwoman" in order to take advantage of their equal opportunities (see also Newell 1993). This was the underlying reason why those women who were getting in, staying in and getting on had typically needed to do more than male peers. Other women were being marginalized. The successful women had needed to struggle and to fight, to be unusual for their sex and, in certain senses, better at their jobs, specifically in terms of commitment, if not technical skill. This was one reason why some male managers had been impressed, while more junior male staff—management trainees and apprentices for example—could feel threatened by high-flying females in predominantly male workplaces.

As explained below, most of the younger women who were interviewed were learning within months how to handle macho workplace cultures and were gaining acceptance as equals among the apprentices, research engineers or whatever their work sections, by demonstrating that they could do an equal job. The ways in which they experienced their work environments were similar to men's experiences in most respects except that the women knew that it would be difficult to take advantage of their nominally equal opportunities. They realized that remaining in the companies for uninterrupted full-time careers would be difficult. The women in management and professional jobs articulated these concerns. Strangely, not a single young woman in the manual grades raised this problem. Maybe it seemed just too obvious to be worth mentioning. However, the older women in the manual grades, the survivors, were often proud of having coped with their difficulties.

Male Shop Floor Culture

'Everyone's Treated Equally.'

Males in skilled manual jobs were far more likely than their managers to express reservations about women entering their occupations. However, they invariably stressed that their objections were not based on straightforward sex prejudice. Rather, they argued that women were less suitable even when they received equal treatment. Several points were made repeatedly. One was that females who had joined the workforces had in fact received at least equal treatment from the men. The latter appreciated that a girl apprentice might feel awkward at first, being the only member of her sex in a group, but they believed that very quickly she could become just part of the crew. "When the girls start off it's hard for them but after a couple of months they settle down" (oil refinery). "Girls probably feel awkward when they start, being the only one in the class, but I think it's all more equal now. A few years ago a man would always get the job. I think they're trying to get away from that" (Electronic). "There're a lot more women than there used to be and I don't think it makes any difference. Some of them swear more than the men. It doesn't bother me, and everyone's trained equally" (Auto Co). The men often commented on how the first women to be employed had faced some hostility and difficulties, but invariably stressed the extent to which things had subsequently changed. "It went down like a lead weight to start with. They weren't readily accepted but that's no longer the case. When I started in 1968 there were attempts to prevent the women coming in.

But good luck to them I say. We're all on equal pay" (Auto Co).

Waste of Training and Skill

A second point, however, was that women would not remain in the crew; they would marry, have children and leave, so their training would be wasted and a man who could have derived and given greater benefit would have missed the opportunity. "The young women on the line are just saving up to get married, buy a new car and that" (Auto Co). Such a remark probably applied equally to, but was never made in respect of young men. "I'm a little bit against it. I don't mind women going into engineering and going to university and doing well. I know this sounds sexist but the job's wasted because in 10 years they're going to have families and leave" (oil refinery). "There's just been a case in this department. They didn't really want to take her because the job can mean travelling abroad. If they train her up ready and she gets pregnant the company will lose. The executive told her straight, but she got on to the union and she got the job in the end" (Electronic). "They have to do shifts and that doesn't appeal to a lot of women. They can't fit it in with family life" (Auto Co).

No one argued that married women or mothers should not be in any paid employment. The men were not arguing that following marriage or motherhood a woman ought to quit the workforce. Rather, it was simply obvious to most of them that such a woman would neither wish nor be able to do a job like theirs. To the men it was just self-evident that it would be difficult, very likely impossible, for a mother to cope with the hours, shifts and pressure of work. Only one shop floor male, a trade union convenor at one of the car plants, mentioned the possibility of modifying the hours of work. The rest took it for granted that jobs such as their own needed full-time commitment. That was simply the way things were. And there was a genuine sense of waste that they should train someone only to see the individual quit before maturing into a fully skilled employee. Older men who had personally trained female apprentices sometimes became keen that they should persist and repay all the time, effort and attention that they had been given. "One of our girl apprentices is due to get married. I've told her that if she gets pregnant before she finishes her apprenticeship I'll be really annoyed. I truly want her to finish. We'll be pulling out all the stops for her to stay on as a fitter" (oil refinery, craft grades).

Physical Requirements

A third point that was raised time and again was that the work required physical strength which women either could not, or should not be expected to display. Maybe technological change had lightened the work but, it was argued, there were still aspects that required power and muscle. According to some of the men, this was a reason why females simply could not be treated just like any other employees but had to be relieved of some normal duties. "I don't agree with them lifting heavy things but otherwise preferential treatment is out. There are certain jobs that I don't think are for women. I'm the old gentleman type. When you've got a girl on the section you try to do a bit more for her" (oil refinery), "I think that on the whole she's treated the same, but there's some aggro from guys who've been here 30 years and who say that she can't turn a valve. There's some big valves out there, some heavy work to be done" (oil refinery). "The girls are treated differently. It's the lad who lifts and carries. That's just natural" (Auto Co). "When there's something heavy it's always the lad who does it" (oil refinery). There were very few references to women disliking oil and grime. In most of the men's view it was the strength requirements rather than the muck that made their jobs unsuitable for women.

Some were obviously determined that any women who joined their work groups would not be allowed to perform the toughest, most masculine tasks. It was not only the older male employees who felt this way. Male apprentices often expressed identical sentiments. The main contrast in male attitudes, or at least those that were expressed, was by occupational class, not generation. However, some shop-floor males admitted to having been surprised by young and older women who had proved that they could do it. "I firmly believe now that females are equal to males in most functions. The only difference is in some physical aspects. When the first female came in here she was small, petite. I admit that I tried to put her off and steer her towards electrical. I showed her the large pieces of equipment but she said, 'Just let me try it and I'll show you'. She competed and was equal if not better than the lads. Now the lass that's coming this year will be able to handle it all because it's less of a physical job now" (oil refinery).

There was always a tendency for women to be channelled away from the heavier production and craft jobs. As explained below, the women did not necessarily resent this. Many shared the view that their own sex was naturally more suited to some jobs. Shopfloor males invariably felt that their sex needed to do the heavier work. At the same time, where significant numbers of women had been part of the workforce for several years it was recognized that, "There's certain jobs that they're better at. If we need someone for the body shop or the overhead conveyor then I'm not sure whether a woman or a slender built guy could do it. On the sealer deck we need dexterity so I wouldn't put a very large man in there" (Auto Co). Women were considered particularly suitable for jobs that needed care and attention, or nimble fingers. So at Auto Co's southern site there were very few women in the body shop, many more on final trim putting sealant in the car engines and carrying out quality checks, and hardly any men doing the cut and sew jobs in soft trim. It was mainly in the car plants and oil refineries that the men insisted that their jobs required strength and endurance that women could not offer. However, in the other industries the male manual employees explained that their jobs were tough in other ways—having to cope with severe weather or aggressive customers for example. Even if women would and could do the work the men insisted that they should not be expected to take it on.

Preferential Treatment

A fourth point was that women were given preferential treatment which most of the men considered patently unfair, except in the case of excusing them from really heavy work. "She'll probably get better opportunities because it's good PR. It was all over the press when she joined. We're all treated the same but she's on a different level. We all have to do an outward bound course, unless you're a girl it seems. She can get away with a lot more" (apprentice, oil refinery). "I've not actually worked with them but the girl told me that she was being treated better, it being a new thing" (Auto Co). Some men believed that the women who were hired were often chosen for the wrong reasons. "At the last intake they recruited 50 per cent of the women who applied (for assembly jobs in one of the car plants). They chose them for what were probably the wrong reasons—that they should be able to stand up for themselves on the shop floor. It should really have been on whether they'd be able to do the job."

There were other ways in which the men believed that women in their workplaces made life difficult. For example, their presence suppressed normal conversation. "When we get girls on a course it throws everything out. Swearing is out and you have to hammer the lads for it" (Service Co). Previous research has drawn attention to a lowering of males' job satisfaction when their occupations are desegregated. They complain of a decline in the quantity and quality of social interaction in their workplaces (Wharton and Baron 1987). Among the male manual employees who we interviewed there were occasional

suggestions that women's presence was a moral danger. "I don't think they should work outside. It's a man's job. Also, I feel that it could be disruptive" (Service Co).

Just two male shop-floor employees spoke of women being given a harder time overall. "I'd say that it's harder for a woman to get on especially if she has children. I can't see many women in this company who've done well for themselves and had kids. The only one I know of left. From what I could make out she was a damn good electrician but they took the mickey and she went elsewhere" (Auto Co).

Women's Experiences

Women in Management

Most of the women managers that we interviewed were in personnel or training departments and nearly all were aged under 30. We would have interviewed more older female production managers, for example, had they been present. Actually one of the oil refineries did have a female manager on a production unit but she was not on the site at the time of our fieldwork. Our attention was always drawn to any such prominent women because we always enquired about the gender composition of different grades. Our interviews revealed how women who embarked into management, which seemed to be nearly always as graduates rather than from the shop floor, were usually being channelled into a limited number of areas, particularly personnel, but sometimes marketing, and the majority of these women looked destined for only short careers in industry. A recently recruited graduate management trainee at one of Auto Co's sites appeared to have encountered considerable difficulty in entering her preferred area, which would have been production. "I told them at the interview that I wanted to go into production. They told me that I'd have to fight like mad to get there. They kept asking me about discipline. They asked how I would discipline 30 big heavy men, so I told them the same way that I would discipline 30 big heavy women. One manager has flatly refused to have me on his shift. He argues that it wouldn't be worth having a female doing the job. I thought that as they'd recruited me they'd give me a fair chance. What's shocked me here is that some people are so open about it. I've been told to go to a tribunal and that I have a good case but I don't want to ruin my career." This was one of the women who did not believe that her sex had been a disadvantage, but she emphasized how she had needed to battle to obtain equal opportunity.

Contrary to the men who believed that "everything is equal now," only one of the women managers whom we interviewed argued that her sex was neither an issue nor any sort of problem, and she did not claim that her own experience was typical. "My boss has been very good but some of the older managers still find it a bit odd to have a woman in this industry. Mind you, you can use it to your advantage. You've got to build up some respect and then you're OK. I did science subjects at school and since then I've been used to being the only girl. It all depends on the area of business that you're in. Technical areas have some very old fashioned values and entrenched views. Those areas would be very difficult to crack but personally I don't see it as a major problem. In the technical areas it isn't going to change until girls start to take the right options at school" (Electronic).

The remainder of the women managers had two major complaints. The first was that they were patronized, and generally taken less seriously than male colleagues. Only two believed that they could use their gender to advantage in these situations. "They always talk about my appearance which they wouldn't do if I was a man but I think I can get away with more. Using my femininity and being small and blonde helps. They do listen to my ideas. Also, the other day I crashed into a manager with a cup of coffee and he just asked if I was alright whereas a man did the same thing last week and got a right rollicking"

(graduate management trainee, Auto Co). Most of the women managers made it clear that they resented any such privileged treatment. "I think most of them look upon me as a daughter. They don't let me get involved in things. They think I won't be interested. Sometimes men are told to curb their swearing because there's a young lady present. That really gets up my nose. They refer to you as a young lady as if you've got a disease" (junior manager, oil refinery). "I don't get treated seriously. They treat me like a daughter. Some of them think it's only a hobby until you get married. They tend to flatter you and they think you're stupid. Just occasionally you come across people who take exception to a female. One manager would pat my head and say 'pretty girl.' I didn't mind because he did it to the fellows as well" (Auto Co). "They're patronizing. Some of them really annoy me, but I don't think it's held me back in career terms. I've not had any direct experience of prejudice or discrimination. However, I've often wondered whether I'd be treated differently if I were a man. I mean things like not listening to you and ignoring what you have to say. On the positive side I think that I can defuse difficult situations. People will be less aggressive because I'm a woman" (Service Co).

The second grievance concerned the incompatibility between the women's likely roles in their families and a long-term career. "I'm constantly surprised at how few women there are in management. The age you are by the time you get there is when many women leave to start families and they're not encouraged to come back unless it's on a full-time basis. I'm thinking about whether to start a family but I wouldn't dream of mentioning it to anyone in here because even the fact that I was just thinking about it, in my view, would damage my career opportunities" (oil refinery). "If I wanted to have a family. Well, in the long-term I'll get to a stage where family commitments get too much. At that point I'll move out of industry, possibly into the civil service. British industry isn't geared to family life, not for women at any rate" (Electronic). None of the women managers complained of blatant discrimination in access to any form of training or promotion. The main problem with promotion for women, as they saw it, was that continuing to climb depended on continuing to work fulltime without interruption. This applied at all the sites. There were no variations in plant or industrial cultures in this respect.

Women as Engineers

The women who were embarking on careers as professional engineers reported slightly different experiences. Very few complained about being patronized or not taken seriously. When they had taken the appropriate subjects at school and college, obtained the necessary qualifications, applied for and been recruited to engineering jobs, relationships with male colleagues and managers in work teams did not seem to be posing special problems for the majority. The two most critical comments on these matters were: "Some of the bosses are great but my first boss was freaked out that he had to teach a girl. I think some of them doubt that I can do the job. I get the impression that they think I'm a bit thick sometimes. It's OK now because of my new boss. He's brilliant. But while there are only three women in a department of 50 I think there'll always be problems" (Electronic). "Most of the men are OK. They're not a problem. There has been the odd occasion of being pestered and a couple of people were very persistent but they backed off when I was really nasty to them" (oil refinery). However, for every female engineer who felt underrated or pestered because of her sex there was another who felt that her gender would work to her own advantage. "To be honest, quite often it's a distinct advantage being a woman. I think I was offered the job because I was female. It's to enhance their equal opportunity policy. They haven't many women so it's given me an advantage if that was the reason" (oil refinery).

Nevertheless, the female engineers shared the female managers' perception that it would be impossible to combine motherhood with career progression. "The talking stops if you say you're not mobile. They have career breaks but I don't know of anyone who has tested that yet. I know one thing, I wouldn't like to be the first" (oil refinery). "The way things are here, if you want to start a family you can forget about promotion to higher levels" (Electronic). "The general attitude is that women will marry and have kids so don't give them any responsibility because they're going to leave or have too much time off. There's a corrective action team looking into flexible working, shorter hours and creches but they're not taken seriously. Starting at 8:30 am is difficult so women have a hard time of it. After you've had kids it's a case of come back full-time or don't come back at all. There are no women in senior management here so I suppose that says it all" (Electronic). These perceptions were uniform across all the sites and industries that were studied.

Women on the Shop Floor

'Protected.'

How did the women experience the shop floor? To begin with, none felt that they really were "just one of the crew." A universal experience was of being protected from some of the harsher aspects of the job, social and physical. Some resented this and had tried to insist on being allowed to do everything whereas others had decided that this was one of several ways in which they could turn their gender to their own advantage. "Really they're alright with me. If they think I'm not physically strong enough to do something they'll automatically do it. I'd prefer to have a go myself first. They tend to look after me more than they do the lads. They make sure that I've got all my safety gear right and they don't like me lifting anything heavy. When I first started they hardly let me do anything. If it was cold and raining they'd make me sit in the van with the heater on. I used to argue with them that I was there to do the job. When they could see that I was determined they started to let me do things" (Service Co). "I think I'm thought of quite protectively. To be a female here has advantages and disadvantages. They treat me with kid gloves. They won't swear or let me lift anything. If I make a suggestion I think they're more likely to advise me if it's been tried before. With a man they'd let him go on" (craft apprentice, Auto Co).

'A Hard Time.'

There were mixed views on whether, overall, women on the shop floor were disadvantaged in career terms. Some believed that they would benefit from positive discrimination. "They (the management) go out of their way to prove that they don't discriminate. I think it's getting to the point of positive discrimination. I think being a woman will definitely help eventually because they're looking for women to go into management" (oil refinery). It was always managers, not shop floor males, who were said to be actively pro-women. The females were more likely to believe that they faced prejudice and were sometimes deliberately given hard times by male shop floor colleagues. "It was a bit strange at first. There was one other female apprentice and we stuck together. At first it was like them and us. Now we all get on great. Mind you, there are still people around the factory who think that we shouldn't be here. You go into some departments and they don't think you can do it. You've got to show them that you can. When I started here someone asked me why they should employ a woman when in a few years she will leave and have children. I said that I thought that attitude stank. All women ask for is six months maternity leave. What would they do if I broke my leg?" (Electronic). "They seemed almost proud when they spoke of a woman who went to work on the shop floor and who had to take so much aggro that she'd disappear into the health centre until

clocking-off time" (Auto Co). "It makes a difference in subtle ways. They don't discuss things with me in the same way. They're very quick to pick up my mistakes. I think that underneath all the time I have to try to prove that I can do the job as well as anyone else. When people ask to do training I've noticed that they will choose to send a man, not a woman, but I have a positive attitude so I know that I'll succeed" (Service Co).

'You Need to Push Yourself and Stick It Out.'

Most of the women interviewees in skilled manual jobs were young, still serving apprenticeships or in training. They had usually applied for the jobs because they had been particularly good at science or technical subjects at school. Quite a few commented that their fathers had engineering or technical jobs, but when such parents had acted as role models this had normally been a passive process. The standard cultural norm seemed to have operated of parents letting the children make up their own minds. Very few reported receiving special encouragement from parents or teachers to seek entry into traditionally men's jobs. It was equally the case that few reported any active discouragement, but it had usually been their own initiative that had made them apply. Only subsequently, once their applications had been successful, did teachers and parents seem to have begun expressing pride in the girls' achievements.

The small number of women in skilled jobs on the shop floor who were aged over 30 all spoke of having had to try exceptionally hard and to push themselves forcefully in order to achieve or retain their present positions. "When the children were older and I was aged 33 I wrote a letter saying that I'd like to be an engineer with this firm and giving the reasons why I thought I'd be a good one. They wrote a letter back saying that there were no vacancies. Then three months later they advertised jobs and I rang to ask what was going on because they had said that they would contact me if a vacancy came up. They sent a form and I got an interview with personnel. The guy asked me why I wanted to be an engineer and disagreed with everything I said. He was very aggressive towards me. Then after about an hour he said that he would recommend me for an engineering interview. At that interview I was asked questions about whether I could lift ladders and how I would cope if a customer came on strong. Then he asked me to wire up a plug. To be honest I think they were trying to find out if I'd be able to stand the barracking. There were further female type questions and that went on for two-and-a-half hours. Finally he offered me a job after coming up with every excuse to put me off. So you've got to be thick skinned. You get hassle from male colleagues and hassle from customers. People are shocked to see a woman. They ask if you'll be alright. Then they want to see your ID card. They wouldn't do that to a bloke and it always annoys me" (Service Co). "I think that if I wasn't the sort of person that I am I would have been neglected. Another woman would possibly not have got to my level. If I didn't have my qualifications I wouldn't have had a leg to stand on. As it is I'm the only person in this department who is really qualified for the job. I was the only woman on the block when I came here and I got a lot of stick. A lot of them said that I should be at home. I didn't think I'd stick it out because the attitude then was that women were taking men's jobs. Also they didn't have facilities for women. The toilets were makeshift and really bad. But I'm the sort of person who sticks things out. It's much better now. You're more equal here today" (team leader, car plant).

The older women who had "stuck it out" often believed that they had made things easier for younger female entrants. Where women had been present in significant numbers for many years, as on the production lines at one of the car plants, much of the hostility said to have been present at that plant in earlier years, and which was still evident elsewhere at the time of our research, seemed to have evaporated. What were once seriously intended male objections had become jokes. "There have been jokes like women should be at home tied to the sink, all of them taking the mickey, but most of it's just for a laugh. It's always the same with new starters. I knew they weren't getting at me. I was always one of the lads down there. We don't get any abuse now or 'bloody woman taking a man's job,' that sort of thing" (Auto Co). "I suppose that when I started some of them were shocked but after three days that went. I don't think sex makes any difference in promotion now. It's a question of the right person for the right job. Some of the work is fairly heavy and you have to get into some awkward places. If you come into this job you have to be prepared to do everything a man does. When I first started I thought, 'How am I going to lift this gear?' Then the instructor showed me the technique, I did it first time, and it was easy" (Auto Co).

Conclusions

Their Way

The advice from experience to young female entrants from the older women who had made it or hung on in skilled core occupations at all levels—on the shop floor, in engineering and in management—was basically to compete with the men at the men's career games. "There used to be a lot of abuse that we shouldn't be here. But once you show them that you are good they cut that out. You have to be determined otherwise you'll give up. My friend couldn't handle it and left the year after she started. I've been through the hurt, the abuse, and now I've made my mark. There was a time when I went home, hit my head on the wall and asked if this was what I really wanted. I find it difficult now to support female workers who are weak. They have to stand on their own feet. Now I don't think that my gender will hinder my own progress" (team leader, Auto Co).

Some of the older women admitted that they deliberately gave younger female trainees a hard time because they needed toughening to survive. The advice was to do everything that the men did, to insist on being allowed to do it all if necessary, not to be put-off by the swearing or girlie calendars, to make the men listen and demand to be trained-up, sent on courses and considered for promotion. This advice was sound in so far as the companies that we studied, even Motor Parts, would deliver equal opportunities if women pushed hard enough and claimed their rights. The older women were probably also correct in their implicit perception that the system and its men would not change of their own accord or just for the sake of women.

A More Equal Future?

Needless to say, the majority of women would be able to compete on men's terms only if men themselves and the domestic division of labour were to change, though the current organization of paid work and domestic arrangements are not really separate, independent matters but different manifestations of the same societal division of labour and expectation by gender. Change in either area would bring about, or be conditional upon, change in the other. A more equal division of domestic labour would require change in male career expectations. If the requirements of work organizations became gender neutral this would create more genuine labour market opportunities for women which would impact on their relationships with male partners. In practice, however, the men who were interviewed who had the power were not seeking change in either area. This was despite the apparently sincere commitment to equal opportunities of the males in management and professional occupations. Were they maintaining the existing organization of work specifically so as to exclude women? There was not a shred of evidence of this in the attitudes that were expressed. However, the men defended the current organiza-

tion of work realizing full well that this excluded most women from core jobs. Most of the men in all grades appeared to regard the current organization of work as simply normal. The justification for its acceptance was that it worked. However, it was equally clear that this organization of work was enabling the men to express and confirm their masculinity. On the shop floors this was evident in the numerous references to the physical requirements, but the male managers and professional staff felt that their careers required comparable qualities of persistence, commitment and resilience. The fact that women were less likely to possess, or to be able to display such qualities in their careers, was not seen as sufficient reason for changing the organizations. Opportunities were judged basically equal because women would, and were in practice being accommodated if they were able to match the career requirements. This was how the men were able to preside in male-dominated work situations while congratulating themselves on their fairness.

Maybe women could and would force change if they had no alternative. However, the younger women whom we interviewed were aware of alternatives, not just full-time permanent domesticity but also switching to occupations where the hours were more convenient and the pressures less taxing. Female school-leavers who are determined to have better careers than their mothers seem prepared to scale down their aspirations when they confront the realities of the labour market and accept that they will need to combine employment with domestic responsibilities that their partners are unlikely to share equally (Chisholm and du Bois-Reymond 1993). The equal opportunities policies that our companies operated were unlikely to deliver real equality because their female employees, including those who displayed exceptional promise on the lower rungs of the career ladders, were likely to need greater career commitment than males if they were to cope with the pressures of remaining in the career mainstreams (see also McRae et al. 1991).

Our evidence suggests that neither the men nor the women who were winning under the existing rules were a likely source of pressure to change their companies' career systems. Moreover, none of the firms had any skill shortages, so straightforward labour market pressures seemed most unlikely to force change. The firms did not need more women in key jobs to solve skill problems. Pervasive patriarchal assumptions remained consistent with organizational requirements (see Walby 1988). So what, if anything, would force change? International comparisons suggest that sex equality within employment is most likely in public rather than private sector businesses, when collective bargaining is centralized and when governments pursue active labour market programmes to achieve equal opportunities (Whitehouse 1992). During the 1990s, the trends in Britain seem more likely to be away from than towards all these circumstances. We suspect, therefore, that even cautious optimism that greater equality is on the horizon for females in Britain's labour markets will prove over-optimistic.

References

Acker, J. 1990. "Hierarchies, jobs, bodies: a theory of gendered organisations." *Gender and Society*, 4:139-58.

Chisholm, L. and M. du Bois-Reymond. 1993. "Youth transitions: gender and social change." *Sociology*, 27:259-79.

Cockburn, C. 1990. "Men's power in organisations: 'Equal opportunities' intervenes." In J. Hearn and D. Morgan (Eds.), *Men, Masculinities and Social Theory*. London: Unwin Hyman.

Cockburn, C. 1991. *In the Way of Women*. London: Macmillan.

Crompton, R., L. Hantrais, and P. Walters. 1990. "Gender relations and employment." *British Journal of Sociology*, 41:329-49.

Crompton, R. and K. Sanderson. 1990. *Gendered Jobs and Social Change*. London: Unwin Hyman.

Hakim, C. 1979. *Occupational Segregation*. Research Paper 9. London: Department of Employment.

Hakim, C. 1993. "The myth of rising female employment." *Work, Employment and Society*, 7:97-120.

Jonung, C. I. and Persson. 1993. "Women and market work." *Work, Employment and Society*, 7:259-74.

Martin, J. and C. Roberts. 1984. *Women and Employment: A Lifetime Perspective*. London: HMSO.

McRae, S., F. Devine and J. Lakey. 1991. *Women into Engineering and Science*. London: Policy Studies Institute.

Newell, S. 1993. "The superwoman syndrome." *Work, Employment and Society*, 7:275-89.

Walby, S. 1988. "Introduction." In S. Walby, (Ed.), *Gender Segregation at Work*. Milton Keynes: Open University Press.

Wharton, A.S. and J. N. Baron. 1987. "So happy together? The impact of gender segregation on men at work." *American Sociological Review*, 52:574-87.

Whitehouse, G. 1992. "Legislation and labour market gender inequality: An analysis of OECD countries." *Work, Employment and Society*, 6:65-86.

Food for Thought and Application Questions

1. Corcoran-Nantes and Roberts' study of women managers, engineers, and "shop floor" workers in male-dominated industries in Britain reveals patterns of male accommodation similar to those described in the previous chapter focused on rapid transit operators. Describe these patterns and give examples from the information presented on the five British firms. Does it appear that patterns of accommodation to the

women's entry vary by occupation level? If so, in what way?

2. Women employees in the male-dominated firms described in this chapter report incompatibility between their family roles and demands for career commitment. Suppose that these firms, in an attempt to accommodate women's family responsibilities, instituted a "mommy track" similar to that described by Chafetz in Chapter 9. How would management be likely to view women on the "mommy track?" Do you think the "mommy track" would prove to be an effective solution for women in these firms? Why or why not? ✦

22

How Women Reshape the Prison Guard Role

Lynn Zimmer

Today, few people would question the ability of women to perform successfully in most occupations in which the workers are predominantly men; however, a number of jobs, such as soldier, police officer, and prison guard retain their male identification, and a decade or more of women's presence in these jobs has not eliminated speculation regarding women's ability to perform them. Both during and after conducting research on women guards who work in men's prisons (Zimmer 1986), the question constantly asked of me was, "Can women really do the job?" Since the job requirements of prison guards seem to be in direct contrast to the traditional norms for women's behavior, the question is not surprising. Expectations for women have changed over the past two decades, to be sure, but not so much that women's ability to perform in jobs traditionally held by men goes unquestioned, especially if the job entails the exercise of power and authority.

What is generally meant when people ask whether women can perform as prison guards is whether their performance is similar to that of their male counterparts. It is assumed that jobs, especially those at the lower ranks, exist as predetermined slots waiting to be filled by workers. Weber

(1964) suggests that the efficient bureaucracy breeds conformity and that individual workers become dispensable, replaceable, and interchangeable. More recently, Hall (1977) has claimed that because the same occupational role constraints operate on each worker, organizational behavior is not dependent on the characteristics of individuals:

> When a new member enters the organization, he is confronted with a social structure . . . and a set of expectations for . . . behavior. It does not matter who the particular individual is; the organization has established a system of norms and expectations to be followed regardless of who its personnel happen to be. (p. 26)

Nieva and Gutek (1981) similarly suggest that when women workers enter jobs traditionally held by men, they will generally not be able to alter work roles so as to reduce the conflict between occupational norms and gender-role norms. Instead, they will have to alter their own behavior:

> Although individuals will always retain some latitude in deciding how to act, social structures heavily shape the options and tools available to them. Individual behaviors adapt to their environment. (p. 132)

Rosabeth Kanter (1977) agrees: "To a very large degree, organizations make their workers into who they are. Adults change to fit the system." (p. 263)

If occupational role restraints are strong in all work organizations, they might be expected to be particularly strong in highly structured, paramilitary organizations like prisons. E. Johnson (1981) describes the rigidity of the guard's job:

> The prison guard must follow the rules and their interpretations made by his superiors; the guard is not free to act toward inmates—either sentimentally or punitively—as he would personally prefer. (p. 82)

Research by Haney et al. (1973), in which student subjects assigned as guards in a mock prison quickly assumed fairly typical guard behaviors, further suggests that the guard's role requirements overshadow any individual characteristics or predispositions.

The work behavior of women prison guards calls these assumptions regarding the rigidity of work roles into question. Based on unstructured interviews with 70 women guards working in men's prisons in New York and Rhode Island, as well as with a high-level personnel in the central administrative offices, mid-level supervisors at the prisons, men guards, and men prisoners,[1] this study explores the ways women have reshaped the guard role and how their presence has an impact on the prisons and the job of guarding. The data indicate that workers, even in highly regulated environments like prisons, can develop innovative and successful ways to perform the job when they find established work roles inadequate or find they are blocked from achieving success using predetermined definitions of appropriate work behavior. Employment roles, like other social roles, offer opportunity for role making as well as role taking (Turner 1962), and women working as guards in men's prisons have, out of both choice and necessity, acted upon this opportunity, creating new ways to do an old job. This pattern of role making may be typical of women in other traditionally male occupations as well. To find out, researchers need to examine more closely the various ways women perform jobs and evaluate their performance on its own terms rather than how closely it resembles that of men.

The Job of Prison Guard

The prison guard is, according to Hawkins (1976), "the key figure in the penal equation, the man on whom the whole edifice of the penitentiary system depends" (p. 105). Because prisons are, in effect, separate societies, guards must perform a wide range of diverse tasks to keep the prison operating, but the most important ones center around their custody and control functions—keeping prisoners inside the walls and following the rules and regulations for inmate behavior that have been established by prison administrators.

The primary mechanism through which guards maintain control in prisons is the constant regulation of inmate movement. On a normal day, most prisoners are released from their cells for meals, work detail, school, medical care, recreation, and visits, but they will constantly be monitored by guards who are stationed throughout the prison. Many guards spend their day checking inmate passes, frisking inmates as they move from one area to another, and unlocking and then relocking gates as inmates pass through. Several times a day, all prisoners are ordered to their cells, allowing guards to take "the count" and make sure no prisoners have escaped.

Guards are also responsible for enforcing the extensive rules that govern inmate behavior. In addition to rules similar to the laws outside of prison—rules that forbid assault, rape, theft, and the like, there are many rules specific to prison life that, for example, prohibit profanity and gambling, regulate smoking, establish grooming and clothing standards, and dictate the items considered contraband. There may also be very general rules for inmate conduct, requiring them to obey direct orders of guards and treat guards with appropriate respect. Not all of the rules are equally important to the maintenance of internal order, and many guards are willing to overlook violation of some petty rules, but for both the guards' own safety and the security of the institution, it is important that most inmates obey most of the rules most of the time. Given the low guard-to-inmate ratio in prisons, there is always the potential for mass violence. Because guards have limited ability to control inmate behavior during a riot or takeover, they must prevent such situations from occurring by controlling inmate movement and obtaining inmate compliance to the most critical rules.

One way guards may obtain inmate compliance with prison rules is through the threat of institutionalized punishment: segregation, loss of privileges (such as commissary, recreation, visitation), and loss of good-time credits. Guards generally cannot implement these punishments themselves, but can write reports to be reviewed by a special disciplinary committee, which may then order appropriate penalties. This threat of formal punishment is an important management tool and guards use it frequently. However, since this process is time consuming and removes punishment from the immediate situation, guards often supplement the formal system with an informal system of rewards and punishments over which they have more direct control.

Prisoners are dependent on guards to provide a wide range of services for them, and although Crouch (1980a) points out that inmate dependency has been reduced by the recent increase in prisoners' legal rights, guards still have the potential to increase substantially the "pains of imprisonment" (Sykes 1958) that accompany incarceration. For example, the inmate who too frequently disobeys the rules may find that he or she is always the last to receive mail or that a written request to make a phone call has been "lost" in the pile of paperwork that cell-block guards accumulate. Guards can also manipulate rewards, and the compliant inmate may be able to obtain a favorable work assignment, a roomier cell, or more freedom of movement. Even small privileges are important to prisoners and, knowing this, guards can grant or withhold privileges as a way of encouraging compliant behavior.

Guards may also obtain inmate cooperation with regard to important rules by agreeing to ignore prisoners' minor infractions, in what Sykes (1956) calls "corruptions of the guard's authority." Such arrangements are potentially dangerous be-cause prisoners may try to "up the ante," asking for even greater concessions from guards for the same amount of compliance. In spite of this danger, most guards do find it advantageous to engage in such mutual accommodations with prisoners; as long as they are used only to supplement and not replace other techniques of control, such "corruption" seems to present no serious threat to prison security.

Finally, guards may use the threat of physical force to control prison behavior; being unarmed and outnumbered, guards cannot use force to control the prison population on a regular basis, but force may be used to punish particular unruly or disrespectful inmates and serve as an example to others (Marquart 1986).

There are many techniques of control, then, that have become part of the guard role as it has traditionally been performed by men. Individual guards may differ in the degree to which they stress some techniques over others, but the overriding strategy is to remain in a position of control vis-a-vis inmates. Concessions and accommodations may be granted, but only if they add to rather than compromise the guards' position of superiority. Crouch (1980b), a noted authority on the guard role, compares guard-inmate interaction to a contest in which the two parties remain in constant competition, each trying to establish dominance. To emerge victorious, the guard must project an image of personal, physical dominance:

> All officers, to maintain some respect and authority must project some degree of physical competence. Regardless of duty assignment, the man who cannot muster some version of this masculine image before both inmates and peers is in for trouble. For example, one rather obese young man I worked with . . . had never been able to gain respect from either [inmates or other officers]. . . . His appearance and behavior did not fit with the informal expectations of this masculine world. (p. 219)

Physical strength, but more important, an image of masculinity and dominance, are crucial characteristics of the traditional guard role. They are characteristics that women entering this profession do not generally possess. To survive on this job, then, it has been necessary for women to redefine the guard role in a way that eliminates the competitive atmosphere and instead utilizes the skills, characteristics, and patterns of interaction that women are likely to bring to the job.

Women in the Guard Role

Most of the women who work as guards in men's prisons have neither the desire nor the capacity to perform the job as it has been traditionally performed by men. Perhaps many of the women have experienced the type of role conflict that Hughes (1944, 1958) suggests occurs when sexual status and occupational status are incongruent. If they have, women guards have not resolved that conflict by embracing one set of role expectations over the other, as researchers have found of women in other occupations (Kanter 1977; Martin, 1980; Nieva and Gutek 1981; Rustad 1982). Instead, women guards, like the women police officers studied by Hunt (1986), have integrated certain aspects of the traditional female gender role into a traditional male occupational role to create new ways of performing the job. Jurik's (1985a) research shows that women and men guards do not differ substantially in their attitudes toward crime and punishment, but my research shows that men and women do behave differently on the job. Not all women guards perform the job alike, but they do, by and large, use strategies different from those used by men.[2]

Women guards who work in direct contact with prisoners[3] use many of the control techniques that are part of the traditional guard role; they maintain control through regulation of inmate movement and use of the formal system of punishment for rule violation. Women guards can also implement informal rewards and punishments, but because they lack the support and cooperation of most of the men guards in the prison (Fox 1982; Peterson 1982; Zimmer 1986), such efforts may be undermined. Women guards have complained, for example, that male coworkers sometimes reverse their decisions, taking away privileges they had granted to inmates or punishing inmates for actions they had approved.

Like the men, women guards can also engage in mutual accommodations with inmates, ignoring some rules in return for inmate compliance to others, a control technique that women find particularly useful. Although not all women guards can be counted on to ignore minor rule violations, inmates often report that the women who guard them are more willing than the men to overlook what inmates consider the petty rules related to clothing and grooming. In return, prisoners agree to comply with the rules that are more critical to prison security.

While utilizing many traditional guard techniques, women guards also use a strategy that is seldom used by men: the development of friendly, pleasant relationships with prisoners as a way of generating prisoners voluntary compliance. Some women play a mothering, nurturing role vis-a-vis inmates, a role that is in direct contrast to the macho, competitive role typical of men guards. Women guards are also more likely to have a social worker's orientation toward the job and to spend a great deal of time listening to inmate problems, discussing their family relationships, assisting them in letter writing, and helping them make plans for their release. Prison administrators are uneasy about the development of friendly bonds between inmates and guards, especially women guards, fearing that the guard's allegiance could shift from the prison to the prisoner and jeopardize security. Many prisons, in fact, have specific rules that prohibit undue familiarity between guards and inmates (May 1981); Toch's (1981) research suggests that when men guards violate these rules, they risk the disapproval not only of administrators but also of their colleagues, many of whom define prisoners as the enemy (Duffee 1974). Because women seldom have the approval of men guards to begin with, they may be freer to use friendship-oriented strategies for gaining inmate compliance with prison rules.

Men prisoners, for the most part, respond positively to women's style of guarding. They follow the daily routine under women's supervision and comply with women's direct orders. Moreover, prisoners tend to behave better in women's presence by, for example, refraining from extensive use of vulgar language. Some men prisoners try to help the women by taking responsibility for control of the more troublesome inmates; in a few instances, men prisoners have even protected women against physical attack.

This style of guarding successfully incorporates aspects of women's traditional behavior into the guard role; as one woman guard put it, "to survive on this job, women have to do what they know best." At the same time, of course, this strategy is successful only because many men prisoners are willing to accept and contribute to the development of friendly, cooperative relationships with the women who guard them. Their motivations in doing so may be complex, and almost certainly contain a large component of self-interest, but it is also the case that men prisoners come into the prison with their own traditional patterns of interacting differently with women and men. No matter how women guards perform the job, most men prisoners will respond to them in gender-specific ways. Many of the women who succeed in this job have found ways of using male responses to their advantage.

Guarding techniques typical of the women, like those of the men, are far from foolproof, and inmate rule violation, sometimes of a serious nature, is common in prisons. Nonetheless, the women's techniques do represent a viable strategy that has allowed many women to remain on a job that they would find difficult to perform in a more traditional, male-defined way. Like the women who broke into the professions at the turn of the century, women guards have used "every creative strategy that could serve their larger purposes of building meaningful careers" (Glazer and Slater 1987).

There are a number of explanations for why most women do not perform the job of prison guard as it is generally performed by men. For one thing, women often fail to receive adequate socialization during the on-the-job training phase of their employment; their trainers are generally men guards, most of whom do not want the women there. They may actively undermine women's ability to succeed on the job by denying them information about both formal and informal techniques for handling inmates. The training assignments of men and women may also differ, so that at the end of their probationary period, many women have had only limited experience in dealing directly with inmates, especially in emergencies. As women continue on the job, they face persistent opposition and sexual harassment from male guards; many women remain skeptical about men's willingness to assist them if needed. In short, women do not receive the kind of support from coworkers that is important to success on any job (Feldman 1976; Terborg et al. 1982; VanMaanen and Schein 1979); without that support, many women find it useful to develop alliances with inmates who will then voluntarily comply with women's orders and even offer to protect women when potentially dangerous situations erupt.

While it is true that women face many obstacles in performing the job like men, it is not at all clear that these obstacles alone are the cause of women's occupational behavior or that the removal of those obstacles would lead women to choose a job performance strategy identical to that of men. There are, of course, many individual differences among women guards and the kind of skills and abilities they bring to the job, but it is important to remember that the women who become guards today have been socialized in a society in which expectations for women are only gradually changing. Women guards therefore tend to bring to this job a set of experiences and, to some extent, a mind-set quite different from men. For most men, growing up in this society has prepared them for confrontational situations; most men who work as prison guards have had considerable experience in competitive exchanges with other men, and they are used to vying for control. Most women who work as prison guards have not had these kinds of experiences and, even if they have, find it difficult to replicate them in the prison, where their ability to compete physically with inmates for control is questionable. So instead, women rely on the qualities and characteristics that have served them well in their relationships outside of prison: skills of communication and persuasion and the ability to generate voluntary cooperation from others.

Finally, it is important to see women guards' job behavior as, in some ways, reflective of male-female interactive patterns outside of prison. If women's style of guarding were based solely on what they bring to the job with them—skills and abilities somewhat different from men—then we would expect women guards to behave the same whether working among men or women prisoners. They do not. Pollock's (1986) research indicates that both women and men change their style of guarding as the sex of the inmate population changes and that each of the four combinations (male guard-male inmate; male guard-female inmate; female guard-female inmate; female guard-male inmate) produces different strategies for managing inmates. Some of the strategies used by women who guard men incorporate role behaviors more typical of women interacting with men than of guards interacting with prisoners (e.g., being friendly, understanding, and supportive). This works for women because most prisoners are willing, in turn, to respond with typically male role behaviors (e.g., being protective). These interactive patterns do not replace those of guard and inmate but are interwoven into them in a way that allows women guards to perform the basic requirements of the job and allows men prisoners to feel comfortable having women in official positions of authority over them.[4]

Impact of Women in Prisons and on the Job of Guarding

Women have shown their ability to perform the job of guarding on a day-to-day basis while remaining less intimidating, less competitive, and less physical than most men guards, but there are some occasions in the prison when intimidation, confrontation, and physical force are needed. In even the best-run prison, fights between inmates are common, inmate attacks against guards occur, and there is always the potential for mass violence should a riot take place; it is guards who must bring these situations under control and, in doing so, may find it necessary to use force and violence themselves. Male administrators and male guards feel that the women working as guards are extremely reluctant to respond to situations in which physical force may be necessary and that they are inadequately prepared to perform this aspect of the job. In their eyes, the presence of women presents a danger to prison security.

In actuality, there has been no reported decrease in prison security or internal order in the decade or more since women began working in men's prisons. Women, of course, do remain a small proportion of the staff in men's prisons, and it is impossible to predict the impact of many more women guards, but current levels do not appear to pose a security risk. An even greater proportion of women might be easily accommodated if prison administrators followed the suggestions of a 1981 American Correctional Association report that special tactical teams be trained and made available in all prisons for response to emergency situations. Rank-and-file men guards may, in fact, act too aggressively in such situations and produce an escalation of violence by those they are trying to control (Attica 1972; Stotland 1976; Toch 1977). The presence of women at the site of erupting violence might do more to reduce aggression by all parties than would any actual physical intervention by them. Several researchers have reported that women workers have a calming effect on men prisoners (Becker 1975; Biemer 1977; Cormier 1975; Flynn 1982; Graham 1981), perhaps because women are less likely to engage in competitive relationships with inmates and do not encourage the "ego-showdowns" that may, themselves, set the stage for violence between inmates and guards.

At some point, the presence of women guards who use different strategies for handling inmates may have an impact on the occupational role itself. Already some men guards use strategies that stress relationship building with prisoners (R. Johnson 1977; Toch 1981), but certainly not to the extent advocated over the years by prison reformers (Bennett 1976; Glaser 1964; Hawkins 1976; Morris and Morris 1980; Schrag 1961). Most men guards have vehemently rejected these suggestions and have, instead, insisted that they need more direct control over inmates to perform the job effectively (Fox 1982). Women's ability to perform the job without reliance on coercive control lends support to reformers' suggestions that the job of guarding itself can be transformed. There is, perhaps, much to be learned from women's adaptations to this job; the guard role may not be as rigid as men guards or some researchers (Haney et al. 1973) have maintained. And as the job is redesigned by women's presence, women entering prison work in the future may find it easier to adjust to the job and to gain the acceptance of their coworkers.

Women in Traditional Men's Jobs

As women have moved into traditional men's jobs, they have usually been evaluated on the basis of how closely their performance approximates that of men. These job roles were originally designed and shaped by men, presumably to fit their own particular skills and abilities, but once created, they have been assumed to be neutral positions that qualified women as well as men should be able to fill. When women have not succeeded (i.e., they have not reproduced men's occupational behavior), coworkers and supervisors, usually men, have felt justified in calling for their removal. Researchers, on the other hand, have often pointed to the structural obstacles in their way, implying that when such barriers are removed, women's work behavior will be more similar to that of men (Jurik 1985b; Kanter 1977; Martin 1980; Rustad 1982). Others have focused on how gender-role socialization has left women unprepared for "men's work" (Hennig and Jardim 1977) and suggest that women themselves need to change—to act, talk, dress, and think like men (Carr-Ruffino 1982; Harley and Koff 1980; Mirides and Cote 1980; Smith and Grenier 1982) or learn to play "the games mother never taught you" (Harrigan 1978).

This study of women guards suggests that there is more than discrimination and structural barriers to prevent most women from performing jobs like men. These factors are important determinants of women's occupational behavior and need to be given serious attention, but also important is the different approach that many women themselves bring to the job. This study also indicates that women need not change themselves nor copy men's behavior to perform traditional men's jobs successfully.

Other research on women working in male-dominated occupations leads to the same conclusion. Loden (1985) claims that a "feminine leadership style," typical of many (but not all) women managers, is just as successful in managing subordinates as is the traditional masculine style and may be more productive under some circumstances. Ramey (1981) finds that women, in general, approach scientific problems differently from men and maintains that the approaches of women scientists should be valued for their difference, because the more varied approaches brought to scientific problems, the more likely it is solutions will be found. Goffee and Scase's (1985) research on women entrepreneurs identifies their successful adaptations to business, some of which successfully incorporate traditional gender roles.

Research on women in policing, an occupation—like guarding— identified with men, has been equivocal. Gross (1981) and Berg and Budnick (1986) have found "defeminized" women officers, displaying "pseudo-masculinity," to be more successful on the job and more accepted by their peers. But others have found women officers with less aggressive personalities to be more successful in defusing potentially violent situations and decreasing the chance of injury to all participants (Bell 1982; Block and Anderson 1974; Remmington 1981; Sherman 1975).

The main reason for such disparity in the evaluation of women police officers is the lack of clear criteria for what constitutes good job performance. Public sector, service-oriented occupations present special difficulties in establishing evaluation criteria (Wholey et al. 1986), and policing, an occupation in which professionals themselves argue over the most important role requirements (Whitaker et al. 1982), is particularly problematic. Morash and Greene (1986) show that most evaluation studies of the police stress the attributes and tasks that are biased toward men and do little more than measure officers' conformity to stereotypical men's behavior. This is true of evaluations of prison guards as well, and such gender-typed evaluations probably occur to some degree in all occupations in which the workers are predominantly men or women.

The evaluation of women (and men) workers, then, by their peers, supervisors, and even outside researchers, continues to contain a great deal of gender bias. When women are evaluated according to occupational standards created for men, many women fail to make the grade. When women do perform like men, they are still not evaluated positively (West 1982). Nor do women receive positive evaluations when they find ways to produce results without duplicating typical men's strategies. Auster (1987) shows that occupational gender bias is particularly prevalent when tasks are unpredictable, complex, or difficult to measure; in the prisons, where accomplishments like reducing tension, de-escalating conflict, and averting riots cannot be quantified, or even observed, the opportunity for bias against women guards is enormous.

Conclusions

This article has focused on the subtle but insidious form of bias against women in the devaluation of their different approaches to their work. This bias occurs in many different social contexts—when women think, act, or approach problems differently from men, the women's approach tends to be undercut and devalued (French 1985; Gilligan 1982; Keller 1985; Oakley 1981).

This article argues that it would be beneficial to women's efforts to achieve equality, and ultimately beneficial to the organizations in which women work, if the different approaches used by women were valued precisely because they are different. If, at some point in the future, there is less distinction between what it means to be a man and what it means to be a woman, some of the differences in how women and men perform jobs may disappear. In the meantime, gender equality may best be achieved through an equal valuing of current differences, both in and out of the workplace. A truly nonsexist society is not only one in which structural barriers and gender discrimination are removed but also one in which women and men have the opportunity to change and reshape the roles they fill.

Endnotes

1. For a more detailed description of the research methodology used in this analysis, see Appendix in Zimmer (1986).

2. There are some women guards who try to perform the job "by the book," but even this is different from the way men generally perform the job. These women have adopted what I call the "institutional role" (Zimmer 1986), hoping that a strict adherence to the rules will provide solutions to all job-related problems and insulate them from any criticism by male coworkers and supervisors. Male guards are much more likely to "bend the rules" when the formal rules seem to them to be inappropriate.

3. There are a number of women guards who do not regularly work in direct contact with men prisoners because they have managed to receive a job assignment in an area of the prison where such contact is minimal (e.g., administrative offices, mailroom, visiting room). These women perform a "modified role" in the prison and, because they have so little contact with inmates, have not developed a style of guarding consistent with that outlined in this article (see Zimmer 1986).

4. Different methods for handling a situation in which gender status is inconsistent with occupational role requirements are outlined by Whyte (1946). He found that the physical environment in the restaurant could be altered to soften the effect of male-female interactions that conflicted with the norm.

References

American Correctional Association. 1981. *Riots and Disturbances in Correctional Institutions*. College Park, MD: American Correctional Association.

Attica. 1972. *Official Report of the New York State Commission on Attica*. New York: Bantam Books.

Auster, E. 1987. "Task characteristics as a bridge between macro and micro research on male-female wage differences." Paper presented at Academy of Management Meetings, New Orleans, LA.

Becker, A. 1975. "Women in corrections: A process of change." *Resolutions*, 1:19-21.

Bell, D. J. 1982. "Policewomen: Myths and reality." *Journal of Police Science and Administration*, 10:112-20.

Bennett, L. 1976. "A study of violence in California prisons: A review with policy implications." In A. Cohen et al. (Eds.), *Prison Violence*. Lexington, MA: Lexington Books:149-168.

Berg, B. and K. Budnick. 1986. "Defeminization of women in law enforcement: A new twist on the traditional police personality." *Journal of Police Science and Administration*, 14:314-19.

Biemer, C. 1977. "The role of the female mental health professional in a male correctional setting." *Journal of Sociology and Social Welfare*, 4:882-87.

Block, P. and D. Anderson. 1974. *Policewomen on Patrol: Final Report*. Washington, DC: Police Foundation.

Carr-Ruffino, N. 1982. *The Promotable Woman*. New York: Van Nostrand.

Cormier, B. 1975. *The Watcher and the Watched*. Plattsburgh, NY: Tundra Books.

Crouch, B. M. 1980a. "The guard in a changing prison world." In B. Crouch (Ed.), *The Keepers, Prison Guards and Contemporary Corrections*. Springfield, IL: Charles C. Thomas:5-45.

————. 1980b. "The book vs. the boot: Two styles of guarding in a southern prison." In B. Crouch (Ed.), *The Keepers*. Springfield, IL: Charles C. Thomas:207-223.

Duffee, D. 1974. "The correction officer subculture and organizational change." *Journal of Research in Crime and Delinquency*, 11: 155-72.

Feldman, D. C. 1976. "A contingency theory of socialization." *Administrative Science Quarterly*, 21:433-52.

Flynn, E. E. 1982. "Women as criminal justice professionals: A challenge to change tradition." In N. Rafter and E. Stanko (Eds.), *Judge, Lawyer, Victim, Thief*. Boston: Northeastern University Press:305-340.

Fox, J. 1982. *Organizational and Racial Conflict in Maximum-Security Prisons*. Lexington, MA: Lexington Books.

French, M. 1985. *Beyond Power: On Women, Men, and Morals*. New York: Ballantine Books.

Gilligan, C. 1982. *In a Different Voice*. Cambridge, MA: Harvard University Press.

Glaser, D. 1964. *The Effectiveness of a Prison and Parole System*. New York: Bobbs-Merrill.

Glazer, P. and M. Slater. 1987. *Unequal Colleagues: The Entrance of Women into the Professions, 1890-1940*. New Brunswick, NJ: Rutgers University Press.

Goffee, R. and R. Scase. 1985. *The Experiences of Female Entrepreneurs*. London: George Allen and Unwin.

Graham, C. 1981. "Women are succeeding in male institutions." *American Correctional Association Monographs*, 1:27-36.

Gross, S. 1981. "Socialization in law enforcement: The female police recruit." Final Report for the Southeast Institute of Criminal Justice, Miami, FL.

Hall, R. 1977. *Organizations: Structure and Process (revised edition)*. Englewood Cliffs, NJ: Prentice-Hall.

Haney, C. el al. 1973. "Interpersonal dynamics in a simulated prison." *International Journal of Criminology*, 1:69-97.

Harley, J. and L. Koff. 1980. "Prepare women for tomorrow's managerial challenge." *The Personnel Administrator*, 25:41-42.

Harrigan, B. 1978. *Games Mother Never Taught You*. New York: Warner Books.

Hawkins, G. 1976. *The Prison—Policy and Practice*. Chicago: University of Chicago Press.

Hennig, M. and Ann Jardim. 1977. *The Managerial Woman*. New York: Doubleday.

Hughes, E. 1944. "Dilemmas and contradictions of status." *American Journal of Sociology*, 50:353-59.

———. 1958. *Men and Their Work*. Glencoe, IL: Free Press.

Hunt, J. 1986. "The logic of sexism among police." Paper presented at American Sociological Association Annual Meeting, New York, NY.

Johnson, E. 1981. "Changing world of the correctional officer." In R. Ross (Ed.), *Prison Guard/Correctional Officer*. Toronto: Butterworths:77-85.

Johnson, R. 1977. "Ameliorating prison stress: Some helping roles for custodial personnel." *International Journal of Criminology and Penology*, 5:263-73.

Jurik, N. 1985a. "Individual and organizational determinants of correctional officer attitudes toward inmates." *Criminology*, 23:523-40.

———. 1985b. "An officer and a lady: Organizational barriers to women working as correctional officers in men's prisons." *Social Problems*, 32:373-88.

Kanter, R. 1977. *Men and Women of the Corporation*. New York: Basic Books.

Keller, E. Fox. 1985. *Reflections on Gender and Science*. New Haven, CT: Yale University Press.

Loden, M. 1985. *Feminine Leadership*. New York: Time Books.

Marquart, J. 1986. "Prison guards and the use of physical coercion as a mechanism of prisoner control." *Criminology*, 24:347-66.

Martin, S. 1980. *Breaking and Entering: Policewomen on Patrol*. Berkeley: University of California Press.

May, E. 1981. "Prison guards in America—the inside story." In R. Ross (Ed.), *Prison Guard/Correctional Officer*. Toronto: Butterworths:19-40.

Mirides, E. and A. Cote. 1980. "Women in management: The obstacles and opportunities they face." *Personnel Administrator*, 25:25-28, 48.

Morash, M. and J. Greene. 1986. "Evaluating women on patrol: A critique of contemporary wisdom." *Evaluation Review*, 10:230-55.

Morris, T. and P. Morris. 1980. "Where staff and prisoners meet." In B. Crouch (Ed.), *The Keepers: Prison Guards and Contemporary Corrections*. Springfield, IL: Charles C. Thomas:247-268.

Nieva, V. and B. Gutek. 1981. *Women and Work: A Psychological Perspective*. New York: Praeger.

Oakley, A. 1981. *Subject Women*. New York: Pantheon Books.

Peterson, C. B. 1982. "Doing time with the boys: An analysis of women correctional officers in all-male facilities." In B. Price and N. Sokoloff (Eds.), *The Criminal Justice System and Women*. New York: Clark Boardman:437-460.

Pollock, J. 1986. *Sex and Supervision: Guarding Male and Female Inmates*. New York: Greenwood Press.

Ramey, E. (in interview with Barbara Coldman). 1981. "Different is not lesser: Women in science." In B. Forisha and B. Goldman (Eds.), *Outsiders on the Inside*. Englewood Cliffs, NJ: Prentice-Hall:42-54.

Remmington, P. 1981. *Policing: The Occupation and the Introduction of Female Officers*. Washington, DC: University Press of America.

Rustad, M. 1982. *Women in Khaki*. New York: Praeger.

Schrag, C. 1961. "Some foundations for a theory of correction." In D. Cressey (Ed.), *The Prison: Studies in Institutional Organization and Change*. New York: Holt, Rinehart, & Winston:309-357.

Sherman, L. 1975. "Evaluation of policewomen on patrol in a suburban police department." *Journal of Police Science and Administration*, 3:434-38.

Smith, H. L. and M. Grenier. 1982. "Sources of organizational power for women: Overcoming structural obstacles." *Sex Roles*, 8:733-46.

Stotland, E. 1976. "Self-esteem and violence by guards and state troopers at Attica." *Criminal Justice and Behavior*, 3:85-96.

Sykes, G. 1956. "The Corruption of Authority and Rehabilitation." *Social Forces*, 34:157-62.

_____. 1958. *The Society of Captives*. Princeton, NJ: Princeton University Press.

Terborg, J. et al. 1982. "Socialization experiences of women and men graduate students in male sex-typed career fields." In H. J. Bernardin (Ed.), *Women in the Workforce*. New York: Praeger:124-155.

Toch, H. 1977. *Police, Prisons, and the Problem of Violence*. Washington, DC: U.S. Government Printing Office.

_____. 1981. "Is a 'correctional officer' by any other name, a 'screw?' " In R. Ross (Ed.), *Prison Guard/Correctional Officer*. Toronto: Butterworths:87-104.

Turner, R. 1962. "Role taking: Process versus conformity." In A. Rose (Ed.), *Human Behavior and Social Processes*. Boston: Houghton Mifflin:20-40.

VanMaanen, J. and E. H. Schein. 1979. "Towards a theory of organizational socialization." *Research in Organizational Behavior*, 1:209-64.

Weber, M. (translated by A. M. Henderson and T. Parsons). 1964. *The Theory of Social and Economic Organization*. New York: Free Press.

West, C. 1982. "Why can't a woman be more like a man?" *Work and Occupations*, 9:5-29.

Whitaker, G. P. et al. 1982. *Basic Issues in Police Performance*. Washington, DC: National Institute of Justice.

Wholey, J. et al. 1986. *Performance and Credibility: Developing Excellence in Public and Nonprofit Organizations*. Lexington, MA: Lexington Books.

Whyte, W. F. 1946. *Industry and Society*. New York: McGraw-Hill.

Zimmer, L. 1986. *Women Guarding Men*. Chicago: University of Chicago Press.

Food for Thought and Application Questions

1. Zimmer argues that job performance is often normed to a male standard, even when women's ways of performing the work are just as effective as men's. Examine the "help wanted" section of your local newspaper for evidence of this pattern. Begin by looking for cases where job requirements consist of male-typed traits or skills (e.g., aggressive leadership ability, ability to lift heavy weight). Then

consider whether the male-typed requirements listed are really necessary for effective performance in the job being described. Discuss any examples of jobs where the male-typed requirements may not be necessary, giving particular attention to any female-typed traits that would be likely to enhance job performance.

2. Reflect upon your most recent employment experience. How did your work shape your behavior? In what ways did you adapt to the work environment? Did any of these changes alter gender-related behaviors? Did your presence on the job and your performance in the work role alter the job in any way? If so, how? Were any changes that occurred gender-related? Explain. ✦

23

'Between a Rock and a Hard Place': Racial, Ethnic, and Class Inequalities in Women's Professional Nursing Organizations

Nona Y. Glazer

In the workplace and in occupational associations, actions by women to protect their jobs may "run counter to unification and solidarity among women . . . workers" (Butter et al. 1985, 44-45). This contradicts feminist theories that explain exclusionary practices by workers first and foremost, if not solely, in terms of gendered interests. Certainly, organizations representing men have often defined their interests as gender based. Women may also define themselves as having common interests with all other women, as did many white, middle-class feminist organizations in the United States in their early stages. However, a Marxist perspective stresses the importance of class relations among workers as well as between capitalists and workers and, therefore, class relations among women workers. Furthermore, many feminists, including Marxists, have argued for the recognition of racial- and ethnic-based interests as a core of social relations between women.

I examine class relations among women workers, how associations representing upper-grade women workers in a female-typed occupation have sought to preserve their jobs against inroads by women workers in lower-grade jobs. In doing so, I examine how associations have used a variety of exclusionary strategies and practice institutional racism. This article describes some of the activities of national organizations of registered nurses (RNs) and nurse educators over the segmentation of nursing personnel. *Segmentation* refers to hierarchically ranked labor markets across which there is virtually no worker mobility; these markets differ from each other in wage levels and benefits, steadiness of employment, job autonomy, and other conditions of employment. The history of nursing in the United States is long and complex and includes many changes, among which segmentation is a critical one. Other changes include the rise in the nineteenth century and the subsequent demise after World War II of diploma-granting schools of nursing and their replacement by community college programs and baccalaureate-granting nursing schools; a shift during the Great Depression of 1929 from private duty to hospital employment; a shift from hands-on delivery of care by private duty and pre-war hospital RNs to RNs' overseeing the delivery of care by nonprofessional nursing personnel, and, finally, a return (beginning in the 1970s) to hands-on care by RNs in hospitals and homes; an uneasy alliance, and at times conflict, between "nursing leaders" (largely educators of RNs) and rank-and-file RNs over professionalization and unionization; and the fight of rank-and-file RNs for such rights as the 40-

hour week, residence outside the hospital, earnings, and job autonomy.

Changes in nursing were interwoven with the efforts of their associations to pursue two occupational goals important to this article: (a) professionalizing RNs by making the baccalaureate of science in nursing degree (BSN) mandatory and (b) preventing the displacement of RNs by licensed practical nurses (LPNs) and nurses aides by restricting the training of these lower-grade personnel and by limiting their work to nontechnical health care tasks. The professional associations of RNs and RN educators have done the second by resisting efforts by private employers, government agencies, and voluntary associations to reduce labor shortages and lower wage costs by training the latter nursing workers. These workers are, of course, less trained and lower paid than RNs.

Within capitalism, associations representing women workers face employers who are concerned with accumulation and profits: employers try to lower their labor costs, for example, by using less-trained and lower-waged workers in place of more trained and higher-waged ones. Registered nurses' associations find themselves "between a rock and a hard place"—trying to prevent their replacement by less-trained workers while upgrading their profession, a process that in engineering, accounting, and teaching has included differentiation into segments. Of course, the organizations have been dependent on the cooperation or acquiescence of their employers in doing so. Associations may resist employer efforts to lower the wages of RNs by accepting the segmentation of nursing or supporting it when it appears to help to professionalize registered nurses: they do so by limiting entry to RN jobs through controlling access to schooling, licensing, and the legal definitions of job responsibilities as specified in "practice acts."

Segmentation is a solution of sorts for registered nurses, protecting the class-based and racial/ethnic privileges of some women workers against inroads by lower-grade women workers. Splitting tasks among different grades enhances the status, earnings, and self-esteem of RNs, because nonprofessional tasks are shifted from them to lower-grade workers. Employers benefit because wage costs shrink as the numbers of the highly paid workers decline, even though lower-paid workers may increase. However, the possibility remains that during periods of crisis, employers may still substitute lower-grade nursing personnel for RNs.

Segmentation may harm licensed practical nurses and nurse's assistants who are disproportionately women of color and from poor households: segmentation freezes them into positions from which they cannot rise through on-the-job experience and provides a rationale for low wages, part-time work, and minimal job autonomy. This process of differentiation, substitution, and shifting among grades is not limited to nursing (Sacks 1988) but also occurs in social work, teaching, and librarian work (Glazer 1988b) and across diverse jobs in factories (Janiewski 1985).

Theories of Segmentation

Segmentation theories help explain the segregation of women workers into female-typed jobs and, because women's jobs average lower earnings than men's, a significant part of the gender gap in earnings. Most important, the theories assume that all men have an identical interest based on their gender that leads them to support the same actions and policies and to do so despite class, racial, and ethnic divisions and conflicts among men. Extensive research documents some of the exclusionary practices used by organizations representing male workers, that is, their efforts to prevent the entrance of women into male-typed occupations (e.g., medicine, plumbing) or industries in which male workers predominate (e.g., printing, construction). These include studies of cigarmaking (Cooper 1987); printing

(Cockburn 1984; Baron 1987); ordinance, railroad, telephone industries, and street-car conducting (Greenwald 1980; Cohn 1985); retailing (Glazer 1984); textiles, engineering, and clerical work (Walby 1986); automotive and electrical production (Milkman 1987); and the postal service (Cohn 1985).

The underlying argument in this research is that, as workers, men gain economic and emotional benefits from the segregation of women's paid work (Strober 1983). For men, gender segregation reduces economic competition from women workers and maintains women in subordinate relations with men both at work and at home (Hartmann 1976, 1981). Segmentation also benefits men of the capitalist class. By segregating women, they gain a productive, low-waged, disciplined, and flexible labor force, and they divide the working class into warring camps along gender lines (Blau and Hendricks 1979; Bonacich 1972).

While significant differences exist among theories of gender segregation, most share one underlying assumption: Women, but not men, are essentially passive in the workplace. Women are nonparticipants in changing the labor process, in influencing who enters their occupation, and in shaping its segmentation. This view of the relative passivity of women finds a complement in feminist views of women as more cooperative and relational, more caring and less aggressive than men (Gilligan 1982), and having a less mechanistic and hierarchical approach to social life (Keller 1982). Presumably, therefore, women workers would be expected to consider the impact of their defense of their job prerogatives on other women workers; also, theories that emphasize gender interests imply that women might be more likely than men to recognize (and respect) the contributions of women in lower-grade jobs to organizational goals and to the success of women in upper-grade work.

I argue to the contrary: My thesis is that in resolving conflicts with employers,

women's organizations may support educational and workplace policies that result in the reinforcement of class and racial/ethnic inequalities between themselves and other women. I assume that employers accept the proposals of RN associations insofar as they see them as compatible with managerial goals.

Method

For my discussion of job grades and social relations among nursing personnel, I draw on the scholarly literature on nursing in the United States, policy papers prepared for nursing associations (e.g., American Nurses Association 1981; Brown 1948, 1970; Fondiller 1983; Winslow and Goldmark 1923) and social histories of nursing (Buhler-Wilkerson 1983; Bullough and Bullough 1978; Langemann 1983; Melosh 1982; Sexton 1981). Although I rely on secondary sources, my interest in women's participation in the segmentation of nursing emerged from 60 interviews I conducted, mostly in 1984-85, on the West Coast. I asked educators of RNs and nursing assistants, union representatives and association officers, middle-level nursing managers, rank-and-file RNs, licensed practical nurses, and nursing assistants in home health care about the changing labor process. In response, many talked about professionalism and nurses' associations. They described tensions among nursing personnel across job grades in hospitals and home health care delivery about job responsibilities, competence, respect, and appreciation; and they described racial and ethnic, as well as class, overtones.

The social agency of women workers is represented by the actions of their professional associations whose membership is mostly white registered nurses and nurse educators of RNs. The associations include the American Nurses Association (ANA), the National League for Nursing Education (NLNE), the National Nursing Council (NNC), and their state associations. Even though staff RNs constitute the majority of the membership (except in associations only for educators), the organizations have been led mainly by educators of RNs and nursing managers (Melosh 1982).

Segmentation in the Nursing Work Force

Although segmentation refers usually to distinctions between occupations, as I have emphasized, it includes differentiation within a profession and the emergence of nonprofessional strata (Richardson 1987). In nursing, the long-term trend has been toward a segmented labor force that includes nursing aides and licensed nurses as well as registered nurses. The training of each segment—lower-grade nursing aides, middle-grade licensed nurses, and upper-grade RNs—has become more formalized and technical. Site specialization increased, with RNs becoming nearly the exclusive nursing force in hospitals, while nursing assistants became concentrated in nursing homes; licensed nurses had difficulty finding jobs as RNs; RNs and nursing assistants became the basic labor force during the late 1970s and 1980s in the expanding home health care delivery sector (Glazer 1988a).

Within each segment nurses are virtually all women: 96 percent of registered nurses, 97 percent of licensed nurses, and 93 percent of nursing assistants (aides, orderlies, and attendants). Segments differ from each other in years of formal schooling, earnings, and the legal right to do certain work as defined by licensing and in state practice acts. Nonetheless, workers in lower grades may do work on one shift or in one workplace that is done by those in higher grades at other times or elsewhere, and they do so without additional pay (Glazer 1988a; Sexton 1981).

Trends in Grades

Nursing shows a recent downward trend in average grades, with more workers in the lower grade than at the top. There has also been a move toward polari-

zation in education, with fewer workers in the middle grades being trained, but many more in the bottom or top grade. Between 1900 and 1940, RNs increased from 11 percent to 73 percent of nursing workers, but in 1940, after reaching 73 percent of all nursing personnel, their percentages began to decline. By 1980, RNs were only 44 percent of all nursing workers. Licensed workers declined from 89 percent of personnel in 1900 to 15 percent in 1980. Workers in the lowest grade, nursing assistants, have grown into the largest segment. Between 1940 (the first year for which national data are available) and 1980 assistants increased from 9 percent to 41 percent of all nursing personnel (U.S. Bureau of the Census 1902, 1914, 1923, 1933, 1943, 1953, 1963a, 1963b, 1973a, 1973b, 1984).

Racial and Ethnic Segregation

Historically, racial and ethnic membership parallels job segments. White women are disproportionately in upper-grade jobs. Black and Hispanic women are disproportionately in the middle and lower job grades, and especially in the latter. Asian women have a higher percentage of workers in upper rather than lower grades, and a larger percentage of them than white women are RNs (U.S. Bureau of Census 1963b, 1973a, 1983). However, most Asian women who are RNs have been recruited from abroad to solve the RN shortage in the United States (Nishi and Wang 1985).

Wages

The segments differ markedly from each other in wages, and the differences increased between 1970 and 1980. In 1970, licensed practical nurses earned between 83 percent (black LPNs) and 72 percent (white LPNs) of the wages of RNs in their racial/ethnic group. White LPNs averaged higher earnings than blacks because the median wages of white RNs ($6,585) was higher than those of black RNs ($5,728). By 1980, the earnings of white LPNs had declined from 72 percent to 68 percent of white RN median earnings ($14,750) while black LPN earnings had declined from 83 percent to 73 percent of black RN earnings ($15,090). Hispanic LPN earnings declined from 76 percent to 69 percent of Hispanic RN earnings ($15,084). The earnings of nursing assistants also showed consistent declines (U.S. Bureau of the Census 1973b, 1984).

Manpower Strategies

Health care delivery in capitalist societies is a commodity like most others—for example, food and housing, clothing repairs and cleaning. Until the mid-1960s, the major sellers of health services for private profit were physicians and proprietary hospitals (owned usually by physicians). In addition, public health agencies provided some nursing services for free or modest fees, and municipalities and religious communities ran free or low-cost hospitals. Since the mid-1960s, through Medicaid and Medicare insurance programs, the federal government has guaranteed substantial reimbursements to sellers of health services, which now include physicians, hospitals, nursing homes, and (since the late 1970s) more home health care agencies. The insurance system attracted corporate investors who have bought hospitals, nursing homes, and home health agencies, resulting in the corporatization of the U.S. health care delivery system (Berthgold 1987). This has meant a new pressure on labor cost, as most investors can be kept only by high and reliable returns. In addition, corporations insure a considerable percentage of workers and their dependents and have attempted to curb their insurance costs.

In capitalism, workers have no right to employment or to a "living" as distinct from a "minimum" wage. On the contrary, workers may lose their jobs or find their wages and benefits reduced as their employers try to reduce the cost of labor. In service industries, labor and costs are central and in health care, nursing personnel are the largest single labor cost. It is diffi-

cult for managers to reduce or eliminate labor in health care facilities by a method used in manufacturing—the substitution of technologies for human labor. Instead, employers use a detailed division of labor or job consolidation, respectively, to degrade jobs or eliminate workers, and thereby to lower wage costs (Braverman 1974). Self-service, which relies on the labor of consumers and their families as a substitute for that of paid workers, is another tactic employers in service industries use to reduce the size of the paid labor force and, hence, their wage bill (Glazer 1988a, 1990).

Manpower Development Strategies

Manpower development strategies include publicly and privately funded training programs outside the workplace, intended by employers to produce a cheaper nursing labor force. The preferred training of nursing personnel is through short courses of several weeks or months rather than through two to four years of training. In the last decades, this has included major state financing of the training of RNs in two-year community college programs and much less support for four-year university-based or three-year nursing school diploma programs. Until after World War II, most training of licensed nurses and nurses assistants was provided by physicians, proprietary schools, and voluntary associations, such as charity and religious societies and settlement houses. In the public sector, LPNs and aides were trained by the armed services, local schools and community colleges, and sometimes in private-public collaborations. In postwar years, federal and state funding, rather than private sources, supported most of this training.

Development strategies have been seen by their proponents as solving various crises, such as acute labor shortages of RNs. Also, there may be increased civilian demand for services, such as when health care insurance becomes more widely available and more RNs are needed. Also, manpower development strategies are supposed to solve problems, such as "too high wages," the loss of charitable contributions to hospitals, increased demands or social services, and the loss of federal and state funds for health services. Also, on occasion, social reform organizations proposed different manpower development strategies, assuming that they would alleviate poverty among women on welfare or establish full employment by training women to be nursing assistants.

Struggle Over Segments in Nursing

Starting in the late nineteenth century, registered nurses established a variety of professional associations: national ones for nursing educators and for RNs working in public health, and statewide ones for other RNs. The associations worked to professionalize registered nursing and to raise its status. They improved the quality of nursing education and advocated longer periods of formal education. Starting in 1903, the RN associations began a state-by-state fight for licensing and "scope-of-practice" acts to define their legal right to do various tasks. Licensing and scope-of-practice acts prevented most nursing assistants, untrained helpers, licensed nurses, and other nontrained workers from (officially, at least) being used as substitutes for RNs. The association also lobbied Congress to fund schools that trained RNs. In addition, they acted as "watchdogs" on manpower development policies, intervening at all levels—from city and county to federal—to improve and protect professional nurses (RNs) from job loss by the extensive training of lower-grade nursing personnel.

Not all RNs belonged to the same associations, nor did all associations have the same goals. Most important, the majority of black RNs were effectively barred from the ANA because of racial segregation in the southern states. Full membership in the ANA was only for members of state chapters, which in the southern states refused to admit blacks. As a result, black RNs formed the National Association for Colored Graduate Nurses (NACGN), which remained active until 1951. In 1948, the Brown Report, commissioned by the ANA, criticized the organization for allowing the exclusion of black RNs and provoked the debate that culminated in voting rights being granted to those unable to join a state chapter (Hine 1989).

In contrast to the ANA, the National Organization for Public Health Nursing (NOPHN) required only national membership. Alone among nursing associations, it acted as a social reform lobby that worked for the betterment of public health, access to health care for blacks, and for the professional concerns of black as well as white RNs (Hine 1989). During the first half of the twentieth century, black RN associations were, understandably, less concerned with preventing the training of lower-grade nursing workers than with eliminating racism: In the southern states, they worked to upgrade nursing education in segregated nursing schools in the South, to eliminate discrimination in hiring and wages of black RNs, and to improve black health care throughout the nation.

Pre-World War I

Beginning in the late nineteenth century, RNs faced repeated efforts by physicians, charities, hospitals, and the government to train lower-grade nurses, and nursing leaders feared these workers would be used to displace RNs (Ashley 1976; Buhler-Wilkerson 1983; Bullough and Bullough 1978, 144-45). Their fears were reasonable: in 1909, for example, Dr. William Stillman proposed to the New York Medical Society that nurses be given different training, depending on the social class of the patients whom they served. Hospital graduate nurses were to serve the rich, and another stratum of women were to be trained in short courses to serve people of moderate means (Ashley 1976, 61).

Until 1930, physicians themselves ran a variety of training courses in "schools," sometimes producing nurses in as little as eight weeks (Ashley 1976). Given the power of physicians, RNs were unable to eliminate such training programs but distanced themselves from the "graduates" by winning state legislation that licensed RNs and reserved the title registered nurse for only graduates of approved schools of nursing. Furthermore, they warned hospitals that the well-being of their patients was threatened when the subnurses were used in place of RNs.

Corporations also tried to substitute lower-grade nursing personnel for RNs. For example, in the early decades the century, Metropolitan Life Insurance (MLA) tried to use licensed nursing in place of RNs in their home care program for chronically ill policyholders. The RNs protested but succeeded only in halting all company visitor programs. Moreover, other corporations and government agencies continued to lower their labor costs by substituting cheaper visiting practical nurses for more expensive public health nurses (Buhler-Wilkerson 1983).

World War I and Aftermath

During World War I, the shortage of RNs prompted the Red Cross to propose to Congress that the agency train a nursing labor force of volunteers, attendants, and practical nurses. Despite protests to Congress, RN associations were unable to prevent the establishment of the programs, and they shifted to gaining control of the training content, licensing, and scope of practice to prevent a large pool of lower-grade nurses from weakening the anticipated poor postwar market position of RNs (Johnston 1966; Winslow and Goldmark 1923).

The efforts to train less-skilled, lower-waged nursing personnel continued after the war, despite a large supply of RNs and the high RN unemployment that nursing leaders had predicted. RNs were attacked for having diverged from some supposed ideal of self-sacrifice by Dr. Charles Mayo of the famous clinic. He called RNs "the most autocratic closed shop in the country" and urged the training of compliant country girls as "sub-nurses." The ANA countered with pleas to protect public health through adequate RN training ("Are Nurses Self-seeking?" 1921, 73-74).

In response to such threats to the employment and status of registered nurses, nursing educators, issued the Goldmark Report in 1923. This was their first formal statement in which a segmented labor force was essentially codified. Leaders urged increased training for registered nursing. They accepted lower-grade nursing personnel but sought to restrict both their training and scope of practice. In addition to urging distinctive training for the three strata (nursing leaders, nursing educators, and staff RNs), the report restricted the training of nursing aides, attendants, and licensed nurses to "non-nursing" tasks (Winslow and Goldmark 1923). Practical nurses were considered deficient compared to graduate nurses, and hospitals were urged not to use student nurses in place of graduate RNs, although the latter were reluctant to help in hospitals (Burgess 1928).

These efforts of nursing leaders to improve the professional status of nursing by state licensing and regulation of scope of practice helped some RNs. But these measures to professionalize did not help black RNs. In most southern states, after training in separate and deplorably unequal schools, they were barred from taking examinations to become registered nurses or given different and easier exams (Hine 1989, 92). Different standards for licensing black RNs effectively prevented them from being offered the occasional job in a white hospital, barred them from postgraduate training, and were used by public agencies and municipal health departments to justify paying lower wages to black RNs than to white ones doing the same work (Hine 1989, 93).

Until 1929, most RNs free-lanced in private duty work. Hence the battle of nursing leaders to prevent the degrading of RNs began when hospitals and the state were relatively minor employers. By the end of the Great Depression, as families lost their incomes and could not afford private duty nurses, RNs began to take low-waged hospital jobs (Wagner 1980).

World War II

To alleviate labor shortages during World War II, the federal government increased funding for nurses' training and encouraged voluntary associations to train more lower-grade nursing workers. Congress funded programs to train licensed nurses and nursing assistants and other non-RNs to care for civilian war workers, stateside members of the armed forces, and their families. The segmentation of nursing was, henceforth, supported by federal funds.

In the postwar years, some social scientists helped to legitimate a segmented labor force in health services. For example, in 1948, Eli Ginzberg explained to the Columbia University School of Nursing that "it is not sound educational and personnel practice to train people to a degree beyond the opportunities they will have to utilize their training effectively in their work. . . . [A] most serious source of discontent among employees is a conspicuous under-utilization of their talents and skills . . . [and] in planning for peace, every effort must be made to avoid it" (1948, 54).

By 1956, segmentation by race and ethnicity was evident. Practical nurses, trained at 395 state-approved schools in the United States, were significantly more likely to be from racial and ethnic minorities and drawn "from a pool of women [with] previously limited opportunity" (Hughes 1958, 24). In contrast, students from 963 diploma schools came predominantly from the white lower middle class. No data were available on the students in the 19 then-new associate degree in nursing (ADN) programs, but community col-

leges do serve working-class students predominantly. Students in nursing baccalaureate programs come from families whose members have lower occupational status and less education than those of other university students but higher status and more education than those of students at diploma schools (Hughes 1958).

In the early 1960s, Congress funded manpower training programs that supported a labor force segmented along racial, ethnic, and gender lines. For example, programs in the War on Poverty typically prepared women from poor families for the lowest-grade service (e.g., nursing aides, welfare aides, teaching aides). Congress authorized training to meet changing manpower needs; in health services that translated into training professionals, including undergraduate and graduate RNs and subsidizing students with low incomes (U.S. Department of Health, Education and Welfare 1967, 29). However, although Congress funded some RN training, it emphasized training a large pool of practical nurses and aides (U.S. Department of Health, Education and Welfare 1967, 32).

Under the Economic Opportunity Act, the nurses' training was intended to put unemployed women to work (Glass and Eisner 1981). Between 1962 and 1967, some 68,000 people entered federally funded programs, the largest numbers of whom were trained as practical nurses and aides and orderlies. The Welfare Administration, which provided rehabilitative programs, family, and other services for the retarded, supported training of additional LPNs and nursing aides from among their clients. Community Action Programs (CAP), directed to healing "the disadvantaged individual unable to gain steady employment," trained health care aides (U.S. Department of Health, Education and Welfare 1967, 34). The Neighborhood Youth Corps, Volunteers in Service to America, and the Job Corps trained youth to be aides, orderlies, and attendants. Working-class poor women were trained for female-typed occupations with substantially lower pay than the occupations for which men were trained (U.S. Department of Health, Education and Welfare 1974), with women being "trained for poverty or near poverty" (National Coalition for Women and Girls in Education 1988, 27).

In the post-World War II period, the National Nursing Council also supported segmentation, using engineers as their model: Registered nurses with graduate training were to plan and direct, less-trained RNs were to care for acutely ill patients, and licensed practical nurses were to care for the less ill (Brown 1948, 64). A follow-up report 20 years later reiterated the council's support for a segmented nursing labor force by proposing that nurse assistants (disproportionately, women of color) be trained for nonnursing functions in order to release RNs for administration and patient education. The report also rejected a career ladder in which further education for nursing assistants could lead to the RN degree (Brown 1970).

Many nursing leaders argued for segmentation even among registered nurses, and in ways that reinforced class distinctions. In 1970 (as earlier in 1923 and 1948), RN educators advocated the division of RNs into *professional* with a four-year university degree, and *technical*, with licenses as practical nurses, and diplomas or an ADN (Brown 1948, 1970; Winslow and Goldmark 1923). Among nursing personnel, only the BSN nurses are taught "nursing theory" and public health administration, which supposedly prepares them, but not their sister RNs and ADNs, to be administrators and to work in home health care. This segmentation was congruent with educators' rejecting the ADN as a step on an educational ladder leading to a BSN degree (Bullough and Bullough 1978, 196). The community colleges thus reproduced class inequalities among women RNs, as working-class students received vocational training. Despite some federal subsidies for RN students, the length and cost

of university training barred most working-class women, white and of color, from professional status as defined by nursing associations. In contrast, middle-class women more easily earned a baccalaureate degree in nursing (BSN), receiving a liberal education in university-affiliated schools of nursing.

RN educator-leaders continued efforts to separate RNs from other nursing personnel. They prevented training programs for practical nurses from locating in diploma schools (Johnston 1966, 52). They defined LPNs narrowly, as "trained to care for sub-acute, convalescent, and chronic patients . . . under directions of licensed physicians or a registered professional nurse" and excluded educators of practical nurses from their association for educators (National League for Nursing 1972, 3, 5). They sought a narrow job description for LPNs and nurses aides, much as physicians did for RNs, and refused to allow these nursing personnel to learn a core nursing knowledge.

Recently, some educational ladders have been established for RNs with diplomas or ADN degrees. However, by 1977, the United States had only 15 programs to serve the 14 percent of all employed RNs who had ADN degrees and who would have been eligible to earn a BSN (Scientific Manpower Commission 1982, 241). Unions in the 1970s won the right of licensed nurses to receive credit for earlier training toward an RN degree.

Congressional preference for two- over four-year training programs ran counter to the goal of the ANA. So did sizable congressional funding of the short and inexpensive training of licensed nurses and nurses aides, such as through the Comprehensive Employment and Training Act and the Manpower Development and Training Act. These programs were intended to remove women from the welfare rolls as well as to meet the nation's manpower needs (Glass and Eisner 1981). Beginning with the Manpower Development and Training Act of 1962, Congress increased financial support for RN brush-up courses only. Subsequently, even though there has been support for RN training, including subsidies of BSN programs in university medical centers, most federally supported training for working-class and poor women has continued to be as licensed nurses and aides.

The average years of schooling of RN graduates began to decline between 1971 and 1984 as more federal funds supported "vocational" rather than university schooling, perhaps because some policymakers believed that higher education resulted in leftist politics. Most important, congressional funding of two-year training community college programs was less than for four-year university ones. The result was that, despite earlier increases, by 1982-83 BSNs had declined from 33.1 percent to 30.8 percent of new RNs (U.S. Department of Health, Education and Welfare 1986: Table 10-1:10-78). The numbers of RNs with graduate and doctorate training increased, but by 1980 they were still only 5 percent of all RNs, employed mainly as administrators and in nursing education (Scientific Manpower Commission 1982: Table LS-M/H-36:241; U.S. Department of Health, Education and Welfare 1986:Table 10-10, 10-87).

Conclusions

This article must not be read as a condemnation of the actions of professional organizations of registered nurses. The various associations acted to professionalize registered nursing and to improve the care of the sick; some of their actions limited the opportunities of other women nursing personnel. Their actions occurred simultaneously with the regularization of training and licensing in other professions, which RNs took as a model, namely, medicine, law, and engineering. Unlike those in these male-dominated professions, however, RNs were not self-employed but depended upon physicians and hospital managers for jobs. Physicians

tried to ensure that the RNs whom they employed or referred to private duty jobs would not be their rivals. Instead, employers tried to keep RNs as a low-cost and subservient labor pool, in part by training rivals of RNs, that is, licensed nurses and nursing assistants. Also, RN associations existed in the context of struggles over and changes in the employment, marital and political rights, and educational opportunities for women and contested views of motherhood, femininity, and female sexuality. My concern is with understanding how class contests over the fights of workers, imbued with institutional racism, lead some white women to protect themselves against the owners and managers while stifling opportunities for women below their own class stratum.

During the differentiation of nursing, associations representing registered nurses tried to control attempts by employers to use less-trained workers as substitutes for RNs. Through professional associations, RN leaders tried "preventive" measures: they argued that practical nurses and nursing assistants were not needed and that their use threatened public health. When the training of subnurses seemed inevitable, associations shifted to limiting training in skills that might have led to their being hired in place of RNs or, with additional training, becoming registered nurses. Furthermore, RN associations won the right to control licensing of lower grades and to limit the work of LPNs and nurse's aides through state practice acts.

Do upper-grade women nursing workers behave "just like men," that is, as white male workers did when faced with the possibility that other workers, men as well as women, might be used by employers to undercut wages and deskill jobs? I think so. The ideology of merit—a presumptive fit between formal education, skills, and rewards—has been accepted as just and fair by most nursing educator-leaders. More important, leaders have assumed that limiting the supply of RNs is an effective defense against the ever-present danger that workers with less training can be used as their replacements. But concerns for other women are sparse. Discussions in journals, books, and reports by leaders about training, job differences, and ranks show no recognition of how creating barriers to training for poor women means that those latter are frozen in dead-end low-wage jobs. This parallels how many white men neglected, ignored, or deliberately marginalized employed women (and other men) in quests to keep their occupational benefits and privileges. So some women, through their professional associations, have neglected, ignored, or marginalized other women, and by their actions helped to constitute these others as a subclass.

Segments in female-typed jobs have been constructed, in part, in the struggles over manpower development strategies: struggles of managers, voluntary associations, and state agencies with nursing leader-educators. Hospital management and the state have tried to control labor markets, to lower wage costs, reduce unemployment, and lessen the reliance of the poor (mostly women, but some men) on public welfare systems and private charities. Especially during the 1960s and early 1970s, others sought manpower training programs, too. Thus social activists in poor people's movements and in universities crafted manpower policies that, ultimately, supported segmentation in nursing. Manpower development programs provided, usually, minimal training for low-income women, which included large percentages of women of color. Nursing leaders sought an opposite goal: the professionalization of nursing through increased formal schooling for entry-level positions, a broader scope of RN practice, and a minimization of differences between themselves and their other rivals (and controllers), physicians. To be sure, RN struggles were also the result of gender-based policies pursued by physicians who were mostly white men. Physicians sought to limit the work, wages, and status of registered nurses. That gender was a major basis of the limits is indicated by the refusal or reluctance of physicians to see the largely female RN labor force as anything but "handmaidens." In contrast, they accepted men who served as medics in the armed services and, subsequently, other men trained formally into the medical fraternity as "physician assistants," although they had far less training than RNs.

I have tried to show how defensive actions against policies imposed by hospital owners, investors, some charities, and the state as well as offensive actions taken by nursing associations (aimed at professionalizing) are exclusionary and parallel those taken by white male workers and professionals. Nursing associations have established barriers to easy access to formal schooling, to on-the-job training, and to the recognition of job experience. Hence they reinforced existing class, racial, and ethnic hierarchies among women in nursing in the United States.

Women in the more privileged stratum of workers, that is, educators and registered nurses, coped with fears about the real experiences of being replaced or otherwise undercut by less-trained workers. They did so by trying to prevent the development of pools of other workers and, when they failed, to establish clear boundaries around the rights and privileges of lower-grade jobs.

Racism is implicated. Black graduate nurses were excluded from southern state nursing associations until well after World War II. Black women remain a small percentage of professional nurses except in cities with large black populations. They and Hispanic women are disproportionately licensed nurses and nurses assistants. The racist consequences of manpower policies have been invisible to RNs or, at least, they were discussed rarely in the nursing literature until the 1970s.

Gender subordination is implicated. The restructuring of the educational composition of nursing has been shaped by gender politics. Decisions made in the private sector and in state institutions about appropriate training, wage levels, and even the reasons given for nursing training programs are premised on gender ideologies. Many working-class poor women have been trained for female-typed jobs that are lower paid than the occupations for which men were trained (U.S. Department of Health, Education and Welfare 1974). An evaluation of vocational education noted that women and girls were trained for jobs with low wages and few chances for upward mobility, so that "a segment of the population [was] being trained for poverty or near-poverty" (National Coalition for Women and Girls in Education 1988, 27).

Women act against other women across subclass and racial and ethnic lines. Working-class resistance to the erosion of the privileges of men in the workplace has been mainly through unions, professional societies, and associations. So has the resistance of the upper-grade nursing workers. Women workers express no special female values or moral concerns about their class relations with other women from lower-class fractions and insubordinated racial and ethnic groups (Gilligan 1982). Instead, women take actions to maintain their own relatively more privileged race- and class-based positions much as men have done.

Women in the United States workplace use an argument similar to that used by men, justifying their exclusionary practices by invoking a *principle of merit*. Ironically, this is the same principle used by liberal feminists to challenge sexism. Merit-based awards assume that rewards flow from differences in training and individual performance and that some fundamental differences among workers prevent the lower-grade worker from *learning* the content of upper-grade jobs.

My case study suggests that women try to defend their job privileges under capitalism, as men do, by using a justification that parallels a fundamental proposition of sexism. Men have argued against equal treatment for women on the grounds that the sexes are unequal. Struggles for equity in the workplace assume the need for fundamental *inequalities* and simply shift the focus from presumptive biological inequalities to presumptive credential and performance ones. Women argue in the frame of "the myth of professional-managerial privilege" that upper-level workers deserve more rewards and privileges because of merit, however tenuous and loose the links really are (Glazer 1987). The struggle of women for *equity with men* became translated by unions and professional associations into militant demands for a "fairer" distribution of rewards among existing job hierarchies, albeit across gender. But the hierarchies themselves, so-called employer classification systems, may be removed from collective bargaining as issues of managerial prerogatives only. Women workers really have no need to invoke racist or class-based prejudices, because the underlying rationales of inequity—sexism, racism, and class privilege—are shared: justice is presumed to mean a correspondence between individual rewards, individual credentials and performance, and of course, the contribution that a job makes to organizational goals and societal well-being. The result is that women may argue against gender differences and matching the differences with rewards.

Emancipation as the alternative legitimating ideology to equity has only a very minor place in the contemporary American women's movement. In its absence, upper-level women workers, as do men, lack a framework for even speculating about the desirability of supporting those in lower strata and other social ethnic groups. In the United States, it seems logical that upper-grade women workers will try to protect themselves from encroachments by lower-grade women workers by acting against rather than with or for those women.

References

American Nurses Association. 1981. *ANA's Economic and General Welfare Program*. Kansas City, MO: ANA.

"Are nurses self-seeking?" 1921. *American Journal of Nursing* 22:73-74.

Ashley, J. 1976. *Hospitals, Paternalism, and the Role of the Nurse*. New York: Teachers College, Columbia University.

Baron, A. 1987. "Contested terrain revisited: Technology and gender definitions of work in the printing industry, 1850-1920." In B. D. Wright et al. (eds)., *Women, Work and Technology*. Ann Arbor: University of Michigan Press.

Berthgold, L. 1987. "Business and the pushcart vendors in the age of supermarkets." *International Journal of Health Services*, 17:7-26.

Blau, F. and W. Hendricks. 1979. "Occupational segregation by sex: Trends and prospects." *Journal of Human Resources*, 14:197-210.

Bonacich, E. 1972. "A theory of ethnic antagonism: The split labor market." *American Sociological Review*, 37:547-59.

Braverman, H. M. 1974. *Labor and Monopoly Capital. The Degradation of Work in the Twentieth Century*. New York: Monthly Review Press.

Brown, E. L. 1948. *Nursing for the Future*. New York: Russell Sage.

_____ 1970. *Nursing Reconsidered*. Philadelphia: J. B. Lippincott.

Buhler-Wilkerson, K. 1983. "False dawn: The rise and decline of public health nursing in America, 1900-1930." In E. Langemann (ed.), *Nursing History. New York: Teachers College, Columbia University*.

Bullough, V. and B. Bullough. 1978. *The Care of the Sick*. New York: Prodist.

Burgess, M. A. 1928. *Nurses, Patients and Pocketbooks*. New York: Committee on the Grading of Nursing Schools.

Butter, I., E. Carpenter, B. Kay, and R. Simmons. 1985. *Sex and Status: Hierarchies in the Health Workforce*. Ann Arbor: University of Michigan School of Public Health.

Cockburn, C. 1984. *Brothers*. London: Pluto.

Cohn, S. 1985. *The Process of Ocupational Sex-typing*. Philadelphia: Temple University Press.

Cooper, P. 1987. *Once a Cigarmaker: Men, Women and Work Culture in American Cigar Factories, 1900-1919*. Urbana: University of Illinois Press.

Edwards, A. 1943. "Sixteenth census of the United States: 1940." *Population: Comparative Occupation Statistics for the United States, 1870-1940*. Washington, DC: GPO.

Fondiller, S. H. 1983. *The Entry Dilemma*. New York: National League for Nursing.

Gilligan, C. 1982. *In a Different Voice*. Cambridge, MA: Harvard University Press.

Ginzberg, E. 1948. *A Program for the Nursing Profession*. New York: Macmillan.

Glass, L. and L. Eisner. 1981. "CETA as a vehicle to recruit welfare recipients and the unemployed into the home care field." *Home Health Services Quarterly*, 2 (Fall): 5-21.

Glazer, N. Y. 1984. "Servants to capital: Unpaid domestic labor and paid work." *Review of Radical Political Economics*, 16:61-87.

_____ 1987. "Questioning eclectic practice in curriculum change." *Signs*, 12:293-304.

_____ 1988a. "Overlooked and overworked: Women's unpaid and paid labor in the American health services 'cost crisis.'" *International Journal of Health Services*, 18:317-39.

_____ 1988b. "The war on poverty and the war on women: Librarianship, social work, teaching and nursing." Paper presented at the annual meeting of the Eastern Sociological Society, Philadelphia.

_____ 1990. "The home as workshop: Women as amateur caregivers in the U.S. health services industry." *Gender & Society*, 4:479-99.

Greenwald, M. 1980. *Women, War and Work: The Impact of World War I on Women Workers in the United States*. Westport, CT: Greenwood.

Hartmann, H. 1976. "Capitalism, patriarchy, and job segregation by sex." *Signs*, 1:137-69.

_____. 1981. "The family and household as the locus of gender, class, and political struggle: The example of housework." *Signs*, 6:366-94.

Hine, D. C. 1989. *Black Women in White: Racial Cooperation in the Nursing Profession, 1890-1950.* Bloomington: Indiana University Press.

Hughes, E. C. 1958. "Report of a study of the co-ordinated program of Radcliffe College and the Massachusetts General Hospital School of Nursing and of its broader implications." Scheslinger Library Archives (BC 778).

Janiewski, D. 1985. *Sisterhood Denied: Race, Gender and Class in a New South Community.* Philadelphia: Temple University Press.

Johnston, D. F. 1966. *History and Trends of Practical Nursing.* St. Louis: C. V Mosby.

Keller, E. F. 1982. "Feminism and science." *Signs,* 7:589-602.

Langemann, E. E. (ed.). 1983. *Nursing History.* New York: Teachers College, Columbia University.

Melosh, B. 1982. *The Physician's Hand: Work, Culture and Conflict in American Nursing.* Philadelphia: Temple University Press.

Milkman, R. 1987. *Gender at Work.?* Urbana: University of Illinois Press.

National Coalition for Women and Girls in Education. 1988. *Working Toward Equity: A Report on Implementation of the Sex Equity Provisions of the Carl D. Perkins Vocational Education Act.* Washington, DC: NCFWGE.

National League for Nursing. 1972. *Licensed Practical Nurses in Nursing Services.* Pub. No. 38-1457:2. New York: National League Office.

Nishi, S. M., and C. P. Wang. 1985. "The status of Asian Americans in the health care delivery system in New York." *New York Journal of Medicine,* 85:153-56.

Richardson, A. J. 1987. "Professionalization and intraprofessional competition in the Canadian accounting profession." *Work and Occupations,* 14:591-615.

Sacks, K. B. 1988. *Caring By the Hour.* Urbana: University of Illinois Press.

Scientific Manpower Commission. 1982. *Professional Women and Minorities: A Manpower Data Resource Service,* 3d ed. Table LS-M/H-36:241. Washington, DC: Commission on Professionals in Science and Technology.

Sexton, P. 1981. *The New Nightingales.* New York: Enquiry.

Strober, Myra. 1983. "Toward a general theory of occupational sex segregation." In B. F. Reskin (ed.), *Sex Segregation in the Workplace: Trends, Explanations, Remedies. Reskin.* Washington, DC: National Academy Press.

U.S. Bureau of the Census. 1902. "Twelfth census of the United States: 1900." *Population.* Vol. 2, Part 2. Table 84:11 4. Washington, DC: GPO.

_____ 1914. "Thirteenth census of the United States: 1910." *Population.* Vol. 4. Table VI:428-431. Washington, DC: GPO.

_____ 1923. "Fourteenth census of the United States: 1920." *Population.* Vol. 4. Table 5:356-358. Washington, DC: GPO.

_____ 1933. "Fifteenth census of the United States: 1930." *Population.* Vol. 5. Table 3:84-85. Washington, DC: GPO.

_____ 1943. "Sixteenth census of the United States: 1940." *Population.* Vol. 10. Table 62:88-90. Washington, DC: GPO.

_____ 1953. "U.S. census of population: 1950." Vol. 4. *Special Reports,* Part 1, Chapter A. Employment and personal characteristics. Washington, DC: GPO.

_____ 1963a. "U.S. census of population: 1960." *Special Report: Occupational Characteristics.* PC(2)-8A. Washington, DC: GPO.

_____ 1963b. "U.S. census of population: 1960." *Special Report: Final Report.* PC(2)-7A, Table 3. Washington, DC: GPO.

_____ 1973a. "U.S. census of population: 1970." *Special Report: Occupational Characteristics.* PC(2)-7A, Table 39:594-809. Washington, DC: GPO.

_____ 1973b. "U.S. census of population: 1970." *Special Report: Occupational Characteristics.* PC(2)-7A, Table 17:18-19. Washington, DC: GPO.

_____ 1983. *Detailed Occupation and Years of School Completed by Age for the Civilian Labor Force by Sex, Race and Spanish Origin.* SR PC (80-SI-8), March. Washington DC: GPO.

_____ 1984. "U.S. census of population: 1980." *Characteristics of the Population.* PC 80-1-D1-A, Section A. Table 281; table 278. Washington, DC: GPO.

U.S. Department of Health, Education and Welfare. 1967. *Health Manpower Source Book.* No. 263, Section 2, Nursing Personnel. Table 49:29, 32, 34. Washington, DC: GPO.

_____ 1974. *Overview Study of Employment and Paraprofessionals.* U.S. Social and Rehabilitation Service (SRS) 74-05417-April. Washington, DC: GPO.

_____ 1986. *Fifth Report to the President and Congress, On the Status of Health Personnel in the United States.* DDDS Pub. no. HRS-P-OD-86-1-March. Washington, DC: GPO.

Wagner, D. 1980. "The proletarianization of nursing in the United States, 1932-1946." *International Journal of Health Services,* 10:271-90.

Walby, S. 1986. *Patriarchy at Work.* Minneapolis: University of Minnesota Press.

Winslow, C. E. A., and J. Goldmark. 1923. *Nursing and Nursing Education in the United States* [The Goldmark Report]. New York: Macmillan.

Reprinted from: Nora Y. Glazer, " 'Between a Rock and a Hard Place': Women's Professional Organizations in Nursing and Class, Racial and Ethnic Inequalities," in *Gender and Society,* 5(3), pp. 351-372. Copyright © 1991 by Sage Publications, Inc. Reprinted by permission.

Food for Thought and Application Questions

1. Compare the behavior of professional registered nurses to that of men in the male-dominated occupations described in the preceding chapters in this unit. How do the two sets of workers compare in terms of the strategies they employ to protect their jobs from perceived threats? How do they compare in terms of the consequences of their "protective" behavior for the groups that represent the threat?

2. Glazer described three "sets" of workers in the medical profession: upper tier physicians and hospital managers (mostly men); middle tier professional registered nurses (mostly women); and lower tier licensed practical nurses (mostly women). Which category of workers is *primarily* responsible for limiting the job opportunities and rewards of the other workers? What prevents workers in the female-dominated jobs from uniting and demanding improved job conditions and higher levels of reward from the male-dominated physicians and managers? Can you think of any way of uniting the workers in the female-dominated jobs so they can pursue their common interests? ✦

24

Gender and the Formation of a Women's Profession: The Case of Public School Teaching

Jo Anne Preston

Despite the burgeoning literature on gender and occupations, little attention has been given to the influence of gender in the formation of professions. For almost half a century sociologists have recognized differences between predominantly female professions and predominantly male professions, but most theoretical and empirical considerations of the professionalization process have failed to account for the development of these differences. Without examining the influence of gender in the formation of professions, sociologists have difficulty explaining how inferior status and wages have become associated with female professions. Employing historical data, this chapter seeks to demonstrate how gender affects professionalization of teaching. Evidence from 19th century school records reveals that the development of gender distinctions in wages, in authority, and in cultural representation was an essential part of professionalization of teaching.

Carr-Saunders and Wilson (1933) first identified common characteristics of pre-

dominantly female professions when they developed the category *semiprofessions* to include all major women's professions. Following Carr-Saunders and Wilson's conceptualization, Simpson and Simpson (1969) recognized that women's professions have been governed by more extensive bureaucratic structures than men's professions. Working within a functionalist framework, they proposed that women workers needed greater bureaucratic control due to their lesser commitment to work. Simpson and Simpson also postulated that a woman's concern for her duties outside the workplace induced her to submit more readily to authority. Gender, in this formulation, has an impact on professionalization by calling forth extensive bureaucratic structures. Although correctly identifying bureaucracy as characteristic of many women's professions, Simpson and Simpson failed to recognize another gender dimension of this development: Men control and often completely make up the bureaucratic structures that govern female professionals.

More recent theoretical considerations of professionalization, eschewing simple ahistorical trait-based views, stress the importance of locating professionalization within its historical period and in reference to external processes. Most, however, do not accord gender much significance. Johnson (1972) conceptualizes professionalization as a process transformed by the growth of the state but ignores the influence of gender in this transformation. He defines professionalization as a process that results in control over an occupation without examining how gender affects that control. Larson (1977), arguing that professions developed as part of the evolution of late-18th-century and 19th-century capitalism, emphasizes the historically bound character of professions as they are locked into broader structural and historical processes. Although she discusses how a category of supervisors was created as a result of the bureaucratization of teaching, she fails to recognize that most of these newly created supervisory positions were filled by men whereas women remained the vast majority of classroom teachers. These gender distinctions, with their attendant wage and power differences, constituted an integral part of the professionalization of teaching.

Abbott (1988) calls for an ecological perspective, viewing professions as a system of continuous, historically located struggles over jurisdictions. In his historical analysis, he concludes that gender had limited significance in the formation of professions. He considers that in cases of occupational transformation gender acts only as a following variable. Like Larson, he discusses the emergence of school supervisors with professionalization without recognizing the importance of the growing number of female teachers to the creation of supervisory positions. The increase in female teachers may not have followed bureaucratization as he suggests; rather, bureaucratic structures may have arisen during and after the increased employment of female teachers. Historical evidence shows that the development of male-dominated bureaucratic structures in New England teaching occurred during the feminization of teaching.

Not all contemporary considerations of professionalization have ignored or minimized the importance of gender. In the last decade two English sociologists, Hearn and Witz, independently proposed models to explain the relationship of gender and professionalization. Hearn (1982) formulated a model for gendered professionalization that places the process within a patriarchal society. Based both on a stage theory of professionalization and the conception of female professions as semiprofessions, his model proposes that occupations achieve full professionalization only when they are completely dominated by men; that is, so long as women make up the rank and file in teaching, nursing, social work, and public librarianship, these occupations will be denied many of the benefits accruing to male professions. As men increase their participation in semiprofessions, Hearn forecasts that they will gain more control until, when men compose the entire workforce, a semiprofession becomes a full profession. In his model, the process of professionalization is equated with process of achieving male hegemony. His analysis, however, conflates patriarchal power and professional power, denying women the possibility of achieving professional power. More problematic is his view of semiprofessions as on a continuum with full professions and eventually becoming entirely composed of men. The historical studies of women's professions, such as nursing (Melosh 1982) and public librarianship (Garrison 1979), reveal no such trend. In teaching, the labor force has remained predominantly female since 1990 (Oppenheimer, 1970).

In contrast, Witz (1990, 1992) views professionalization as a process that is profoundly altered by the dynamics of gender relations. Using a neo-Weberian framework, she argues for a model of gendered closure strategies in which men as a dominant social collectivity seek to exclude or to control women who, in turn, respond either by challenging the male monopoly of an occupation or by creating a related, exclusively female occupation. Closure practices—exclusionary, inclusionary, demarcationary, and dual—have gendered dimensions. Gendered agents choose specific closure strategies and bring gender-determined differential power to bear upon specific professionalization projects. Male doctors, for example, choose to exclude women from medicine by employing their greater power over credentialing institutions and the state. Female nurses and midwives, on the other hand, engage in a dual closure strategy which contains both usurpationary and exclusionary activities; they resist domination from male doctors and, at the same time, restrict entry to their own professions. Gendered agents, therefore, can construct women's professions through dual closure strategies. Although Witz's model may explain the development of medical professions, it is less revealing in the case of school teaching, in which state officials have always prevailed and teachers have had little success in influencing the social construction of their profession.

Borrowing from Witz's conception of gendered agents, however, this chapter considers the actions of those gendered agents who influenced the professionalization of teaching, chiefly school reformers Horace Mann and Henry Bernard. In addition to considering the influence of these gendered agents and rather than simply confining their influence to closure strategies, it recognizes that gender "is present in the processes, practices, images and ideologies, and distributions of power" (Acker 1992, p. 567). According to Acker, gender is "the patterning of difference and domination through distinctions between men and women that is integral to many social processes" (p. 565). I argue, therefore, that gender is integral to the process of professionalization. Thus gender, as a part of the process of professionalization, affects both the dynamics and the outcome of the process in a variety of ways. This study employs this broader conceptualization of gender.

The definition of professions and professionalization is more problematic, with little consensus among sociologists. Abbott (1988) defines professions as "exclusive occupational groups applying somewhat abstract knowledge to particular cases" (p. 8). He explains that he arrives at this conceptualization because of its relevance to answering his theoretical questions on how professions control skill and knowledge in relation to one another. The process of professional development of any occupation, he demonstrates, is influenced by jurisdictional conflicts. Abbott proposes that professionalization theory should focus on work rather than the structure of occupations. This study focuses on how gender influences the devel-

opment, structural as well as ideological, of one profession; my conceptualization of professionalization follows from those theoretical formulations that concentrate more extensively on these changes within an occupation. This chapter considers professionalization as a process that can result in the development of bureaucracy (Larson 1977), in the evolution of cultural legitimation (Bledstein 1976), in the establishment of formal training and credentialing with the related raise in material rewards (Wilensky 1964), and in changes in workers' autonomy and control over their occupation (Johnson 1972).

Using these formulations, this study examines the case of the professionalization of teaching in 19th-century Massachusetts. In the United States, school teaching became professionalized first in Massachusetts, which later served as the model for other states. Over the course of the 19th century, driven by the same social and economic forces that professionalized law and medicine (Larson 1979; Starr 1982), it evolved from an undesirable occupation to a more highly regarded profession, experiencing all the changes enumerated above. At the beginning of the century, teaching was a low-status, low-paid occupation demanding little expertise or training. By the end of the century, it was a higher-paid, higher-status profession governed by bureaucratic structures and requiring education in teacher-training colleges and additional formal credentials. Each of these changes was affected by another important transformation in teaching, feminization. As teaching became increasing female through the first half of the century, the changes wrought by professionalization were shaped by the increasing presence of women in the classroom. In the second half of the century, when women composed the vast majority of teachers, gender had even a more powerful impact on workers' control over the profession and workers' autonomy.

I have analyzed the causes of feminization of teaching in New England extensively elsewhere and will not discuss them here at length. My empirical work has demonstrated that the transformation of teaching from a male occupation to a female occupation was a process that took more than 200 years and was finally completed in the 19th century with structural and ideological changes in teaching, both driven by the school reform movement (Preston 1982, 1989, 1993). The new hierarchical job segregation by sex, increased supervision, and a female representation of the ideal teacher all reduced the prejudice against female teachers, the greatest impediment to feminization. Strober and Landford (1986), analyzing 19th-century quantitative school data in six states for the years 1850-1880, also found that feminization was associated with structural changes in teaching. Specifically, they found higher percentages of female teachers in counties where teaching was formalized, where it was calculated by length of the school year and teachers per school, and where women's earning were a small fraction of men's. These changes were also developments in the professionalization of teaching and as such were, in turn, extensively transformed by the increase in female teachers. In related work, Strober and Tyack (1980) identified the development of sex-segregated, male-dominated bureaucratic structures in schooling. Empirical evidence from the history of teaching cited below demonstrates that these sex-segregated bureaucratic structures arose with professionalization and increased the gender gap in absolute wages.

In the following sections, the chapter presents some empirical evidence from the history of teaching demonstrating the impact of gender on professionalization. The evidence reveals that professionalization, rather than being a gender neutral process, was profoundly influenced by gender. The first section explores changes in teachers' autonomy. Freidson (1986), who considers an increase in autonomy critical to professionalization, defines autonomy as "the

right to use discretion and judgment in the performance of their work" (p. 184). Similarly, Jaffe (1989) measured autonomy by "the extent to which employees exercise self-direction and discretion over the execution of their jobs" (p. 381). Others define autonomy as the absence of supervision imposed on the worker. For example, Forsyth and Danisiewicz (1985) conceptualize professional autonomy as a phenomenon "manifested by freedom from the client and employing organizations" (p. 61). To explore the various dimensions of autonomy, this section employs these definitions to examine 19th-century changes in teachers' capacity for self-direction and the degree to which they have control over their work.

The second section presents historical data on the changes in teachers' control over their occupation during professionalization. Johnson (1972) defined a profession as "not an occupation but a way to control an occupation" (p. 45). In contrast, as teaching evolved from a male occupation to a female profession, male administrators assumed more control over recruitment, licensing, and training. Despite the efforts of male and female teachers and prominent female educators, the male leaders of the school reform movement gradually transferred teacher training from female academies to state-dominated normal schools and successfully lobbied for greater state control over credentialing teachers.

The third section of this chapter discusses changes in wages during professionalization. During professionalization wages rose for both men and women teachers. Although not extensively discussed in the work and occupations literature, professionalization customarily elevates financial rewards by creating an elite occupation. Despite feminization, which is associated with declining wages (Reskin and Roos 1990), professionalization caused teachers' wages to rise. More significantly, the gender difference in absolute wages of teachers also increased, with men benefiting more economically from professionalization than did women. The causes of the gender gap in wages are not well-explained by neoclassical economic theories; the problems with these approaches are extensively discussed elsewhere (Marini 1989; Stevenson 1988), and they will not be reviewed here. In spite of the failure of various theoretical approaches to fully account for the gender gap in wages, empirical studies have found a relationship between the gender gap in wages and job segregation by sex (Bielby and Baron 1984; Treiman and Hartmann 1981). Data presented in this section suggest that the increase in the gender gap in teachers' wages was caused, in part, by the creation of sex-segregated bureaucratic structures.

Gender, however, was not expressed solely by structures. A specific cultural representation of the female schoolteacher evolved during professionalization of school teaching, and this representation had a direct effect upon the process. Professions acquire sex-specific ideologies, like all occupations, as they are socially constructed, and these constructions are informed by gender ideology—that is, a set of ideas that consider either men or women better suited to do the work required of an occupation because of their supposed innate qualities. Milkman (1987) identifies these ideas as the "idiom" of an occupation. Although the idiom of every female profession prescribes that women are best suited for that type of work, the content of each idiom is idiosyncratic and not necessarily related to women's domestic roles (Crompton 1987; Milkman 1987); neither is it always shared by the professional workers themselves (Preston 1989, 1993). The construction of the idiom may well be part of image building during the professionalization process and may act to limit the aspirations of the female professionals (Forsyth and Danisiewicz 1985; Hearn 1982). Ideology is crucial to the professionalization of occupations because professions need cultural legitimation (Bledstein 1976). As part of that legitimation process, the public must be convinced that the service rendered is "essential, exclusive, and complex" (Forsyth and Danisiewicz 1985, p. 64). They must view the professional worker as competent to perform the professional service. Section four examines the evolution of a gendered professional image of the school teacher.

The final section of this chapter discusses the findings of limited autonomy and control over the occupation, gendered bureaucratic structures, increased gender gap in wages, and sex-typed ideology. It then speculates on the implication of these findings in light of current understandings of professions and professionalization.

Autonomy in the Teaching Profession

The autonomy of the teacher, whether measured by capacity for self-direction or by degree of control over the work process, declined over the course of the 19th century. In the 18th century, when the occupation was predominantly male, little supervision was exercised over Massachusetts teachers. Teachers' diaries and correspondence reveal that teachers could open and close their schools as their needs dictated. Thomas Robbins, teaching in Torringford in 1798, felt entitled to close his school when he had a pain in his jaw (Tarbox 1886-1887). After he heard of a disturbance in Cambridge in 1775, Scituate schoolmaster Paul Litchfield (1881-1882) closed his school for two and one half days to check on his rooms at Harvard. Earlier in the same week he chose to miss one morning of school because of "rainey weather." Likewise, female teachers had some control over their schedules. Elizabeth Bancroft, a teacher in Groton, freely dismissed her school for funerals and barn raisings during her 1773 summer session (Bancroft, 1793-1799). In these accounts, use of the term *schoolkeeping* rather than *school teaching* indicates the control 18th-century teachers had over their workplace.

From the second decade of the 19th century, when feminization of the winter session began, changes in schooling increased the supervision of teachers. Towns had traditionally reserved the winter sessions, usually equivalent to the summer sessions in length and content, for male teachers while appointing only women to summer session schools. As towns began to hire women for winter session positions, they directed male supervisors to assume more control over schoolteachers' work, curtailing their freedom to execute their job as they chose. The timing of the increase in supervision, coincident with the feminization of the winter sessions, suggests that the state and towns perceived a need to assume more control over an increasingly female workforce. The frequency and character of the selectmen's visits changed in the 1820s with the passage of state legislation granting more powers to the selectmen and requiring more stringent supervision of teachers. The Massachusetts acts of 1826 and 1827 conferred on local school committees, which comprised male leaders of the community, powers to appoint and certify teachers, to visit and inspect the classroom work of the teacher, to direct and supervise the teacher's work, and to select textbooks. Authority to certify and appoint gave the committee the power to decide what personal qualifications and training made an applicant an acceptable teacher. Selection of textbooks allowed the committee to influence the curriculum but not yet the course of study or teaching methods, changes which were to come later (Suzzallo 1906). More importantly, the school committee now had general charge and "superintendence" over the teachers' work. To assure that the school committeemen carried out their new function, the 1826 and 1827 acts stipulated that they visit the classroom once a month without advance notice to observe the teacher and question the students. Superintendence of

the teacher, therefore, increased the control of the administrators, all men, over the standards of teaching and, consequently, diminished teachers' autonomy.

The new superintendence of the teachers is well described by a Massachusetts teacher writing home in 1826:

Dear Achsah,

. . . I am almost tired to death. . . . I have engaged a school. . . . Oh I have been brought under the most rigid laws this season than I ever was in New York State. The Legislature of this state has adopted a new system in regard to public schools. This is that each town choose a committee of five or more to superintend the schools in town . . . that is to process the teacher, select the books and direct the studies and everything concerning the schools. No teacher is entitled to their pay unless they are examined by the committee. . . . They also visit the school the first or second week after commencement and give the teacher notice before coming after that once a month without previous notice to the teacher until the last week when they are there to let them know they are coming. . . . I have been under their contract since the first of May when I went before them for inspection since then they have visited my school six times—sometimes one at a time, sometimes two or more just as they choose but thank fortune I am almost done with them a week from Monday comes my exam on Tuesday I close my school and I think I shall rejoice if I ever did [school] has almost worn me out. . . . It has made my fat checks look rather hollow. (Brammer 1826)

In addition to reporting the changes in Massachusetts school laws, Electa Snow's account also illustrates the resentment generated by the selectmen's expanded authority over teachers' work.

By the 1830s, Massachusetts towns hired male teachers in the winter to supervise female teachers, thereby seeking to lessen their residents' resistance to hiring female teachers for the exclusively male-taught winter session. Towns, for example, often consolidated two district schools during the winter session, assigned the younger students to a female teacher and the older students to a male teacher, and placed "the whole school" under the male teacher (Massachusetts school reports, 1833-1834). These districts often referred to the man as teacher and the woman as assistant teacher. The town of Sunderland, for example, reported that it incorporated two female teachers into the winter session schools as follows:

> District No. 3 and 4 lying near each other unite and in winter have a central school attended by the scholars in each district over ten years of age. This school is taught by a man. Those under ten attend schools in each district taught by a woman. (Massachusetts School Reports 1833-1834)

Sunderland then granted the male teacher authority over the female teachers. Restructuring schooling along gender lines thus maintained male dominance of the winter sessions.

The subsequent proliferation of managerial positions, which accompanied professionalization, further constrained teachers' autonomy. Towns evolved a structure of control and supervision that included a school committee, a superintendent, and one or more principals, all of whom were male, with the exception of principals of female high schools. The most developed of these systems were the fully bureaucratized school systems of cities and large towns. In the bureaucratizing urban school systems that developed with professionalization, full-time administrators, all male, supervised teachers, who were primarily female. In addition, grammar masters began to supervise female assistant teachers.

As shown in Table 24.1, Boston in 1852 hired 37 male grammar schoolmasters and submasters to supervise 138 female "assistants." In 1866, the Boston School

Table 24.1
Hierarchy and Annual Wages of Boston Teaching Positions by Sex, 1852

Position	Number	Wages
Male (N = 82)		
Supervisory		
Superintendent	1	$2,500
High School		
Masters	2	$2,400
Submasters	3	$1,500
Ushers	5	$800-$1,200
Grammar Schools		
Grammar masters	23	$1,500
Writing masters	5	$1,500
Submasters	9	$1,000
Ushers	13	$800
Female (N = 315)		
Grammar Schools		
Head assistants	3	$400
Assistants	135	$250-$300
Primary Schools		
Primary mistresses	177	$300

Source: Report on the Boston Schools, 1852; Massachusetts State School Returns, 1851-1852.

Committee also extended the powers of the grammar masters to include overseeing the primary mistresses in their respective districts. In 1875, new legislation abolished the school committee, created a school board of 24 members, added six new supervisors, and formed a board of supervisors to be chaired by the superintendent (Katz 1987)—actions that definitively placed most of the power in the superintendent's office. Table 24.2 shows the new configuration of hierarchy in the Boston schools. Female and male teachers were segregated not only by job title but also increasingly by the degree of autonomy conferred by the title. By 1876, 48 men held administrative posts as principals whereas one woman occupied the recently created position of assistant principal of the normal school, an institution attended by a majority of female students.

Other female positions in the primary, grammar, and high schools had been divided into first, second, third, and fourth assistants. Boston now gave all women the rank of assistant—assistant principal; first, second, and third assistant in the high schools; normal school assistant; first, second, and third assistant in the grammar schools; and fourth assistant in the primary schools. Gone were the female positions that implied some independence, such as head assistant or primary mistress. All of these changes in job titles accompanied the increase in supervision and the resulting decline in autonomy experienced by teachers. Significantly, the erosion of autonomy was greater among female teachers.

In these bureaucratized school systems, the resident principal and various members of the school committee made frequent, unannounced visits to each classroom to assess the progress of the teacher by examining the students. These evaluations were more extensive than those of the 1820s. In her diary, Lynn, Massachusetts, school teacher Mary Mudge (1854) described one visit as follows:

> Dr. Callaupe and Mr. Ambler into the school this P.M. . . . Heard the 1st class read . . . asked many questions not in their lesson. Harriet Brown got confused and could not spell Alcohol. 2nd class read "The Father" . . . did very well in reading and spelling. 1st class in Colburns recited on division of mixed numbers . . . 1st Class in Geography did well but could not tell what year Greenland was discovered. Dr. [Callaupe] made a few remarks; . . . said he had been well pleased . . . they did well in Geography and Arithmetic and would be excellent readers if they kept their voices up at the comma.

Although female teachers privately lamented the encroachment on their work by the extended, intrusive classroom visits of supervisors, the historical record reveals no direct opposition. Finding no meaningful means of protest, female and

Table 24.2
Hierarchy and Annual Wages of Boston Teaching Positions by Sex, 1876

Position	Number	Wages
Male (N = 124)		
Supervisory		
Superintendent	1	$4,500
Supervisor	6	$4,000
Principal	48[a]	(wages for teaching rank)
High schools		
Master	40	$1,700-$4,000
Submaster		
Usher		
Grammar schools		
Master	87	$1,700-$3,200
Submaster		
Usher		
Female (N = 962)		
High schools		
Assistant principal; first, second, and third assistant; normal school assistant	46	$1,000-$2,000
Grammar schools		
First, second, and third assistant	493	$600-$1,200
Primary schools		
Fourth assistant	423	$600-$800

Source: City of Boston Abstract of Semi-Annual Returns, January 31, 1876.
[a]Principals are also enumerated in high school and grammar schoolmaster categories.

male teachers' most common recourse was to seek alternative employment. Men sought and gained employment in the emerging exclusively male professions of law and medicine. Women, more limited in their options, moved from teaching job to teaching job in search of more suitable employment. For example, in the mid-19th century, Massachusetts school teacher Aurelia Smith, constantly dissatisfied with her work, taught in five towns during her 6-year teaching career. Work biographies of 19th-century Mount Holyoke graduates show that female teachers continually moved from one teaching position to another (Preston 1982).

Even more central to workers' autonomy is the capacity to determine how the work is done. In 18th-century Massachusetts, pedagogy, the method of teaching, remained primitive. Teachers developed what teaching methods they had idiosyncratically. Although they frequently followed a series of texts, teachers could choose the lessons or recitation exercises. Supervisors rarely imposed a method of teaching. Most 18th-century teachers taught alone in one-room schoolhouses; supervision consisted of occasional visits by one or more town selectmen. Because the average selectman had less education than the teacher, he usually concerned himself only with decorum and the physical appearance of the classroom (Suzzallo 1906). Teachers had control over how teaching was done and over other conditions of their work.

Nineteenth-century male administrators, at more elevated positions, began to assume responsibility for developing teaching methods. The science of pedagogy was almost nonexistent in Massachusetts until the first decades of the 19th century, when Horace Mann and other leaders of school reform began to advocate teaching methods. Mann's second annual report (1838) included a treatise on methods of instruction. But even before Mann published his directives, Samuel Hall (1829), founder of the first teacher-training institution in America, published his *Lectures on Schoolkeeping*. In his lectures, he spelled out the teacher's appropriate presentation of lessons, the proper curriculum to be taught in each type of school, and the correct relationship between the teacher and the student. Such instructions, when followed, may have improved teachers' performance in the classroom. From the standpoint of the autonomy of the worker, however, teaching methods imposed by managers reduced teachers' control over the work process. Later developments in curriculum reform further restricted teachers' decision making in the formulation of the content and methods of teaching (Apple 1986). Consequently, the mid- to late-19th-century teacher became less autonomous as a result of the professionalization of teaching.

Thus changes in the structure and content of teaching during the professionalization of the occupation curtailed the professional workers' control over their work. Significantly, I argue, the professional workers were increasingly women. Because 19th-century women's low social status and subordination to men in all other aspects of their lives allowed school reformers to create male-dominated bureaucratic structures to control female teachers and because women's limited employment opportunities curtailed their options, teaching evolved as a profession that was structured by a sex-segregated system of hierarchical control and supervision. This hierarchical restructuring of teaching permitted reformers to achieve their goal of making schooling a more influential social institution without granting power to the growing number of female teachers. Gender, then, rather than having an influence after the fact, determined important and enduring characteristics of the teaching profession. These changes are in contrast to those occurring in the 19th century male occupations of law and medicine. The professionalization of these occupations resulted in greater power for the individual worker and for the profession in general (Larson 1977; Starr 1982). The much more limited autonomy of the teachers resembled that experienced by workers in other female professions. For example, the development of managerial positions primarily held by men can also be found in the professionalization of librarianship (Garrison 1979). Although nursing did not develop a male-dominated managerial structure, control was exercised by a related male profession—that of medicine (Hearn 1982; Witz 1990).

Control Over the Teaching Profession

Teachers never achieved control over the development of their emerging profession. During the course of professionalization, the state took over the responsibility of training teachers, denying teachers authority over the training of the new members of their profession. This further constraint on female teachers' autonomy came about as state-financed and state-controlled normal schools replaced the female academies as the educators of teachers. Normal schools, first established in the late 1830s, became the primary institution for teacher training by the end of the Civil War. The state legislature also mandated criteria for certification and employment (Woody 1929).

Female academies were first established in New England in the 18th century and proliferated during the antebellum period. Most academies were not specifically aimed at training women to become teachers; rather, they were devoted to educating young women in liberal arts, science, and religion. Many academy founders explicitly saw themselves as committed to improving the situation of women, who were barred from studying at men's colleges (Woody 1929). Some academies even conferred explicitly female degrees. The Springfield Female Collegiate Institute, for example, awarded an M.E.L., or Mistress of English Literature, an L.B.A., or Lady Baccalaureate, and an M.L.A., or Mistress of Liberal Arts (Springfield Female Collegiate Institute 1860-1861).

Less concerned with intellectual development, the curriculum at normal schools prescribed methods of teaching developed by male administrators. When the first normal school was established in 1839, female academies were the main educators of female teachers. By 1860, with the founding in Massachusetts of five more normal schools, school committees—with the encouragement of the state legislature—hired normal school graduates over female academy graduates (Magnum 1928). Increasingly, more teachers prepared for their work at normal schools with their state-mandated course of study rather than at female academies. Because normal schools emphasized methods and most female academies taught only subject matter, leaving choice of method to the prospective teacher, the transition from female academies to normal schools gave the state control over the training of new workers.

The state also usurped any power teachers may have possessed over recruitment and standards of the profession. By passing legislation requiring training in state-run normal schools and setting criteria for certification, the state, rather than a professional organization, assumed control of entry to the profession. Town school committees still retained the power to hire teachers; these committees, however, were directly influenced by the voters—not by teachers' associations. How voters conceived of the proper role of the teacher in any particular historical period can further dictate what the school committee sets as professional standards (Freidson 1986).

Teachers made repeated unavailing efforts to influence the development of teaching. In 1830, 45 men met in Topsfield to form the Essex County Teachers' Association, whose express purpose was "the improvement of teachers and the system of education generally." By the 1850s, the organization allowed women to attend their lectures but reserved all policy making to male members. In its first 3 decades, the organization sponsored lectures on timely educational issues, petitioned Congress for federal support of education, and established a fund to aid disabled teachers. It expressed its dissatisfaction with the current system of supervising teachers through published essays in *The Massachusetts Teacher*. Unfortunately, the association's recommendations on this issue and other matters were spurned by state officials. Norfolk County also formed an all-male teachers' association in 1830 for "mutual improvement, with reference to professional duties." It too failed to shape the profession. Later teachers' organizations, such as the American Institute for Instruction, an organization also dominated by men, suffered a similar fate (Messerli 1972).

Promoters of female education were also enthusiastic supporters of the professionalization of teaching, perceiving it as a way of increasing the status and wages of female teachers and ultimately elevating them to a position equal to that of male professionals. Prominent educators Catherine Beecher and Emma Willard advocated professional status for female teachers (Lutz 1964; Sklar 1973). Catherine Beecher (1851), for example, argued for upgrading teaching to a "profession for women, as honorable and lucrative for her as the legal, medical, and theological professions are for men" (p. 79). Rather than establishing separate teacher-training schools run by the state, Beecher recommended adding teaching departments to already existing female academies (Beecher 1835). Correspondence of female teachers describes similar aspirations for their new profession (Preston 1989). These women, however, lacked the power to control the development of the profession. It was the school reformers and the state legislatures with their greater political power who ultimately determined its shape and content. Teachers became the objects of school reform: Having found no effective means of gaining political influence, they were excluded from active participation.

Furthermore, with the development of bureaucratic structures during professionalization, male administrators directly oversaw the implementation of state- or local-mandated educational policy. As managers, they had decision-making power over the formulation of classroom instruction. Frequent supervision of classroom instruction ensured that certain pedagogical techniques were followed. Formal and impromptu oral examinations of students,

as in the case cited in Mary Mudge's diary, guaranteed that teachers adhered to certain curricular directives. By 1880, the very content of teaching became determined and enforced by male administrators, not teachers, the vast majority of whom were now women.

Professionalization and the Gender Gap in Wages

Massachusetts teachers' wages rose from 1840 until the end of the century. Yet many studies of feminized occupations find that wages decline (Reskin and Roos 1990). Thus, in teaching, the effects of professionalization must have outweighed those of feminization. When broken down by sex, however, the data show that men benefited more from professionalization than did women. The average monthly wages of Massachusetts teachers from 1840 to 1870, inclusive of board, are presented in Table 24.3. Men's wages rose from $33.08 in 1840 to $74.24 in 1870, whereas women's wages rose from $12.75 in 1840 to only $30.24 in 1870. The gender difference in absolute wages grew from $20.33 to $44. Relative wages, however, remained nearly the same; women continued to make approximately 40% of what male teachers earned.

Towns exploited the gender gap in pay to contain the cost of the wage bill. By hiring female teachers, they could raise teachers wages without significantly increasing the school budget. If, for example, a town hired three male teachers and one female teacher in 1840 at the respective average wages, the cost of wages would be $111.99. By hiring one female to replace one male teacher in 1850, at the average wages paid for that year, the town expense for teachers' wages would be only $98.62. In 1860, if the same town replaced one more male teacher with a female teacher, paying the higher average wage, the cost to the town would be $110.50, less than the 1840 figure. Thus feminization contained or even lowered the total cost of wages to the towns, even as professionalization increased the wages of both male and female teachers.

Even with the gender gap in wages, 19th century women sought teaching positions. Although female teachers continued to earn less than male teachers, increasingly they earned more than other categories of female workers. In 1840, textile corporations in Massachusetts paid female operatives approximately the same wages as Massachusetts towns paid female teachers. After 1840, female teachers' wages rose while female textile workers' wages plummeted; by 1960 female teachers earned twice the wages of millgirls (Gitelman 1967). Other women's occupations, such as shoe binder, seamstress, tailoress, and domestic service, paid even less than factory work (Abbott 1910). In comparison to other forms of employment available to women, school teaching, despite the gender gap in pay, represented a remunerative opportunity (Carter 1986).

Although women schoolteachers were relatively well paid, the gendered wage differential still denied women the full advantages of professionalization. Towns that were willing to pay higher wages for professional workers paid more to male teachers. Data from local school reports indicate that the greater gender gap may be related to the establishment of hierarchical structures during professionalization. In bureaucratized school systems, where qualifications for teachers were the most

stringent, school committees hired men as supervisors of female teachers. Men not only held different jobs from female teachers but ones that were regarded as clearly superior and that paid higher wages. The wage structure in the Boston school system in 1852, for example, indicates a clear relationship between hierarchical structure and the gender gap in earnings: Men hold all the higher-paying, supervisory positions and women predominate in the lower-paying teaching positions (see Table 24.1). With the increased number of supervisory positions, all filled by men, and the greater preponderance of female teachers in lower-level teaching positions in 1876, the gender gap widened. In 1852, the average male wage was $1,134 and the average female wage, $290. In 1876, the average male wage rose to $2,654 while the average female wage increased to only $840 (see Table 24.2).

Even in those towns that did not report by job title a special supervisory role for men, male teachers may have acted as supervisors to female assistant teachers, a practice discussed earlier and a rationale for differential pay. To further complicate matters, some towns routinely included the wages of their male principals and superintendents in their calculations of the average male teacher wage, thus inflating the wage of regular male teachers (Preston 1982). Much of the gender gap in wages, therefore, may be accounted for by the assignment of supervisory tasks to male

Table 24.3
Average Monthly Wages (inclusive of Board) of Massachusetts Teachers, by Sex, 1840-1880

Year	1839-40	1849-50	1859-60	1869-70
Males	$33.08	$34.89	$50.56	$74.24
Females	$12.75	$14.42	$19.98	$30.24
Female wages as percent of male wages	39%	41%	40%	41%

Source: Massachusetts Board of Education, 1839-1870.

teachers, a practice which became widespread during professionalization.

The wage differential was not wholly due to men's supervisory positions in teaching, however. Evidence from antebellum Massachusetts shows that where the professionalization and feminization of teaching had yet to have much impact, male teachers, segregated from female teachers only by the season in which they taught, earned higher wages. In 10 towns that continued under the district system, male teachers, all of whom taught in the winter season, earned on average higher wages than did female teachers—almost all of whom taught in the summer session. Because most towns did not hire female teachers for the winter session and because each male teacher taught alone in a one-room district school, the male teachers could not have been supervisors. Female teachers who taught in the winter session made on average more than females teaching in the summer but less than their male counterparts. The higher wage for female teachers may have been due to their participation in the winter session, which was considered "men's work."

Prevailing attitudes toward women workers may also have contributed to women's lower wages. Many state and local school officials announced in their annual reports their intention of paying female teachers, yet to be hired, lower wages than male teachers. School reformer Henry Bernard, for example, argued that "a female teacher could be hired for twelve weeks for the same price as hiring a male teacher for five weeks" (Rhode Island Board of Education 1846, p. 144). Massachusetts town school reports are replete with remarks on the economic advantages of hiring female teachers. Gardner reported "Females may be procured for sixteen dollars per month . . . males [for] . . . twenty dollars a month" (Massachusetts Board of Education 1845, p. 128). Northbridge stated that "A female might be employed . . . at an expense of nearly one half a male" (Massachusetts Board of Educa-

tion 1845, p. 150). The savings realized by paying female teachers less than males for the winter session, Ashburnham calculated, "would hire a competent man for six months" (Massachusetts Board of Education 1840-1841, p. 85). Significantly, the wage was determined by the gender of the worker, because no other differences between the two workers were known to the school committeemen. This evidence suggests that women's work was devalued independent of its structural position in the occupation. Moreover, it shows that jobs became female jobs as women were hired for them; that is, a teaching job acquired a woman's wage as women were hired.

The absolute wage gap between male and female teachers increased over the 19th century. As shown in Table 24.3, male teachers earned on average $21.33 a month more than female teachers in 1840 and by 1870, male teachers earned on average $44.00 a month more than female teachers. Many of the male workers in this category were administrators, and by 1870 their numbers had increased, a possible cause for the widening the gender gap in absolute wages. The further development of hierarchical structures in teaching, then, may have been the cause of the change in absolute wages.

Centralized, bureaucratic school systems also created the conditions for collective action. In the Lynn school system, female teachers organized to improve their wages. In 1854, Lynn schoolteacher Mary Mudge recorded the following in her diary: "about 8 1/2 o'clock Miss Row, Miss Nickerson, Cook, and Dodge called to get me to sign a petition to have the Female Teachers' salaries raised. Called with them on Misses Newhall, Neal and Anna. They all signed." Their campaign was unsuccessful. Lynn schools records report no increase in female wages in the next year (Lynn [MA] School Committee 1855). An examination of 92 female teachers' writings revealed no other collective endeavor to improve wages (Preston 1993). As discussed above, most female teachers strove to improve their situation by seeking alternative employment.

Undeterred by female teachers' complaints or brief tenure, school committees continued to appoint male supervisors at superior wages. Thus, the material gains from the professionalization of teaching continued to affect male and female workers differently. Higher-paying supervisory positions for men amplified the existing gender gap in wages caused by sex segregation by season and by discriminatory attitudes. These attitudes were strengthened by the association of gender ideology with the newly constructed jobs within teaching, a development that also influenced the creation of a gendered image of the professional teacher.

Professionalization and the Cultural Representation of the Female Schoolteacher

During the professionalization of school teaching, Horace Mann, Henry Bernard, and other school reformers created a representation of the ideal professional teacher to persuade towns to increase the wages and status of female teachers. Like other aspects of the professionalization process, this cultural representation was gendered; the conception of the professional teacher as female constituted an integral part of the social construction of the profession. The reformers argued that women possessed gender-specific characteristics that enabled them to do the work required of professional teachers: that the characteristics attributed to women in the 19th century, qualities of nurturance and moral rectitude, gave women a special expertise in teaching.

The school reformers, all men, actively created and propagated a new cultural representation of the female teacher that later became firmly implanted in the educational and popular literature of the second half of the 19th century. The ideology of woman's domestic sphere, ideas that emerged with the advent of industrial capitalism, furnished the basis for this new representation. Both reformers and female advocates of women's education—Catherine Beecher, Mary Lyons, and Emma Willard—borrowed selectively from this dominant ideology to argue that the ideal teacher must be a woman. Catherine Beecher strove for 40 years to advance the cause of women by advocating that women's domestic duties necessitated improving female education and hiring women as public school teachers (Sklar 1973). Because women lacked access to political power, especially within the male-dominated state administration, the view of the female teacher promoted by Beecher and other female educators, one that stressed a capacity for intellectual achievement and merited high wages, failed to predominate. Instead, the representation provided by the reformers, which attributed to women a lack of interest in wages and little intellectual ability, became the 19th-century cultural image of the female schoolteacher.

The school reformers had one primary goal: They sought to create a school system that would socialize students to the changing requirements of work in industrial society by instilling habits of obedience and respect for authority (Bowles and Gintis 1976; Katz 1971). Whether school reform created an appropriate workforce for New England factories, or more generally quelled social disorder by producing more obedient citizens, the school reformers' rhetoric leaves no doubt that they perceived a new school system as critical to the smooth transition from an agricultural to an industrial society. In achieving this goal, the reformers concluded that professional female teachers were essential. To promote public acceptance of women as professional teachers and to encourage school committees to hire them, the school reformers created a new conception of the female teacher, which they propagated by using lectures, essays, and reports widely disseminated throughout New England (Preston 1989, 1993).

Four supposedly innate qualities of 19th-century women made them the appropriate teachers for the new school system: high moral character, disregard for material gain, limited intellectual capacity, and a natural love of children. The first quality, high moral character, was congruent with their mission to instill in children appropriate values. Horace Mann, the most eminent of the school reformers, argued in his numerous essays and lectures that female teachers were more qualified to teach because "by nature" they possessed purer morals (Massachusetts Board of Education 1841). Another school reformer, Henry Bernard, proclaimed that women were ideal teachers because, among "their peculiar talents," were "purer morals" (in Rhode Island Board of Education, 1845, p.11). Drawing on this supposed natural quality of women, the reformers hoped to reduce the use of corporal punishment in the schools, substituting instead moral control. They advocated that "moral influence should be substituted, as far as possible, in place of mere coercion" and that "it must follow that women are, in most respects, preeminently qualified to administer such a discipline" (Bernard in Rhode Island Board of Education 1852, p. 6). School reformers, then, sought to persuade the 19th-century public that purer morals, as assumed characteristics of women, uniquely qualified them to assume professional positions in the new school systems.

School reformers also ascribed to 19th century women a lack of ambition, especially for financial gain. Mann first proposed this self-serving belief in the 1841 school report: "As a class, they [women] never look forward as young men invariably do, . . . to build up a fortune for themselves; and hence the sphere of hope and of effort is narrower, . . . and the whole forces of the mind are more readily concentrated upon present duties." He cited this as one of the characteristics that make "females incomparably better teachers for young children than males" (Massachusetts Board of Education 1841, p. 45). Although this quality is consistent with moral purity, it contradicts the notion of the monetary value of expert labor. Here one must consider that the development of professional ideology, as a part of the professionalization process, is gendered: Among the emerging 19th-century professions, the desire for financial remuneration consistent with the value of their expert knowledge is acceptable for male professionals in law and medicine, but not for female professionals in teaching and nursing. As part of the professionalization of teaching, school reformers represented female teachers as morally pure, self-sacrificing professional workers. Accordingly, towns could pay female teachers low wages and still regard them as professionals.

Third, school reformers argued that female teachers, like all women, had limited capacity and interest in intellectual endeavors. Since the colonial period, the predominant view was that women had little intellectual capacity. Contrary to popular thinking, the reformers asserted that women did have enough mental ability to teach school, but they did not go so far as to claim that women's intellect was equal to men's. Women, "although deficient in natural brilliance and literary attainments," could acquire enough knowledge to teach children (Rust in New Hampshire Board of Education, 1848, p. 8). Their lack of intelligence was compensated for by other qualities. In the "female character there is always a preponderance of affection over intellect," which, reasoned Mann, "made the female . . . the guide and guardian of young children" (Massachusetts Board of Education 1842, p. 9). The limited intellectual abilities ascribed to female schoolteachers were sufficient for teaching. Their claim to expert knowledge, however, lay not in their intellect but in their unique relationship to children.

Women's "natural" association with children proved the most compelling reason for school committees to consider women the ideal teachers. Transformations in 19th-century gender ideology prescribed a more intense relationship between mother and child. Elaborating on this new conception of motherhood, school reformers extolled the special ability of women to teach children: "Women's stronger parental impulse makes the society of children delightful [for them], and turns duty into pleasure" (Mann in Massachusetts Board of Education 1841, p. 45); "The influence of the mother on the young mind is far greater than even the father" (Cembe in Rhode Island Board of Education 1853, p. 87); "Heaven has plainly appointed females as the natural instructors of young children, and endowed them with those qualities of mind and disposition . . . a greater measure of the gentleness so winning and grateful to the feelings of a child, and of . . . patient forbearance" (Bernard in Connecticut Board of Education 1840, p. 6). This special relationship extended to the ability to control children "by the silken cord of affection, [which has] led many a stubborn will, and wild ungovernable impulse into habits of obedience and study" (Bernard in Connecticut Board of Education 1840, p. 7). Drawing on the dominant gender ideology of the mid-19th century, the school reformers portrayed female teachers as possessing unique talents enabling them to become superior teachers. These talents were not acquired through rigorous professional training; they were bestowed on women "by nature."

My examination of 92 female teachers' correspondence found that these 19th-century women held different self-conceptions (Preston 1993). Their correspondence is replete with discussions of wages. Instead of eschewing the material rewards of teaching as claimed by Mann, Massachusetts women constantly bargained for better wages and, if the school committee was unyielding, sought better-paying teaching positions. Female teachers, rather than limiting their intellectual goals, read poetry, studied foreign languages, attended public lectures, and wrote compositions. Although the woman concerned themselves with moral questions, especially as related to religious doctrine, they did not conceive of moral behavior as a means of managing unruly children. Spurning "moral suasion," female teachers maintained discipline by employing various forms of corporal punishment. Although some demonstrated affection and concern for their students, many others, shocked by their first contact with the bedraggled and underfed children who populated 19th-century public schools, expressed disapproval and disdain.

In spite of female teachers' self-conceptions, the four qualities of the ideal 19th-century schoolteacher—moral rectitude, limited intellectual ambition, disregard for material gains, and a natural love of children—constituted the popular cultural representation. All were derived from the prevailing mid-19th-century gender ideology, which postulated separate spheres for men and women. Because this ideology consigned male and female qualities to mutually exclusive categories, only women could fulfill the social ideal of the professional teacher. The evolution of this social ideal of the professional worker was, therefore, necessarily a gendered process.

Once in place, the cultural representation of the ideal worker is difficult to modify and hence acts as a conservative force upon an occupation (Milkman 1987). In the present case, it principally affects the actions and attitudes of the employers and the public, although, as stated before, not the female schoolteachers themselves (Preston 1989). This incorporation of a certain conception of the female teacher in the social construction of the teaching profession offers a compelling explanation for the persistence of sex-typing in teaching. Moreover, it may account for why certain negative characteristics of teaching—low wages, limited intellectual content, restricted upward mobility—are so resistant to change.

Conclusions

Gender influenced historically specific changes in teaching during the process of its professionalization, including sex-segregated structures of supervision and bureaucratic control. These structures allowed male administrators and state legislatures to curtail the autonomy of female teachers and limit their collective control over the teaching profession. By examining changes in wage levels, one finds that whereas professionalization raised the wages of both male and female workers, men benefited more from the increase. The gender gap in teachers' pay was associated with sex-segregated hierarchical structures and job location, and with discriminatory attitudes. Finally, the chapter identifies and discusses four qualities of the ideal professional schoolteacher and shows how the evolution of this ideal, based on 19th-century gender ideology, specified that women would make the best professional teachers.

The evidence presented shows that men came to dominate teaching during professionalization—a finding that confirms the models proposed by both Hearn and Witz. Other findings of this investigation are not accounted for in either model. Witz (1992) ignores the influence of gender ideology. Hearn (1982), although acknowledging the importance of gender ideology, limits its power to persuading women to enter a women's profession—a contention that has been contradicted by empirical studies (Preston 1989, 1993). Moreover, Hearn attributes the content of gender ideology to women's domestic roles, an assertion disputed by Milkman's study of the electrical and automobile industries (1987). Both ignore the gendered effect professionalization has on wages. Witz accords women's actions the power of usurping a portion of a profession from men while, through closure, also denying entry to other workers. Hearn disregards the agency of women in professionalization. In 19th-century Massachusetts, women attempted to shape teaching so it would be a profession equal to men's; their efforts, however, were overpowered by those of male state officials. A complete model of gendered professionalization should therefore consider how gender affects wages, professional ideology, and actions of agents.

Even without a comprehensive model, the empirical findings of this investigation support the proposition that professionalization is a gendered process: that occupations in the process of becoming female professions undergo unique changes that in time may differentiate them from male professions. The transformations occurring in the teaching occupation during professionalization included formation of male-dominated bureaucratic structures restricting autonomy, wage restructuring leading to greater gender differences in absolute wages while increasing wages overall, and the creation of a cultural representation of the female teacher. The evidence suggests that female professions may not be occupations in a state of arrested development, stalled on the road to full professionalization, as the category semiprofessions implies; rather, they may be in many respects qualitatively different from male professions, acquiring these differences during the process of professionalization.

The generality of this interpretation will remain unclear until the results of investigations on the influence of gender on professionalization of other occupations can be assessed. Furthermore, comparative data based on historical studies will enable sociologists to determine if the social construction of all female professions differs from that of male professions. Such findings would have important theoretical implications for the sociology of the professions because they would indicate that current conceptions of a profession and of professionalization should be revised to consider gender as constitutive of the process.

References

Abbott, A. 1988. *The System of Professions.* Chicago: The University of Chicago Press.

Abbott, E. 1910. *Women in Industry: A Study in American Economic History.* New York: Appleton.

Acker, J. 1992. "From sex roles to gendered institutions." *Contemporary Sociology,* 21(5):565-569.

Apple, M. W. 1986. *Teachers and Texts: A Political Economy of Class and Gender Relations in Education.* New York: Routledge and Kegan Paul.

Bancroft, E. 1793-1799. *Diary.* Boston: Massachusetts Historical Society.

Beecher, C. 1835. *Essay on the Education of Female Teachers.* New York: Van Nostrand & Dwight.

_____. 1851. *True Remedies for the Wrongs of Women.* Boston: Phillips, Sampson.

Bielby, W. T. and J. N. Baron. 1984. "A woman's place is with other women: Sex segregation within firms." In B. F. Reskin (Ed.), *Sex Segregation in the Workplace: Trends, Explanations, Remedies.* Washington, DC: National Academy Press:27-55.

Bledstein, B. J. 1976. *The Culture of Professionalism.* New York: W. W. Norton.

Bowles, S., and H. Gintis. 1976. *Schooling in Capitalist America: Educational Reform and the Contradictions of Economic Life.* New York: Basic Books.

Brammer, E. S. 1826. *Correspondence, 1818-1838.* Berkeley: Bancroft Library. University of California.

Carr-Saunders, A. M., and P. A. Wilson. 1933. *The Professions.* Oxford: Oxford University Press.

Carter, S. B. 1986. "Occupational segregation, teachers' wages and American economic growth." *Journal of Economic History,* 46(2):373-383.

Connecticut Board of Education. 1837-1860. *Connecticut School Reports.* Hartford: Author.

Crompton, R. 1987. "Gender, status, and professionalism." *Sociology,* 21(3):413-428.

Essex County Teachers' Association. 1830. *Journal, 1830-1888.* Salem, MA: James Duncan Phillips Library, Peabody and Essex Institute.

Forsyth, P. B. and T. J. Danisiewicz. 1985. "Toward a theory of professionalization." *Work and Occupations,* 12(5):59-76.

Freidson, E. 1986. *Professional Powers: A Study of the Institutionalization of Formal Knowledge.* Chicago: University of Chicago Press.

Garrison, D. 1979. *Apostles of Culture: The Public Librarian and American Society, 1876-1920.* New York: Free Press.

Gitelman, H. M. 1967. "The Waltham system and the coming of the Irish." *Labor History,* 8:227-253.

Hall, S. R. 1829. *Lectures on Schoolkeeping.* Unpublished manuscript, Boston.

Hearn, J. 1982. "Notes on patriarchy, professionalization and the semi-professions." *Sociology,* 16(2):184-202.

Jaffe, D. 1989. "Gender inequality in the workplace autonomy and authority." *Social Science Quarterly,* 70(2):375-390.

Johnson, T. J. 1972. *Professions and Power.* London: Macmillan.

Kanter, R. 1976. "The impact of hierarchical structures on the work behavior of women and men." *Social Problems,* 23:415-430.

Katz, M. B. 1971. *Class, Bureaucracy and Schools: The Illusion of Educational Change in America.* New York: Praeger.

_____. 1987. *Reconstructing American Education.* Cambridge, MA: Harvard University Press.

Larson, M. S. 1977. *The Rise of Professionalism.* Berkeley: University of California Press.

Litchfield, P. 1881-1882. Diary July 1 to March 23, 1775, Massachusetts Historical Society. *Proceedings of the Massachusetts Historical Society,* 19:376-379.

Lutz, A. 1964. *Emma Willard: Pioneer Educator of American Women.* Boston: Beacon.

Lynn [MA] School Committee. 1855. *City of Lynn School Report.* Lynn, MA: Author.

Magnum, U. L. 1928. *The American Normal School: Its Rise and Development in Massachusetts.* Baltimore: Warweek & York.

Marini, M. M. 1989. "Sex differences in earnings in the United States." *Annual Review Sociology,* 15:343-380.

Massachusetts Board of Education. 1839-1880. *Massachusetts School Reports*. Boston: Author.

Massachusetts School Reports. 1833-1834. Manuscripts, 1830-39. Boston: Massachusetts State Library, Special Collections.

Melosh, B. 1982. *The Physicians' Hand*. Philadelphia: Temple University Press.

Messerli, J. 1972. *Horace Mann: A Biography*. New York: Knopf.

Milkman, R. 1987. *Gender at Work: The Dynamics of Job Segregation by Sex During World War II*. Urbana: University of Illinois Press.

Mudge, M. 1854. *Diary*. Cambridge, MA: Schlesinger Library, Radcliffe College.

New Hampshire Board of Education. 1848-1867. *New Hampshire School Reports*. Concord: Author.

Oppenheimer, V. K. 1970. *The Female Labor Force in the United States* (Population Monograph Series No. 5). Berkeley: University of California Press.

Preston, J. A. 1982. *Feminization of an Occupation: Teaching Becomes Women's Work in Nineteenth-Century New England*. Unpublished doctoral dissertation, Brandeis University.

_____. 1989. "Female aspiration and male ideology: School teaching in nineteenth-century New England." In A. Angerman (Ed.), *Current Issues in Women's History*. London: Routledge:171-182.

Preston, J. A. 1993, December. "Domestic ideology, school reformers, and female teachers: Teaching becomes women's work in nineteenth-century New England." *New England Quarterly*:531-561.

Reskin, B. and P. Roos. 1990. *Job Queues and Gender Queues: Explaining Women's Inroads Into Male Occupations*. Philadelphia: Temple University Press.

Rhode Island Board of Education. 1845-1860. *Rhode Island School Reports*. Providence: Author.

Simpson, R. L. and I. H. Simpson. 1969. "Women and bureaucracy in the semi-professions." In A. Etzioni (Ed.), *The Semi-Professions and Their Organization: Teachers, Nurses, Social Workers*. New York: Free Press:196-265.

Sklar, K. K. 1973. *Catherine Beecher: A Study in American Domesticity*. New York: W. W. Norton.

Springfield Female Collegiate Institute. 1860-1861. *Catalogue*. Cambridge, MA: Special collections, Gutman Library, Harvard University.

Starr, P. 1982. *The Social Transformation of Medicine*. New York: Basic Books.

Stevenson, M. H. 1988. "Some economic approaches to the persistence of wage differences between men and women." In A. H. Stromberg and S. Harkness (Eds.), *Women Working: Theories and Facts in Perspective*. Mountain View, CA: Mayfield:87-100.

Strober, M. H. and A. G. Landford. 1986. "The feminization of public school teaching: Cross-sectional analysis, 1850-1880." *Signs: Journal of Women in Culture and Society*, 11(2):212-235.

Strober, M. and D. Tyack. 1980. "Why do women teach and men manage? A report on research on schools." *Signs: Journal of Women in Culture and Society*, 5(3):494-503.

Suzzallo, H. 1906. *The Rise of Local School Supervision in Massachusetts*. New York: Columbia University Press.

Tarbox, I. N. (Ed.). 1886-1887. *Diary of Thomas Robbins*. Boston: Connecticut Historical Society.

Treiman, D. and H. Hartmann (Eds.). 1981. *Women, Work, and Wages: Equal Pay for Jobs of Equal Value*. Washington, DC: National Academy of Sciences.

Wilensky, H. L. 1964. "The professionalization of everyone?" *American Journal of Sociology*, 70:137-158.

Witz, A. 1990. "Patriarchy and professions: The gendered politics of occupational closure." *Sociology*, 24(4):675-690.

Witz, A. 1992. *Professions and Patriarchy*. London: Routledge.

Woody, T. 1929. *Women's Education in the United States*. New York: Octagon Press.

Food for Thought and Application Questions

1. Select a female-dominated semi-profession other than teaching (e.g., librarian, social worker, registered nurse). First, locate recent data on the percent female in the job category you selected. (The *Statistical Abstract of the United States* is a good source.) Then describe the cultural representation of the "ideal" professional in this job category. Does this cultural representation consist of gender-linked traits? Discuss. Do you think the cultural representation you described influences the percent female in the occupation?

2. Preston argues that male-dominated bureaucratic structures developed in the nineteenth century to limit the autonomy and professional status of public school teachers. Do these male-dominated bureaucratic structures still exist? In order to answer this question, you must collect information on women's representation in educational administration. One way to find the information you will need is to collect data from sources such as the U.S. Department of Education on the percentages of women who are principals, superintendents, members of school boards, etc. Another option is to gather data on your local school district. This may require that you interview an employee of the district. ✦

25

Dilemmas of Organizing Women Office Workers

Joan Keller Burton

In the past decade, clericals working in banks, insurance companies, universities, libraries, and law firms have joined unions or become members of nonunion working women's organizations founded by activists (Foner 1980; Glenn and Feldberg 1984; Seifer and Wertheimer 1979; Tepperman 1976; Wertheimer 1984). By its tenth anniversary in 1983, for example, 9 to 5 had grown from a small group of discontented office workers in Boston to a national association with a membership exceeding 12,000. Women Employed claimed to represent 1,000 members in the Chicago area and 2,000 nationwide (White Collar Report 1983, p. 373).

Although deteriorating office-work conditions may act as a stimulus to office-worker activism (deKadt 1979; Glenn and Feldberg 1984; Tepperman 1976; West 1982), few studies have examined the process by which discontented office workers are drawn into workers' organizations. Goldberg (1983) found that recruits joined Baltimore Working Women, a local affiliate of 9 to 5, because of discontent with work conditions, such as low pay, limited training opportunities, and a lack of respect from those in higher positions. Participation heightened their awareness of common problems, taught the value of collective protest, and strengthened commitment to improving work conditions. In Goldberg's terms, the actives developed "job consciousness," an awareness that work-related problems were political, not personal, and required collective solutions.

The transformation of discontent into activism through the acceptance of new ideologies that question the legitimacy of an inequitable system has occurred in other movements (Gamson 1968; Orum 1974; Turner 1981; Zurcher and Snow 1981) in which taking the role of an active was an important first step (Bromley and Shupe 1979; Mueller 1984). The conditions that facilitate potential recruits in forming or joining an organization are unclear, however. This study explores the relationship between discontent, consciousness, and activism by examining the recruitment process, focusing on members' own experiences and their efforts to recruit others and identifying similarities and differences in very active and less active members' and nonmembers' perceptions of, and responses to, poor working conditions.

Research Design

Baltimore Working Women was founded in 1978 through the efforts of a group of politically active professional women who worked for the city government. Media coverage of clerical organizing and personal contacts with organizers in Chicago aroused their interest in founding a local organization that would address clericals' problems. From the start, their goals were to "win rights and respect for all office workers" by pressuring government agencies and corporations to abide by existing laws and to change unfair practices. By 1979, when BWW's members voted to affiliate with Working Women, National Association of Office Workers (renamed 9 to 5, National Association of Working Women, in 1981), the founders no longer played an active role (Goldberg 1983).

Like all local chapters of 9 to 5, BWW recruits office workers on a citywide, rather than job-site, basis. At the time of the study, the organization claimed a dues-paying membership of 100 office workers and a mailing list of 1,500 supporters. Staff and active members expressed concern that membership had decreased by a third since BWW was founded in 1978. Convinced that the decrease was due to insufficient attention to recruitment, plans were made for a membership drive to be held during 1983.

Several months prior to the beginning of the membership drive, I received permission from BWW staff and officers to study the organization's recruitment strategies and to interview its members. I observed recruitment strategies from the December 1982 general meeting announcing the recruitment drive, to September 1983, when awards were presented to the top recruiters. During this nine-month period, I participated in the activities expected of any active member, such as attending weekly committee meetings and workshops, soliciting funds, demonstrating against local companies, and planning media events.

Since I was interested in exploring recruitment to a working women's organization from the point of view of potential and actual recruits, I also interviewed 72 office workers. My first interviews were with actives who were most involved in BWW and nonmembers who attended meetings and events or whose names were on BWW's phone lists compiled from attendance sheets, surveys, and phone calls to the office. Following guidelines for snowball sampling (McCall and Simmons 1969), I asked those interviewed for one or two names of other office workers. I continued interviewing until no new names were suggested and I had contacted all office workers on my phone lists who had currently listed local numbers.

The 72 respondents were categorized by level of activism as defined by paid staff members who worked regularly with BWW's members: *actives* (14)—held an office for at least one year or had been actively involved for five or more years; *less active members* (16)—participated only sporadically; *inactives* (14)—infrequently attended meetings; *nonmembers* (28).

The interview lasted about two hours and elicited data on family, work history, and association with BWW. I obtained data on marital status, number and ages of children, present and past occupations, work conditions, employee-boss and co-worker relationships, date members had first heard of BWW, reasons that they joined the organization, and descriptions of involvement in its activities.[1] These data are summarized in the tables below.

Recruitment Patterns and Involvement in BWW

Of the early recruits who remained in BWW, 46 percent were actives who had joined "to fight for the rights of all office workers" and expected "the battle" to be a long one (see Table 25.1). Another 37 percent had joined because of their own work-related problems that kept them participating at a less active level over the years. No one had to "sell" these early recruits on joining. After learning about BWW through leaflets, surveys, advertisements, or news reports, they recruited themselves and began participating in BWW's activities.

By 1982, the pool of ready recruits had diminished, and patterns of recruitment and involvement had changed. Half of the recent recruits were recruited through the efforts of members who spent considerable time and energy persuading them to come to a meeting. One active explained, "I've been talking to some office workers about joining since 1979. I'm always selling the organization." During the 1983 membership drive, all members were urged repeatedly: "Go out and look for someone just like the woman you were, someone with a problem, who needs help from an organization like BWW."

The strategy of recruiting through members' friendship networks attracted recruits seeking social activities, rather than an opportunity to address working women's issues. Very few recent recruits were active, and 50 percent were inactive (see Table 25.1). Members who successfully coaxed a coworker into joining were disappointed at the new recruit's failure to participate actively. Others grew angry and discouraged by their coworkers' lack of interest or feared they would lose their friends if they tried too vigorously to recruit them. They described coworkers as "turning cold" or "rolling their eyes when they see you coming." Even the actives, who were committed to "spreading the word," mentioned being turned down so often they had lost count. The expectation that members use their friendship networks as a source of new recruits had sig-

Table 25.1
Level of Involvement in BWW, by Period of Joining

	%	N
Early Recruits: August 1978-October 1981		
Active	46	(11)
Less active	37	(9)
Inactive	17	(4)
Total	100	(24)
Recent Recruits: November 1981-September 1983		
Active	15	(3)
Less active	36	(7)
Inactive	50	(10)
Total	100	(20)

nificantly increased the costs of participating in BWW.

Reactions to Working Conditions

Although potential recruits were less likely to recruit themselves to BWW after 1981, office-worker discontent had not disappeared. All members were dissatisfied with low salaries, absence of opportunities for advancement, and lack of respect for clericals, which managers and professionals conveyed through bursts of unexplained anger, harsh and undeserved criticisms, or nasty jokes (Fox and Hesse-Biber 1984; Glenn and Feldberg 1982, 1984; Goldberg 1983; Seidman 1978). These problems were exacerbated by company reorganizations following automation. Clericals were laid off as soon as the computerized system was installed, creating competition among coworkers for decreasing numbers of jobs and an atmosphere of distrust and hostility. Members' responses to discontent with work conditions depended on their understanding of working women's issues, job security, employee-boss and coworker relationships, and commitment to protesting work-related inequities.

Actives

Although actives were likely to have worked less than five years for their present employers (see Table 25.2), they were sufficiently secure in their jobs to question company policy openly and raise issues that affected all clerical workers. They had joined BWW to work toward the goal of the national organization, 9 to 5, "winning raises, rights, and respect for all office workers." In 63 percent of their comments about joining, they stressed wanting to fight for a variety of issues, including comparable worth, job reclassification, and safety legislation to protect office workers using video display terminals (see Table 25.2).

Through their participation in BWW's activities, they hoped to set an example for coworkers and bosses and educate them about the collective nature of the inequities clericals faced. For example, an active

Table 25.2
Work Conditions and Marital Status, by Level of Activism

	Active (N = 14)		Less Active (N = 16)		Inactive (N = 14)		Nonmember (N = 28)	
Salary (in dollars, modal categories)	12,001 15,000	–	12,001 15,000	–	8,500 12,000	–	8,500 12,000	–
Years in present job (means)	4.6		6.9		3.0		6.8	
Had direct experience with automation	36%	(5)	31%	(5)	57%	(8)	21%	(6)
Work relationships: bosses described in negative terms	43%	(6)	38%	(6)	57%	(8)	29%	(8)
coworkers described in negative terms	36%	(5)	69%	(11)	71%	(11)	69%	(19)

employed by a large insurance company described the considerable distress she and coworkers experienced witnessing a series of wholesale layoffs and demotions. At first, because those in her department were angry and "ready to do something, to organize," she sought the advice of BWW and union organizers. Within a week, the anger and willingness to cooperate that accompanied the first wave of cuts had turned to fear. Those who still had jobs "didn't want to rock the boat." Realizing there was little support for open protest, the active concentrated on convincing management to adopt safety standards to protect clericals working at video display terminals.

Because actives were issue-oriented and convinced their activism could make a difference, they defined participating in BWW as an integral part of their lives as clerical workers. However, over half said they felt comfortable in their active role because they worked for "tolerant" bosses (see Table 25.2). Those who were not so fortunate in their office relationships felt their visibility as active members of BWW was a form of protection. Their bosses might not approve of their activities, but they were reluctant to punish arbitrarily someone they knew would officially protest such an action.

Of all respondents, actives were the least likely to describe coworkers in negative terms, such as petty, bitchy, hostile, jealous, or overly competitive (see Table 25.2). Their participation in BWW's efforts to organize clericals had heightened their awareness of the need for clericals to cooperate, not compete. Picketing employers, publicly representing BWW, and teaching others about working women's issues enhanced the solidarity they felt with all clericals facing similar problems.

Since few actives were married, they did not have to consider a spouse's needs or responses to his wife's activism (see Table 25.2). Half were single parents, however, and sole providers for their families. When family commitments competed with BWW for their time and energy, their strong interest in collectively addressing work inequalities helped them effectively juggle these demands (Turbin 1984; Wertheimer and Nelson 1975).

Table 25.3
Members' Reasons for Joining BWW, by Level of Activism

Type of Response	Active (%)	(N)	Less Active (%)	(N)	Inactive (%)	(N)
Issue-oriented: work on "the issues," ready to help others	63	(24)	31	(15)	6	(2)
Career-oriented: get assistance, skills, or information to solve problem at work	16	(6)	34	(16)	27	(9)
Socially oriented: make new friends, use spare time, support a "good cause"	21	(8)	35	(17)	67	(23)
Total responses	100	(38)	100	(48)	100	(34)

Less Active Members

Less active members were career-oriented women who had worked for their present employer for an average of nearly seven years (see Table 25.2). They had job security and worked for supportive bosses who did not object to their involvement in BWW as long as they were "discreet" and participated on their own time. In contrast to the actives who joined BWW "on the spot," however, less active members "flirted with the idea of joining" or "tested the waters" for several months before actually becoming members. They were concerned about working women's issues, but they joined BWW to address their own problems, rather than to improve conditions for all office workers (see Table 25.3). The following comments were typical:

Oh yes, I remember why I joined. I hadn't gotten a promotion in eight years and I was angry. I joined because I hoped BWW could help me.

When I first joined, I was having job problems. It was the typical thing with secretaries. I didn't think my work was appreciated. I wasn't respected, and I didn't have any promotional opportunities. The boss was in charge and the secretary was supposed to do whatever he asked of her. And everyone thought that was the way it should be. This bothered me and I thought an organization like BWW could help me. At least I could learn how I might make my own situation better.

As members, they took part in the activities directed toward solving these problems and tended to cut back on their involvement in BWW when the focus shifted away from their specific interests. They were also less willing than the actives to call attention to their dissatisfaction with company policy. Coworkers who had addressed inequalities had found their work situation intolerable, as the following incident illustrates:

One woman filed a pay discrimination suit with EEOC because she got a 10-cent an hour raise while another woman doing the same work got 25 cents. The case took one and one-half years, but she finally won. A few months later she was gone. All her coworkers had turned against her. The company asked everyone to testify, and they all did so willingly. Everyone resented her, but she was a loner and somewhat isolated. It was easy to label her a troublemaker and just shun her. Shortly after that, another woman filed an age discrimination suit, but she just left immediately. She didn't want to go through all of that.

Less active members were more likely than actives to be critical of coworkers, describing them as jealous, petty, and hostile (see Table 25.2). Despite their positive relationships with bosses, they blamed those in higher-level positions for encouraging competition and suspicion among clericals. During company reorganizations, employers accomplished this through demotions and layoffs that increased anxieties and distrust among those forced to compete for the remaining jobs. At the publishing company where a less active member worked, for example, automation meant overtime, shift work, and increased workloads for clericals who were not laid off. Management reclassified all remaining jobs and implemented a new rule, "Don't fraternize with those you supervise," ending friendships that had lasted as long as 20 years.

Clericals were also pitted against each other in subtler ways. A state employee observed, for example:

> On several occasions one of the professors showed me a paper another secretary had typed and complained that periods were left out or were in the wrong place. At first I thought it was terrible that she was so sloppy. And I was angry that she had the same position I did, but didn't work as carefully or as hard. Then I happened to be looking at one of the journals and found that she was just following a correct journal format. When I mentioned this to him, he said, "I doubt it, not her."

Working in such an atmosphere discouraged less active members from approaching coworkers about shared problems and running the risk of losing the support of those in higher-level positions. They were less likely than the actives to be dependent solely on their own earnings to support a family and could quit if conditions became intolerable, but they did not want to jeopardize their careers by being labeled as "troublemakers."

Inactives

Although inactives were more critical of their work conditions than other members, they lacked any clear sense of how collective action could help. They had worked an average of only three years for their present employers and were lower paid and less secure in their jobs than other members (see Table 25.2). The worst work conditions were described by inactives whose employers had installed computer systems and, expecting the work to go faster, had laid off clericals. For example, a typist employed by an investment company recalled:

> It didn't matter how long you had worked for the company or how hard you worked. They didn't seem to care about loyalty. You would come to work not knowing who would be let go next.

Her coworkers discussed protesting, but fear of reprisals ended the discussions:

> Management did just what they wanted and no one did anything. We just accepted it.

Worsening job conditions aroused inactives' interest in BWW, but most came to meetings because they were curious, had a vague desire to support a good cause, or hoped to meet friendly office workers (see Table 25.3). Where layoffs had raised fears of being replaced by their own coworkers, inactives were reluctant either to identify publicly with BWW or to discuss common problems with other clericals. For example, one said, "I felt a tremendous need for an organization like BWW because things went bad for me at work, recently. But I can't become involved because I'll lose my job." Another thought it made more sense to align with those higher up:

> I make sure I get along with my immediate supervisor. I've begun to make myself noticed by the right people higher up. I've gotten assigned to some special projects and done a good job on them. I've already been informed,

unofficially, that when the cuts come, I'll be taken care of.

Few inactives had this option, however. Of all members, they were the least likely to work for supportive bosses (see Table 25.2).

Like the less active members, inactives described their coworkers as competitive and suspicious of each other, and they were aware that bosses created this atmosphere through overt actions, such as wholesale layoffs, and in subtler ways. Relations among clericals working in a university hospital deteriorated, for example, when a head secretary was fired and three secretaries were offered the position:

The doctor didn't tell any of them that he had asked the others. They were all flattered because they would be supervising everyone else. One who planned to quit decided to stay and she lost the job opportunity. Another told her parents she was going to be the supervisor. Then he decided to hire someone from outside and told everyone in the department no one had the right qualifications for a supervisory position.

Despite the poor quality of their office relationships, a few inactives had attended meetings organized by coworkers to discuss work-related problems of particular interest to them, but they thought these meetings accomplished very little. Bosses always knew exactly what had been discussed as soon as the meeting ended, proving to them that coworkers could not be trusted. The knowledge that bosses encouraged competition and jealousy among coworkers did little to relieve inactives' suspicions of those who shared their deteriorating work conditions.

Of all members, inactives were the most in need of any assistance BWW could offer, but, lacking the protection offered by a supportive boss or by long-term visibility as an activist, they rightfully feared reprisal if they took action to remedy their situations. They admired the courage of their outspoken coworkers but were not ready

to emulate them by actively pursuing working women's issues.

Nonmembers

Typically, nonmembers began discussions of work conditions by commenting: "I've never had cause to complain" or "I guess you want to hear about how bad things are, but I just can't think of anything I dislike about my work." Later, they would mention low salaries, lack of promotions, unfair treatment of clericals, and unpleasant coworkers. They recognized that these problems affected most of the clerical work force, but did not consider the possibility of addressing them through collective action. The attitude most frequently expressed was, "I just keep my mouth shut and go directly to my boss for raises and promotions."

Most nonmembers expressed a commitment and loyalty to their employers, which had developed over a long-term association lasting an average of seven years (see Table 25.2). They were secure in their jobs and turned to their bosses for support, protection, and rewards. Typical comments included: "I can go to him with anything"; "she looks out for me"; "he doesn't ask me to do anything he doesn't do"; and "he sticks up for me when I complain." A positive working relationship with those in higher-level positions involved being invited to social gatherings or asked to assume nonclerical responsibilities.

Not only did they value special treatment that set them apart from coworkers, nonmembers frequently expressed considerable hostility and resentment toward outspoken coworkers (see Table 25.2). Those who protested unfair work conditions were "chronic complainers" who failed to do their work properly or who "just antagonized those in higher-level positions and made things worse for everyone." Because nonmembers accepted management's version of equitable work conditions, they did not speculate about the legitimacy of a coworker's complaint. They had the same advice as their bosses for troublemakers: "If you aren't happy, there's the door."

Nonmembers did question company policy when it was clear they would be hurt by it, however, For example, a nonmember and her coworkers learned that a Xerox machine they all used frequently was to be placed in a room with hazardous waste materials. On the advice of a coworker actively involved in BWW, they approached the doctors they worked for, threatened to inform the Maryland Committee on Occupational Safety and Health (an organization of workers, unions, and health and legal professionals) of their situation, and succeeded in getting the machine moved to a safer location. They resisted the active's efforts to recruit them to BWW, however, because the benefits of participating were not clear. Like most nonmembers, they wanted to know whether BWW's activities would get them a raise, promotion, or some comparable benefit (Olson 1965; Zald and Ash 1966).

Although half of the nonmembers worked for the same employer as a member, none had been recruited. The disinterest they expressed in BWW reflected a different set of priorities in their work and personal situations, as well as loyalty to employers and disapproval of clericals who raised issues that criticized company policy or affected all office workers. Over half were married women who spent their time away from the office on family activities. The rewards for doing so were clearer than those associated with fighting for working women's issues. Those who were working outside the home to pay for a child's education, buy a new appliance, or pass the time until their husbands retired were neither issue- nor career-oriented and had little understanding of the single-parent actives who juggled their work, family, and BWW activities.

Conclusions

Potential recruits to working women's organizations are rational actors who weigh the rewards and costs of volunteering their time to any organization (Zald and Ash 1966). For the members in this study, becoming active fostered commitment to working women's issues, which increased the rewards of further activism (Bromley and Shupe 1979; Goldberg 1983; Mueller 1984). However, activism also entailed costs—the need to recruit members among less interested, and sometimes hostile, coworkers. Contrary to previous studies of recruitment that identified friendship ties between members and nonmembers as effective sources of new recruits (Lofland and Stark 1965; Lynch 1977, 1979; Snow et al. 1980; Stark and Bainbridge 1980), this study found that most members feared being rejected by the friends they tried to recruit.

Actives felt comfortable with their activism because of secure jobs, tolerant bosses, and a commitment to protesting work inequities collectively. Less active members were in similar work situations but less comfortable with collective action. They hoped to benefit from participating in BWW's activities as a solution to their own work problems. The least active members were in precarious and intensely competitive work situations and feared being labeled troublemakers and fired if they questioned company policies. They joined BWW when recruited by member-friends and participated sporadically and socially, not for assistance with work-related problems. Nonmembers dealt with work-related problems by aligning with management and doing whatever was necessary to be seen as a good worker (Kanter 1977; Tepperman 1976). They had little interest in working women's issues, strong family commitments, and a tendency to be hostile toward outspoken coworkers.

While organizations of collective action will ordinarily not be able to compete with family commitments and personal efforts to secure good working conditions just for oneself, at a time of extreme crisis the nonmembers, too, may come for help to a women's group that has been successful in collective action. However, even those who do not see the need of or who are afraid of the consequences of collective action may join for friendship. Since recruits who joined for friendship's sake participated the least, it may not be worth the effort to recruit those who do not see the need for collective action, although most organizations depend on these inactive members for fundraising.

Endnote

1. If nonmembers knew of BWW, I asked why they hadn't joined. Those who had not heard of BWW sometimes viewed my questions with suspicion and thought the interview was a gimmick for signing them up. In this way, I gained insight into the recruitment process as it was often experienced by members.

References

Bromley, D. G., and A. D. Shupe, Jr. 1979. " 'Just a few years seems like a lifetime': A role theory approach to participation in religious movements." In L. Kriesberg (ed.), *Research in Social Movements, Conflicts, and Change: A Research Manual*, Vol. 2. Greenwich, CT: JAI Press:159-185.

deKadt, M. 1979. "Insurance: A clerical work factory." In A. Zimbalist (ed.), *Case Studies on the Labor Process*. New York: Monthly Review Press:242-256.

Foner, P. 1980. *Women and the American Labor Movement: From World War I to the Present*. New York: Free Press.

Fox, M. F. and S. Hesse-Biber. 1984. *Women at Work*. Palo Alto, CA: Mayfield.

Gamson, W. A. 1968. *Power and Discontent*. Homewood, IL: Dorsey Press.

_____. 1975. *The Strategy of Social Protest*. Homewood, IL: Dorsey Press.

Glenn, E. N., and R. L. Feldberg. 1982. "Degraded and deskilled: The proletarianization of clerical work." In R. Kahn-Hut, A. K. Daniels and R. Colvard (eds.), *Women and Work: Problems and perspectives*. New York: Oxford:202-217.

_____. 1984. "Clerical work: The female occupation." In J. Freeman (ed.), *Women: A Feminist Perspective*. Palo Alto, CA: Mayfield:316-352.

Goldberg, R. 1983. *Organizing Women Office Workers: Dissatisfaction, Consciousness, and Action*. New York: Praeger.

Kanter, R. M. 1977. *Men and Women of the Corporation*. New York: Basic Books.

Lofland, J. and R. Stark. 1965. "Becoming a world-saver: A theory of conversion to a deviant perspective." *American Sociological Review*, 30:862-75.

Lynch, F. R. 1977. "Toward a theory of conversion and commitment to the occult." *American Behavioral Scientist*, 20:887-908.

_____. 1979. " 'Occult establishment' or 'deviant perspective'? The rise and fall of a modern church of magic." *Journal for the Scientific Study of Religion*, 18:281-98.

McCall, G. J., and J. L. Simmons (eds.). 1969. *Issues in Participant Observation*. Reading, MA: Addison-Wesley.

Mueller, C. 1984. "Women's movement success and the success of social movement theory." Paper presented at the American Sociological Association Annual Meeting, San Antonio, TX.

Olson, M. 1965. *The Logic of Collective Action*. Cambridge, MA: Harvard University Press.

Orum, A. 1974. "On participation in political protest movements." *Journal of Applied Behavioral Science*, 10: 181-207.

Seidman, A. 1978. *Working Women: A Study of Women in Paid Jobs*. Boulder, CO: Westview Press.

Seifer, N. and B. M. Wertheimer. 1979. "New approaches to collective power: Four working women's organizations." In B. Cummings and V. Schuck (eds.), *Women Organizing: An Anthology*. Metuchen, NJ: Scarecrow Press:152-183.

Snow, D., L. Zurcher, and S. Eckland-Olson. 1980. "Social networks and social movements: A microstructural approach to differential recruitment." *American Sociological Review*, 45:787-801.

Stark, R. and W. Bainbridge. 1980. "Networks of faith: Interpersonal bonds and recruitment to cults and sects." *American Journal of Sociology*, 85:1376-95.

Tepperman, J. 1976. Not Servants, Not Machines: Office Workers Speak Out. Boston: Beacon Press.

Turbin, Carole. 1984. "Reconceptualizing family, work and labor organizing: Working women in Troy, 1860-1890." *Review of Radical Political Economics*, 16:1-16.

Turner, Ralph H. 1981. "Collective behavior and resource mobilization as approaches to social movements: Issues and continuities." In L. Kresiberg (ed.), *Research in Social Movements, Conflicts and Change: A Research Annual,*. Vol. 4. Greenwich, CT: JAI Press:1-24.

Wertheimer, B. M. 1984. " 'Union is power': Sketches from women's labor history." In J. Freeman (ed.), *Women: A Feminist Perspective*. Palo Alto, CA: Mayfield:337-352.

———— and Anne H. Nelson. 1975. *Trade Union Women: A Study of Their Participation in New York City Locals*. New York: Praeger.

West, J. 1982. "New technology and women's office work." In J. West (ed.), *Work, Women and the Labour Market*. London: Routledge & Kegan Paul:61-67.

White Collar Report. 1983. "Occupational segregation, wage bias listed as major barriers for women." Volume 57:17. Washington, DC: Bureau of National Affairs.

Zald, M. N. and R. Ash. 1966. "Social movement organizations: Growth, decay and change." *Social Forces*, 44:327-40.

Zurcher, L. and D. A. Snow. 1981. "Collective behavior: Social movements." In M. Rosenberg and R. Turner (eds.), *Social Psychology: Sociological Perspectives*. New York: Basic Books:447-482.

Reprinted from: Joan Keller Burton, "Dilemmas of Organizing Women Office Workers," in *Gender and Society*, 1(4), pp. 432-446. Copyright © 1987 by Sage Publications, Inc. Reprinted by permission.

Food for Thought and Application Questions

1. According to Burton's data, marital and parental status are associated with union membership and levels of activism. Which women are most likely to join and become active? Discuss how their family status may motivate this activism. Which women are least likely to join and become active? How might their family status hinder participation in unions?

2. Burton discusses factors that inhibit worker activism in gender-segregated clerical occupations. What do you think would happen if these obstacles to activism were circumvented and broadbased activism occurred? How might the high level of gender segregation in these occupations affect activists' success? If employers refused to concede to the workers' demands, where might they turn for new workers to staff the jobs? ✦

26

Waitering/ Waitressing: Engendering the Work of Table Servers

Elaine J. Hall

A rich body of literature addresses the question of how work organizations construct and maintain gender relations. Answers to this question have taken two forms. Work organizations structure gender relations by placing male and female workers in different work positions (Bielby and Baron 1987; Feldberg and Glenn 1983; Sacks and Remy 1984; Stratham, Miller and Mauksch 1988; Talbert and Bose 1977) and by attaching gender meanings to the work performance (Benson 1984; Cockburn 1985; Rollins 1985). In other words, waiting on tables is defined as typical "women's work" because women perform it and because the work activities are considered "feminine."

Reskin and Roos (1987) see work positions and meanings as complementary approaches, suggesting that different mechanisms operate to produce gender inequality at different levels. Focusing on who does the work, positional mechanisms include allocating male and female workers to different firms or to different jobs within the same firm. Appearance norms and interactional styles differentiate between male and female workers doing the same job in the same work setting,

creating *gender meanings* of the work. A gendered meanings approach can differentiate between men and women holding the same position, doing the same work. In addition, focusing on gender meanings may mean ignoring the individual sex category of workers to see the common gender processes they share when performing a gendered type of work.

This article addresses positional integration of men and women in the same restaurant and shows how integrated restaurants continue to load gender meanings onto work performance, specifically the prescribed style of service. A *formal* service style requires servers to appear dignified and reserved and is gendered as masculine, whereas *home-style* service promotes a casual, familial form of interaction and is gendered as feminine.

The process of gender integration includes changes in both positions and meanings. In terms of position (who holds the job), the occupation of table server historically has been and currently is female dominated; 82% of all servers were women in 1991 (U.S. Department of Labor 1992). However, this occupation has always contained two legitimate work roles: one for waiters and one for waitresses. Waiters have traditionally performed a craft-based formal style of service in high-prestige restaurants, whereas waitresses have performed a familial service style in family restaurants and coffee shops (Cobble 1990; Howe 1977; Mars and Nicod 1984). The existence of segregated styles of service means integration can consist of various processes—the proportion of male servers could increase in home-style service positions, female servers could gain greater access to upscale restaurants, or integrated staffs could develop overall. Historical evidence shows that waitress unions have struggled for four decades to gain entrance to prestigious restaurants (Cobble 1988, 1990; Howe 1977), but success has been limited, and work roles remain gender typed. Only a couple of years ago, a waitress successfully working as a wine steward, a traditional male role, was a newsworthy item for a restaurant trade journal (Draper 1986).

The two service styles, formal and familial, are gendered by association with the persons who conventionally do each style of work. If waiters previously performed *waitering* in upscale restaurants and waitresses performed *waitressing* in low-prestige restaurants, what are the integrated staffs performing? This article explores whether gender integration of positions changes the gender meanings of the work activities. I propose that, even when male and female servers are working side by side in the same restaurants, one form of table service is interpreted as waitering and the other is waitressing; waitering remains the higher-status work.

Literature Review

Separating the gender category of the role incumbent from the gender meanings given to the work role is theoretically justified by the definition of gender as behavior in a social context and empirically grounded in recent case studies of the experience of gender-atypical workers in integrated workplaces. I address each of these literatures in turn.

Gendered Modes of Behavior

Following West and Zimmerman (1987), I define gender as something people *do*, an emergent feature of social settings, rather than an identity people *have*, a property of individuals. Gender is an action occurring between people in a particular setting. West and Zimmerman (1987) emphasize how individuals in interactions organize their behaviors to express gender and perceive the behavior of others in terms of gender (p. 127). In this article, I emphasize how work organizations are gendered social contexts that provide work roles loaded with gender meanings. Instead of assuming that workers "bring" gender to their jobs, I assume workers "do gender," performing their jobs in certain

ways because their jobs are structured to demand gender displays.

A doing-gender conceptualization differs from a gender roles definition (sometimes called sex roles). In the latter view, "supposedly dichotomous, internally consistent, and complementary, 'sex roles' [are] presumed to be internalized early in life and expressed by individuals in a variety of social settings" (Ferree 1990, 867). Critics (Connell 1987; Lopata and Thorne 1978; West and Zimmerman 1987) of sex role or gender role language point out that these terms misapply the concept of *role*. Social roles, such as teacher or daughter, refer to expectations and appropriate behavior in particular settings, but the concept of gender roles incorrectly implies that all women, all white women, or all middle-class white women know and enact the same gender role. Although gender scripts may exist for many social contexts, critics argue that no one gender role exists that is universally applicable to all contexts (Connell 1985; Lopata and Thome 1978; West and Zimmerman 1987). Furthermore, gender roles inappropriately locates gender in the individual, assuming that women enact a culturally defined gender role that overrides the structural conditions of each social context.

In contrast to the gender role approach, my article focuses on the *work roles* of servers—the behavioral scripts that servers are expected to exhibit to give "good" service in a particular restaurant. I argue that table servers do gender by enacting a work role that is loaded with gender meanings. Because table servers do gendered work, that is, do either waitering or waitressing, the individual's performance on the job involves managing both the gendered work activity and an individual gender category. Hagemann-White's (1987) notion of gendered modes of behavior is particularly helpful here. She argues that individuals do not apply gender meanings to supposedly abstract or ungendered behaviors but that the behaviors themselves are culturally "loaded" with gender.

As she states, "When actors differentiate and identify the actions of themselves and others, they attribute meaning to them, and in doing so implicitly attribute gender to the *mode of action*. Gender is not external to behavior but is part of its meaning in interaction" (Hagemann-White 1987, 13-14, emphasis added). When we see the behavior itself as gendered, we can talk about gendered behavior as distinct from the sex of the actor; "any gendered mode is potentially available to persons of both sexes" (Hagemann-White 1987, 14).

Some aspects of the way gender meanings are loaded onto work behaviors are captured in the term *women's work*. Occupations such as cocktail waitresses (Spradley and Mann 1975), flight attendants (Hochschild 1983; Nielsen 1982), and secretaries (Pringle 1988) are considered typical women's work, partially because they involve activities that are culturally understood as extensions of femininity—serving, supporting, and deferring to men. At the occupational level, to give service by waiting on tables is to perform work tasks typically cast as feminine.

A more complex and interesting picture of gendered work roles emerges when we focus on specific work settings within the occupation of table servers. Given the historical segregation of service styles into different kinds of restaurants, both a male way of waiting on tables and a female way of waiting on tables exists. Both men and women could perform a male style of service in some work settings, doing what I call waitering, and a female style of service, waitressing, in other work settings. Leidner's (1991) research comparing two service occupations—counter servers in a fast-food restaurant and insurance salespersons—reminds us that gendered work roles arise from the contextual meanings of the work site and are not inherent in the work tasks themselves. Both counter servers and insurance salespersons must cope with the customer's reactions, but the service style is cast as feminine for women

counter clerks and masculine for men sales representatives.

In this article the terms *waitering* and *waitressing* refer to the gendered work roles, whereas workers as gendered individuals are called *waiters* and *waitresses*. To refer to both genders, I use the terms *table service* for the work role and *servers* or *wait staff* for the workers.

Case Studies of Engendering

Integration of previously gender-typed occupations challenges the gender meanings loaded on the work performance. Previously, male workers performed work roles that were gendered as masculine; men who were subway conductors (Swerdlow 1989), marines (Williams 1989), police officers (Martin 1980), and correction officers (Zimmer 1987) were doing gender by performing the tasks of their occupations. And female workers as nurses (Williams 1989) enacted work roles gendered as feminine. But when gender-atypical workers successfully perform the same occupational tasks, incongruity between the worker's gender and the gendered work role prompts a reinterpretation of the gender meanings embedded in the work role. For example, female rapid transit operatives challenge the ideology of supremacy, which is "based in important part on the view that *the work* that men do is beyond the inferior capacity of women" (Swerdlow 1989, 386, emphasis added).

Reinterpreting the gender meanings of work usually includes a heightened importance of gender displays. One way to maintain the gender meanings loaded on the work activities and work role is to define any interlopers as distinct workers who perform the job differently. Thus male transit operatives collectively redefine women workers as performing the tasks in a "feminine" manner (Swerdlow 1989), and the marines institutionalize an exaggerated emphasis on femininity among the women marines (Williams 1989). Training programs require women marines to take classes in grooming, poise, and makeup;

military studies probe the possible "masculinization" of women officers, and drill instructors seek to make female recruits into "feminine" women (Williams 1989). Male nurses actively promote themselves as masculine workers by selecting specializations, such as acute care or psychiatric nursing, that provide greater autonomy and authority, closer collaboration with physicians, and higher pay (Auster 1978; Williams 1989).

Gender integration in all these settings leads to splitting the work role into two gendered forms. For example, women who become police "are forced to choose between two polar patterns of behavior" (Martin 1980, 185). They choose to emphasize their gender identity by enacting a feminine police WOMEN work role or to submerge their individual gender in the masculine work role of professional POLICE women (Martin 1980, 186). Male nurses distance themselves from the female gendered work role by developing a "masculine" kind of nursing that emphasizes physical "stevedoring" tasks, such as lifting and moving patients, instead of "soft" expressions of care.[1] When "the *work itself* was redefined and in the process made into a legitimate *activity* for 'masculine' men" (Williams 1989, 142), male nurses carved out a masculine niche for themselves in a female gendered work role.

When integration challenges the gender meanings loaded onto the work activities of these case studies, two role performance scripts develop, one gendered female and one male. In contrast to these occupations, table service in the preintegration stage consists of two work roles segregated into different kinds of restaurants; male servers performed a formal service style in upscale restaurants, and female servers gave friendly service in family restaurants. Thus studying table service provides a unique opportunity to consider how integration affects the gendering of work roles. Are the gender meanings abandoned or diluted when wait staffs are integrated, or do

integrated wait staffs perform waitering in some restaurants and waitressing in others? Or is each gendered work role split?

This research focuses on the way restaurants use job titles and uniforms to reaffirm the gendered service style that workers are expected to perform and the way servers use them to negotiate the gender meanings of their jobs. Traditional language patterns and dress codes subordinated all servers; forms of address based on their job and uniforms associating them with servants in private homes (Howe 1977, 119; MacDougall 1929) demark the subservient status of waiters and waitresses alike. But terms of address and uniforms also traditionally differentiate services by gender, especially by treating waitresses as sex objects. Although male servers are called "waiters," female servers are called "girls" or "broads" by male coworkers (LaPointe 1987) and "honey," "cutie," or "sweetie" (Howe 1977,114) or the "immature adult" term of "miss" by customers (Elder and Rolens 1985, 32; Howe 1977, 114). Although male servers typically wear a "refined" tuxedo-style uniform, female servers have been required to dress as sex objects in striped hot pants uniforms (Elder and Rolens 1985, 127), miniskirts or "sweet but sexy milkmaid" uniforms (Howe 1977, 106), or uniforms depicting "hip but sweet" women (Creighton 1982, 61).

Method

I used a nested research design that combined quantitative and qualitative data to capture the range of gender processes operating. I began by conducting a telephone census of all restaurants having table servers listed in the yellow pages of the telephone book for Hartford, Connecticut. Ninety surveys were completed in the summer of 1988, for a completion rate of 77%.[2] Quantitative data from the telephone survey were used to evaluate between restaurant segregation of waiters and waitresses (Hall 1990) and to construct a purposive sample of restaurants from which qualitative data were collected on the way managers and servers give gender meanings to the work process.

Based on information from the telephone survey, 55 restaurants that serve dinner and employ an integrated wait staff were selected for further analysis. Because the price of meals is generally considered to be directly associated with service styles ranging from mass catering to individualistic (Mars and Nicod 1984), this subsample was stratified into five prestige ranks measured by the price of an average dinner. For the case studies, one restaurant was selected from each of the five prestige ranks. Each was purposively chosen to represent the key organizational features of restaurants having that level of prestige and to provide diversity in the range of organizational types. Because the quantitative analysis (Hall 1990) showed that organizational features outweighed prestige in the mid range, I discuss these case studies as representing three prestige types.

The low-prestige restaurant, which I call the Sandwich Shop, is a franchise restaurant serving breakfast, lunch, and dinner from a standardized menu that features hamburgers and ice cream. Each of the three middle-prestige restaurants provides a distinctive dining ambience and work environment. A three-generation family business, the Family Italian, caters to a downtown clientele with a full bar and a lunch and dinner menu featuring Italian dishes and seafood. At the Trendy Café, customers sit at brightly painted chairs surrounded by modern art and bouncy music, have full-bar facilities, and choose from a menu that features individual-size pizzas and mesquite-smoked meats. The Downtown Formal serves lunch and dinner from separate menus for wine, dessert, and food in the subdued ambience of pastel tablecloths and decor. The highest-prestige restaurant and the area's only three-star restaurant, the Elegant Nouveau, presents a French menu as "the chef's choices," a sorbet course to "clean the palate," and buspersons who stand "waiting to serve" with hands behind their backs.

I collected three types of qualitative data from each of the five selected restaurants. First, I interviewed the dining room manager who directly supervised the wait staff. Second, I repeatedly observed typical meal service in each restaurant. In an initial two-hour formal session, I ate a lunch, a dinner, or both in each restaurant to observe typical work tasks and interactions. Subsequent informal observations occurred as I scheduled interviews, before and after interviews, and during periodic meals eaten in each restaurant. These informal observations were particularly worthwhile, as when I observed a new waitress being trained or ate lunch at the staff table with three workers discussing their new uniforms.

Third, I interviewed the wait staff in each restaurant. A total of 57 servers worked in the selected restaurants; staffs range in size from 7 to 22. Access was channeled through the managers, who permitted me to interview off-duty servers on the restaurant's premises. I completed formal interviews with a total of 19 waiters and waitresses, each approximately an hour in length, using a guided interview schedule.[3] In addition, I had numerous informal contacts with the dining room staff during the data-collection period.

Findings

I begin by briefly reviewing the extent of positional integration in the Hartford-area restaurants, which provides the context in which restaurants and servers negotiate the gender meanings of service. Then, I examine the way job titles and uniforms embody the gendered service styles that integrated staffs perform.

Positional Gender Stratification

The traditional form of gender stratification is intraoccupation firm segregation: all-male staffs in prestigious restaurants and all-female staffs in family restaurants and coffee shops. Assuming the traditional pattern would persist, I expected that all-female staffs and all-male staffs would predominate in my sample of 90 restaurants and that men and women would be working in organizationally different kinds of restaurants. Contrary to these expectations, two-thirds have integrated wait staffs. Specifically, 65% (59 restaurants) have waiters and waitresses, 28% (25 restaurants) have only waitresses, and 7% (6 restaurants) have only waiters. Although occurring more frequently in middle-prestige restaurants, integrated wait staffs are found in restaurants of all prestige ranks, including the high-prestige ranks previously associated with only waiters. The few all-male staffs work in nontraditional contexts (middle-prestige restaurants not serving liquor), and the all-female staffs continue to work in low-prestige restaurants where breakfast is served and liquor is not available.

A second positional issue is within-restaurant stratification. The traditional form of within-firm stratification among single-sex staffs has been to differentiate servers functionally by the allocation of work shifts, serving stations, and the amount of nontipped sidework. I expected this traditional pattern to be mapped onto gender in integrated staffs. However, most of the case-study restaurants have developed mechanisms that reduce or prevent intrastaff stratification. The Family Italian does functionally differentiate among servers to some degree; two "very senior" servers have a higher status than the other servers, who rotate their shifts and stations. Although requiring servers to rotate shifts, the Downtown Formal does stratify servers by skill and serving function (see below). But the other restaurants consciously attempt to remove most forms of functional differentiation among servers by permitting workers to choose their days off (Trendy Café), by rotating servers among the serving stations (Sandwich Shop), or by allocating sidework to an already equalized station system (Elegant Nouveau). Instead of stratifying servers by gender, most of these restaurants have instituted highly complex structures to institutionalize equality among the integrated staffs.

In some restaurants, the emergence of these complex equalizing mechanisms is part of the response to gender integration. For example, the prestigious Elegant Nouveau, traditionally the most hierarchically structured, now avoids functional differentation among servers by scheduling all servers to one hour of sidework per meal, by rotating servers through a weekly sequence of stations, and by allocating sidework tasks by serving stations. When waitresses first joined the staff, however, they were subjected to functional differentiation by gender; managers gave the "best" tables and stations to male waiters and permitted waiters to act as "prima donnas" by dumping their share of sidework on the waitresses. Removing gender from the allocation of shifts, stations, and sidework was a conscious and explicit strategy to keep waitresses from being second-class servers. The waitresses themselves struggled to change the rules and be treated equally. They found that the best way to alter the gender bias in the stratification system was to remove most, if not all, status differences among servers.

Positional mechanisms of gender appear to be minimal in the Hartford-area restaurants. Waiters and waitresses now serve side by side in most of these restaurants of almost every combination of organizational characteristics, and the allocation of shifts, stations, and sidework in four of the five case-study restaurants were designed to remove differences of any kind, especially those based on gender. Such restructuring, important as it is, does not address the operation of gender via the gendering meanings of the work process itself. In the next section, I consider how job titles and dress codes embody a gendered service style.

Gendered Meanings of Waiting

Job titles and dress codes have long reflected two legitimate work roles performed by single-sex staffs in different kinds of restaurants. Called waitresses, female servers wore feminine and even sexy uniforms in family-style restaurants and coffee shops; male servers, called waiters, wore tuxedo or formal uniforms in fine-dining restaurants. Some occupations that had sex-typed terms and uniforms have developed gender-neutral job titles and dress codes with integration (e.g., the term *stewardess* was changed to *flight attendant*.)Is the same process occurring for waiters and waitresses?

Job Titles

Gender-neutral titles for male and female servers are uncommon. Researchers and authors tend to use the term, *server*, or perhaps, *wait person*, and one training manual included the term, *waitron* (De Voss 1985, 124). Few restaurants in this research use *waitron*.[4] Instead of developing gender-neutral terms, restaurants continue to use sex-typed terms. This language persists because the label is linked to the kind of service being provided and not just the workers who serve.

Even though I was careful to avoid gender-specific language, most managers and servers I interviewed used gendered job titles of waiter and waitress. The manager of the Sandwich Shop, for example, referred to all servers, male and female, as "waitresses." Even after I commented on his choice of job titles, he referred to the occupation as "waitressing" (e.g., "It's a physically demanding job . . . waitressing"), and he consciously corrected his use of gendered titles (e.g., "Everyone in the store seats customers including the waitresses . . . the . . . er . . . wait . . . ugh . . . staff"). The female managers of the Downtown Formal and the Elegant Nouveau referred to all servers as "waiters." In fact, the manager of the Elegant Nouveau recently changed from gender-neutral titles to "waiter"; "I used to use 'wait person' and

sometimes conversations get lengthy when you use waiter and waitresses . . . so I just use 'waiter.' " What is revealing is that this manager never considered calling the male and female servers waitresses, whereas, the Sandwich Shop manager never thought in terms of waiters.

Servers were careful to avoid what they identified as sexist terms. A female server at the Trendy Café, for example, comments "waiters and waitresses now . . . generally we're trying to be called 'servers' now . . . to get rid of that waitress, coffee-shop, diner type of image." Even so, their language suggests that servers perceive the occupation or the work activities as gendered. Female workers in the lower-prestige restaurants—the Sandwich Shop and the Family Italian—generally refer to the occupation as "waitressing" and their wait staff as a whole as "waitresses," but to individual servers as "waiters" or "waitresses." In these restaurants, to provide quick service in a busy restaurant where servers seat their own customers, fix their own desserts, and clean their own tables is to "waitress." In contrast, some servers in the high-prestige restaurants (the Downtown Formal and the Elegant Nouveau) call the occupation "waitering" and the collective staff "waiters." Interviews with servers at the Elegant Nouveau are sprinkled with such phrases as "most people here, the waiters, are . . ." and "rules are made mostly by the staff, the waiters . . ." when referring to integrated staffs composed of equal numbers of waiters and waitresses. Furthermore, some female servers refer to themselves as "waiters." For example, one waitress stated, "I've never gone to a table and found a person was [acting superior] to me because I'm their server, a waiter." For these servers, to cater leisurely to customers in a formal restaurant where the staff stand waiting with their hands behind their back is "to waiter."

The way job titles encapsulate engendered work roles is illustrated by the comments of a waiter at the Downtown Formal who differentiates the kind of service performed by food servers from that performed by waiters. A food server is someone who "takes your order and brings your food and just throws it on the table," but a waiter is "someone who sells wine . . . who makes you a table-side salad . . . that's a waiter . . . what we call a waiter." To be a waiter means the server interacts in a charming and informative manner, engages in "selling," but remains reserved and "professional." The kind of service a food server performs is generally called waitressing by other respondents. Because both waitering and waitressing refer to gendered service styles, male and female servers can perform waitering, and a male server may alternate the two kinds of service with the same customers during a single meal.

Although one could argue that these linguistic patterns are a meaningless legacy of gender-typed role incumbents, I believe these workers understand their current work in gendered terms. This interpretation explains the use by two servers (one in the Sandwich Shop and one in the Elegant Nouveau) of the term, *male waiter.* Because *waiter* is already a historically male term, the addition of *male* is unnecessary unless the term *waiter* in this expression refers to the work being done, and not the person who is doing it. The gendering of the work activities is also being assumed by the server discussing a customer's reactions to a slow server he or she has requested.

> Male customers when they request a waitress will put up with the waitress if she takes too long to get something . . . but a woman customer will get upset with a *male waiter* she requested if he takes too long to get something because she wants that *type of service* and she wants it to be good. (emphasis added)

Uniforms

Three restaurants use uniforms that differentiate between male and female coservers. At the Sandwich Shop, wait-

resses wear a blue-and-white dress, and waiters wear blue-and-white shirts with blue pants. Servers at the Family Italian wear white blouses or shirts with black pants if they are males and black skirts if they are females. Staff at the Downtown Formal wear tuxedo-type uniforms, but men wear pants and women wear skirts.

Servers provide two interpretations of the gender meanings symbolized by these gender-differentiating uniforms. On one hand, workers in these restaurants accept the societal definition of men and women as different kinds of people who wear different kinds of clothing. What mattered to the waitresses at the Family Italian was that the uniforms be color coordinated and that they have a "professional" look; they saw no need to have everyone wear pants. Waiters at the Downtown Formal described women in skirts as more attractive than women in pants; waitresses did not perceive women wearing skirts and men wearing pants as uniforms to be an indication of gender stratification. On the other hand, some waitresses at the Sandwich Shop argued that dressing like a woman by wearing a skirt provided financial rewards. "In a way it sounds sexist . . . but I'd rather be in a skirt or dress because it brings better tips . . . [I'm] more comfortable in pants but [I'd] rather wear a dress . . . money, that's why I started waitressing."

Two restaurants prescribe a generic male uniform for male and female servers. At the Trendy Café, servers wear black pants and knit tops that have the restaurant's name as an artistic decoration. At the Elegant Nouveau, servers wear a tuxedo-style uniform consisting of black pants, black aprons, and a white tuxedo shirt with black studs, cuff links, and a bow tie. All servers interviewed in these two restaurants stated that workers holding the same position should wear the same uniform. Waiters did not consider this important and could envision scenarios in which a consistent professional appearance could exist with women wearing skirts.

In contrast, the waitresses explicitly associated the uniform policy with gender equality. At the moderate-prestige Trendy Café, young servers cater to yuppies and hip customers who enjoy the arty decor and music. Servers perceived the Trendy Café as a progressively organized restaurant creating new dining trends. In this unconventional work setting, a unisex uniform and nonsexist language are associated with professional service. When asked about women wearing skirts and men wearing pants, a waitress at the Trendy Café commented "I'd never work in a place that does that. . . . I can't think of many servers who would at this point . . . because it's unprofessional."

At the Elegant Nouveau, where a waitering service style is most entrenched, waitresses are aware and fearful of the interactional and structural status differences that could emerge if they wore skirts. In the words of the first female server to work at the Elegant Nouveau, customers would treat female servers wearing skirts differently.

> I don't think there should be a distinction in uniform with the waitresses and waiters because there's not a distinction. But if you dress them differently, people think they can treat them differently. . . . Everyone in the same uniform means that we're all the same. . . . [If I wore skirts] you never know if they [the customers] would say "I want a waiter" or if they might treat you as if . . . you're not a server.

According to another waitress, wearing the same uniform also reminds the staff that the waiters and waitresses are doing the same work.

> I wouldn't mind skirts [but] I know it's a good thing that everybody wears the same thing because then there's no differing. There's not the men wearing tuxedo jackets and the women wearing just shirts, or whatever. . . . I like everybody having the same because that means everybody is the same. You're not going to take a party out of my sec-

tion and give it to one of the guys. . . . And that's what some of the girls are afraid of. It would be a sexist thing starting with if we didn't wear the same uniforms.

Both the Elegant Nouveau and the Downtown Formal are prestigious restaurants that promote a waitering service style, and both prescribe a tuxedo-style uniform. But female servers wear skirts at the Downtown Formal and pants at the Elegant Nouveau. These differences in the dress codes may emerge from other organizational features. In contrast to the Elegant Nouveau, servers at the Downtown Formal are placed in a hierarchy based on skill and seniority, consisting of captains, trainers, front waiters who manage the service, and back waiters who assist other servers. Uniforms may function to mark this status hierarchy. For example, a waiter suggested that captains should wear a different uniform; "a matador's costume . . . something distinctive [to] show this person is a professional . . . just like the captain of a hockey team . . . visible." In contrast to the Elegant Nouveau, the organizational structure of the Downtown Formal has been imposed by the management. Servers at the Elegant Nouveau talked about the "rules coming from the staff" in problem-solving discussions, but servers at the Downtown Formal talked about the permanence of the current procedures, and about owner-managers who present themselves as restaurant experts.

In sum, the structural transformation of the restaurant industry has placed male and female workers in positions as coservers in the same restaurants, but these positions retain their gender meanings. Job titles and the meaning of uniforms illustrate the way work roles are negotiated to carry gender in different work settings. In low-prestige restaurants, the integrated staff members are more likely to be called waitresses, and gender-differentiating uniforms are accepted as appropriate and even advantageous to female servers. In more prestigious and trendy restaurants, the integrated staff members are more often called waiters, and generic male uniforms areperceived by female servers as an important aspect of gender equality. The gender meanings incorporated in the language of job titles and dress codes suggests that to wait on tables in a fine dining restaurant is to do waitering and to wait on tables in a coffee shop is to do waitressing, regardless of the sex or gender of the worker.

Conclusion

When we say waiting is women's work, we mean that most of the workers are women and that the work tasks have been gendered as female. Gender-atypical workers experience more than being a different sex; they encounter a gendered work role that may conflict with their gender behaviors in other roles. Male and female servers in integrated restaurants continue to do gender, but the gender embedded in their work role may no longer match their own individual gender. Both the role incumbent and the meanings of work carry associations with womanhood, and both aspects must be part of any program to promote gender equality in the workplace.

Male workers remain scarce in many female-dominated occupations or work settings. Usually they are differentiated from female workers and the kind of work females perform. Waiters in low-prestige coffee shops or ethnic family restaurants work with waitresses performing waitressing, but they are distinguished from female servers by being men who waitress.[5] Male servers in restaurants that prescribe waitressing retain their higher status as males in the society in part by gender-differentiated uniforms. They fit in as exceptions to the rule, and they are perceived as different kinds of workers. Male workers in devalued female-dominated occupations seldom are catalysts for social change. Blaming the negative status of their occupation on the women who perform it (Williams 1989, 126), male workers

tend to congregate in the prestigious ranks of the occupation or to leave for better jobs. In a patriarchal society, doing work that requires performing feminine-associated tasks remains women's work and therefore devalued work, even when males perform it.

In addition to the material benefits attached to men's jobs, women in male-dominated occupations and work sites experience increased status as workers. But on whose terms and at what costs? For female workers, integration means entering male turf, which usually requires implicit, if not open, acceptance of the gendered male work role. Women cooks, for example, must choose to be "one of the boys" by engaging in sexual banter and enacting a "macho" work pattern or to "act like the female other" by being the brunt of sexual jokes and by accepting sexual approaches (Fine 1987). Either way, the male definitions of the work role and the work site are maintained as appropriate and legitimate.

Female table servers have higher status when they can enact waitering by performing the work role as all-male staffs have in the past. The male form of work performance, as waitering (or as executive), is still the more highly valued activity. An engendering approach suggests that we may need to reevaluate the literature on women executives as "Iron Maidens" (Kanter 1977, 236) and women bosses as "dragons" (Pringle 1998, 57). Instead of expressions of individual workers' personalities or even reactions to structural forces such as tokenism, such behavior may be better conceptualized as the enactment of masculine work roles. In a context in which caring and nurturing are devalued feminine activities, women entering male careers may actively do gender by adopting work styles that are assertively masculine and avoiding modes of behavior that are gendered female.

Because integrating the work sites of restaurants did not automatically remove the gender meanings of table service, this article suggests that a more entrenched and subtle form of sexism is the engendering of work roles, job tasks, and service styles. Although individual women benefit financially from performing waitering, the positive evaluation of male work may go unchallenged. Restaurants continue to hire for and customers remain willing to pay for the formal waitering style associated with professional service in fine dining restaurants. Although individual men may now do waitressing, sumptuary and etiquette norms maintain their higher status as men, and the familial waitressing service style of family restaurants continues to be devalued. Along with desegregating occupations and work sites, programs to achieve gender equality need to address the devaluation of the work that comes from gendering a feminine work role. In a patriarchal society, changing the gendered aspect of women's work may be the most important way we can remove the inequality that occurs when doing one's work is doing gender.

Endnotes

1. A male nurse interviewed by Williams (1989) commented, "I just can't go with the mellow, mothering type of things of a floor nurse" (p. 114). Male nurses do not "touch" their patients or offer "soft, kind words" as female nurses do; they provide a more overt form of caring in contrast to the "warm fluffy" care that female nurses give (Williams 1989, 120). Cockburn (1985) found a similar pattern of engendering work roles along a "caring" dimension among radiology specialists; women emphasized physical and emotional contact with the patients while men stressed the technical skills of maintaining the X-ray machinery.

2. Of the 117 restaurants having table servers, 19 restaurants (16%) were not available because of language limitations, incorrect telephone listing, and unavailability after four calls back. Only eight restaurants (7%) refused to complete the survey.

3. Complete background information is available for 16 of the 19 interviewed servers.

The typical server in this sample was young (all under the age of 35) and single without dependents (12 were single; 13 had no dependents). They were well educated; only two servers had not attended college and five had graduated from college. The length of employment at the selected restaurant ranged from as little as four months in the low-prestige restaurants to as long as eight years in a fine-dining restaurant. Waiting on tables was the only job for three-fourths of the sample, but just over one-half of the sample did not describe waiting as their "regular occupation and/or career."

4. Managers and servers I interviewed did not volunteer the term *waitron* during interviews, and some servers were unfamiliar with the term when directly asked. One waiter at the Elegant Nouveau stated that "waitron is fairly common among people in the business . . . more of a humorous description," and another waiter at the Trendy Café talked about the mechanistic connotation as appropriate for the repetitive and rountinized service in high-volume, middle-prestige restaurants.

5. The gender meanings embedded in the two roles of parenting are evident when we talk about men who are primary caregivers to minor children as "men who mother," (Risman 1987) and when we cast "women as fathers" if they enact the traditional parenting privileges (Rothman 1989).

References

Auster, D. 1978. "Occupational values of male and female nursing students." *Sociology of Work and Occupations*, 5:209-33.

Benson, S. 1984. "Women in retail sales work: The continuing dilemma of service." In K. Sacks and D. Remy (eds.), *My Troubles are Going to Have Trouble With Me: Everyday Trials and Triumphs of Women Workers*. New Brunswick, NJ: Rutgers University Press.

Bielby, W. and J. Baron. 1987. "Undoing discrimination: Job integration and comparable worth." In C. Bose and G. Spitze (eds.), *Ingredients for Women's Employment Policy.*

Albany: State University of New York Press.

Cobble, D. S. 1988. " 'Practical women': Waitress unionists and the controversies over gender roles in the food service industry, 1900-1980." *Labor History*, 29:5-31.

_____ 1990. " 'Drawing the line': The construction gendercd workforce in the food service industry." In A. Baron (ed.), *Work Engendered*. Ithaca, NY: Cornell University Press.

Cockburn, C. 1985. *Machinery of dominance: Women, men and technical know-how.* London: Pluto.

Connell, R. W. 1985. "Theorizing gender." *Sociology*, 19:260-72.

Creighton, H. 1982. "Tied by double apron strings: Female work culture and organization in a restaurant." *Insurgent Sociologist*, 11: 59-64.

De Voss, L. 1985. *How to Be a Professional Waiter (Or Waitress).* New York: St. Martin.

Draper, P. 1986. "Why I love serving wine." *National Restaurant Association News*, 6:26-27.

Elder, L., and L. Rolens. 1985. *Waitress: America's Unsung Heroine.* Santa Barbara, CA: Capra.

Feldberg, R. and E. N. Glenn. 1983. "Technology and work degradation: Effects of office automation on women clerical workers." In J. Rothschild (ed.), *Machina ex dea: Feminist Perspectives on Technology.* New York: Pergamon.

Ferree, M. M. 1990. "Beyond separate spheres: Feminism and family research." *Journal of Marriage and the Family*, 52:866-84.

Fine, G. 1987. "One of the boys: Women in male-dominated settings." In M. Kimmel (ed.), *Changing men: New directions in research on men and masculinity.* Newbury Park, CA: Sage.

Game, A. and R. Pringle. 1983. *Gender at Work.* Boston: Allen & Unwin.

Hagemann-White, C. 1987. "Gendered modes of behavior—A sociological strategy for empirical research." Paper presented at the Third International Interdisciplinary Congress on Women, July, Dublin, Ireland.

Hall, E. J. 1990. *Waiting on Tables: Gender Integration in a Service Occupation.* Ph.D. dissertation, University of Connecticut, Storrs.

Hochschild, A. R. 1983. *The Managed Heart: Commercialization of Human Feeling.* Berkeley: University of California Press.

Howe, L. K. 1977. *Pink Collar Workers, Inside the World of Women's Work.* New York: G. P. Putnam.

Kanter, R. Moss. 1977. *Men and Women of the Corporation.* New York: Basic Books.

LaPointe, E. 1987. "Waitressing: The politics of the labor process." Paper presented at the annual meeting of the American Sociological Association, August, Chicago, Illinois.

Leidner, R. 1991. "Serving hamburgers and selling insurance: Gender, work, and identity in interactive service jobs." *Gender and Society*, 5:154-77.

Lopata, H. and B. Thome. 1978. "On the term 'sex roles.'" *Signs: Journal of Women in Culture and Society*, 3:718-721.

MacDougall, A. F. 1929. *The Secret of Successful Restaurants.* New York: Harper.

Mars, G. and M. Nicod. 1984. *The World of Waiters.* Boston: Allen & Unwin.

Martin, S. E. 1980. *Breaking and Entering: Policewomen on Patrol.* Berkeley: University of California Press.

Nielsen, G. P. 1982. *From Sky Girl to Flight Attendant: Women and the Making of a Union.* Ithaca. NY: ILR Press.

Pringle, R. 1988. *Secretarial Talk. Sexuality, Power and Work.* New York: Verso.

Reskin, B. and P. Roos. 1987. "Status hierarchies and sex segregation." In C. Bose and G. Spitze (eds.), *Ingredients for Women's Employment Policy.* Albany: State University of New York Press.

Risman, B. 1987. "Intimate relationships from a microstructural perspective: Men who mother." *Gender and Society*, 1:6-32.

Rollins, J. 1985. *Between Women: Domestics and Their Employers.* Philadelphia: Temple University Press.

Rothman, B. K. 1989. "Women as fathers: Motherhood and child care under a modified patriarchy." *Gender and Society*, 3:89-104.

Sacks, K. and D. Remy. 1984. *My Troubles are Going to Have Trouble With Me: Everyday Trials and Triumphs of Women Workers.* New Brunswick, NJ: Rutgers University Press.

Spradley, J. and B. Mann. 1975. *The Cocktail Waitress: Women's Work in a Man's World.* New York: Alfred A. Knopf.

Stratham, A., E. M. Miller, and H. O. Mauksch. 1988. "The integration work: A second-order analysis of qualitative research." In A. Stratham, E. Miller and H O. Mauksch (eds.), *The Worth of Women's Work.* Albany: State University of New York Press.

Swerdlow, M. 1989. "Men's accommodations to women entering a nontraditional occupation: A case of rapid transit operatives." *Gender and Society*, 3:373-87.

Talbert, J. and C. Bose. 1977. "Wage-attainment processes: The retail clerk case." *American Journal of Sociology*, 83:403-24.

U.S. Department of Labor. Bureau of Labor Statistics. 1992. *Employment and Earnings*, 39(1), Table 22. Washington, DC: GPO.

West, C. and D. Zimmerman. 1987. "Doing gender." *Gender and Society*, 1: 125-51.

Williams, C. 1989. *Gender Differences at Work: Women and Men in Nontraditional Occupations.* Berkeley: University of California Press.

Zimmer, L. 1987. "How women reshape the prison guard role." *Gender and Society*, 1:415-31.

Food for Thought and Application Questions

1. Go out to eat at an establishment that employs table servers and collect the information required to answer the following questions. What is the prestige level of the establishment? What is the sex ratio of the table servers present? If there are servers of both sexes present, does it appear that positions are gender segregated by type? If so, describe the pattern. Ask your server his or her job title. Does it conform to the pattern described by Hall? Describe any indications you observe of gender embedded in the performance of your table server's work role. Is the gendered work performance you observe aligned with the gender of the table server? Discuss.

2. If you have ever been employed as a table server, answer the questions in number one above as they pertain to your own employment experience. Were you aware that you were "doing gender" as you performed your work role? Discuss. If you have never been employed as a table server, locate a friend or acquaintance who has and interview him or her so that you can answer the same questions. Discuss any information that confirms patterns described by Hall as well as any information that deviates from those patterns. ✦

27

Chicanas Modernize Domestic Service

Mary Romero

Introduction

Domestic service may once have carried "the shreds of genteel respectability," but as Lewis Coser pointed out, in 20th century America it has been an occupation "so stigmatized that it can hardly attract potential recruits among ordinary citizens and must increasingly turn to a pool of otherwise 'undesirable' foreigners" (Coser 1974, p. 39). Along with the stigma of servitude and low-status, David Katzman noted two other characteristics that make the occupation unattractive to workers: it "offers no opportunities for mobility and it is highly personalized in both tasks and employer-employee relationships" (Katzman 1978, p. 378). Both the shortage of domestic workers and the declining need for servants caused by labor saving-devices in the home are factors that, Coser argued (1974, p. 39), make the servant role obsolete. Future household workers, he predicted, will become a new profession in which "families will no longer be able greedily to devour the personality of their servants." "Servants" may indeed be obsolete. But the need for household workers is expanding to keep pace with increasing numbers of women in the labor force.

Several researchers have identified one structural change that has modernized the occupation of domestic service. Historical studies by Katzman (1978) and Clark-Lewis (1983) identified the shift from live-in to live-out as contributing to major changes in working conditions. Glenn (1986, p. 143), in her study of Japanese-American women in the Bay Area, attributed non-residential jobs to the modernization of domestic work by bringing it closer to industrialized wage work: "Work and non-work life are clearly separated, and the basis for employment is more clearly contractual—that is, the worker sells a given amount of labor time for an agreed-upon wage." Katzman (1978, p. 378) characterized the "hourly 'cleaning lady,'" as replacing "the uniformed maid who was part of the household." Even with the change to hourly work, though, the relationship between domestics and mistresses have retained characteristics of the master-servant relationship. Recent studies on the experiences of minority women employed as domestics indicate that the extraction of emotional labor, described by Coser as obsolete, still persists.[1] My own work on Chicana domestics supports these findings by showing that the occupation still has traits of servanthood. The mistress maintains a benevolent attitude towards "her" domestic, demanding loyalty and deference. She will treat the employee with the type of kindness reserved for domestic animals or pets and children, or at times even as a "non-person." Interpersonal relationships continue to be the major factor in job satisfaction and job tenure. However, my findings also suggest a broader range of relationships co-existing in the occupation.

The focus of this paper is to identify modernizing trends in domestic service and to explore how domestics can create a meaningful work environment. Chicanas engaged in domestic service find that the occupation poses a paradox: on one hand, cleaning houses is degrading and embarrassing; on the other, domestic service can be higher paying, more autonomous, and less dehumanizing than other low-status low-skilled occupations available to them. The challenge is to manage this paradox in everyday life and to modernize the working conditions. Analysis of 25 Chicanas' work histories show how each weighed her options and made choices based on the work situation that provided the most advantages.

The data were derived from participant observation, in-depth interviews, and collecting life histories of current and former domsetic workers. I analyzed the experiences of Chicanas employed as private household workers in a major western urban area. Two current and one former domestic worker known to the researcher provided entry into an informal network. Each interview subject was asked to recommend other potential interviewees. Churches and social service agencies were also used to identify domestics. Interviewees ranged in age from 29 to sixty-eight. All but one of the women had been married. Four of the women were single heads-of-household. The other women were currently living with husbands employed in blue collar jobs, such as construction and factory work. All of the women had children. The smallest family consisted of one child and the largest family had seven children. At the time of the interview, the women who were single heads-of-household were financially supporting no more than two children. Nine women had completed high school, but seven had no high school experience. One interviewee had never attended school at all. The remaining eight had at least a sixth grade education. All of the women were U.S. citizens. None of the women in this study belonged to a union.

In analyzing their work histories, in particular the reasons given for leaving or returning to domestic service, I was struck by the way Chicanas make the most of their options. Domestic service is only one of several low-paying, low-status jobs the women held during their lives. They had been hired as waitresses, laundresses, janitors, farmworkers, nurse aides, fast food servers and various types of line workers in poultry farms and car washes. In general, these were jobs with no benefits or where workers are subject to frequent layoffs and little chance for promotion. In comparing domestic service to other available work options all of the women identified certain advantages. Mrs. Rojas, for example, concluded that domestic service offered independence:

> When you work like in a hospital or something, you're under somebody. They're telling you what to do or this is not right. But housecleaning is different. You're free. You're not under no pressure, especially if you find a person who really trusts you all the way. You have no problems.

Unable to find employment offering job security, advancement, or benefits, these Chicanas made a calculated attempt to modernize the one occupation offering some advantages by minimizing control and personalism. Domestics use several strategies in their struggle for control: (1) increasing opportunities for job flexibility; (2) increasing pay and benefits; (3) establishing and maintaining an informal labor arrangement specifying tasks; (4) minimizing contact with employers; (5) defining themselves as expert housekeepers; and (6) creating a business-like environment. The critical locus of their struggle is to define the work on the basis of a contract—by the house or apartment—not as hourly work. Examination of the strategies used by the Chicanas reveal differences from the experience of other contemporary women of color employed as domestics. Unlike many of the black domestics studied in the East, these Chicanas were not sole supporters of the family, nor union members. Unlike the Japanese-American women in Glenn's study, most of the Chicanas were second or third generation and were much younger. The Chicanas that I interviewed had more formal education, and for the most part were not being replaced by newly arrived immigrants.[2] The most important difference is that the Chicana domestics have restructured the work by transforming it from wage labor to labor services.

The Restructuring of Domestic Service

Job Flexibility

Chicanas, like other women employed in domestic service (Glenn 1981, 1985), work for several employers. Having a different employer every day allows domestics more independence than having only one employer.[3] This alternative provides domestics with the leeway to quit, replacing employers without affecting the rest of the work week.

The women experience great latitude in negotiating both a flexible schedule and the length of the working day. Personal arrangements and verbal contracts between employer and employee make it easy to negotiate a half day's work or to skip a day. As Mrs. Garcia, a 54-year-old domestic, explained:

> You can change the dates if you can't go a certain day and if you have an appointment, you can go later, and work later, just as long as you get the work done. . . . I try to be there at the same time, but if I don't get there for some reason or another, I don't have to think I'm going to lose my job or something.

The flexibility of day work is important to women with small children who need to attend to illnesses and school schedules. The cost of day care can be a burden for middle class women; it is especially onerous for low-paid workers. In many cases, the issue of child care for preschool children can be resolved by taking them to work, as in the case of Mrs. Rivera, a 33-year-old mother of two:

> I could take my kids with me. There were never any restrictions to the children. Most of the people I've worked for like kids, so I just take the kids with me. It's silly to have to work and pay a sitter. It won't work.

Flexibility was not limited to rearranging a particular day or week; domestic workers could easily rearrange the work week to fit their needs during a particular period in their life. For instance, many of the older women had reduced their work week to three or four days a week, whereas the younger women who needed more income were more likely to be cleaning two apartments a day and working six days a week. A few women, like Mrs. Lovato, used the flexibility to work as a domestic part-time during times of economic crisis:

> I worked for Coors (brewery) for about three years and I would still do housecleaning, sort of part-time in the morning.

Payment and Benefits

Older women recalled earning $1.25 an hour in the early '60s and $3.25 in the '70s, but most of the women are now averaging between seven and eight dollars an hour—a lot more than other jobs they have had. For many women, the higher pay earned in domestic service reduced the financial need to work six days a week.

Payment in cash was frequently cited as an important aspect of domestic work. As with so many working-class families, even when there is a working husband, many live from pay check to pay check, with little if any money left over for unplanned or extra expenses. Extra cash is particularly important to families with school-age children who need lunch money or cash for class trips, gym clothes, or school supplies. Also, extra cash is important in supplementing the families' meals, especially towards the end of the week. Without the ready cash, end-of-the-week cooking ingredients are frequently limited to flour and beans.

In all but two cases, employment in domestic service was not reported to the IRS and these women expressed relief that income tax was not filed. Underreporting income to the IRS appeared to be partially the result of their husbands' fear of raising the family into a higher tax bracket. But it is also the case that the women did not know how to file income tax and felt uncomfortable about requesting employers to do so. However, three women expressed concern about social security and urged their employers to submit the required paper work. Two of the oldest women were receiving social security benefits as a result of their long-term employers' concern over their welfare.

One third of the women received benefits unknown to other domestics or other holders of low-status jobs. Nine Chicanas who had worked for years for particular employers reported paid vacations. This benefit usually involved no more than one or two paid days per employer. Christmas bonuses were more common than annual raises. However, nine reported annual raises and three of the women increased their wages annually by requesting raises or quitting one employer and raising the cost for new employers.

Negotiating Specific Tasks

Chicanas established verbal contracts with employers. When starting a new employer, the domestic would work one day, and if the employer was satisfied with the work, the two would agree upon a work schedule and the specific tasks to be accomplished. Mrs. Rodriquez describes the ideal situation:

> Once the person learns that you're going to do the job they just totally leave you to your own. It's like it's your own home.

The ideal is similar to informal arrangements reported by Glenn. However, half of the women explained the ideal situation was achieved after some supervision and negotiation. Such an experience is alluded to in Mrs. Portillo's explanation of why she left an employer:

> I don't want somebody right behind me telling me what to do. I will not work like that and that's why I didn't stay any longer with this lady.

Fifteen of the Chicanas interviewed made a practice of carefully distinguishing specific tasks considered part of the agreement from other tasks which would only be undertaken for additional pay. While informal work arrangements frequently implied a set number of hours the typical arrangement was referred to as "charging by the house" or a "flat rate." Mrs. Salazar explained the verbal contract as follows:

> When you say you're going to clean a house, after you find out how big it is, you tell them (the employer) "I'll clean it for say 60 dollars." You're not saying how long you're going to be there. To me, that was just a contract between you and the customer and after awhile when you've been there awhile you know how fast you can work and I was doing it in less than eight hours.

Mrs. Lopez expressed her preference for "charging by the house":

> I never liked to work by the hour because if I would work by the hour the lady would just go crazy loading me up with work, with more work and more work to do.

Similar to the dialectic between employer and employee described by Glenn, there was an ongoing negotiation as the domestic attempted to maintain the agreement while the employer attempted to lengthen the working day or add more tasks. Unlike the report on Japanese-American domestics, however, Chicana domestics developed procedures for handling "extras." One way to avoid extra tasks was to prepare a monthly or bimonthly schedule for rotating particular tasks, such as cleaning the stove or refrigerator. Another practice was to establish an understanding with the employer that if one task was added, one would be eliminated. If the employer did not identify the tasks to be eliminated, the employee simply selected one and explained that there was not enough time for both.

> My cousin said, "do the same thing every time you come in, as far as

changing the sheets, vacuum and dust, and window sills, pictures on the walls, and stuff like that unless they ask you to do something extra. Then, maybe don't clean the tile in the bathroom, or just do the windows that really need it, so you can have some time to do this other stuff that they wanted you to do extra." And she said, "never do more than what they ask you to do, because if you do then you're not really getting paid for it."

Employers feared that domestics were cheating on their time. Three women reported that past employers insisted they work until the very last second, leaving little if any paid time for putting away appliances or cleaning materials and ignoring the additional time required to complete a task. One domestic recalled employers bringing her lunch to her on the stairs or elsewhere in the house so that she would not take a lunch break. However, domestics, like Mrs. Sanchez, viewed the work as "averaging out":

> Suppose one day they (employers) may be out of town and that day you go to work. You won't have much work to do, but you'll get paid the same. And then maybe some other time they're going to have company and you end up working a little more and you still get paid the same. So it averages about the same, you know, throughout the month.

Chicana domestics, not unlike black and Japanese-American domestics (Rollins 1985; Coley 1981; Dill 1979; Katzman 1981; Glenn 1986), did not necessarily find an affective relationship the ingredient for a satisfying working relationship. In fact, the opposite was the case, because affective relationships provided more opportunities for exploitation. Frequently, close friendships resulted in fictitious kinship references, such as a young employer adopting the domestic as a surrogate mother. Redefining the work obligation as a "family" obligation placed the domestic in a difficult position. One older domestic

explained how the personal nature of the relationship created an atmosphere conducive to manipulation: "Some people use their generosity to pressure you." Maintaining the conditions of the verbal contract became difficult because requests for extra work were made as requests from a friend rather than an employer.

Minimizing Contact With Employers

In order to create meaningful work, domestics needed to remove employers from controlling decisions that structure the work and reduce the domestic to unskilled labor and housecleaning to mindless hourly work. Furthermore, the domestics wanted to eliminate the stigma of servitude, or being "hired help," which implies unskilled labor. The Chicanas defined their work as being different from maid's work. Mrs. Fernandez, a 35 year-old domestic, pointed to the distinction in the following account:

> They (the employer's children) started to introduce me to their friends as their maid. "This is our maid Angela." I would say "I'm not your maid. I've come to clean your house and a maid is someone who takes care of you and lives here or comes in everyday and I come once a week and it is to take care of what you've messed up. I'm not your maid. I'm your housekeeper."

Domestics commonly reported conflict over the work process. Some employers gave detailed instructions on how to clean their home: washing the floor on hands and knees, using newspaper instead of paper towels on the windows, or even which direction to scrub the wall. Mrs. Portillo, a retired domestic with 30 years experience, expressed the frustration of such a situation:

> I used to have one lady that used to work right along with me. I worked with her three years. I found it hard. I was taking orders. I'm not the type to want to take orders. I know what I'm going to do. I know what general house cleaning is.

Mrs. Sanchez voiced the general consensus that the less interaction with employers the better the working conditions: "The conflicts have been mostly with people who stay at home and really just demand the impossible." Five domestics even commented that they select employers on the basis of whether the employer worked outside the home.

Chicanas argued that working women are more appreciative of having the housework done, and are relieved to turn over the planning and execution of cleaning to the domestic. Unemployed women were perceived as "picky" and not willing to relinquish control. Three domestics made the analysis that unemployed women feel guilty because they are not doing the work themselves and, thus, have to retain control and responsibility for the housework.

I think women that weren't working were the ones that always had something to complain about. The ones that did work were always satisfied. I've never come across a lady that works that has not been satisfied. Those that are home and have the time to do it themselves, and don't want to do it, they are the ones that are always complaining, you know, not satisfied, they always want more and more. You can't really satisfy them.

Mrs. Lopez classified the type of employer she was working with by their attitude in the first few minutes of their first encounter:

I have had ladies that have said "I know you know what to do so I'll leave it to you" or they pull out their cleaning stuff and tell you "this is for this and this is for that" and I say "I know I've done this before. Oh, ok, I'll let you do it."

Supervision and the monitoring of workers not only control the work process but reminds the worker of her subordinate position in society. Offering unsolicited advice about cleaning techniques, such as scrubbing floors on hands and knees

rather than with a mop, or the safest way to bend while picking up the vacuum cleaner and moving heavy furniture, symbolizes a level of servitude. Asking a domestic to scrub floors on hands and knees, not a common practice of housewives today, is experienced as demeaning. The inferior status of the domestic is also evident in the employer's instructions on how to bend instead of offering assistance.

Becoming an Expert

The Chicana domestics' strategy of defining themselves as expert cleaners or housekeepers was one more step forward in modernizing domestic service. It is a unique strategy not found among the blacks studied by Rollins or the Japanese-Americans in Glenn's study. This strategy served to modernize the employee/employer relationship, creating an ideal situation in which employers turned over responsibility for the housework to the domestic. Establishing themselves as expert house-cleaners involved defining a routine set of tasks that did not include personal services such as babysitting, laundry, or ironing.[4] Mrs. Montoya's statement illustrates the equation of personal services with maid's work:

I figure I'm not there to be their personal maid. I'm there to do their housecleaning—their upkeep of the house. Most of the women I work for are professionals and so they feel it's not my job to run around behind them. Just to keep their house maintenance clean and that's all they ask.

The women interviewed considered themselves experts. They were aware of the broad range of knowledge they had acquired from cleaning a variety of homes. This knowledge included the removal of stains on various surfaces, tips for reorganizing the home, and the pros and cons of certain brands of appliances. A source of pride among the women was the fact that they had introduced a labor-saving device or tactic into the employer's home. Mrs. Garcia's experience in removing stains illustrates the assistance that domestics give employers:

> They (employers) just wipe their stoves and then complain "this doesn't come off anymore." They never took a SOS pad or a scrub brush to scrub it off. They expect it just to come off because they wiped. . . . Their kitchen floors would have kool-aid stains or they would have it on the counters, so I would just pour Chlorox on it and the Chlorox would just bring it right up and they would say "but you'll ruin it!" "No it will be alright." "Are you sure?" I never ruined anything from helping them out.

Mrs. Cortez's habit of providing cleaning hints illustrates how many employers willingly accept the expertise of the domestic.

> I cut out pieces of cleaning (information) that tell you how to do this an easy way . . . I'll take them and paste them on like their pantry door and I'll put them there and then when they go to open (the pantry door) they say "Oh, that's a good idea." So then they start doing it that way.

As expert cleaners, the women take responsibility for all decisions regarding the structure of the work process, the pace of the housework, and the selection of work materials. Ideally the domestic would enter the employer's home, decide where to begin, and arrange the appliances and cleaning products accordingly. She would pace herself to finish in a certain number of hours. If she needs to leave early she can speed up and not take a break; in other cases, a more leisurely pace would be indicated.

Half of the women recalled offering employers advice on the care of appliances and the best detergent or cleaning utensil for a particular surface. The Chicanas also attempt to routinize and rationalize the housework by reorganizing family practices and introducing new methods, perhaps cleaning neglected areas of the house to create additional space or rearranging the furniture. Mrs. Rodriquez described her approach as follows:

> I take one room and give it a full general cleaning which was walls, windows, everything, and from there I would do the rest light housework. Then the next week, I would take another room and give that a general cleaning and go to the rest lightly until I had all the house done real good and after that it was just a matter of keeping it up.

Taking responsibility frequently included finding replacements during their absence.

> I worked for my mother-in-law sometimes and if she was sick or if she was going out of town, I'd do some of the houses that she does every week and she really couldn't leave without somebody going to do something because it would be really a mess when she came back and it would be more work on her. So I would go and fill in for her.

The domestics did not view themselves as "one of the family." They also retained a separation between tasks completed for their employers and the "work of love" given to their families. The Chicanas attempted to enforce a new set of norms modernizing the domestic-mistress relationship into a customer-vendor relationship. In their struggle to transform the occupation, the Chicanas altered the employer's role from mistress to client or customer. This new definition of the relationship lessened the opportunity for psychological exploitation and the extraction of emotional labor. Chicanas identified particular tasks that would add to the problem of psychological exploitation. For instance, cooking Mexican food for employers was a request refused by all but two of the women. Their reasons for refusing the request suggest that they made a division between paid tasks and "work of love" and took precautions against selling their personhood.

I only cook for my family, I didn't want to share my culture with them (employers).

In order to convince employers to accept the new working relationship, private household workers had to present the advantages. One strategy used to convince the employer that she did not want to be a supervisor was to create a situation on the part of the employer that demanded more detailed supervision. This included such tactics as doing only the tasks requested and nothing else, not bothering to inform the employer that the worker had used the last vacuum bag or had used up cleaning materials, and refusing to offer the employer assistance in fixing a simple mechanical problem in an appliance. Consequently, employers who refused to shift control and responsibility were confronted with domestics who took no interest in or responsibility for completing the housework.

To redefine their work as skilled labor, Chicanas capitalized on the fact that working women are no longer interested in supervising the work of private household workers. Women hiring domestics to escape the double day syndrome cannot reap the benefits of the work if they supervise the activities of a "menial laborer." Acknowledging housework as skilled labor affirms the worth of the housewives' housework. In shifting housecleaning to "expert housekeepers," the housewife fulfills her responsibility to the family by obtaining skilled services; and, in doing so, she defines the work as difficult and time consuming, requiring skilled labor.

Creating a Business-Like Environment

Just as in other female-dominated occupations, such as nursing and teaching, private household workers lack authority (Spencer 1987; Ritzer 1977; Corley & Mauksch 1987) and must therefore rely on the employers' cooperation in accepting them as expert housekeepers. Rios' account of an employer's daughter expecting her to subordinate illustrates the role some employers play in eliminating any aspects of servitude in the occupation.

I told a young lady something about leaving her underclothes thrown around, and she asked me what was I there for? I went straight in, called her mother and told her the situation. Her mother came home from work and let the young lady have it. She (the mother) was thoroughly upset. I was not there to be her (the daughter's) personal maid and she was told that in no uncertain terms.

Analysis of the informal networks used by both employees points to a key role in establishing a business-like enviroment. The informal network between employers and employees serves to socialize employers and employees to the value of modernizing trends in the occupation. Chicana work histories revealed that, particularly for younger workers, the introduction to domestic service involved an informal apprenticeship. The new recruit accompanied a relative to work for several days or weeks until deciding she was ready to work alone. Domestics identified these training sessions as providing experience in cleaning, learning about new products or appliances, and discovering the pros and cons of structuring the work in particular ways.

She would go look it over and see if I missed anything or like in the bathroom you have to polish all the chrome and I didn't know that so I cleaned it and it was clean but she's the one that gave me all these tips on polishing up the chrome and stuff.

Most important, new workers were socialized to expect certain working conditions, and wages, and they learned ways to negotiate with employers.

Employers were similarly tied to the network. Employers asked domestics for the names of interested persons to work for neighbors, while domestics asked employers for the names of their friends interested in hiring housekeepers. Domestics were often very careful in their recommendations:

> They'll (friends) call and see if I know anybody that needs help but I have to know the person, and if I don't think the person is going to do the job, I will not send them . . . I'm very careful who I send—who I recommend.

In assisting friends and neighbors in finding workers, employers informed potential employers of existing conditions and thereby helped to create certain expectations. In using the network, Chicanas could be reasonably assured that new employers were socialized to appropriate expectations.

> I right away tell them what I do and what I expect to get paid and they already know because of their friends because they have already discussed my work.

Employers' involvement in modernizing the occupation may not be limited to exposing new employers to contemporary expectations. Two domestics reported that employers actually applied pressure on other employers to upgrade working conditions. Both domestics worked for employers who set standards of fairness and urged their friends and neighbors to conform—for instance, by complying with federal regulations by filing income tax and social security forms. Mrs. Salazar had such an employer:

> I don't ask for raises anymore. I have one woman who kind of sets the pace and she's given me a raise almost every year and then she hints around to some of the other ones that she knows what I work for and then they all bring it up to her standards.

The controlled environment created by the use of the informal network provides the avenue for Chicanas to establish their self-defintion as experts and their informal work arrangement as a business-like relationship.

Conclusion

Faced with limited job opportunities, Chicanas turned to domestic service and restructured the occupation to resemble a business-like arrangement. The Chicana domestics defined themselves as expert cleaners hired to do general housework. They urged their employers to turn over the planning along with the execution of the work. They considered themselves skilled laborers who were well-able to schedule tasks, determine cleaning techniques, select appropriate work materials, and set the work pace. Verbal agreements specifying tasks served to minimize supervision and increase the degree of autonomy. Eliminating the employer from a supervisory role removed the worker from a subordinate position. Domestics' ability to select and change employers became a critical source of autonomy and control in what would otherwise be a powerless, subservient position.

Chicanas employed as day workers in private households are moving away from "wage work" and selling their "labor time," toward a "flat rate" in which a "job" is exchanged for a specific amount of money. In this situation, any efficiency realized by the worker saves her time and can sometimes be converted to profit that will accrue to her. The Chicanas are modernizing domestic work in the direction of a petty bourgeois relation of customer-vendor rather than the preindustrial relation of mistress-servant or even the capitalistic relation of wage worker-employer. This arrangement is most successful with employed housewives who readily accept the skills of domestics. The strategy to modernize domestic service by selling labor services rather than labor power is also useful in eliminating potentially exploitative aspects of the domestic-mistress relationship.

Endnotes

1. Recurring themes in the mistress/maid relationship that appear in recent studies

are: the extraction of emotional labor, maintenance of status and control with an informal and companionable relationship, and the struggle for control as a crucial source of conflict. Cock (1980) and Rollins (1985) identified the personal nature of the relationship between domestics and their employers as primarily one of psychological exploitation. Exploitation is most visible in the expectation of emotional cheap manual labor, and is a common experience among black women in the East (Rollins 1985; Coley 1981; Dill 1979), Japanese-American domestics in the Bay area (Glenn 1985), West Indians in New York (Colen 1986), and Chicanas in the Southwest (Romero 1986; 1987).

2. Presently Mexican immigrants do not represent competition, but the Chicanas indicate they are incorporating Mexican women into their networks and urge them not to lower standards. Several women expressed concern over the willingness of Vietnamese immigrants to work for less pay, and do gardening along with household chores. For the most part, Chicanas experience a domestic's market and, therefore, have the latitude to select employers that show respect and professional behavior.

3. In recent years some of the women were working for two employers in one day, cleaning two houses. This pattern was particularly common when employers lived in condominiums or apartments.

4. Older Chicanas recalled babysitting, ironing, cooking and doing laundry, but in recent years they rarely did such tasks. Even younger Chicanas in their thirties, some with 12 years experience, only did ironing or laundry for employers they started with 10 years ago.

References

Clark-Lewis, E. 1983. "From 'servant' to 'dayworker': A study of selected household service workers in Washington, D,C., 1900-1926." Ph.D. Dissertation, University of Maryland.

Cock, J. 1980. "Maids and madams: A study in the politics of exploitation." Johannesburg: Raven Press.

Colen, S. 1986. " 'With respect and feelings' voices of West Indian child care and domestic workers in New York City." In J. B. Cole (Ed.), *All American Women: Lines That Divide, Ties That Bind*. New York: Free Press:46-70.

Coley, S.M. 1981. "And still I rise: An exploratory study of contemporary black private household workers." Unpublished Ph.D. Dissertation, Bryn Mawr College.

Corley, M. C. & H. O. Mauksch. 1987. "Registered nurses, gender, and commitment." In A. Statham, E. M. Miller and H. 0. Mauksch (Eds.), *The Worth of Women's Work: A Qualitative Synthesis*. Albany: State University of New York Press:135-149.

Coser, L. 1974. "Servants: The obsolescence of an occupational role." *Social Forces*, 52:31-40.

Davidoff, L. 1976. "The rationalization of housework." In D. L. Baker and S. Allen (Eds.), *Dependence and Exploitation in Work and Marriage*. New York: Longman:121-151.

Dill. B. T. 1979. "Across the boundaries of race and class: An exploration of the relationship between work and family among black female domestic servants." Ph.D. Dissertation, New York University.

Glenn, E. N. 1985. *Issei, Nisei, War Bride; Three Generations of Japanese American Women in Domestic Service*. Philadelphia: Temple University Press.

_____. 1981. "Occupational ghettoization: Japanese-American women and domestic service, 1905-1970." *Ethnicity*, 8(4):352-386.

Grossman, A. S. 1980. "Women in domestic work: Yesterday and today." *Monthly Labor Review*, (Aug.):17-21.

Katzman, D. M. 1981. *Seven Days a Week: Women and Domestic Service in Industrializing America*. Chicago: University of Illinois Press.

_____. 1978. "Domestic service women's work." In A. H. Stromberg and S. Harkess (Eds.), *Women Working; Theories and Facts in Perspective.* Palo Alto: Mayfield Publishing Company:377-391.

Ritzer, G. 1977. *Working: Conflict and Change.* Englewood Cliffs, New Jersey: Prentice-Hall, Inc.

Rollins, J. 1985. *Between Women: Domestics and Their Employers.* Philadelphia: Temple University Press.

Romero, M. 1987. "Day work in suburbs: The work experience of Chicana private housekeepers." In A. Statham, E. M. Miller, and H. 0. Maukoch (Eds.), *The Worth of Women's Work; A Qualitative Synthesis.* Albany: State University of New York Press:77-91.

_____. 1986. "Domestic service in the transition from rural to urban life: The case of la Chicana." *Women's Studies*, 13(4):199-222.

Spencer, D. A. 1987. "Public schoolteaching: A suitable job for a woman?" In A. Statham, E. M. Miller and H. 0. Mauksch (Eds.), *The Worth of Women's Work; A Qualitative Synthesis.* Albany: State University of New York Press:167-186.

Food for Thought and Application Questions

1. In Chapter 8, Amott and Matthaei argue that in order to understand women's disparate work experiences it is necessary to examine the interaction of gender, race, and class in the context of both history and place. Identify the particular combination of statuses and circumstances that enabled the Chicana domestics studied by Romero to successfully modernize their work while many other workers in low level occupations were unable to do so. What aspects of Chicana domestics' *work situation* were associated with successful attempts at modernization? What *personal characteristics* affected their success?

2. Compare the strategies used to improve work conditions, job security, and pay described in this chapter to those used by registered nurses (Chapter 23) and teachers (Chapter 25). How do gender, race, and class appear to affect the "activist" strategies employed? ✦

28

Women in Direct Sales: A Comparison of Mary Kay and Amway Sales Workers

Maureen Connelly
Patricia Rhoton

Women who work in direct sales do not get involved as a result of a lifelong dream to enter that field. Their entry could be explained more readily by the concept of "occupational drift" than "occupational choice" Working in direct sales is a "choice" heavily influenced by the fact that this is an occupation requiring little or no preparation or experience, no or few geographical restrictions, and in most cases a minimum amount of financial investment. Some contact with a direct sales organization seems to be almost a universal experience among adult American women—be it coerced participation in a neighbor's Tupperware party or merely occasional purchases from a local "Avon lady." For a significant number of women, however, this casual involvement leads to some formal affiliation. According to the Direct Selling Association (1984) the sales forces of these companies encompass approximately five million individuals, 80 percent of whom are women working part time.

The social science literature has directed scant attention to this phenomenon. Given the number of women estimated to be involved in this activity (four million), part time direct sales work is clearly an important area of study.

This paper looks at the experiences of women in direct sales, particularly women involved in two major sales organizations—Mary Kay Cosmetics and Amway Corporation. These two corporations were selected because their organizations and day to day operations seem to reflect differences between a "masculine" and "feminine" work culture. These differences appear in the structural aspects of these organizations as well as in the motivation for women's involvement. Analysis is based on participant observation of these organizations and their activities over a three-year period and a series of in-depth interviews with a sample of 20 women who had participated or were currently involved in Mary Kay or Amway.

Relevant Literature

The sociology literature has devoted little attention to the direct sales phenomenon. (See Green and D'Aiuto 1977, Taylor 1978 for the few existing studies.) Most discussions have appeared in business publications (e.g., Bage 1980, Coburn 1982, Koil 1981). The literature on similar occupations, for example, on self-employment, does not provide useful insights, particularly regarding women. This literature deals with the specific nature of self-employment; i.e., the characteristics of those who attempt to start their own businesses or the characteristics of those successful and nonsuccessful in their self-employment ventures (Daum 1984). Most of this research concentrates on men, limiting its relevance for women in direct sales. Other works in this area have either looked at the nature of direct sales organizations in general while concentrating on Tupperware specifically (Peven 1968) or looked at women historically in the more structured setting of retail sales in department stores (Benson 1983).

Sex differences in occupations have been neglected partly because of a reluctance in the social sciences to explore general sex differences, given the political impact of this scholarly work. The first major wave of social science research concerned with differences coincided with the rebirth of the women's movement in the 1960s. Research during that wave seemed either to downplay the existence of sex differences (see Maccoby and Jacklin 1974), or to argue for the socialized basis for observed differences. This wave of research aimed at distinguishing between biological sex, which for the most part is unalterable, and gender or sex roles, which are variable, socialized and therefore alterable.

Friedan's "second stage of the women's movement" (Friedan 1981) appears to parallel a comparable second stage of research and writing emerging in the 1980s. Exemplified in the work of Gilligan (1982), this research reexamines issues of sex differences. Rather than denying that any differences exist, it affirms a distinct women's culture, a distinct female experience. It deemphasizes questions of causality and argues for the legitimization of sex differences and the valuation of the distinctly feminine.

Methodological Approach

Information on the two direct sales organizations under consideration here has been gathered in a number of ways. Participant observation with the Amway organization, the organization studied more extensively, included attendance at rallies or group meetings (24 within a 12 month period), reading Amway motivational literature, listening to tapes on a weekly basis and becoming involved in numerous discussions with Amway distributors. For comparative purposes, contact was also established with Mary Kay consultants. This contact consisted of attendance at Mary Kay parties, training meetings and regional gatherings.

During the summer of 1985, more formal interviews were undertaken. Twenty women (ten from each organization) were interviewed. Snow ball sampling procedures were used to generate interviews in Columbus, Ohio and Frostburg, Maryland (i.e., initial contacts were asked to provide names of two other potential interviewees). The instrument used was an open-ended questionnaire focusing on aspects of the women's motivation for participation; satisfaction and problems encountered; information detailing her life cycle stage and standard demographic data. Interviews were conducted in the women's homes using tape recorders. Although written notes were made during the taping, the interviews were later transcribed for more detailed analysis. The discussions and analysis that follow incorporate responses from these interviews as well as material from the participant observations.

Two Major Direct Sales Organizations

Direct selling can be seen as "the marketing of products or services directly to a consumer, on a one-to-one or small group (party plan) basis" (Juth 1985: 1). Companies such as Shaklee, Avon, Tupperware, Fuller Brush, Home Interiors, Amway and Mary Kay are examples of direct sales organizations currently operating in the United States and in some cases internationally. Mary Kay and Amway were chosen because of a number of similarities between the two. Both were formed by charismatic leaders who remain intimately involved in the current operation of the organization. Both are appropriately classified as multilevel marketing organizations in which the individual entrepreneur is both wholesaler and retailer. Both require that the worker engage in selling the corporation's products and recruiting other "salespersons." Both distribute products that are readily available locally considerably cheaper. Although the product lines carried by these two organizations are very different, both distribute products that are at the upper end of the scale in terms of price and quality. Mary Kay has a number of different products all related in some way to skin care or makeup. Amway started out with a single line of soaps, but now has a wide range of products such as water treatment systems, vitamins, safety equipment, satellite disks and a "personal shopper's catalog" similar to but smaller than Sears' or J.C. Penney's.

Certain work is basic to all direct sales organizations—selling the company's products and recruiting others to do the same. Yet numerous and important differences exist between these two organizations. First, aspects of the reward system vary. Amway emphasizes cash incentives for both sales and recruitment. Successful movement up the Amway distributor ranks results in an increasing profit percentage. While this system exists as well in Mary Kay Cosmetics, emphasis is placed on nontransferable goods-in-kind as rewards. Success in Mary Kay is motivated by incentives of furs, jewelry, and cars which the company gives to successful consultants.

Structural links between the individual and the corporation also differ. Amway emphasizes a rigid hierarchical structure, and a distributor's link to the corporation is mediated by various levels. Bookkeeping on product sales and distribution of profit checks and other routine aspects of Amway "work" are routed through the upline sponsors or downline recruits. Distributors are counseled to be cognizant of the hierarchical structure even in disclosing their personal frustrations as Amway Distributors. Frustrations and complaints are never to be shared with subordinates downline; rather, the distributor is instructed to take problems upline and to share successes downline. The first direct contact the individual has with the

corporation beyond filing the initial application does not occur until the person reaches the status of direct distributor—a position obtained with monthly sales of $7,000 plus and achieved by relatively few in the distributor ranks. In contrast, consultants in Mary Kay have a more direct and unmediated link to the corporation. Admittedly, a hierarchical structure exists in Mary Kay. Subordinate to each consultant are those they have recruited—termed "offspring." Yet routine aspects of the work, such as orders, are not routed through the hierarchical structure but carried out by each individual consultant, who is directly linked to the company.

While both organizations strongly support the ideal of the traditional family, the two differ in the way that a woman functions within the organizational structure. Women working in Amway are most often involved initially by their spouse. A traditional division of labor exists and is perpetuated within the Amway family, with the wife performing the secretarial and bookkeeping functions in the home while the husband goes out and shows the plan and sponsors new recruits. The value system emphasizes achievement and success as traditionally defined by how much money an individual is making. In contrast, Mary Kay seems to reflect a uniquely feminine work experience. Spouses of consultants have peripheral involvement in their wives' work. There is also a great deal of emphasis placed on nurturance and support, which coexists and even dominates the emphasis on success.

Getting Involved in Direct Sales

Reasons for engaging in direct sales are varied. Women often seek this essentially part time employment for its convenience. They can make extra money, perform most of their work at home, structure the work day and fit the work into the confines of their existing life and its associated constraints.

The route to involvement varies in the two organizations. Mary Kay consultants make their own choice to become involved. Although they may have been encouraged to participate by family or friends, particularly if these are Mary Kay consultants, their decisions have not been precipitated by their husbands. In contrast, in Amway the husband in the family is usually the first person approached as a potential recruit.

The Amway woman is more often than not unmotivated to participate. She usually does not share her husband's vision of immediate and dramatic financial success. Rather, she often anticipates the extra work of their involvement—the products that need to be transported and the paperwork that needs to be completed and transmitted. When women are motivated initially to join Amway, it is often for reasons other than the expected financial gain. For example, the wife may see this work as a way of improving the family's and the couple's relationship. She thinks she can become involved in her husband's work in a way not possible in his traditional job. Amway can be seen as a way of improving her relationship with her husband, as something they can "share together."

Additional motivators for participation are evident in the company's suggestions for appealing to potential recruits. Amway emphasizes the "democratic" nature of participation: no individual can buy into the Amway corporation—movement up the hierarchy must be earned. Furthermore, Amway equalizes traditional social class advantages: formal education is not a prerequisite for success. Anyone can be successful so long as they follow the plan and work hard. Mary Kay stresses the concept of flextime; young mothers can stay home with their children during the day and schedule their parties at night, while mothers with older children can schedule their parties during the day and be home when the children return from school.

The Work of Direct Sales

Some physical labor is involved in the selling of both organizations' products, but the two companies vary in the amount of physical labor required. This difference is related not only to the type of product sold but also to the organization's procedures for distributing products and processing paperwork. Physical labor is more intense in the Amway organization: the product comes in larger quantities and larger containers, and distributors must pick up their orders at the home of the upline distributor. The order is broken down as downline distributors arrive to pick up their portions of the consolidated order, and this pattern is repeated until the product is delivered to a consumer. Within Amway "families," a standard pattern of division of labor exists in which these tasks are relegated to the wife. Mary Kay has a more "refined" approach to product distribution: orders are smaller in bulk and are delivered by UPS to each consultants' home. The physical labor consists of unloading the smaller size boxes and taking them to individual customers.

The distribution of the products is, however, only a minor aspect of the labor involved in selling. Getting people to use the products encompasses emotional and mental labor and impression management. Both companies purposefully socialize their workers for these various activities. In Mary Kay consultants are instructed to offer potential customers a "free facial" as a vehicle for introducing the product line. These facials can be performed on an individual basis or in a group party setting. Regardless of the setting, the facials are carefully structured—consultants are trained to introduce each product in a precise and standard fashion. Once a product has been purchased consultants are advised in ways to maintain contact with the consumer and encourage continued consumption. For example, they are advised to send each customer a birthday card and to allow the person a product discount as a birthday present.

The selling of Mary Kay products is couched in a nurturance ideology. At meetings for current and potential consultants, the altruistic nature of their work is often emphasized. Selling Mary Kay is defined as important work since "you are helping other women become more beautiful."

In discussing the work of selling in the Amway organization, it is important to distinguish between the official company position and that articulated by various "groups" within the Amway organization. The term "group" refers to large organizational structures which have emerged around key people within the organization. Technically, all direct distributors have their own groups as soon as they sponsor someone. Their group consists of persons they have sponsored directly and the people that their recruits have sponsored. While all distributors can have their own groups, some are considerably more active than others. An indication of the size and the prominence of a particular direct distributor and the resultant group is whether or not the group is referred to by that direct distributor's name.

The official position of the Amway Company regarding selling and recruitment is quite similar to that of Mary Kay. Distributors are to perform two major tasks, selling products and recruiting other members into the organization. Furthermore, distributors are encouraged to sell their products by demonstrating the product's use. As with Mary Kay, the person is instructed to do so using a structured presentation, either before individual potential customers or groups of customers.

Some of the more prominent groups within the Amway organization, however, de-emphasize selling to customers. Rather they suggest that Amway work consists of merely recruiting other families who will consume approximately $100.00 worth of Amway products per month. Instead of selling products the recruit only has to sell the idea of selling the idea.

Furthermore, Amway distributors are encouraged to become the ultimate Amway consumers: members of some groups are encouraged to purge themselves of all "poison products" from their homes—i.e., those not available through Amway. Distributors often point with pride to their attire reassuring their potential recruits that all items on their body are available from the Amway catalog. "If Amway doesn't sell it you don't need it." Sponsoring or recruiting other members is the second major task in multilevel direct sales organizations. All such organizations encourage their members to recruit other members, and they provide monetary incentives for doing so. In each organization, the sponsor receives a proportion of the sales generated by recruits. Amway and Mary Kay differ, however, in some important aspects of this recruitment.

The two organizations seem to differ in how sponsorship relates to the hierarchical structure of the sales force. Lineage and hierarchy appear to be reinforced in the Amway organization. "Downline" and "upline" are omnipresent in the Amway vocabulary. The organization reinforces this hierarchy in its incentive operation: if the recruit's immediate sponsor should drop out of the organization, their percentage of the recruit's sales goes to that sponsor's sponsor. No similar mechanism exists in Mary Kay; there, when a consultant drops out of the company, the 3 percent portion of recruit's sales reverts to the parent organization.

In Mary Kay, a nurturance theme seems to be reflected in sponsorship and the language used to describe aspects of it. Individuals sponsored are called "offspring"—a marked contrast to the term "downline" used in Amway. Should a Mary Kay consultant be geographically distant from her sponsor, the emotional support and training provided by this relationship can be acquired from a surrogate. In such a situation, the "offspring" gets "adopted" by a consultant working in the same geographic area. This geographically proximate consultant receives no monetary compensation for "adopting." However, a strong norm encourages her to provide the same services and support to her adopted offspring as to her own offspring, whose sales she directly profits from. This policy is in marked contrast to the Amway procedure, in which reliance is put solely on the upline person. Regardless of geographic distance, the sponsor is required to perform the training and motivational function. This expectation applies even to the mechanics of the product distribution. A distributor, for example, even at a great geographic distance, must still channel their downline's orders, if necessary, mailing the products down line. The Amway organization has a mechanism for switching groups, but the procedure is formal in nature and rarely used. A distributor can switch to a geographically proximate group only with the agreement of all parties involved. Since this switch will result in the termination of the original sponsor's percentage of the recruit's sales, there is little incentive for the sponsor to agree to this arrangement.

Furthermore, the members in the two organizations differ in their emphasis on the sponsorship function and, seemingly, their degree of comfort with this activity. We have seen that in some Amway groups, sponsorship is presented as the only work involved in participation and as work entailing very little labor. Although the Amway corporation itself repeatedly warns against using this "chain letter" approach in the presentation of the plan the strength and regularity of such warnings are evidence of the frequency of such patterns.

At Mary Kay meetings, sponsorship is down-played. Recruiting other women is mentioned, yet the fact that a person financially profits from such activity is not emphasized. A number of women we interviewed talked of sponsorship as the "least attractive" aspect of their experience. One individual has been working as a Mary Kay consultant for four years. Throughout the interview, she outgoingly discussed how Mary Kay "changed her life." Yet, when talking of recruitment of others she became uncomfortable, shy, hesitant and said "I guess I need to work on that . . . but I don't know . . . somehow I don't feel right asking other people to join," and was unable to articulate why she was uncomfortable recruiting others. She has four "offspring," and talked at length of the satisfaction she got working with them—and yet, she hesitated to recruit and viewed herself as "needing to work on this." In hearing women like her talk of recruitment, we felt their hesitancy was tied to unarticulated issues of exploitation, and somehow recruiting others and financially profiting from their recruits' work seemed unnatural and not quite right.

A final aspect of sponsorship is what could be termed the secondary market aspect of this activity. Both Mary Kay and Amway make a multitude of training and facilitating products available to the recruit. The products range from motivational tapes and books to a computer designed for the direct sales home office. These products, designed to enhance the recruit's success as a direct sales worker, are consumed by the sales force, and they need them solely because of their involvement in Mary Kay and Amway. The two companies differ in the extensiveness of this secondary market and its relationship to the sponsorship activity.

Mary Kay's secondary market products are fewer in number and are purchased directly from the parent company. An Amway distributor is exposed to a much larger array of motivational products and these are often retailed by the distributor's group as well as by the company. Certain Amway groups produce and market their own motivational materials. For example, one such group distributes for purchase by its downline a motivational "book of the month," "tape of the week," and "rally of the quarter." The upline in this group profits then not only from their downline's sales of Amway products, but also from the downline's consumption of the motivational aids.

Impression Management

Impression management occurs throughout both of these organizations. Each encourages conformity to an organizational dress code coupled with a positive attitude and outlook on life. Subtly, each seems to justify these behavioral and attitudinal presentations of self in light of other aspects of the organization's ideology.

Mary Kay stresses that the well-groomed woman never leaves her house without being "made up." "Looking Good and Feeling Great" is a term used by various consultants to summarize this norm. In her autobiography, the organization's founder, Mary Kay, articulates the justifications for and functions of this activity. Positing a link between outward experience and emotional state, she writes "A tremendous change comes over a woman when she's looking good and knows it. A woman's psychology is such that when she looks attractive, she becomes more confident" (Ash 1981, 129). Cultivation of a consultant's grooming is then encouraged not merely as a vehicle for advertising the company's products, but as a technique for promoting the growth of the women involved. Like the dissonance theorists, Mary Kay posits the need to change behavior first, with the idea that internal changes will automatically follow. She describes, for example, a consultant who initially struggled with her sales. The woman was encouraged to buy a new dress and then almost immediately increased her sales. "The secret was that at long last she was confident that she looked good. And, with her new self confidence, she was able to project more enthusiasm and conviction in her presentation" (Ash 1981, 130).

A similar justification is given for the organization's emphasis on a positive outlook. "Mary Kay Enthusiasm" and the idea "You Can Do It" are keynotes in the presentation of self. Again the emphasis is on the ramifications these ideas have for the women involved. "For me, the most meaningful thing about the growth of Mary Kay Cosmetics has been seeing so many women achieve. All of us here thrive on helping instill in other women the 'You can do it' spirit. So many women just don't know how great they really are. They come to us all vogue on the outside and vague on the inside. It's so rewarding to watch them develop and grow" (Ash 1981, 8). Thus impression management in Mary Kay is tied to personal growth as well as being a tool for the sale of the products.

Amway also has a dress code for its distributors. Men are expected to wear suits and ties; women are expected to wear dresses, heels and makeup. Sports jackets on men and pants on women are viewed as not adequately conveying the Amway image—one of a professional albeit an at-home entrepreneur. Concurrent with this code of dress, distributors are expected to convey a positive and enthusiastic attitude when dealing with the world. Uplines, for example, will coach recruits on the appropriate response to the inquiry "How are things going?" Amway distributors are instructed to respond with a "Great, never been better" and to do so with conviction and enthusiasm. In some of the Amway interviews, the women involved expressed their initial discomfort with this policy. One distributor described her distrust and perception of it as being "phony." "It's not normal to be that 'up' all the time." Distributors are instructed never to reveal their doubts and concerns to those below them in the organization, "Never say anything negative downline." Rather, if feeling less than enthusiastic and great, the recruit is to bring these concerns upline.

Division of Work Time Within Direct Sales

For most of the women interviewed, work in direct sales organizations is essentially a part time activity. Asking them to articulate how they divided their time, for example, how many hours they devoted to attending rallies and meetings, seemed a fruitless activity. They were often stunned by this question, would struggle with it for a while and then would almost lament "I can't really say. . . . That's so difficult to answer."

There are a number of explanations for this difficulty. Often, the total amount of time devoted to the direct sales organization fluctuated during their phases of involvement. "Are you talking about the time I spend now or when I first joined or when I was most into Amway?" one woman asked. Furthermore, one of the prime motivators these women often had for being involved in direct sales is the very irregularity of the time allocation and the possibility of their controlling their own allocation. In contrast to traditional nine-to-five jobs, direct sales can be "fitted" into the day and other rhythms of life. One successful Mary Kay distributor, for example, varies her schedule seasonally. A golf enthusiast, she works more than full time during the colder months of the year. During the summer, she takes a vacation from Mary Kay. Other distributors and consultants "fit" their work into the demands of their family life and other employment if they are already in an employment situation. The Mary Kay organization specifically states that Mary Kay work should be subordinate to family demands—"God first, family second, career third" (Ash 1981, 56). In discussing her own experience with other direct sales work, Ash writes:

> . . . One of the nicest things about my flexible hours was that I could always be home to give my tender loving care if one of the children was ill. There was very little I ever let interfere with my work—except my family. Employers need to understand that these are a woman's priorities. I've seen women with nine-to-five jobs come to work when they had a very sick child at home. In my opinion, their employers would have been better off to tell them

to stay at home and take care of the child. There's no way a mother can keep her mind on her work when she's worried about a sick child. (1981, 60)

The Pleasures of Direct Sales

Motivation for seeking particular employment is related to, but not synonymous with, the pleasures of the work. Often when selecting a type of work, motivation comes from the anticipated pleasures of the work, from what the person discerns as its pleasures. At times, however, the pleasures of work are emergent phenomena—almost unexpected by-products of the employment. In our interviews, we asked for both the reasons for choosing direct sales as well as what the interviewee saw as "the most attractive aspects" of her work. Often, the women interviewed linked these two, They referred back to their motivation when addressing the pleasures. Yet at times, the question regarding pleasures elicited very different information. One woman, for example, talked of the impact Mary Kay work has on her children. Since becoming involved in direct sales, she sees her family as being affected by the company's "You Can Do It!" philosophy. Thus, she described her children as becoming more positive, confident and enthusiastic as a result of her work.

Not only was a range of pleasures articulated, but they often differed from those articulated by the organizations. The Amway organization, for example, in its motivational tapes and rallies, emphasizes the pleasure of new found wealth. A typical plan presentation found in some Amway groups starts by asking the potential recruits to fantasize their dream home or vacation. Commenting on the gestalt of an Amway rally, *60 Minutes* concluded "What they are really selling is—the hope of getting rich beyond your wildest dreams" (1983, 2). Some of the Amway women interviewed mentioned that this idea of making "easy money" was one of their initial reasons for getting involved. Those who dropped out of Amway often linked their dissatisfaction to their failure to achieve this dream of unlimited and easy wealth. Most of the women detailed pleasures often not addressed by the Amway organization. For example, they met friends through the rallies and meetings, they got to spend some time traveling with their husbands without their children, or they came in contact with a group of people who "looked together." Interestingly, one theme promoted by sponsors and at rallies was never mentioned by the women we interviewed. Amway is often touted as a means of getting free from the clock—the successful distributor gets to "throw the alarm clock out," often in the midst of a celebration specifically for that purpose. Yet, none of the women interviewed mentioned this, even those who have worked or were working in more traditional and time structured employment. Perhaps this is a pleasure or a theme more suited to the male Amway recruits. Perhaps women, particularly those encumbered by the demands of child care, cannot fathom a life in which work-related demands are ever entirely restricted to certain times of the day.

Mary Kay similarly attempts to attract with a vision of material success. Furs, jewelry, and the ultimate, a pink Cadillac, are pleasures to be reaped by the successful consultants. Some of the women interviewed mentioned that working for Mary Kay resulted in "things I'd probably never buy for myself." However, the theme most addressed in the interviews was the flexibility they had with respect to the time afforded by their work—"I can fit Mary Kay in."

The Problems in Direct Sales

In a similar vein, in our interviews, we asked the women to articulate the "least attractive aspects" of their work. As one might expect, more problems were addressed by those who had aborted or curtailed their involvement prior to our interviews. Former Amway women seemed more bitter in their discussions. They often saw the problems they experienced as externally caused and linked to some deception by sponsors and the Amway corporation. One woman, for example, focused on the effort involved to be successful. She initiated involvement, thinking that it would entail very little time, and dropped out when she realized "more time was needed." Others complained that they discovered that they weren't making enough money. When their dream for unlimited wealth was not realized, they became disenchanted with the work.

In our Mary Kay interviews, the women more often talked of their own personal problems in executing the work. A number discussed their problems recruiting, their reluctance to approach friends or family, or their fears and anxieties regarding "cold bookings" (approaching complete strangers).

These problems seem to be both intrinsic and extrinsic to the work per se. Sales and recruitment by their very nature entail some imposition upon others. Mary Kay women, as previously stated, often addressed this and their difficulty in doing so. When asked to speculate on what types of people are more successful in direct sales, they often described people who were more aggressive than they. Amway complaints often were extrinsic to the work per se—the previously discussed discrepancy between their promised "easy money" and the reality of their commission checks.

Our analysis also suggests that there are problems in the rules and roles of the organization. Within the direct sales normative structure, a paradox exists. The worker is viewed as free, an independent, at-home entrepreneur. Yet within both organizations, workers experience extensive normative constraints. Codes of dress and set routines for presentation of products and recruitment of other members are restrictions on one's freedom. Although these structures can aid in making the transition into sales, they also limit the worker's options.

A model of the perfect family unit is fostered by some of the more successful Amway groups. Their rallies and tapes presented the specialization of functions within the family unit as a requisite for success. The husband in such a family functioned in the public arena—charged with the tasks of presenting the plan and recruiting others. The wife in such a family functioned in the background. Ever supportive, she performed the "clerical" aspects of the work—did the bookkeeping, and moved the products through the various distributor channels. Although it was agreed that singles can do it too, the suggested route to success consistently portrayed this ideal family unit.

In Mary Kay, this traditional division of labor does not exist. This organization recruits women, not family units. Although at the yearly meetings there are some activities for Mary Kay husbands, the organization has minimal expectations regarding their actual participation. At best, the husband is expected to be emotionally supportive of his wife's work. He may babysit the children while she does facials and encourage her involvement, but rarely does he participate in the work itself.

Solving the Problems in Direct Sales

A variety of coping mechanisms exist for solving the problems extrinsic and intrinsic to this work. Getting out or "sneaking out" of the organization appears to be the dominant solution used by individuals as a response to problems. Becoming involved in direct sales, in contrast to other forms of work, often entails minimal investment from the individual. One does not undergo a formal education as training for this work, and setting up the business can be done with a minimal monetary investment, ergo, when confronted by problems, a relatively easy solution exists in

getting out—deciding to no longer be a direct sales worker. Mechling, for example, estimates that three out of four Amway sales distributors quit after the first year (1980, 462). This was the strategy used by almost half of the women we interviewed. Some severed their ties to the organization. Some "snuck out," maintaining a nominal affiliation, but viewing themselves as no longer "working" in direct sales. One woman, for example, described herself as now merely being "a good customer." She maintains her official affiliation as an option for her retirement years.

Criticism of direct sales organizations often focuses on former members who have large inventories which cannot be returned to the company. This is a function of inventory loading—a practice in which the direct sales entrepreneur is coerced into purchasing large quantities of products in order to qualify for certain incentives. A recent court case in California (Barlett versus Patterson et al.) addressed such an occurrence. The plaintiffs charged that their Amway upline coerced them into purchasing over $50,000 in products to qualify for the status of "direct distributor" (Juth 1985, 16). None of the women we interviewed had this experience.

Aside from this coping mechanism, our interviewees did not directly address the issue of their coping strategies. However, we thought that coping mechanisms were reflected in their discussions. Lack of success, for example, is often coped with in one of two ways. Some women blamed the parent organization and deemed themselves as having been misled when they were originally recruited. Some of the elements that seemed most attractive in the beginning were ultimately blamed for failure. Workers are afforded unlimited flexibility in the amount of time devoted to their work, yet this flexibility and the fact that the worker determines it seems to relieve the organization from responsibility for individual failure. Success is often, even by the workers, equated with effort. If the recruit is not doing well—not making the fortune one had come to anticipate—failure to do so is often attributed to not putting in enough time. Such internalization of responsibility and blame seems to be reflected in their analyses regarding success. They seem to believe that if only they had been more aggressive or invested more effort they might have realized their dream.

Conflicts Between Direct Sales and Other Aspects of the Women's Lives

Our interviews and observations suggest that in contrast to other types of work, direct sales is less likely to create problems in other spheres. By its very nature, this work can be fit into one's existing life demands and constraints. In fact, given the ideology of both Mary Kay and Amway—that family is important—women in direct sales were unlikely to say that they experienced conflicting role demands. Women in Mary Kay, for example, often quote the organization's prioritization—God first, family second, Mary Kay third—when asked to address this issue. They often described how legitimate it is in Mary Kay to cite family obligations as a reason for not doing some Mary Kay work.

A few of the women we interviewed described some conflict with their extended family and friends. These conflicts revolved not around the issue of competing demands but rather around the perceived legitimacy of their work. Thus, they described their family as being critical of the direct sales organization and not supportive of their work. One respondent said she would never forget what her mother said when she got into Mary Kay, "You have a college degree and you're peddling lipstick!" Such conflicts seemed to be dealt with by avoidance. The women talked of avoiding the issue—not mentioning the organization and their involvement when interacting with these individuals.

The Realities of Direct Sales from an Economic Standpoint

While prescribed recruitment material tells the recruiter to stress the positive aspect of self-employment, it has little to say about the start-up costs involved in establishing such a business. Costs involved in purchasing special telephone equipment such as an answering machine or a device to record phone conversations can be considerable. Even if the recruit decides to start out with just the basics, not investing in office and storage equipment, there are still numerous items as product handouts, samples, customer gifts, and supplemental literature. All of these items are designed to bring the products to potential purchaser's attention and to keep the products in their minds. However the cost of these items has to be taken out of whatever profit is made by the individual doing the direct selling.

Money is made in two ways in a direct sales organization. First the difference between what the worker pays for the product and what the worker sells the product for is profit; however, this amount is affected by a number of factors. Each organization has built-in incentives to increase the volume of products sold so the more product that the individual purchases from the company the less the products cost. This practice can have serious consequences for the recruits of an individual who is trying to build volume quickly since they may encourage their recruits to purchase a large inventory irrespective of the recruit's ability to sell.

Purchased inventory can be an incentive to a recruit in the sense that the large amounts of money tied up in inventory can certainly motivate one to do some selling. However, if the recruit decides that he or she no longer wants to be involved in the organization it may be awkward to return the products. Some women seem to feel that it is easier to withdraw from the organization if they do not try to return the products they have purchased. In some cases this is because the products have some use to the individual—some can be used by the household, some can be given away as gifts or some can be sold either at cost or at a loss. Others are left with larger quantities of products that they cannot use or feel comfortable trying to sell. Since both organizations have a very liberal return policy it seems that the reason individuals end up with large unsold inventories of goods is not the actual difficulties of returning the goods but the difficulty of facing their sponsor and announcing their intention to quit. In order to avoid this, it becomes easier to keep the inventory and so avoid any confrontation.

In both organizations there is a financial advantage to be gained in a situation in which the sponsor has a number of recruits who make regular sales to a small group of individuals. This advantage occurs because the recruit who sells the item to a customer absorbs the cost of the sale and yet may make only a 3 percent or 6 percent bonus or profit on the transaction because their overall volume is below a certain level. If the sponsor has enough volume to be at a higher profit level then the difference in profit percentage goes to the sponsor, rewarding the sponsor for the time, energy, and money spent on training and motivating recruits.

From the company's perspective there are a number of advantages in using this type of sales personnel. First, the company invests absolutely no money in the salesperson until that individual has risen far enough in the organization to have already made a firm commitment to the company itself. If the individual does not make any sales, the company is under no obligation to give any money to the salesperson. Nor does the company have to worry about such costly and/or time-consuming items as pension plans, social security taxes, unemployment compensation, workman's compensation or health plans. This is different from a situation where the salesperson works on a draw until their sales are high enough to work for straight commission.

Also, each recruit provides his or her own warehouse space, office, office help, supplies, typewriters, phones, file cabinets, shelving and photocopying equipment. They purchase the forms needed to do the paperwork that the company requires, from the company itself. In actuality these companies have two related lines, one involving the sale of the actual products and a secondary business of selling sales and motivational support material to the salesperson. This material can be used either to make the sales process easier or more professional or keep the level of interest and effort high.

Noneconomic Returns from Participation in Direct Sales

The heart of the direct sales organization is the distribution system. This system itself has many advantages for the distributor. Its basic appeal lies in the ready made support network of individuals who are not going to make any money unless the new recruit succeeds in selling the product at some level. Unless the person sponsored either buys the product for their own use or sells the product to others, no money changes hands. Thus sponsors will make a concerted effort to help their recruits to the very best of their ability. In many cases the training period is a pleasant time of constructive dreaming of what if, of goal setting, meeting new people, sharing new experiences, and in some cases traveling to new places.

This participation in direct sales can also precipitate a change with respect to the women's entry or reentry into other parts of the labor force. One woman who is a makeup and wardrobe consultant became involved in Mary Kay as a side to her existing business. Others found outside jobs when they realized that they were not making enough money through their sales work. Some went into direct sales when they could not find a job they wanted in their geographic area. The most successful Mary Kay woman interviewed had left a job that she had begun to dislike intensely.

Conclusions: Direct Sales and a Female Work Culture

The primary analysis of direct sales presented here suggests a number of themes related to larger issues relevant to women and work: integration of work and family, a distinct female work culture or experience, and exploitation of women workers.

Traditionally women more than men confront the need to balance work with family or home responsibility. Women who are employed outside the home often do a "double day." While these women allocate fewer hours daily or weekly to household responsibility than do full time homemakers, they spend more time on these tasks than do their spouses. Blumstein and Schwartz, for example, conclude from their study of American couples, "working women . . . still do the vast bulk of [housework]" (1983, 145). Furthermore, they see women interweaving their work and family concerns; wives allow their relationships to affect their jobs and their jobs to affect their relationships (1983, 155). For example, when women select their place of employment they often use criteria that reflect their family responsibility. They choose a particular job because it is convenient to the house, daycare, or their children's school.

Direct sales work then seems almost ideally suited to the interweaving of work and family. The ideology of direct sales companies often espouses consideration of family concerns and, if anything, allows family responsibility to override work. The flexible hours of direct sales pragmatically facilitate this balancing of work and family.

The idea that women have a distinct culture, a mode of experiencing, that distinguishes them from men is the thesis advocated by Gilligan (1982) and others. Gilligan suggests that relationships are pri-

mary considerations for women, that female solutions to moral problems, for example, tend to emphasize the ethics of care, human attachment, and the resolution of conflict through communication and cooperation. That this distinct culture might be reflected in the world of work seems plausible and seems to integrate numerous findings and speculations regarding women and their work. The low status professions of teaching, nursing, and social work—professions which women have historically dominated—all emphasize nurturance and helping.

The idea of a distinctive female work culture and perhaps a distinctive female work experience have been present throughout our analysis. It is our thesis that Mary Kay is different from Amway in some important ways, and that these differences reflect a female work culture. A number of aspects of Mary Kay work seem to echo this culture: the theme of nurturance; the less rigid hierarchical structure; the ambivalence regarding exploitation; and the nature of the reward system.

Nurturance, caring for others, appears as a dominant theme in Mary Kay work. The work itself is touted as nurturing— "You are helping other women become more beautiful." Caring for and helping others was mentioned or alluded to so frequently that an uninformed observer might have concluded that the usual Mary Kay meeting was a meeting for social workers or others in the "helping" professions. Not only is nurturance emphasized in the relationship with customers, it also permeates the organization's internal relationships. The terminology of "offspring" and "adopters" symbolically conveys a maternal and nurturing relationship, particularly when these terms are compared to their Amway equivalent, "downline." That adopting exists as a viable alternative to overcome problems of geographical distance likewise suggests the importance of support within the organization.

The nurturing aspect of the company's founder is also emphasized. A highlight of the yearly meeting in Dallas is the invitation to Mary Kay's home. During this visit to her residence, consultants are given cookies that she has baked herself in her own kitchen.

Similarly, this theme of nurturance is reinforced by the lack of hierarchical structure in Mary Kay. Amway emphasizes one's position within a hierarchical chain of command even in the routine work of placing orders. In contrast, Mary Kay emphasizes a closer link between each consultant and the parent organization. Meetings are held on the basis of geographic proximity rather than a chain of command.

Perhaps here our analysis is on more tentative and speculative ground, but we think that exploitation of others is less acceptable within the Mary Kay world. As we have seen, a number of the Mary Kay consultants talked about their hesitancy in recruiting others. While they realized that this activity was important and necessary for success, they experienced difficulty doing so. Consistently, they were unable to articulate the reasons surrounding this difficulty. At times, they merely said it "didn't feel right" to them. Given that some of these women are quite comfortable with other aspects of their direct sales work—meeting customers and giving facials to groups of strangers, we thought that their hesitancy reflected something other than their self-perceived lack of aggression.

Finally, the nature of the reward structure in Mary Kay seems more compatible with a traditional female experience. Rewards and incentives in the organization often are in the form of nontransferable goods. Cash incentives exist, but these are not emphasized to the extent that they are in Amway. Meetings do not symbolically display the checks received by successful consultants. Reference is made to money, how much one can earn in Mary Kay, but such references are more fleeting and veiled. Rather, the incentives and rewards touted are the luxury items "given" away by Mary Kay. The bumble bee pins, furs,

jewelry, and cars are often the motivators—the "prizes" received for performance. Thus, working for Mary Kay seems to reinforce the wage structure of a traditional homemaker role.

In contrast the typical scenario presented on Amway motivational tapes illustrates a far different sequence of events. There the enthusiastic husband brings his reluctant and often antagonistic wife into the "family" of Amway work. Although the husband's motivation is not the focus of concern in this paper, the prominent place given to money in the motivational literature suggests that for them the freedom of choice afforded by the money that will be made is a large part of the attraction. The promise is access to the good life—luxurious housing, expensive cars, and exotic vacations—all while freed from the constraints of traditional employment. Furthermore, this work allows for the participation of the spouse in the earning process without interfering with her primary function as homemaker.

Direct sales in general, whether performed by females or males, is a grey area in the labor force. As a means of making money, there seems to be a wide range of success. Only three of the women involved made enough money in direct sales to consider it the equivalent of a full time source of income, yet the majority of the women interviewed on the whole were more positive about their experiences than we expected that they would be. In the majority of the interviews, the women or household either lost money or made very little in terms of what they had expected to make originally. Yet in most cases they either continued to use the products or continued to sell the products to friends, relatives and neighbors even though they were not making a large amount of money by doing so. Most of them focused on the growth that they had experienced on a personal level. Their experiences had resulted in their feeling better about their lives, their spouses, or themselves. Even the women who expressed some bitterness (always those involved in Amway, never those involved in Mary Kay) found more positive than negative things to say about their experiences. It may be that in direct sales organizations the product is only a vehicle for the social interaction that takes place, and the financial losses that occur are not very important in terms of what the participants perceive themselves to have gained. As one respondent said, "It's the women in it, they are very good people."

References

Ash, M.K. 1981. *Mary Kay*. New York: Barnes and Noble Books.

Bage, T.J. 1980. "Selling to farmers." *Advertising Age*, 51 (November): S4-S5.

Benson, S.P. 1983. "'The customers ain't God': The work culture of department-store saleswomen, 1890-1940." In M. H. Frisch and D. J. Walkowitz (eds.), *Working Class America: Essays on Labor, Community, and American Society*. Urbana, Illinois: University of Illinois Press.

Blumstein, P., and P. Schwartz. 1983. *American Couples*. New York: William Morrow.

Coburn, M.F. 1982. "Direct's sleeker sell." *Advertising Age*, 53 (March 1): M18.

Daum, M. 1984. *Correlates and Consequences of Salaried and Self-Employment in Middle and Late-Life*. Brookdale Center on Aging: New York.

Friedan, B. 1981. *The Second Stage*. New York: Summit.

Galginaitis, C. 1980. "What do farmers think?" *Advertising Age*, 51 (November 24): 55-57.

Galluccio, N., and A. Lappen. 1979. "Avon calling . . . with acquisition still on her mind." *Forbes*, 123 (April 16): 142-45.

Gilligan, C. 1982. *In a Different Voice*. Cambridge, Massachusetts: Harvard University.

Green, J. and R. D'Aiuto. 1977. "A case study of economic distribution via social networks." *Human Organization*, 36 (Fall): 309-15.

Koil, M. 1981. "Racing the competition." *Advertising Age*, 52 (May 4): S14-SI5.

Jobin, J. 1982. "Direct sales." *Women's Day*, 45 (May 18): 20-25, 143.

Juth, C. 1985. "Structural factors creating and maintaining illegal and deviant behavior in direct sales organization: A case study of Amway Corporation." Paper presented at the 80th Annual Meeting of the American Sociological Association, August 26-30, Washington, D.C.

Maccoby, C., and N. Jacklin. 1974. *The Psychology of Sex Differences*. Stanford, California: Stanford University Press.

Maxa, R. 1977. *Dare to be Great*. New York: William Morrow.

McElena, J.K. 1978. "Motivate distributors by tickling competitive nerve!" *Advertising Age*, 49 (October 16): 2-6.

Mechling, T 1980. "Patriotism, capitalism and positive thinking." *Commonweal*, 29 (August 29): 459-62.

Peven, D.E. 1968. "The use of religious revival technique to indoctrinate persons: The home-party sales organization." *Sociological Quarterly*, 9 (Winter): 97-106.

Richmond, E. 1975. "On the road to riches." *Harpers Magazine*, 250 (February): 12.

Rubin, L. 1983. *Intimate Strangers*. New York: Harper and Row.

Rudnitsky, H. 1981. "The flight of the bumblebee." *Forbes*, 127 (June 22): 104-06.

60 Minutes. 1983. "Soap and Hope." Volume XV, Number 1-7 as broadcast over the CBS Television Network Sunday, January 9, 7:30-8:30 EST:2-7.

Taylor, R. 1978. "Marilyn's friends and Rita's customers: A study of party-selling as play and work." *The Sociological Review*, 26 (August): 573-94.

Wedemyer, D. 1975. "There's a tupperware party starting every 10 seconds . . ." *Ms.*, 4 (August): 71-4, 82-5.

Food for Thought and Application Questions

1. Discuss any apparent relationship between the product lines offered by the two firms described in this chapter and the gendered work cultures that exist

within them. Does there appear to be a relationship between the types of client served by the two firms and their gendered work cultures? Discuss.

2. List several different types of products that are commonly sold through direct sales. Based on your own experiences with direct sales workers and your knowledge of cultural representations of them, indicate whether the product is more likely to be sold by men or women. Also estimate the price of each product/type of product. If accurate estimates are difficult, simply categorize products as expensive, moderately expensive, and inexpensive. Which products cost more, those sold by men or those sold by women? Do you think there is a relationship between cost of the product and direct sales workers' earnings? If so, which sex has greater earning potential? ✦

Index

Index

A

Abortion, 23
Accountants, 234, 238, 301
Accounting clerks, 77, 91
Adolescents, 17, 26-27, 43-51
Affirmative action, 67, 88-91, 93, 162, 223, 257
  comparative worth and, 88-91
Africa, 101
  Africans, 104, 105, 106
  See also Slavery
African Americans. *See* Blacks, Women of color
Agassis, Louis, 101
Age, 8, 9, 75-76, 101, 126, 251, 253, 254
  discrimination by, 69
  old age, 135, 136
  See also Elder care
Agricultural societies, 4-5
Airlines, 226
Alternative work styles. *See* Flextime, Job sharing, Leave, Part-time work, Telecommuting
American Association of University Women (AAUW), 17, 43-52
American Correctional Association, 294
American Federation of State, County and Municipal Employees, 91
American Indians, 7, 102, 103, 104, 105, 106, 107, 226, 229, 241, 244
American Institute for Instruction, 325
Amway Corporation, 369-384
Anatomy, 53
Androgyny, 19
Anthropology, 53, 103
Antidiscrimination legislation, 88
Asians, 8, 55, 70, 101, 105, 106, 108, 226, 227, 228, 229, 241, 244, 303
AT&T, 153
Athletic scholarships, 22
Autonomy, 126, 366
  See also Independence
Avoidance, 153
Avon Company, 370

B

Badore, Nancy, 182
Bakker, Jim: Jim Bakker-Jessica Hahn affair, 157
Banking, 6, 71, 189, 226, 227, 335
Bartending, 71
Basset Report, 189
Beecher, Catherine, 325, 328
Benefits, 110, 121, 122, 243, 361
Bernard, Henry, 317, 327, 328, 329, 330
Biology

and gender role, 15-16, 19-23, 101-102, 134, 161, 206-207, 370
  biological clock, 153
  field of study, 53
  race-ethnicity and, 101-102, 104-105
Birth order, 25-26, 33
Blacks, 4, 7, 8, 33, 70, 74-75, 77, 78, 103, 107, 108, 109, 114, 226, 227, 249, 261
  affirmative action and, 88-89
  Black middle class, 97, 235, 236, 242
  Black Power movement, 102
  Black professional women, 11, 228, 234-246
  Black underclass, 97
  Black upperclass, 106
  domestic service and, 5, 362
  education and, 236, 237
  job ceilings for, 234-246
  nursing field and, 303, 304, 306-307, 308, 310
  stereotypes of, 234
  work experience, compared to that of whites, 101-112, 222
  See also Occupational segregation, Race, Racism, Slavery, Women of color
Blue-collar jobs, 66, 109, 223, 260, 261, 269
Bonuses, 189, 361
Bookkeeping, 28
Broadcast reporting, 71
Brothers, 26
Brunson, Dorothy, 182
  Brunson Communications, 182
Bureau of Labor Statistics, 153, 221
Bush, George, xiv, 226
Business owners, xi, 126, 127

C

California State Employees Association, 89
Canada, 186, 187, 189
Capitalism, 97, 102, 107, 108, 235, 301, 304, 315
Careerist women, 250, 253, 256, 257
Career placement counselors, 11, 125
Catalyst (research organization), 174
Chicanas, 103, 106, 225
  domestic service and, 358-368
Child-care centers, 153
  See also Day care
Childless women, 132, 135-137, 147, 193, 274
Children, 9, 93
  altering child-rearing ideologies, 143-148
  child care, 24, 66, 103, 109, 114, 118, 128, 152
  child custody, 83
  child support, 83
  learning of roles and, 19
  pre-school age, 7, 8, 116, 117, 121, 146, 153
  physically challenged, 155
  school and, 2, 8
  sickness of, 119, 120, 122, 155, 190
  See also Families, Schools, Work-family conflict
Children's literature, 27-28
Chinese, 7, 226
City Women for Advancement, 90, 91